THE Litigation MANUAL

Special Problems and Appeals

Third Edition

John G. Koeltl
John Kiernan
Editors

Section of Litigation
American Bar Association

Cover art and interior art by Will Park.
Cover design by Catherine Zaccarine.

The materials contained herein represent the opinions of the authors and editors and should not be construed to be the action of either the American Bar Association or the Section of Litigation unless adopted pursuant to the bylaws of the Association.

Nothing contained in this book is to be considered as the rendering of legal advice for specific cases, and readers are responsible for obtaining such advice from their own legal counsel. This book and any forms and agreements herein are intended for educational and informational purposes only.

© 1999 American Bar Association. All rights reserved.
Printed in the United States of America.

03 02 01 00 99   5 4 3 2 1

The litigation manual / [edited by] John G. Koeltl, John S. Kiernan.
     p.   cm.
  ISBN 1-57073-639-1
  1. Trial practice—United States.   2. Civil procedure—United States.   I. Koeltl, John G.   II. Kiernan, John S., 1954–   .
KF8915.A2L57   1998
347.73'75—dc21   98-52430
                                                                                 CIP

Discounts are available for books ordered in bulk. Special consideration is given to state bars, CLE programs, and other bar-related organizations. Inquire at Book Publishing, ABA Publishing, American Bar Association, 750 North Lake Shore Drive, Chicago, Illinois 60611.

www.abanet.org/abapubs

TABLE OF CONTENTS

ix   Foreword

I. BEFORE THE APPEAL

2   Preserving and Assembling the Record for Appeal: Getting Through the Mine Field
James F. Hewitt

13   Appealing Evidence
James Harris

24   Standards of Appellate Review
George A. Somerville

34   Dangers, Toils, and Snares: Appeals Before Final Judgment
Luther T. Munford

46   Interlocutory Appeals and Mandamus
Walter J. Bonner and William D. Appler

60   Posttrial Alchemy: Judgments As a Matter of Law
Franklin A. Nachman

72   New Counsel on Appeal?
Dennis J. C. Owens

79   The Elusive Appeal
Elizabeth A. Phelan and Theresa J. Collier

II. STRATEGY OF THE APPEAL

96   Issues, Facts, and Appellate Strategy
Jordan B. Cherrick

107   Twenty Pages and Twenty Minutes
John C. Godbold

118   Points on Appeal
Arthur L. Alarcon

125   Some Nuts and Bolts of Appellate Advocacy
Jim R. Carrigan

134   Tips for Appellate Advocates
Robert L. Stern

142   Reality on Appeal
James L. Robertson

152   **Winning on Appeal**
      Daniel M. Friedman

165   **Second and Third Chances on Appeal**
      Dennis J. C. Owens

177   **Appellate Judicial Notice: Oasis or Mirage?**
      Paul Mark Sandler and Francis B. Burch, Jr.

183   **Jumping at Constitutional Questions Is Risky Business**
      Abner J. Mikva

187   **How to Appeal to an Appeal Judge**
      Leonard I. Garth

III. LANGUAGE OF THE APPEAL

200   **Why Can't Lawyers Write?**
      Christopher T. Lutz

212   **The Ba Theory of Persuasive Writing**
      Miriam Kass

221   **The Language of Appellate Advocacy**
      Bryan A. Garner

230   **The Art of Brief Writing: What a Judge Wants to Read**
      Albert Tate, Jr.

241   **How to Write a Good Appellate Brief**
      Andrew L. Frey and Roy T. Englert, Jr.

258   **Anatomy of the Written Argument**
      Gary L. Sasso

264   **Strategy of the Brief**
      Girvan Peck

278   **Building a Brief**
      John E. Nelson III

IV. ORAL ARGUMENT

286   **Time for Oral Argument**
      David W. Peck

291   **Preparing for Oral Argument**
      Steven F. Molo and Paul P. Biebel, Jr.

303   **Appellate Advocacy, Modern Style**
      Murray I. Gurfein

310   **The Don'ts of Oral Argument**
      Roger J. Miner

316	Appellate Oral Argument Gary L. Sasso	
326	Questions, Answers, and Prepared Remarks Stephen M. Shapiro	
337	Moot Courts: Scrimmage for the Appellate Lawyer Charles G. Cole	
345	Brush Up Your Aristotle Robert F. Hanley	

V. THE SUPREME COURT

356	An Invitation to State Courts William J. Brennan, Jr.
363	Certiorari Petitions in the Supreme Court A. Raymond Randolph
371	Petitioning for Certiorari in the Big Case Charles G. Cole
380	Opposing Certiorari in the U. S. Supreme Court Timothy S. Bishop
392	Amicus Briefs in the Supreme Court Stephen M. Shapiro
401	Supreme Court Advocacy: Random Thoughts in a Day of Time Restrictions E. Barrett Prettyman, Jr.

VI. SPECIAL PROBLEMS OF THE CRIMINAL CASE

414	What to Do Till the Plumber Comes Jill Wine-Banks and Carl S. Nadler
421	Heading Off an Indictment Andrew J. Levander
436	The Grand Jury: An Overview James M. Kramon
448	Representing a Grand Jury Witness William L. Osterhoudt
463	Getting Immunity and Using Privileges Andrew R. Rogoff
476	Basic Strategy in Federal Criminal Defense Litigation George J. Cotsirilos and Robert M. Stephenson

483   **Dealing with the Prosecutor**
Howard Wilson

496   **Criminal Discovery: Leveling the Playing Field**
Jeffrey E. Stone and Corey B. Rubenstein

508   **Joint Defense Agreements**
Michael G. Scheininger and Ray M. Aragon

526   **Criminal Discovery for the Civil Litigator**
Candace Fabri and Rebecca Cochran

539   **Unconventional Strategies in White-Collar Criminal Investigations**
Vincent J. Connelly and Tyrone C. Fahner

551   **Staying Clean**
Donald H. Beskind and David S. Rudolf

556   **Creative Defenses and Desperate Defenses**
Juanita R. Brooks

566   **Making the Most of the Multiparty Defense**
John J. E. Markham II

581   **White-Collar Crime: The Defendant's Side**
Boris Kostelanetz

591   **Sentencing the Corporation**
Edward F. Novak and Randy Papetti

600   **The Hidden Penalties of Conviction**
Elkan Abramowitz

VII. SPECIAL PROBLEMS IN CIVIL LITIGATION

610   **Avoiding Problems in Joint Defense Groups**
Mark D. Plevin

627   **Defending the Multiparty Civil Conspiracy Case**
W. Donald McSweeney and Michael L. Brody

634   **Thinking About Class Actions**
Christopher T. Lutz

643   **Checkmate: Takeover Litigation Strategy**
Jonathan J. Lerner

655   **Derivative Litigation: A Primer**
Robert J. Kopecky

666   **Patent Litigation**
Laurence H. Pretty

680   **Planning Fees Fights**
Christopher T. Lutz

Table of Contents

695   **Representing a Victim of Employment Discrimination**
Barry L. Goldstein

705   **Remedying Sexual Harassment: A Primer**
Michael B. Reuben and Isaac M. Zucker

719   **What to Do When a Defendant Goes Bankrupt**
Martin L. Grayson and Douglas D. Dodd

726   **Bankruptcy Litigation: More Than Voodoo**
Robert A. Julian

734   **The Client's Suffering**
Kenneth P. Nolan

744   **Litigating Cases Before Adminstrative Law Judges**
Lawrence P. Postol

754   **Collecting a Judgment**
James J. Brown

761   **Humanizing the Corporation**
Elizabeth Runyan Geise and David J. Katz

771   **Simple Lessons from a Complex Case**
Norman J. Wiener

FOREWORD

This is the third edition of *The Litigation Manual*, which was published first in 1983 and updated in 1989. Each succeeding edition has significantly expanded on the size of its predecessor, as the number of new articles that seemed worth adding has greatly exceeded the number that seemed to have become outdated.

All of the articles that appear in this edition of the Manual—like those that appeared in the first two editions—originally appeared in *Litigation*, the quarterly journal of the Section of Litigation of the American Bar Association. All of the articles ultimately accepted for presentation in this edition either reflect authors' updates to take account of developments since their articles were originally published, or have a timelessness of subject matter or quality that does not need updating.

This edition is presented in three volumes: *Pretrial, Trial,* and *Special Problems and Appeals.* Many of the articles in the *Special Problems and Appeals* volume appeared earlier in the *Appellate Practice Manual*, edited by Priscilla Anne Schwab of Washington, D.C., which this new volume expands and updates. Our move to three volumes is calculated to present the most comprehensive possible array of perspectives on each step in the litigation process, in a way that serves as a practical guide for all practitioners—whether neophytes or veterans—who are involved in the litigation process.

Litigation was the brainchild of Charles H. Wilson, a former journalist and practicing lawyer in Washington, D.C., who was its first editor-in-chief. Charlie set the standards for *Litigation*, which have prevailed ever since—a readable, practical magazine that shuns footnotes, advertisements, and ponderous writing. *Litigation* concentrates on practical wisdom from those who have actually experienced litigation. The objectives for *Litigation* are reprinted in every issue:

> A serious journal does not have to be dull, and scholarship need not be presented with a long face. *Litigation* seeks to be practical and concrete, not abstract and theoretical, lively and readable, not sober and sesquipedalian. The editors want *Litigation* to come to a halt on its journey across the desks of busy lawyers and not to flow past like a leaf on a stream, unnoticed and untouched.

Each of the editors-in-chief who have followed Charlie has spent extraordinary time assuring that each issue of *Litigation* continues the standards of readability and practical wisdom that Charlie set. Like Charlie, each has been a practicing lawyer who has taken the time from his or her practice. Charlie was succeeded by Doug Connah of Baltimore, F. Wallace Pope, Jr., of Clearwater, John G. Koeltl of New York, William Pannil of Houston, James McElhaney of Cleveland, Bart Schwartz of Los Angeles, Jean Maclean Snyder of Chicago, Christopher T. Lutz of Washington, D.C., Miriam Kass of Houston, Mark A. Neubauer of Santa Monica, Kenneth P. Nolan of New York, and Lawrence J. Vilardo of Buffalo. Each has been helped by the great dedication of the editors and editorial staff of the American Bar Association.

The success of *Litigation* has also depended on the judges and trial lawyers who have taken the time from their own schedules to share their experience with their co-venturers in this process. *Litigation* has additionally been helped by the foresight and assistance of the leadership of the Litigation Section who have supported the magazine and given it the editorial freedom that is essential for responsible journalism.

All of those who have been involved with *Litigation* for some or all of the past twenty-three years dedicate this edition to Charlie Wilson, *Litigation*'s first editor-in-chief, and to the dedicated editors-in-chief who have followed him. As editors of this latest edition, we also extend our gratitude to the authors, to the ABA staff who performed all of the tasks of assembling this edition with their customary energy, attention to detail, and good humor, and to Kristen K. Sauer, who worked long hours maintaining contacts with authors, assisting with editing issues, and managing the logistics of putting our three volumes together.

John S. Kiernan
John G. Koeltl
New York City
January 1999

PART I

Before the Appeal

Preserving and Assembling the Record for Appeal: Getting Through the Mine Field

James F. Hewitt

There are many depressing moments in a trial lawyer's life. Few compare, however, with reading this in an appellate opinion: "Trial counsel's failure to make timely objection precludes our review except for plain error affecting substantial rights."

Such a charming observation can make you feel like a public fool, even though we all know from bitter experience that the court probably would have affirmed anyway—even if you had meticulously objected, excepted, and filed written affidavits on the error. Your client, however, takes the court at its word and is now convinced you would have won the appeal if you had made a proper objection at trial.

There is an acute frustration in this. Properly objecting at trial may not be *sufficient* to obtain reversal, but it is almost always *necessary*. There may be a thousand things you must do, but doing all of them may not be enough.

In thinking about trial objections and record preservation, many lawyers misconceive the appellate process. They believe that appeals courts have an independent supervisory duty to ensure that a just result was reached at trial. Things do not work that way. You may feel with every fiber of your being that the trial was unfair, and you may be right, but unless you can specifically identify errors committed by the *court* below, you will lose on appeal.

Procedural rules in days gone by made this explicit: They required formal specification of errors made by the trial court. Appeals were referred to as "writs of error." The old rules of the Ninth Circuit, in fact, required "specification of errors in numbered paragraphs," and God

---

James F. Hewitt was formerly the federal public defender for the Northern District of California and is now a consultant with Heller, Ehrman, White & McAuliffe in San Francisco. He served for 12 years on the Advisory Committee on Criminal Rules of the Judicial Conference of the United States.

help the lawyer who failed to comply. In those musty unopened old volumes of appellate reports, there are cases dismissing appeals for lack of jurisdiction simply because no errors were specified.

Although this practice no longer prevails, it is crucial to understand the point it is based on: To prevail on appeal, you must identify errors that were committed by the trial judge and not merely by trial counsel. Usually this can be done only when the trial judge has done something directed at your client—usually ruled against him. Seldom will *inaction* by the trial judge warrant reversal. To preserve your appeal, you must therefore make unmistakably clear on the record below that the trial court has considered and rejected your client's position.

Unfortunately, some trial judges think careful lawyers are setting a trap whenever they object. But wise judges know the importance of preserving issues for the appellate court. They have enough confidence in their own judgment to let counsel object if they wish. All judges, however, are not wise; and some lawyers are not careful. If the appellate court needs a scapegoat, we know who it will be.

Just as there are few invariable rules for trying a case, there are few for preserving the record. But one principle is paramount. It is *trial counsel's* duty to perfect the record in the trial court. You will seldom get much help from the court or opposing counsel. In fact, you may often feel they are dedicated to preventing you from making an adequate record. Fight back. Overcome them. Make sure that every item necessary to your case gets into the record, in proper form. If you don't do it, it won't happen.

Before going on, I will say that some experienced trial lawyers think an article like this is just wasted space. They denigrate the importance of preserving a trial record and have many reasons for their view. You must try your case to the trier of fact, they say, not to the appeals court. Juries do not like lawyers who object. If you become wrapped up in petty record preservation, you will miss the forest and preserve the trees. You will become a pest to the trial judge, who does not like ruling on objections. You will distract the jury and break the cadence of the trial. Everyone eventually will get the impression that you have a weak case and are simply trying to screw up the record.

That is a formidable list of criticisms. Some of them do have a grain of truth, but together they are just a few grains, and not a whole beach. Only a fool does not provide for the future, and today's trial record may become tomorrow's record on appeal. In fact, you are not a skilled trial lawyer unless you can simultaneously preserve your record and try your case.

Start with the most fundamental question. What is this record you are trying to preserve? Primarily, it is the trial court pleadings (including motions germane to the appeal), orders, transcript, and exhibits. The verdict and judgment must be included and usually a statement of docket entries as well. Jury instructions offered and refused should also be made part of the record.

But the record is not always every scrap of paper in the lower court case file. The rules of some appellate courts limit the contents of the record and must be consulted; the rules of the Ninth Circuit, for example, require that relevant motions be included but not supporting memoranda of law. In addition, a limited record can be assembled by agreement of the parties.

The reporter's transcript in the record should include testimony and all oral matters incident to it. Opening statements and arguments may be excluded, unless designated as part of the record by the parties. There is usually little need for such material. Before you order deletions of parts of the transcript, however, be sure you know what the court reporter will do with your instructions. While you may not need closing arguments, you *will* want arguments on objections and motions during trial. Once we told a new reporter not to include "arguments." As a result, the transcript contained only testimony—no motions, objections, or arguments—only testimony!

Jury Instructions

Incorporating the instructions to the jury can be tricky. You want to get in the record the instructions *actually given*. Many judges will stick a packet of written instructions in the court file, and some send a packet into the jury room. Such documents do not always agree with the oral instructions given from the bench. Because the oral instructions control, make sure they agree, at least in substance, with the written. This can be difficult. There may be gross discrepancies between the two versions. If your trial judge wants to send written instructions to the jury room, suggest this approach: Have the court reporter transcribe the instructions actually given and then send in copies of that transcript to the jury.

Whether to include pretrial and posttrial material in the record depends upon the issues on appeal. If this paper is germane, it should be included; if not, leave it out. Be aware that pretrial motions can create a trap for even the most diligent record assembler. You may file a pretrial motion, have argument, and hear the judge say he will rule later. When he does rule, be sure that the decision is contained in a memorandum or a minute order; the record *must* reflect the ruling. At the very least, submit a proposed order for filing in the record. If you allow the ruling to be informal and unrecorded, you may have nothing to appeal.

Exhibits fall into two categories: those admitted and those refused. You must be sure that any objection to an exhibit's admission is stated on the record, emphasizing the unfair prejudice to your client from its admission. On the other side of the coin, exhibits that are offered and refused should be marked for identification and made part of the record. The relevance and materiality of the evidence should be stated at the time of the offer, preferably in writing.

If, despite your diligent efforts, you are left with an incomplete, inadequate record, you must move in the trial court to augment the record on appeal—a thoroughly unpleasant task. It is much easier to do it right the first time.

A prime area of record inadequacy is the transcript of trial proceedings. Reporters vary in competence and experience, and lawyers often find themselves in a strange forum with a strange court reporter. Always remember that the reporter reports only what he or she hears, and then may proceed to "clean up" even that. Nods, mumbles, grimaces, loudness, tone, pointing, shrugs, sneers, and snickers rarely find their way into the record unless someone puts them there. If you need them, that someone must be you.

There are many ways to note such prejudicial events in the record. The simplest is to stand up and ask the record to reflect the event. But do not be surprised or dismayed if the judge facetiously comments: "The record will reflect what it reflects." You have made your point—on the record.

Standing Firm

If the trial judge will not permit you to make an adequate record, you must stand your ground. Whether orally or in writing, you must state on the record that the court is preventing your making a proper record. This takes courage, but it must be done. Whatever happens, however, do not preface your courageous stand by saying, "Just for the record, Your Honor. . . ." This catch phrase—vastly overused by lawyers—implies that you are not serious about your objection—that it is just a formality. With such an apparently casual approach, you may be hard-pressed to argue prejudice later. Remember that the point of your objection is to prevent the court from committing a serious error that will unfairly prejudice your case. Treat the matter seriously.

Most transcript problems arise from human weaknesses: unskilled reporters, simultaneous speech, and the usual distractions inherent in attempts at oral communication. There are infinite variations among reporters. Many follow the rule that "if in doubt, leave it out." Some are too shy to speak up; a few are too lazy. Most really want to get everything down accurately, but they need your help.

There are ways to help get the record right from the outset. Give the reporter a list of difficult names or places. In cases involving technical terms, prepare a glossary for the reporter. Keep your voice and the voices of your witnesses up. Always keep one eye on the reporter to catch the quizzical or pained look that is a cry for help. Learn to recognize the frantic, drowning expression that says things are going too fast. If in doubt, ask, "Did the reporter get that last answer?" If an answer is significant and likely to be referred to later, ask the reporter to mark the notes.

There is no question that reporters love lawyers who help them do their jobs. In return, your hesitant, disjointed phrases may appear in the transcript as eloquent as the words of Daniel Webster. The court reporter can be your friend.

Every now and then, you will find the record mysteriously deletes or alters comments by the judge that could be embarrassing. What you remember—a stinging rebuke or impatient explosion—is not there or has been toned down. This happens on those occasions—fortunately rare—when the trial judge has edited the transcript before it is filed. If you are before a judge with a reputation for editing, consider asking the reporter to keep a verbatim tape backup of the proceedings, for which you will pay. This can be a delicate matter. The possibility of judicial anger is obvious. You should avoid tape backup unless it is absolutely critical. But where it *is* critical, recording the proceedings seems to have a chilling effect on judicial transcript alteration.

No matter how carefully you assemble the record, it will be useless for appeal if you have not played your part at trial. That brings up the subject of objections.

Making proper objections is fundamental to preserving the record. In fact, if you are the appellant, objections are the precise tool you use to save points for appeal. The reason is self-evident: An appellant argues that the trial court erred. But he cannot make that argument if he did not alert the trial judge to his disagreement. A proper objection is how that notice is given. What it involves therefore merits careful consideration. In reading what follows, remember this: An objection serves two audiences. It must be sufficient for appellate purposes, while giving the trial judge fair notice of your disagreement without gumming up the trial itself.

Just what is an objection? As noted, it is how a lawyer expresses disapproval of some aspect of the proceedings. It may be directed, among other things, at:

- the form of a question put to a witness;
- the substance of a question;
- the substance of the answer;
- the competence of the witness to answer;
- the failure to lay a proper foundation;
- the propriety of a proposed exhibit;
- the conduct of counsel or the jury;
- the jury instructions.

Many objections have their genesis before trial. If you can anticipate that an objection will be made to the admissibility of important evidence, or on some other point, you should prepare a pretrial brief. Never assume that the trial judge understands all the rules of evidence. Proceed on the assumption that you must cite the rules and law, chapter and verse. Like it or not, trials are a battle of wits between you and your opponent. There is a natural tendency for the judge to trust the litigant who displays the better grasp of what is going on.

The best way to state an objection is the simplest. Say loudly, "Objection!" Then state the grounds. That is preferred practice, but there are variations. One longtime San Francisco criminal lawyer with whom I tried many cases had his own style of objection: "Object, Your Honor. Calls for hearsay, is irrelevant, incompetent, and immaterial, calls for an opinion and conclusion of the witness, is speculative and highly prejudicial to the defendant." It usually worked, but we always wondered what would happen if the trial judge had tried to pin him down.

Precision is always better, but there are times when the precise objection does not come immediately to mind. In these cases, do not refrain from objecting, or even hesitate. Use a general objection to stop the testimony. As long as you object, you have interrupted the proceedings, and then you have time to think of the proper basis. The easiest (and perhaps most often used) general interruption technique is the "I don't understand [or didn't hear] the question, please repeat it" ploy.

Keep in mind that if you make a general objection and it is sustained, the appellate court will presume that you and the court knew the specific grounds, even though not stated. However, if your general objection is overruled, no correct specific ground will be presumed. Therefore, whenever possible—and especially if you think the judge will be unsympathetic—you should state the specific ground when you object.

When objecting, it is good practice to rise, unless local practice forbids it. That calls attention to *you* and takes the focus from your opponent and the witness. It may even be wise to raise your hand if the witness appears to be ignoring your objection. Whatever you do, however, you must stop the flow of testimony. After all, the whole point of the objection is that you do not want the offending question answered. Once the witness stops, wait for the ruling, and if it is unclear, ask whether the reporter got it.

If, despite your diligent efforts, the witness answers an objectionable question, ask that the answer be stricken and that the jury be admonished to disregard it. This is a weak remedy. It has been likened to "throwing a skunk into the jury box and admonishing the jury not to smell it." Therefore, if the answer was clearly prejudicial, you must move for a mistrial.

If argument is required on an objection, it should be out of the jury's presence. If at all possible, get the judge to have the jurors leave the courtroom. Of course, many judges prefer sidebar conferences for convenience; they hate delay and do not want the jurors to feel like so many jacks in the box. But bench arguments are unsatisfactory in many ways. They make the jurors impatient and suspicious. With *sotto voce* murmuring and counsel elbowing for position, there is often a bad transcript. In addition, the acoustics in many courtrooms are such that whispers can be heard at great distances. Heated exchanges go up in volume, and the jury often becomes privy to many matters best left to lawyers and judges.

If you do succeed in getting the jury excused for arguments on an objection, you may also wish to exclude the witness from the stand. Your arguments may tip the witness to the problem with his testimony. We have all had witnesses regain or reshape their recollection after listening to pieces of arguments about a pending question.

One of the most difficult objection problems is caused by the trial judge who has a habit of not listening to the testimony. When an objection is made, the judge invariably has the reporter read back the question, sometimes more than once. Such repetition, and emphasis, of the improper question attaches a severe penalty to objecting in jury trial. In an extreme case, it might be appropriate to call the court's attention to the practice and point out the hazard. The judge might be unaware that he or she is creating a problem and may be prompted to pay better attention.

Offers of Proof

Another critical means of perfecting the record—if your opponent has an objection sustained—is the offer of proof. Few procedures have been more neglected, especially in criminal cases. An offer of proof is the most effective means of telling the trial court why evidence should be admitted and of preserving the record for appeal. If the evidence is important and its exclusion can be anticipated, the offer should be in writing, supported by a legal memorandum and filed with the court. You should state that a written offer of proof is being made and summarize its contents on the record.

Many times, however, offers of proof are oral. You cannot foresee every objection, and—even if you could—you cannot brief all such problems in advance. Instead, like any good trial lawyer, you must think on your feet. If your opponent objects to the relevance of evidence or the competence or qualifications of the witness, you must be prepared to explain what the evidence will be and why it is proper. As with arguments on objections, it is better practice to ask to have the jury excused.

If you are on the other side of an offer of proof—if your objection is sustained—you should know this: Offers of proof can be used for less benign purposes than preserving the record. Your opponent may try to use one to influence the trial judge with evidence of dubious admissibility.

This is a real risk in criminal cases where evidence of prior similar conduct is offered supposedly as evidence of intent, motive, identification, knowledge, method of operation, and so forth. *See* Federal Rule of Evidence 404(b). In fact, such proffers are sometimes made to suggest a propensity to commit the crime charged—a prohibited reason. Even though such evidence may not be admitted, and even though the prior acts may not have resulted in a conviction, the trial judge—having heard the offer—now may think the defendant is a bad person.

If such an offer is patently untrue, object and challenge its accuracy, even though the court sustains your objection to its admissibility. While it is almost impossible to show bad faith on the part of your opponent—or prejudice—you cannot permit such offers to be used as character assassination tools.

What if proffered bad act evidence is admitted over your objection? Then you must act decisively: Move the court to instruct the jury on the limited use of the evidence, preferably at the time of its admission. And be sure that the supposed limited purpose of the evidence, such as proof of intent, really concerns an issue in the case. The Supreme Court has said that undue prejudice in Rule 404(b) cases may be avoided by (1) admitting the similar act evidence only for a proper purpose; (2) requiring that it be relevant to the issues; (3) balancing the probative value of the evidence against its potential for unfair prejudice; and (4) instructing the jury that consideration of the evidence be limited to the proper purpose. *Huddleston v. United States*, 485 U.S. 681 (1988). Trial counsel must invoke all these protections.

As noted earlier, sometimes the best time to object is before trial. Often the best way to do it is through a motion *in limine*. Such motions are usually made to prevent disclosure of facts in opening statements when admissibility is in question. The procedure can also be used in any situation where a preliminary ruling will prevent prejudice or where the existence of a pretrial order will minimize the chance that improper evidence will "accidentally" slip out.

Prior Acts

The admissibility of prior acts evidence is a common subject of a motion *in limine*, but there is no real limitation on its use other than common sense. Such motions are usually straightforward, but confusion can sometimes arise. If there is a pretrial offer of proof, the limiting motion may be denied—and the evidence provisionally approved—on the condition that the actual proof during trial satisfy the offer. This is a variation of the pretrial motion trap. In such cases, you must renew your objection during trial if the promised facts are not developed. The court may forget the pretrial contingency; you must remember it and put it on the trial record.

Sometimes a court will conditionally admit evidence "subject to being connected up." There are few hazards in the record preservation mine field as perilous as the offer to "connect up." Here is why: Evidence that must be connected up is by definition inadmissible standing alone. Nonetheless, it is admitted provisionally. The court and jury hear it. Later, when the time comes for a connection, it may be skipped or made inadequately. In an ongoing trial, when you have your hands full just objecting to material that is coming in right now, it can be hard to object to something that does *not* happen—namely, the connection.

An offer to connect is thus doubly difficult: It helps get in possibly improper evidence and it greatly complicates protection of the record. Given these pitfalls, you should always object to the connect-up procedure, proposing instead a variation in the order of proof. If that does not work, ask that an offer of proof be made—now—on just how counsel will connect up the objectionable evidence. Of course, if that evidence is not connected up, your objection must be renewed and a motion made to strike all evidence conditionally admitted. If the prejudicial effect of the unconnected evidence cannot be expunged by admonition, move for a mistrial.

What about nonevidentiary objections? From time to time, misconduct of counsel requires an objection, but be careful. Technically, if a lawyer does anything during trial other than questioning witnesses, offering exhibits, and making objections and motions to the court, he has engaged in objectionable conduct. Still, it is foolish to object to all objectionable conduct. The important question is, "How objectionable is it?" If the conduct does not badly prejudice your case, let it pass. But if there is serious misbehavior or if you detect a pattern of objectionable conduct by your opponent, call it to the court's attention. Again, however, you must be careful. Many times, lawyers wish their venom had been released in the corridors during a recess rather than in an unsuccessful motion for a mistrial.

I can offer only this advice: If you are going to attack your opponent for misconduct, be sure of what you are doing and go for the heart. Do not be surprised if the trial judge does not share your indignation, especially in criminal cases. Considerable latitude is allowed lawyers to ensure that the guilty do not go free.

If you think opposing counsel has dealt improperly with jurors, you must, again, make every effort to verify your suspicions. Having done so, you *must* act promptly to preserve your record. Many lawyers wait until they lose and then complain about jury tampering. The longer you wait, the more diluted your claim will be. You will not be able to answer the judge's inevitable question: "Why didn't you say something at the time so I could correct it?" More than that, a long-delayed jury-tampering charge may be viewed with what might euphemistically be called skepticism. Courts are inclined to think that jury tampering attacked only after a loss must not have been serious and may not have happened at all.

Jurors can also misbehave without any help from opposing counsel. You may overhear them discussing some aspect of the case during a lunch recess, or reading newspapers in violation of the court's instruction. Again, be sure you are on solid ground, that the misconduct is serious, and that a mistrial is in your best interest. Remember, you may have misunderstood. Most of my own complaints on this point over the years have done little more than antagonize at least one juror. In addition, judges are reluctant—especially in major cases—to declare a mistrial if any allegation of juror misconduct can be resolved in the juror's favor. In other words, don't make waves unless it is essential, but if you do, splash for all you are worth.

The formulation of jury instructions is also something that can cause objection problems. Many courts prefer to thrash out jury instructions in chambers. If a reporter is present, make your objections to particular instructions then and there. If no reporter is present, you must later restate your objections on the record, and you must be sure that instructions offered but refused are included in the court record. The easiest way to do this is to request an opportunity when court next convenes, out of the jury's presence, to state your objections.

In federal criminal cases, some courts require strict compliance with Federal Rule of Criminal Procedure 30; it provides for the stating of objections after the instructions are given and just before the jury retires. This means you must keep accurate notes of the instruction conference. Even though Rule 30 suggests that one objection is enough, it is better to object both when instructions are settled and after they are given. This is because, from time to time, the instructions actually given will vary from those promised.

In thinking about objections to instructions, remember that, in federal criminal cases, jury instructions are subject to the Fifth Amendment requirement that felonies be prosecuted by indictment of a grand jury, unless waived. Giving instructions that broaden an offense's scope may improperly amend the grand jury's indictment. Here is an example: A defendant is charged in an indictment with violating the Hobbs Act by extortion involving the shipment of sand into Pennsylvania. The proof at trial shows that he also interfered with the shipment of steel from Pennsylvania to Ohio. The trial court instructs the jury that the defendant could be convicted if the jury found that he obstructed either the shipments of sand or steel. In such a situation, the Supreme Court reversed; it held that the expanded instructions amended the indictment to permit conviction of a crime for which the defendant was not charged: namely, extortion concerning the steel shipments. *Stirone v. United States*, 361 U.S. 212 (1960). The lesson is this: When making objections to instructions, don't rely on just the text you proposed; double-check the indictment.

There is a critical reason for concentrating on instruction objections in criminal cases. Experience has shown that instructions are often used by an appellate court to reverse convictions that seem sufficient but leave the court with the feeling that the trial was somehow unfair. It is easier to order a new trial based on an inadequate instruction, or the refusal to give a requested instruction, than it is to comb the record for cumulative errors.

Though it can be difficult to identify and preserve errors for review, pointing out mere mistakes is not enough. Because of the harmless error rules, you can be right about a court's mistake and still lose. You must therefore constantly be alert to the potential application of such rules. If a particular ruling will substantially prejudice your case, say so. In doing this, you may face long odds. Most evidentiary rulings are routine. Most rarely will affect the outcome of the case. Occasionally, the cumulative effect of otherwise innocuous rulings can be sufficiently harmful to constitute reversible error, but not often.

It is your job to show how a particular ruling, by itself, will unfairly prejudice your case. Allow the trial judge to evaluate his rulings in that light. Equally important, by pointing out the harm flowing from the error, you have already begun to talk to a higher court, even though there is yet no appeal. Be specific about the steps the court should take to ensure a fair trial. The remedy you request—for example, a cautionary instruction or continuance—may be as important as the objection you make.

The same principle applies to objections to instructions. If the trial court refused to give an instruction in a criminal case on a theory of the defense, you must object and state how you will be prejudiced in your closing argument. Be sure to pin the court down as early as possible. You need to know *before* closing argument whether the court will give defense instructions. Many judges are reluctant to say much in advance beyond the general substance of the instructions. Make a clear record that you cannot adequately argue your case without the instruction. Otherwise, any error will probably be held harmless.

On all these points, you must afford the trial court every opportunity, before final submission of the case, to correct serious mistakes affecting the fairness of the trial. Appellate courts are more sympathetic to litigants who call the trial court's attention to the impact of its ruling in time to permit modification than they are to counsel who do not complain until the opening brief on appeal.

There is no perfection in life, or in the practice of law. You will never object with perfect eloquence and crystal clarity. But, however inelegant, objections help keep you alive to fight another day. Making timely objections may not assure correction of the problem at trial or ultimate reversal on appeal, but failing to do so virtually guarantees that your first shot will be your only one.

Appealing Evidence

James Harris

It's your worst nightmare as a defense lawyer. The jury has just come in with a huge verdict against your biggest client. You're depressed. You're angry. You want to quit the practice of law. Then reality sets in. You must save this client. You are certain an injustice was done. You're determined to turn it around on appeal. But how can it be done?

A similar question from quite a different perspective is bothering your adversary on the other side of the courtroom. She is thrilled with the jury's result. But she cannot help but be concerned about it slipping away on appeal. The judge made several controversial evidentiary rulings. Some seemed, and seem, critical to the outcome of the case. You ponder whether any of these will allow you to salvage your pride and your client. Your adversary is trying to figure out what to do to prevent it.

Figuring out which of you has more reason for concern, and hope, requires an understanding of the process by which appellate courts review evidentiary issues. At bottom, the task is not a difficult one. The substantive law of evidence varies widely from jurisdiction to jurisdiction. But appellate review of evidence works about the same way in almost all cases. For virtually any evidentiary issue on appeal, there are three, and only three, issues you will need to analyze and brief. But these three issues present a host of problems and many traps for the unwary.

What are these issues that hold the keys to your future?

First—did you properly preserve the evidentiary issue in the trial court?

James Harris is a partner at Sidley & Austin in Los Angeles.

Second—what standard of review applies to your issue or, as is often the case, what standards apply to the several components of your issue?

Third—was the error prejudicial or harmless?

Even experienced appellate counsel frequently overlook one or more of these issues, most often the standard or standards of review. It pays to focus methodically on each of these issues as you prepare your appeal, regardless of whether you are attacking or defending. In particular, you must identify and argue to the correct standard of review to maximize your chances on appeal.

First, the bad news for losing counsel. Your fate on appeal is in part already sealed by what happened in the trial court. Get rid of the popular misconception that appellate review permits you, as the losing party, to present your entire case for a second time. Rather, appellate review is about whether the trial court committed one or more specific errors. If so, were they of sufficient magnitude to warrant reversal?

This has important consequences. Most immediately, you cannot have waited until the appeal to litigate issues that should have been the subject of an objection at trial. You must have made your record in the trial court. Some appellate courts, such as the Ninth Circuit, will even require you to specify in your brief exactly where the issue presented on appeal was preserved below by making a proper objection before the trial court.

Preserving the Record

If you failed to preserve the trial record, you are likely facing a second disaster with your client. If you did not object at trial, the appellate court may well deem the supposed evidentiary error as simply "waived." At best—though hardly "best"—the court will address the merits under a "plain error" standard of review. This will require you to establish that the error materially affected the result of the trial. You are still alive, but your situation is far from desirable.

Why do appellate courts strictly enforce the requirement that counsel provide the trial court with the specific basis for an objection? For several reasons. Perhaps the most important is to provide the trial court with an opportunity to correct the error at the time it occurs. Trial, not the appeal, should be the "main event" in litigation.

There is also an institutional unfairness and inefficiency in allowing an appellate court to reverse a trial court if trial counsel never explained the basis of its objection at the time it was made, or perhaps stood mute as the evidence came racing in. Trial judges are not and should not be required to gaze into their crystal balls to determine counsel's thought process and the unexplained basis for the objection. Finally, by requiring a specific objection, the courts ensure that trial counsel will not receive a windfall if, in the interval between trial and appeal, he is able to formulate a basis for the objection and present it for the first time to the appellate court.

How do you do it? Have you done it? The answer depends on the nature of the particular issue. At least one of the following, which are the most common ways of preserving the record, should be available to you:

1. You objected to the introduction of evidence at the time it was admitted;
2. You objected to the exclusion of evidence at the time it was excluded;
3. You moved to strike evidence from the record if it was improperly admitted;
4. You provided the court with an offer of proof supporting your argument if the court excluded certain evidence.

Assume, for example, that your adversary's witness testified about inadmissible hearsay statements. You could have preserved the record by making an objection on the basis of hearsay. You were not required to embark upon a lengthy explanation of the hearsay rule and should have avoided doing so. But you also cannot have merely objected without specifically informing the court of the particular basis for the objection. "Objection, hearsay" will do it. Then move to strike any testimony admitted after the objection.

What do you do if you are the victim of an objection sustained by the trial court on testimony critical to your case? The answer is an "offer of proof." When making the offer of proof, either explain to the court why the testimony is not hearsay, or if it is, set forth the specific exception to the hearsay rule and its application to the testimony at issue. The offer of proof should be made either at a sidebar conference or at a hearing outside the presence of the jury, depending on the length of time required. Even if you are unable to convince the trial judge that the testimony should be permitted by making the offer of proof, at least you will have properly preserved the trial record for appeal. Keep in mind, though, that offers of proof do have a tendency to interrupt the flow of a trial and may frustrate both the court and the jury. Use them sparingly to avoid being held responsible for prolonging the trial unnecessarily.

Let's say you or other trial counsel failed to properly object or otherwise assert error before the trial court. Are you finished? The court has discretion to decide if that issue is deemed "waived" and not entitled to appellate review. But the rule regarding waiver of issues on appeal is not jurisdictional. The appellate court can, and under the right circumstances will, consider whether waiver is appropriate.

The outcome will probably depend upon whether the issue is factual or legal in nature. For example, if the issue on appeal concerns a factual matter, such as a witness's testimony, the appellate court's willingness to apply the waiver doctrine depends principally upon the significance of the testimony for the trial as a whole. Follow this rule: The more significant the testimony, the more reluctant the court will be to apply the waiver rule. The best guaranty of success is for you to demonstrate persuasively that the testimony at issue is critical in the context of the entire trial. As should be obvious, this determination requires that the court conduct some kind of inquiry into the merits of the issue. In this sense, the concept of waiver is somewhat of a misnomer.

If you convince the court that the witness's testimony was significant, the court might exercise its discretion and consider the factual question on appeal, even though no objection was made at trial. But you are still not out of the woods. Because there was no objection at trial, the appellate court will probably apply the "plain error" test to determine if reversible error occurred. Plain error is not easy to come by. You must convince the appellate court that the error was highly prejudicial, and that there is a high probability that the error materially affected the outcome of the trial. This imposes a much heavier burden than you would face with the "clearly erroneous" test, which is the standard that would have been applied if trial counsel had objected to the testimony.

So much for "factual" issues. What happens if the issue raised for the first time on appeal is a pure question of law? Did the insurance company have a duty to defend? In such a case, the court may, but is not required to, exercise its discretion and resolve the issue. Will it do so? It depends on several factors, including:

1. Does the resolution of the legal issue require the development of a factual record in the trial court?
2. If the issue requires a factual record, has the record been adequately developed to permit meaningful review?
3. Would the resolution of the issue result in prejudice to the party against whom the issue is raised?

An appellate court will exercise its discretion and resolve the legal issue only if the record is either adequately developed or is unnecessary to the resolution of the issue. The opposing party also must not be prejudiced. Prejudice would exist, for example, if the party would have presented its case differently had the legal issue asserted on appeal been raised before the trial court.

All of this adds up to one fundamental conclusion. The conduct of trial counsel is critical to the success of securing a favorable result on appeal. Objections are critical. They must be timely and specific. And, offers of proof are invaluable and sometimes essential. If you have not performed these tasks at trial, your chances on appeal cannot be rated very high. The first rule for success on appeal, then, is: preserve the trial record.

On the other hand, suppose that you have taken care of business as a trial lawyer. You have carefully preserved your record. Your objections are crisp and clear. The judge's rulings are apparent. You have made your offers of proof. You can now turn your attention to the real task at hand: persuading the reviewing court that the trial court's rulings were erroneous.

Missteps are all too common at this point too, and usually for a single reason. As trial counsel, you have preserved the record, and, as appellate counsel, you are prepared to show the palpable defect in the trial court's reasoning. But have you asked what the proper question is on appeal? Have you stopped to consider what the standard of review will be? How much deference will the appellate court give to the trial court's decision? If you do not consider this question, you will never frame your arguments in light of the real issue on the appellate court's mind.

The phrase most commonly sounded in this context is "abuse of discretion." *Rogers v. Raymark Indus., Inc.*, 922 F.2d 1426, 1429 (9th Cir. 1991). Trial courts have "wide latitude" in making decisions to admit or exclude evidence, and their decisions are ordinarily reviewable, it is said, if they abuse the discretion that this implies. *Kenekoa v. City of Honolulu,* 879 F.2d 607, 613 (9th Cir. 1989). It is important, however, to understand where this general statement comes from, for it applies less frequently than many counsel realize.

In reality, the standard of review turns in the first instance on whether the underlying evidentiary issue is one of fact or of law. If the underlying issue is purely legal, such as the proper construction of a rule of evidence, review is de novo. This is the least deferential standard, the one most favorable for the appealing party. *U.S. v. Manning,* 56 F.3d 1188, 1188 (9th Cir. 1995). On the other hand, if the issue is purely factual, review is for clear error. Here the responding party is in full control, with a standard of review most conducive to defeating an appeal. *U.S. v. Ford,* 21 F.3d 759, 763 (7th Cir. 1994). Between the two extremes are the cases requiring discretionary determinations on whether a particular piece of evidence should have been admitted. These include assessments of the probative value (relevance and reliability) of the evidence versus the danger of unfair prejudice, confusion of issues, misleading the jury, and needless presentation of cumulative evidence on the other.

Hence, the "abuse of discretion" standard. Because the majority of evidentiary issues on appeal fall into the discretionary category, some counsel and courts tend to think automatically in terms of "abuse of discretion." In precise terms, though, the standard applicable to many issues encompassed by the trial court's rulings may be either far less or far more deferential.

This has important implications for you when you are formulating arguments or writing any portion of your brief. Consider carefully whether, based on the record below, the true basis of the trial court's ruling is legal or factual or must be admitted to be in the middle ground described as discretionary. Seize the opportunity to gain an advantage by framing the issue on appeal in a way that will trigger the standard of review you want. You may win your appeal just by being more discerning than your counterpart.

How does all this work? Some legal questions are easy to spot. Suppose the trial court's ruling rests simply on the construction of an evidence rule. The standard of review appears to be straightforward. The appellate court will not defer to, but will independently evaluate, the trial court's construction of the rule.

But there is more than one kind of construction issue, any of which will give rise to the de novo standard. One is the question of which evidence rule applies. Examples are whether the evidence is "other acts" evidence subject to the requirements of Fed. R. Evid. 404(b), hearsay (subject to the appropriate limitations and exceptions), expert testimony subject to Rule 701, or documentary or demonstrative evidence subject to the requirements of Fed. R. Evid. 901 and those following.

Arguing Evidentiary Rulings

To bring this issue to the reviewing court's attention, you must argue that the evidence does not fit within the rule under which the trial court analyzed it. For example, suppose the trial court excluded testimony on the ground that it is hearsay not within a recognized exception. Your argument should be that, as a matter of law, the testimony was not hearsay. It was not offered to prove the truth of the matter asserted, or perhaps it was "not hearsay" as defined in Rule 801.

But there is another kind of construction issue: the proper interpretation of the legal requirements of the applicable rules. Here, you must identify the requirement and show how the trial court overlooked or misapplied it.

Suppose, for example, that the trial court has admitted, under Fed. R. Evid. 404(b), a party's prior misconduct to prove intention to commit the act for which he is being sued. In support of its ruling, the trial court has concluded that all the requirements of Rule 404(b) have been met. There is sufficient evidence that the prior act occurred, it is offered to prove a material element of the present cause of action, and the prior act is sufficiently similar to the conduct alleged at trial. But the trial court's consideration of the elements has fallen one short. You should emphasize that Rule 404(b) contains an additional requirement that the prior act not be too remote in time. The trial court has committed an error of law in overlooking this requirement. *American Home Assurance Co. v. American President, Ltd.*, 44 F.3d 774, 779 (9th Cir. 1994).

Use a similar approach if you want to challenge the exclusion of evidence. Identify a requirement for admission not specified in the rule but nevertheless imposed by the trial court. For example, suppose the trial court has excluded a business owner's personal diary as hearsay. The diary, she said, cannot fit within the business record exception because it is not a commercial record maintained by someone under a duty to do so. Personal records can fit within the business records exception, however, so long as they are systematically checked and regularly and continually maintained. If you put in evidence during the trial that the business owner did these things, then the diary qualified under Fed. R. Evid. 806(6). *Keogh v. C.I.R.*, 713 F.2d 496, 499 (9th Cir. 1983). You are entitled to de novo review to correct the trial court's error of construction.

Bear in mind that de novo review does not mean reversal. In either of the above situations, the appellate court will not overturn the ruling on the basis of an error in construction if it can find another basis in the record to affirm. *See, e.g., American Home Assurance Co.*, 44 F.3d at 779. You must show that the trial court's ruling would have been different under the correct construction of the rule. If you are challenging the admission of evidence, you must show that the requirement for admission ignored or misapplied by the trial court was not met. In the Rule 404(b) example, the prior conduct must in fact have been too remote in time to have been admitted under the rule.

If you are challenging the exclusion of evidence, you must show that the correct construction of the rule would not have resulted in the evidence being properly excluded for some other reason. This would include a showing that the required preliminary facts were not established, or perhaps that the trial court would have exercised its discretionary power. In the above Rule 806(6) example, the record evidence must show that the personal diary was systematically checked and regularly and continually maintained. This type of showing may not be available if the trial court rested its decision exclusively on its construction of a rule, and did not reach any other issues. In occasional cases, a limited remand for further development of the record may be required.

Factual and Discretionary Issues

Note that even where the primary ground for appeal is the construction of a rule, the factual and discretionary issues may surface as well. Such factual and discretionary determinations pose real obstacles to the appealing party. More than a few courts have avoided the construction problem entirely by applying these default principles.

Factual determinations affecting evidence frequently pose thorny problems on appeal. Are there foundational facts that the proponent had to establish by a preponderance of the evidence before the trial court could exercise any discretion to admit the evidence? Examples of such facts include whether a declarant was conscious of imminent death, as required under the dying declaration exception to the hearsay rule, *Herrera v. Collins*, 904 F.2d 944, 949 (5th Cir. 1990); whether a conspiracy existed, as required under the coconspirator exception to the hearsay rule, *Stauffacher v. Bennett*, 969 F.2d 455, 459 (7th Cir. 1992); and whether a witness possessed the qualifications to be classified as an "expert" within the meaning of Fed. R. Evid. 702, *Cook v. American Steamship Co.*, 53 F.3d 733 (6th Cir. 1995).

Ordinarily, the trial court's findings on these facts are reviewable only for clear error, Fed. R. Evid. 104(a); *Cook*, 53 F.3d 733. In some cases, however, you may be able to redefine these factual questions as a legal issue. If issues are properly presented to the appellate court, you may be able to gain much closer scrutiny and a possible reversal of the trial court's decision.

One way to turn a factual issue into a legal one is to argue that the trial court has misconceived the preliminary facts that must be shown under the applicable rule. Suppose the trial court admits a hearsay statement under the dying declaration exception, finding only that the declarant was conscious of imminent death. The appellant should point out the additional preliminary finding required under Fed. R. Evid. 804(b)(2)—that the declarant believed there was no reasonable chance of recovery, *Herrera*, 904 F.2d at 949. Your appeal stands a better chance if you emphasize that the trial court erred as a matter of law in failing to make this finding.

Suppose, on the other hand, that the trial court excluded the dying declaration. The declarant was conscious of imminent death and believed there was no reasonable chance of recovery, but did not die. The court held that the dying declaration exception did not apply. Because this is not a preliminary fact required by Rule 804(b)(2), you can argue that the court's error was a legal one, entitling you to tougher review of the record below.

A second legal issue that may lurk beneath an apparent factual question is whether the trial court applied too high or too low a burden of proof for the preliminary fact. If the trial court, for example, required only a prima facie showing of a conspiracy—enough evidence that a reasonable factfinder could find a conspiracy existed—you should emphasize to the appellate court that the correct burden is preponderance of the evidence, *Stauffacher*, 969 F.2d at 459. The trial court committed not a factfinding, but a legal error.

So far, so good. But again, your job is not complete until you also show that the error of law infected the court's ruling. If challenging the admission of evidence, you must still show that the preliminary facts required under the rule were, under the correct burden of proof, not established. To challenge the exclusion of evidence, you must show that all required preliminary facts were established. As a result, the evidence could not properly have been excluded under the court's discretionary power.

Outside this relatively controlled world of legal and factual determinations is the great universe of discretionary conclusions. It is tempting to describe this as the great catch-all, a none-of-the-above category. It includes all of those determinations that must be made after the legal and preliminary factual requirements are met. Probative value versus prejudicial effect. The phrase is familiar to all trial lawyers. It is critical on appeal. Examples include whether otherwise admissible "other acts" evidence is sufficiently probative to justify admission, whether otherwise admissible expert testimony will assist the trier of fact, and whether otherwise admissible hearsay is sufficiently reliable to go to the jury.

The trial court has wide latitude to make these discretionary determinations. The reason is its familiarity with the facts of the case and its opportunity to evaluate first-hand the quality of the evidence presented. It's hard to beat. But don't give up too soon. As in the case of preliminary factual conclusions, seeming cases of discretion often raise legal issues. Two such issues are particularly common and, if properly emphasized to the appellate court, can trigger de novo review of an otherwise discretionary ruling.

The first of these issues is whether the district court has exercised any discretion at all. In some instances, the district court is simply wrong in believing that its decision is required under a rule. When this happens, the appellate court will not treat the decision as if it were discretionary. *U.S. v. Rahm*, 993 F.2d 1405, 1410 (9th Cir. 1993).

Suppose, for example, that the trial court finds the requirements of Rule 404(b) are met. There is sufficient evidence that the prior act occurred, the prior act was offered to prove a material element, and the prior act was sufficiently similar to the alleged conduct in the present case. On the basis of these findings, the court concludes the prior act must be admitted. In challenging the ruling, you should argue for de novo review on the ground that the trial court has failed to exercise any discretion to weigh the probative value of the evidence against the danger of unfair prejudice.

Discerning whether the trial court has exercised its discretion is often complicated by the trial court's failure to state thoroughly the rationale for its ruling. Perhaps trial counsel failed to ask for a statement. Ambiguity in the record makes your job more difficult on appeal but, at the same time, creates an opportunity. Each party has a shot at shaping the standard of review in its favor. Look for such opportunities; they may make the difference between success and failure—especially where the appellate court disagrees with the trial court's ruling on the merits.

The second legal issue sometimes hiding in a seemingly discretionary ruling is whether the trial court, in making a discretionary determination, has relied upon improper factors or has failed to consider factors that must be considered. Suppose the trial court exercises its discretion to exclude expert testimony on the ground that the expert has based his opinion on materials not reasonably relied upon by other experts in the same field. But the court conducts no inquiry into what experts in the field actually rely on. Instead, the judge considers whether the materials are within the expert's immediate field of expertise;

whether the materials, in the court's own view, are reliable; and the extent to which the expert acknowledges the flaws in those materials when testifying. *See In re Japanese Electronic Products Antitrust Litigation*, 728 F.2d 238, 277 (3d Cir. 1983). You should point out that the trial judge has erred as a matter of law in considering several improper factors and failing to seriously consider the one factor—what experts in the field actually do—that should have guided her inquiry.

Again, this is not enough to win on appeal. You still must show that the ruling would have been different had the trial court properly exercised its discretion. If the appellate court can, based on the findings and evidence in the record, independently resolve the discretionary question, it may do so. *Rahm*, 993 F.2d at 1412, 1414. If, however, the record contains insufficient information to allow an independent determination, the court may be forced to remand for further development of the record.

Standard of Review

In sum, simply arguing that the trial court was right or wrong is the shortest path to failure. Instead, frame your arguments in light of the standard of review. Keep the following rules in mind:

1. Appellate review focuses on legal errors, not factual disputes. Therefore, wherever possible, frame challenges to evidentiary rulings in terms of legal issues.
2. Where the trial court's ruling appears to rest on its construction of an evidence rule, try to identify either a requirement for admission overlooked by the trial court or a requirement for admission not specified in the rule but nevertheless imposed by the trial court. Also look for those relatively rare cases where the trial court has analyzed the evidence under the wrong rule entirely.
3. Where the trial court's ruling rests on findings of preliminary fact, try to frame the challenge to those findings in terms of a legal issue such as whether the trial court has misconceived what preliminary facts must be shown or imposed the wrong burden of proof for those preliminary facts.
4. Where the trial court's ruling rests on a discretionary determination of the probative value versus the prejudicial impact of evidence, try to rest the challenge on a legal ground such as the trial court's failure to exercise its discretion or the trial court's reliance on improper factors.
5. Where it is unclear whether the basis for the trial court's ruling is legal, factual, or discretionary, seize the opportunity created by the ambiguity to characterize the trial court's rationale in a way that will trigger the standard of review you want.
6. Don't leave out the final step in the process. It is not enough to show that the trial court has committed a legal error in construing a rule, making a preliminary factual finding, or making a discre-

tionary determination. You must go on to show that the trial court would have properly reached a different ruling had it not made the error of law.

While preserving the record and identifying and arguing to the correct standard of review are essential stages in the appellate process, they are inconsequential to the appellant if the trial court's error did not result in prejudice, i.e., the error was harmless. An error is not considered prejudicial unless it is more probable than not that it affected the verdict.

The rationale for the harmless error rule is similar to that underlying the popular sports euphemism "no harm, no foul." In other words, appellate courts are not concerned about errors that don't matter to the outcome of a case. Obviously, based on the low percentage of cases that are reversed on appeal, appellate courts consider most errors, including those based on evidentiary rulings, to be of the harmless variety.

There are essentially two broad categories of evidentiary errors. The first category consists of those in which the appellant contends the trial court erroneously excluded certain evidence. Errors in this category are generally considered harmless for a number of reasons, including: (1) the evidence was of little or no value in determining the merits of the case; (2) the evidence was cumulative; (3) the evidence was inadmissible for a reason other than that ruled on by the trial court; and (4) the failure to admit the evidence was cured by the court's jury instructions.

The second category consists of errors in which the appellant contends that the trial court erroneously admitted certain evidence. Errors in this category might be considered harmless for a number of reasons, including: (1) the fact established by the erroneously admitted evidence was supported by other, admissible evidence presented at trial; (2) any prejudice in admitting the evidence was cured by a jury instruction; and (3) the evidence supported a proposition which was true as a matter of law.

It is generally quite difficult for the appellant to establish that a particular evidentiary error warrants reversal. Therefore, an individual evidentiary error must address a central issue in the case in order to be prejudicial. However, it may be easier for the appellant to establish prejudice if he or she can demonstrate that the court committed a number of errors, which, when taken cumulatively, are sufficient to demonstrate prejudice. Thus, almost always argue that the cumulative effect of multiple errors resulted in prejudice, even if the errors, when considered individually, do not warrant reversal.

Because most evidentiary errors are not prejudicial, consider adopting a strategy of conceding the existence of an obvious evidentiary error, and instead, focus your argument towards explaining why the error was not prejudicial. By adopting this approach, you avoid looking foolish by denying the existence of an obvious error, while at the same time protecting your client's interest and arguing about what really matters.

Standards of Appellate Review

George A. Somerville

You are about to appear in federal court to oppose a citizens' group that wants to stop clearing and construction on your client's prized commercial property. You have prepared carefully. You are confident that your client has complied with all legal requirements. The plaintiffs' standing is questionable, and nothing in their affidavits remotely suggests an irreparable injury. The plaintiffs' "public interest" argument seems especially thin; it earnestly points out the importance of some rather mundane archaeological finds (from around 1880). Your brief magnanimously suggests that, although old artifacts have some importance, promotion of economic activity and employment, together with protection of reasonable, investment-backed expectations, tips the balance of the equities heavily in your favor. It looks like an open-and-shut case.

At the hearing, you quickly realize that the court is not of the same opinion. A cold, heavy feeling grows in your stomach as the judge tosses plaintiffs' counsel a few softballs: "This injury really would be irreparable, wouldn't it? I mean, each of these things is handmade, am I correct? So each is unique and therefore irreplaceable?" Plaintiffs' counsel just mumbles a grateful "Yes, Your Honor."

By the time you take the podium, you expect to be chewed to shreds for your client's insensitive refusal to consider donating the property to the plaintiffs for their archaeological studies. You are not disappointed. The judge signs and hands down his order as you stand there: Your client is enjoined from disturbing the property, pending trial.

After calling your client with the bad news, your thoughts turn to appeal. The judicial code provides a right to review of interlocutory injunctive orders, and for many lawyers, the decision is quick and easy.

George A. Somerville is a partner with Mays & Valentine, L.L.P., in Richmond, Virginia.

"I'll show that antibusiness judge," they think. After the client has added a few "go-get-ems," the notice of appeal goes out the door.

You may end up wishing you had saved the filing fee. The problem is that in your haste to take an appeal, any appeal, you may have gotten yourself a ruinous standard of review. An appellate court reviews a preliminary injunction primarily for abuse of discretion. It will (and should) be predisposed to affirm the trial judge; getting a reversal will be difficult. Most trial courts will at least pay lip service to the usual factors for entering a preliminary injunction. This avoids reversal for simple legal error, and showing abuse in the weighing of those factors can be close to impossible.

The problem is more than just a likely loss, however. A hasty decision to take an interlocutory appeal that you then lose can hurt in the ultimate resolution of the merits. The fact that the standard of review is abuse of discretion reflects an appellate judgment that some decisions are best left to the trial court. Still, declaring the law is what appellate courts principally do; so, when they review the "likelihood of success" criterion in injunction appeals, they often announce in controlling dicta the rules for later proceedings. *See, e.g., West Publishing Co. v. Mead Data Central, Inc.,* 799 F.2d 1219 (8th Cir. 1986).

Unfortunately for you, the appellant, an appeals court's legal pronouncements may be affected by the sparsely developed record, especially if your opponent has shown unequal hardships and genuinely equal harms. In addition, the abuse of discretion standard, by enforcing deference to the trial court, may incline the court to fashion case-controlling legal standards that help justify the trial court's action.

Consider Not Appealing

This then is the possible penalty for a hasty interlocutory appeal: Partially blinded by the standards of review, the court will be inclined to affirm the preliminary injunction in a way that virtually precludes a later decision in your favor.

Therefore, if your client can live with the status quo through the trial, and probably through an appeal, he should do it. After the trial and judgment, the lower court's legal conclusions will be reviewed on a full evidentiary record; they will not be protected by any deference or presumption of correctness. Avoiding the abuse of discretion standard will allow (and require) the court of appeals to make an *independent* judgment, at least of the legal issues. One of the real consolations of appellate practice is that appellate courts usually are willing to do so.

At first glance, standards of review questions may seem obvious or boring. Why not just look it up? In reality, however, complex and subtle questions—of both law and tactics—are present in considering standards of review. One good reason for assessing these issues carefully is that the Federal Rules of Appellate Procedure (Rules 28(a)(6), 28(b)(4)) and some state counterparts require parties to state in their briefs the standards of review applicable to the issues presented. More important, a practical understanding of the standards of appellate review will improve your written and oral presentations and enhance your chances of obtaining a favorable judgment on appeal.

"Standard of review" refers to the strictness or intensity with which an appellate court will evaluate a trial court's actions. To understand *standards* of appellate review, however, is to move toward an understanding of the very *nature* of such review. The principles developed in the federal system, which are the focus here, are readily transplanted elsewhere.

The strictest standard of review is plenary, or de novo, review, usually for legal error. Under this standard, the trial court's determination is entitled to little, if any, presumption of correctness. The other most common standards of review, arrayed from the stricter to the more forgiving, include abuse of discretion, clearly erroneous review of trial court fact-findings, and rational basis review of jury findings. Standards of review for administrative action follow the same general pattern and add a few categories unique to the agency context, chiefly arbitrary or capricious and substantial evidence on the record as a whole.

Going Up the Ladder

The reason for understanding and being able to use such standards is this: If you represent the appellant, you want to move the standard of review up the ladder to a stricter, less deferential level; if you represent the appellee, you want a standard more generous to the trial judge. More than that, you need to know that there are varying levels of review even within a single standard. They too may be used to your advantage.

To know how to move an issue up or down the review ladder, you must understand why review is structured as it is, and you must appreciate the variations within virtually every individual level of review.

Legal error is the standard of review the appellant wants. When an appellate court reviews on this basis, the theory is that it accords the trial court decision no presumption of correctness whatever. In practice, however, legal error review has its variations. Sometimes, even when the standard is legal error, the lower court opinion will have advantages. If you do not understand these advantages, your appeal will be handicapped.

On a mundane level, for example, a well-written trial court opinion is every appellant's worst enemy and every appellee's best friend. It creates its own presumption of correctness by the force of its reasoning and the quality of its examination of law and precedent. If you are an appellant stuck with a good opinion, there is not much you can do about it except advise your client and press the attack.

The intensity of legal error review also will depend on what the appellate court is asked to do. Will the court have to select a legal rule? Interpret an existing rule? Or merely to apply recognized legal standards to the historical facts?

Most cases require only application of settled law to the facts. As cases, statutes, or regulations define an area of law, trial court decisions become more accurate and more predictable. Even though legal error is ostensibly the standard, decisions in such circumstances are more likely to be affirmed by per curiam opinions or unpublished orders. Appellate judges know that trial court errors occur less often in the application of settled law than in other kinds of cases where review for legal error is exercised. In effect, there is a presumption that the decision below is correct. Therefore, when you represent the appellee and face a legal error standard, you should try to argue that the case requires only application of settled law to the facts.

At the other end of the spectrum is the relatively rare case where a court must select or fashion a new legal precept, both for the case on appeal and as a precedent for future cases. Such cases ordinarily consume much of appellate judges' time and attention, and they tend to occupy many pages of the reports.

There is a reason why law selection cases occupy more judicial attention. Cases requiring the choice of a rule of law represent the core of the appellate function. As a result, this is the category of cases in which any deference to the trial court's rulings is likely to be at a minimum. These cases also are those in which the quality of advocacy can be most influential, particularly when the trial court's opinion is weak or nonexistent. When new law must be fashioned, legal error review is truly de novo.

A final category of legal error review, interpretation, lies between application and choice. In this broad category is most of our statutory and constitutional jurisprudence. But the lines between interpretation and its brothers are wide and gray. For example, when the question is which of two conflicting rules controls, choice and interpretation essentially merge. *See, e.g., Fitzpatrick v. Bitzer*, 427 U.S. 445 (1976). In the other direction, interpretation may become indistinguishable from application of the law in a particular case. The precise categorization is not critical, however. The point is that if what the trial judge did lies between the extremes of selecting a brand new rule and applying obvious law to obvious facts, then the legal error review will be intense, but there will be some deference to the trial court.

For an appellate advocate, the significance of these seemingly subtle distinctions lies in how the brief is written. Characterizations of what the lower court did, or what the appeals court should do, are often matters of opinion, or even semantics. How you describe what was done will depend on how intense you want the review to be. As appellant, for example, you would be better off saying that the trial judge adopted "an entirely new and erroneous legal standard" than to say the court applied the wrong rule of law to this case.

The standard that many appellants fear most is abuse of discretion. It often seems as if appeals courts think that a decision left to a trial judge's discretion is none of their business. Even findings of fact, which are subject to a clearly erroneous review, seem at times to be scrutinized more closely than discretionary decisions.

Such fears are not always right. As with legal error, there are several varieties of discretion. Though review of discretion can be more forgiving than clearly erroneous review, some kinds of discretionary review are in fact stricter. Careful analysis of the particular exercise of discretion in a case may convince a court to apply a tougher standard.

A warning before proceeding: It is never easy to obtain reversal of a pure exercise of discretion. The odds are against you. The point is this: Do not give up—actually or emotionally—merely because a decision against you is discretionary. A careful and discriminating argument sometimes can overcome the unhelpful standard.

Consider a few examples: A ruling on a discretionary matter involving admission of evidence or discovery rarely is reversed. These kinds of questions—especially in discovery—are committed to the strong discretion of the trial court. That commitment is a recognition of the trial judge's superior knowledge of the issues, the record, the proceedings, and the personalities. It also is based on the tremendous variety of situations in which such questions arise, making formulation of legal rules difficult or impossible. Furthermore, there is the principle that a litigant is entitled to a fair trial but not to a perfect one; decisions on subjects such as discovery may be wrong, but they rarely affect the basic fairness of the trial.

Compare this with questions that are not committed to trial court discretion because trial courts are in a better position to decide, but because such questions present novel issues. Committing certain decisions to trial court discretion provides a period of flexibility—almost experimentation—while appellate courts develop expertise from a series of cases. Sometimes, however, things change. Decisions move from the substantial to the limited discretion of the trial court, or even become prescribed by a rule of law. Lawyers' fees awards under fee-shifting statutes have followed that pattern. At first there were only general legal standards with much left to the trial judge. Gradually, appellate courts adopted more and more specific guidelines. These cases often present opportunities for review and reversal not found in cases in which decisions are permanently committed to lower court discretion. In such experimental discretion situations, yours may be the case where the basis for decision moves from the trial court's discretion to a rule of law—or it may be the case that confirms the wisdom of leaving certain issues to the discretion of the courts below.

Close Review of Discretion

There are two other categories in which matters committed to trial court discretion may get meaningful review. In the first, the exercise of discretion must conform to standards announced in prior opinions; appellate courts may reevaluate lower courts' applications of the standards. In this category are cases seeking a preliminary injunction, a declaratory judgment, or an exercise of supplemental jurisdiction under 28 U.S.C. §1367. The second category involves subjects on which previous cases have established a preferred outcome. This includes motions for a voluntary dismissal or approval of a settlement. Even though ostensibly committed to trial court discretion, departures from the usual outcome are tolerated rarely, and only for good reasons persuasively articulated by the trial court.

There is another reason why almost all exercises of discretion may actually get meaningful review. A discretionary judgment often has legal components. *See, e.g., Pratte v. NLRB*, 683 F.2d 1038, 1040 (7th Cir. 1982) (de novo review where a normally discretionary question "turns on interpretation of the law"). Legal error can be embedded in an apparently discretionary decision when the trial judge fails to recognize that a question *is* discretionary; if he thinks himself bound by a rule of law, he should be reversed for legal error and instructed to exercise his discretion on remand. *Compare United States v. Williams*, 407 F.2d 940 (4th Cir. 1969) with *United States v. McCoy*, 517 F.2d 41, 44–45 (7th Cir.), *cert. denied*, 423 U.S. 895 (1975).

More commonly, particularly in a developing area, a lawyer attuned to the substantive law may be able to persuade an appeals court that the trial court considered impermissible factors or failed to consider factors that should have been evaluated. *E.g., Kern v. TXO Production Corp.*, 738 F.2d 968, 970 (8th Cir. 1984). Though appellate courts in such cases may say that the trial court did or did not abuse its discretion, in fact its choice of factors usually presents a question of law, subject to review for error and not for abuse of discretion. Once again, the aim for an appellant is to see through an apparently discouraging abuse of discretion standard, identify an issue of law, and obtain a more intense appellate review.

Was the Decision Explained?

There is another point for those facing an appeal of a discretionary decision. How well did the trial court explain its decision? This can be important, but it is hard to evaluate. Even though a thoughtful trial court opinion should be an appellant's worst enemy, some judges have complained that the opposite is true. They believe that a trial judge who explains in detail the reasons for an exercise of discretion is more likely to be reversed than one who states no reasons at all. The problem is that the more that is said, the more there is to criticize. To the extent this is true, it is lamentable. Also, it may be true that if the trial judge stated no reasons and the exercise of discretion is attacked, an appellee will have a freer hand in suggesting proper factors that may have influenced the decision. Nonetheless, an opinion that states no reasons is usually good news for the appellant. Your opponent can talk all day about what the trial judge thought, but the talk inevitably will be hamstrung by a lack of any visible support from the ruling below. *See, e.g., Northcross v. Board of Education*, 412 U.S. 427 (1973).

If you must attack an exercise of discretion, and the trial judge acted without explaining any reasons, you can argue that the appellate court's institutional interest in reviewability demands articulation of the trial court's reasons. *E.g., Farmington Dowel Products Co. v. Forster Mfg. Co.*, 436 F.2d 699, 701–02 (1st Cir. 1970). The point is obvious. If the trial judge said nothing, the appeals court will have no basis for its review. Such an argument may be effective—especially in a delicate or developing area—but a reversal is likely to be cold comfort. The usual result is a remand to the trial court for a statement of its reasons or, worse yet, a decision announcing a prospective rule that is not applied to your case.

Review of Findings of Fact

What about review of findings of fact? Most litigators know that appellate review of fact-findings is exceedingly forgiving. Most of us have told clients that chances for an appeal are slim because the trial judge "killed us on the facts."

A common response is to characterize an issue of fact as a question of law, or as a mixed question of law and fact. The line between law and fact is not always sharp. It wavers and can be moved. Courts sometimes will characterize matters that appear factual as legal, usually to permit them to reach what they consider a just result. As an appellant you want to take advantage of this malleability.

What *is* the standard for findings of fact? In federal *civil* cases, Rule 52(a) forbids appellate courts from setting aside trial court fact-findings unless "clearly erroneous." The Supreme Court has explained this standard as follows:

> [a] finding is "clearly erroneous" when although there is evidence to support it, the reviewing court on the entire evidence is left with the definite and firm conviction that a mistake has been committed. . . . If the district court's account of the evidence is plausible in light of the record viewed in its entirety, the court of appeals may not reverse it even though convinced that had it been sitting as the trier of fact, it would have weighed the evidence differently.

Anderson v. City of Bessemer, 470 U.S. 564, 573–74 (1985).

This is a tough standard, and perhaps as a result, it has had exceptions and odd wrinkles. For example, until recently many federal courts employed a much stricter standard of review, often virtually de novo, of findings based on documentary evidence. The idea was that no credibility concerns were involved. This view was firmly put to rest in *Bessemer City* and by the adoption a few weeks after that case of the 1985 amendment to

Rule 52. In *Bessemer City*, the Supreme Court observed that the clearly erroneous standard applies "even when the district court's findings do not rest on credibility determinations, but are based instead on physical or documentary evidence or inferences from other facts." 470 U.S. at 574. The Rule 52 amendment added the italicized phrase in the following: "Findings of fact, *whether based on oral or documentary evidence,* shall not be set aside unless clearly erroneous, and due regard shall be given to the opportunity of the trial court to judge of the credibility of the witnesses."

The credibility clause deserves attention. In *Bessemer City*, the Supreme Court said that clause was not merely a justification of the clearly erroneous rule. Instead, it defined an occasion for even more stringent application of the standard: "[W]hen findings are based on determinations regarding the credibility of witnesses, Rule 52(a) demands even greater deference to the trial court's findings. . . . when a trial judge's finding is based on his decision to credit the testimony of one of two or more witnesses, each of whom has told a coherent and facially plausible story that is not contradicted by extrinsic evidence, that finding, if not internally inconsistent, can *virtually never* be clear error." 470 U.S. at 575 (emphasis added).

Language like that makes it obvious why parties to an appeal often spend much of their time tussling over whether the issue in dispute is a factual or legal conclusion.

Criminal Findings

Review of fact-findings in federal *criminal* cases is not as well defined, because the Federal Rules of Criminal Procedure (unlike the Rules of Civil Procedure) do not prescribe a standard. Most courts apply the clearly erroneous standard in criminal cases, but sometimes they add the qualification that the "ultimate finding" of guilt will be reviewed only for "substantial evidence" to support it. *E.g., United States v. Delerme,* 457 F.2d 156, 159–60 (3d Cir. 1972).

In considering review of factual findings in criminal cases, remember the difference in evidentiary burdens between civil and criminal cases. Since *Jackson v. Virginia*, 443 U.S. 307 (1979), it has been clear that a reviewing court must determine whether the evidence is "sufficient fairly to support a conclusion that every element of the crime has been established beyond a reasonable doubt." *Id.* at 313–14. Thus, a finding not clearly erroneous under the civil "preponderance of evidence" standard might be found clearly erroneous in a criminal case. The same principle applies to review of facts that must be proved by clear and convincing evidence in a civil case. *Anderson v. Liberty Lobby, Inc.,* 477 U.S. 242, 252–55 (1986).

Given this law, what can you do if you are an appellant attacking a judgment based largely on factual considerations? First, learn to recognize lost causes. If your case arises in a settled area of the law and you lost at trial because the court found that the historical facts favored the other side, you have almost no chance on appeal. Such pure findings of fact generally can be attacked successfully only where they lack any rational connection to the record—where they seem to have materialized out of thin air—or occasionally when the vast weight of the evidence persuades the appellate court that a finding is surely wrong. Such circumstances are exceedingly rare. Appellate courts seem to take the view that while puzzling or questionable findings *may* reflect confusion or prejudice, they far more often are the product of the trial judge's hands-on familiarity with the case.

But clear errors sometimes do occur. Chiefly this happens in areas where the trial court's greater familiarity is a weakness and not an asset—for example, when a fact has been pleaded and asserted in briefs, and repeated so often it is almost second nature to the judge. The party asserting the fact may forget to support it with evidence, and the court may just assume it was proven. Absent such a special situation, however, you will have a hard time attacking the findings below.

Criminal cases may be an exception. Some skillful practitioners argue that sufficiency of the evidence should be challenged in a criminal appeal whenever possible, consistent with professional ethics. At the very least, this will help avoid having the appeals court reach the easy conclusion that legal errors were harmless. *See* M. Tigar, *Federal Appeals Jurisdiction and Practice*, § 5.06 (1987).

Mixed Questions

Better than attacking findings of fact is trying to turn them into conclusions of law. Isolating the legal components of the critical findings is what you want to do. Judge Aldisert described the process well in *Universal Minerals, Inc. v. C.A. Hughes & Co.*, 669 F.2d 98, 103 (3d Cir. 1981), where the issue was whether personal property had been abandoned:

> Abandonment is not a question of narrative or historical fact but an ultimate fact, a legal concept with a factual component. . . . It is "a conclusion of law or at least a determination of a mixed question of law and fact," . . . requiring "the application of a legal standard to the historical-fact determinations." . . . In reviewing the ultimate determination of abandonment, . . . we are therefore not limited by the "clearly erroneous" standard, . . . but must employ a mixed standard of review. We must accept the trial court's findings of historical or narrative facts unless they are clearly erroneous, but we must exercise a plenary review of the trial court's choice and interpretation of legal precepts and its application of those precepts to the historical facts.

See also Ornelas v. United States, 116 S. Ct. 1657, 1661–63 (1996); *United States v. McConney,* 728 F.2d 1195, 1200–04 (9th Cir.) (*en banc*), *cert. denied,* 469 U.S. 824 (1984). Many of the findings that burden appellants will, on close analysis, be seen to have a legal component. If a factual finding troubles you, look for a facet that reflects issues of law.

Do not waste much time analyzing jury verdicts, however. Appellate challenges to jury findings rarely succeed. In federal courts, the Seventh Amendment's proscription of reexamination of jury findings except "according to the rules of the common law" limits review of jury verdicts even more than Rule 52 already restricts review of trial court findings. A jury's verdict should not be set aside unless it has no rational basis in the evidence. *See generally* 9A C. Wright & A. Miller, *Federal Practice and Procedure* §§ 2524–2529 (2d ed. 1994). Showing *that* is an uphill path so steep it is almost vertical. If you do want to undertake the daunting climb, pay careful attention to Rule 50's procedural requirements for judgments as a matter of law.

There is a limited exception to the appellate protections accorded findings of fact. Appellate courts occasionally exercise independent judgment on pure questions of fact, despite Rule 52(a) and the Seventh Amendment. In *Bose Corp. v. Consumers Union*, 466 U.S. 485, 499 (1984), for example, the Court said that "in cases raising First Amendment issues we have repeatedly held that an appellate court has an obligation to 'make an independent examination of the whole record' in order to make sure that 'the judgment does not constitute a forbidden intrusion on the field of free expression.'" In *Ornelas v. United States*, 116 S. Ct. 1657 (1996), the Court held that reasonable suspicion for an investigative stop and probable cause to make a warrantless search present "ultimate questions" and mixed questions of fact and law requiring de novo appellate review. Appellate courts generally are quite reluctant to risk opening these floodgates, however, and it seems likely that these rules will be extended slowly and cautiously, if at all, and only when stricter appellate review is deemed necessary to assure protection of constitutional rights.

The final frontier is review of administrative agency action. Unfortunately, it is a wilderness too complex and vast to be mapped here. Suffice it to say that the standards for such review are set out in the federal Administrative Procedure Act (and state equivalents). *See* 5 U.S.C. § 706. They include every standard explained thus far in this article, and then some. As complicated as they may seem, these statutory catalogs simply hide further complexities. When agency action is involved, there are at least two kinds of legal error review, two kinds of abuse of discretion review, and three kinds of review of findings of fact. It would take many pages to sketch this out, much less to explain how to use it. It is a subject for another day.

Dangers, Toils, and Snares: Appeals Before Final Judgment

Luther T. Munford

Just as big oaks grow from little acorns, thorn hedges of appellate complication can spring from simple lawsuits. The main difference is timing. Oaks take decades to grow, but you can be in appellate brambles before you know it. Here is an example: You have filed a simple contract suit for Goodco in federal court against Breach Corp. But Breach Corp. has earlier sued Goodco in state court on the same dispute. Trying to preserve what it sees as a state court advantage, Breach Corp. moves the federal court to stay all its proceedings pending the outcome of the state suit. The judge grants Breach Corp.'s motion. Because you do not want to be hometowned, you decide to appeal the stay. The path may seem clear, but, in fact, you have just jumped into a briar patch.

The snares of the law of interlocutory appeals lie in wait whenever you try to appeal from an order rendered before entry of a judgment that settles all the rights and liabilities of all the parties. Fed. R. Civ. P. 54(b). A judgment that does fully resolve all claims will, of course, be appealable as a final decision under 28 U.S.C. § 1291. Short of that, complications abound.

Many problems confront a prospective interlocutory adventurer. First, the law on interlocutory appeals is not codified in a single place. In fact, even if you find all the applicable statutes and rules, you still will not have all the law you need. Chances are you will not even find it all in the precedents in your circuit. There is some good news, however. A number of well-organized books and treatises set forth most of what you need to know. *See, e.g.*, 9 J. Moore, *Federal Practice* ¶ 110 (1996); M.

Luther T. Munford is a partner in Phelps Dunbar, L.L.P., Jackson, Mississippi, and he is a member of both the Advisory Committee on Appellate Rules to the Judicial Conference of the United States and the Lawyer Advisory Committee of the U.S. Court of Appeals for the Fifth Circuit. He also teaches appellate practice as an adjunct professor at Mississippi College School of Law.

Tigar, *Federal Appeals Jurisdiction and Practice*, §§ 2.01–3.17 (2d ed. 1993); 15, 15A, and 16 C. Wright, A. Miller & E. Cooper, *Federal Practice and Procedure* (1992 & 1996).

Armed with the knowledge in such books, you can take the steps and make the tactical choices needed to maximize your chances of getting into a higher court, while controlling what happens in the meantime in the lower court.

Your research will teach you that you may be able to obtain interlocutory review in at least five ways. Each has different requirements, imposes different burdens, and may have different consequences. There is a lot of variety. Under certain statutes or doctrines, your client may be entitled to take an interlocutory appeal as a matter of right. Under other precepts, however, the client's fate may rest on that most precarious of all legal perches: the discretion of the trial court, or court of appeals, or both. You need to know about all of this and more.

A word of caution before marching into the thicket. What follows is, in places, complicated and technical. Illusion and reality are hard to distinguish. It provides the kind of excursions into legal history and abstract analysis that can drive practical litigators crazy. Much of it is the sort of stuff you thought you had sworn off the day you left law school. But there is no choice. Faced with the intensely practical job of relieving your client from what it believes is interlocutory outrage, you must master the arcane.

Is There a Right to Appeal?

As you do your research on behalf of Goodco, your practiced eye is alert for things that give a *right* to an interlocutory appeal. A sure thing is better than some overworked judge's discretion.

One of the first things you notice involves injunctions. A statute, 28 U.S.C. § 1292(a)(1), permits interlocutory appeals as a matter of right from orders "granting, continuing, modifying, refusing or dissolving injunctions, or refusing to dissolve or modify injunctions." The statute permits appeals when irreparable harm threatens. There is some history behind it. Historically, equity allowed interlocutory appeals, and law did not. In Dickens's day, the law court could place a criminal on the gallows long before equity had resolved the first interlocutory appeal in the *Bleak House* estate dispute.

In Goodco, you may take heart from § 1292(a). The district court's stay order certainly *seems* like injunctive relief, or at least preliminary injunctive relief. After all, it orders a case not to proceed. What could be more injunctive than that?

On this point, however, appearances often deceive. The courts have construed § 1292(a) narrowly. It does not apply to a court's stay of its own proceedings or refusal to stay those proceedings. *See Gulfstream Aerospace Corp. v. Mayacamas Corp.*, 485 U.S. 271 (1988) (overruling prior cases, which had developed a jurisprudence of unbelievable impenetrability). This means § 1292(a) is no help to Goodco. The section also does not apply to injunctionlike orders unrelated to the substantive relief sought in the case—such as an order sealing a deposition or granting an attachment—or to temporary restraining orders that can be reconsidered before they do much harm.

Appearance and Reality

The appearance-reality divide for injunctions can get even more fuzzy. Appellate courts have not let the label a district court uses control the application of § 1292(a). Just as orders that seem like injunctions may not be, so too orders not called injunctions may qualify. For example, § 1292(a) *will* support an appeal from an order rejecting a settlement agreement that includes injunctive relief.

And there are other problems. Even if—unlike with Goodco—you have the right to take an interlocutory appeal under § 1292(a), you may not want to do it. Taking an appeal from an order on preliminary injunctive relief can be a bad bet because an appeals court may defer to the district court's discretion. Worse yet, in sustaining the district court's orders, the court of appeals might compound your problems by making comments that will jeopardize your prospects for ultimate success. It might, for example, announce that your opponent has a "probability of success" on the merits. Sure, such an observation will not technically control the district court's ultimate ruling. But how do you think a trial judge is likely to rule if his appellate court has said you will probably lose? Beginning litigation with such an adverse observation compares to kicking off from your own end zone.

Two housekeeping matters concerning § 1292(a): First, under Federal Appellate Rule 4(a), a party presumably has 30 days after entry of an injunctive order to pursue an appeal under § 1292(a). The courts have not, however, construed that rule to bar a delayed appeal of the interlocutory order taken at the conclusion of the case when a final judgment is entered. A party has an option, and may decide to forgo an interlocutory appeal while preserving its right to attack the injunction when it appeals the final judgment.

Second, if you can and do take an appeal under § 1292(a), you must think about the impact of that appeal on the proceedings in the district court. It is possible that a district judge may grant a stay pending an immediate appeal, even if the judge were unwilling to grant a stay for the longer period required to conduct a trial on the merits. Unless the district court grants a stay, however, an appeal under § 1292(a) does not stay the injunction attacked, nor does it stop other proceedings in the case. *See* Fed. R. Civ. P. 62(a) and (c). You may find yourself fighting on two fronts at once, with your mind making factual decisions in one forum contingent on proceedings in the other.

If Goodco cannot say it is appealing from an injunction, does it have any other basis for an appeal of right? The answer may be yes.

The Supreme Court has identified a small class of orders that are treated as final and appealable under 28 U.S.C. § 1291, even though some claims remain to be resolved. These are known as "collateral orders."

A good example—in fact, the first example—of an appealable collateral order is one denying a motion to require a plaintiff to post a security bond. In *Cohen v. Beneficial Industrial Loan Corp.*, 337 U.S. 541 (1949), the Supreme Court held that such an order was final and appealable because it had certain important characteristics (further defined in succeeding cases). It (1) conclusively decided a disputed question, (2) resolved an important issue completely separate from the merits of the action, and (3) was effectively unreviewable on appeal from a final judgment. Applying such standards, appeals have been permitted from orders denying such motions as a request to record pretrial proceedings verbatim; a nonparty witness's motion to quash a subpoena; and a public official's motion for summary judgment based on official immunity from suit.

Fortunately for Goodco, the collateral order doctrine also applies to some stay orders. In fact, the Supreme Court has specifically sanctioned an appeal from a district court's order staying further proceedings pending the disposition of parallel state court litigation. *Moses H. Cone Memorial Hosp. v. Mercury Const. Corp.*, 460 U.S. 1 (1983). The Court determined that such an order met the collateral order tests. It was meant to be conclusive, it did not involve the merits, and it would otherwise have been unappealable because of the res judicata effect of a state court decision.

Given this, the *Cone* case may well get Goodco into appeals court. As a sidelight, and as an illustration of the significance of slight differences in this area, it is worth pointing out that if Breach Corp. had lost—if the federal case had *not* been stayed—it could not have appealed. Such an order would not be regarded as conclusive, because the district court could revise it at any time, depending on the relative progress of the state and federal cases.

Before getting lost in the tangles of collateral order law, practicing litigators should know this: It may be a dying doctrine. In recent years, the Supreme Court has repeatedly rejected attempts to classify new classes of orders as collateral. The Court has ruled, for example, that an order refusing to certify a class—sounding what had become known as the "death knell" for the case—is not an appealable collateral order. Likewise the collateral order doctrine does not apply to an order denying a motion to disqualify a lawyer, or to an order denying a motion to dismiss on grounds of immunity from process or *forum non conveniens*. See *Van Cauwenberghe v. Baird*, 486 U.S. 517 (1988).

Again, some history may help explain all this. The Supreme Court created the collateral order doctrine before the 1958 enactment of 28

U.S.C. § 1292(b). As discussed later, that section permits a district court to certify interlocutory orders for appeal without engaging in the fiction that they should be deemed final judgments. More recently Congress has given the Supreme Court the authority to adopt rules recognizing classes of interlocutory appeals, 28 U.S.C. §§ 1292(e), 2072(c). With these statutes in place, there is little reason to think that the recent trend narrowing the collateral order doctrine will be reversed. In fact, these statutes have been cited as one reason not to recognize additional categories of collateral order or other interlocutory appeals. *Swint v. Chambers County Comm'n*, 115 S. Ct. 1203, 1209–10 (1995); *Digital Equipment Corp. v. Desktop Direct, Inc.*, 114 S. Ct. 1992, 2004 (1994).

If you, like Goodco, can use the collateral order doctrine, time and trial court matters must be kept in mind. When the district court enters an order final under the collateral order doctrine, you must take an interlocutory appeal within 30 days. If you choose not to appeal, however, you will not waive your right to attack the order after final judgment. Of course, if it truly *is* a collateral order, and is therefore "effectively unreviewable," there may be nothing to attack by the time the case ends.

When appealing a collateral order, you have no right to a stay pending appeal. You have to ask for one from the district court or court of appeals, and either may deny it. In many instances, however, compelling grounds will exist to support a stay. As the order is, by definition, an important, separate decision that may dispose of the case, a judge may want to await its final resolution before proceeding. An example is a case in which a public official claims immunity from the burden of trial. He or she must have a stay pending appeal, or the right the official asserts will be destroyed before the appeal is resolved.

If you do not have a right to appeal under § 1292(a) or the collateral order doctrine, you must journey down other discretionary avenues to interlocutory review. Even if you think that you have a right to appeal, but some doubt exists, you should pursue discretionary routes as back-up insurance.

One possibility is Federal Rule of Civil Procedure 54(b). Rule 54(b) is helpful if the trial court has made a ruling that affects only part of the case. The rule provides that, when a case presents more than one claim for relief or involves multiple parties, "the court may direct the entry of a final judgment as to one or more but fewer than all of the claims or parties." The rule permits a judge to do this "only upon an express determination that there is no just reason for delay and upon an express direction for the entry of judgment."

Rule 54(b)

Orders subject to Rule 54(b) differ from decisions appealable under either § 1292(a) or the collateral order doctrine. A § 1292(a) decision involves only one element of relief, an injunction, whereas Rule 54(b) certification requires judgment on an entire cause of action. On the other hand, collateral orders, by definition, are separable from the merits, but Rule 54(b) judgments *are* judgments on the merits. As a result, if Goodco had not been able to rely on the collateral order doctrine, Rule 54(b) would not have helped. The district court's stay order did not involve the merits and did not resolve a cause of action.

In a way, Rule 54(b) exists to prevent unfairness that can arise from combining the final judgment rule with the liberal joinder provisions of the Federal Rules. Under the joinder rules, many separate, although related, claims—almost separate lawsuits—can be resolved in one action. Were it not for Rule 54(b), decisions on none of these could be appealed until all were resolved. But Rule 54(b) applies only to separately enforceable claims. It does not, for example, permit an appeal from the dismissal of an element of damages or an appeal from a successful motion in limine.

The trick in seeking Rule 54(b) certification is convincing the trial judge that a small, self-contained dispute has been disposed of within the larger litigation. Point out the separateness of the claim the order covers. Demonstrate that the remaining trial level case will be affected little, if at all, by the outcome of the appeal you want. If the order you want to attack resolves the only claim affecting your client in a multi-party dispute, say so. What you want the trial judge to believe is that someone, or something, will be spinning its wheels if an appeal is not allowed.

If the trial court certifies partial judgment under Rule 54(b), the court of appeals will review the certification only for an abuse of discretion. *Curtiss-Wright Corp. v. General Electric Co.*, 446 U.S. 1, 10–12 (1980). The standard of review for the merits of the appeal is, of course, a different matter. It is therefore important that the record reflect a reasoned certification decision by the district judge. To help ensure this, the best approach is to file a written motion stating the reasons Rule 54(b) certification is needed, and to support the motion with a brief. Even that is no guarantee of a perfect outcome. Providing a written discussion of the factors contained in the rule, however, increases the likelihood that the judge will write a defensible opinion.

If you get Rule 54(b) certification, watch the time. You must appeal within 30 days. As important—and unlike injunction or collateral order appeals—once you get a certification, you do *not* have the option of waiting until the entire case is resolved before appealing.

Nothing in life is perfect, and even the Rule 54(b) certification you want can have unhappy collateral consequences. Certification makes a judgment final for purposes other than appeal. For example, if you represent a defendant taking an appeal under Rule 54(b), certification will give the plaintiff a lien created by the judgment you have gotten certified, the power to execute on that judgment, and the accrual of interest at the judgment rate. A stay of the judgment is possible under Rule 62(b), but complications abound. *See Curtiss-Wright,* 446 U.S. at 13 n.3.

Suppose the stay entered against Goodco were not a collateral order. Rule 54(b) is no help because the merits are not involved. Is there any other route to interlocutory relief?

Yes. Under 28 U.S.C. § 1292(b), a district court may certify that an order involves a "controlling question of law" about which there is a "substantial ground for difference of opinion," and that immediate review will "materially advance the ultimate termination of the litigation."

Getting such trial court certification is only half the battle. Unlike Rule 54(b), § 1292(b) gives the court of appeals independent discretion to deny the appeal. Some of those who drafted § 1292(b) believed that certification under it should work like a decision on a grant of certiorari by the Supreme Court. An appellate court can refuse to take a certified appeal for any reason or no reason. It can even turn one down because of its caseload. This means that, when seeking certification, you should brief the issue thoroughly and forcefully in the district court. You need a thoughtful opinion from the trial judge. If the appeals court thinks the judge was cursory or casual, the chances of the appeal being turned down increase.

District judges have certified all kinds of questions under § 1292(b) in all kinds of circumstances. In contrast to Rule 54(b), no claim need be finally determined. In fact, questions concerning subject matter jurisdiction or failure to state a claim have been certified under § 1292(b), as have issues concerning disqualification of counsel and discovery. The Supreme Court has said that the section may be used even to review *forum non conveniens* or res judicata rulings in appropriate cases. Although there are no guarantees under § 1292(b), the playing field is broad.

There is no magic formula for fashioning an argument seeking § 1292(b) relief. Relying on the statute's language is a good starting place, but only a start. What you want to do is to convince both courts (trial and appellate) that the issue for appeal is important, hotly contested, and crucial to the outcome of the case. If it is a matter on which district judges in the circuit, or different circuits, disagree, point that out. Be certain to demonstrate how resolution of the issue will critically affect the lawsuit. Also, it never hurts to convince the appellate court that your probability of success on appeal is great.

In doing all this, remember the district court and appeals court will have slightly different perspectives on the appeal. The trial judge's principal interest will be case management—that is, whether appeal will move the case along. He or she will already know about the importance of the issue and the possibilities for disagreement. The appeals court, on the other hand, may be more concerned with the degree of dispute over the question, and the need to resolve it as a matter of law within the circuit.

Although it is helpful, you need not necessarily make a strong showing on all of the § 1292(b) factors. The courts have shown a willingness to relax one of the criteria if others weigh heavily in favor of appeal. For example, the ground for difference of opinion on a key jurisdictional issue need not be as strong if the district court's order permits future litigation that would be pointless if the district judge has decided the question incorrectly.

Section 1292(b) requires that an application for leave to appeal be made to the court of appeals within ten days from the certification order in the district court. Unlike Rule 54(b) certification, § 1292(b) certification does not require an immediate appeal. An aggrieved party can ignore the certification and wait until the end of litigation to seek review of the question. If a party perfects a § 1292(b) appeal, however, counsel should be aware that the appellate court is not limited to the question framed in the application and may address "any issue fairly within the certified order." *Yamaha Motor Corp., U.S.A. v. Calhoun*, 116 S. Ct. 619, 623 (1996). Also, while failure to take a § 1292(b) appeal does not bar later review, the failure may allow the opponent to cure the error, even if it was jurisdictional. *Caterpillar, Inc. v. Lewis*, 117 S. Ct. 467, 475 (1996).

Federal Appellate Rule 5(b) controls the content of the § 1292(b) petition in the court of appeals. You must specify in the petition the question to be reviewed and the reasons certification is proper. You must attach to the petition the order that you want to appeal, along with any findings or opinions relating to it. Although you must state why a substantial basis exists for a difference of opinion with the trial court's ruling, you need not brief the merits fully. Nor need you file the record with the petition. If the appellate court grants the petition, it is treated simply as a notice of appeal, and the case proceeds according to standard appellate rules; thereafter, the record is certified and briefs are filed.

Use § 1292(b) as a Backup

Because of its breadth and flexibility, § 1292(b) certification might also be considered as a backup to other grounds for interlocutory review. You may encounter a time bind, however, in using § 1292(b) to back up an attempted appeal under § 1292(a), "injunctive" appeals, or the collateral order doctrine. A notice of appeal from an injunction or collateral order must be filed within 30 days of entry of the order. If you also request § 1292(b) certification after entry of an order, the district court may not rule on that request before the 30-day appeal period has run. There are two possible solutions. First, appeal in two stages: within 30 days and then within ten days of whenever the § 1292(b) motion is decided. Second, ask the district court for an extension of time for filing a notice of appeal at the same time that you request § 1292(b) certification. However, given the fact that appeal periods are generally regarded as jurisdictional and rarely can be extended beyond what is permitted by Federal Appellate Rule 4(a)(5), the second option should be approached with great caution.

Section 1292(b) does not provide for an automatic stay of trial court proceedings. You must seek a stay in the trial court or from the court of appeals under the procedures generally governing stays. Although such requests can be refused, the risk of a two-front war is usually slight. A district court willing to certify a question for interlocutory appeal will usually also be willing to limit its proceedings until the appellate court can rule on the question.

If all else fails, and if Goodco is unable to rely on the provisions and theories already described, there are extraordinary writs. You may have thought special writs—mandamus, prohibition, and the like—live only in law schools and textbooks. In fact, the courts of appeals' power to issue special writs to review trial court matters is another way to get immediate review of interlocutory orders.

Under 28 U.S.C. § 1651(a), the courts of appeal can issue extraordinary writs. There has been a steady expansion of the use of such writs to review interlocutory trial court decisions. Do not be misled by the cases on such writs. They are usually couched in restrictive language: The right to a writ must be "clear and indisputable." The only function of a writ is to confine an inferior court to the lawful exercise of its prescribed jurisdiction or to compel it to exercise its authority when it must do so. The writs are "extraordinary" in the sense that a party seeking one must have exhausted all options in district court and must show it has no other means of effective relief.

In practice, however, these grudging limits are not quite so stringently applied. One recent treatise contends that the flexible nature of common law writs has enabled appellate courts to use them to do justice in individual cases, despite the writs' technically restrictive characteristics. M. Tigar, *Federal Appeals Jurisdiction and Practice,* § 3.04 (1993). In this view, there are—despite the usual restrictions—really four tests for the grant of an extraordinary writ:

1. Would a federal appeals court have jurisdiction over an eventual appeal in the case? This prevents a court from issuing a writ to a district court in another circuit, for example.
2. Is there an adequate remedy by ordinary appeal or otherwise? This means a petitioner must exhaust all nonwrit remedies. The case for a writ is strongest if the petitioner has exhausted all other methods of interlocutory appeal or shown why they are not available.
3. Is the district court order in question erroneous as a matter of law?
4. Is the question a recurring one, or significant and novel? This is critical. A litigant seeking extraordinary writ review should demonstrate that the court has "an opportunity to solve a knotty prob-

lem and avoid future litigation." Tigar, *supra,* at 150. The importance of the question proposed for review may be as important as the inadequacy of ordinary appeal routes.

Use of extraordinary writs can have many forms. Courts of appeal have ordered a district court to hear a transfer motion, to provide an opportunity for the opposing party to respond to such a motion, and to use the proper test in deciding it. Writs have also been used to protect the rights of nonparties—the news media and witnesses particularly—in the conduct of trials. And writs have been granted to prevent loss of the right to trial by jury.

Writ practice is flexible almost to the point of being standardless. No rule prescribes a time limit for seeking an extraordinary writ. But you should move with dispatch. One rule of thumb is that you should seek an extraordinary writ within the time you would have for taking an appeal if the district court order had been a final judgment. It is probably better to move even faster. A litigant who seems to dawdle may have trouble convincing an appeals court that there is an "extraordinary" problem.

Research on Writs

Because general writ principles do not provide much guidance in specific cases, you need to look laboriously for factually similar cases. Such research can be tricky. Computerized case search services can be used to locate cases involving the same issue in which the court *granted* the writ. A party *opposing* the writ, however, may not be able to do this. Here is why: Courts tend to write opinions when they grant a writ but not when they deny one. If there is a denial, the case simply goes back to the trial court, after issuance of a one-page unpublished appellate order. There are few extended explanations of denials of extraordinary writs.

Opponents of writ applications are not, however, without resources. They should look for decisions in which the legal issue was resolved by means other than an extraordinary writ. A string citation of cases resolving questions after a final judgment would surely call into question the petitioner's claim that the issue must be decided immediately and through the use of unusual procedures.

Federal Appellate Rule 21(a)(2) governs the contents of a petition for a writ of mandamus or prohibition. It states that the petition must contain not only the order to be reviewed but also "parts of the record that may be essential to understand the matters set forth in the petition." If the court of appeals grants the petition, the parties file briefs on the merits at a later date set by the court.

Because Rule 21 requires that part of the record be sent to the court with a petition, extraordinary writ review can have a speed advantage over other methods of interlocutory review. You may not need to wait for the preparation of a more complete record, and the court can more readily expedite the briefing schedule.

Just knowing the five main roads to interlocutory review does not mean you understand all the byways and dead ends. Consider this: Suppose that, having done your homework, you got interlocutory review of the order staying Goodco's suit. Suppose further that, against all odds, you got the stay reversed. However, after a bench trial, before the same district judge, Breach Corp. prevailed on the merits against Goodco's claims and also obtained a judgment for damages and unspecified lawyers' fees against Goodco on its counterclaim. You want to oppose the amount of fees Breach Corp. has requested.

By now, of course, you think you are thoroughly familiar with the law on interlocutory appeals. You have considered taking immediate appeal from the judgment on liability and damages; however, solicitous of the interests of justice and Goodco's cash resources, you decide to avoid piecemeal appeals. You know that Rule 54(b) provides that a merits judgment can be revised at any time until all rights and liabilities are determined, and that seems to you a good test for whether your judgment is final. Because the lawyers' fees claim of Breach Corp. remains unresolved, you conclude that the judgment on the merits remains interlocutory and that you may postpone your appeal from it until the whole case—merits *and* fees—is resolved.

Wrong. The problem is that the order you thought was interlocutory was in fact final, and it started the time running for taking an appeal. You have been fooled by an "illusory" interlocutory order. This trap exists because the Supreme Court, author of Rule 54(b), ignored that rule in *Budinich v. Becton Dickinson & Co.*, 486 U.S. 196 (1988), and adopted a new test for determining when a judgment is final. Under *Budinich,* a judgment disposing of everything *except* lawyers' fees is final and must be appealed even though the request for lawyers' fees remains for adjudication.

Budinich prompted a 1993 amendment to Fed. R. Civ. P. 58 that leaves you with three options. First, you can seek an order from the district court directing that your fee motion be treated as a motion under Fed. R. App. P. 4(a)(4), which extends the time for filing a notice of appeal until after the motion is decided. You must, however, persuade the district court to issue its order before it rules on the motion. Second, you can file a timely notice of appeal on the merits and then immediately move to stay action on the appeal until the fee question is resolved. In some circuits, the clerk can grant this motion if it is unopposed.

Finally, you can simply appeal and fight in two courts; that, of course, can turn out to be wasteful. If you win on appeal and the merits judgment is reversed, any right to fees may well evaporate. Even a modification on appeal may affect fees entitlement. This means that time spent litigating fees at the trial level may have been wholly or partly wasted.

Budinich leaves few avenues of escape for the lawyer who fails to take these precautions and allows the time for appeal to expire. Appeal periods are jurisdictional; they are rarely equitably extended. Letting them run out is big trouble. One option would be to request relief from judgment under Fed. R. Civ. P. 60(b) in the hope of obtaining a new judgment from which an appeal can be taken. Such a request is beyond the intended scope of Rule 60(b); however, a party making it would, in the words of Professor Moore's treatise, be "truly in extremis."

The moral of our final example is this: In your zeal to learn if you *can* take an appeal, do not forget to consider whether you *must* take an appeal. To borrow from the hymn, taking an appeal—particularly an interlocutory one—requires contemplation of many "dangers, toils, and snares." Even the most seasoned litigator may need "amazing grace" to survive.

Interlocutory Appeals and Mandamus

Walter J. Bonner and William D. Appler

No less an authority than the late Justice Hugo L. Black pointed out that the use of interlocutory appeals and the writ of mandamus is reserved for "exceptional circumstances." *Will v. United States*, 389 U.S. 90, 108 (1967) (concurring opinion). Yet the exceptional case, like beauty, tends to be in the eye of the beholder (or his counsel), and appellate courts frequently find that, in the words of a Fifth Circuit decision reversing an interlocutory order, "one way or another, this case is properly before us." *Hines v. D'Artois*, 531 F.2d 726, 732 (5th Cir. 1976). This article explores the ways for bringing the appellate process to bear upon various trial court rulings that would otherwise be unappealable because they are not final orders.

The receptivity of appellate courts to reviewing interim rulings may stem from the fact that the final judgment rule has always appealed more to the head than the heart. By cutting off review of important but preliminary rulings, it operates to deny substantial justice in many circumstances where the trial court's decision affects important rights that cannot be recovered even by successful appeal of the final judgment. Since appellate courts are invariably more concerned with dispensing justice than relying on technicalities, it is not entirely surprising that *well-taken* requests for relief from arbitrary interlocutory orders are frequently successful, even in circumstances where the decision is nominally adverse.

Walter J. Bonner is a senior partner in the Washington, D.C., firm of Michaels, Wishner & Bonner, where he specializes in the defense of complex white-collar criminal as well as civil cases. Mr. Bonner was lead counsel for Maurice Stans in the Stans-Mitchell trial discussed in this article. William D. Appler no longer practices law. Mr. Bonner gratefully acknowledges the invaluable assistance of his partner, Thomas A. Guidoboni, and that of Anne M. Kurtz, a third-year student at the Catholic University of America, Columbus School of Law, in preparing this article.

This is illustrated by an experience in the Second Circuit where review was sought of the refusal by the district court in the *Stans-Mitchell* case to extend the trial date to allow defense preparation. The district judge had consistently denied our requests for additional time, relying on grounds that could not withstand appellate scrutiny, if such scrutiny were available. But, it is hard to imagine a decision more completely within a trial judge's discretion, more outside the usual function of appellate courts, than establishing a trial date.

A majority of the circuit court panel felt that the setting of trial dates could not be reviewed through an interlocutory appeal, by mandamus or otherwise. But their opinion made it clear that they disagreed completely with the district court's refusal to grant the defense additional time to prepare, and explained that it

> state[d] these views so that [the judge] may again consider the matter as we hope he will. . . . If, on further reflection, the judge should adhere to his determination, a course we hope he will not follow, defendants, if convicted, will be able to raise the issue on appeal. . . .

Stans v. Gagliardi, 485 F.2d 1290, 1292 (2d Cir. 1973).

This pointed advice, supplemented by Judge Lumbard's dissenting view that mandamus could issue, led the trial court to grant the requested extension.

If *Stans-Mitchell* was one of Justice Black's "exceptional" cases (though it hardly involved an exceptional issue), there are any number of situations trial counsel face in ordinary litigation where interlocutory orders may seriously affect the case, but appear unreviewable before final judgment. Consider these hypothetical but not uncommon situations. A trial judge:

- refuses to dismiss a case although jurisdiction is lacking or a meritorious preliminary defense exists;
- stays trial proceedings pending arbitration, exhaustion of some administrative remedy, or resolution of a related case in another forum;
- quashes writs of attachment or garnishment filed before trial to ensure any judgment can be satisfied;
- denies permission to file a cross-claim or other pleading amendment, or refuses to permit intervention;
- refuses to permit depositions of certain individuals, or grants permission to take inappropriate depositions, or improperly limits or conditions depositions;
- enters orders limiting or denying discovery, or requires the production of privileged material;
- denies class action status, or consolidates or severs two trials, or refuses to do so;
- refuses to recuse himself.

While reviewing these orders would certainly amount to what Judge Godbold has colorfully described as "halting the orderly process of a case in midstream to review incidental matters which cross the current of the litigation," *Carr v. Monroe Manufacturing Co.*, 431 F.2d 384, 386 (5th Cir. 1970), federal appellate courts have reached the merits of nonfinal orders in all these circumstances.

They have done so by using the basic jurisdictional tools contained in Title 28, §§ 1291, 1292, and 1651 to develop a generally consistent body of law governing interlocutory appeals, with some variation among the federal circuits. These tools include (1) exceptions to the final order rule, (2) appealable injunctions and other specific types of orders, (3) permissive or discretionary appeals from interlocutory orders, (4) the writ of mandamus and related writs, and (5) sanctions that render an order appealable. While these approaches are sometimes said to be exclusive, more often they can be utilized together, or in successive stages where the initial approaches are unsuccessful.

The starting point for any counsel facing the question of how to appeal a nonfinal interlocutory order is a review of the judicially created exceptions to the final order rule, 28 U.S.C. § 1291, which grants the courts of appeals jurisdiction over "final decisions of the District Courts. . . ." While all decisions that do not terminate the litigation are not really final, some types of decisions—to paraphrase George Orwell in *Animal Farm*—"are more final than others." Those decisions are treated as final decisions, even when they are obviously not, thereby giving the unsuccessful trial party an absolute right to appeal them.

Certainly the best-known and most commonly used exception is embodied in Rule 54(b), Fed. R. Civ. P., which permits a district court to enter an appealable final judgment on fewer than all the claims, or in favor of fewer than all the parties, where the court makes "an express determination that there is no just reason for delay and upon an express direction for the entry of judgment." If the trial court issues a Rule 54(b) certificate, the losing party has an absolute right to appeal any issue relating to that judgment. Conversely, the court's refusal to grant a certification may be reviewable under the Cohen rule, described below, as one court of appeals has said, or possibly by mandamus.

While Rule 54(b) is commendably clear, its reach is limited, embracing only those orders that, because they dispose of one or more issues or parties, have a greater than usual claim to finality anyway. Thus, the rule is primarily a housekeeping device that allows the successful party to remove himself from the continuing litigation and enables the unsuccessful party to appeal that part of the order while trial proceedings continue.

A more important, if much less clear, second exception to the final order rule is the collateral order doctrine generally known as the Cohen rule. *Cohen v. Beneficial Industrial Loan Corp.*, 337 U.S. 541 (1949). This exception permits appeal of right from a small class of orders that adjudicate issues collateral to and clearly separable from the main action, where the issue involved is (1) too important to be denied review and (2) lost if review is delayed until final judgment. *Cohen* itself involved review of an order imposing security requirements that could not be met as a condition of the litigation, and its application has often involved such collateral matters.

The collateral order rule has been applied in other situations, however, to allow review of orders regarding trial consolidation and severance, disqualification of counsel, various orders relating to counsel fees, bail orders, and orders denying counsel to indigents. Indeed it is this versatility of the Cohen rule that accounts for some reluctance by appellate courts to apply it in circumstances where the collateral order under review does not involve access to the judicial system. Therefore, unlike most other approaches to interlocutory appeals, *Cohen*'s use may be expected to decline, perhaps in favor of broader use of "supervisory mandamus," discussed below, where there is no right to appeal and the appellate court has the discretion not to hear the case.

The Cohen rule may also be diminished by use of a third exception to the finality rule that has only recently emerged. The Gillespie rationale, still too infrequently applied to be described as a rule, stems from *Gillespie v. United States Steel Corp.*, 379 U.S. 148 (1964), where the Court concluded that orders of "marginal finality" involving issues "fundamental to the further conduct" of the litigation would be reviewed as final orders under § 1291. Alternatively, *Gillespie* can be read as permitting appeal without a § 1292(b) certificate where it is apparent that one should have been issued.

Gillespie involved, on its facts, questions relating to the extent to which state damage law concepts survived under the Jones Act, where the trial court had ruled all such issues out of the plaintiff's case. As such, the order clearly was not final for purposes of appeal, although the trial court might properly have certified it under Rule 54(b), and, generally, it has not been thought that the inconvenience of a further trial on damages, if the trial court's determination was wrong, justified appellate interference at this stage of the proceedings. Presumably, the Supreme Court's interest in the matter resulted from the fact that the question on the merits was a novel one obviously important to the conduct of all Jones Act litigation.

Thus, the *Gillespie* rationale conceivably will be applied only where the issue presented by the interlocutory order is fundamental, not only in the conduct of the particular litigation, but also in the context of general federal law. This apparently had been the Court's intention in the *Cohen* case, where the Court had noted that it was dealing with a small class of cases essentially of first impression.

A comparison of *Cohen* and *Gillespie* suggests that while the issues warranting advanced appellate review under *Gillespie* need not be collateral

(Mrs. Gillespie's claim went to the heart of her case), they may have to be more final than *Cohen* suggested. It may be that *Gillespie* reaches only circumstances where the order terminates a definite part of the litigation, such as the state damages claims involved in the latter case.

There are two additional exceptions to the final order rule that counsel must consider, although their application is not widespread. The Second Circuit proposed a "death knell" exception for orders that effectively preclude continued litigation by imposing substantial barriers to a party's proceeding. This exception is intended to deal with situations where, for example, denial of class action certification means that the remaining individual plaintiff or plaintiffs cannot reasonably be expected to pursue the case. In other words, "when a plaintiff's action is effectively dead, the order which killed it must be viewed as final." *Hines v. D'Artois*, 531 F.2d 726, 730 (5th Cir. 1976).

Even in this limited sphere, however, the Second Circuit apparently is having some doubts about the propriety of making class action certifications appealable of right, depending on whether the amount claimed by the individual plaintiff would induce counsel to take the case. Its approach has led to situations like *Korn v. Franchard Corp.*, 443 F.2d 1301 (2d Cir. 1971), where the court held that a party with a three-figure claim could appeal denial of a class action certification, while a party with a four-figure individual claim could not. This has seemed a rather arbitrary result, and most other federal appellate courts have rejected or greatly limited the death-knell doctrine, even where the remaining individual claim was so insignificant that continued litigation was most unlikely. *Hacket v. General Host Corp.*, 455 F.2d 618 (3d Cir. 1972).

It seems likely this trend will continue, given a growing judicial distaste for class actions and a concomitant absence of any perceived need to accord denials of Rule 23 certificates special appellate treatment. *See* Fed. R. Civ. P. 23. Any further expansion of the death-knell exception to broader areas is probably unnecessary because there are other available avenues to appellate review that do not involve an absolute right to appeal.

Finally, the Forgay-Conrad exception (*Forgay v. Conrad*, 6 How. 201 12 L. Ed. 404 (1848)) has more lineage than application today. It covers situations where the order entered is interlocutory because damages have not been calculated or an accounting completed, but where title to property is annulled or transferred. In these circumstances, the party receiving the property might dispose of it so the appellant's interest could not be recovered if the judgment of liability is reversed, so the courts treat the underlying order as appealable.

It is simply the existence of irreparable injury, if the unsuccessful party must wait to appeal, that accounts for the Forgay-Conrad rule. Similar notions of irreparable injury, which would result if the appellate court did not review the interlocutory order, underlie the general mandamus requirement that no alternative avenue of relief exist before the writ will issue. It would seem that treating orders as certifiable questions under Rule 54(b), or as injunctions under § 1292(a), or even as collateral orders under *Cohen,* would make the Forgay-Conrad rule unnecessary.

These five judicial exceptions to the finality doctrine reflect the practical rather than technical construction the courts have given the language of § 1291. Other exceptions will doubtlessly be developed as the courts continue to measure, in the context of particular factual situations, the policy disfavoring piecemeal appeals against the denial of justice that can occur when review of interlocutory orders is postponed. For example, one of the authors, while employed by the Department of Justice, handled a case where a district court ordered the government, under Federal Rule of Civil Procedure 30(b)(6), to produce an aircraft accident report for use in private tort litigation. Such discovery orders are ordinarily not appealable, but on being ordered to produce the report, the Secretary of the Navy raised a claim of executive privilege, which the district court ruled was untimely asserted.

Since production of the documents would destroy the privilege, the government successfully contended that the interlocutory discovery order was appealable. On the merits the court of appeals reversed the district court and concluded that the report need not be produced under the Rule 30(b)(6) procedure. *Cates v. LTV Aerospace Corp.,* 480 F.2d 620 (5th Cir. 1973). Arguably, then, discovery orders that overrule claims of privilege by private parties or involve compulsory production of documents from individuals not party to the lawsuit are subject to interlocutory appeal, although a § 1292(b) certificate, as discussed below, could also be sought.

In sum, even though appellate courts are understandably chary about delaying trials and further crowding appellate dockets, which have expanded far more rapidly than trial dockets in recent years, they can be expected to turn an understanding ear to those cases where justice is not served by the final order doctrine.

Section 1292 deals with orders frankly recognized as interlocutory but either specifically or generally appealable when the conditions laid down by Congress are met, including (in the case of § 1292(b)) the granting of permission to appeal by the trial and appellate courts.

Therefore, the second approach to appealing interlocutory orders lies in coming within the class of order expressly made appealable by § 1292(a). For the most part, such orders are specifically limited to those involving the appointment of receivers and details of the receivership, and those involving admiralty cases where appeals from decrees are allowed. There is rarely any dispute about whether a particular order falls within these categories.

Section 1292(a)(1) also permits appeals from interlocutory orders "granting, continuing, modifying, refusing, or dissolving injunctions, or refusing to dissolve or modify injunctions" unless direct review is permitted in the Supreme Court. Initially, the scope of this authority had been somewhat uncertain, since most affirmative relief involves some aspect of the injunctive power. But it is now clear that even though an order purports to enjoin, it is not considered an injunction for purposes of § 1292(a) appeal regardless of how mandatory or prohibitory its language may be, unless it *grants* or *denies* all the relief requested. 9 Moore, *Federal Practice*, ¶ 110.20[1], at 214.

Several questions have arisen as to the effect of § 1291(a) in particular areas. While temporary restraining orders are not injunctions within the meaning of the statute, they may become appealable if the trial court extends them substantially beyond the 20 days authorized in Rule 65(b). And, although the failure to act upon a motion for an injunction is not usually viewed as a denial, there may be circumstances where the trial court's delay will be equivalent to a denial if the right to the injunction is overwhelmingly clear. In such circumstances, the failure to act becomes a denial that is appealable.

The third route for appealing interlocutory orders is § 1292(b), which authorizes the district court to certify that an order (1) involves a controlling question of law, (2) as to which there is substantial ground for differences of opinion, and that (3) immediate appellate resolution will materially advance the litigation. Within ten days of the certificate's issuance, a party may petition the court of appeals to hear the case.

Most of the questions involving § 1292(b) have centered around the first requirement, since there is rarely any dispute about whether the certified issue is fairly debatable, and it is comparatively easy to determine whether the issue, when answered by the court of appeals, will advance the litigation. Indeed, if a question is "controlling" under the first requirement, its resolution will perforce advance the litigation.

The issue must be a controlling, though not necessarily dispositive, question of law. If the relevant facts are unknown or disputed, a § 1292(b) certificate may not properly issue, and if issued will be remanded by the court of appeals. *Slade v. Shearson, Hammill & Co.*, 517 F.2d 398 (2d Cir. 1974). However, when this happens, mandamus may be an appropriate route to early appellate review.

Section 1292(b) reaches only those issues not otherwise specifically appealable, under the other subsections of § 1292. Thus, when added to these routes, § 1292(b) allows virtually all interlocutory orders to become appealable if the criteria are met.

Certificates have been issued and appeals heard on orders only partially granting or denying motions for summary judgment or dismissal; orders involving the statute of limitations, jurisdiction over the person, or the correctness of class action denials; and orders involving such common legal issues as tort liability in advance of a determination of damages, the application of collateral estoppel, and whether an oral contract was enforceable. Jurisdictional questions involving pendent jurisdiction over state claims, primary jurisdiction between a federal agency and the courts, and exhaustion of administrative remedies in civil rights and other cases have been resolved in this way.

While the reach of § 1292(b) is extensive, the statute reposes the broadest discretion in the district court, and denial of the certificate is not appealable under any theory, even mandamus. *Leasco Data Processing Equipment Corp. v. Maxwell,* 468 F.2d 1326 (2d Cir. 1972). However, after such denial a mandamus petition can be filed to bring up the correctness of the disputed order. Similarly, review in § 1292(b) cases is entirely discretionary with the court of appeals, even where the certificate issues, although the trial judge's determination should and does carry considerable weight with the appellate court.

The fourth approach to obtaining review of interlocutory orders is by writ of mandamus. If none of the preceding methods of appealing an adverse interlocutory order—judicial and procedural exceptions to the finality rule affording appeal as of right under § 1291, specific interlocutory orders appealable as of right under § 1292(a), and certified interlocutory orders appealable only with appellate courts' consent under § 1292(b)—is appropriate, or if they have been tried unsuccessfully, the proper course of action is to pursue a writ of mandamus authorized by 28 U.S.C. § 1651, the All Writs Act. This statute permits "all courts established by Act of Congress [to] issue all writs necessary or appropriate in aid of their respective jurisdictions and agreeable to the usages and principles of law."

Mandamus thus stands essentially as an exceptional remedy in exceptional circumstances to provide appellate review of otherwise nonappealable interlocutory orders. It also may be the only remedy for interlocutory orders in criminal trials when these orders do not fit an exception to the finality rule, since § 1292(b) does not apply to criminal trials. But it must be used with care, since there is (even among some appellate judges) an instinctive hesitancy to apply a remedy intended for "usurpations of power" to a particular district judge.

Traditionally, mandamus was limited to those extreme circumstances where a trial judge assumed power he clearly lacked, or contumaciously refused to exercise power he had when there was a clear duty to do so. Its scope was thus limited to errors of "jurisdictional" proportions, consistent with the language of § 1651. Gradually, however, the definition of "jurisdiction" has expanded so that appellate courts will sometimes correct actions where the trial judge only seriously misused, rather than entirely lacked, the powers he exercised. Occasionally, the Supreme Court has felt it necessary to remind the lower courts that mandamus must be limited to the exceptional case, *Will v. United States, supra.*

Because the successful mandamus cases typically involve nonrecurring situations, there is little point to listing the variety of circumstances where the writ has issued. In our practices we have sought mandamus where a trial court refused to extend a trial date, refused to stay depositions to allow new counsel to be obtained, ordered the deposition of an official not subject to deposition, or refused to dismiss a case clearly brought in the wrong forum. In each situation, the trial court's error was virtually beyond dispute, and in each case we obtained the relief sought, though not in all cases through the issuance of the writ.

At the same time the Supreme Court has noted the limitations upon traditional "jurisdictional" mandamus, it has broadened the opportunity to appeal certain orders by establishing the concept of "supervisory" mandamus. It has done so in cases where the action taken was concededly well within the scope of the trial court's power, but where the issue involved was novel and important for the administration of the federal judicial system. *LaBuy v. Howes Leather Co.*, 352 U.S. 249 (1957); *Schlagenhauf v. Holder*, 379 U.S. 104 (1964).

The theory underlying supervisory mandamus is that the appellate court acts pursuant to its authority to supervise lower courts within its jurisdiction. By deciding significant and potentially far-reaching issues that usually are not brought up by appeal from a final order—such as the permissibility of ordering an examination of the defendant under Rule 35 in *Schlagenhauf*—when they are first presented, the matter is resolved for all future cases. In a sense, the court of appeals is using the happenstance of an interlocutory appeal to issue advisory opinions to all district courts in its circuit.

Supervisory mandamus will have its greatest effect as a vehicle for reviewing discovery orders that present unresolved and important issues. So far, its expansion beyond this has largely been in the area of criminal rather than civil issues, where opportunities to appeal by other means are much more restricted than in civil cases. For example, supervisory mandamus was used for review of trial court orders refusing to act on an indictment, ordering the government to disclose certain monitored conversations, and prohibiting the government from using statements of particular witnesses, all in criminal trials.

Whatever the type of mandamus relief sought, jurisdictional or supervisory, its invocation has frequently been useful even where the writ does not issue. Often the court will review the merits of the request, state how it believes the trial judge should have decided the issue, but decline to issue the writ for technical reasons, as it did in the *Stans* case discussed above. It is rare that the district court does not "get the message" and grant the relief voluntarily.

The Supreme Court followed this course in *Kerr v. United States District Court*, 426 U.S. 394 (1976). In that case the district court ordered a parole board to provide certain prisoner information to plaintiffs, refusing the board's request for a prior in camera inspection, and the court of appeals affirmed. While the Court would not issue the requested writ of mandamus, since no novel issue was involved in this routine discovery order, it stated that in camera review "is a relatively costless and eminently worthwhile method" that the Court itself had long considered proper. Therefore, it was "confident that the Court of Appeals did in fact intend to afford the petitioners the opportunity to . . . receive in camera review."

This rather common practice of announcing the lower court's error, but refusing to issue a writ not meeting the technical requirements for mandamus, was the focus of a dissenting opinion by Justice Rehnquist in *Connor v. Coleman*, 425 U.S. 675, 680–81 (1976). He suggested that by assuming the lower court would act consistently with the language employed in denying the writ, the Court was using the "iron fist which shows so clearly through the Court's velvet glove. . . ." Thus, even where mandamus may not seem technically appropriate, but is an attempt to rectify a potentially disastrous interlocutory order, the practitioner will surely welcome the iron hand of the appellate court, however gloved.

There is a fifth method for obtaining review of interlocutory orders that may be used when no other approach is successful. The party may respectfully decline to comply with the nonappealable order, and suggest the trial court impose as a sanction dismissal of the action, or a contempt citation. If the court does so, appeal becomes proper from either of these orders. This practice has been used in some earlier government cases, where documents were ordered produced in discovery, but no claim of privilege could be asserted, and no important question justifying supervisory mandamus was presented.

This approach must be carefully used, since if the trial judge was correct, dismissal of the case will be affirmed, or the contempt penalty sustained. Moreover, a contempt citation is appealable only where it is criminal rather than civil contempt. Although the distinction between the two is somewhat blurred, a criminal contempt sanction punishes past conduct, while civil contempt penalties are generally intended to bring about the desired action, ceasing when the action is taken. Even a corporate fine of $150,000 per day has been held to involve civil contempt, and therefore not to support appeal of the underlying order that had been disobeyed.

Regardless of which of these methods for reviewing interlocutory orders is used, there are certain tactical approaches the practitioner should keep in mind. First, interlocutory review is not likely to be successful unless the court of appeals can be shown that justice is truly being denied by the particular trial court action. Even more than with requests for injunctions, interlocutory appeals must be aimed at the court's sense of fairness and equity. Arguments that center around technical rules of law and convoluted doctrines from ancient cases, however flawlessly reasoned, are not the route to successful interlocutory efforts, particularly where the court of appeals has discretion not to hear the appeal (such as under section 1292(b) or by mandamus.)

Second, the denial of justice to the appealing party has to be shown, with unmistakable clarity, in the brief's statement of facts. The noted appellate expert Frederick Bernays Wiener (*Briefing and Arguing Federal Appeals*) stresses the importance of the factual presentation in all appellate efforts, pointing to the example of a former Supreme Court justice who allowed his law clerks to draft his legal opinions but always wrote the factual portions of those opinions himself.

In our office, we have applied the rule that a brief is not properly done unless it is possible to cut out the argument portion, file only the statement of facts, and be reasonably sure that nothing more need be submitted to the court. Frequently, more time is spent combing the record for the facts, and polishing them through repeated sentence-by-sentence editing, than is spent researching the relevant case law. Appellate courts can distinguish cases when convinced by the facts, and this is nowhere more true than in interlocutory appeals.

Third, it is axiomatic that you cannot have an effective statement of facts unless you have taken care to make a proper record in the trial court. While counsel usually are well aware of getting the material necessary for ultimate appeal into the record at trial, much less thought is commonly given to making a record for appeal of an adverse interlocutory order. This means that counsel must consider the areas where he or she might lose important preliminary points from the beginning of the case.

For example, it was apparent to us early in the *Stans-Mitchell* case that we were going to have difficulty getting the time needed to prepare this complex case. Accordingly, at every opportunity, we put our requests for more time on the record, with appropriate supporting documentation. The trial judge's repeated refusals, despite the well-justified requests before him, made an effective presentation in our petition for mandamus, where their recitation took 17 of the 29 pages. Because we convinced the court of appeals on the facts, we were ultimately successful even though a majority felt mandamus could not issue.

When the trial court issues an unexpected order, so that counsel has not had the opportunity to put in important factual material, it is essential to move for reconsideration of the decision and submit whatever evidence or other items are available with the motion, before seeking appeal. The interlocutory appeal then can be taken from the denial of reconsideration with as favorable a record as possible. This is the course followed in the *Cates* case, described above, where the trial court ordered the government to produce documents, and a motion for reconsideration was made to assert a claim of executive privilege. The district court felt the claim was raised too late, but the court of appeals concluded that it was the assertion of the privilege (whenever raised) that made the interlocutory order appealable as an exception to § 1291.

It is most helpful if the underlying legal issue for which review is sought is, or can be made to appear, important or of first impression. Casting the issue in some way as exceptional, as was done by interweaving Rule 30(b)(6) and Rule 45 in the *Cates* case, increases the likelihood that the court of appeals will hear the case.

Thus, the practitioner must be flexible in selecting his method for reviewing an interlocutory order, careful in presenting the issue to stress the denial of justice, aware of the need to present the facts convincingly (prepared by constructing the necessary record), and skillful in framing the issue as uniquely as possible. When this is done, the final order rule is certainly not the final word for interlocutory orders.

Final word or not, the practitioner should be aware that Congress has delegated rulemaking authority in the area of interlocutory appeals to the Supreme Court. Since 1988, when the Federal Courts Study Committee was established to study United States courts and report its findings to Congress, there has been a movement to deal with the murkiness of appealable orders and the final judgment rule. After much study, the committee suggested that Congress delegate to the Supreme Court the authority to define what constitutes a final decision, and to define circumstances in which an otherwise nonfinal interlocutory order could be appealed to a circuit court.

Congress adopted both of these recommendations. In 1990, it passed the Federal Study Committee's Implementation Act. Section 315 of the act added subsection (c) to 28 U.S.C. § 2072, giving the Supreme Court the rulemaking power to define a "final" decision under § 1291. Then, in 1992, Congress passed the Federal Courts Administration Act. Section 101 of the act added subsection (e) to 28 U.S.C. § 1292, giving the Supreme Court the power to define circumstances in which an otherwise nonfinal interlocutory order could be appealed. Subsection (e) states the "[t]he Supreme Court may prescribe rules, in accordance with § 2072 of this title, to provide for an appeal of an interlocutory decision to the courts of appeals that is not otherwise provided for under subsections (a), (b), (c), or (d)." This language is intended to empower the Court to enlarge the list of appealable interlocutory determinations, but not curtail it. H.R. Rep. No. 1006 (Part I), 102 Cong., 2d Sess. 18 (1992).

One commentator, who likens existing exceptions to the final judgment rule to a "patchwork" created by Congress and the courts, believes, with the passage of 28 U.S.C. §§ 1292(e) and 2072(c), "that the time has come to unstitch this crazy quilt so that litigants can spend more time arguing about the merits of their cases and less time arguing about when they can argue." John C. Nagel, "Replacing the Crazy Quilt of Interlocutory Appeals Jurisprudence with Discretionary Review," 44 *Duke L.J.* 200, 201 (1994).

While the Supreme Court has yet to devise a list of appealable interlocutory determinations under § 1292(e), it has acknowledged that it is the *only* Court that has the rulemaking authority to expand the list of appealable interlocutory determinations. *Swint v. Chambers County Com'n.*, 115 S. Ct. 1203 (1995). In *Swint*, the proprietors, an employee, and a patron of a nightclub sued, among others, police officers and a county commission for alleged civil rights violations that occurred during a raid on the nightclub. *Id.* at 1204. The district court denied the summary judgment motions of all defendants, ruling that the police officers were not entitled to qualified immunity from suit, but stating that it would rule dispositively on the county's liability before jury deliberations. *Id.*

The police officers, invoking the rule that an order denying qualified immunity is appealable before trial, *Michell v. Forsyth*, 472 U.S. 511, 530 (1985), immediately appealed. *Id.* The county commission also appealed, arguing that "denial of its summary judgment motion" was immediately appealable as a collateral order satisfying the test in *Cohen v. Beneficial Industries Loan Corp.*, 337 U.S. 541, 546 (1949) ("decisions that are conclusive, that resolve important questions apart from the merits of the underlying action, and that are effectively unreviewable on appeal from final judgment may be appealed immediately"). The county commission argued, alternatively, that the Eleventh Circuit had "pendent appellate jurisdiction." *Id.* While disagreeing with the county commission's initial argument, the Eleventh Circuit decided to assert "pendent appellate jurisdiction" to review the commission's liability. *Id.* It described this "pendent appellate jurisdiction" as "discretionary" and "concluded that judicial economy warranted its exercise in the instant case. . . ." *Id.* at 1208.

The Supreme Court disagreed, holding that "[t]he Eleventh Circuit's authority immediately to review the District Court's denial of the individual police officer defendants' summary judgment motions did not include authority to review at once the unrelated question of the County Commission's liability." The Court went on to say that the district court's preliminary ruling regarding the county did not qualify as a "collateral order," and that there is no "pendent party" appellate jurisdiction of the kind the Eleventh Circuit purported to exercise. *Id.* at 1212.

Justice Ginsburg, writing for the Court, rejected the Eleventh Circuit's procedural actions, stating that there will be no further "expansion of appellate jurisdiction in the manner endorsed by the Eleventh Circuit." *Id.* at 1210. She went on to say that, by enacting § 1292(e), Congress has "empowered *this Court* to clarify when a decision qualifies as 'final' for appellate review purposes, and to expand the list of orders appealable on an interlocutory basis." Having so stated, Justice Ginsburg made clear, however, that the procedure Congress ordered for such changes is not expansion by court decision, but by *rulemaking* under § 2072." *Id.* At 1211 (Emphasis added). Judge Ginsburg emphasized that the Court's rulemaking authority is constrained by statute and requires, "among other things, that meetings of bench-bar committees established to recommend rules ordinarily be open to the public . . . and any proposed rule be submitted to Congress before the rule takes effect."

Thus, the Court has invoked its power under § 1292(e) and § 2072 to stymie the growth of exceptions to the final judgment rule by court decision. It has stated emphatically that it is the only entity by law possessing power to cut through the murkiness of interlocutory appeals. However, litigators must still question when, and if, the Court will, as Nagel described it, "unstitch the crazy quilt" of exceptions. To date, although the Court has pronounced its power to clarify when a decision qualifies as "final," pursuant to § 2072(c), it has failed to prescribe rules that would expand the list of orders appealable on an interlocutory basis pursuant to § 1292(e).

Posttrial Alchemy: Judgments as a Matter of Law

Franklin A. Nachman

Here is a nightmare you do not want to experience. I have lived it twice.

On first reading, the complaint against your client looks extremely doubtful. You investigate the facts and conclude that no sane person could expect to recover. The legal theories are out of *Alice in Wonderland*. Even if they had substance, they are hopelessly misapplied to the factual allegations. In short, the case is a sure winner for your side. You may have even told your client that there is nothing to worry about.

Things begin to unravel a strand at a time. Your well-founded motion to dismiss for failure to state a claim is denied. Undaunted, you take extensive discovery and file a thoroughly convincing motion for summary judgment, which the court also inexplicably denies.

Still confident of eventual success, you go to trial. The evidence proceeds as expected. But, keeping your streak intact, the court denies your motion for judgment as a matter of law (known as a "directed verdict" before the 1991 amendments to the Federal Rules). The jury receives the case for deliberation. Several agonizing hours later, the jurors file back in; none will look you in the eye. With a surprised expression, the judge reads the verdict form. The jury tells your client to find its checkbook and start writing large numbers.

Now is the time for posttrial alchemy. You give your horrified client the usual advice: "Don't worry, we'll win on appeal." But you wish it were simply a matter of turning the base metal of an adverse jury verdict into the gold of a judgment in your client's favor. In fact, it may be just that, through the use of a successful motion for a posttrial judgment as a matter of law.

Until the 1991 amendments to the Federal Rules of Civil Procedure, Rule 50(a) "motions for judgment as a matter of law" made during trial

---

Franklin A. Nachman practices law with the firm of Littler Mendelson in Denver, Colorado.

were designated "motions for directed verdict." Rule 50(b) "motions for judgments as a matter of law" made after the jury returned its verdict were designated "motions for judgment notwithstanding the verdict" (JNOV). The commentary to the 1991 amendments as well as subsequent case law confirm that the standard for granting these motions has not changed. One court has held use of the former terms was not fatal to such a motion. *Fleet Nat. Bank v. Anchor Media Television, Inc.*, 45 F.3d 546 (1st Cir 1995). Because courts were required to apply the same standards to motions for directed verdicts and posttrial judgments as a matter of law, a change in terminology was reasonable to avoid confusion.

The orthodoxy on posttrial judgments as a matter of law is not encouraging: They are sparingly granted. Still, juries can and do make mistakes, and trial courts will sometimes correct them.

Some cases are better candidates for a successful posttrial motion for judgment as a matter of law than others. Obviously, if the evidence in a case was closely balanced, a judge will not disturb a jury's verdict. If the verdict turned on the credibility of witnesses or resolution of disputed evidence, you may get an *A* on your posttrial motion for judgment as a matter of law, but it will mean the verdict is Acceptable. Conversely, where the evidence was largely undisputed and witness credibility was not an issue, a posttrial judgment as a matter of law is more likely.

It is not just the balance of the evidence that governs whether a verdict can be turned around. Suits in which the plaintiff's burden of proof is especially heavy generate more than their share of successful posttrial motions for judgment as a matter of law. These include fraud cases requiring proof by clear and convincing evidence, civil rights cases involving proof of intentional discrimination, and public figure defamation cases where malice must be proven.

Other likely posttrial judgment as a matter of law candidates are cases involving emotional factors that can overwhelm the merits. Examples are Age Discrimination in Employment Act cases, in which the plaintiff is an older, long-term employee and the apparent victim of unfairness, although not necessarily of age discrimination. Similarly, large verdicts may disappear at the stroke of a judge's pen in product liability cases involving inherently unbelievable expert testimony. Posttrial judgments as a matter of law are also sometimes granted in cases where the court concludes it has erred by submitting to the jury issues that should have been resolved as matters of law; an example is governmental immunity defenses in civil rights cases. Finally, complex cases such as antitrust, patent, and copyright suits may be candidates for posttrial relief because their complexity may have completely confused the jury.

Judgment During or After Trial?

In cases where evidence of liability is thin, there is another reason why posttrial judgment as a matter of law may be granted. Appellate decisions tell trial courts to deny motions for judgment as a matter of law even if there is limited evidence, and to give the case to the jury. Thereafter, if the jury still finds for the plaintiff, the trial court may dispose of the case by a posttrial judgment as a matter of law. The theory behind this is judicial economy: An improperly granted preverdict judgment as a matter of law requires a new trial, but an improperly granted posttrial judgment as a matter of law will merely result in the jury's verdict being reinstated. *See, e.g., Konik v. Champlain Valley Physicians Hospital,* 733 F.2d 1007, 1013 n.4 (2d Cir. 1984).

There is an old saying that "if you're going to be in the race, you've got to have a horse." So it is with postverdict motions. Obtaining posttrial relief starts at the beginning of the case, not after the verdict is rendered. Several procedural and substantive obstacles impede obtaining a posttrial judgment as a matter of law. To improve your chances of getting a posttrial judgment as a matter of law if you need it, you must anticipate an unreasonable adverse jury verdict as part of your trial preparation.

You begin by understanding the case; try to determine what factual and legal issues are strong enough to bring judgment in your client's favor if a jury finds your case less than irresistible. Nothing is more frustrating than learning—after discovery is over—that you have not covered an important element of the opposition's case because of incomplete research. Emphasize the other side's weak points: If the opposition's case rests crucially on evidence that may not be admissible, seek its exclusion before and during trial. In addition, to the extent that arguments about factual issues can be avoided, the possibility for overturning an adverse verdict increases.

Another midtrial consideration: You cannot understand how to get a posttrial judgment as a matter of law without understanding preverdict judgments as a matter of law. Under Rule 50(b) of the Federal Rules of Civil Procedure (and analogous state rules), motions for a preverdict judgment as a matter of law at the close of the adverse party's evidence *and* at the close of all evidence are prerequisites to a motion for a posttrial judgment as a matter of law. (The previously recognized exceptions to this rule are no longer valid.)

Stringent Standards

The standard for granting a judgment as a matter of law is stringent: A court will grant a judgment as a matter of law only when, without weighing the credibility of the witnesses or otherwise considering the weight of the evidence, there can be but one verdict reached by reasonable jurors. Wright & Miller, *Federal Practice and Procedure: Civil* § 2524. A "mere scintilla" of evidence supporting a verdict is not enough.

If you anticipate that a plaintiff's case will be weak and believe a judgment as a matter of law motion looms on the legal horizon, you should consider educating the court *before* trial. Even an unsuccessful summary judgment motion can alert the court to flaws in the opposition's evidence and legal theories. Such a summary judgment motion can act as a trial brief, addressing the facts and law and emphasizing that only one verdict is reasonable, even if the jurors later fail to follow your arguments.

There is a kind of logic behind making a judgment as a matter of law motion a prerequisite to a posttrial judgment as a matter of law request. Spelling it out may clarify what you should be thinking about during trial. The idea—slightly overstated—is this: In considering a posttrial motion for judgment as a matter of law, a trial judge must discount defense witnesses and evidence so much that it is almost as if they were never offered; that is, he can grant a posttrial motion for judgment as a matter of law only if the plaintiff's case, essentially standing alone, would not have supported a plaintiff's verdict from a reasonable jury. (Ignore the rare case where the defendant blunders and introduces evidence improving the plaintiff's case.)

Given this standard, here is the reason a motion for judgment as a matter of law is a prerequisite to one for a posttrial judgment as a matter of law: If, discounting the defense case, the jury's verdict is unreasonable, then the plaintiff's case should have appeared insufficient when it closed. To put it another way, if you did not give the judge a chance to dump an inadequate plaintiff's case when it ended, you cannot ask him to turn around the jury's verdict after days of additional trial time.

Procedural details are important in this area. By rule, motions for judgment as a matter of law may be made at any time before the case is submitted to the jury. If the motion is made before the close of evidence, it can be renewed after the verdict by filing a motion no later than 10 days after the entry of judgment. If the motion is made at the close of all the evidence, though, the court "is considered to have submitted the action to the jury subject to the court's later deciding the legal questions raised by the motion." See Rule 50(b).

It is particularly easy to forget renewal of a judgment as a matter of law motion at the close of evidence. It is a busy time. A lawyer may be preoccupied with questioning the crucial witnesses, cross-examining rebuttal witnesses, and preparing jury instructions or final argument. He or she may assume that the court's denial of the motion for judgment as a matter of law at the close of the opponent's case would make renewing the motion fruitless. Do not fall into that trap. Though some courts may rescue counsel who fail to renew the motion, the best course is to assume nothing. Renew the motion, either orally or in writing.

Also pay attention to the form of your judgment as a matter of law motion. Rule 50(a)(2) requires that a motion for judgment as a matter of law "shall specify the judgment sought and the law and the facts on which the moving party is entitled to the judgment." This language suggests that technical compliance will no longer be excused when the moving party has objected to jury instructions on the basis of insufficient evidence or when resolution of the issue is strictly a matter of law and no formal motion has been made.

If all else fails, and you have neglected to renew a motion for judgment as a matter of law, hope that opposing counsel fails to point out your oversight when you seek a posttrial judgment as a matter of law. This may bar him from raising the waiver issue on appeal. *Collins v. State of Illinois*, 830 F.2d 692 (7th Cir. 1987).

Despite these possible safety nets, it is better to do things right. Relying on procedural twists and hoping for appellate liberality can be avoided by advance preparation. The issues germane to a motion for judgment as a matter of law should have been addressed in a trial brief; little additional time and effort should be required to draft written motions arguing the reasons the case should not be submitted to the jury. There is no good excuse for not reading the rules or not following them.

Though you may still be in shock from the jury's verdict, the first step after trial (assuming you have made the appropriate motions during trial) is to calculate the deadline for filing your posttrial motion for a judgment as a matter of law. Rule 50(b) of the Federal Rules of Civil Procedure requires the motion to be filed no later than ten days after entry of the verdict. The requirement is stringent: The ten-day period cannot be extended. *Johnson v. New York, New Haven & Hartford R.R. Co.*, 344 U.S. 48 (1952).

A posttrial motion for a judgment as a matter of law can be combined with a motion for a new trial, and doing that makes good sense. Since the standard for granting a new trial because of insufficient evidence is less stringent than for a posttrial judgment as a matter of law, a conditional request for a new trial is always a wise backup. There is another benefit even if you succeed in getting a posttrial judgment as a matter of law. In granting your posttrial motion for a judgment as a matter of law, the trial court can also decide whether you would be entitled to a new trial if an appeals court reverses the posttrial judgment as a matter of law. This means you can carry your backup protection with you on appeal.

Even if a lawyer seeking a posttrial judgment as a matter of law has cleared all procedural hurdles, the depressing fact remains that opposing counsel holds most of the cards. The Seventh Amendment, and other factors, mean that jury verdicts will have a certain sanctity. The jury system would be subverted if judges could freely substitute their judgments for those of juries. Therefore, the standards for granting a posttrial judgment as a matter of law favor the nonmoving party. In fact, before Rule 50 was passed in 1937, some doubt existed about whether granting a posttrial judgment as a matter of law was even constitutional. *See* 5A *Moore's Federal Practice* Rule 50.07[1].

The standard for granting a posttrial judgment as a matter of law has been stated in many different, but essentially similar, formulas. (A passing note: In diversity cases, courts disagree whether a federal or state standard should be applied to deciding a posttrial motion for a judgment as a matter of law. This rarefied debate is, however, largely academic; no case has involved federal and state standards distinct enough to make any difference.) Trial and appellate courts ordinarily consider *all* the evidence and not just the evidence that supports the nonmoving party's case. Such evidence is evaluated by indulging in all reasonable inferences most favorable to the party opposing the posttrial motion for judgment as a matter of law. If such evidence and inferences point so strongly in favor of the moving party that the court believes a reasonable jury could not arrive at a contrary verdict, the motion is granted. Conversely, if the evidence is such that reasonable and fair-minded jurors might reach different conclusions, the motion will be denied, and the jury verdict will stand. Again, a "mere scintilla" of evidence is insufficient to support a verdict.

These are broad—but not very informative—pronouncements. How do you make motions based on such vague, but demanding, standards succeed? You must spend the entire trial not only putting on your case but also fortifying your strong points: an unanswered bit of key evidence; total lack of critical proof by the other side; a fatal admission by an opposing witness. Long before you file a posttrial motion for a judgment as a matter of law, you must remind the judge of these points.

In this respect, trials are like athletic contests. Regardless of their length, the outcome is often decided during a small percentage of the respective proceedings. A few plays in a football game, or a few minutes of testimony from a crucial witness, may decide everything. Two personal experiences in litigation illustrate this.

Jailed in Saudi Arabia

Gregory Crossman spent 11 months in a Saudi Arabian jail for theft. He wanted someone to pay for this unpleasant experience. He chose Trans World Airlines, which originally had hired him to work for Saudi Arabian Airlines (Saudia) as a technician. The basis for his claim was an alleged promise by TWA that "TWA would always be there should . . . employees ever need any assistance, [and] that TWA would not abandon their American partners or people." Since TWA had failed to extricate him from a foreign jail, Crossman brought a five-count complaint for breach of contract, fraud, and outrageous conduct.

Motions practice started immediately. The court dismissed one breach of contract count and the outrageous conduct count, leaving one count for breach of contract and two for fraud. Following an unsuccessful summary judgment motion by TWA, the parties went to trial.

The court had been informed of TWA's defenses in the summary judgment motion, but more was needed. I therefore submitted an extensive pretrial brief outlining what Crossman had to prove to prevail. The point was to demonstrate how much he had to show, but how little he could show on key points. His fraud claims appeared especially weak. They required Crossman to prove *all* of the following elements: (1) that TWA made a promise of future conduct with a present intention not to perform; (2) that TWA knew or should have known the promise was false or that it made the promise without knowing its truth or falsity; (3) that TWA made the misrepresentation with an intent to induce Crossman to rely on it; and (4) that Crossman was proximately injured by TWA's conduct.

Discovery had revealed—and the trial brief reminded the judge—that Crossman could not satisfy any of these elements. In particular, discovery showed these facts as undisputed: The question of what TWA would do if an American employee were jailed in Saudi Arabia was never discussed before Crossman took the job. In fact, Crossman admitted that he never thought about the matter. Correspondingly, because no American employee had ever been jailed for theft before Crossman, the TWA employee making the alleged misrepresentation could not have anticipated the crime or the result. Furthermore, Crossman signed an agreement absolving TWA of responsibility for employee criminal conduct abroad.

And that was not all. Crossman did not attempt to contact TWA when he was arrested; instead, he called the American Embassy, an entity more likely than an airline to influence a foreign government. Finally, TWA was not involved in Crossman's arrest, and the evidence suggested Crossman did what he was accused of.

It seemed an inescapable conclusion that (1) an unequivocal promise had *not* been made to keep Crossman out of jail; (2) any vague statement about "always be[ing] there" could *not* have been made with an intent to breach it; (3) in acting as he did at the time, Crossman did *not* rely on anything TWA had said; and (4) there was *no* proof of injury from anything TWA did. The trial brief and the summary judgment motion extensively covered these points, but the judge was not moved. We moved on to trial in the federal courthouse in Chicago.

Crucial Testimony

A key point in the trial came when Crossman testified about the supposed promise. His testimony made clear that, if made at all, TWA's promise was extremely vague. Crossman was, in fact, uncertain that a promise really was ever made. The questioning proceeded as follows:

Q: And the dealings with the government, . . . were those discussed?
A: No, not that I can remember, not particularly.

Q: And you didn't ask what that meant—"looking after dealings with the government"—whatever it was that you said?
A: I *assumed* in any dealing. [emphasis added]
Q: That was an assumption that you made, is that right?
A: That was the representation that I believe was made.

I argued (unfortunately unsuccessfully) that Crossman's misunderstanding of the alleged avuncular statement by TWA—or his private assumptions—did not add up to a promise, and certainly could not make any presumed promise fraudulent.

After Crossman's evidence was in, I followed the prescribed steps of Rule 50 and moved for judgment as a matter of law at the close of plaintiff's case. The court granted the motion on the breach of contract count. More than that, though he submitted the fraud counts to the jury, the judge said he would have a difficult time upholding a plaintiff's verdict on them.

The jury deliberated nearly eight hours; it returned a verdict for Crossman on one of the two fraud counts. I quickly reminded the judge of his statement at trial, and I filed what I thought was a cogent motion for posttrial judgment as a matter of law. Despite this, the judge denied my motion and allowed the verdict to stand. It was time to ride the elevator to the top floor of the Dirksen Federal Building and begin a two-year appellate journey.

The Court of Appeals for the Seventh Circuit heard the same evidence and legal arguments but arrived at a different conclusion. *Crossman v. Trans World Airlines*, 777 F.2d 1271 (7th Cir. 1985). Because the appeals court could not weigh the evidence, it assumed as fact that the "we'll be there for you" statement was made, despite TWA's denial. Still, even though it assumed the statement was made, the court found no proof that Crossman relied on that promise to his detriment. I had emphasized Crossman's post-arrest thinking and actions—his call to the embassy, not TWA, for example—in my Rule 50 motions, and it finally paid off in the Seventh Circuit. The appeals court held that the trial court should have granted posttrial judgment as a matter of law and entered judgment for TWA.

The swing vote in the *Crossman* case (a 2-to-1 decision) was cast by a senior district judge. His first question at oral argument implied that I was asking the appeals court to decide disputed factual issues. My response, which he apparently accepted, emphasized the lack of *any* probative evidence to support the four elements of proof. It did not matter whom you believed, I suggested; there was *nothing* to support Crossman's claims.

The *Crossman* case illustrates why fraud suits are overrepresented among posttrial judgment as a matter of law decisions. The plaintiff must prove a number of demanding elements to establish his case. Often—

despite the jury's feeling that something should be done—there is no evidence on one of those elements. See also *Colonial Lincoln-Mercury, Inc. v. Musgrave,* 749 F.2d 1092 (4th Cir. 1984); *Aaron Ferer & Sons v. Chase Manhattan Bank,* 731 F.2d 112 (2d Cir. 1984); *Liberty Leather Corp. v. Callum,* 653 F.2d 694 (1st Cir. 1981).

A bizarre product liability case provided my second experience with the vagaries of juries and Rule 50. Robert "Bo" Rein was hired in 1979 as the head football coach of Louisiana State University. Unfortunately, he never lived to coach a game at LSU, much to the sorrow and disappointment of Tiger fans.

On the evening of January 10, 1980, Coach Rein boarded an almost new Cessna Conquest airplane in Shreveport, Louisiana, for a short flight to Baton Rouge. Because of thunderstorms between the two cities, air traffic controllers routed the pilot east, and then south, to avoid the weather. The aircraft headed east but exceeded its 25,000-foot altitude clearance. At that point, air traffic control tried unsuccessfully to contact the pilot, as did a commercial pilot in the area. The Cessna continued flying at an altitude of approximately 40,000 feet. Air Force jets dispatched to follow the plane observed no signs of life in the cabin, although the aircraft appeared intact. Several hours after departure, the plane plunged into the Atlantic Ocean. Neither the Cessna nor the bodies of the pilot and passenger were recovered.

All sorts of theories, including sabotage, were offered to explain the tragedy, but none could be proven. Suits by the estates of the pilot and passenger, and by the company that insured the aircraft, were consolidated for discovery and trial. After the wrongful death case was settled, the subrogation suit of the insurer against two product manufacturers and the seller of the aircraft went to trial. There was a glaring weakness in the plaintiff's case: no direct evidence of any component's failure in the brand new Cessna. The aircraft was never recovered; the pilot never radioed any medical emergency or equipment failure to air traffic control; and those observing the aircraft saw no signs of structural damage. To this day, the cause is a mystery.

Mere lack of evidence did not deter the plaintiff's expert, however. He was a jack-of-all-aviation-trades who had gone from the desert of aeronautical engineering to the promised land of the consulting expert. He may have been the inspiration for Ishmael Reed's novel *The Freelance Pallbearers*. He traveled the country helping to bury opposing parties.

Unhampered by facts, the expert had a theory. It began with a simple, but uninformative, proposition: If a plane crashes, something must have gone wrong. Then, based on the scant evidence, the expert opined that the Cessna's pressurization system had failed. Finally, he fingered the cabin pressure outflow valves, manufactured by my client, as the specific culprits, even though he admitted he could not say for sure how the cabin pressurization system, checked and found functional on the very day of the tragedy, failed.

The expert's limitations surfaced during discovery. An extensive trial brief was filed, arguing that his pyramiding of inferences, and the insufficient basis for his opinion, violated Rules 702 and 703 of the Federal Rules of Evidence. The brief cited several analogous product liability cases arising in Louisiana and the Fifth Circuit as justification for granting judgment as a matter of law.

Despite these fatal shortcomings, the court allowed the expert to testify. To his credit, the expert was consistent with his deposition testimony; he was just as inconclusive at trial as in discovery. In court, the crucial failing was the expert's repeated inability to say which of two mutually exclusive product failures was more likely to have occurred. The questioning proceeded as follows:

Q: The [cabin outflow] valve failed to operate properly?
A: That's correct.
Q: Then it failed in an open position?
A: I said either one, open or closed.
Q: I thought that you said that it was open, that you felt it failed open.
A: One failure mode will fail it in the open position [i.e., pressure will escape directly through an open valve] and the other failure mode in the closed position, pressuring the aircraft and resulting in structural damage in the aircraft, then the loss of pressurization as a result of the structural failure [i.e., the closed valve will overpressurize the plane, causing structural damage and then loss of pressure].
Q: So you have two scenarios?
A: That's correct....
Q: Which happened? You don't know which one happened?
A: No, I don't know, sir.
Q: You don't know whether it failed opened or closed?
A: No, I don't.
Q: You don't know whether there was an initial underpressurization or an initial overpressurization?
A: That's correct....
Q: Under the scenario of having the closed valve failure you would have to assume that you had a double failure? [I.e., the valve sticks closed and then there is structural failure.]
A: That's correct.
Q: Do you have anything to show that it happened in this case?
A: No, sir....
Q: Which of those two is more likely in your opinion, sir?

A: Well, I have difficulty which is the most likely . . . the best I can say either one of them could happen. . . .
Q: As you sit here today, you can't tell the jury or us which one of those is more likely?
A: No way I could do that.

After a two-week trial, the jury returned a $964,000 plaintiff's verdict. Apparently, they thought that because something went wrong, someone should pay.

Attacking the Expert

The expert's testimony became the core point on which to attack the verdict. After I filed the usual posttrial motions, the district court ordered and reviewed the transcript of the expert's testimony. The judge correctly reasoned as follows: The expert's testimony did not comply with the Federal Rules of Evidence; the expert's opinion was the sole evidence on proximate cause; and, therefore, the jury's verdict was based on guesswork and speculation. He granted the posttrial judgment as a matter of law.

Three years later, the Court of Appeals for the Fifth Circuit affirmed the posttrial judgment as a matter of law. *Nichols Construction Corp. v. Cessna Aircraft Co.*, 775 F.2d 1325 (5th Cir. 1985), *opinion withdrawn and republished on denial of rehearing*, 808 F.2d 340 (5th Cir. 1986). This outcome is similar to that in other product liability cases in which expert testimony was the sole support for an essential element of the case. E.g., *Calhoun v. Honda Motor Co.*, 738 F.2d 126 (6th Cir. 1984); *Fenner v. General Motors*, 657 F.2d 647 (5th Cir. 1981); *Fairley v. American Hoist & Derrick Co.*, 640 F.2d 679 (5th Cir. 1981). This illustrates a general principle. Where the plaintiff's case depends on a single evidentiary link that is weak in ways a jury may ignore, a posttrial judgment as a matter of law is a distinct possibility.

My two experiences with Rule 50 demonstrate that cases in which posttrial judgment as a matter of law may be possible should be cultivated by early concentration on crucial and uncontroverted facts and the relevant law. Forget broad-brush arguments about sufficiency of evidence. Focus instead on a single element where proof may be lacking; this avoids any need to argue about which witnesses to believe. Examples of such single weak links come up in many contexts: *Selle v. Gibb*, 741 F.2d 896 (7th Cir. 1984) (failure to prove copying in a copyright infringement case); *Barber v. American Airlines*, 791 F.2d 658 (8th Cir. 1986) (age discrimination plaintiffs failed to show that persons replacing them were younger than 40), *Marcone v. Penthouse*, 754 F.2d 1072 (3d Cir. 1985) (journalist's misunderstanding of a footnote in a law enforcement agency report was held not to constitute legal malice in a libel suit).

Jurors are fallible. They are as prone to error as all of us, especially when the plaintiff is an individual allegedly victimized by a corporation. In addition, jurors may dislike a party personally and simply ignore uncontradicted evidence. Complex cases with extraneous evidence and voluminous jury instructions may also confuse jurors. Irrelevancies may be given undue weight. (In *Nichols Construction,* for example, defense counsel still swear that jurors' knowledge of the wrongful death settlement made them believe the defendants were liable, but were just putting the plaintiff through the exercise of trial.) Worst of all, the lawyers' personalities might influence the outcome. Posttrial judgments as a matter of law exist to correct these human failings.

It is, of course, better to learn the law of posttrial motions for judgment as a matter of law as the victorious party at trial. But using Rule 50 to snatch victory from the jaws of defeat is one of the great events a litigator can experience, provided he can survive the hard times that precede ultimate success. You can only hope that the people—especially clients—to whom you reported the jury's adverse verdict are still around when it is time to tell them that justice has finally prevailed.

New Counsel on Appeal?

Dennis J. C. Owens

Should you get a new lawyer when a case goes up on appeal? I believe the answer is almost always yes. Of course, because I am an appellate lawyer, my conclusion may not seem surprising, but more than self-interest, I have reasons for my view.

It is important to begin by defining terms. First, who is the "you" I am urging to get a new lawyer? It is *not* the client. Whether a client decides to change horses for appeal often depends on personal or emotional factors, and not strategy. Perhaps it is anger—possibly irrational—over the loss. Perhaps it is a conviction that the trial performance was bungled, even by the lawyer who won. Perhaps there was a personal falling-out.

Clients can decide those things for themselves. However, I want to address a different audience. The "you" I am talking to is lead trial counsel. Win or lose, you are still in the case. You still retain the confidence of your client, but what you must realize is that replacing yourself on appeal—for most lawyers anathema—will probably help your client prevail.

You must also understand what "get a new lawyer" means. In small firms, it may mean farming the case out to another firm. But, at big firms, it may not; one of your colleagues may be the new lawyer you need. Two things, though, are critical: First, the appeal lawyer is not you, and second, the lawyer is a specialist, someone who concentrates on appeals and whose name shows up frequently in F.2d and the state appellate reports.

Why change lawyers? The chief reason is simple: An appellate lawyer can do a better job because he or she is a specialist. Such a lawyer knows the appellate court's rules, customs, and judges. More importantly,

---

Dennis J. C. Owens, *a fellow of the American Academy of Appellate Lawyers, practices appellate law in Kansas City, Missouri, and is of counsel to DeWitt & Zeldin.*

appellate lawyers know how to write a brief and make an oral argument, and do both efficiently and quickly. There is more to this than just repetition and familiarity. The way you argue and write for appeals is different from the same tasks at the trial level. An emotional, almost visceral, approach can work at trial, but appellate work is usually more restrained and academic. A person at home with one style may not be comfortable with the other.

The arguments for new counsel on appeal parallel those for a general practitioner's referring litigation to a trial lawyer, or a trial lawyer's referring tax work to a specialist. No one can do everything well. It takes concentration and training to master a specialized part of the law, and appellate practice is just that.

The argument for appellate specialization finds support in the organization of government law offices. Most large United States lawyers' offices have appellate experts. Most state prosecutors do not handle their own appeals; that work is instead given to the appellate lawyers of the state attorney general's office. And appellate specialization reaches its zenith in the office of the Solicitor General of the United States, which—in terms of skill, experience, and success—may be the greatest law firm in the country.

Despite these facts, many private lawyers continue to handle the appeals of cases they try. Their reasons deserve attention.

Some lawyers believe law school prepares them to handle appeals. This belief seems to grow out of the "case method," the principal educational technique in law schools. The notion is that, because a person begins to think like a lawyer by studying appellate opinions, he or she will surely be at home in courts of appeal. While that may be an accurate characterization of law school teaching, it is not right to think that intensive study of appellate decisions is the best training for appellate advocacy. Reading case books and being skewered in a Socratic exchange *may* help you analyze facts and understand legal concepts. But, skillful appellate advocacy requires much more.

Think about it this way. Just knowing the geology and geography of the Rockies does not mean you can climb Pike's Peak. Information about the rocks and terrain is helpful, but actually scaling a cliff also makes demands on your personality, character, and physical ability. Technique and experience are more important than merely knowing how the rocks are arranged and the physics that holds them in place.

In a similar way, the job of an appellate lawyer is more than just reading and analyzing opinions. It is certainly not *writing* opinions. An appellate lawyer works to persuade those who will write the opinions, not to write those opinions himself. Advocacy and law school case analysis are just not the same.

Another reason many lawyers do not bring in an appellate specialist is rarely discussed, but a clue to it appears in one fact: Most appeals lose.

Very often, the decision to appeal was a mistake—a waste of the lawyer's time and the client's money. Why do so many smart people take such dumb appeals?

Appellate Catharsis

Appellate judges know the answer: Most appeal briefs are written to convince the client that the case was a good one and ably tried. The losing lawyer pursues and keeps the appeal for himself so that he can justify (to the client and himself) the decision to push the case through the ordeal of a jury trial. The losing lawyer is, in a way, berating the trial judge, the evidence, and the opposition for the client's edification.

Such appellate catharsis is another reason many lawyers handle their own appeals. They want to make up for their disappointments at trial. They feel bad about losing, and suffer for their clients. Handling the appeal is a way to expiate their sense of failure and to restore their confidence.

Unfortunately, the psychic boosts an appeal can provide have nothing to do with success. Read a few briefs written by those seeking appellate atonement and you will understand why it is wise to involve a specialist with no emotional stake in the case. Such filings adopt a tone and address issues that have little to do with what appellate judges need to know.

Of course, having a specialist does not guarantee success on appeal. In fact, it may lead to no appeal at all. Review by a trained, objective outsider may persuade the client—and the trial lawyer—to accept defeat. Careful, unemotional evaluation may indicate that atonement is just not available in a higher court. Curse the judge and jury at the tavern, not in the court of appeals.

This underscores the narrow purpose of an appellate brief: to persuade the court. The objectivity of a new lawyer will help restore the brief to its proper function. The past emotional baggage, and continuing demands, of the lawyer-client relationship will not get in the way, and the appellate courts will not be used in professional self-defense.

Probably the most frequent reason given by trial lawyers for handling appeals is something like this: "I know the case better than anyone ever could. I have lived and sweated with it for years. Why have someone else learn the case from scratch?" The view commonly held is that only trial counsel can be aware of all the case's nuances. Only this lawyer can answer appellate questions about why this evidence was offered, or how that motion was resolved.

To a degree, this is true. No one will know a case better than trial counsel; some things about the litigation are not in the written record. But, like other objections to bringing in a specialist, this reasoning is unrelated to success. A trial lawyer may know too much, and may have lived too long with the case. His or her mind may be cluttered with facts and ideas, relevant and not so relevant, background and foreground.

Such overfamiliarity can be harmful in two ways. First, an appeal is not decided or presented on a complete case history. It turns instead on the formal record. There can be a big difference between the record and everything that happened, but trial counsel may confuse the two. An afternoon's testimony by an expert that was ultimately stricken may have had a substantial emotional impact on trial counsel, even though, for appeal purposes, it is as if the words were never spoken. A new lawyer, reading only the written record, will not be muddled by these things.

A second problem is that a lawyer who knows it all may not be selective, or may be selective for the wrong reasons. Viewing the facts through a filter of emotional commitment, remembering all the minutiae of trial strategy, and burdened by the emotional ups and downs of the trial, a trial lawyer may not properly pick the parts of the record that will best persuade an appeals court.

Though trial counsel may know the entire case better than anyone, the formal record *can* be mastered by others. In fact, appellate specialists may do it best because, unlike trial counsel, they do not have to unlearn any facts. Consider this: The longest trial in Missouri history was the Progressive Farmers Association, or *PFA* case. It was a criminal prosecution that consumed almost eleven months of trial time. There were more than 500 exhibits and many volumes of transcript. I represented on appeal two of the five defendants who were convicted after that trial. They, and two of their co-defendants, won reversals. The *PFA* record was mastered. If it can be, any can.

What About Loyalty?

Loyalty is another reason some lawyers choose to fight rather than switch. They say to themselves, "I have battled this all the way, and I will see it to the end." Though loyalty is admirable, there is nothing *disloyal* about bringing in an appellate specialist. The client is still yours. You are simply being loyal to his cause by bringing in the right expert at the right time.

In fact, loyalty and dogged devotion to the bitter end can have unhappy consequences. By the time a case comes up for appeal, the trial lawyer may have been with it too long. Staleness sets in. The arguments become pat. Inclusion of a thousand details—known for years and presented for the twentieth time—produces a dull, ponderous presentation. True loyalty to the client may consist of getting a new lawyer, with a new perspective, new vigor, and a new grasp of the issues.

A few paragraphs back, I said the client remains yours when a new lawyer comes in. Doubt about that is another reason trial counsel sometimes go it on their own. They fear their client will become charmed by the skills of a slick appellate expert and never return.

Such fears are generally unfounded. It would be stupid for an appellate lawyer to recruit general practice clients from appellate referrals.

When word of such raiding got around, the referrals would dry up. Besides, the dynamics of the situation guard against client loss. If the appeal loses, the client will blame the appellate lawyer, not you. If it wins, you will share in the credit because you were wise enough to suggest an expert.

The arguments for changing lawyers depend on a fundamental proposition: A great trial lawyer and a wonderful appellate advocate rarely exist in the same body. Consider why this is so.

The reason is that the two types of lawyer are different breeds. It is like the difference between bomber pilots and fighter pilots, swimmers and divers. They work in the same kind of place but perform very differently.

Trial lawyers are impassioned and focused on the facts, actors before a silent jury audience, living by their wits, thinking on their feet, selling themselves with sincerity and a warm voice to six or twelve strangers. By contrast, appellate advocates are cooler—laborious rewriters and self-editors who disappear into the law library and delight in reconciling apparently conflicting precedents. Such lawyers are reflective, making up for their lack of showmanship through a love of artful, persuasive language. It is not surprising that such divergent activities often must be done by different people.

Nonetheless, the objections persist. At a recent seminar, a respected trial lawyer offered two more. First, he suggested that having a new lawyer might be a sign of weakness to the appeals court. Appellate judges, he thought, might be offended (or suspicious) that trial counsel didn't care enough, or was too skeptical of the merits, to handle the appeal. Inquiries to such judges, however, have failed to reveal even one who holds that view.

The sage trial lawyer's second objection to new counsel on appeal is this: Having a trial lawyer handle his own appeals is a good way for him to train. Learning to be aware of the record and to identify the crucial issues are certainly by-products of appellate work. But who is paying the trial lawyer's "tuition" for this education? The client is, with his claim or defense at risk. That makes as little sense as trying a case rather than taking an attractive settlement merely because a lawyer needs trial experience. The client's interests come first. With appeals, the client's best interest is usually to entrust the matter to an appellate lawyer, rather than to a trial lawyer who needs the experience. Lawyers who handle appeals should try to win solely for their client, not to learn how to be a better trial lawyer in the future for someone else.

If you accept these reasons, and the time comes for an appeal, do not rush blindly to any specialist. Make sure you are able to get new counsel and that you do it right.

Determine first whether it is permissible to change lawyers. Sometimes a trial lawyer wants to refer a case to an appellate lawyer because of fatigue. He may be exhausted by a difficult case. Maintaining a relationship with a client during litigation can be hard, and sometimes trial counsel may just want to end it. But care is essential. A retainer agreement may explicitly commit the lawyer to handle an appeal, or it may fail to limit his duties to trial only. In that case, you can face trouble if your client is unpersuaded by the reasons outlined in this article and commands you to proceed. If that happens, you *cannot* get a new appeal lawyer, even though it might be wise to do so.

A case illustrates the perils of this situation. When a trial lawyer refused to handle an appeal despite contractual requirements to do so, a bankruptcy judge denied payment of any lawyer's fees for a seven-week trial *and* ordered trial counsel—not the client—to pay appellate counsel $5,625 in fees. In making these orders, the judge observed that "when you contract to represent a client, you contract to do so until the bitter end." *In re Bough* No. 84-00204-S-2-11 (Bankruptcy Court, W.D. Missouri, April 17, 1986).

The opposite situation—where, rather than ignoring or accepting reasoned advice to get a new lawyer, the client fires you—also has risks. The client has become disenchanted, perhaps because of bad trial work or just the bad result. More often, the causes are unrealistic expectations, poor communication, or the lawyer's displeasing personality. In these circumstances, the lawyer—hurt, bitter, angry, or worse—may be just as happy to see the client go elsewhere.

But beware. You must be ethically careful. No matter how difficult or unpleasant the situation, you must do nothing to prejudice the client's case. ABA Model Rule of Professional Conduct 1.7. For example, if the deadline for posttrial motions or an appeal notice is approaching, a trial lawyer cannot ignore it just because the client talked about getting another lawyer. Still less can he let spite or anger stop him from taking essential steps. A trial lawyer must protect the client until the client is well represented by another lawyer. Model Rule 1.16.

Serving the client even if he fires you is another aspect. You must cooperate in a number of ways with appellate counsel—even if things have gotten so bad that the client has stopped paying your bills. Here the rules can be tricky. If you have not been paid the cost of a specific item—an exhibit or a deposition transcript, for example—you can withhold it from the client. But you cannot withhold case files from a new lawyer. If your bills are not paid, you may have a lien on any proceeds of the case, but in most states you do not have a lien on the case files themselves. In thinking about this, do not confuse the evidentiary privilege of lawyer work product with a supposed right to withhold work product from a client because of nonpayment or a desire that he not appeal. The privilege exists; the "right" does not.

The overriding ethical consideration is this: When the client's interests (in an appeal) conflict with the lawyer's interest (in payment), the client wins. So, even if you are still not persuaded that you need an appellate specialist, you must cooperate with a new lawyer if your client gets one. Any lawyer who withholds such cooperation to his client's detriment is not only jeopardizing the case; he is threatening his license to practice law.

The Elusive Appeal

Elizabeth A. Phelan and Theresa J. Collier

Your journey into the thickets of posttrial motions and Rule 4 of the Federal Rules of Appellate Procedure begins with a simple phone call.

The federal district court has issued an order granting summary judgment, disposing of all asserted claims and awarding damages on the counterclaim. Would you be willing to handle the appeal? Happy to have been asked, you accept and begin drafting the notice of appeal.

You know that Rule 4(a)(1) requires the notice of appeal to be filed within 30 days after the entry of judgment unless the United States or one of its officers or agencies is a party, in which case the rule allows 60 days. As the opponent is not the federal government, your notice of appeal must be filed within 30 days. You recall that the time requirements of Rule 4(a)(1) are mandatory and jurisdictional. *Griggs v. Provident Consumer Discount Co.,* 459 U.S. 56, 58 (1982); *Pinion v. Dow Chemical U.S.A.,* 928 F.2d 1522, 1525 (11th Cir.), *cert. denied,* 112 S. Ct. 438 (1991). You resolve to file your notice on time, a goal that seems simple enough at the outset.

You are grateful that Rule 3(c) of the Federal Rules of Appellate Procedure was amended in response to *Torres v. Oakland Scavenger Co.,* 487 U.S. 312 (1988). There the Supreme Court held that former Rule 3(c) required each appellant to be specifically named in the notice of appeal, that the use of *"et al."* to refer to would-be appellants did not satisfy this requirement, and that a failure to meet the specificity provision required dismissal of the appeal on behalf of the insufficiently identified appellants. Under amended Rule 3(c), you are permitted to name each appellant either in the caption or in the text of the notice of appeal, and

---

Elizabeth A. Phelan is a partner in the firm of Holland & Hart in Denver, Colorado. Theresa J. Collier is a lawyer at the firm of Baker & Hostetler, L.L.P., in Denver, Colorado.

to use phrases such as "all plaintiffs," "the defendants," "the plaintiffs A, B, *et al.*," and "all defendants except X" to designate multiple appellants. Fed. R. App. P. 3(c). You also must file a representation statement specifically naming each of the appellants you represent, within 10 days after filing the notice of appeal. Fed. R. App. P. 12(b). You confirm that the two related entities through which your client does business were both parties to the suit; you name each of them as appellants, both in the text of the notice of appeal and in the representation statement.

You also wonder whether the specificity requirement of Rule 3(c) applies to appellees as well as to appellants. You find that both before and after the amendment to Rule 3(c), the circuit courts have applied the specificity requirement only to appellants. *See, e.g., International Union v. United Screw & Bolt Corp.*, 941 F.2d 466, 470–71 (6th Cir. 1991); *MIF Realty v. Rochester Assoc.*, 92 F.3d 752, 757–58 (8th Cir. 1996); *Thomas v. Gunter*, 32 F.3d 1258, 1262 (8th Cir. 1994). By designating the judgment as the order from which the appeal is taken, you ensure that you will be able to raise "all preserved claims of error. . . ." *Sanders v. Clemco Industries*, 862 F.2d 161, 170, & 164–65 n.3 (8th Cir. 1988).

You mail both the notice of appeal and the representation statement one week before the 30 days expire, confident that the pleadings will arrive on time because the customary mailing time from your office to the district court is only one or two days. You enclose an extra copy of the notice of appeal and a self-addressed, stamped envelope, requesting the district court to return a file-stamped copy to you.

The 31st Day After Judgment

Upon receipt of the notice of appeal, a court clerk file-stamps it and forwards copies of it, with the docket sheet, to the circuit court and to all counsel of record. You receive your copy, along with the file-stamped copy of the notice of appeal that you requested, a few days after the deadline for the notice. You also receive a copy of the formal judgment, entered on a separate document, and a motion for prejudgment interest filed by your opponent.

The notice of appeal catches your eye first. The district court's filing stamp indicates that the clerk did not receive and file the notice of appeal until the 31st day after judgment was entered, even though you had allowed ample time for delay in mail delivery. The docket sheet confirms that the notice of appeal was filed on the 31st day.

You try not to panic. You know that mailing the notice of appeal within 30 days is not enough. The notice must be *filed* with the district court within 30 days of entry of judgment. *See Fink v. Union Central Life Ins. Co.*, 65 F.3d 722, 723 (8th Cir. 1995); *Ramseur v. Beyer*, 921 F.2d 504, 505–06 n.1 (3d Cir. 1990). Unless you can remedy the untimely filing, your appeal will be dismissed for lack of jurisdiction. Rule 4(a)(1) "means what it says: if an appellant does not file his notice of appeal on time, [the appellate court] cannot hear his appeal." *Varhol v. National Railroad Passenger Corp.*, 909 F.2d 1557, 1561 (7th Cir. 1990) (*en banc*). Accord *Hope v. United States*, 43 F.3d 1142 (7th Cir. 1994).

You anxiously review the Federal Rules of Appellate Procedure for a solution. Rule 4(a)(5) offers one. It authorizes the district court to grant an extension of time to file a notice of appeal, as long as you file a motion not more than 30 days after expiration of the initial period for appeal, provide notice of the motion to all opposing parties in accordance with the district court's local rules, and make a "showing of excusable neglect or good cause."

Greatly comforted, you review the related case law. You discover that the "good cause" standard was added to Rule 4(a)(5) in 1979. The Advisory Committee Notes to the 1979 amendment can be read to suggest that the "good cause" standard was intended to apply only to motions filed before expiration of the initial time for appeal, and that "excusable neglect" was to be the standard for motions filed during the 30-day grace period. A majority of circuits have adopted this reading; only the First Circuit has rejected it as inconsistent with the plain language of the rule. *See, e.g., Thompson v. E.I. duPont de Nemours & Co., Inc.*, 76 F.3d 530, 532 (9th Cir. 1996) (following the interpretation of "the overwhelming majority of our sister circuits"). *But see Pontarelli v. Stone*, 930 F.2d 104, 109–10 (1st Cir. 1991) (adopting contrary interpretation).

You also find that before *Pioneer Investment Services v. Brunswick Assoc.*, 113 S. Ct. 1489 (1993), the circuit courts had concluded that excusable neglect is a strict standard, met only in "extraordinary cases." *Marsh v. Richardson*, 873 F.2d 129, 130 (6th Cir. 1989); *Reinsurance Co. of America, Inc. v. Administratia Asigurarilor de Stat*, 808 F.2d 1249, 1251–52 (7th Cir. 1987). In *Pioneer*, however, the Supreme Court held that as used in Bankruptcy Rule 9006(b), the phrase "excusable neglect" permits courts, "where appropriate, to accept late filings caused by inadvertence, mistake, or carelessness, as well as by intervening circumstances beyond the party's control." *Pioneer*, 113 S. Ct. at 1495. The fact that Bankruptcy Rule 9006(b), not Rule 4(a)(5) of the Federal Rules of Appellate Procedure, was at issue in *Pioneer* is not significant: All of the circuit courts that have considered the issue have held that *Pioneer*'s definition of excusable neglect applies to Rule 4(a)(5). *See Thompson*, 76 F.3d at 533 (citing cases). *See also Stutson v. United States*, 116 S. Ct. 600, 602 (1996) (acknowledging "the unanimous view of the six courts of appeal that have held that the *Pioneer* standard applies in Rule 4 cases," i.e., cases under either Federal Rules of Criminal Procedure 4(b) or Federal Rule of Appellate Procedure 4(a)(5)).

Despite this more favorable interpretation of "excusable neglect," you cannot predict how the district court would analyze your reliance on the mail under this interpretation. For instance, in the context of a different kind of error, two courts applying *Pioneer* have reached conflicting conclusions. Compare *Advanced Estimating System, Inc. v. Riney*, 77 F.3d 1322, 1323 (11th Cir. 1996) (counsel's erroneous belief that untimely posttrial motions had tolled time for appeal might constitute excusable neglect) *with Prizevoits v. Indiana Bell Tel. Co.*, 76 F.3d 132, 133–34 (7th Cir. 1996) (counsel's erroneous request for extension of time to file posttrial motions cannot constitute excusable neglect).

You are somewhat heartened by the Supreme Court's decision in *Stutson*, 116 S. Ct. at 602–03. There, the defendant in a criminal case challenged the dismissal of his appeal, where the notice of appeal was filed by mail and arrived one working day late. The Supreme Court granted *certiorari*, vacated the circuit court's decision, and remanded for reconsideration in light of *Pioneer*. *Id*. You note that *Stutson* has several unique features that may limit its reach, *id*. at 602–03, and you turn to other post-*Pioneer* circuit court decisions.

You find that the Fourth Circuit, applying *Pioneer*, refused to find excusable neglect where appellant's counsel mailed the notice of appeal three days before the deadline and it arrived three days late. *Thompson*, 76 F.3d at 531–32, 534–35. By contrast, the Eighth Circuit recently declined to follow "the unduly strict standard" that it had applied in an earlier case, factually similar to yours, on grounds that it was "in conflict with *Pioneer*." *Fink*, 65 F.3d at 724 (declining to follow *Vogelsang v. Patterson Dental Co.*, 904 F.2d 427 (8th Cir. 1990), where no excusable neglect was found when the notice of appeal was mailed six days before the due date but never arrived). You decide to recalculate your initial appeal period just to determine whether a Rule 4(a)(5) motion is really necessary.

The Other Pleadings

Then you recall the other pleadings that came with the notice of appeal—the formal judgment and the motion for prejudgment interest. The docket sheet indicates that the motion for prejudgment interest was filed the day after you filed the notice of appeal and that two days later the district court issued the separate judgment, which the clerk entered on the docket the next day.

You know from Rule 77(d) of the Federal Rules of Civil Procedure that failure to receive a copy of the judgment when it was entered would not have affected the due date for the notice of appeal, "except as permitted in Rule 4(a) of the Federal Rules of Appellate Procedure." Fed. R. Civ. P. 77(d). Under Rule 4(a)(6) of the Federal Rules of Appellate Procedure, a district court may reopen the time for appeal in certain circumstances when a party has not received notice of entry of judgment from either the clerk or another party within 21 days after its entry. Fed. R. App. P. 4(a)(6). Rule 77(d) and Rule 4(a)(6) therefore altered prior practice, where appeals were dismissed as untimely after parties did not receive notice of entry of judgment within the 30-day appeal period. *See*, *e.g., Polylok Corp. v. Manning*, 793 F.2d 1318, 1320–21 (D.C. Cir. 1986) (dismissing as untimely an appeal by a party who did not receive 30 days' notice of entry of an order dismissing the action); *Hassett v. Far West Sav. & Loan Ass'n (In re O.P.M. Leasing, Inc.)*, 769 F.2d 911, 914–15, 918 (2d Cir. 1985).

After further study, you realize that you will not have to use this new procedure. Reviewing Rules 58 and 79(a) of the Federal Rules of Civil Procedure, you find that the original summary judgment order was not effective as a final judgment because it was not set forth on a separate document and entered on the docket. *Meadowbriar Home for Children, Inc. v. G. B. Gunn Corp.*, 81 F.3d 521, 527–28 (5th Cir. 1996). *Accord Powell v. Georgia-Pacific Corp.*, 90 F.3d 283, 284 (8th Cir. 1996). Under Rule 4(a)(2) of the Federal Rules of Appellate Procedure, the order became appealable upon entry of final judgment, and the notice of appeal would be deemed to be filed on the day judgment was entered. *See FirsTier Mortgage Co. v. Investors Mortgage Ins. Co.*, 498 U.S. 269, 272–77 (1991). The motion for prejudgment interest, however, is still outstanding, and you want to know how this might affect your appeal.

For this inquiry, you turn to Federal Appellate Rule 4(a)(4), which was substantively amended in 1993. The rule now provides that the time for appeal is tolled by the timely filing of any of the following motions under the Federal Rules of Civil Procedure:

(A) for judgment under Rule 50(b);
(B) to amend or make additional findings of fact under Rule 52(b), whether or not granting the motion would alter the judgment;
(C) to alter or amend the judgment under Rule 59;
(D) for lawyers' fees under Rule 54 if a district court under Rule 58 extends the time for appeal;
(E) for a new trial under Rule 59;
(F) for relief under Rule 60 if the motion is filed no later than 10 days after the entry of judgment.

Fed. R. App. P. 4(a)(4). You recognize immediately that the motion for prejudgment interest is *not* a motion for judgment as a matter of law under Rule 50(b), a motion to amend or make additional findings of fact under Rule 52(b), a motion for lawyer's fees under Rule 54, or a motion for a new trial under Rule 59(a).

Deciding whether a posttrial motion is a motion to alter or amend the judgment under Rule 59(e) proves to be a more difficult task. You discover that the issue often arises in the context of distinguishing a motion to alter or amend a judgment under Rule 59(e) from a motion for relief from judgment under Rule 60. Since the 1993 amendments to Rule 4(a)(4), the classification is not as critical for purposes of calculating the time for appeal. *See United States v. Duke*, 50 F.3d 571, 574 (8th Cir.), *cert. denied*, 116 S. Ct. 224 (1995). Like a motion to alter or amend a judgment under Rule 59(e), a motion for relief from judgment under Rule 60 now tolls the time for appeal if the motion is filed no later than ten days after entry of judgment. *Id. See also* Rule 4(a)(4)(C) & (F). If filed outside the ten-day period specified in Rule 4(a)(4)(F), however, motions under Rule 60 do *not* toll the time for appeal of the underlying judgment. *See* Fed. R. Civ. P. 60(b) (motions must be filed within a "reasonable time" and, with respect to certain grounds for relief, "not more than one year" after the judgment was entered); *Williams v. Chater*, 87 F.3d 702, 704–05 (5th Cir. 1996); *Duke*, 50 F.3d at 574.

Any attempt to cure the untimely filing of a Rule 59(e) motion by having it classified as a Rule 60(b) motion ultimately will be of limited value. An appeal from a ruling on a Rule 60(b) motion does not result in full appellate review of the original judgment; it triggers review only of the order granting or denying Rule 60(b) relief. *See, e.g., Knapp v. Dow Corning Corp.*, 941 F.2d 1336, 1338 (5th Cir. 1991); *Vanornum*, 912 F.2d at 1025; *First Nationwide Bank v. Summer House Joint Venture*, 902 F.2d 1197, 1200–01 (5th Cir. 1990). Moreover, a Rule 60(b) ruling "is reviewable only for abuse of discretion so that such motions do not become a means of circumventing the requirement of a timely appeal." *Chater*, 87 F.3d at 705 n.2.

Rule 59(e) Motions: A Functional Test

In fact, the Supreme Court has adopted a broad, functional test for identifying Rule 59(e) motions. "[A] postjudgment motion will be considered a Rule 59(e) motion where it involves 'reconsideration of matters properly encompassed in a decision on the merits.' " *Osterneck v. Ernst & Whinney*, 489 U.S. 169, 109 S. Ct. 987, 990 (1989) (quoting *White v. New Hampshire Dept. of Employment Security*, 455 U.S. 445, 451 (1982)).

The circuit courts have adopted a similar test: "Regardless of how it is styled, a postjudgment motion filed within ten days of entry of judgment that questions the correctness of a judgment is properly construed as a Rule 59(e) motion." *Venable v. Haislip*, 721 F.2d 297, 299 (10th Cir. 1983); *Finch v. City of Vernon*, 845 F.2d 256, 258–59 (11th Cir. 1988) (postjudgment motion that raised a "substantive issue going to the heart of the judgment" is a Rule 59(e) motion); *A. D. Weiss Lithograph Co., Inc. v. Illinois Adhesive Products Co.*, 705 F.2d 249, 250 (7th Cir. 1983) (a "motion to reconsider summary judgment" was a Rule 59(e) motion: "[O]ne must look to the body of the motion, and see what the movant wants").

It will not be necessary to resort to these functional tests in the instance of your opponent's motion for prejudgment interest. In *Osterneck*, the Court expressly held that a motion for prejudgment interest is in substance a Rule 59(e) motion. 109 S. Ct. at 992. *Accord Havinga v. Crowley Towing and Transp. Co.*, 24 F.3d 1480, 1490 (1st Cir. 1994); *McNabola v. Chicago Transit Auth.*, 10 F.3d 501, 520 (7th Cir. 1993); *Schake v. Colt Ind. Operating Corp. Severance Plan*, 960 F.2d 1187, 1192 (3d Cir. 1992).

The fact that the motion was filed before entry of judgment does not matter. Rule 59(b) was recently amended "to include postjudgment motions that sometimes are filed before actual entry of the judgment by the clerk." Fed. R. Civ. P. 59(b); Advisory Committee Notes, 1995 Amendments. *Accord Wagoner v. Wagoner*, 938 F.2d 1120, 1123 (10th Cir. 1991); *Dunn v. Truck World, Inc.*, 929 F.2d 311, 312–13 (7th Cir. 1991).

In addition to the tolling provision, Rule 4(a)(4) provides that a notice of appeal "filed after announcement or entry of the judgment but before disposition of any of the above motions is ineffective to appeal from the judgment or order. . . . specified in the notice of appeal, *until the entry of the order disposing of the last such motion outstanding*" (emphasis added). The rule was amended in 1993 to eliminate the "trap" for the unwary litigant that was created by its predecessor, which nullified any notice of appeal filed before disposition of all posttrial motions. *See generally Burt v. Ware*, 14 F.3d 256, 257–60 (5th Cir. 1994). *See also Schroeder v. McDonald*, 55 F.3d 454, 458–60 (9th Cir. 1995); *Barber v. Whirlpool Corp.*, 34 F.3d 1268, 1273–74 (4th Cir. 1994). Your pending notice of appeal therefore will be held in abeyance until the district court decides the motion for prejudgment interest. After the ruling on the Rule 59(e) motion, you *must amend* your notice of appeal if you want to challenge the order that resolves the motion. Fed. R. App. P. 4(a)(4). The amended notice of appeal must be filed "within the time prescribed by . . . Rule 4 measured from the entry of the order disposing of the last such motion outstanding." *Id.* You are pleased to see that this additional filing will not require your client to pay another fee; Rule 4(a)(4) specifically provides that no additional fee will be imposed for an amended notice of appeal.

You wonder whether the entry of judgment two days after the motion was filed may be deemed to deny the Rule 59 motion. The answer depends on whether the judgment can be understood to have denied the motion, either expressly or implicitly. In *American Security Bank, N.A. v. John Y. Harrison Realty, Inc.*, 670 F.2d 317 (D.C. Cir. 1982), an order denying the posttrial motions was entered on the same day as the judgment on the jury verdict. Thus, "no tolling occurred as a result of such motions." *Id.* at 319–20.

In contrast, when the circumstances show that the entry of judgment was not intended to dispose of a pending posttrial motion (any of those listed in Rule 4(a)(4)), the entry of judgment is not deemed to deny the posttrial motion. *Greater Houston Chapter of the ACLU v. Eckels*, 755 F.2d 426 (5th Cir. 1985), *cert. denied*, 474 U.S. 980 (1985). For instance, in *Eckels*, the district court ordered briefing on the motion for a new trial on the same day judgment was entered, and the court subsequently issued a decision on the motion. Therefore, the motion for a new trial did toll the time for appeal. 755 F.2d at 427–28.

From these cases, you are ready to conclude that the entry of judgment in your case, without any reference to the motion for prejudgment interest, probably did not serve to deny the motion. Then you read *Dunn v. Truck World, Inc.,* 929 F.2d 311 (7th Cir. 1991). There the court stated that when a motion for a new trial is filed before judgment has been entered, "the judgment itself is the order 'denying a new trial.' " *Id.* at 313 (quoting Fed. R. App. P. 4(a)(4)).

But *Dunn* also holds that "when . . . the Rule 59 motion seeks prejudgment interest, a subsequent judgment that does not address the subject is not final." *Id. Dunn* reasons that "[i]nability to appeal follows not from Rule 4(a)(4), but from 28 U.S.C. § 1291, limiting appeals to final decisions." *Id.* It is not clear from the opinion why the court's reasoning would not apply to any other motion within the scope of Rule 4(a)(4) and pending at the time judgment is entered.

Fortunately, you do not have to resolve this issue or pursue your reservations about *Dunn's* rationale. You recognize that an implied denial of your opponent's request for prejudgment interest would not injure your client, and that the previously filed notice of appeal is still valid, although held in abeyance pending resolution of the motion for prejudgment interest. Fed. R. App. P. 4(a)(4). You conclude that an amended notice of appeal is not necessary at this time. If the court grants the motion, however, you will have to file an amended notice of appeal in order to appeal from the award of prejudgment interest.

As you are considering these options, your client calls. She has decided that one of the court's findings of fact is erroneous, and she wants to file a motion to correct it. You recognize that such a motion would be a motion to alter findings of fact or conclusions of law, subject to Rule 52(b) of the Federal Rules of Civil Procedure. As with other posttrial motions listed in Rule 4(a)(4), a timely Rule 52(b) motion will toll the time for appeal.

The Rule 52(b) motion, like the other motions listed in Rule 4(a)(4) of the Federal Rules of Appellate Procedure, must be filed within ten days of entry of judgment. *See* Fed. R. Civ. P. 50(b), 52(b), 59(b), and 59(e). *See also* Fed. R. App. P. 4(a)(4)(F) (Rule 60 motion *filed* no later than 10 days after entry of judgment tolls the time for appeal). In addition to filing, the motion must be served; Rule 5(d) of the Federal Rules of Civil Procedure requires that when a pleading is filed, it must contain a certificate of service on other parties. *See* Fed. R. Civ. P. 59, Advisory Committee's Note (1995 amendments). A motion that is not filed *and* served within 10 days of entry of judgment may not toll the time for appeal. *See Havinga,* 24 F.3d at 1490. The requirement of service, however, is easily satisfied because Rule 5(b) of the Federal Rules of Civil Procedure provides that service is complete upon mailing. Thus, your motion will be timely if it is filed and mailed within 10 days after judgment was entered.

You check the calendar and find that even though entry of judgment was delayed, it is still 12 calendar days since judgment was entered. Although the clerk mailed a copy of the judgment to you, the "three-day mailing rule" set forth in Rule 6(e) of the Federal Rules of Civil Procedure does not apply in calculating the time deadlines for postjudgment motions. *See, e.g., Parker v. Board of Public Utilities*, 77 F.3d 1289, 1291 (10th Cir. 1996); *Cavaliere v. Allstate Ins. Co.*, 996 F.2d 1111, 1113–14 (11th Cir. 1993). You remember that the computation of time under Rule 6(a) of the Federal Rules of Civil Procedure excludes intermediate Saturdays, Sundays, and certain legal holidays when the time period is less than 11 days. You count the days again and discover that Rule 6(a) permits you to exclude four of the 12 days that have gone by, leaving you with two more days to file your Rule 52(b) motion and serve it on all other parties. *See Wright v. Preferred Research, Inc.*, 891 F.2d 886, 890 (11th Cir. 1990).

The timely filed motion further tolls the time for appeal and delays the effective date of your previously filed notice of appeal, which is being held in abeyance pending resolution of the posttrial motions. Fed. R. App. P. 4(c)(4). Once again, you recall that you may need to amend the notice of appeal if the court denies your Rule 52(b) motion.

Within ten days after entry of judgment, you receive a copy of your opponents' motion for a 30-day extension of time to file an application for lawyers' fees and a bill of costs. Although the motion for extension of time does not reference Rule 59, your experience with the prejudgment interest motion makes you question whether posttrial requests for lawyers' fees and costs are also Rule 59(e) motions. If so, your opponent has asked the district court for an extension that the court simply has *no power* to grant. Fed. R. Civ. P. 6(b). Other appellants who have requested and relied on such extensions in calculating the time for appeal have lost their right to appeal on jurisdictional grounds. *Pinion*, 928 F.2d at 1524–26. *See also Varhol*, 909 F.2d at 1561; *Gribble v. Harris*, 625 F.2d 1173, 1174 (5th Cir. 1980).

Costs, Lawyers' Fees, and Rule 59(e)

Your review of the case law indicates that, to the extent your opponent seeks recovery of taxable costs pursuant to Rule 54(d)(1), the request is not a Rule 59(e) motion and does not toll the time for appeal. *Buchanan v. Stanships, Inc.*, 485 U.S. 265, 268–69 (1988). The question concerning lawyers' fees, however, is less certain. In *Budinich v. Becton Dickinson and Co.*, 486 U.S. 196 (1988), the Supreme Court adopted a "uniform rule that an unresolved issue of lawyers' fees *for the litigation in question* does not prevent judgment on the merits from being final." 486 U.S. at 202 (emphasis added). Nonetheless, subsequent cases interpret the "uniform rule" differently.

For instance, the Eighth Circuit has found significance in the language in *Budinich* that refers to "fees for the litigation" and "fees attributable to the case." *Budinich*, 486 U.S. at 202–203. In *Justine Realty Co. v. American National Can Co.*, 945 F.2d 1044 (8th Cir. 1991), the Eighth Circuit held that a motion for lawyers' fees that sought not only "fees for the litigation," but also fees "provided by the contract and incurred in prelitigation performance of the contract" was a Rule 59(e) motion to the extent that it requested prelitigation fees. 945 F.2d at 1047–49. Thus, the motion tolled the time for appeal. *Id.* The Fifth, Seventh, and Ninth Circuits, however, have expressly rejected the *Justine Realty* approach to *Budinich*. *See United States for Use & Benefit of Familian Northwest, Inc. v. RG & B Contractors, Inc.*, 21 F.3d 952, 954–55 (9th Cir. 1994) ("*Justine Realty* ignores *Budinich's* emphasis on the need for a bright-line rule to determine appealability, and we decline to follow the Eighth Circuit's lead"); *Continental Bank, N.A. v. Everett*, 964 F.2d 701, 702–03 (7th Cir. 1992) (rejecting *Justine Realty* and finding that an "open issue about legal fees, contractual or otherwise, does not affect our jurisdiction"); *First Interstate Bank v. Summer House Joint Venture*, 902 F.2d 1197, 1200 (5th Cir. 1990) (rejecting *Justine Realty*).

Yet other cases have determined that *Budinich* applies only to postjudgment motions for lawyers' fees and does not apply when the judgment authorizes an award of fees but does not quantify them. *See Ragan v. Tri-County Excavating, Inc.*, 62 F.3d 501, 505 (3d Cir. 1995); *Maristuen v. National States Ins. Co.*, 57 F.3d 673, 676–79 (8th Cir. 1995). These courts hold that, under these circumstances, the judgment is not final and appealable until the amount of the lawyers' fees is determined. *Ragan*, 62 F.3d at 505; *Maristuen*, 57 F.3d at 676–79. Moreover, in the Fifth Circuit, *any challenge* to an original judgment regarding the denial or award of lawyers' fees tolls the time for appeal: "[A] motion to reconsider a judgment will be considered a Rule 59(e) motion *even where the request for reconsideration encompasses only that part of the judgment regarding lawyer's fees.*" *Ramsey v. Colonial Life Ins. Co. of America*, 12 F.3d 472, 478 (5th Cir. 1994) (emphasis supplied).

The Tenth Circuit, by contrast, has analyzed these issues differently. *See Utah Women's Clinic, Inc. v. Leavitt*, 75 F.3d 564 (10th Cir. 1995), *cert. denied*, 116 S. Ct. 2551 (1996). In *Leavitt*, when the district court entered judgment, it *sua sponte* awarded prevailing defendants their lawyers' fees and did not quantify the fees. 75 F.3d at 566. Plaintiffs filed a "Rule 59(e)" motion challenging only the court's decision to award fees, and did not file a notice of appeal from the merits of the judgment until after the lawyers' fees issues were decided. *Id.* The Tenth Circuit held that, under *Budinich*, there was no jurisdiction to review the merits because "a Rule 59(e) motion, challenging only the award of costs and attorney's fees, does not toll the time for a merits appeal." *Id.* at 567.

In search for certainty, you notice that Rules 54 and 58 were amended in 1993 to provide a procedure for requesting lawyers' fees. *See* Fed. R. Civ. P. 54–58, Advisory Committee's Notes (1993 Amendments). First, unless provided otherwise by statute or court order, all motions for lawyers' fees must be filed no later than 14 days after entry of judgment. *See* Fed. R. Civ. P. 54(d)(2)(A). Second, when a timely motion for fees is made under Rule 54(d)(2), the trial court "may order that the motion have the same effect under Rule 4(a)(4) of the Federal Rules of Appellate Procedure as a timely motion under Rule 59." Fed. R. Civ. P. 58. Such a determination tolls the time for appeal until the lawyers' fees issues are decided. *See* Fed. R. App. P. 4(a)(4)(D).

You conclude that under Rule 54(d)(2)(A), the district court has power to grant your opponent's motion for extension of time to file a request for lawyer's fees. However, your review of the post-*Budinich* case law has convinced you that further analysis of this issue is futile—outstanding issues concerning an award of lawyers' fees *may or may not toll the time for appeal*. You decide that unless the district court directs that the lawyers' fee request be treated as a Rule 59(e) motion—*see* Fed. R. Civ. P. 58—your analysis of the appellate time deadlines will not be affected by how the motion for extension of time is resolved. You must follow the most conservative approach, i.e., you must calculate the time for appeal from the merits of the judgment independently of any appellate procedural issues that may be raised by the motion for extension of time or by the application for lawyers' fees.

While the motion for extension of time is pending, your opponent files a brief in support of its motion for prejudgment interest, together with a motion to amend the motion for prejudgment interest. The motion to amend asks the district court to consider, in addition to the claim for prejudgment interest, your opponent's claim that newly discovered evidence warrants additional compensatory damages. You recall the cases that hold that the district court has no power to extend the time to file posttrial motions. *See, e.g., Pinion,* 928 F.2d at 1524–26. Perhaps the court also has no power to consider grounds raised in an amended motion filed after the ten-day mandatory time period.

Amended Posttrial Motions

Rule 59(d) of the Federal Rules of Civil Procedure permits a district court to grant a motion for a new trial on grounds not raised in the motion. Relying on this power of the district courts under Rule 59(d), some circuits have allowed parties to seek leave to file an amended motion for a new trial outside the ten-day period. *See Pate v. Seaboard Railroad, Inc.,* 819 F.2d 1074, 1083–86 (11th Cir. 1987) (citing cases).

But a motion for prejudgment interest is a Rule 59(e) motion, not a new trial motion. At least one circuit court has held that in ruling on a timely Rule 59(e) motion, a district court may consider matters not raised in the motion. *Varley v. Tampax, Inc.,* 855 F.2d 696, 699–700 (10th Cir. 1988). Another circuit has held that the district court does not abuse its discretion in refusing to allow an amendment to a new trial motion when the amended Rule 59(e) motion is simply filed, without seeking leave to amend and without explaining why the new grounds were not raised in the original motion. *Dotson v. Clark Equip. Co.,* 805 F.2d 1225,

1228–29 (5th Cir. 1986). *See also Abbott v. The Equity Group, Inc.*, 2 F.3d 613, 628–29 (5th Cir. 1993) ("The district court certainly did not abuse its discretion [in denying motion to supplement new trial motion], considering the basis for the motion, the length of delay, and the lack of explanation for not having timely raised the issue"), *cert. denied,* 510 U.S. 1177 (1994).

Perhaps challenging the motion to amend on this procedural point would be unsuccessful for another reason. The new ground asserted—newly discovered evidence—is a ground for relief under Rule 60(b) only as long as the evidence could not have been discovered in time to move for a new trial under Rule 59(a). The proposed amendment may be permissible because it is not seeking relief under Rule 59(e) but rather under Rule 60(b). If so, you know the motion is timely because your earlier research showed that Rule 60(b) motions are not subject to the strict ten-day limitation for other posttrial motions. Rule 60(b) motions that are based on newly discovered evidence may be filed "within a reasonable time" and, with respect to certain grounds for relief, "not later than one year after the judgment . . . was entered." Fed. R. Civ. P. 60(b).

You also recall that a Rule 60(b) motion does *not* toll the time for appeal of the underlying judgment if filed more than ten days after the entry of judgment. Fed. R. App. P. 4(a)(4)(F). The nontolling aspect of such a Rule 60 motion probably is of no consequence in your case, because the motion for prejudgment interest and the Rule 52(b) motion have tolled the time for appeal.

The district court grants the motion for extension of time to file the application for lawyers' fees and bill of costs. Before the application for fees is filed, the district court enters an order granting the motion for prejudgment interest, denying the motion to amend the motion for prejudgment interest, and denying your Rule 52(b) motion. You know that this is a key order. Assuming that the application for lawyers' fees does not toll the time for appeal, the tolling effect of the posttrial motions has ended and the 30 days for appeal begin to run anew. Fed. R. App. P. 4(a)(4).

Three days later, you learn of a new case addressing the availability of prejudgment interest in circumstances that are similar to those in your case. You believe that the new decision may persuade the district court to reverse itself, and you prepare a motion for reconsideration of the order granting prejudgment interest. Before filing the motion within ten days after entry of the order, you change the title to "Motion to Alter or Amend" the order, consistent with Rule 59(e).

You wonder whether a second Rule 59(e) motion will toll the time for appeal. You find that it will do so "where the motion for reconsideration represents the movant's *first attack* on the trial court's judgment" (emphasis in original). *Wright,* 891 F.2d at 889. In other words, when an order deciding a posttrial motion substantively changes the original judgment, a motion for reconsideration of the posttrial order may be the movant's "first attack" on the revised judgment and, therefore, may toll the time for appeal. *Id.* at 889–90. *Accord Charles v. Daley*, 799 F.2d 343, 348 (7th Cir. 1986). *See also Venable*, 721 F.2d at 299 (when the first postjudgment motion was a Rule 60(b) motion and did not toll the time for appeal, motion for reconsideration of the order ruling on the Rule 60(b) motion is the first motion to toll the time for appeal and therefore is a Rule 59(e) motion).

On the other hand, if the motion for reconsideration states substantially the same arguments as raised in the first posttrial motion or requests rehearing of an amended order that does not expand a previously reconsidered order, the motion for reconsideration is not a Rule 59(e) motion and does not toll the time for appeal. *Wright*, 891 F.2d at 889. You conclude that because the prejudgment interest order is a substantially new judgment and because your motion to alter or amend is your first attack on the new judgment, your motion probably has tolled the time for appeal.

Nevertheless, you plan to file an amended notice of appeal on the 30th day after entry of the order awarding prejudgment interest and denying your client's Rule 52(b) motion. This amended notice of appeal protects against the risk that your motion to alter or amend the judgment may *not* have tolled the time for appeal and ensures that the rulings on prejudgment interest and the Rule 52(b) motion are, in fact, appealed. You calculate the time for this amended notice of appeal in accordance with Rule 4(a)(1) and Rule 4(a)(4): Under Rule 4(a)(1), the time for appeal in your case is 30 days and under Rule 4(a)(4), the 30-day period is "measured from the entry of the order disposing of the last such [tolling] motion outstanding."

The district court resolves a bit of this uncertainty by denying your motion to alter or amend, and it does so within the 30-day period following the prejudgment interest and Rule 52(b) order. Hence, as long as you calculate the due date for the amended notice of appeal from the entry of the original posttrial order—rather than from the entry of the order concerning the motion to alter or amend (which may not have tolled the time for appeal)—you can safely file just one amended notice of appeal.

An amended notice of appeal filed within 30 days of the prejudgment interest and Rule 52(b) order, but after the order on the motion to alter or amend, will be effective to appeal from both posttrial orders, as well as from the underlying judgment. At the same time, the notice will render moot any questions about the orders from which the appeal is taken and any possible impact that the motion to alter or amend may have had on the time for appeal.

Your opponent also files a timely notice of appeal from the order denying the motion to amend the motion for prejudgment interest.

Under Rule 28(h) of the Federal Rules of Appellate Procedure, the party who filed the first notice of appeal will be deemed the appellant for purposes of Rules 28, 30, and 31 of the Federal Rules of Appellate Procedure unless the parties otherwise agreed or the court otherwise ordered. (If both parties had filed notices of appeal on the same day, the plaintiff in the district court would be deemed the appellant unless the parties otherwise agreed or the court otherwise ordered.)

After filing the amended notice of appeal, you recall that the district court has not entered an amended judgment or separate order pursuant to Rule 58 of the Federal Rules of Civil Procedure that reflects the rulings on the posttrial motions. You wonder whether that omission affects the appealability of the posttrial orders and whether your amended notice of appeal is premature.

On this issue, the law is sparse. *Wright v. Preferred Research, Inc.*, 937 F.2d 1556, 1559 (11th Cir. 1991), *cert. denied*, 502 U.S. 1049 (1992). It is also conflicting. *See, e.g., Chambers v. American Trans Air, Inc.*, 990 F.2d 317, 318 (7th Cir. 1993) (noting split among the circuits). As to orders *granting* posttrial motions, some circuits require a separate judgment issued pursuant to Rule 58, *see Marre v. United States*, 38 F.3d 823, 825 (5th Cir. 1994), but others do not, *see Wright*, 937 F.2d at 1560–61. The Seventh, Ninth, and Eleventh Circuits have determined that a separate document issued pursuant to Rule 58 of the Federal Rules of Civil Procedure is *not required when the posttrial motion is denied. See Marre v. United States*, 38 F.3d at 825 (citing cases); *Chambers*, 990 F.2d at 318. Nonetheless, the First Circuit requires compliance with Rule 58 with respect to *every order* granting or denying a posttrial motion. *See Fiore v. Washington County Community Mental Health Ctr.*, 960 F.2d 229, 232–36 (1st Cir. 1992) (*en banc*).

These conflicting decisions are troublesome because you are appealing from one order *denying* posttrial relief, the Rule 52(b) motion, and another decision *granting* posttrial relief, the award of postjudgment interest. You take some comfort in the fact that the appellate courts usually apply the separate document requirement to *preserve* the right to appeal, not to defeat it. *See Meadowbriar*, 81 F.3d at 528; *Barber*, 34 F.3d at 1274–75. Thus, the appealability of the orders should be maintained, despite the trial court's possible failure to comply with Rule 58.

Your Opponent's Motion

The district court awards only a portion of the lawyers' fees that your opponent requested. You give some thought as to whether you need to amend the notice of appeal. Cases such as *Justine Realty, Ragan*, and *Maristuen* suggest that the judgment may not be final until the lawyers' fees are quantified. If so, then your previous notice of appeal is premature. You determine that the award of lawyers' fees is subject to challenge on appeal. Erring on the side of caution, you decide to file an amended notice appealing from the decision on the merits, the posttrial rulings, *and* the award of lawyers' fees.

While confronting this quandary and attempting to decipher the conflicting case law, you take a second look at *Pinion*. Reviewing *Pinion*, you become intrigued by its discussion of the "unique circumstances" doctrine. You read the three cases that gave rise to the doctrine: *Wolfsohn v. Hankin*, 376 U.S. 203 (1964) (per curiam); *Thompson v. INS*, 375 U.S. 384 (1964) (per curiam); and *Harris Truck Lines, Inc. v. Cherry Meat Packers, Inc.*, 371 U.S. 215 (1962) (per curiam).

In *Harris Truck*, the district court had granted an appellant's timely motion for an extension of time within which to file a notice of appeal, and the appellant had relied on the extension. The circuit court dismissed the appeal, holding that the district court had erred in finding the requisite excusable neglect. The Supreme Court reversed, holding that the appellate court should have given "great deference" to the district court's finding of excusable neglect, "[i]n view of the obvious hardship to a party who relies upon the trial judge's finding of 'excusable neglect' prior to expiration of the 30-day period and then suffers reversal of the finding. . . ." 371 U.S. at 217. The Court held that the record established "a showing of unique circumstances sufficient that the Court of Appeals ought not to have disturbed the motion judge's ruling." *Id.*

In *Thompson*, 12 days after entry of judgment, Thompson gave notice of his intent to file a motion for a new trial. The INS did not object. The district court expressly stated that the motion was filed "in ample time," and the court decided the motion on the merits. Thompson filed the notice of appeal within 60 days of the order denying the motion for a new trial, but not within 60 days of the judgment. The Supreme Court recognized that the appeal was untimely under a strict application of the Federal Rules of Appellate Procedure but held that the case "fit[] squarely within the letter and spirit of *Harris*." 375 U.S. at 387.

In *Wolfsohn*, the district court entered judgment and four days later granted the plaintiff an extension of time within which to file a motion for rehearing. *See Wolfsohn v. Hankin*, 321 F.2d 393 (D.C. Cir. 1963) (providing procedural history of case). The motion was filed more than 30 days after entry of judgment. The notice of appeal was filed within 30 days of the order denying the motion for rehearing but more than five months after judgment was entered. The court of appeals dismissed the appeal, holding that the order granting the extension of time within which to file the petition for rehearing was invalid and the motion was untimely. The Supreme Court summarily reversed without opinion, citing *Thompson* and *Harris Truck. Wolfsohn v. Hankin*, 376 U.S. 203 (1964) (per curiam).

Updating *Harris Truck, Thompson,* and *Wolfsohn,* you find that the Supreme Court referred to the unique circumstances doctrine in *Oster-*

neck. The Court stated that *"Thompson* applies only where a party has performed an act which, if properly done, would postpone the deadline for filing his appeal and has received specific assurance by a judicial officer that this act has been properly done." *Osterneck*, 489 U.S. at 179. Compare *Moore v. South Carolina Labor Bd.*, 100 F.3d 162, 164 (D.C. Cir. 1996) (unique circumstances doctrine held inapplicable because statements by clerk's office staff "cannot fairly be characterized as official judicial action") with *Prudential-Bache Securities, Inc. v. Fitch*, 966 F.2d 981, 985 (5th Cir. 1992) (district court order that was stamped "ENTERED" on a date certain was an affirmative representation of the court, for purposes of applying unique circumstances doctrine). You also find circuit court decisions questioning the current validity of the unique circumstances doctrine. *Pinion*, 928 F.2d at 1529–30; *Varhol*, 909 F.2d at 1562. These cases note that *Osterneck* referred to the unique circumstances doctrine and distinguished *Thompson*, but did not overrule it. *Pinion*, 928 F.2d at 1530; *Varhol*, 909 F.2d at 1562. Thus, the doctrine appears to be viable, at least until the Supreme Court specifically rules otherwise. *Schwartz v. Pridy*, 94 F.3d 453, 456 n.3 (8th Cir. 1996).

In any event, the doctrine is little comfort. It does not provide relief from an erroneous interpretation of the confusing maze of appellate rules and case law. Moreover, reliance on the orders of a district court does not necessarily provide protection. Any reliance on the district court must be reasonable, which cannot occur when an order conflicts with the express provisions of a rule of procedure. Once again, you conclude that persistent vigilance is the only safe course when navigating this labyrinth.

Merits of Appeal

After this intensive focus on procedure, you are relieved finally to shift attention to the merits of the appeal. As you turn to the files, one of the lawyers in your office stops to see you. He has copies of a district court judgment entered eight days ago and an order granting his client a 30-day extension within which to file posttrial motions. He wants to know whether you would be willing to handle the motions and the appeal. Undaunted, you begin again.

PART II

Strategy of the Appeal

Issues, Facts, and Appellate Strategy

Jordan B. Cherrick

There are many kinds of litigation strategy. A trial lawyer must have a general plan, of course, but trying a lawsuit is a fluid, dynamic enterprise. New facts are discovered, witnesses change their minds, and the opponent shifts course. A trial lawyer must constantly shift his strategy, like a quarterback calling an audible at the line of scrimmage.

Appellate strategy is more fixed. Appeals concern a known, usually unchanging, factual record. Briefing is confined by more rigid rules, and appeals court is a more controlled place than the local courthouse. Appellate strategy is therefore more like participating in a formal debate. Rules and advice have wider, more certain application.

The keys to successful appellate advocacy might, in fact, be expressed in a one-word acronym: PASS—Preparation, Anticipation, Selectivity, and Style.

Preparation: An attorney's mastery of the record, the law, and the rules of the appellate court.

Anticipation: A briefwriter's effort to determine how to frame the issues and develop appellate strategy in a way that will best influence the judges who decide the case.

Selectivity: Choosing the facts, events, and legal arguments likely to control the outcome.

Style: The ability to persuade by writing and thinking well.

A lawyer's performance in every aspect of the appellate process—from briefwriting to oral argument—depends on his ability to follow the

---

Jordan B. Cherrick is a partner of the St. Louis office of the law firm Armstrong, Teasdale, Schlafly & Davis, and a member of the American Law Institute. Mr. Cherrick is a winner of the Missouri Bar Foundation's David J. Dixon Appellate Advocacy Award for outstanding achievement in appellate practice.

elements of PASS. This is particularly true when a lawyer is framing the issues and describing the facts in a brief. These may seem like easy assignments, but they are critical. Mapping out the presentation of the issues and the facts is where a successful appeal begins.

It bears repeating: This planning process is *not* the same as developing a trial strategy. Trial skill and appellate skill are different. Many trial lawyers mistakenly send an inexperienced associate to the library to write an appellate brief and then provide no supervision. These mistakes are usually compounded when the trial lawyer presents the oral argument after spending little time on overall appellate strategy or the brief. This approach is wrong. Although it is important to consult with the trial lawyer, do not duplicate trial strategy on appeal.

A successful appellate strategy must start with an understanding of the nature of the appellate process. The most basic, and most often ignored, point of departure is this: Appellate courts and trial courts do different things. A court of appeals corrects the trial court's legal errors; it does not decide questions of fact. Its principal job is not to determine whether conduct was reasonable or outrageous, and it rarely shares the sympathy or indignation born of direct exposure to witnesses. Jury arguments—purely emotional pitches—will not impress a court oriented toward protecting the rule of law.

Finding Themes

Having in mind the appellate court's role, a lawyer must first identify overall themes for his appeal. These themes must be incorporated into the brief's statement of issues and should continue throughout.

Choosing themes is one of the most difficult aspects of briefwriting. It begins with sound thinking. Irving Younger, a great teacher of legal writing, once argued that good writing is based on good thinking. See "Bad Writing = Bad Thinking," 73 *A.B.A. J.* at 90 (January 1987). If you rush headlong into an appeal brief, the odds are it will be confusing or illogical. What seemed forceful and compelling at trial before a jury can be picked apart intellectually in a judge's chambers.

The first step to good thinking is thorough preparation. Start by reading, analyzing, outlining, and digesting the trial court record. This includes the lower court's opinion, the trial exhibits, the transcript of the proceedings, and the pleadings. Speak with the trial lawyer to clarify questions about the record. Throughout this process, write notes of all your ideas or observations. Besides getting down the basics, the point is to understand the tone and tenor of the case at trial. What was it like? What were your client's main themes? What was the trial court atmosphere?

Next, think about a question that should stay with you during the entire appeal: How will the appellate judges view the factual and legal issues in this case? Try to anticipate their reactions. Sit in their places. Analyze their opinions and study their books and articles. Listen to their speeches. Then, like an actor studying a new role, try to become an appellate judge and think about the case.

Only by doing all that can you identify case-dispositive issues and arguments that may win the day. The challenge cannot be overstated: Framing appellate issues often demands a fundamental reorientation of the case. A lawyer must extract crisp, well-defined legal questions from a proceeding that was mostly a welter of competing facts. The unrestrained, visceral trial battle must be converted into an emotionally controlled and intellectual exercise on appeal.

Appellate judges apply different standards of review to decisions of the trial court or jury. An appellate lawyer must understand these standards when choosing his strategy and framing the issues. An appellant who cannot identify a legal error even in a factually intensive case will likely lose. Conversely, when an appellee can persuade the court of appeals that his opponent is merely relitigating fact findings, the court will likely affirm.

Prune the Issues

Once you identify issues, limit them. Present no more than three or four of your strongest claims that the trial court erred. State them in order of their importance, unless the organization of the brief dictates otherwise.

Most appeals turn on just one or two issues. It is a serious mistake to spatter issues in a brief like shotgun pellets in the hope that a few will hit the court. Fight the instinct to list every conceivable error. Appellate judges are not law school professors. They do not give high grades to lawyers who can spot all the issues. Your client will be best served if you have the confidence to present only the important issues.

Appellate judges also urge selectivity. Listen to Senior Eighth Circuit Judge Myron H. Bright: "If an appellant can't win on the strength of the strongest claim or claims, he stands little chance of winning a reversal on the basis of weaker claims. . . . The court needs to know just where the heart of the matter lies; distracting attention from the most important issues can hardly help an appellant's cause." Bright, "Appellate Briefwriting: Some 'Golden' Rules," 17 *Creighton Law Review* 1069, 1071 (1983–84).

Many lawyers have difficulty identifying the important issues in an appeal. This usually stems from a poor understanding of the appellate decision-making process. Lawyers should know that appellate judges have two major goals: (1) to apply the law correctly; and (2) to reach a just result that is fair to the litigants. The key issues you select as an appellant should keep both goals in mind and should have these characteristics:

- They involve errors of law by the trial court.
- The errors of law are important; their correction is likely to have an impact on this case and others.

- The errors are not dry technical points (unless your appeal involves a procedural question and you have no other choice); discussing them will tap basic notions of equity and justice.
- The errors actually affected the outcome of the case. (Many appellants complain about actions that, if done differently, would not have changed the result.)

Working with such elements (or their converse if you represent appellee), a lawyer must create a theme and frame the issues. He hopes to argue that the court will satisfy the ends of justice and adhere to established legal principles if it rules his way. Throughout, the trial record is a limit. In some cases, the record will compel emphasis on principles of equity and fairness. In others, the best strategy is to appeal to the rule of law and the related policies of certainty, predictability, continuity, and precedent.

Once you have issues and a theme in mind, the next job is writing the brief—beginning with a description of the issues or questions presented. Careful drafting is essential. The way the issues are written will govern the court's first impression of the merits. Whatever the theme, each issue statement should incorporate specific facts and legal principles in a simple, concise, and accurate manner. The briefwriter must try to put the issues persuasively, but must not lose credibility by being strident or overstated.

How do these principles work in practice?

Suppose you have a case in which the jury returned a $10 million verdict for your client, the husband of the late Karen Smith. Dr. Smith, a brilliant young physician, was killed when the airplane in which she was traveling exploded over the ocean. Your problem is that the trial court granted the defendant's motion for a judgment notwithstanding the verdict. The court concluded that your case was insufficient because your expert witness was not competent to testify that the explosion was caused by defective engines manufactured by the defendant.

What is your appellate strategy? You decide to concentrate on two issues: the ample evidence supporting the jury's verdict and the trial court's failure to apply the proper standard in setting aside the verdict. Argument on the first point will show that an injustice occurred. The second will identify the legal error at stake.

With this general approach, you begin to write, starting with the question presented. Here are two ways it could be done:

> Should the trial court's posttrial judgment as a matter of law (known as a "judgment notwithstanding the verdict" or "JNOV" before the 1991 amendments to the Federal Rules) be reversed because plaintiff's expert witness, an aviation mechanic with more than 20 years of experience, was not competent to render an opin-

ion "based on reasonable scientific certainty" that the explosion that killed Dr. Smith was caused by defendant's defective engines?

or

> Should the court of appeals conclude that the trial court erred in granting defendant a posttrial judgment as a matter of law?

The first version is far better. It outlines the equitable heart of the appeal and implies the legal problem involved. The second formulation just sits there, arid and lifeless. It makes the case indistinguishable from all other appeals of posttrial judgments as a matter of law—most of which are affirmed. Your statement of issues must do more: It must, from the first page, acquaint the court with why your case is different.

How do you frame the case for the appeals court if you represent the appellee? Again, there are good and bad ways to do it. Compare this statement:

> Did the trial court properly enter posttrial judgment as a matter of law for the defendant because plaintiff's expert, a mechanic with no engineering training, was not competent to testify that electronically complex jet engines caused the airplane's explosion?

with this one:

> Should the trial court's posttrial judgment as a matter of law be affirmed because the court properly concluded that the plaintiff's expert was not competent to testify about the accident?

Again, the first version is better. It conveys the trial court's primary reason for entering a posttrial judgment as a matter of law in forceful terms. Reading it, the appeals court knows, at one glance, the essence of the appellee's argument. The second version is much inferior. It merely asks whether the posttrial judgment as a matter of law should be affirmed. This statement ignores the real problem in the case: Was the plaintiff's expert witness competent to opine on causation, and how did his dubious competence affect the plaintiff's case?

A word of warning on framing the issues. Though it is wise to weave the facts through the legal question, do not go overboard. It is one thing to convey crisply what the case is about. It is another to engage in strident special pleading. In our crash case, this would *not* be good form:

> Did the trial court's reversal of the jury's careful verdict wrongly depend on the conclusion that plaintiff's expert was incompetent to testify that a jet engine's slipshod design caused a shattering explosion that, in a searing flash, snuffed out the life of a brilliant young physician over the chilly waters of the Atlantic?

That is not a statement of the issue on appeal. It is part of a jury summation.

Sometimes you cannot capture the core issues in a single sentence. Even the examples given are cumbersome. A complex case may require the briefwriter to begin with a short introductory statement that will help the court understand the issues. An example of this technique is contained in the Fifth Circuit's guide on appellate practice:

> The defendant was charged with conspiracy to import cocaine. The judge was requested to charge the jury that the prosecution must prove that the defendant had the intent to join a conspiracy and did so knowingly. The court refused to do so. Was this error?

"Fifth Circuit Reporter," July 1985, quoted in M. Tigar, *Federal Appeals—Jurisdiction and Practice* at 240 (Shepard's/McGraw-Hill, Inc., 1987).

There are advantages to this two- or three-sentence approach, even in a simple case. The custom of a single-sentence issue statement is usually just that—a custom. It is rarely mandatory. Sometimes, straying from custom will avoid having your brief start with blocks of text that might be more at home in *Finnegan's Wake*.

The range for creativity in stating issues is not limitless, however. Some jurisdictions have local rules that dictate a special style in which counsel must draft the issues. Missouri Supreme Court Rule 84.04(d), for example, states that the "points relied on shall state briefly and concisely what actions or rulings of the court are sought to be reviewed and wherein and why they are claimed to be erroneous, with citations of authority thereunder." Various federal circuits have other rules on style and positioning of issue statements. Not all are the same. Appellate lawyers must comply with these rules. The price may be rejection of your brief or even dismissal of the appeal.

Refining the Arguments

Your first draft of the issues will likely change. As the remaining sections of the brief are written, you will refine your view of how the arguments work. That improved view, and particularly apt phrases developed during briefwriting, will be filled back into the statement of issues. An appellate lawyer must revise and edit the issues until they constitute the best, most succinct, and most accurate statement of the questions facing the appellate court.

After getting focused by preparing a first draft of the issues, a briefwriter is ready to write the statement of facts. This is without question the most important part of a brief. Successful appellate advocates know that most appeals are won or lost on the facts, not the law. This may seem ironic, because, as noted, appeals courts correct legal errors. So it is. But rely on John W. Davis, as close to the ultimate authority on appellate practice as has lived in this century:

> [I]t cannot be too often emphasized that in an appellate court the statement of facts is not merely a part of the argument, it is more

often than not the argument itself. A case well stated is a case far more than half argued. . . . The court wants above all things to learn what are the facts which give rise to the call upon its energies; for in many, probably in most, cases when the facts are clear there is no great trouble about the law.

John W. Davis, "The Argument of an Appeal," 26 *A.B.A. J.* 895, 896 (December 1940). Davis capsulized the essential elements of a factual statement into the "[t]hree C's—chronology, candor and clarity":

Chronology, because that is the natural way of telling any story, stringing the events on the chain of time just as all human life proceeds; candor, the telling of the worst as well as the best, since the court has the right to expect it, and since any lack of candor, real or apparent, will wholly destroy the most careful argument; and clarity, because that is the supreme virtue in any effort to communicate thought from man to man.

Id. at 897. By carefully selecting and organizing facts from the record, an appellate advocate tries to create an interesting story for the appellate judges. Although he should not, in the statement of facts, comment on the evidence or argue the legal implications of the facts, a briefwriter can convey the equities of his client's position by presenting the facts in an interesting, compelling way.

Tragic Facts

In our hypothetical case about the airplane explosion, appellant's counsel should, to a degree, describe the life, promising future, and tragic death of the young physician. He should explain the mechanical failure of the engines that caused the explosion. Special emphasis should also be given to the experience and knowledge of the plaintiff's expert witness who provided the crucial testimony on causation.

Appellee's counsel, on the other hand, should highlight the evidence that indicates the engines did not cause the accident. Little time should be spent on the plaintiff or other inessential matters. The critical facts undermining the competence of the plaintiff's expert must be examined. This can be done by emphasizing the technical complexities of the engine's components and the expert's lack of professional education or training in aeronautical engineering.

In presenting their cases through the statement of facts, appellate lawyers must understand the essential elements of a good story: chronology and plot.

A chronology is the essence of a story—one fact following another in time sequence. More times than many might believe, fact statements in briefs skip from one event to another in a disorganized way. Almost always, this approach will frustrate the judges and lose their attention.

Briefwriters should proceed more logically: Start with the earliest events and move forward to the present.

Every rule has exceptions, of course. In rare, complicated cases, a thematic rather than a chronological presentation is more effective. If you do this, each unit of the discussion should be chronological, and you should provide cues in the text for what you are doing. If, for example, the appeal involves the parallel but unconnected conduct of three companies over a period of time, you might first describe what firm A did. The transition sentence could then be "During precisely the same period, company B was engaged in a similar course of conduct." Such cues are essential. Even with them, an out-of-sequence narrative requires skill.

Novelists weave facts out of their imaginations. Lawyers must work with the facts they are given in the record. Both writers and lawyers, however, must display ingenuity in developing the plot. A plot explains why events occurred. It links them together by outlining cause and effect, motivations, and emotions.

In the hypothetical defective engine case, the plot underlying the statement of facts can explain whether the physician was killed by defective engines, pilot error, or lightning striking the airplane. This involves more than reciting the facts in an orderly sequence. It requires linking them together and explaining how some events imply or underpin others. This cannot be accomplished with summaries of testimony or long quotations from the record; those are inadequate substitutes for good writing. In developing a plot, a writer of fiction emphasizes or arranges events so that the reader will be intellectually interested and emotionally moved by the story. The lawyer-writer must do this but has the added task of persuading the court that his client acted properly.

Appellate lawyers face two other hurdles: the demands of candor and plausibility. Judges are persuaded by lawyers whom they can trust. As Aristotle and Quintilian have taught, an advocate's character or "ethos" is an essential element of the art of persuasion. *See* Aristotle, *The Art of Rhetoric* (Harvard University Press 1982); Quintilian, *The Institutio Oratoria* (Harvard University Press 1980).

An appellate court forms an initial opinion of a lawyer's credibility and trustworthiness by reading the brief. The judge will ask: Have any facts been misrepresented? Do the citations to the record support the factual recitation? Is the lower court's ruling characterized properly?

Answering these questions involves more than supporting all factual statements with specific citations to the record, though that is essential. The downfall of many briefwriters is that they ignore the factual or legal problems in their cases. Adverse facts must be acknowledged and explained in the brief. If you do not deal with such items, opposing counsel will surely highlight them. As Justice Robert H. Jackson observed, "[T]o delay meeting these [difficult] issues is improvident; to attempt evasion of them is fatal." "Advocacy Before The United States Supreme Court," 37 *Cornell Law Quarterly*, 1, 5 (Fall 1951).

Worse than ignoring harmful facts is misstating them. If a lawyer is inaccurate about the facts in a brief, his opponent's most effective strategy is to inform the court of these inaccuracies at the beginning of his answering submission. Appellate judges do not easily forgive advocates who misrepresent the record.

The demands of candor, however, involve more than dealing accurately with all the important facts. The requirement is hard to describe, but it might be called achieving a balanced tone. Though written by an advocate, the statement of facts in an appellate brief should not seem overly adversarial. The narrative should flow in an apparently inevitable fashion, avoiding overstatement and special pleading. It should seem as natural as relaxed breathing—with no panting, sweating, or screaming. The narrative should be economical, with no excess facts or gratuitous references. Achieving this tone is one of an appellate lawyer's greatest challenges. You must be a committed advocate while setting out the facts in an objective, but nonetheless persuasive, way.

Another Imaginary Case

Again, an imaginary case can help illustrate these ideas. Suppose you are in a case involving a business dispute over a computer licensing agreement. A privately held company, Applied Science, Inc., has developed an outstanding software package that helps small businesses and consumers prepare their tax returns. Applied Science negotiates a licensing agreement with American Computers, Ltd., a national computer marketing company. The agreement provides that American Computers will market the tax software nationwide and that Applied Science will receive 25 percent of all profits. American Computers also agrees to make bimonthly royalty payments and to provide an accounting of the number of software packages sold in each state.

Several years after the agreement is signed, Applied Science files a lawsuit against American Computers in which it seeks actual and punitive damages for breach of contract and fraud. Applied Science claims that American Computers intentionally misrepresented the number of tax software packages sold and failed to pay $1 million in royalties due. American Computers denies these claims. Alternatively, it contends that if sales figures were inaccurately reported, it was an unintentional accounting error not justifying punitive damages.

The case is sent to the jury, which returns a verdict for Applied Science of $1 million actual and $4 million punitive damages. American Computers appeals and hires your firm as appellate counsel.

The breach finding may be hard to overturn, but you are confident that the punitive damages award is vulnerable. There is a good chance that the appellate court will vacate it. You therefore recommend that the focus of the appeal be directed toward the punitive damages award. The client agrees.

Then you set a strategy for your brief. First, you choose a theme. The basic concept is this: Even if the court accepts the jury's finding of a breach, there is nothing to indicate that American Computers' conduct constituted fraud. In your jurisdiction, a party may not recover punitive damages for simple breach of contract, and so, you will argue, the fraud and punitive damages issues should not have been submitted to the jury.

Even though your theme is, in a phrase, "It was only a breach," you should *not* concede the breach finding on appeal. To the contrary, it should be an important battleground in the brief. You want at least to convince the court that the breach issue was close at the trial level. The more the appellate judges see that it was almost not a breach at all, the less it will look like fraud and an occasion for punitive damages.

Your statement of facts as appellant should incorporate these themes. Emphasize the details of the contract dispute. Stress American Computers' good faith belief that it accurately reported sales and royalty data. Your strategy is to persuade the court that the plaintiff masqueraded its breach of contract claim as a fraud claim so that it could recover punitive damages.

What if you were the appellee's counsel? Then you would focus your theme on the fraud claim. The statement of facts would emphasize the evidence that supported each element of fraud. American Computers' intentional disregard of its duty to report properly the sales and royalty data would be highlighted. The briefwriter would also stress Applied Science's complete dependence on American Computers to provide accurate accounting information. Such a statement of facts might well incline a court to conclude that American Computers committed fraud in addition to a breach of contract, and that the jury's award—actual *and* punitive damages—should be affirmed. By changing the theme, the same set of facts and record can serve two opposing ends.

Finally, a few words on writing skill. The problem is this: A lawyer cannot persuade a court unless he can effectively communicate facts, law, thoughts, ideas, and feelings. If a lawyer is not an excellent writer, he should assign the appeal to a skilled appellate practitioner. The best theme and most carefully selected issues will count for little if mired in vague, cloudy prose. The fundamental principles of clear writing have been articulated time and again, but are rarely followed. Strunk and White's *The Elements of Style* is still the best short guide to writing. Get it and use it. Accomplished advocates will revise, rewrite, and edit the brief until it is polished and precise.

The final rule of briefwriting style is brevity. If appellate judges are reading this article, they will likely pause here and rejoice. Work hard to make your brief as short as possible.

Of course, all the strategy, polishing, and brevity in the world do not guarantee victory. Fourth Circuit Judge J. Braxton Craven, Jr., once said in an address to the North Carolina Association of Trial Lawyers that there is only one rule of appellate advocacy that guarantees success in every case: Choose the right side.

Absent such foresight, an appellate advocate can only do as well as he or she can. By remembering PASS—preparation, anticipation, selectivity, and style—you increase the chance that the right side will be your side.

Twenty Pages and Twenty Minutes

John C. Godbold

The subject of effective appellate advocacy has been thoroughly worked over, but it always deserves renewed discussion. New lawyers enter the practice. Times change. Courts continually reexamine their procedures and habits with cold and critical eyes. Judges are less and less willing to do something, and do it in a particular way, because it has always been done that way.

Appellate practice itself is also changing. Bench and bar are learning to get to the bare bones of disputes with less concern for the fat. There is an overall air of "no nonsense." At the same time, the picture of the typical appellate advocate—a wily veteran of many cases and a master of rules, tactics, and wit—is changing. Appointment of counsel in indigent criminal appeals brings to the appellate courtroom lawyers who otherwise might not be there. I do not imply that today's advocates are less effective than their predecessors. Many are superb. But all of them need all the help they can get.

Nowadays, the written brief in particular must aim for maximum effectiveness. A brief may be the only shot that counsel gets at the appellate court. The Eleventh Circuit, for example, assigns more than 50 percent of its cases to the Non-Argument Calendar, where they are decided on the briefs and the record. Other courts are moving in the same direction with procedures such as affirmance by a simple order and without argument. Some panels occasionally require no argument by appellee when they have not been swayed by appellant's argument. Today's advocate must use to his full potential the tools available to him.

John C. Godbold is senior circuit judge, Eleventh Circuit Court of Appeals. A longer version of this chapter appeared in the Southwestern Law Journal *of the Southern Methodist University School of Law.*

My comments are from the side of the bench that reads what advocates write and listens to what they say. I therefore cover both brief writing and oral argument. The comments are solely mine. I cannot even say that all my former colleagues on the circuit courts agree with me. I have not asked them.

I have discussed this subject many times with practicing lawyers in speeches and seminars. An article reducing these informal dialogues to writing may appear simplistic, but I prefer the risk of oversimplification to even a whisper of unnecessary complexity. Communication in simple, understandable terms is a central theme for me.

Presentation of an appellate case on the calendar for oral argument involves assembling a group of actors at a formal meeting place under the rules of a highly structured system. Gathered together are (1) the lawyers (and the parties if they want to come); (2) the record of the case; (3) advance written statements of the parties' positions (the briefs); and (4) a body of official deciders (the judges). Following this assembly, and a short, reasoned discussion of the case, the official deciders reach a decision, and sometimes provide a written statement explaining how it was reached.

Counsel's role in this assembly is communication and persuasion, first by the briefs and then by oral argument. When the meeting occurs, the judges ordinarily will have done their homework. They will be sufficiently acquainted with the matters under discussion so that they can understand what is said and perhaps participate in the dialogue. Counsel's participation is specifically defined and rigidly constricted; skills of communication and persuasion must be brought to bear in a few pages and a few minutes.

Inform and Persuade

There are two steps for you, as counsel, to consider when convincing the court that what you advocate is correct. One is impressing your will upon the judges so that they accept what you urge; you cannot win until the deciders who read what is written and who listen to what is said move off dead center. However, before counsel can convince, you must inform. You must cause the court to understand. The process of linguistic communication has been described in this way:

> [T]he gulf that often separates sender and receiver [of communications], spanned at best by a bridge of signs and symbols, is sought to be narrowed yet further so that ultimately the intended communication may have the same meaning, or approximately the same meaning, for those on the left bank as those on the right.

I. M. Mehler, *Effective Legal Communication* 3 (1975).

It is not enough that counsel understands perfectly what is written and spoken. All is in vain unless the court also understands. But in many cases the advocate is so intent upon the ultimate aim of persuasion that the threshold step of making clear to the court what is complained of, how it came about, what the court should do about it, and why, is overlooked. I recall with pain and amusement the comment of a colleague, seated beside me, after 15 minutes of argument by an impassioned lawyer in a significant en banc case: "Do you have the remotest idea what he is talking about?"

The appellate judge has an interest in having the advocate perform effectively the double-barreled task of informing and persuading. The judge wants lawyers to get maximum mileage from the few pages and few minutes allotted to them. True, cases are won on the facts and the law, not on the eminence, polished writing, oratory, or personality of counsel. A lawyer can, and often does, lose with a good performance and win with a poor one. Courts give no medals for good briefs and arguments and seldom exact penalties for a poor performance.

Nonetheless, judges need help. They are neither all-wise nor all-seeing. Whether in the library or on the bench, the judge is trying to traverse the path from issue to answer. Every intellectual pore is open to receive help and guidance from what the lawyers say and write. This help is most effective when there are no artificial obstacles and irrelevant diversions impeding communication. Unfortunately, lawyers erect their own obstructions to the judge's progress from issue to answer.

Courtroom lawyers are endowed with at least a little more ego than the average person. Few are shrinking violets. In the adversary system, where someone must win and someone must lose, the loser is tempted to use the appellate court as a forum to soothe his or her bruised self-esteem. The winner is equally tempted to seek additional elevation of an already triumphant ego. Each lawyer wants the approval of the appellate body. The lawyer is filled with the case, proud if the winner, unhappy if the loser. Both sides feel better if they can share the experience with the court. Like a participant in a divorce case, the lawyer wants to tell everything that has ever happened, particularly if it is unpleasant.

Ego building and esteem repairing, however, are counterproductive when they interfere with the essential tasks of communication and persuasion. And sometimes they do interfere, with a vengeance. I keep a file of examples of poor appellate advocacy. One exhibit is a 58-page brief, of which 19 pages (one-third of the brief) are devoted to complaints about rulings and events before and at trial, followed by a statement that *none* of these matters is claimed to be reversible error. The crucial question in the case, the basis for appellate decision, is given three pages of superficial and incomplete discussion. Counsel squandered his time and his client's money to compose and print a litany of bruises to his emotions. The court lost the benefit of the guidance and assistance it wanted, needed, and should have had in those wasted pages.

Picking Issues

Each year I tell my law clerks that the most valuable by-product of clerking is grasping the fact that the dispositive issues in appeals are highly predictable. As Justice Robert H. Jackson wrote:

> One of the first tests of a discriminating advocate is to select the question, or questions, that he will present orally. Legal contentions, like the currency, depreciate through over-issue. The mind of an appellate judge is habitually receptive to the suggestion that a lower court committed an error. But receptiveness declines as the number of assigned errors increases. Multiplicity hints at lack of confidence in any one.

Jackson, "Advocacy Before the Supreme Court: Suggestions for Effective Case Presentation," in *Advocacy and the King's English* 216 (G. Rossman ed. 1960).

It is a lawyer's job to pick with a dispassionate and detached mind the issues that common sense and experience suggest will likely be dispositive. Other issues must be rejected or given short treatment. In oral argument, counsel may have to be even more selective. Eight or ten issues cannot be treated in 20 or 30 minutes.

The great advocate John W. Davis made this same point in different terms. He spoke of the "cardinal rule" that one must, in imagination, change places with the court.

> [T]hose judges who sit in solemn array before you, whatever their merit, know nothing whatever of the controversy that brings you to them, and are not stimulated to interest in it by any feeling of friendship or dislike of anyone concerned. They are not moved as perhaps an advocate may be by any hope of reward or fear of punishment. They are simply being called upon for action in this appointed sphere. They are anxiously waiting to be supplied with what Mr. Justice Holmes calls the "implements of decision." These by your presence you profess yourself ready to furnish. If the places were reversed and you sat where they do, think what it is you would want first to know about the case. How and in what order would you want the story told? How would you want the skein unraveled? What would make easier your approach to the true solution? These are questions the advocate must unsparingly put to himself. That is what I mean by changing places with the court.

Davis, "The Argument of an Appeal," in *Advocacy and the King's English* 216 (G. Rossman ed. 1960).

I recall an especially effective presentation by a young lawyer, formerly a law clerk for another circuit judge, who walked to the podium and said simply: "My name is So-and-So, from Houston, Texas. The issue in this case is whether *Chambers v. Maroney* is retroactive." The effect was electric. In two sentences, he had identified himself and precisely targeted the dispositive issue on which discussion would be centered and the case decided. The room came alive. Everyone was mentally on the edge of his chair. In seconds, counsel had riveted the attention of all on the critical question.

Contrast this with a brief I have in my file from a civil case in which there were either five or six issues, depending on how one might want to slice them. The appellant's brief stated them as 22 issues. There are few absolute rules in life, but here is one: There is no case in which 22 issues should be raised on appeal. Unfortunately, the appellee's brief did little better: It restated and regrouped the issues into 16. Appellant's reply brief in turn disagreed with appellee's restatement and contained a partial third regrouping. In appellee's brief, each restated point began with a statement similar to this: "This point covers appellant's points 2, 5, and the first half of 7, and the second half of 14."

To make our way through this maze, my clerk and I prepared a mammoth chart with lines, arrows, and boxes, making the necessary consolidations and separations and rationally redefining the issues. It looked like the organizational chart for the Department of Health and Human Services. In the box where each issue is described is a notation like this: "Read pp. 4–6, 14–17 and 42–44, Brief I; pp. 19–22 and 31–35 of Brief II; pp. 2–3 and 10 of Brief III." Counsel in this case were engaged not in communication but in saying things that were not communicated. The communicatee—me—had to devise his own system to understand what the two communicators were trying to tell him.

Clear and Simple Language

The need to be selective is just one aspect of a more general requisite: You must communicate with the court, by pen and by voice, in terms as simple and as easily understood as the subject matter permits. I used to tell my clerks a story told about General Stonewall Jackson. Pressed for a reason he kept on his staff a not-too-bright officer, Jackson replied: "When I have written a field order, I have him read it. If he can understand it, anybody can understand it." Write and talk that way to judges. Some are brilliant, some are bright, some pedestrian, but all want to understand, and understanding is the condition precedent to persuasion.

Speak to the court in conversational tones. The day of oration is gone. The great Chief Justice Vanderbilt put it this way: "The orotund quality, the accent of declamation, are as foreign to a good argument as they are to a prayer." Argument is more and more a Socratic dialogue between informed and interested persons.

For a guide to written simplicity, every lawyer, in fact every writer, can profit from Professor William Strunk, Jr.'s timeless little book *The Elements of Style* (3d ed. 1995). Priceless fundamentals of writing are crammed into its few pages. If I were still in the practice, I would get a copy for the desk of each lawyer in the firm. E. B. White, himself a craftsman with words, studied college English under Professor Strunk and edited later editions of the book. In the introduction to the 1972 edition, White referred to Strunk's "attempt to cut the vast tangle of English rhetoric down to size." Then he said:

> In its original form, it [the book] was a forty-three page summation of the case for cleanliness, accuracy, and brevity in the use of English. Today, fifty-two years later, its vigor is unimpaired, and for sheer pith I think it probably sets a record that is not likely to be broken.

In fact, *The Elements of Style* is so terse and full of wisdom that its key points cannot be shortened by paraphrases. It must be read.

Pared-down writing is so important that I cannot resist a few examples. Rudolf Flesch's book *The Art of Plain Talk* (1946) points out on pages 36–37 that the following language "is hard even on lawyers":

> Sick leave shall be granted to employees when they are incapacitated for the performance of their duties by sickness, injury, or pregnancy and confinement, or for medical, dental, or optical examination or treatment, or when a member of the immediate family of the employee is affected with a contagious disease and requires the care and attendance of the employee, or when through exposure to contagious disease, the presence of the employee at his post of duty would jeopardize the health of others.

He suggests this formulation instead:

> Employees shall be granted sick leave for these four reasons:
>
> (1) They cannot work because of sickness, injury, or pregnancy and confinement;
>
> (2) They need medical, dental, or optical treatment;
>
> (3) A member of their immediate family is affected with a contagious disease and needs their care and attendance;
>
> (4) Their presence at their post of duty would jeopardize the health of others through exposure to contagious disease.

His restatement is not substantively perfect, but unquestionably it is more quickly and easily understood.

Another example. Compare these two versions of an appellant's contention:

> (1) The plaintiff was not contributorily negligent when, as plaintiff was on his way to church, defendant's six-ton Mack truck thundered through the red light and upon plaintiff's Pinto automobile at the intersection of 8th and North streets in Savannah, Georgia, on February 2, 1974.

(2) The trial judge was plainly erroneous in entering a finding of fact that the plaintiff was guilty of contributory negligence.

Everything is wrong with the first version. It is mostly needless detail. Whether the truck ran the light and struck plaintiff's automobile, or plaintiff ran the light and drove in front of the truck, was a disputed question of fact on which the issue of contributory negligence turned. The references to defendant's six-ton truck, to plaintiff's Pinto automobile, and to plaintiff's being on the way to church, were sophomoric appeals to prejudice and sympathy. These things had already been set out in the statements of the facts, and none was relevant to the contributory negligence issue. There was only one accident, so the date and the name of the city and streets were of no significance.

The greatest fault in the first statement, however, is that the reader cannot tell what the writer is trying to communicate. Does he mean that the trial judge found contributory negligence and that this finding was plainly erroneous? Or does he mean that there was a jury finding of contributory negligence not supported by sufficient evidence? Or does he mean that there was no evidence of contributory negligence, so that as a matter of law plaintiff was not guilty of it? Or is he attempting to say that there was some evidence of contributory negligence but not enough to submit to a jury? Compare all this to the second statement, in which the court is told everything it needs to know, and no more.

Like other professionals, lawyers love, or fall into, professional jargon. Some words of the profession carry their own credentials and are invaluable: "proximate cause," "self-incrimination," and "impeachment." Other jargon adds nothing and can obscure meaning. In this "no value" category is the following example from my file:

> Without waiving any point heretofore made but expressly relying upon each and all of them, separately, severally and collectively, and without reflecting upon the able judge below, The Honorable _____, United States District Judge for the _____ District of _____, who ordinarily is fair, able and well informed but nevertheless is subject to normal human error, I am constrained to say, respectfully but firmly, that the District Judge committed error to the substantial prejudice of the plaintiff when he declined to accept the argument made in Part IV of plaintiff's trial brief relating to par. 7 of the complaint and instead accepted the contrary argument of the defendant and ruled accordingly.

This is irrelevant nonsense, except for the concluding effort to describe the error, and that effort conceals rather than describes the point. Only when the reader reaches into the body of the actual argument is he able to piece together what the writer means.

The author of this fog of words is an intelligent man. If asked on the street how to get to the nearest gasoline station, he would say: "Turn right at the second stoplight, go four blocks, and you'll see it on your left." But put a pencil in his hand and place him in his law library, and he lapses into the noncommunicative patois of his profession.

Some writers describe issues in a form similar to the jurisdictional statement required by the Supreme Court. Jurisdictional statements can serve an important function, but they are poor devices for transferring information from writer to reader. The writer who uses this format tries to crowd everything into one sentence. He strings out clauses independent and dependent, modifiers, qualifications, parenthetical phrases, and exceptions to the exception, all punctuated with citations. Here is a result.

> In an action brought by the last assignee and holder of a negotiable promissory note transferred to him by an assignor in good faith and upon valuable consideration but after maturity, can the maker of the note who is sued establish a setoff or counterclaim, whether matured, or not, if mature when pleaded, which setoff or counterclaim existed in favor of the maker against the assignor of the party suing, before notice to the maker of the assignment?

This is a fit example for *The New Yorker*'s "The Legal Mind at Work."

My file contains another striking example of how not to say it short and plain. The case was complex, and the brief writer had used up all allowable pages after being denied permission to file an overlength brief. One of the major parties was United States Fidelity & Guaranty Company, known to everyone who has done much trial practice, and surely to the brief writer, as USF&G. In every instance from the beginning of the brief to the end—more than 200 times—USF&G is referred to as "defendant-appellant United States Fidelity & Guaranty Company, a Maryland Corporation." Similarly, in every instance the trial judge is described not as "the judge," "the court," "the trial judge," "Judge Roe," or even "he," but as "Honorable Richard R. Roe, United States District Judge for the _____ District of _____." This is an example of how it went:

> The Honorable Richard R. Roe, United States District Judge for the _____ District of _____ , erred when he overruled, denied and failed to grant the objection of defendant-appellant United States Fidelity & Guaranty Company, a Maryland Corporation, to the admission into evidence of this exhibit, which exhibit was irrelevant, incompetent, immaterial, prejudicial and shed no light on any of the issues in the case.

Motivated by frustration and curiosity, I made a word count of the excess baggage consisting of the description of USF&G and of the trial judge. (Of course there was more flab than that.) This verbiage alone used up 16 pages, space precious to both the writer and the court.

The indiscriminate use of dates is another Linus blanket for the writer, but cruel and unusual punishment for the reader. I quote from a brief:

> The grand jury returned the indictment March 2, 1974. Defendant was arraigned March 17, 1974. He was tried beginning August 7, 1974. The jurors began deliberating August 9, 1974, in the late afternoon, and returned a verdict at midday August 10, 1974, after deliberating for six hours. The motion for new trial was filed August 18, 1974, argued September 10, 1974, after one continuance and denied by an order entered September 15, 1974. Defendant timely appealed September 20, 1974.

As I read, I assumed those dates and events were given for some purpose. I attempted to file each in my mind for future recall. Like a person watching a striptease, I assumed that when all the layers had been successively removed I would see something, but there was nothing to see. There was no issue of timeliness or delay in the case. No date—in fact not a word or figure of this entire recital—served any useful function.

There is a corollary to the principle of "tell it short and plain." It is "tell it once—or twice at most." Erosion by repetition is a poor way to convince. Most judges will catch the point the first time it is developed. Almost all will understand when it is run by the second time. They are more likely to understand if told early. The court blesses the lawyer who steps to the podium and, zap, like an arrow to the center of the target, strikes the heart of the controversy.

Many lawyers also spend too much space and time framing alternative arguments. Every appellate court understands the use of an alternative argument. Judges know that by suggesting an alternative, the advocate does not waive his initial contention. "Even if" or "alternatively" is enough. Using a phrase like "without waiving anything heretofore said to the contrary by specifically insisting thereon" is a trite formalism. It almost implies that the court has neither good sense nor good faith.

Tell the Whole Truth

Besides writing simply, every appellate advocate must state facts and law candidly and accurately. This is an uncompromising absolute. Every sentence must shine with the whole truth. Even when it has been misled, the court may find the correct path, but a lawyer who is inaccurate or less than candid interferes with the objective of persuasion. Lawyers come to the court saying "please believe me and be persuaded," but if what is said cannot be believed, the confidence that he or she seeks to create is forfeited.

Telling the facts accurately does not mean stopping with just those facts favorable to your side. It especially does not mean stating inferences as though they were facts. In an appeal in which everything turned on whether the accused was inside or outside a car when arrested, the statement of facts in the defendant's brief said, without qualification or reference to pages of the record, that the accused was inside the car. The government's brief, with equal assurance and without reference to what the defendant had asserted, baldly stated that the defendant was outside the car. This sent me to the record to read pertinent testimony. I discovered, as you might expect, that some witnesses said the defendant was inside the car, and others said he was outside.

Both counsel misled the court. Neither told us that the evidence was in conflict and that the real issue was whether permissible inferences had been drawn from the conflicting testimony. This is inexcusably bad advocacy.

Both brief and argument should reflect the dignity and professional competence of the spokesman and a respect for the courts, trial and appellate. Improper tone is a self-created impediment. Courts are uncomfortable with a lawyer who recklessly accuses his adversary of misleading the court or misstating the facts. Casting aspersions on an adversary casts a shadow on a lawyer's own standards and on the strength of the presentation. No one expects a good lawyer to roll over and play dead. But firmness and preservation of one's own points and rights seldom require stridency or discourtesy.

Besides keeping the court comfortable, appropriate moderation is also persuasive. I say "appropriate" because a case may call for forceful hard-hitting statements. But not every mosquito must be killed with a sledgehammer. Appellate judges, except brand-new ones, have already heard, and rejected, more ad hominem arguments than any one lawyer can think up. A judge who has normal sensibilities and loves the law will react on his or her own to events that call for outrage.

Answers to Questions

Finally, there is the matter of responding to questions from the bench. In an assemblage where the purpose is to inform and persuade, it should be like manna from heaven for the potential persuadee to say to the persuader: "Here is what troubles me about the subject on which you are trying to convince me." This is an opening into the mind of the listener. It is the most valuable piece of information the persuader can get. Most advocates understand this principle and welcome questions from the bench. They know how to capitalize on them. Other counsel unwisely resent questions as intrusions into a carefully prepared and organized presentation. But the court has its own responsibility to reach the correct decision, and only the judge knows what still troubles him or her.

I have been surprised at the number of experienced advocates who believe that they are overquestioned during oral argument. Though questioning sometimes is overdone, and the judge may ask for help too soon, usually it is essential and inevitable. Judges enjoy lively dialogue, but they too can, and do, impede the communicative process. The solution lies, I believe, in moderation on both sides of the bench. Counsel can recognize and accept why questions are valuable to the court. The court can exercise restraint through fewer and better-thought-out questions, and can be a little less quick on the trigger.

In the written words in the brief and spoken words at the podium, the advocate should try to leave some parting impression fixed in the minds of the judges who have read and listened. There is no better impression to leave than this: "I understood what he said. He did not say too much. I have confidence in what he said. I am persuaded by it and am compelled to rule with him."

Points on Appeal

Arthur L. Alarcon

Using the language of the business world, it is the lawyer's job to sell or communicate the righteousness of his client's cause in the midst of many other earnest competitors for our attention. Those of you who practice in the federal courts are aware of our rising caseloads. In the last two years, case participation per judge has increased from 184 to 350. At the same time, the number of cases filed in our court has increased by 19 percent. The result of our increased output, in response to an overpowering caseload, is that we have less time to spend on your cases than did our predecessors.

Until you file fewer appeals, or we get more judges, all of us will have to accommodate ourselves to this reality—an increasing workload, given the same number of workers, means less time available per unit.

This condition, in turn, places a greater burden on appellate lawyers to produce briefs of the highest professional standards to assist judges in producing dispositions that are well reasoned and correct. Because of crowded argument calendars and mounting filings, you have an ever-increasing responsibility to your clients to write carefully, clearly, and briefly to gain our concurrence in the justice of your cause.

With the foregoing solemn sermon in mind, I will proceed to set forth some of my observations after several years of reading briefs and hearing oral argument as a circuit judge.

First, make a record. Justice Tobriner of the California Supreme Court once observed in a luncheon speech in Los Angeles that trial judges spend their careers searching for the truth, while appellate judges look only for error. We simply cannot reverse a judgment unless error appears on the record.

Arthur L. Alarcon is United States circuit judge in the Ninth Circuit Court of Appeals. Judge Alarcon's chapter also appeared in the June 1984 issue of ABTL Reports, *published by the Association of Business Trial Lawyers.*

Those of you who confine your labors to litigation exclusively and leave to others the handling of the appeal should be mindful that many errors can be disregarded by appellate judges if a proper objection is not made in the trial court. Let me set forth some examples of trial omissions we see frequently.

1. Affirmative defenses and matters in evidence such as immunity and res judicata must be pleaded and proved in the trial court. Failure to do so results in waiver. *See Santos v. Alaska Bar Association*, 618 F.2d 575, 576–77 (9th Cir. 1980) (immunity and res judicata may not be raised for the first time on appeal).
2. Error in the admission or exclusion of evidence cannot be raised on appeal unless a timely objection or motion to strike appears on the record, stating the specific ground of objection, unless the ground is apparent from the record. Fed. R. Evid. 103(a) (1). (Do not rely on your assessment that anything is apparent from the record—we may not agree with you.)
3. Evidence improperly received under one theory at trial may not be successfully defended on appeal on alternate grounds where a finding of the existence of requisite foundational facts must be made by the trial court before admission. *See Giordenello v. United States*, 357 U.S. 480, 488 (1957) (A party cannot support admissibility on a theory raised for the first time on appeal because it would unfairly deny the other side an adequate opportunity to cross-examine the government's witnesses or adduce rebuttal evidence). *See also Sims v. United States*, 405 F.2d 1381, 1383 (D.C. Cir. 1968) (consideration of alternative bases for the admissibility of evidence received at trial refused because the argument was not presented to the trial court).
4. Alleged lawyer or judicial misconduct cannot be raised on appeal without a proper objection or motion unless it is so flagrant that the plain error rule applies. (Again, I would not gamble that an appellate court will clean up behind you by holding that your silence is excused by the plain error rule.)
5. Error in the giving or failure to give an instruction may not be raised on appeal unless a timely objection setting forth the specific grounds therefor has been made in the trial court. Fed. R. Civ. P. 5.

Appellate courts are tolerant of the errors described above based on the theory that it is unfair to the trial judge and opposing counsel to sit back until an unfavorable judgment is rendered before raising issues that could have been cured by swift remedial action. If you fail to make a proper objection you risk an adverse ruling from an unsympathetic panel holding that had you done your job, the trial court would have ruled properly and your client would not have suffered.

Writing Briefs

Second, brief writing. My concerns about brief writing are not new. Unfortunately, the same problems continue to recur.

1. *Use simple, clear language.* Don't obfuscate or pettifog in setting forth your contentions in an effort to show your command of the English language. I may be too busy to look up a polysyllabic term you have used to impress us. (For example, don't use words like obfuscate, pettifog, or polysyllabic. Why not say confuse or imprecise?)
2. *Be blissfully brief.* State your point concisely and once. Nothing is more irritating than to have the same question stated again and again in varying ways for forty-five sleep-inducing pages of redundancy. Let me add an incentive to the production of short and pertinent briefs. The longer you make your brief, the more likely that most of the preargument analysis of your case will be turned over to a law clerk who just finished the bar exam.
3. *Be accurate in summarizing the facts.* A brief writer should summarize facts with scrupulous accuracy. If you slant the facts, or ignore evidence that hurts your position, you can be sure your opponent will highlight in outraged detail the facts you have distorted or omitted. Misstating the record can irretrievably damage your credibility with the court. You don't want to waste precious time at oral argument trying to rehabilitate yourself.

Another rule frequently overlooked is one that requires appellate courts to accept as true every fact that supports the judgment and to disregard contradicting evidence submitted by the losing party. We read many briefs that set forth only the evidence presented at trial by the appellant. We are then asked to reverse on the ground that the trier of fact erred in entering judgment for the appellee in the face of such overwhelming evidence. That type of brief lightens our workload. We must summarily affirm—although in the hands of competent counsel, reversible error might have been readily demonstrable.

Please don't misunderstand me. When you can demonstrate that error was committed, it is vitally necessary for you to present a fair summary of the evidence on *both* sides. If the evidence at trial was evenly balanced, then the impact of error in the admission of evidence, or the instructions on the theory of the case or the defense, or misconduct in closing argument may have been more damaging than in a case where the evidence in favor of the prevailing party was overwhelming.

In setting forth the facts, *always* refer to the page and line of the record where the testimony appears. If you fail to do so, you place the burden on the appellate court to search through the entire transcript to find some verification for your claim. That is not our job. We may fail to do it for you, or we may try and be unable to locate support for your position. Now, let me hasten to add that most of us will in fact search the transcript for the facts you rely upon even if you do not refer us to the record. We do so, however, with some discontent and lingering doubts about your competency and the integrity of your arguments.

4. *Always cite and analyze those authorities that do not appear to support your position.* You have an *ethical* duty to do so. Rule 3.3(a) (3) American Bar Association, Model Rules of Professional Conduct, Rule 3.3(a)(3); Cal. Business and Professions Code § 6068d (West 1974). *See Shaeffer v. State Bar,* 160 P.2d 825, 829 (Cal. 1945) (counsel must direct the court's attention to a decision that contains a decision contrary to his position).

If you fail to do it, you can be assured that your opponent will cite and discuss all the law that undermines your contention, with enthusiasm. If opposing counsel misses it, one of my law clerks will probably find it. If we discover these cases *after* argument, you have lost your opportunity to persuade us that these cases are either distinguishable, or should not be followed because of faulty reasoning, or that recent developments in the law support your position.

I once worked on a matter in which we were asked to adopt the law of another circuit. Counsel failed, however, to point out that the Ninth Circuit Court of Appeals had expressly rejected this precise suggestion four times in the last twelve years. Opposing counsel enjoyed the opportunity to expose this appalling and fairly obvious dereliction of duty. Counsel's lack of candor placed a great strain on our collective judicial temperament. We are, unfortunately, human.

5. *Limit your issues on appeal.* In every long trial, error is committed by one of the participants. With very few exceptions, only prejudicial error will result in a reversal. Use a scalpel and not a shotgun in shaping your appeal.

If, after combing the record, you find thirty-seven errors that range in gravity from minimal to devastating, don't argue with equal vigor and passion that each one, standing alone, was prejudicial. You devalue your argument if you assert that error in overruling an objection to a compound or leading question compels reversal if you also argue that damaging hearsay evidence was admitted. (Has any court reversed because a trial judge erroneously permitted a witness to answer a leading or compound question?)

Try to limit your appeal to the three or four most serious issues in the case that you feel best demonstrate prejudicial error.

Present your strongest argument first. Don't hide it in the midst of a collection of your weakest points. If you put your best contention last, the court may lose confidence in your ability to recognize prejudicial error when you see it before they reach that issue.

6. *Do not give a long string of citations for relevant case authority that clearly supports your position.* It is a waste of your time. Just cite the earliest case in point and the most recent in order to demonstrate the continuing vitality of the principle you are espousing. Be sure that you read the case you cite.

   Recently, I read a brief that cited a case for a principle of law that was important to the writer's client. No jump citation was given to the page where the legal question was discussed by the court. In reading the case, I learned the reason. The favorable proposition appeared in a headnote but not in the text. Always refer the court to the exact page where your point is covered. Do not rely on us to read the entire case to ferret out the discussion that you believe supports your view.

7. *In citing a case that you believe contains helpful language in a matter involving comparable facts, always give the court a brief statement of the facts.* By so doing, you can state with accuracy and confidence that the law expressed in the cited case should be applied to your cause because the facts are analogous. Too often, counsel find themselves in the embarrassing position of being unable to answer the court's question, "Counsel, what were the facts before the court in that case?" A citation without some discussion of the treatment of the issue is not very helpful.

8. *Avoid the use of footnotes.* Avoid the temptation of parading the brilliance and depth of your research into related areas of the law by crowding your brief with footnotes. If the point advances your client's cause, put the discussion in the text. Do not bury it. If the discussion is not relevant, leave it out.

   Footnotes force the reader to break his concentration on your discussion of an issue to chase after an often extraneous diversion. One of my colleagues has stated publicly that he never reads footnotes before oral argument. If you want our undivided attention, you should put your comment in the text.

9. *Long quotations are exasperating and distracting.* Further, they sometimes appear to be a lazy person's substitute for analysis. If you must quote, select the precise sentence that advances or supports your discussion of the law. If you use an ellipsis to show that you have omitted part of the quotation, do not cheat. If you leave out language that hurts you, we will find out. Whenever I see an ellipsis, I check to see what you have omitted. Your deliberate omission may emphasize what you may have tried to avoid.

10. *If you are relying on a statute, rule, or regulation, include the relevant text in the body of your discussion.* Do not assume that the judges have memorized 18 U.S.C. § 651(3)(c) or that they will enjoy being assigned the job of looking up the law and picking out the portion that advances your position. Make it easy for the judge to rule in your favor. Don't take the chance that a tired, aging judge may decide that your citation must not be too important or you would have set it out.

    Remember also that most federal judges become generalists. Do not assume that we are as familiar with the buzz words or the numbers of the statutes or regulations that are commonplace in cocktail conversations among the experts in your specialty. (My wife has pointed out that it is not very charming for me to ask my California criminal defense lawyer friends in her presence if they are going to pursue their *Rost* motion and 995 (Cal. Per. code section 995) before the 1368 hearing.) *See Rost v. Municipal Court,* 184 Cal. App. 2d 507, 512 (1960) (a warrant of arrest must be shown within a reasonable time after the filing of the complaint). Do not do the same kind of thing to a judge who may not have heard of or visited a "scenes a faire" before reviewing your copyright case. Err on the side of explaining too much. We need your help in getting to the heart of your problem.

11. *The rules of our circuit require that you set forth the standard of review on appeal.* 9th Cir. R. 13(b)(2). On each calendar we have at least one lawyer who has no notion of the standard that limits our review of his appeal.

12. *Conclude your brief with a half-page summary of your argument and a clear statement of the precise relief you want from the court.* If you want us to instruct the trial court to do something upon remand, suggest to us the precise direction we should give to serve your client's interests.

13. *Do not duck any of your opponent's contentions or arguments.* You may think it is so weak it deserves no answer. We may find it persuasive after a first reading. If you ignore it, we may be persuaded that it is irrefutable.

Oral Argument

Third, oral argument. After listening to oral arguments for many years, I have compiled the following list that I would try to follow if I were to return to the practice of the law.

1. Do not waive oral argument unless you have abandoned all hope or would be willing to guarantee reimbursement to your client if your confidence in the ultimate success of your position is wrong.

2. Do not waste time in summarizing the facts. The judges have read the briefs.
3. Start by advising the court you will be happy to address any questions before you proceed with your argument.
4. Begin your argument by outlining the dispositive issues you wish to address.
5. Do not argue every issue with equal fervor. Choose your sure winners. If you cannot tell, you are in trouble.
6. Be ready to concede that some of your contentions may not be as compelling for reversal or affirmance as the rest.
7. Do not get angry at the judge who attacks your position. He may be your best supporter on the appeal.
8. Respond to the court's questions. If you are caught by surprise—admit it and ask for the opportunity to file a letter brief. Do not wing it.
9. Speak up if you wish to be heard. We are getting older.
10. Make your argument as interesting as possible. Do not read and do not quote. Use your own words.
11. Quit if you sense you are ahead. You do not have to argue the allotted time.
12. Never argue credibility if you are the appellant. The court may view any contested facts or inferences in favor of your opponent.
13. Know your record and the exhibits. Be ready to cite exact pages and lines or exhibits by number to support your argument.
14. Be prepared to tell the court how you would like the dispositive paragraph to read if you could write the opinion.
15. Ask the court if there are further questions before you sit down. It is OK to thank the court for its courteous attention to your cause. Surprisingly, few lawyers do.

Some Nuts and Bolts of Appellate Advocacy

Jim R. Carrigan

While the rules governing briefs and oral argument in state courts of last resort differ substantially, the tactics, skills, and techniques of persuasion are universal. Yet even with the most arduous research, law books will not produce many workable pointers in this field. Some practical hints on appellate advocacy from a recently "benched" trial lawyer might, therefore, be helpful. My views are based on personal observations from "the other side of the bench."

An appellate judge soon learns that friends and former colleagues approach him or her with awkwardness when greeting the former litigator "off the bench." Some who have always been on a first name basis suddenly begin using titles like "Your Honor." The problem for the lawyer is how to walk the line between stiff formality on the one hand and obsequious servility on the other. One should not be overly friendly, yet not disrespectful. There are a few judges who have a taste for ermine and would prefer to be called "Your Worship," but, generally speaking, the best course is to do what comes most naturally and not worry about it.

What then is the proper attitude, frame of mind, and tone of communication for a lawyer to cultivate in arguing to an appellate court? For some lawyers, especially the young, arguing before a state supreme court is a fearful experience calculated to humble, mortify, and confuse. The very setting—with the lawyers down in the pit before several black-robed "wise men"—is awe-inspiring. The atmosphere is not a congenial setting for communicating ideas.

The persuader should begin with a mind-set that will facilitate concentration on the ideas involved in the argument without being distracted by

---

The Honorable Jim R. Carrigan is a U.S. district judge of the Colorado Supreme Court in Denver. A similar version of the article originally appeared in THE COLORADO LAWYER. *The article is reprinted by permission of* THE COLORADO LAWYER *from Vol. 8, No. 5 (1979). © The Colorado Bar Association, 1979. All rights reserved.*

the personalities present or their elevated status. One highly successful Colorado lawyer says that as he stands to begin his oral argument, he visualizes all the justices sitting on the bench in red "long johns." Thus, he pierces the barrier of dignified pomposity and gets down to telling these other lawyers—who happen to be wearing black robes—about his case.

By whatever means, the lawyer's attitude must be to seek to *communicate*. This entails concentrating on the *content* of the legal issues involved in his presentation, in his opponent's argument, and in questions raised by the court. The demeanor most likely to facilitate communication is one of mutual respect and civility due to co-professionals working together to solve a problem.

The question frequently arises: Who should handle the case on appeal—the lawyer who tried it, or an appellate specialist? In an earlier era there was perhaps more specialization in appellate advocacy, and there are still many lawyers who follow this specialty. Some of the best briefs and oral arguments are the work of specialists in the appellate divisions of the public defender's office and the attorney general's office. But, by and large, there are many advantages to having the same lawyer who tried the case write the brief and argue the appeal.

Obviously there are substantial savings for the client in *not* familiarizing a new lawyer with the vast detail of the trial record. The lawyer who tried the case has lived intimately with it—its facts and law, its bone and marrow—for a year or two. The issues on appeal must have been raised at trial. The lawyer who lived with the case in the lower courts can explain it better—give more life to those issues and their complexities. Very often a justice will ask a specific question about something that occurred at trial—and it is frustrating for everyone in the courtroom when the response is, "I don't know, I didn't try the case."

Moreover, the lawyer who tried the case is less likely to misstate the record accidentally. Misstating the record is a cardinal sin that raises the hackles of the justices and totally undermines the credibility of counsel. There is just no way to know for sure whether such a misstatement of the record is blameless, negligent, or intentional.

One less obvious aspect cannot be overlooked. The lawyer who tried the case is certainly more likely to be able to communicate—nonverbally—that critical sense of injustice that makes appellate courts scrutinize cases closely. Arguing an appeal of someone else's trial must be, emotionally, a little like kissing your sister.

A caveat must be kept in mind. The appellate lawyer's function is primarily intellectual. Too much emotionalism can be counterproductive, in bad taste, and downright offensive. Therefore, if the lawyer who tried the case cannot overcome and put aside any *hostility* toward the trial judge and *bad* feelings toward opposing counsel that the trial may have generated, it is probably better for the lawyer who tried the case not to brief and argue the appeal.

Brief means what it says. Court rules regarding the number of pages allowed in briefs set *maximums,* not minimums. Lawyers should not feel that they have to use all the pages allowed. Briefs are not graded by length or weight, as we sometimes suspected in law school.

Anyone acquainted with the caseload problems in most appellate courts must realize that as briefs grow in girth, the chances of their being read decrease. For example, our court typically hears six or seven cases on each oral argument day. In each case, assuming only one party on each side and no amici curiae, we have to read at least one opening brief, one answer brief and one reply brief. Often, multiple parties and amici file extra briefs. Thus, each justice is expected to read and digest at *least* three briefs for each case. In the seven cases set for each oral argument day, each justice must plow through at least twenty-one briefs. Our court hears cases four days during the week of each month that we devote to oral argument. This means about eighty-four briefs (plus amici and extra party briefs) must be read in preparing for oral argument week. In addition, many courts have their law clerks or staff lawyers prepare, and circulate in advance of oral argument, memoranda highlighting the points raised in the briefs.

The point is simple. To be persuasive, a brief must be read. Its chances of being read and assimilated are in inverse proportion to its length. Briefs should be edited and "boiled down" to eliminate repetition and surplusage.

Points or issues to be covered in the briefs, and on oral argument, should be carefully selected. The fewer points raised, the greater will be the court's concentration on each. The rifle shot, rather than the scattergun, is likely to hit the bull's-eye—or at least the judge's eye.

Similarly, oral argument should concentrate only on the strongest points raised. Oral argument time is far too precious to be spread thinly over many issues. The weaker points should be submitted on the briefs. As Mr. Justice Jackson said, "The mind of an appellate judge is habitually receptive to the suggestion that a lower court committed an error. But receptiveness declines as the number of assigned errors increases. . . ."

If I were to advise lawyers when to waive oral argument, my advice could be stated in one word: Never! Waiving oral argument inescapably carries the implication that counsel feels the case is not important enough to justify argument. Even worse, waiver may cause some judges to infer that counsel feels the arguments set out in the brief are so weak or doubtful that counsel is embarrassed to appear personally to express them. Waiver thus marks the case, in the minds of some judges, as a pro forma appeal of a hopeless cause that the lawyer is processing because the client demanded an appeal or because he has a sense of duty to exhaust all possible avenues of relief.

Oral argument is far too important to be waived. Impersonal persuasion—or selling of ideas—through a brief is useful. But its efficacy compared to a vigorous, personalized argument is much like that of a salesman's letter compared to his personal sales call to present his pitch to the prospect.

In today's busy, overscheduled courts, oral argument is critical to assist the judges in focusing on the really important issues. Moreover, a scheduled oral argument date acts as a deadline to stimulate the judges to read the briefs. In many courts, oral arguments are tape-recorded and any judge may play back any part or all of the argument.

Oral argument is usually followed immediately the same day by a brief conference at which each argued case is discussed and a tentative vote taken. All the justices who heard the argument participate fully.

By contrast, a case submitted on the briefs without oral argument may be assigned to one judge. His job is to study the briefs, then write and circulate to his colleagues a proposed opinion. Such a decision, and opinion, tends to be the product of only one judge instead of the collegiate product of the whole court.

The importance of oral argument is also illustrated by the fact that the tentative vote taken immediately after oral argument is seldom changed. After that vote is taken, the case is assigned to one of the justices who voted in the majority to write an opinion. It is usually weeks, or even months, later when that opinion is circulated and set for discussion at the court's regular, weekly opinion conference. Those justices who did not write the opinion will not remember the case in great detail and will tend to be persuaded by the views of the justice to whom the opinion was assigned. Thus, for practical purposes, the "tentative" vote taken immediately after oral argument, which is greatly influenced by the oral argument, generally decides the case.

In planning oral argument, it is important to know whether the court will be a "hot bench" or a "cold bench." A hot bench is one composed of justices or judges who read the briefs prior to oral argument, and a cold bench is one composed of those who do not. Many appellate judges feel that it is better not to read the briefs in advance of oral argument.

If the case is being presented to a cold bench, the appellant who opens the case has a considerably heavier burden of stating the facts and the issues of the case in a clear, cogent manner. Even if the case is being presented to a hot bench, it is safe to assume that few, if any, of the judges have had time to give really careful study to all the briefs. Moreover, to be on the safe side, counsel should assume that none of the judges has read the transcript of the record in advance of oral argument. Thus, the task of stating the case should be approached with the attitude that the lawyer is trying to explain the facts and issues to legal peers who want to know and understand all they can about the matter.

Counsel should not read from briefs or other documents, except when short quotations will add emphasis or authority. For the nervous lawyer, it may be helpful to write out the first sentence or two of the oral argument, and perhaps the planned "closer" that emphatically summarizes the matter. Otherwise, concise notes or an outline should be relied upon, and there should be a maximum of both voice and eye contact so that there can be real communication of ideas.

A great appellate advocate, John W. Davis, suggested that the lawyer arguing an appeal should mentally change places with the judges on the bench. He should say to himself, "If you were up there and had a job to do deciding this case and wanted to do the best job you could, what would you want to hear from counsel?"

Counsel must choose the most persuasive points to raise. There is no need for reciting detailed citations unless one of the justices asks for them. Transcript and case citations should be available in the event a judge requests them. If not readily at hand, counsel should not spend time leafing through the brief, but should inform the court that they are in the brief and available by consulting the table of authorities.

Where counsel will rely on authorities not in the brief, they should be listed, filed with the clerk, and served on the opponent a day or two before the oral argument.

Before the argument, the lawyer should visit the court and sit through the argument of another case. He should become familiar with the physical layout, especially with the space available on the podium for notes, files, and other records. If the podium is a modern one—adjustable in height—counsel should know how to operate it. The lawyer should note the location of the clock or other timing device and find out how the court indicates time limits and warns when time is about to expire. Counsel must also know how to arrange to reserve part of the allocated time for rebuttal and how the court will signal when opening argument begins to encroach on rebuttal time.

Part of oral argument preparation is getting into the proper frame of mind. Counsel should be well-rested and alert, tense and sharp, quick rather than tranquilized or too relaxed. Oral argument can be an exciting and stimulating intellectual exercise, as well as one of the highest forms of the advocate's art.

Innovation and creativity are not confined to the trial level, but also may be most helpful on appeal. For example, demonstrative aids may be very persuasive in appellate argument. Thus, briefs should not attempt to explain or describe facts that can be illustrated by reproducing maps, blueprints, plans, photographs, or drawings. In a products liability case, photographs of the product, scale drawings, and photographs of the warning label involved or the part that allegedly failed can be very important. Since these items cannot be included in the brief or presented at oral argument unless they were admitted into evidence at the trial, the brief should refer to their exhibit numbers.

Even where not included in the brief, it may be helpful to display such demonstrative evidence exhibits to the court while arguing an appeal. For example, our court recently heard a criminal case in which the defense was mistaken identification. There had been a photo lineup in which the victim had been shown five photographs. Four depicted balding, middle-aged men, some with glasses. The other was of the rather young-looking defendant who had a full head of hair and no glasses. Such a demonstration is very persuasive to the appellate court. Similarly, a lawyer should show the appellate court actual aerial photo blowups, mock-ups, and models, as well as charts of accident scenes and other demonstrative evidence.

Every case is different, and each lawyer's style is individual. What works for one lawyer or one case may not work for all. But a few fundamental suggestions may be generally useful.

A straightforward, narrative style is probably the most useful to fit all that must be said into the brief time allotted. For example, an appellant who has twenty minutes to present his opening argument, with some additional time for rebuttal, should plan to state the case on the opening argument as if he were at the airport seeing off a lawyer friend whose plane leaves in twenty minutes. Given that twenty minutes to relate to the friend everything about this important case, how should the case be presented?

Rebuttal time should be used for rebuttal. Many judges resent as unfair tactics the raising, in rebuttal time, of issues that were not discussed by the opponent and were not mentioned in the opening argument.

The side entitled to rebuttal should *always* reserve at least a few minutes for rebuttal. If no rebuttal is required, the time need not be used, and counsel will receive a "gold star" from the court for concluding the argument in less than the full time allotted. If no rebuttal time has been saved, however, and opposing counsel misstates the record or miscites a case, there is no opportunity to respond. If nothing else, reserving rebuttal time acts as a healthy deterrent to an opponent who otherwise might be tempted to stretch the record a bit in argument.

Timing the argument is extremely important. Be sure to understand who keeps track of the time and what, if any, warnings about time are given. In our court, for example, each side is given 30 minutes in the typical case. There are three lights on the podium. A green light comes on when the lawyer begins his argument. After 20 minutes, a yellow light comes on to warn that only ten minutes remain. At the end of that time, a red light comes on. It has its usual meaning and is strictly enforced. One who wants to be informed when five minutes remain should make that request at the beginning of the argument.

A frequent tactical question is whether to divide one's precious allotment of oral argument time among two or more lawyers. In the typical case, dominated by a single major issue, this is probably not advisable, because it tends to diffuse concentration. In multiple issue cases, however, or those involving considerable public interest, different considerations may apply. For example, if an amicus curiae has been permitted to file a brief, and represents an important public interest group, it may be wise to grant the amicus some portion of your oral argument time. This adds not only persuasiveness to your case, but adds importance to the case itself as viewed by the court.

One generally neglected weapon in the appellate advocate's armamentarium is the opinion written by the court below. It seems ironic that lawyers search far and wide for similar cases from which to quote judicial reasoning, yet almost never quote the often scholarly, well-reasoned, and persuasive opinions of the trial court and the intermediate appellate court in the very case at issue. Mr. Justice Marshall has noted his Court's disappointment in counsel's common failure "to use a beautiful opinion by the lower court, scholarly done, bursting with research."

Our state has been blessed with an excellent court of appeals and many superb trial judges. Their work product in the form of opinions commands high respect in our court. Even a dissenting opinion in the intermediate appellate court can be most persuasive. In fact, a well-written dissent is frequently determinative of our decision to grant certiorari. A lawyer who fails to mention or quote from the dissent in that situation surely forfeits a real opportunity to persuade.

Just as there is a time to speak up, there is a time to be silent. If the trial judge whose decision you seek to uphold is highly regarded, surely he or she should be mentioned in your oral argument. In every state, however, there are a few trial judges whose decisions are as "reversible" as some jackets. Past experience with their work has taught appellate judges to scrutinize it with special care and to exercise less than the usual reluctance about reversing. If such a judge rendered the trial court decision in your favor, the less said about it the better.

The question of questions is troublesome to some lawyers. How should counsel respond when oral argument is interrupted by questions from those stolid, black robes on the bench? The first response should be rejoicing! A question proves that at least one of the judges is awake. If by chance the question is relevant to the argument, it may even demonstrate that the interrogator is following the argument and you have captured the interest of the judge.

Most questions can be taken at face value and ought to be answered promptly and forthrightly. Evading an immediate, candid answer by putting off the question to be dealt with later not only irritates the judge who asked the question, but also may provide an opponent an opportunity to answer it on rebuttal.

Counsel should realize, however, that every question is not necessarily what it seems. Some appellate judges question counsel to persuade their colleagues on the bench. Such questions are really directed *through*, not *to*, counsel, and it is through the content of the judge's question, not the answer, that the interrogating judge intends to assist his slower-witted confreres to see the point of the case. The lawyer must be "tuned in" to the question and its real purpose. If the questioner's attitude, and the sense of the question, seem favorable, a very brief, congenial response is appropriate. Above all, counsel should avoid becoming combative with a judge whose question is helping the cause. All too often, a lawyer bites the helping hand.

Some appellate judges succumb to the temptation to "play lawyer" at oral argument. Thus, counsel may be bombarded by probing questions as if he or she were a witness undergoing cross-examination. The victim of this form of lawyer abuse has no real remedy, except in the other judges' sense of fair play, but that remedy is usually sufficient.

The appellate lawyer must learn to deal with the "straw man" questions employed by some judges. Such a judge usually has made up his mind against the position being advocated on a particular issue. He steps into the argument with a question or a statement logically extending the argument to a ridiculous extreme, states an example in the form of a question, and tries to attribute the example to the lawyer by a statement such as, "Is that what you are arguing?" The lawyer must firmly—but as graciously as possible—state that he did not intend to make such a statement, then move quickly to another subject. He must not allow himself to be lured into wasting valuable time jousting the straw man.

In planning oral argument, an important consideration is the *order* in which the issues will be discussed. Lawyers differ on whether the most important issue should be treated first, last, or somewhere in the middle. For several reasons, I advise discussing it at the outset. First, the court is freshest, most receptive, and most interested in the case at the beginning of your argument. Second, the principle of primacy teaches that the point first argued makes the deepest and most lasting impression. And, third, if the most important issue is reserved until last, the court's questions may use all the time allotted and there may never be a chance to discuss it.

Appellate advocacy requires that the lawyer be flexible and adaptable. One who mechanistically adheres to a previously plotted "game plan," in spite of unforeseen developments in the course of the argument, is not likely to communicate well. For example, when it is obvious from the court's questions that a majority has decided one issue in your favor, switch to other issues. There is always the danger of flaying a dead horse back to life with your tongue.

Lawyers differ on whether it is wise to bring the client to an appellate argument. Generally, that practice may influence one to engage in a more emotional, jury-type argument to impress the client. But it is not the client one needs to impress in oral argument. Nor are the justices likely to be swayed by the style that would sway the typical client. Therefore, for most cases, the better rule is probably to leave the client at home.

While not wishing to encourage emotionalism in oral argument, I must stress that the persuasive appellate advocate should communicate in bearing, tone of voice, and general attitude a strong feeling of the innate justice of the cause. Stated conversely, counsel must make the court feel a sense of injustice in what has happened to the client in the court below—or in what would happen to the client if that court were reversed. In short, a little restrained and tasteful righteous indignation will not hurt. Most judges who choose careers on appellate courts have given up highly lucrative pursuits to be there because they really care about justice. Thus it helps to "have a little justice on your side" and to be able to communicate that feeling. If you do not feel strongly a sense of the fairness of your case, and a sense of injustice in the opponent's position, perhaps it is a case someone else ought to argue.

Tips for Appellate Advocates

Robert L. Stern

Many aspects of appellate advocacy often escape lawyers' attention. Some of these considerations are subtle, some are incompletely understood, and some seem so obvious that no one talks about them. But, inattention does not come from unimportance. In fact, these overlooked features can greatly affect, and sometimes even determine, the outcome of an appeal.

A good example is the caseload in most appellate courts. Many lawyers have a general idea that appellate work has gone up, but few know how great the increase has been or how much it affects what courts must do in handling appeals.

First, the facts: The number of appeals in most state courts has doubled every ten years since the 1940s. The number of cases decided by the federal courts of appeals has grown from 3,900 in 1960 to more than 41,000 in 1990. Cases docketed in the United States Supreme Court, including petitions for review by certiorari and appeal (and not merely the small number heard on the merits), have jumped from about 1,200 in 1950 to 5,500 in 1990. Of course, the number of justices in that Court and in almost all state supreme courts has remained unchanged. By no coincidence, the Supreme Court decides approximately the same number of argued cases on the merits each year—150—as it has for some time. Thus, especially for the highest courts in the state and federal systems, this is not an increase; it is an explosion—both absolutely and per judge.

As these bare statistics show, appellate judges now have much heavier workloads. One effect has been the creation of intermediate appellate courts in 38 states. Only one state with a population exceeding

---

Robert L. Stern practices law with Mayer, Brown & Platt in Chicago. He is co-author of Stern, Gressman, Shapiro & Geller, Supreme Court Practice *(7th ed. 1993) and author of* Appellate Practice in the United States *(2d ed. 1989), from which the material in this article comes.*

2 million, Mississippi, does not have such a court, and that is not for lack of need, but for lack of money.

The changes are not just structural, however. A number of them involve restrictions now routinely imposed on appellate lawyers. For example, the federal appellate courts and most of the state courts now limit the number of pages in briefs. Fifty typewritten pages is the most common limit. About ten states allow even fewer. Only a few states still fix no limits. In many cases, keeping briefs short makes the writing more difficult and requires more, rather than less, time from the lawyers.

For the same reasons, the time for oral argument has been cut to a usual maximum of 30 minutes per side in most courts, including the United States Supreme Court; often it is less. Some courts, including a number of the federal courts of appeals, fix argument time on a case-by-case basis, and the times fixed are rarely generous. Indeed, many appeals courts now refuse to allow any oral argument in numerous cases when they believe the questions presented are frivolous, insubstantial, or covered by recent authority, or that oral argument would not be helpful.

These restrictions contrast starkly with the absence of any argument limit in the United States Supreme Court during its early years. An argument might have gone on for days. Such unlimited arguments still continue in places less burdened by a caseload explosion, such as the British House of Lords, the Canadian Supreme Court, and the Australian High Court. But the caseload problem is spreading.

Limits on Lawyers

For appellate lawyers, these restrictions drastically limit how much can be said, both in the briefs and in oral argument. In particular, the limitations do not permit nearly as much to be said orally as in a written brief: Approximately one-third as much can be spoken in 30 minutes as can be written in a 50-page brief, and much less in ten or 20 minutes.

What this all means to the appellate advocate is that he or she must do more with less. Unfortunately, speaking and writing less are more difficult, requiring more time and skill. And familiar bromides are not always helpful. It is easy to say, as most commentators do, that counsel should emphasize the strong points, omit the weak ones, and get speedily to the heart of the case. All that seems obviously desirable. It is even more important to concentrate on the points essential to winning the case. Unfortunately, what is seldom recognized is that these simple generalizations do not always point in the same direction.

In some cases, a party must prevail on most or all points in the case to win, while the opposing party need win on only one of the several possible grounds. For the first party, the weakest point—not the strongest—will be the most critical, because it poses the greatest threat of loss. In such circumstances, beginning with or spending much time on the strongest point could be dangerous. Such considerations, as well as the court's probable interest in having certain issues—jurisdiction, for example—treated at the outset, must guide counsel in deciding the sequence of the points to be briefed and argued.

Put Complex Points in Writing

In planning a presentation, remember that some arguments are too complicated in fact or law to be caught easily on the fly in oral argument. Scientific details or lengthy analysis of authorities should be left to the brief, with only a cursory oral summary, if any at all. Still, there is always the risk that a judge may ask for enlightenment on just such complicated points, which, if fully explained, would use up all available time. The safest course if this happens is to describe the point briefly, and then refer the questioner to details in the brief.

The above negative observations suggest that few formal rules control, except that counsel should apply their best judgment to the problems presented in a particular case. An unexpressed rule, however, is that counsel must condense and condense—in writing and orally—to meet the restrictions caused by burgeoning caseloads.

A related point is that, in these days of limited time and resources, only one lawyer should argue one side of a case. There are rare exceptions involving co-parties with different interests, but the fact that several counsel on the same side want to appear, or that their clients want them to, is not enough. Experienced advocates and judges, such as Robert H. Jackson (who was both), have repeatedly pointed out that separate arguments are likely to be overlapping, repetitious, and incomplete, and that the judges "have a highly developed perverse instinct for putting . . . questions" to one lawyer on points another is prepared to argue. Some courts, such as the United States Supreme Court, enforce this precept by rule; they allow only one counsel without leave of court. Other court rules, such as the Federal Rules of Appellate Procedure, merely state that divided arguments "are not favored."

The dangers of dividing arguments have grown as the time available has become shorter. Occasionally counsel or the parties reasonably believe that permitting another party or amicus, particularly a representative of the government, such as the solicitor general, to share in the argument will help the client. But think twice. The same goal can often be achieved simply by the filing of an amicus brief.

Lawyers preparing to argue a case face a common dilemma that is rarely discussed at length: Should the argument be written out, based on notes, or left to memory alone? In my view, only one part of the answer is obvious: Relying on memory alone is too dangerous for most arguers, no matter how bright they are or how good their memories. Appellate questioning will throw even the most skilled off the memorized path. Nerves can do the same thing. It is one thing to memorize a text and then recite it straight through. It is quite another to begin a prepared speech, get diverted by a question, or many questions, and then hop back to memory. There must be a backup. A lawyer should not dispense with some written assistance unless he or she absolutely *knows*, from rehearsal, moot court, or prior experiences, that he or she is up to it. Even then, be wary. I have known very few lawyers who should take such a chance.

It may be surprising to learn that there is a sharp division of opinion about whether an arguer should go to the other extreme: that is, whether a full written text should be prepared. The orthodox view is well known. Most commentators insist without qualification that writing a text for an oral presentation is deplored. They depict it as the worst kind of mistake, one that will stultify argument and reduce persuasiveness. I was surprised at the firmness of these generalizations. I have prepared arguments both ways myself, and I know many top-notch advocates who have written out their arguments.

My surprise led me to survey approximately 100 lawyers who I had reason to believe were skilled advocates. They divided almost evenly between those who wrote a text and those who relied on notes alone. Each group was firmly convinced that its technique was greatly superior.

Those who never went beyond making notes often used strong language. One of them said that "writing out a complete statement and memorizing as much of it as possible . . . is the worst type of preparation" and "a waste of time." All those who take such a harsh view, however, seem to assume that anyone who writes out an argument will read it to the court—or memorize and recite it. I think such objections miss the mark: Everyone agrees that reading is a no-no. In fact, it is explicitly forbidden by many court rules. And, as I have indicated, hardly anyone memorizes.

Why Write Your Argument?

The truth is that the lawyers who produce and use a written text insist that they do not read the text, much less memorize it. Many of them, including me, do not even have it before them while arguing. Instead, after writing out an argument, many convert it back to notes, often by inserting catchwords or phrases between the paragraphs, then using only those insertions as their notes during the argument. Others may have the text before them while arguing, but they do not look down any more than do lawyers who have only their notes before them.

Going from notes to text and back to notes may seem cumbersome during the course of preparation, but it has distinct benefits. Writing produces a better, more accurate flow of language. It should be less windy and more compact, an important factor in these days of short arguments. But there is more than just terseness. There are points in every argument that you want to put just the right way. They may be complicated legal concepts or involved facts. They may be summaries of key points that you want to come out crisply or forcefully. You cannot achieve such precision and effect without writing things down. You may not end up saying things just as you wrote them, but, by writing and editing, you can master the basic phrasing that puts things best.

The Value of Rereading

There is another factor. Reading a written presentation a number of times—always making changes to improve the impact—plants it firmly in the speaker's mind even though it is not memorized. Furthermore, by timing the oral recital of a written argument, the arguer can determine how much time it will take without questions. This way he or she can determine just how much must be eliminated, and also what can best be omitted if time is consumed answering questions.

Those who oppose writing out a draft contend that it will cause the arguer to lose eye contact with the judges. They say the text will be too formal and stilted. Again, this incorrectly assumes that the text will be read. And, a writer for oral presentation knows that spoken words can and should be more informal than words that appear only in writing.

Whichever method of presentation an advocate adopts, whether notes, a text, or both, he or she should review it a number of times before the argument, usually making changes every time. This makes it unnecessary to glance too often at papers.

Two final mundane but important suggestions about written aids: Anything you think you may want to read to the court should appear verbatim in your notes, so that you won't have to take time to find even a tabbed passage in a record or brief. In addition, you should put your notes, text, or outline on the largest pages possible. Put them in capital letters or large type if necessary for you to read them easily when you glance down. Use underlining and different colors of ink to highlight essential points. Visibility is critical. Cards, or small pages, are hard to see, require more shuffling, or may even get dropped. The fewer pages you must turn, the better.

The issue of visibility leads naturally to the topic of visual aids. Not many lawyers think about using maps, charts, and other such material to aid an appellate court in understanding an oral argument. Those devices seem to be the stuff of the trial court. It is true that such external aids are not used or needed in most cases. But, in special instances—a dispute over the course of a river, or real estate boundaries, or an accident scene—they may be crucial. If you use such aids, focus only on points at the heart of the case. Otherwise, a chart or map might lead the judges to give disproportionate weight to matters of little importance.

Remember also that whether and how visual material is presented may depend upon the logistics of the particular court and courtroom. As several distinguished judges have warned, appellate judges are likely to be elderly or nearsighted. A lawyer must be sure that the document he or she wants to use is large enough for them to see from where they sit. Apart from personal visual acuity is the matter of simple visibility: The Clerk of the United States Supreme Court discourages the use of maps and charts because, no matter how big a visual aid is, the judges on such a wide bench may have difficulty seeing the document clearly. In addition, counsel may turn away from the bench—and the microphone—to point to and explain the document; this may make it difficult for the court to hear and understand. To prevent these troubles, the Supreme Court clerk's office suggests that instead of relying on enlarged exhibits, counsel should submit copies for each member of the Court (as well as the clerk and opposing counsel). These copies may be larger than the pages of briefs and other court documents, but small enough for a person to handle.

While lawyers may not often rely on charts and maps during oral argument, they frequently will, and should, discuss cases. Too many citations and overly long quotations in both briefs and oral arguments should be avoided. But how many is too many? How long is too long? The answers will depend on the situation and the case.

Principles Instead of Citations

Obviously, an admonition to reduce reliance on cases applies more strictly to oral arguments than to briefs. This is not just because less can be said in oral argument, but also because judges, like most people, cannot immediately grasp or remember oral descriptions of the details of many cases, and certainly not of many quotations. Both in brief and oral argument, but particularly in the latter, the arguer should concentrate on principles and reasons, and not merely authorities, except perhaps for a few recent decisions of the same or a higher court. Supreme courts are adept at giving decisions, including their own, great or little weight as they choose. Judges have often said they want to know *why* certain principles or decisions should be applied, followed, or distinguished, and not merely what the cases say.

All this does not mean that courts will decide cases purely on the basis of personal preference. But the consequences of deciding one way or another, or the effect of a ruling on a constitutional or legislative purpose, can be very important.

Quotations from cases or anything else should be as short as possible. A lawsuit may turn on the precise language of a statute, contract, or will, or even the language of a decision. If so, quotations may be appropriate, but keep them short. Simplify citations, if you use them at all orally. Say "the Reynolds case in 468 U.S.," or "decided in 1987," not "*Reynolds Whiskey Distributing Company v. Robert J. Harrison Milling Co.,* 468 U.S. 693 (1987)."

As the discussion on writing oral argument shows, conventional wisdom is not always wise or right. Another example involves use of the record. In particular, the question of whether the record must always be adhered to is complex.

All lawyers know the basic rule. Appeals are to be decided on the basis of the trial court record; going outside the record is improper. Most lawyers have seen themselves or others skewered in oral argument because they relied on something not in the record. But there are exceptions to this rule; some facts are subject to judicial notice. What are they?

Some examples are obvious, but rare. Appellate courts *expect* lawyers to advise them of some extra-record facts: those that make a case or an issue moot. If a party has died or no longer is in office, or if a law has been amended or repealed, tell the court quickly or expect to be chastised, as has happened in the United States Supreme Court.

Another well-known, but also unusual, situation that goes beyond the strict limits of noticeable facts of common knowledge is the "Brandeis brief." The technique was originally used by Brandeis as a lawyer in 1908 in *Muller v. Oregon*, 208 U.S. 412 (1908), to show the reasonableness of a statute—in that case, to show that the state legislature could reasonably have concluded that excessive working hours could harm women's health.

I suspect the Brandeis brief is often employed, as it was in *Muller*, because a new lawyer brought in to handle the appeal had ideas that did not occur to trial counsel and were therefore unsupported by evidence. Obviously, it would be better to get all the theories and facts in the trial court record in the first place. If that has not happened, think about a Brandeis brief.

Such facts, which relate to the impact of interpretations of a law or constitutional provision, are now commonly described as legislative (those a legislature might consider) as distinct from adjudicative (the facts of the case itself). Such legislative facts may or may not be indisputable or matters of common knowledge. This is not the place to try to clarify these fuzzy definitions. What is important is that any lawyer who wants to dispute the treatment of facts as judicially noticeable should promptly notify the court of his position in writing. A preliminary phone call to the clerk may be appropriate if time is short.

Finally, reference to facts not in the record is also often necessary for an amicus curiae. Such participants frequently want to show the court the effect of its decision upon persons whose situations are different from those of the parties. This can be especially important in disputes over certiorari petitions or other discretionary review, where the granting of review may depend on whether the court believes that the case will have a serious effect on the public. An amicus brief may call attention to such extra-record facts, which often will not be subject to notice.

Answers in Oral Argument

The subject of responding to questions in oral argument has been covered in articles for decades. There is no need for a new detailed treatment, but two isolated points deserve emphasis.

First, if you don't know the answer to a question, just say so. If the point is important, ask for leave to file a supplemental memorandum. Do not bluff. Trying to guess at the answer is dangerous and may be disastrous. It would be nice always to be perfectly informed, but that is unattainable. If you feel it is necessary, you can try to protect yourself by admitting that you are not sure of the answer you are giving and do not want to bind your client by it.

Second, remember you will never know how much time the questions will take in any particular case. The best you can do is try to learn in advance whether the judges before whom you appear ask many or few questions. In some courts, however, counsel will not know in advance who the judges will be. A rule of thumb in the United States Supreme Court is that the questioning will take one-third of the time, and sometimes much more. In some state courts, where questioning is not so intense, counsel can often reasonably predict that it will only take one-tenth of the time. Careful counsel will try to determine in advance—and perhaps mark—the parts of the prepared argument that can be omitted if the questioning becomes unexpectedly intense.

Fittingly, my last point concerns what classical rhetoricians called the peroration. Many lawyers want to close an argument or a brief with a persuasive bang. Seldom will there be time or space. Use what remains of your time in argument for rebuttal instead. And do not worry if you do not close things with a neat conclusion; if the court is not already persuaded, such a conclusion will seldom make a difference.

The same is true of briefs. Many court rules governing briefs require a statement at the end of what relief is requested. By that time, there should seldom be any doubt about what you want. In most cases, a sentence or two will suffice. Detailed amplification will rarely be necessary.

Always, in thinking about your closing—as in thinking about so many aspects of appellate advocacy—remember that courts continually urge counsel to keep their arguments short. So my advice, which I shall follow here, is don't perorate. Just stop.

Reality on Appeal

James L. Robertson

If I were back in the free world, I would get the "book" on every judge on every appellate court I (or my firm) regularly appeared before.

I would want to know more than just voting records. I would want to know each judge's conscious intellectual process in receiving and probing argument. But perhaps more important, I would want to know the subconscious forces at work—the hidden agendas the judge would vehemently deny, but a perceptive observer would easily recognize.

Finally, I would want to know the personal interaction among the judges of the panel—the group psychology, if you will.

My premise is that an appeal is essentially a communicative enterprise that succeeds best when the communicants know each other—totally.

This is not to say that the functions or attitudes of court and counsel are complementary or even approximately so. The job of counsel is candid and competent advocacy, within limits. The Constitution charges that courts adjudge justly, but in an institutional setting that imposes forces counsel may not fathom or accept.

Lawyers are permitted, if not obligated, to do things courts are obligated to try to keep them from getting away with. The legal system is not a smoothly operating machine. It yields at its best but a crude approximation of justice, a fact we must not forget.

Oliver Wendell Holmes, Jr., once said, "The prophecies of what the courts will do in fact, and nothing more pretentious, are what I mean by the law." It was one of his most controversial utterances.

Every lawyer provides clients with prophecies about what the courts will do in fact. And I believe every lawyer also fantasizes that skill in

---

James L. Robertson, a former associate justice of the Supreme Court of Mississippi, is a partner at Wise Carter Child & Caraway in Jackson, Mississippi.

advocacy will have much to do with whether the prophecy is fulfilled. A lawyer's sense of self-worth compels that fantasy, regardless of courtroom reality.

What is the reality? On the docket of any appellate court are many cases that probably never should have been appealed and can only be affirmed. Others can only be reversed.

Maybe 50 percent could go either way. A professionally competent appellate judge could write an opinion either affirming or reversing these cases—an opinion that would strike a learned lawyer as being reasonably correct. I write here about these borderline cases.

How do you move the court toward writing that opinion your way? By the principle of total communication, I believe. From the appellate judge's point of view, the communication is in briefs and arguments. I'll make some suggestions about those later. But first, why lawyers need the book and what should be in it.

I must begin by attacking the practice of so many lawyers who develop a preplanned argument to be delivered wholly without regard to the makeup of the panel or the identity of the judges sitting on it. They prepare for argument by anticipating the questions from the bench and developing answers on the assumption that there is a lone, legally correct answer to each such question. Even lawyers who know better, who know something of the personalities and idiosyncrasies of the individual judges, do this.

It is not the way to win.

Lawyers must individualize their arguments to the particular panel. They must understand as well as possible the psychological and communicative dynamics at work on appeal. That is why they need the book.

It would include as much personal background data as I could find—the same sort of information we regularly get on jurors. Because judges are public figures, the information on them is more available than it is for jurors, which makes it all the more surprising that lawyers do not collect or use such information systematically.

I refer to where judges come from, where they went to college and law school, what kinds of clients they represented, religious and political affiliations, and all of the other factors that go into a psychological profile.

But, not just the obvious ones. What are the cases they lost as lawyers and have never gotten over? We all have a few of those. And what about the judge's self-image?

Include the judge's (family's) financial and investment interests. Who are the principal social acquaintances? Has he or she been in the military service? If so, what did he or she do and for how long?

Anyone who knows the judicial career of Justice Oliver Wendell Holmes, Jr., knows well that his three years as an officer in the Twentieth Massachusetts Regiment deeply influenced his entire life. That experience was the origin of his skepticism toward lawyers who would argue the legal equivalent of eternal truths.

Every appellate judge has something you should know. For example, for seven years I taught admiralty law. Each year I spent an hour on early admiralty jurisdiction, particularly on a case called *The Genessee Chief*.

Several years ago our court heard a case in which both parties argued *The Genessee Chief*. It was painfully obvious that neither lawyer knew I was familiar with the case. "Painfully," I say, because neither realized I knew *The Genessee Chief* had little to do with the case at bar. Their ignorance did not bias me, of course—equal as it was. But then, I do remember it. And them.

Experiences Shape Attitudes

I would like to think I was equally unbiased in another case—on the potential liability of parole officials for "negligent parole" of a paroled prisoner who violently assaulted a citizen.

One of the lawyers was aware that through much of the 1970s as a lawyer I had defended state prison officials on charges of abuse and negligence in the prison system. The other apparently was not.

Of course, we judges strive mightily to shed our past partisan advocacy. But who among us has not at some point unearthed the brilliant brief that, alas, did not carry the day (often to learn how time dims brilliance)? We are mere humans.

Without calling names or going into specifics, I suggest that there are experiences in the background of each of my eight colleagues that have an impact upon their respective attitudes toward particular types of cases.

Several served for years as lawyer for the principal county government in my state. Most were once trial judges. One had substantial litigation experience in eminent domain cases several decades ago. These facts can easily be discovered and cataloged.

Where do you get the information? First, from the judge himself—but take what the judge says about himself or herself with three or four grains of salt. Second, former law clerks. They are often the best source, though you'll need a single grain of salt to temper their loyalty/hero worship. Former partners and colleagues at the bar are frequently talkative, willing to tell all for reasons sometimes less than pure. Your imagination can conjure up other sources.

The book should also contain opinions, reflecting decisions each judge has made as the writing judge and, to a lesser extent, as a panel member.

If you have a collateral estoppel case before my court, it is not enough to know our collateral estoppel cases. You should know what a particular judge has written and how that judge has voted in collateral estoppel cases.

If you have an insurance bad-faith refusal case before our court, it would be inexcusable not to know what each judge has written on that topic. With today's technologies a lawyer should never begin argument without the complete book of every judicial utterance of every judge on the panel.

Another chapter of the book should reflect each judge's values about the legal process. Each of us has such values or prejudices, and they have an impact on how we vote, especially in cases that we have not had the opportunity to study as fully as we would like.

You do not have to be too smart to figure out that we have several judges on our court who do not like Rule 56 and summary judgment. Ignore their public prejudices at your peril.

One judge tends to exalt property rights. Several have little sympathy for insurance companies, large corporations, and, particularly, utilities.

It is easy to recognize in my opinions and other expressions a theology that all forms of law should be seen together as a part of an organic whole, my penchant for objective standards, and my disdain for arguments that ignore "the myth of legislative intent" or "the tyranny of labels."

I teach jurisprudence and have for years. I read Holmes and Dworkin. On important points such as statutory or contract interpretation, I see an affinity between those writers; I try to mine it. I have left a paper trail of my values and prejudices.

The work habits of each judge also belong in the book. How do the judges read or use the trial record? How do they use their law clerks? How much do they listen to them? (Especially in a case that doesn't much interest the judge, the law clerk may have enormous influence.) To what extent do they do their own research and write their own opinions?

Knowing the raw data is only the beginning. You must evaluate it carefully and in perspective.

For example, I practiced for fourteen years with what is commonly called an insurance defense firm. But that tells only part of my story. A lawyer arguing to me should also know I assiduously avoided participating in the Federation of Insurance Counsel or the Defense Lawyers Association (although I did once break down and write an article for the latter's journal). Couple those facts with a careful reading of my opinion in *Hartford Accident and Indemnity Co. v. Foster*, 528 So.2d 255, 288–92 (Miss. 1988), if you really want to know my thinking about the role of insurance counsel.

Two judges on our court are former district lawyers. That fact will start you out, but it won't get you where you need to go. If you delve deeper you will learn that out of their (at least superficially) common experience, each acquired a different attitude about the prosecution of criminal cases.

Putting it all together takes thought and effort. Consider, for example, an opinion that has attracted some attention in my state, the dissent of Judge Edith Jones in *Reserve Life Ins. Co. v. Eichenseer*, 894 F.2d 1414 (5th Cir. 1990). It is a bad-faith refusal case involving substantial punitive damages against an insurance company.

Anyone who has followed Judge Jones knows she is very conservative. Her opinion criticizes judicial activism and employs many catch phrases of judicial conservatism.

I think Judge Jones is mistaken in her philosophy. Yet, I find her criticisms of my court's decisions on bad-faith refusal to be right on target—in fact, substantively congenial with my own dissenting and concurring opinions.

I wonder how many who have read Judge Jones's views in *Eichenseer* and my own opinions on the same subject realize how close we are on our decisions in specific cases. Few, I suspect. In fact, if they have only a superficial awareness of our respective jurisprudence, they probably consider us light years apart. (I believe competent judges who carefully study cases will draw the same conclusions most of the time, despite radical philosophical differences.)

The book should also cover the appellate court's internal decision-making processes.

Every appellate court I know anything about has internal operating procedures. Hardly any court regards these as proprietary information any longer. Some are available to the public. More to the point, all courts have "commonlaw" internal processes that most judges are willing to discuss at bar meetings or in print.

For example, most courts conference most cases the day they are argued. In my experience a high percentage of cases—perhaps more than 80 percent—are finally decided in a "tentative" vote taken a few hours after argument. If you know this, you know that you should rarely (if ever) spend your oral argument time urging the judge to read more before deciding the case.

You should also have a place in your book for the way writing assignments are made within the court. In many appellate courts, the presiding judge assigns the opinion after argument and conference.

In my court (and others, I am told) the cases are assigned well before argument. Each panel member knows who will write the opinion, provided that the majority goes that judge's way. A prominent part of the panel conference is the writing judge's recommendation about how the case should be decided. It behooves the lawyer to figure out who "has the case" in order to subtly cast the lure toward that fish at oral argument.

Many courts still try to conceal the identity of the judges on the panel, but there are usually ways a resourceful lawyer can find out ahead of argument. Even if you can't find out until, say, an hour before argument, you can still adjust your thinking to the particular judges on the panel. (I think we should abandon any effort to keep panels secret. I know the policy reasons for it, but let's face it, the practice doesn't work.

It only gives an occasional advantage to the lawyer who learns who the panel members are and has a less resourceful opponent.)

You should also know how each judge regards oral argument. Some (like me) like it. Others regard it as a chore. Does Judge X generally come to oral argument well prepared? How does Judge Y prepare for argument? One judge on our court sincerely believes a lawyer has a natural right to argument—though I often doubt argument has much impact on his vote. Another almost never asks a question, but he listens intently and in conference often raises issues the lawyers argued. Still another is prone to sharp questioning that does not necessarily predict his vote.

So much for the overview. Now for your first contact with the court—the brief. The appellate court has a finite and quite limited amount of time to spend on one case. A lawyer ignores that point at his or her peril. For better or for worse, the court is simply not able to study to its collective hearts' content the facts and law of each appeal, no matter how earthshaking lawyer and litigant may consider it.

Before putting the first words on paper, try to think like a judge. But not just any judge. Crawl into the minds of *the* judges who will hear and decide your appeal. Ted Williams always got into the pitcher's mind, not just hours, but days before the game; you must do the same with your judge. Ask yourself, "If I were Judges Nasty, Brutish, and Short, of the Court of Appeals, how would I view these facts and this law?"

I think the most important part of the brief is the Summary of the Argument. I invariably read it first. It is almost like the opening statement in a trial. From clear and plausible argument summary, I often get an inclination to affirm or reverse that rises almost to the dignity of a (psychologically) rebuttable presumption.

Work on the Reader's Mind

I do not mean to denigrate the importance of a fully developed and technically sound argument. But, I read the subsequent argument in a "show me" frame of mind, testing whether it confirms my impression from the summary of the argument.

Like the initial summary, labels and headings should work on the reader's mind. Consider this heading, for example:

> Should *Enmund* be applied retroactively, or should the state be permitted one last cruel and unusual punishment before *Enmund* takes effect?

Jones v. Thigpen, 741 F.2d 805, 811 (5th Cir. 1984).

As for labels, I remember a case from my days in practice. One of my partners represented a fish bait business that had employed the Orkin Exterminating Company to kill off certain insects that were killing the crickets raised by the bait farm. As fate would have it, Orkin managed to kill the crickets as well; hence, a wrongful death suit for the death of a million crickets.

My partner began all trial and appellate papers with "Orkin Exterminating Company, hereinafter referred to as 'Exterminator,'" and with effect.

I also recall two hotly contested cases in which I cannot help but believe our success in labeling had a beneficial effect.

The first was a challenge of overly restrictive outside-speaker regulations on Mississippi's college campuses. We managed to get everybody talking about the case as "the speaker-ban case."

The second was an action challenging gross inequities in Mississippi's property tax system. The media called it the property reappraisal case, raising the unnerving specter of tax increases. We managed to get the court talking about it as "the tax equalization case."

Within my own court, judges are not supposed to be advocates but, if they are honest, will often admit they are. We had an important case regarding the Mississippi legislature's usurpation of powers constitutionally committed to the executive branch. The case arose in the context of a political power play between the attorney general and legislative leaders. Chief Justice Neville Patterson changed the tone of the case as he got everybody thinking of it as "the separation of powers case," rather than "Bill Allain's suit against the legislature."

It is impossible to measure the impact of such subtleties. I suspect it is small, but real.

Of course, how the facts are stated in the brief itself is important. Judges like to think of themselves as caring for the people who appear before them. Behind every lawsuit is a story of living and breathing people. Humanize your client. It is something the lawyer routinely does before the jury, but seldom thinks to do before the judges.

Tell your story so that a fair-minded and reasonably intelligent reader would instinctively think your client was in the right if there were no law. Do not overstate the case. That could produce an adverse effect.

You want the judge who reads your statement of facts to conclude, "If there's any justice in the world, this party should win; now let me see if there is any law that allows me to decide this way."

Include extensive record references. Although we have all had experience to the contrary, I tend to assume that no lawyer is going to cite me to a record reference if it doesn't support the proposition or fact being stated.

Don't waste your time and pages trying to score points upon opposing counsel, especially if you are the appellee. After deciding a case for my client, a trial judge once told me he looked upon me as "his" lawyer.

The appellee's brief should tell why the trial court should be affirmed, not why appellant's brief is all wrong.

Do not raise every error the trial court may technically have committed. An appellant raising two or three strong issues has a better chance of success than one raising ten or twelve issues where only two or three possess real merit.

Many counsel brevity in briefing, and rightly so. But if you use the Summary of the Argument correctly and effectively, I see no harm—and much profit—in a thorough and detailed explication of your point. I would much rather have a fifty-page "law journal article" that is helpful than a ten-page brief that isn't.

The way you cite and discuss cases is also important. Rarely will an appellate court feel the force of stare decisis so strongly that the lawyer can argue "*Smith v. Jones* is on all fours" and expect to be persuasive. Explain why the principal cases you rely on were decided correctly. In the end, your brief should transcend authority. It should explain why the case should be decided in favor of your client as if it were a genuine case of first impression.

Finally, this often overlooked reality about briefs: The judicial reader will perceive but a small part of the soul and being you pour into your brief. Briefing (when done right) is an intense experience marked by intellectual insight and careful crafting and massaging of every word, phrase, sentence, and thought. The reader never gets it all. Your stylistic subtleties may be missed if they are too subtle.

Effective Oral Argument

Now to oral argument. I think its value is real, though (candor forces me to confess) not high. There have been cases where oral argument changed my mind, though more often it confirmed my preargument impression.

In a sense, style and tactics at oral argument are peculiar to the individual lawyer. In baseball the batting stance that works well for one player does not always work well for another. Certain batters will ignore accepted norms completely from time to time, yet be inordinately successful. The same is true in advocacy.

One indispensable requisite to effective oral argument is complete mastery of the case. Know in detail the record, the procedural history, and arguments made at different stages. Nothing impresses me more than to ask for a point of fact and to have counsel answer in substance and add, "That may be found at page 389 of the record."

Conversely, except for a bluff that fails, nothing more effectively discredits an argument than "I simply don't know" in response to a question about the record.

Judges also hate to ask a question of one lawyer only to be told that co-counsel is going to handle that point. That is the conventional reason for not dividing an argument between two lawyers. I agree with the advice, but for a different reason. I simply do not think two lawyers can cover a case as effectively in ten or fifteen minutes each as a single lawyer can cover the case in twenty or thirty minutes. It is true that four sprinters can run a mile faster than a single runner. But because of the shortened time requirements, oral argument is more like running a twenty-yard dash with a relay team instead of a single runner.

As appellant, I would never reserve time for rebuttal. I think you can use twenty or thirty minutes more effectively in a single block of time than in broken-up blocks. In the days when I used to do rebuttal, I would invariably repeat points I had made on my affirmative argument or get on the defensive and concentrate on my opponent's argument.

As a judge, I have never seen an appellant's counsel use rebuttal effectively, and I have never seen the decision turn on anything said in rebuttal.

A lawyer should approach oral argument as a particular and unique opportunity to discuss the case with the court. Opposing counsel is a necessary evil in this process, to be treated fairly and courteously and otherwise ignored.

There is inevitably a certain amount of time in which the lawyer can control the content of the argument. The question is what to say and how to say it.

As a lawyer I was advised to forget about the facts and go straight to the legal argument. True, repeating the traditional statement of the facts is a waste of time. On the other hand, most controlling issues on appeal are not pure questions of law. Therefore, devote about half of your "free" time to the facts central to the appeal so that the court can get a clear understanding of them and the legal premises.

Spend the rest of your time arguing the law of the case as though the case were one of first impression. Explain why as a matter of principle your client should win. Then reason by analogy to other settled premises of law, and show that your client's victory would be consistent with established law.

Finally, cite few, if any, cases in oral argument. They go in the brief. If you do cite cases, think about your book and the opinions written by judges on the panel. Use opinions with great care and finesse.

Don't say, "As Your Honor, Judge X, wrote last year in *Smith v. Doe*, . . ." Nine times out of ten, Judge X will remember *Smith v. Doe*. If by chance it is forgotten, you will merely embarrass the judge.

Moreover, singling out Judge X is hardly likely to endear you to Judges Y and Z. You never know whether Judge Y or Z joined *Smith v. Doe* reluctantly. Judges Y and Z are as vain and egotistical as Judge X and may resent instruction in the law according to Judge X.

Finally, a caveat: From what I have said, you may think me a cynic or merely a realist (or, God forbid, a Realist). I see myself as a judicial idealist. I aspire to impartial, principled justice in the noblest view of what Karl Llewellyn called the Grand Manner of the Common Law Tradition.

In the depth of my being I believe with Ronald Dworkin that "it matters how judges decide cases." I want desperately to excise from my judging all legally impermissible thoughts. I concede here only my suspicion that I am as fallen in my judicial duties as in other dimensions of my life.

I see in this no cause for despair, for Robert Browning reminds me daily, "Ah, but a man's reach should exceed his grasp, or what's a heaven for?"

To reach for the heaven of adjudication, I seek and badly need the aid of the lawyers who appear before me. I can receive that aid only through the intense, though brief, communication, the intellectual and interpersonal interaction of argument. I can reach for the heaven only if they know whence I come.

Winning on Appeal

Daniel M. Friedman

This is a how-to-do-it piece. There is no adequate substitute in appellate advocacy for doing it. Thus this article will set forth practical considerations and suggestions based on a quarter century of my experience. This time was spent exclusively in appellate work, most of that in the Supreme Court of the United States but also in the United States courts of appeals.

First, a few general observations about appellate practice:

- Perhaps the most important requirement—and one that many lawyers ignore—is to present your own affirmative case. A well-constructed and well-written brief should leave no doubt in the mind of the reader that the position is correct. It is not enough for the appellant to show that the lower court erred. That court's grounds for decision may be vulnerable, but even to invalidate that reasoning does not necessarily mean that the court's judgment will be reversed. The appellate court may discern other grounds on which the judgment should be upheld.

    Similarly, to refute your opponent's argument does not ensure victory, since there may be other grounds for upholding the position. It is therefore essential to an effective brief that it affirmatively establish the party's case.

    Of course, while establishing the affirmative case, the errors in the other side's position will be exposed. The appellant will also expose the errors committed by the lower court. Frequently, an effective presentation of one side's case will go a long way toward refuting the other side's and permit rather brief treatment of its arguments.

Daniel M. Friedman is a senior circuit judge on the U.S. Court of Appeals for the Federal Circuit.

- Do not simply reargue the case you presented in the lower court. A brief or oral argument that convinced a trial court may be unsuccessful before an appellate tribunal. The roles of the two courts are different. The trial court determines the facts and applies the law to those facts. The appellate court reviews the decision of the trial court to ascertain whether the latter committed reversible error. In the appellate court, the lawyer's function—depending on which side he or she represents—is to convince the tribunal that the lower court did or did not commit reversible error.
- Avoid significant emotional involvement in your case. Under our adversary system, the function of the lawyer is to make the most effective presentation on behalf of his client. It is not his role to decide whether his client is right; that is the function of the court, not the lawyer.

  An effective presentation of a case requires the lawyer to examine not only its strengths, but also its weaknesses, as well as the strengths of the other side. To deal with them, you must be aware of them. If a lawyer becomes convinced that his client's position is totally correct and his opponent's case totally without merit, he loses the objectivity essential to effective advocacy.

  A good brief, therefore, must take account of the weaknesses as well as the strengths of both sides. If a lawyer becomes so convinced of the rectitude of the client's position that he or she can see no merit in anything the opponent argues, a substantial degree of effectiveness in representing the client will be lost.

  In preparing the brief and oral argument, a lawyer inevitably becomes convinced of the soundness of his or her position, and there may be times when it is difficult to understand how the decision could go other than in his or her favor. A lawyer whose brief and oral argument do not carry the stamp of conviction and certainty is not an effective advocate. But every good advocate is aware of the weaknesses in his or her case and the strengths in his opponent's, and presents a case to reflect those considerations.
- Do not make personal attacks upon your opponent, the lawyer, or the lower court that decided against you. Although such comments may give you and your client personal satisfaction, they will harm rather than aid the cause. They add nothing to the analysis of the case, are likely to antagonize the court, and may create sympathy for your opponent. If you are the recipient of a personal attack, whether on your skill or your integrity, it is best to ignore it and stick to arguing the case before the court.
- In the United States Department of Justice, different lawyers usually handle a case on appeal. To some extent this reflects the huge volume of litigation the department handles and the increased efficiency that specialization permits. But the handling of appeals by

lawyers not involved in the trial of the case also reflects the judgment that other benefits result from the process.

By the time a case reaches the appellate court, the lawyer who has been involved in it from its inception usually has fixed views about its theories and presentation. If the same lawyer handles the case on appeal, he or she probably will continue to urge the theories argued—whether successfully or unsuccessfully—in the lower court. A new lawyer taking a fresh look at the case on appeal, however, may view it somewhat differently and use fresh insight to shift the theories and approaches, at least in emphasis. This change in approach may avoid some of the pitfalls that led to a loss in the lower court or strengthen the grounds upon which an affirmance is sought.

Of course, the lawyer handling the case on appeal cannot function in a vacuum; he or she should work closely with the person who handled the case below and give the lawyer the opportunity to review the brief before it is filed. New or altered arguments that seem effective to the second lawyer may have to be dropped or changed because of factual problems or events at the trial level of which only the trial lawyer is aware. Moreover, for individual practitioners and small firms, such a shift in responsibility may not be feasible. But where it is possible—in larger firms or in government agencies—the practice has substantial advantages.

A brief must be carefully and thoroughly organized before it is written. There is nothing worse than a rambling document that sounds as if it had been dictated off the cuff and filed virtually without change. That kind of brief is difficult to follow, frequently repetitious, often internally inconsistent, and always unpersuasive.

The basic organization of the brief should be developed at the outset. If the case is complicated and has a number of issues, an outline of the brief can be helpful in organizing the material and presenting it most effectively. Often the preparation of the outline discloses flaws in the tentative order or structure of the argument. That leads to changes that sharpen the presentation. If the facts are lengthy or complicated, an outline of them, broken down into subdivisions, either chronologically, by subject, or by a combination of the two, may be helpful in writing the statement portion of the brief.

Poor Writing

Good writing is the key to an effective brief. Good ideas are frequently lost or buried in poor writing.

Write simply and clearly. Avoid long and complicated sentences; short simple sentences are best. If necessary, break a complicated sentence into several separate sentences. A period followed by a new sentence is often better than an "and." Write in the active rather than the passive voice. "The court held" is both shorter and more effective than "It was held by the court."

1. *Facts.* The facts are often the most important part of a brief. If the court can be persuaded to take a particular view of the facts, the legal conclusions may follow almost automatically.

   The facts must be stated with absolute accuracy. They cannot be overstated. If the record shows that three people attended a meeting, do not say "a large number" or "many." Do not state as a fact something that is only an inference to be drawn from the facts. If the record shows only that three people were in Chicago, do not state that they met there. The latter conclusion is an inference that perhaps may be drawn from their presence in that city, but if the point is important, it should be made in the argument portion of the brief, not in the statement. The statement should be wholly objective, not argumentative.

   The facts, accurately stated, should be organized to present the most effective case. They should be marshalled selectively. If there are adverse facts that the other side will stress, bring them out yourself, and explain them away or minimize their significance. That is better than to permit the other side to present them first and then accuse you of ignoring them. It also creates a good impression with the court, since the judges see before them a candid and forthright advocate.

   State only the relevant facts. That the appellant is a New Jersey corporation, chartered in 1923 and with its principal place of business in Cleveland, may well be irrelevant to any issue in the case. Detailed dates may be unnecessary. It may be immaterial whether suit was filed on January 23 or January 29, 1961, or whether suit was filed in January or February, or whether it was filed in 1961 or 1962.

2. *Statutory materials.* If dealing with a statute, explain what it does and describe its various elements and requirements. If the statute is complicated, it should be summarized and simplified. Quote the critical language; it is ineffective merely to summarize in the text what the statutory provision does, and then append as a footnote a lengthy paragraph of statutory text. The reader is likely to ignore the footnote, and then be unable to follow the argument. If only a sentence or two of a lengthy statutory provision is involved, quote only those words; the entire provision may then be set forth in a footnote if it will be helpful to the reader.

   In any case involving a statute, the starting point should be the statutory language. A brief that ignores or casually passes over the language of the statute and goes directly to the legislative history or statutory policy suggests that the language does not support the argument and therefore is being ignored. Although it is sometimes difficult to make the language support the argument, it is a rare case in which at least a plausible contention cannot be based on the language. If the language is so clear that there is not room for argument, the case will probably not be in court.

There naturally are exceptions: If the language unequivocally points in one direction but the legislative history is directly contrary, the language cannot be relied upon. But the situation should be explicitly stated at the outset.

3. *Captions.* Appropriate headings and subheadings increase clarity. They explain where the brief is going and provide signposts along the way. The captions should be as brief as possible, but sufficiently explicit to describe the point. Numbering the subpoints may also be helpful. That tells the reader that the brief is turning to a different but related aspect of the same subject.

4. *Underlining and other emphasis.* Effectiveness is lost by extensive capitalization, underlining, boldface type, or italics. These devices are helpful only if used on those rare occasions that emphasis dramatically drives a point home or draws an important contrast. But if every third sentence is underlined, there is no emphasis at all. The strength of an argument ultimately depends on its force, logic, vigor; a weak argument does not gain strength by undue emphasis of particular portions.

5. *Quotations.* Quotations from cases are effective only if used sparingly. Quoting at length from opinion after opinion is a lazy way of writing a brief, and the finished product is likely to be unconvincing. Long before the brief approaches its end, the reader has begun to skip over the quotations. If used with discretion, however, pertinent quotations from judicial opinions give a brief force and emphasis.

Quotations must be accurate and not taken out of context. Avoid the cropped quotation, with critical qualifications omitted, or an ellipsis of language that significantly alters or limits the language quoted. Not only will the other side point out the omission, but this technique also will likely destroy the court's confidence in the lawyer and make the court doubt other statements in the brief that are not similarly flawed.

6. *Unnecessary adjectives and adverbs.* Frequent use of colorful adjectives and adverbs does not make an argument more effective. The claim that a particular statutory provision covers the case does not gain strength by stating that it "clearly," "plainly," or "patently" does so. Nor is the phrase "the purpose of the rule" improved by inserting the word "plain" or "clear" before the word "purpose." Indeed, words like "patently" or "obviously" suggest that what follows is the *ipse dixit* of the writer, rather than a necessary conclusion.

7. *Weak arguments.* Do not make every argument possible. A poor argument is easily demolished. Its very presence suggests weak-

ness, on the theory that the lawyer's case cannot be good if he is forced to rely upon unsound contentions.

8. *Technical material.* Technical material must be presented with sufficient clarity that someone not expert in the field can understand it. Too often, lawyers who work in specialized areas fail to realize that the judges to whom the arguments are made do not have a similar knowledge and expertise in the field. Avoid technical jargon. Simplify and explain complicated concepts in specialized areas. Explain them in terms that laymen can understand.

9. *Abbreviations.* The current practice of using initial letters of lengthy titles as a shorthand reference can become extremely confusing. Use of NLRB for the National Labor Relations Board presents no problems. But it is not unusual to read a sentence such as this in a brief:

> The Port Association of Freight Forwarders (PAFF) entered into an Agreement Covering Loading Practices in the Inner Harbor (ACLPIH) with the Seattle Chapter of the Union of Warehousemen and Stevedores (SCUWS).

Two pages later the following appears:

> Under the ACLPIH, SCUWS was required to consult with PAFF before taking that action.

This problem could be avoided if, instead of using these initials, the writer employed shorthand terms, such as "Association," "Agreement," and "Union." In place of the gibberish just quoted, the sentence would be fully comprehensible and succinct:

> Under the Agreement, the Union was required to consult with the Association before taking that action.

10. *Footnotes.* Footnotes have a place in a brief, but only a limited one. They may be used for citations, although it distracts the reader to shift his eye constantly from text to footnote. At some point, he is likely to stop reading the footnotes altogether. A large number of case citations ordinarily is unnecessary. The two or three pertinent cases cited for a proposition are more likely to be noticed if in the text.

Footnotes also may properly be used to block off areas of a case or to note issues that the case does not involve. But the lengthy "talking" footnote, which runs on for paragraphs and even pages, should be avoided. Those footnotes usually involve either lengthy discussion of issues that are not in the case and therefore need not be discussed, or demonstrations by the author of the research he has done (which, unfortunately, has proven unnecessary), or his erudition. This type of footnote, although the staple of a scholarly law review article, has no place in an appellate brief. Busy judges, who must read a large number of briefs, are unlikely to read footnotes that are discursive and argumentative and contain intricate arguments.

11. *Anticipating the other side's arguments.* Often it is dangerous to anticipate the other side's arguments and answer them in the opening brief. Those arguments may be made better than the other side would state them. Or, they may be made in a way that enables the other side to restate or refine the arguments so they are more difficult to answer. Moreover, a well-presented affirmative case may remove all need to answer the other side's contentions in any detail.

    Of course, there are some cases in which it is so clear that the other side will make certain arguments that they safely may be anticipated and answered. But generally the practice is not wise.

12. *Length.* The story of the lawyer who explained that he filed a 50-page brief because he did not have time to write a 25-page brief reflects the reality that tight writing is time-consuming. But it is so much more effective that it is worth the additional time and effort.

    Briefs should be as brief as possible. Many are too long. Excessive length results from making unnecessary arguments, stating unnecessary factual detail, giving too many lengthy quotations, repeating points needlessly, and failing to think the case through and organize it carefully before beginning to write. There are complicated and difficult cases that require lengthy exposition, but most briefs could be improved by tightening and sharpening. The shorter the brief, the more effective it will be.

    The Conclusion section of the brief should be a simple and clear statement of what you want the court to do. For example, "The judgment of the district court should be affirmed," or "The judgment of the district court should be vacated, and the case remanded to that court to make additional findings regarding the notice of the alleged breach of contract." There is no need, however, to use your conclusion to summarize your entire argument—a summary that too frequently sounds like a summary of the summary of the argument given earlier. If the court is not familiar with and does not understand your position when it reaches the Conclusion section, the brief is seriously deficient.

There are lawyers who file a reply brief in every case. Those briefs usually merely restate, in shorter form, the arguments made in the opening brief. If the arguments have been fully and effectively presented in the opening brief, there is no reason to restate them in a reply brief.

There are situations, however, where a reply brief is necessary. If the other side makes strong arguments that were not anticipated or answered, or cites pertinent authorities not previously considered, a response is in order. Sometimes additional legislative history is presented for the first time in the case and must be dealt with. A reply brief also is useful in answering technical or detailed arguments—such as those involving complex mathematical calculations—that cannot effectively be dealt with in oral argument.

A reply brief should be short, punchy, and incisive. Do not file a reply brief that is primarily concerned with correcting minor errors the other side has made. Such a brief is a sign of weakness: it suggests that you have no good answers on the merits, and therefore are nit-picking at the periphery.

In recent years, the Supreme Court has been flooded with amicus curiae briefs in most major cases involving important constitutional or statutory issues. Many of those briefs contribute nothing significant to the case, but merely repeat, in varying form, the arguments already made. Their major function seems to be to enable the organizations submitting them to gain publicity and to advise their memberships after the decision that the Court adopted their views.

Sometimes an amicus curiae brief can make a real contribution to a case. If the amicus has important factual material that is not available to the parties, the brief is likely to aid the court in reaching a correct decision. Occasionally an amicus will develop a persuasive argument that the parties have overlooked. There are instances where the brief of one of the parties is inadequate and a good amicus curiae brief will clarify the issues. Generally, however, such briefs contribute little or nothing to the decision of a case and require the court to do considerable unnecessary reading.

Oral Argument

The oral argument is the capstone of the appellate process. All that has gone before comes to a head in a short period of spoken exposition and exploration. It is the only occasion that the court can question counsel, test his or her position to determine its strengths and weaknesses, and determine the implications and consequences of the arguments. It is the one chance the lawyer has to find out what is troubling the court and to assuage those doubts. It also is the single occasion when the opposing parties can be forced to face up to the difficulties in their positions. In the briefs, the parties may pass each other without ever meeting, but at oral argument they can be forced to lock horns and determine which one must give way.

Virtually all judges who have written on the subject attest to the importance of oral argument. Although recently many courts have limited or eliminated oral argument in a substantial percentage of cases, they have done so not because of doubt about the desirability of oral argument, but because the step was necessary to deal with the great increase in appellate litigation.

An oral argument should not repeat the brief. It must focus upon the critical points in the case and expound them simply and effectively. A good oral argument should be a dialogue between the advocate and the court in which, through joint exploration of the case, the court gains information about the critical facts and issues and insight into the policy judgments that must illuminate and shape the decision.

A friend once suggested that the function of oral argument is to make the court want to decide in your favor, and that of the brief is to provide the court with the tools to do so. An effective oral argument will reflect this distinction.

Thorough preparation is the key to a good oral argument. Advocates have different methods of preparation, but all good ones know their case completely when they stand up in court. The advocate must be completely conversant with the record. There is nothing worse than a lawyer who, when asked where something is in the record, fumbles around in the document, desperately turning the pages, and finally answers: "I know it's there, but I can't put my finger on it." Similarly distressing is the lawyer who, when asked whether the record shows so-and-so, responds: "I think it does, but I cannot cite you the page." Even worse, of course, is the lawyer who is forced to answer the question whether the record shows a particular fact with: "I don't know." There is no excuse for an advocate not knowing what is in the record, and inability to answer questions about the record creates a bad impression with the court.

Knowledge of the record also is necessary to answer factual misstatements of the other side. After the other side has stated that the record contains no evidence on a particular point, nothing is more effective for an opponent than giving a couple of record references to the evidence the other side has overlooked.

It is the rare lawyer who can know the record well enough not to need some aids to help find critical portions. Some tab the record to identify various items. Others make a summary of significant portions, which can quickly furnish the necessary citations. Still others make notes of particular items they may want to have quickly available, such as important testimony or findings. Some use a combination of these techniques. Each advocate must find the devices most suitable, but some method of identification and recall is essential.

Methods of preparation also vary greatly. Some lawyers first read the record, then the briefs, then the cases, and only then prepare the actual argument. Others reverse the procedure. Hybrid methods are also used. Again, the proper procedure depends upon the needs of the particular lawyer.

Some lawyers have their colleagues conduct a moot court. Others talk the argument out, presenting it to the walls of the office. Going through the argument orally is helpful, because a presentation that seems fine on paper or in the mind may disclose flaws when spoken.

An important part of preparation is thinking through the implications of the position and developing answers to anticipated or possible questions from the bench. All too often a lawyer makes what sounds like a plausible contention, only to stand mute when a judge points out to him a difficulty that he apparently had not recognized and cannot answer.

Thorough preparation is also necessary to give the lawyer sufficient flexibility to be able to alter the order of presentation in response to questions. Early in the argument the court sometimes asks counsel to discuss a point he had planned to treat with later on. Only a well-prepared lawyer can quickly shift course and argue the point as effectively as if permitted to follow the original order of presentation.

Presentation of Content

To be effective, an oral argument must explain and argue the case simply and clearly. It may be necessary to oversimplify in order to make the issues and arguments easily comprehensible. Complicated issues are difficult to understand when presented orally. Figures are hard to follow when spoken; a string of percentages and dollar amounts quickly becomes meaningless to the court, no matter how convincing it may be after detailed study. If you must use figures, give one or two, not a large number.

At the beginning, tell the court in a few words what the case is about, what issues it must decide, and how the case reached it. If a statute is involved, read the critical language; do not just talk in generalities about the legislation. If the statute is complicated, with repeated cross-references between different sections, take it step-by-step, summing up at appropriate points to ensure that the court understands the legislation.

Do not try to cover every point in the case in oral argument. Select the two or three strongest points, and focus on them. If the court is concerned with other issues, it will ask about them. If a point is highly technical and difficult to expound orally, tell the court so and that it is fully covered in the brief. Again, if the court has questions about it, one of the judges will let you know.

In some cases it may facilitate presentation to use large maps, charts, or tables on an easel in the courtroom. If the route of a particular motor carrier is important, a map properly marked may explain the situation with greater clarity than any oral description. Instead of a large chart or map placed before the court, small copies of those documents may be distributed to the court before the argument, with the statement that counsel will refer to them.

An oral advocate must speak clearly, not too fast, and loudly enough to be heard. It is embarrassing when a judge asks a lawyer to speak louder. A staccato delivery in which arguments cascade from the advocate's mouth in an uninterrupted flow is difficult to follow and ineffective. Similarly, it is ineffective if a lawyer delivers his entire argument at a high pitch of passion; emphasis is telling only if used occasionally.

There are a few lawyers who can present an argument without any notes. That is the best technique, but unfortunately it is the rare advocate who has this skill. Notes, as detailed as necessary and with suitable underlining, are the best method of presentation. Key sentences and phrases may be written out when it is important to state a point exactly.

An oral argument should never be read. It sounds stilted, no matter how skilled the speaker. Contact between the court and lawyer is lost when the lawyer's eyes are glued to the page and do not face the court.

In recent years a severe reduction in time has somewhat changed the character of oral argument. In many courts each side frequently is allotted only 10 or 15 minutes. This means that the appellant's lawyer no longer can make a fairly extensive presentation of the facts. Many appellant courts announce at the opening of the day's session that the court has read the briefs and is familiar with the facts, and admonishes counsel to get right to the legal issues. Even in that situation, however, the lawyer for the appellant may, in relatively few words, state one or two important facts that are critical to the case and effectively color the argument. The lawyer for the appellee has more flexibility and may use the facts in greater detail in developing his argument.

Facts must be stated accurately and not overstated. If opposing counsel has misstated the facts, correction of his errors is likely to destroy his credibility with the court. Similarly, if you are inaccurate and the other side exposes the flaw, the court will lose confidence in you.

Do not discuss cases at length, or read copiously from them. The lawyer who drones on with a series of statements that "In *Smith vs. Brown*, the court stated as follows," followed by a lengthy quotation, quickly loses the court's attention. If there are one or two controlling or pertinent authorities, discuss them briefly. But be familiar with the principal cases cited in the briefs, so that you can answer questions about them.

Cases often have serious problems and difficulties. If your case has them, it is better for you to bring them out and explain them away than for the other side or, even worse, the court to raise them. The difficulties will not just go away if you ignore them. By bringing them out yourself, you can discuss them in the context and with the emphasis you want, and also take some of the wind out of the other side's sails.

If you are the appellee, a good opening is important. Sometimes the other side provides the opportunity. In answer to questions, or in the zeal of advocacy, a lawyer may overstate his case or exaggerate the breadth or reach of his opponent's position. Setting the case back on course often is an excellent way to begin.

Questions from the bench usually put the advocate to his hardest test. Many lawyers dislike questions, on the theory that they interfere with a prepared presentation. Lawyers should welcome questions. It is the one opportunity to find out what is troubling the judges, and to answer them.

Although counsel engages in a lengthy colloquy with a single judge who seems hostile to his or her position and unconvinced by the answers, even that exercise may not be in vain. Other judges who have not said anything may have similar doubts, and the answers to their colleague may have satisfied them.

When a question is asked, answer it immediately. Do not say, "I'll get to it later." Often the lawyer never does get to it, and the problem that was bothering the judge continues to do so. Moreover, questions are most effectively dealt with when asked, not later on. If the question requires a detailed explanation that the lawyer was planning to give subsequently, the question may be answered briefly when asked, with the statement that it will be discussed in detail later.

If a question is embarrassing or exposes a weakness in the case, do not give an evasive answer. Answer it directly, with whatever explanation can best extricate you. Judges are quickly aware when counsel is evading a direct answer, and are likely to call you on it. Courts become irked with a lawyer who tries to avoid answering difficult questions. Conversely, they respect a lawyer who faces up to difficult problems questions pose and answers the inquiries forthrightly and directly.

If a lawyer does not know the answer to a question, he or she should not try to bluff through it. It is likely to be caught and to be seriously embarrassing. There is nothing wrong with saying "I don't know"— provided you do not have to say it too often. If you are unclear about what the judge is asking, so indicate.

While a professor at Harvard Law School, Justice Frankfurter told his students that cases rarely were won in oral argument before the Supreme Court but often were lost. A case can be lost at oral argument if the lawyer is unable to give a satisfactory answer to a difficult question. Sometimes counsel makes a concession—indeed, perhaps, without being aware he or she is doing so—that gives the case away or make a position untenable.

When the red light of the lectern goes on, your time has expired. Sit down as quickly as possible. Go ahead and finish your sentence and answer any questions. Some lawyers, unfortunately, ignore the red light and continue to speak as though there were no time limit at all. That conduct irks the judges and frequently leads the presiding judge to state, sometimes quite testily, "Your time has expired."

Divided Arguments

Arguments in which more than one counsel appear generally are a mistake and sometimes are a disaster. Although the lawyers have arranged what appears to them to be a suitable division of the case, often the court questions the first lawyer about points the second is to cover, and vice versa. Unless each lawyer has fully prepared the entire case—including the portions he or she is not to argue—the result is confusing and usually the lawyers fail to make an effective presentation.

It is even worse when three or four lawyers argue a single case, popping up and down as one follows the other to the lectern. Barely has one gotten into the subject when it is time to yield to a colleague. When there are several parties, each represented by separate counsel, it may be difficult for all to agree to let one of them make the entire argument, but that is the best course. Some lawyers have solved the problem by retaining an outstanding person to make the oral argument for all of them, thereby insuring that no feathers are ruffled and no pride injured.

Rebuttal can be extremely useful, but it can also be dangerous. If there are effective answers to significant points the other side has made, make them. Rebuttal should be short and vigorous; do not waste time with correcting minor errors or making peripheral points. It can be extremely effective to show in rebuttal that the other side has misstated the record or important decisions.

The danger in rebuttal is that once the lawyer stands up, he or she is open to further questioning. That questioning can lead to trouble that would have been avoided had the lawyer remained silent. If, at the close of the appellee's case, the court appears sympathetic and unimpressed by the other side, there is no need to rebut. On the other hand, a good rebuttal can change the whole atmosphere of a case. One thing is certain: do not rebut unless you have something really important and telling to say, and unless you say it vigorously and effectively.

Second and Third Chances on Appeal

Dennis J. C. Owens

A party is entitled to one appeal. A second chance is possible, but it is not a matter of right. The idea of a second review runs contrary to one of the basic tenets of the jurisprudence of the appeal: Once fairness in procedure and uniformity of the application of the law are assured, the controversy should be laid to rest. Rehearings, either by the same panel or *en banc*, and transfers to a higher appellate court make the matter unsettled once again. Further, the second appeal—and the third and fourth—make the first effort a waste of energy. These additional appeals may put at risk a result that was obtained from a jury and a competent judge and that has been approved by three more jurists.

Usually, we could have confidence in that result. In fact, at that point, the aggrieved party has exhausted his or her right to a jury trial and the right to an appeal. Is it fair to allow yet another chance to reverse the results?

The answer is yes; it is fair. Not only is it equitable, it is jurisprudentially necessary. The philosophy underlying appeals of right (the first appeal) is different from the legal theories underlying rehearings (or second appeals). The purpose of the appeal of right is twofold: to ensure that the process of determining the *facts* was fair and to ensure that the rules of the *law* were applied appropriately. The goals are fair trials and the uniform application of the law. This is the work of the intermediate appellate courts. This work is done in three-judge panels both in the district benches of our state courts of appeals and in the various circuit benches of the federal courts of appeals.

Dennis J. C. Owens, a Fellow of the American Academy of Appellate Lawyers, practices law in Kansas City, Missouri, and is of counsel to DeWitt & Zeldin.

Rehearings by those panels, rehearings en banc, and supreme court review have different functions, both at state and federal levels. The discretionary review presumes that the facts were properly determined. The goals of these secondary or tertiary appeals are these: to reconcile conflicts in appellate decisions; to amass the maximum resources of the appellate systems for questions of exceptional importance; to reconsider the state of the current law, in light of an apparently unjust result of the application of that law; and possibly to realign the law by overruling precedents. If the goals of these secondary and tertiary appeals were merely the same as those for the primary appeals, jurisprudential policy would compel us to abolish the "second chance."

The presumption that the facts are properly determined is a rebuttable one. But, it is not very rebuttable.

In the intermediate courts of appeals, rehearings by the panels and hearings en banc following panel opinion serve other functions for those courts. They avoid the pitfalls of the panel systems. Three judges speak for the court. What if the three judges just happen to be a very bad combination for this case? Such things happen. What if there is a polarization on that bench? Two panels could contradict each other. Again, such things happen. En banc hearings are the theoretical solution to this problem.

Rehearings and en banc hearings also help the intermediate court avoid embarrassment. A rehearing can provide an opportunity to replace an opinion that the superior appellate court surely would reverse with one that it would not. Being human, appellate judges are displeased when their decisions are nullified by the supreme court. A revised opinion in the original appellate court may cure some problems before the case can be taken by the higher court.

An appeal in the court of appeals is the first appeal. If there is a rehearing, that is a second appeal. If the case is transferred to the supreme court, that is the third appeal. The supreme courts will only rarely rehear cases. This is because the functions of secondary reviews should have been fulfilled by then. Just as important, the supreme courts believe that they have too many other important cases, and they do not want to redo work that has already been reworked once. They do not have time for fourth appeals.

When should you ask for a rehearing by the panel or for an en banc hearing? Not very often. No one likes to lose. Embittered by defeat, lawyers frequently file an appeal, and then begin to look for some grounds to support it. How many appeals have been demanded by aggrieved clients, regardless of merit, expense, or likelihood of success? Just as frequently, lawyers have led their clients into the appellate thicket because of a wounding of their own professional pride or because of unprofessional, petty anger. An appeal presents an opportunity for disappointed advocates to blame the judge, thereby exonerating their case, their client, and their own trial skills. Appellate judges will tell you that many briefs seem to have been written to convince the client of the beauty of the case and not to convince the appellate judge of the errors below. This is even more true of rehearing motions.

You should seriously consider seeking a rehearing when: the panel opinion never addresses some crucial fact; an entire question is not resolved and that question survives the disposition on the other issues; conflicting precedents are germane, but not distinguished; or the law is clearly misstated.

If there was no dissent on the panel, the odds are overwhelmingly against you. On the other hand, do *not* seek a rehearing every time there is a dissent. Remember, a dissent is the forlorn loser in the battle of opinions. Further, if a point is considered in a dissent, the majority has not overlooked that point, and the majority believes that it has not misconstrued it.

A set of workable guidelines for when to seek rehearing should encompass the following two questions: Can the author of the opinion be convinced that a mistake was made? Is this decision out of line with the law as developed or developing in this jurisdiction? Those are two very high standards. Usually, the answer is "not this time." And remember, the standards of the Federal Rules of Appellate Procedure are different and more demanding.

One good admonition was advanced by Missouri Appellate Judge George Flanigan: "Make sure your motions for rehearings are not reargument. If it is reargument, and you have nothing else, don't file a motion for rehearing." "Tips for the Appellate Lawyer," 41 *J. Mo. Bar,* 183, 186 (Apr.–May 1985).

When you ask for a rehearing in a state intermediate appellate court, the odds are against you. In one Missouri state court of appeals, 500 motions for rehearing or for transfer to the state supreme court were filed within a two-year period. In only ten cases, just 2 percent, did that intermediate court either sustain the motion for a rehearing or overrule the motion but withdraw the opinion and resubmit the case on its own motion (usually, the court does not hear oral reargument in those cases). The statistics from the other Missouri appellate districts were similarly bleak for the advocate seeking another chance.

Should you bother? A 98-percent chance of failure suggests that you should not. But, in the same two-year period, the local court filed 900 opinions. That means that in 55 percent of these cases, rehearing motions were filed. Why?

Occasionally, the losing lawyer figures that the motion is no big deal, and the decision to prepare it is not made with much concern. Sometimes the losing lawyer is mad. But, most of the time, the losers want to ask the state supreme court to give them a second appeal, and a motion for rehearing in the court of appeals is a procedural requirement before applying in the state capital.

If you have decided to seek a rehearing, begin by reading the applicable rules. Heed what the typical state rule advises: A motion for rehearing shall be brief and succinctly state the grounds upon which a rehearing is sought.

What is the purpose of a motion for rehearing? To call attention to material matters of law or fact overlooked or misinterpreted by the court, as shown by its opinion.

What is the biggest mistake of moving counsel? Rearguing issues determined by the opinion.

Should you file suggestions? Yes. If you do not have any suggestions to file, you probably should not file the motion itself. You should point out (with precise legal file or transcript references) facts that were ignored or overlooked, or point out that an entire issue in your brief was ignored.

In reading the first appellate opinion, some lawyers discover how poorly they had examined the issues. Only after the decision do they come to grips with the hard issues. Unfortunately, this work was supposed to be the function of the brief, not the motion for rehearing. If you find yourself in this predicament, do not expect your motion to be successful. If you attempt to raise a new issue at this juncture, including a constitutional issue, it will be disregarded. So will reargument of issues determined by the opinion.

If you win and the opposing party files a motion for rehearing, do not be overconfident (98 percent odds or not). *Do* file suggestions in opposition. Remember, there will be judges reading the motion who have not paid much attention to this case before. They need your help to understand why to deny the motion.

If a motion for rehearing is granted, the case typically stands as if it had never been heard. At rehearings the issues usually are determined by what was preserved in the record and not by what was argued in the first submission. In most states if the motion for rehearing is denied, it may not be renewed or refiled.

Do not despair just because the odds are overwhelmingly against you. Your case may be within that 2 percent. Someone's case has to be.

En banc rehearings in state intermediate courts are rare, of course. My hometown appellate court has transferred only two cases to the court en banc after decisions were rendered by a three-judge panel. During that period, more than 1,600 cases were filed before that bench. (One reason that en banc work is so rare is that some courts have no specific rules that mention a motion for rehearing en banc, and therefore, lawyers do not think of it.) But the most important reason for the paucity of en banc treatment is that the judges do not like to rehear cases en banc. They have enough to do already.

When a litigant successfully bucks the odds and convinces the court of appeals that, indeed, material matters were overlooked or misinterpreted, a rehearing en banc is a misnomer. Generally, oral argument is not reset and new briefs are not sought. The challenged opinion is withdrawn. The author of the errant opinion will address the overlooked matter or will now correctly interpret the point previously mishandled, and a new opinion is handed down without the necessity of a "rehearing."

State intermediate court transfers to the state supreme court are possible—but rare. Of the 500 applications filed in my local appellate court to transfer an action to the state supreme court, three were granted; the other districts' numbers are similar. So, good luck.

Upward transfers of cases to the state supreme courts are based on standards wholly different from those for rehearings. Transfers to the highest courts generally are predicated on the general interest or importance of a question involved in the case or for the purpose of reexamining the existing law.

Most state supreme courts may order transfer *before* an opinion of the intermediate appellate court on their own motion, or a party can move for an expedited transfer before an intermediate opinion is rendered. But, these types of transfers are rare.

Most of the work load of the state supreme courts arises out of cases that the courts transfer to themselves after an opinion has been handed down by the intermediate court of appeals. In Missouri, for example, 658 applications for transfer were filed in the supreme court in one recent year, yet only 70 were granted, about 11 percent. Next to what we have seen in the intermediate appellate courts, the percentage sounds relatively good. But, batting .110 will not get you to the major leagues, unless you are a shortstop for the Royals.

If you have ever wondered what law clerks really do in your state's appellate courts, here is one answer: They study your applications for transfer and make recommendations.

After transfer by whatever method, a case is before the state supreme court as though it had been appealed to that court originally. Thus, the supreme court may choose to consider plain error that was not raised in the intermediate appellate court. It also can ignore the opinion below, if there is one. Indeed, the court may very well ignore it since its order of transfer possibly indicates some dissatisfaction with that opinion. But, the opinion below is sometimes fondly quoted by a dissenting supreme court judge.

The typical guidelines for the exercise of discretionary review by a state supreme court in a two-tiered system are set forth in Houts and Rogosheske, *Art of Advocacy: Appeals*, at 7-3, § 702 (1986). The authors suggest that the higher court will take a case if:

- it presents a substantial constitutional problem;
- it presents a new question of law or statutory construction, so that an opinion will have important precedential value;
- it presents a legitimate challenge to existing law or precedent;

- disposition of the appeal appears to be controlled by a prior decision, but its application to the facts at hand requires amplification, so that gaps in the law can be filled;
- the case represents a question of significance to the entire jurisdiction, not merely to the litigants;
- the case has received extreme notoriety (a sensational murder or divorce case); or
- the media's interest in the outcome of the case (as in an election contest) demands that the full court rule on the case to assure the public that the court is performing its proper constitutional function.

It is questionable whether these last two factors really play a significant role in most transfer decisions of state supreme courts.

Typical grounds for a state supreme court to order a transfer are that: (1) the case is of general interest or importance; (2) it requires reexamination of the law; or (3) the opinion filed is contrary to a previous decision of an appellate court.

The least effective way to apply for transfer is to complain that the lower appellate court did not view the law correctly or that it did not analyze a legal concept properly. The rules do not mention a "bad decision." Most applications do.

Reexamination is called for when the law was well applied to the facts, but the result is patently unfair. Your application based on this ground is really a call to explore public policy, a plea to make new law. Reexamination applications should cite legal scholars, law review articles, the restatements, federal cases, and cases in other states, all with a view to establishing that the state is not in line with current legal reasoning.

Conflicts Are Overrated

While alluring, the ground of conflicting opinions is overrated. Conflicts are fairly common. The state supreme courts have tolerated some conflicts between the various districts of the intermediate court for considerable lengths of time. It is better to base an argument for supreme court review on conflict coupled with general importance.

Although an application should not be solely grounded on an allegation of appellee error below, factual errors should not be disregarded. State supreme courts want the important, troublesome cases, but a few factual errors also can help secure a granting of transfer.

Nothing is more important than a firm grasp of the facts, the legal arguments, and the opinion below—paired with clear, powerful writing.

Obtaining a rehearing in the state supreme court is harder yet. The Missouri Supreme Court filed 114 opinions within a one-year period. In 54 of those cases, the losing party moved for rehearing. Not a single request was granted. In three cases, however, the opinion was modified after the motion was filed. In one other case, submissions were set aside on the court's own motion. As these figures reflect, the chance of getting a rehearing in Missouri is slim. It is slender in other states as well.

The many motions for rehearing that are filed often are prepared in ignorance or disregard of their possibility for success. A lawyer should ask for a rehearing in a state supreme court only if the opinion overlooked or misinterpreted material matters of fact or law. Disliking the court's statement of the law does not justify asking for a rehearing. Instead, go to the Supreme Court of the United States. There is no requirement in that federal court that you have moved for a rehearing in the state court.

The only practical justification, such as it is, for seeking a rehearing in the state supreme court is to extend the time for petitioning for a writ of *certiorari* in the United States Supreme Court. Such an extension may permit the time for a more deliberate decision—or for seeking the financing of further appeal.

Where do you go if you are aggrieved by an order of a bankruptcy judge? You may appeal the order either to the circuit court of appeals or to the district court. After the appellate decision, a rehearing can be obtained within ten days under Rule 8015 of the Bankruptcy Code.

Unfortunately, the rule does not provide guidelines for when a rehearing should be granted. The best advice is to rely on Rule 40(a), Fed. R. App. P. That rule directs that petitions for rehearing in the circuit courts of appeals "shall state with particularity the points of law or fact which . . . the court has overlooked or misapprehended."

The filing of a motion for rehearing in the district court in bankruptcy cases does not toll the time for taking an appeal to the court of appeals from the district court. *See* the Advisory Committee Note on Rule 8015. The format of a motion for rehearing should follow Rule 32(a), Fed. R. App. P., since that rule is explicitly invoked by Rule 40(b).

What are your chances? In a recent five-year period, 172 bankruptcy appeals were disposed of by the United States District Court for the Western District of Missouri. During that five-year period, only two appeals were reopened. The three-year batting average is .012. That is not good even for a Royals shortstop.

What about obtaining a rehearing in the United States courts of appeals? Almost all the decisions of these courts of appeals are rendered by three-judge panels. The pertinent rule for rehearing *en banc* is Rule 40, Fed. R. App. P. In addition, every circuit has a local rule.

The key point is that a "petition for rehearing by a panel should not be routinely filed." If a party insists on proceeding, filing should be done within 14 days, using Rule 32(a), Fed. R. App. P., for the format.

The rules require that the petition state with particularity "the points of law or fact" (the federal rule) or "significant issue" (the circuit rule) that was overlooked, misapprehended, or misconstrued. Make your argument now.

The committee comment to the Eighth Circuit rule reminds counsel:

> A petition for rehearing is not a prerequisite to the filing of a petition for writ of certiorari in the Supreme Court. The court encourages the parties to limit the filings of petitions for rehearings. If an error has been made, an informal letter or a motion for technical correction often suffices and obviates the filing of a formal petition for rehearing.

They mean it.

Justice Frankfurter wrote in *Western Pacific RR Corp. v. Western Pacific RR Co.*, 345 U.S. 247, 270 (1953):

> Rehearings are not a healthy step in the judicial process; surely they ought not to be deemed a normal procedure. Yet one who has paged the Federal Reporter for nearly fifty years is struck with what appears to be growth in the tendency to file petitions for rehearing in the courts of appeals. I have not made a quantitative study of the facts, but one gains the impression that in some circuits these petitions are filed almost as a matter of course. This is an abuse of judicial energy. It results in needless delay. It arouses false hopes in defeated litigants and wastes their money. If petitions for rehearing were justified, except in rare instances, it would bespeak serious defects in the work of the courts of appeals, an assumption which must be rejected.

Frederick Wiener calls petitions for rehearing "Love's Labor Lost." F. Wiener, *Briefing and Arguing Federal Appeals,* at 365 (1967). While highly discouraging, Wiener suggests that the question of jurisdiction is always open and certainly would be a "significant issue" meriting rehearing.

Other valuable materials on rehearing practice are Stern, *Appellate Practice in the United States* (1981), particularly Chapter 9. Rehearings and Mandates, Louisell and Degnan, "Rehearing in American Appellate Courts," 44 *Cal. L. Rev.* 627 (1956); and Lynn, *Appellate Litigation* (1985), especially Chapter 11, Rehearings.

Knibb, in his treatise, *Federal Court of Appeals Manual,* at 280 (1981), describes the standard for granting a rehearing as "obvious error." He believes that petitioning for rehearing is frequently abused and finds encouragement only in cases where the law has changed since the case was briefed.

Petitions for rehearing often are a medium for invective. More than once, counsel have been taken to task for this. *See Olympia Equipment Leasing Co. v. Western Union Telegraph Co.,* 802 F.2d 217 (7th Cir. 1986), and a highly critical response to that opinion in Gutman, "A Posnerian Trilogy," 13 *Litigation* No. 3 at 51, 52 (Spring 1987).

The best suggestion is not to indulge in invective. (If you must, write out the diatribe and throw it away or mail it to your client.)

Although most commentary on these petitions and the statistics on denial are depressing, some humor remains. Former Chief Justice Schaefer of the Illinois Supreme Court wrote in "Appellate Advocacy," 23 *Tenn. L. Rev.* 471–472 (1954):

> The allotted number of days passes; the petition for rehearing is filed; (the judge) learns that he has grossly misunderstood the facts, shockingly misapplied the law, and, underneath it all, there is an unmistakable current that hurts worse than anything else. This gross error that he has perpetrated, it becomes clearer as he reads the petition again, is ascribed not so much to his stupidity and ignorance as to his abandoned and malignant heart! . . .
>
> Those things have become in our court a peculiar set of engines of destruction. During all the centuries and across all the lands man has produced a great many devices for inducing humility. Fasting, prostration, the French guillotine are great levelers, but I insist that as a means of reducing the spirit of man to its lowest common denominator, I would bank the 20th century Illinois petition for rehearing against any of them.

As for en banc hearings in the federal courts of appeals, the statutory authority is 28 U.S.C. § 46(c) and the applicable procedural guide is Rule 35, Fed. R. App. P.

Here are several observations about this practice:

- There is no "motion" for en banc treatment, only "suggestions by counsel." The court may ignore the suggestions.
- In a recent one-year period, the Eighth Circuit received 167 suggestions for en banc rehearings. Only 12 submissions were heard en banc. (Counting multiple appeals and cross-appeals in the same case, these submissions involved a total of 28 appeals.) The following year, the court reheard only eight cases in response to 205 suggestions out of a total of some 2,000 cases. Thus, only about 10 percent of cases generates "suggestions" for rehearing and less than 1 percent of the "suggestions" is accepted.
- Rule 35 explicitly states that such a rehearing en banc is "not favored" and requires a question of exceptional importance or a conflict of decisions.
- Eighth Circuit Rule 16(d) requires your signed statement that you believe the case qualifies under Rule 35 and how so. Of course, take this certification very seriously.
- Frivolous petitions in the Eighth Circuit may cost you $250 in "costs" paid to the opposing party. As I said, "very seriously." 8th Cir. Rule 35A(c)(3).
- A petition for a panel rehearing may be treated as "a suggestion" for a rehearing en banc.

- Suggestions in opposition to a hearing en banc should not be filed unless specifically invited by the court.

Chief Judge Markey of the United States Court of Appeals for the Federal Circuit has noted, with great surprise and distress, that 87 of the first 89 cases decided by that court were promptly followed by suggestions for rehearing en banc! "We could not have been that wrong eighty-seven out of eighty-nine times!" Proceedings of the First Annual Judicial Conference of the United States Court of Appeals for the Federal Circuit, 100 F.R.D. 499, 503–4 (1983).

En banc consideration is designed for cases where a panel decision is not only wrong, but where that error may set a precedent on an issue of broad public importance or is in direct conflict with another decision of the circuit or of the Supreme Court. Error in applying state law, in applying the facts of the case, or in applying the correct precedent to those facts may justify a panel rehearing, but these types of flaws do not warrant en banc consideration.

One last thought on en banc rehearings. They involve all active judges of the circuit. With many cases, that will exclude one, two, even all three of the original panel. Senior judges, visiting judges, district judges, and Supreme Court justices sitting by designation all are excluded. Rule 35, Fed. R. App. P.

Has your day arrived for petitioning the United States Supreme Court for a writ of certiorari? Send off for admission to the bar of the Supreme Court. You need three years' law practice, two sponsors who already belong to the bar, and a fee of $100. Rules 5 and 45(e), Rules of the Supreme Court of the United States. The certificate is beautiful. There probably are ten lawyers admitted for every one who actually has had a case in the Supreme Court, so if your case may finally bring you to the marble palace, enjoy the opportunity. Now, down to work.

Each year, the Supreme Court receives about 4,200 applications for review. This figure grows a bit every year. Only about 180 cases receive plenary consideration each term, a number that remains constant year to year. Your job is to get your case from the 4,200 to the 180. That is tough, but not impossible.

Of the 8,762 cases disposed of by the Eighth Circuit in a five-year span, petitions for 903 writs of certiorari were filed in the Supreme Court. Certiorari was granted in only 52 of these cases, barely 5 percent.

The latest edition of the bible for this area, L. Stern, E. Gressman, S. Shapiro & K. Geller, *Supreme Court Practice* (7th ed., 1993) costs about $100 and is worth every cent. This handbook has no competitors, but there are other helpful materials. For instance, *see* Prettyman, "Petitioning the United States Supreme Court—A Primer for Hopeful Neophytes," 51 *V.A.L. Rev.* 582 (1965).

A Winning Petition

The art of preparing a winning petition for writ is subtle, technical, and difficult. F. Wiener, *Briefing and Arguing Federal Appeals,* flatly argues for new counsel on appeal. Whether old carries forth or new counsel takes over, a few directions are in order:

- The Supreme Court is not a judicial body that sits to correct errors. The allegation that a decision is wrong will not persuade the Court to take that case to correct it.
- Intra-circuit conflicts do not concern the Supreme Court.
- High financial stakes do not intrigue it.
- Stating that the case is unique is counterproductive. If it is truly unique, the facts are not likely to be repeated in the future, and no precedent will be established. The judges do not want weird cases.
- Do not bother to find a federal question belatedly. If you did not find it when the case was in the state supreme court, it is too late.
- The Supreme Court has a high level of tolerance for inter-circuit conflict. It now seems to require long-standing conflicts involving several circuits on each side to invoke its review.
- An effective petition for writ of certiorari should not tell the Court why the petitioner should have won below. Instead, it should tell the Court why it should hear this case. It should convince the judges that the questions are important and the facts of this case present those questions squarely.
- Always keep in mind the guidelines set forth in part one of the Supreme Court's Rule 17 on considerations governing review on certiorari:

    A review on writ of certiorari is not a matter of right, but of judicial discretion and will be granted only when there are special and important reasons therefor. The following, while neither controlling nor fully measuring the Court's discretion, indicate the character of reasons that will be considered.

    (a) When a federal court of appeals has rendered a decision in conflict with the decision of another federal court of appeals on the same matter; or has decided a federal question in a way in conflict with a state court of last resort; or has so far departed from the accepted and usual course of judicial proceedings; or so far sanctioned such a departure by a lower court, as to call for an exercise of this Court's power of supervision.

    (b) When a state court of last resort has decided a federal question in a way in conflict with the decision of another state court of last resort or of a federal court of appeals.

    (c) When a state court or a federal court of appeals has

decided an important question of federal law which has not been, but should be, settled by this Court, or has decided a federal question in a way in conflict with applicable decisions of this Court.

The Supreme Court does rehear cases. The Court has reversed itself on rehearing more than once. *Reid v. Covert,* 354 U.S. 1 (1957), a 6-to-3 vote, overturned *Reid v. Covert,* 351 U.S. 487 (1956), and *Kinsella v. Krueger,* 351 U.S. 470 (1956), (5-to-3 vote) (companion cases). Another example of reversal after rehearing is the five-to-four decision, *Jones v. Opelika,* 316 U.S. 584 (1943), overturned by the five-to-four vote in *Jones v. Opelika,* 319 U.S. 103 (1943).

In a six-year span, the Court granted six rehearings of the 735 sought by nonindigents. Again, a batting average below 1 percent.

When should a petition for rehearing be filed in this Court? Supreme Court Rule 51.2 provides the answer:

. . . its grounds must be limited to intervening circumstances of substantial or controlling effect or to other substantial grounds not previously presented.

At least four of the nine justices must vote to grant certiorari. A rehearing is much harder. It requires both the support of a justice who concurred in the judgment or decision as well as the votes of five of the nine justices. Rule 51.1, Rules of the Supreme Court of the United States. Traditionally, new appointments to the Court are not allowed to play a role in considering these rehearing petitions.

In sum, rehearings and transfers to a superior appellate court after an appellate decision are not a matter of right. The party losing on appeal is not likely to win a second chance. These discretionary rehearings, however, may be granted if the very high standards are met and if counsel skillfully presents the request.

And if you don't succeed, don't feel too depressed. You might try out for the Royals. They always seem to need a shortstop who can hit .100.

Appellate Judicial Notice: Oasis or Mirage?

Paul Mark Sandler and Francis B. Burch, Jr.

The trial is over after two weeks. Coupled with two weeks of preparation time, it destroyed your Christmas vacation and, as usual, disappointed your spouse and family. The fact that you lost only aggravates the situation. Your client insists on appeal. The stakes are high, and intensity is great. Fortunately, you asked the court's stenographer to prepare daily transcripts for your review, and you waste no time in reviewing them in preparation for framing the issues on appeal. You know that the cardinal rule of appellate practice is to preserve the record, and you usually prove or proffer all essential facts during trial.

Then it hits you. A fact, which you now think is crucial, was not proved or even proffered. Your throat begins to dry, your forehead becomes hot, and you feel like a forlorn traveler in the desert: lost, aching from the heat, and intensely looking for help. Suddenly, you see it—what appears to be an oasis in the distance—appellate judicial notice. Quickly you begin to cool off, and with new excitement you begin to plot your course.

Unfortunately, you will not know whether it is an oasis or a mirage until you arrive at your destination. That is the way it is with appellate judicial notice in our legal system. Scholars discuss it; lawyers occasionally attempt to use it; and, like obscenity, the courts know it when they see it; but the appellate advocate rarely knows whether it is an oasis or a mirage until after the court has decided his case.

Imagine yourself counsel for appellant in the case of *Gaither v. District of Columbia*, 333 A.2d 57 (D.C. 1975). Your client, an inmate at the Lorton Reformatory in Virginia, was injured when a gas burner, which he was ordered to light despite his protest that he could smell escaping gas,

---

Paul Mark Sandler is a member of Freishtat & Sandler in Baltimore. Francis B. Burch, Jr., is a member of Piper & Marbury, L.L.P., in Baltimore. Glen K. Allen, an associate at Piper & Marbury, L.L.P., assisted with this chapter.

exploded in his face. You brought an action against the District of Columbia, which you alleged owned and operated the correctional facility. You called only the plaintiff and his mother to testify, after which you rested your case. The defendant moved for a directed verdict on two grounds: that there was no evidence of any negligence for the jury to consider and that you did not establish that the defendant owned and operated the facility. To your astonishment the trial court agreed with both of the defendant's arguments and directed a verdict against you.

You file an appeal resolute in your belief that the trial court erred in holding the evidence of negligence legally insufficient, but you are devastated by the prospect that the question might never be reached as you offered no evidence at the trial to show that the defendant did own and operate the Lorton facility.

Fortunately for the appellant in *Gaither*, his plight did not prove hopeless. The District of Columbia Court of Appeals took judicial notice that the defendant owned and operated Lorton. The court was satisfied that:

> [a] reasonable person with reasonable knowledge of the District of Columbia community would understand that the District owns and operates its own reformatory. *Id.* at 59.

Additionally, the court cited a congressional statute giving the District of Columbia control of the Lorton facility, and it recognized that the trial judges sitting in the Superior Court of the District of Columbia had actual knowledge of who owned and operated Lorton because a great majority of the persons incarcerated by the Superior Court had been sent there.

After disposing of the issue of who owned the facility, the court of appeals also reversed the trial court on the sufficiency of the evidence and granted a new trial.

The willingness of the *Gaither* court to judicially notice that the District of Columbia owned Lorton Reformatory underscores that judicial notice may be an important and effective appellate tool. It may prove useful as either a sword or a shield, and it may miraculously surface, unsolicited, in the appellate opinion. Unfortunately, the cases do little to assist the appellate advocate in determining, in advance, whether the court will take judicial notice of a fact.

Rule 201 of the Federal Rules of Evidence and the Advisory Committee's Note to the rule capsulize much of the common law and the commentators' views on the subject.

The rule provides that to be judicially noticed, a fact must not be subject to reasonable dispute in that it is either (1) generally known within the territorial jurisdiction of the trial court or (2) capable of accurate and ready determination by resort to sources whose accuracy cannot reasonably be questioned. The rule permits the court to notice facts on its own or on the motion of a party, and it requires that the party be afforded an opportunity to be heard on the propriety of taking notice before or after judicial notice has been taken.

Rule 201 regulates judicial notice only of adjudicative facts, not legislative facts. Adjudicative facts relate to the parties in the case. Legislative facts have relevance to legal reasoning and to the law-making process in general. The distinction was drawn by Professor Kenneth Davis in his well-known article "An Approach to Problems of Evidence in the Administrative Process," 55 *Harv. L. Rev.*, 364, 404–07 (1942). An example of an adjudicative fact, frequently used by Judge Younger in his lectures on evidence, is that the radar device used on a police vehicle accurately reflects the speed of a passing motorist. A legislative fact involves a court's recognition that adverse testimony by a spouse in a criminal case would likely destroy a marriage. This example is drawn from the Advisory Committee's Note to Rule 201. Unlike Rule 201, the common law generally does not distinguish between adjudicative and legislative facts.

Subdivision F of Rule 201 states that the judicial notice may be taken at any stage of the proceedings, and the Advisory Committee's Note makes it clear that this includes the appellate level. *Accord In re Appeal No. 504*, 24 Md. App. 715, 332 A.2d 698 (1975). As an abstract proposition, therefore, an appellate court can take judicial notice of any matter in the same manner as the trial court. As a practical matter, however, the appellate advocate often must overcome the additional hurdles of many appellate judges' instinct not to consider a matter that is not part of the record. Counsel's ability to justify the omission from the record may be an important factor in the appellate court's decision whether to notice the fact. For example, a court may be more willing to notice a fact not proven at the trial because it did not yet exist, than a fact not proven because the lawyer neglected to prove it.

In those situations where a lawyer simply forgets to prove an important fact, the appellate court still may be persuaded to take judicial notice of it. Judge Soper, in *Morse v. Lewis*, 54 F.2d 1027 (4th Cir. 1932), first articulated the exception to the settled rule that the appellate court will not travel outside the record:

> But in exceptional cases . . . the dictates of logic will yield to the demands of justice, and the courts, in order to reach a just result, will make use of established and uncontroverted facts not formally of record in the pending litigation. *Id.* at 1029.

This test was embraced by the Maryland Court of Appeals in *Fletcher v. Flournoy*, 198 Md. 53, 81 A.2d 232 (1951), and has been applied several times thereafter.

A good example is *James v. State*, 31 Md. App. 666, 358 A.2d 595 (1976). During the trial the defendant took the stand in his own defense, and on cross-examination the prosecutor elicited testimony that the conditions of his parole prohibited firearms possession. The prosecutor then introduced the order for release on parole, which revealed not only the conditions of parole but also the defendant's conviction for robbery with a deadly weapon in 1963. The prosecutor did not ask the defendant whether he had the benefit of counsel or had knowingly waived representation back in 1963. On appeal, the Maryland Court of Special Appeals criticized the prosecutor for not establishing the status of the defendant's representation in 1963, but nevertheless affirmed after taking judicial notice that at that time it was the standard operating procedure for the criminal court of Baltimore to provide counsel or advise a defendant of his right to counsel.

Of course, for every case like *James*, there are many others in which advocates could not persuade the appellate court to take judicial notice of a fact they had neglected to establish at trial. In *Jones v. State*, 29 Md. App. 182, 348 A.2d 55 (1975), for example, the Maryland Court of Special Appeals declined to take notice of "court records and statistics" not reflected in appellate opinions.

In *Fletcher v. Flournoy*, 198 Md. 53, 81 A.2d 232 (1951), the court of appeals declined to take notice of lower court records in a different case involving the same parties. The court concluded that justice did not require a departure from the settled rule against traveling outside the record, as the appellant could have simply and inexpensively entered the records into evidence at trial. Of course, the Court of Special Appeals could have employed the same rationale to decline to take judicial notice in *James* because the prosecutor could have proven that the defendant had been represented by counsel at his prior conviction simply by asking him the question.

The equities sometimes cut differently when the fact that counsel wants the appellate court to take judicial notice only develops after the trial. This was the situation in *Creative Development Corp. v. Calhoun Bond, Trustee*, 34 Md. App. 279, 367 A.2d 566 (1976). After a trial in which the grantor of a deed of trust unsuccessfully attacked a trustee's foreclosure sale, counsel for the trustee requested on appeal that the court take judicial notice that the purchaser at the posttrial foreclosure sale was the beneficiary of the deed of trust who then sold the property securing the deed of trust. The court did so and found that the case was therefore moot.

If a court will consider facts developing after the trial to hold an appeal moot, it should also consider the same facts for other purposes. The Supreme Court of the United States did so, albeit reluctantly, in *Trailmobile Co. v. Whirls*, 331 U.S. 40, 67 S. Ct. 982 (1947). There, relevant matters that had occurred after the ruling below were set out in the respondents' brief and raised at oral argument. The court made clear that while such consideration was not to be encouraged, it would consider the facts in deciding the case.

The appellate advocate might also be wise to consider seeking judicial notice when the appeal is from a judgment on the pleadings alone with no opportunity to present evidence to the lower court. For example, in *Phipps v. General Motors Corporation*, 278 Md. 337, 363 A.2d 955 (1976), the Maryland Court of Appeals considered for the first time whether to adopt the doctrine of strict liability in tort. The issue had been certified to the court of appeals from the United States District Court for Maryland, and the entire record consisted of the plaintiff's complaint and the defendant's motion to dismiss. The defendant, who was designated as the appellee by agreement, suggested in its brief that the adoption of strict liability might entail certain harmful economic consequences, and it sought to support that argument by referring to statistical data compiled by the census bureau. These matters were addressed at oral argument, and the court did not make an issue of their absence from the formal record.

Occasionally, courts will take judicial notice of facts not in the record, *sua sponte*, leaving counsel dazed at their creativity. For example, in *Davidson v. Miller*, 276 Md. 54, 344 A.2d 422 (1975), the court of appeals relied on judicial notice of significant shifts in Maryland's population since the latter half of the 19th century in finding no rational basis grounded in population differences for applying different removal rules to civil litigants in Baltimore City than to those in two nearby counties. The court acknowledged that such issues are normally decided on the basis of testimony or documentary proof, but justified its excursion beyond the record:

> [E]ven though petitioners here presented no such evidence on the point, this issue so peculiarly involves the judicial process about which . . . it is our responsibility to have a particular familiarity that we here take judicial notice of the essential facts which assail the conclusion that there exists a rational basis for this States' unequal constitutional automatic right of removal. 344 A.2d at 347.

Perhaps no case better illustrates the scope of appellate courts' judicial notice license than the Maryland Court of Appeals' decision in *Kelley v. R.G. Industries, Inc.*, 304 Md. 124, 497 A.2d 1143 (1985). There, in a case certified from the United States District Court for Maryland, the court of appeals recognized a new theory of strict liability for manufacturers and marketers of Saturday night special handguns. In a paradigmatic instance of taking notice of legislative facts, the court relied extensively on testimony relating to handgun control before several Senate subcommittees. But the court also took notice of adjudicative facts relating to R.G. Industries. The court quoted an R.G. salesman as having allegedly said of an R.G. handgun, "This sells real well, but between you and me, it's such a piece of crap I'd be afraid to fire the thing." The source of the quote was an article in *Harper's* magazine.

In the last few years, several federal courts, including a circuit court of appeals, have taken judicial notice of facts about acquired immune deficiency syndrome (AIDS) and its relationship to the human immunodeficiency virus (HIV). *See Chalk v. U.S. District Court for Central District of California*, 840 F.2d 701 (9th Cir. 1988) (observing Surgeon General's report that HIV cannot be spread through casual contact); *see, e.g., Kozup v. Georgetown University*, 663 F. Supp. 1048 (D.D.C. 1987) (observing the combined 100 percent effectiveness of the two HIV antibody tests). The Maryland Court of Appeals, in *Rossi v. Almaraz*, 329 Md. 435, 620 A.2d 327 (1993), followed the lead of these courts and took extensive judicial notice of what it characterized as well-established and scientifically understood facts about AIDS and its transmission. The court endorsed the trial court's judicial notice of most, but not all, of these facts, while noting that it had previously taken judicial notice of basic facts about the sexually transmitted disease of herpes in *B.N. v. K.K.*, 312 Md. 135, 538 A.2d 1175 (1988).

Appellate courts will sometimes demand that judicial notice be taken of all related facts. Thus, in *Barsalo v. Barsalo*, 18 Md. App. 560, 308 A.2d 457 (1972), the trial court refused to modify a child custody decree to allow the child to visit her father in Panama, taking judicial notice that air piracy and hijacking were prevalent at the time and posed a danger to the child. The appellate court, in reversing, observed that the lower court should also have taken judicial notice of the fact that all airlines that permit minors to travel unescorted take special care of such passengers.

You may not know whether judicial notice is an oasis or a mirage until you or your adversary tries it. Either way, it may be important to remember that the trial court record will not always be the only resource from which the appellate court derives its facts.

Jumping at Constitutional Questions Is Risky Business

Abner J. Mikva

When I started my tenure in Congress, I held some rather naive notions about how a legislator should approach questions of constitutionality. Reasoning that the very first act of a member of Congress is to take an oath to "support and defend the Constitution of the United States," I resolved that I would sit as a court of one and pass on the constitutionality of every bill before voting on it.

It soon became clear, however, that the fastest way to empty out the House chamber was to take the floor and raise questions about a bill's constitutionality. "That's what we have the courts for," some of my former colleagues would grouse. Others would loudly complain that "the lawyers" were jamming up the legislative process again. I quickly learned that constitutional excursuses were not the coin of the realm in the House of Representatives.

When I arrived on the bench, the prevailing attitude was quite the reverse. Perhaps it is because the constitutional buck stops here—judges do not have Congress's easy out that someone else will look at the constitutional questions; perhaps it is simply that judges and lawyers have been trained their whole professional lives to look for issues of this sort. For whatever reason, I repeatedly have been struck by how eager lawyers and judges are to toss aside traditional judicial canons of restraint and to wage constitutional battle.

One of the judicial restraints that appears to have fallen loose in recent years is the traditional canon of construction that instructed judges to avoid unnecessarily reaching constitutional questions. This canon required a court whenever possible to find an interpretation or application of a statute that would obviate the need to reach a constitu-

---

Abner J. Mikva is retired as chief judge, U.S. Court of Appeals, District of Columbia Circuit, and is a former member of Congress, 10th District, Illinois.

tional question. Today, however, judging by the arguments made by counsel and the decisions made by my colleagues, there is enthusiasm about putting the Constitution in issue, whether necessary or not.

A second judicial restraint that seems to have popped loose is the canon that requires judges to give maximum deference to legislative competence in order to reduce the tension between legislative action and constitutional limitations. This canon rightly ensures that legislation comes to a court with a presumption of constitutionality that is not easily overcome. A corollary of this canon of deference to Congress is one requiring a court to limit any constitutional infirmities that it does find to as small a portion of the statute as it can.

These restraints are not hoary relics of a "less activist" bench. Rather, they are based on premises that are as valid today as they were when those canons emerged. The first such premise is that the less often courts wander into the political thicket the better. Although courts sometimes fail to realize it, every time they strike down a congressional statute or an act of the President, they are throwing down a gauntlet to the political branches. Lawyers and judges may have accepted the principle of judicial review as laid down in *Marbury v. Madison*, 5 U.S. 137 (1803), but Congress and the President still find that decision burdensome.

Looming over all such political decisions is an ominous question: What would happen if the political branches forced a confrontation? Judicial decisions are not self-executing. President Jackson touched the Achilles heel of the judicial branch with his famous, if perhaps apocryphal, retort to the Supreme Court's decision in *Cherokee Nation v. Georgia*, 30 U.S. 1 (1831): "John Marshall has made his decision. Now let him enforce it." The implications of such an attitude from the political branches are devastating.

Suppose President Eisenhower had expressed similar views about *Brown v. Board of Education*, 347 U.S. 483 (1954), and refused to call out the troops in Little Rock? Or suppose President Nixon had heeded the counsel of some of his advisors and "stonewalled" when the Supreme Court ordered him to turn over the Watergate tapes. One need not quarrel with the correctness of either *Brown* or *U.S. v. Nixon*, 418 U.S. 683 (1974), to be concerned about the strain that such decisions put on our nation by the danger of noncompliance. The image of the Supreme Court's marshal and an unarmed assistant going forth into the land to enforce the Court's decrees is not a comforting one.

The practical fears of political branch defiance reflect the essential fragility of the power of the third branch. The high bench and the black robe create a mystique of strength, but the reality is more like the Wizard of Oz. Behind the curtain and the smoke and the loud voice is a force that relies almost exclusively on faith and tradition. Those qualities ought not to be put to the test too often in as pluralistic and fractious a society as ours.

There is a second reason, beyond the risk of noncompliance, for courts to avoid constitutional pronouncements whenever possible. Judicial determinations of constitutionality have a finality to them warranting that they be wielded with considerable caution. When a court misinterprets a statute, either Congress or a court can correct the mistake. When a court misinterprets the Constitution, however, only a court can make the correction. Leaving a question beyond the reach of the legislative branch risks ossification of an area of law, threatening the nation's progress and perhaps even survival.

This was precisely the danger posed by the Supreme Court of the early 1930s, which used the due process clause to strike down much of the early New Deal agenda. This brand of judicial activism endangered both the Court and the country. The "switch in time" saved not only the nine Justices, but quite possibly our free economic system as well. If the Court had persisted in its activist ways, fundamental changes in the Court or the Constitution likely would have ensued that would have been far more profound than the New Deal programs that eventually emerged.

If it seems that I am advocating some form of "strict constructionism," I suppose I am. But as we have seen in the recent debates on interpretivism, qualities like "strict constructionism" and "judicial activism" are in the eye of the beholder. The "strict constructionism" that I advocate differs from that of former Attorney General Meese. Mine states simply that judges ought to write fewer and narrower constitutional decisions, particularly when such decisions would limit the power of the first branch of government, the Congress.

The willingness of the courts, acting in the name of the Constitution, to infringe on Congressional power was illustrated by the Court's decision in *I.N.S. v. Chadha*, 462 U.S. 919 (1983). Mr. Chadha had been done in by a House of Representatives veto of an administrative law judge's decision permitting him to remain in the country. The notion of Congress "vetoing" a judicial decision (albeit a non–Article III court's decision) is as bad an idea as the Supreme Court said it is.

The *Chadha* majority went on, however, to strike down the entire concept of a legislative veto and the numerous statutes containing such a provision. I am not sure that all of these statutes were equally vulnerable to constitutional challenge. I am very sure that Congress reacted with more than a little testiness at the broad sweep of the Court's ruling. The post-*Chadha* hearings on the Hill encompassed everything from suggestions of a constitutional amendment overruling *Chadha* to mutterings about an amendment overruling *Marbury v. Madison*. Certainly some of the reaction was simply Congress letting off steam, but some of the animosity and proposals for reform that the decision engendered posed a potential threat to the delicate balance between the courts and the political branches.

A second example of this sort of judicial overreach was the three-member court decision in *Bowsher v. Synar*, 106 S. Ct. 3181 (1986), 478 U.S. 714 (1986), the case striking down some provisions of the Gramm-Rudman balanced budget law. Congress had authorized the comptroller-general to effectuate the substantive budgetary provisions when Congress failed to agree on a budget. The three-judge court struck down this procedure, and then went on to draw into question the constitutionality of all the independent agencies from the Federal Communications Commission to the Federal Trade Commission.

The Supreme Court, although painting with a somewhat narrower brush, did not remove all the doubts cast on administrative agencies by the decision below. This uncertainty, again coupled with testiness on the part of a Congress whose independence from executive-branch meddling has been threatened, has not been good for the delicate balance.

I am not criticizing the Supreme Court's decisions. As an "inferior court" judge, I do not have that option, nor do I seek it. Yet I can deferentially suggest that all courts should contribute to the comity each branch of government owes to the others. We can ensure such comity by not invoking constitutional limitations on Congress except when necessary, and then only to the extent necessary. Broad dicta about the meaning of the Constitution can only create problems for all three branches.

When I was in the state legislature in Illinois, we had a House speaker who had little use for courts, lawyers, or constitutional limitations. Whenever some legislator would raise a question about whether a legislative initiative could withstand challenge under the state constitution, he had a very pragmatic response. "Let's just attach it to the appropriation bill for the Supreme Court, and there won't be any constitutional problems."

While the Illinois speaker probably exaggerated the frailties of the judicial system—even in Illinois at that time—he was not entirely wrong. Courts are by their nature frail institutions. We cannot and should not always avoid friction with the political branches. Yet we ought not to seek it out unnecessarily. Nor should we wage any wider war than is required to undertake the constitutional obligations imposed on the courts.

Even the most outspoken legislative court-bashers do not really contemplate a world without the reviewing presence of the courts as provided by *Marbury v. Madison*. But the courts have neither purse nor sword to enforce their judgments. When the courts are dealing with the branches of government that do wield those powerful instruments, discretion dictates that we exercise appropriate restraint. The Constitution made the courts the third branch of government. That ordering is due to more than mere happenstance of constitutional structuring, and we must respect it.

How to Appeal to an Appellate Judge

Leonard I. Garth

I have always been drawn to the analogy expressed by the former great appellate advocate, John W. Davis, who wrote:

> Supposing fishes had the gift of speech, who would listen to a fisherman's weary discourse on fly casting, the shape and color of the fly, the size of the tackle, the length of the line, the merit of different rod makers, and all the other tiresome stuff that fishermen talk about, if the fish himself could be induced to give his views on the most effective methods of approach? For after all, it is the fish that the angler is after and all his recondite learning is but the hopeful means to that end.

John W. Davis, "The Argument of an Appeal," *26 A.B.A. J.* 895 (1940).

To carry this further, I suspect that the average brook trout would not waste much time or energy analyzing the techniques of the fly fisherman seeking to hook him. Rather, the trout's eye is out for a juicy, succulent dinner that he can snap up and digest. Once you have learned what the trout is looking for, and where, when, and how he expects to find it—your task as an angler has become much easier and more effective. Here is how to land this appellate judge when you go fishing in my court.

First, let me emphasize that each federal court of appeals judge is confronted annually with an overwhelming caseload that keeps growing—and growing—and growing—much as the Energizer Bunny keeps going, and going, and going. The number of appeals filed in the U.S. Courts of Appeals has increased dramatically in recent years. The Administrative Office of the United States Courts reports that more than 50,000 federal appeals were filed in 1993—a 25 percent increase over

---

Leonard I. Garth was appointed to the U.S. Court of Appeals for the Third Circuit in 1973.

1989 filings. After a slight dip in 1994, the number of appeals rose by 4 percent in 1995. In 1996, more than 52,000 new federal appeals were filed.

Why should this concern you?

Because, if a circuit judge is to sit on roughly 280 cases a year (40 cases a sitting, seven sittings annually)—in addition to writing opinions assigned from earlier sittings, reading and deciding motions, reading and deciding *pro se* briefs, reading intra-court circulating opinions, reading petitions for rehearing, studying habeas corpus petitions, preparing circuit administrative reports, as well as preparing judicial conference memoranda, as required—your brief and your arguments, in order to catch and hold the judge's attention, must be direct, to the point, easily understood, in compliance with the Federal Rules of Appellate Procedure and the local rules of the circuit, and must be, hopefully, brief!

Second, you should recognize that if you have a 90 percent losing case, even if your advocacy skills match those of Clarence Darrow and John W. Davis combined, you will undoubtedly still lose the appeal. By the same token and conversely, if you have a 90 percent winning case, you will undoubtedly prevail—even if you read no further, and even if you eschew each and every one of my suggestions.

If you have such a small impact, why bother refining your advocacy talents? The answer is simple: Most appeals fall within the 45 percent to 55 percent "win/lose" category. If that is where your appeal is lodged, you will be well advised to hone your advocacy skills.

Third, although these observations are written from the viewpoint of a federal court of appeals judge, the same appellate advocacy guidelines can be applied in your own state courts. The court rules may differ, but the principles are essentially the same.

But having mentioned court rules, let me add quickly that no appellate advocate should put his hand to paper without having first become familiar with the court's rules and, in the federal courts in particular, the individual circuit's local rules. Filing a brief and preparing an argument before a court without regard to that court's rules is as risky as driving from Portland, Maine, to Baja, California, without a road map: If you veer too far off course, you may never reach your objective.

Fourth, be aware that the era in which oral argument was the main feature of appellate advocacy has now passed. It has gone by the board largely because of the volume of appeals and because the brief itself, for the most part, carries the burden and message of the appeal, both before and after we have heard oral argument. This is not to say that oral argument is unimportant—it is indeed essential for many of us in deciding the outcome of an appeal, but it is not necessarily needed in every case.

Consider, for example, the following three appeals reported in a *New York Times* story on the flood of prisoner rights suits that have swamped the courts. All three appeals claimed infliction of cruel and unusual punishment in violation of the Eighth Amendment. One case, seeking $1 million in damages, charged that a prison guard refused to refrigerate a prisoner's ice cream, causing it to melt. Another prisoner claimed that it was unconstitutional for the prison not to provide him with lamb, veal, and oysters—a deprivation of which contributed to his ulcer. In the third case, the prisoner brought action after he received a jar of *creamy* peanut butter when he had ordered *chunky* peanut butter. *See* Ashley Dunn, "Flood of Prisoners Rights Suits Brings Efforts to Limit Filings," N.Y. Times, Mar. 21, 1994, at A1. Would any of you, sitting as an appellate judge, have granted 30 minutes of oral argument to hear any of these claims?

Tooling the Brief

Thus, it is the brief that is the main tool of the appellate advocate, and it is, therefore, the brief that occupies the better part of my attention here.

Before turning to the *presentation* of an appeal, however, I must emphasize the importance of the *preservation* of the appeal. Technically, an appeal starts with the filing of a Notice of Appeal; realistically, an appeal starts with the filing of an indictment or a complaint. The record that is developed in the district or trial court is the record on which your appeal will be decided.

A bad record below—i.e., a record where specific contemporaneous objections or offers of proof are not made; where issues later deemed significant are abandoned at trial; where crucial motions are made, or crucial discussions are held "off-the-record"; where counsel fails to call the court's attention to prejudicial matters or fails to submit desired points for charge—must necessarily result in a bad appeal.

Indeed, where you have not preserved error, not only will you be prosecuting a bad appeal, but unquestionably you will be pursuing a losing appeal. Without preserving your points for appeal, you will be remitted to "plain error" (a doctrine that has a dozen different meanings to every judge), and the chances of the court reaching the merits of your arguments are unlikely.

The preservation of error is an essential principle of appellate advocacy, yet one that is consistently overlooked and almost always fatal to an appeal where overlooked. That reality is illustrated by the following example:

A few years ago, the Third Circuit had before it a wrongful death appeal. A police officer had seen a suspicious young man running down an alley with a TV set at 2 A.M. The officer first shouted warnings and then fired two shots in the air. A third bullet struck and killed the young man. His estate sued. The jury held for the officer and the city, both of whom were defendants.

On appeal, the primary issue urged was that the district court judge had abused his discretion by denying the plaintiff estate's motion for a bifurcated trial. Argued the estate: The decedent had a most unhappy, extensive, and lurid criminal record. Evidence of his record would not have come out during the liability phase if the trial court had ordered bifurcation, even though the same evidence would have been relevant and preserved to the jury on the issue of damages. By failing to bifurcate, the estate argued, decedent's criminal record had to have influenced the jury, which resulted in a defendants' verdict.

Unfortunately from the estate's standpoint, the record was completely barren of any bifurcation motion, as well as the district court judge's reasons for ruling against it. Why? The motion to bifurcate was made in the judge's chambers without a court stenographer present. We, as appellate judges, decide cases only on the record. When the record is silent, the party bearing the burden loses.

The moral is, don't ever, ever, ever, go off the record. A fully developed record is the greatest ally a lawyer can have.

Another example of counsel's losing an appeal by failing to preserve error is reported in a Tenth Circuit case, which calls attention to the need for counsel to pinpoint the grounds of objection with specificity in order to preserve the issue for appeal. In that case, *Fenstermacher v. Telelect,* Inc., 21 F.3d 1121 (Nos. 92-3283 and 92-3297) (10th Cir. Mar. 28, 1994), a lineman for a power company was severely injured when the bucket in which he was working came into contact with the power line. His co-workers had not seen the accident, but they nevertheless testified to and about a re-enactment staged months later. The product liability defendant, the manufacturer of the bucket, claimed that neither the re-enactment photographs nor the witnesses to the re-enactment had been revealed until just before trial and long after the pretrial conference, and the time to disclose witnesses had expired. The district court admitted the evidence over this objection, and the majority of the court of appeals panel affirmed the $7 million verdict for the plaintiff. The Tenth Circuit majority held that the defendant's ambiguous and unspecific objections did not suffice to preserve the issue of "surprise" and "expert" testimony for appeal.

Raising an issue for the first time on appeal is another "no-no"! Appellate courts will generally not entertain an issue raised for the first time on appeal, although they have the discretion to do so. *See, e.g., United States v. Benjamin,* 995 F.2d 19, 21 n.2 (3d Cir. 1993). If you have developed a good record, a record that has preserved error, and if you are not raising issues for the first time on appeal, you are on your way to a successful appeal—even though it may not be a winning appeal.

I should point out that, at least in the Third Circuit, our Local Rule 28(1) requires the appellant to designate that part of the record where the error is preserved. Certainly, if the appellant does not do so, the appellee should. It should not be necessary to take time at oral argument to answer a judge's questions as to how and where the particular issue was preserved on the record.

Nor is it ever satisfactory for an appellate judge to hear, as I have, the explanation that an appellate lawyer does not know where in the record the particular objection was taken because, "I didn't try the case below." Neither did the judges hearing the appeal! We expect you to know the record, backwards and forward, and certainly far better than we do. If your task is to educate, teach, and persuade us, the very least we can expect is that the foundation of the appeal—that is, the record—is as familiar to you as the back of your own hand.

I receive two sets of briefs in my chambers for each appeal. One set is destined for my law clerk, and the other for me. Over the years, I have established standing rules that require my law clerks to look first at whether we have jurisdiction—both subject matter and appellate jurisdiction—and then, and only then, to note how the appeal reaches us, e.g., from a dismissal of the complaint, from a summary judgment, from a bench trial, or a jury trial. This latter exercise, of course, also requires a study of the standard of review specified for each issue in the brief.

Protecting Jurisdiction

Obviously the federal courts, where subject matter jurisdiction stems from congressional enactments, present a different problem from state court jurisdiction where the power to act is not so restricted. When the jurisdictional question involves *appellate* jurisdiction, however, many of the same principles are pertinent in both state and federal courts. For years, the Third Circuit's local rules required the jurisdictional requisites to be spelled out in each party's brief, along with the appropriate standards of review. Now, Fed. R. App. P. 28(a)(2) and (6) require counsel to specify both the basis of jurisdiction and the standard of review.

So make certain that the court where your appeal is filed has jurisdiction—and that you acquaint the court with that fact, up front in your brief and with an explanation. If you want to make the judge who is reading your brief a very unhappy jurist, just fail to provide jurisdictional information the judge needs to act on and decide your appeal. Time and again, I have seen no more than the term "final order" appear in the jurisdictional statement of a brief—when indeed a jurisdictional issue of some moment was involved.

Was the order from which the appeal was taken a collateral order? Did it satisfy the criteria for a collateral final order? *See Cohen v. Beneficial Indus. Loan Corp.*, 337 U.S. 541, 546 (1949). Did the order that was entered dispose of all the parties and all the issues? See Fed. R. Civ. P. 54(b). Did it provide the reasons required for a Federal Rule Civil Procedure 54(b) certification? *See Allis-Chalmers Corp. v. Philadelphia Elec. Corp.*, 521 F.2d 360, 364–65 (3d Cir. 1975). Were the necessary certifications prepared authorizing an interlocutory appeal pursuant to 28 U.S.C. § 1292(b)? Will I, reading your brief at home at 2 A.M., be in a position to resolve these questions?

To ensure that other judges and I have the answers that we need when we need them, do not skimp on the jurisdiction section of your brief. Provide us with a citation supporting your position whenever possible. In other words, do not leave it for the judge to struggle with the jurisdictional issue. After all, if we do not have jurisdiction, we cannot act. We are obliged sua sponte to examine our power to act at every stage of every proceeding. If jurisdiction is lacking, we can do nothing except dismiss the appeal—certainly an unhappy result for your client.

Obviously, not every jurisdictional statement needs a brief of its own. For the most part, if your appeal is from a final order, no more need be said than, "Jurisdiction vests in the Court of Appeals pursuant to 28 U.S.C. § 1291." But, please do not shortchange us by failing to provide when required the particulars of the order from which the appeal was taken.

Standard of review is the element of appellate advocacy that distinguishes the good appellate advocate. We, as judges, approach an appeal that arises from the dismissal of a complaint completely differently from an appeal that arises from a summary judgment—or a trial—or a preliminary injunction—or a bench trial. Because our standard of review differs depending upon how the issues reach us, we look for different things in each instance.

Where the complaint has been dismissed, we look to allegations of the complaint itself. Does it state a cause of action, accepting all of its allegations as true? If the appeal arises from a bench trial, we are generally presented with findings of fact that, unless clearly erroneous, may dictate the appeal's disposition. An appeal arising from a summary judgment requires us to look at the same sworn submissions as those the district court considered to determine if there are material facts in dispute; only if there are none, do we then look to see whether the district court erred in the law applied.

A few years ago, I heard a prisoner appeal in which the prisoner complained that the district court granted summary judgment for the prison warden instead of the prisoner. The complaint alleged that the warden denied the prisoner access to his lawyer and to the court because a telephone was not available. The brief on appeal was larded with constitutional quotations and citations. *Bounds v. Smith,* 430 U.S. 817 (1977), and all of its progeny were cited to a fare-thee-well. However, we could not find one sworn statement of fact that refuted the warden's affidavit, which was to the effect that: (a) the prisoner was held in a maximum security cell; (b) to get to the telephone, three separate sections of the prison had to be traversed with two guards at each section transporting the prisoner; (c) security considerations prevented transportation and attendance at the telephone more than three times a week for each prisoner; (d) no other telephonic means could be made available to the inmate without sacrificing security, although mail was always available.

The prisoner's counsel disclaimed any knowledge of the prison facility's transportation arrangements, security concerns, and the like, explaining that as a volunteer lawyer he had never contemplated taking the warden's or the guards' depositions, nor had he prepared an affidavit of his own client that might have disputed the facts set forth in the record before us. Needless to say, in the face of an uncontradicted record of security considerations, we were obliged to hold for the state and for the warden.

All of us, that is, the three judges on the panel who unanimously affirmed the judgment of the district court, came away from the oral argument quite disturbed. We were bothered by counsel's failure to comprehend and implement what we regard as the most elementary concepts of summary judgment—obtaining either affidavits or depositions—and by counsel's failure to do something other than cite Supreme Court and Third Circuit opinions, something which, if the record had been developed as it should, might well have resulted in a different disposition of the appeal.

Focus on the Facts

Most judges are familiar with the relevant cases and law, but have to be educated as to how those cases and law are to be applied to the facts of the appeal before them. When I sit on a case presenting a *Brady* issue (the government must disclose to defense counsel any exculpatory material known to the government), I do not need an extensive discussion of the law or the *Brady* principle, nor do I need 63 citations of cases applying *Brady*, all of which say the same thing. What I do want to know is how the facts of this case fall, if they do, within the *Brady* doctrine, and whether the facts of this case satisfy each of the *Brady* requirements.

For an effective appeal, both the brief and the oral argument should be structured around the appropriate standard of review. If, for example, the issue on appeal is whether the district court judge abused his discretion in denying a continuance, then both the brief and the oral argument should emphasize that abuse of discretion standard. It is the particular standard of review that should be the take-off point for a discussion of the facts and the reasons giving rise to the exercise of the judge's discretion.

One of the best appellate arguments I ever heard concerned a discretionary ruling in favor of a major utility. The case and the appeal were thoroughly unsympathetic so far as our court was concerned. Yet counsel for the utility kept reminding us that, even though we might not have ruled the same way as the district court had we been the initial decision-maker, the record supported the lower court's ruling. In conference after the argument, we were all disposed to reverse the district court, but none of us could responsibly write an opinion that discounted the district court's reasoning or that could legitimately hold that the district court judge had abused his discretion. The utility prevailed—but it did so because of the tenacity and advocacy of its counsel, who structured his argument on just one issue, the standard of review, and would not let us escape from it.

If we, as judges, think that it is important to fashion and draft our opinions within the framework of the relevant standard of review, then you too should ascribe the same importance to that unique feature of appellate lore. Pick up just about any appealable opinion, and you will find at the outset of that opinion an explanation of jurisdiction and then a statement of the standard review of the issues involved.

It is also likely that the opinion repeatedly refers to the particular standard of review as a means of explaining why the facts of the case either do or do not satisfy the standard. We may conclude that the facts found are not clearly erroneous; that the district court did abuse its discretion by denying a continuance so that the judge could attend the Super Bowl championship game; or that the district court erred because a material issue of fact was disputed when the parties' depositions were compared. The very conclusion of the court's opinion may recite the standard of review. I can only reiterate: If it is important enough for us to include the standard of review in our opinion, framing your argument in terms of the standard of review ought to be important to you.

I assume that you have now studied both the Federal Rules of Appellate Procedure and the local rules of the circuit in which your appeal is filed; that, if the particular circuit requires an appendix, you have complied with Fed. R. App. P. 30(a) and the local rules respecting appendices; that your brief has the necessary references to the appropriate appendix pages; that the cover of your brief conforms to the Federal Rules of Appellate Procedure; and that in all other particulars you have complied with the rules for briefs and the local rules pertaining to brief preparation.

A word first about color coding. The Federal Rules of Appellate Procedure require that an appellant's brief be covered with a blue cover and an appellee's brief with a red cover. The appendix is assigned a white cover, the reply brief, a gray cover, and the amicus brief, a green cover. It is quite distracting and irritating for a judge, who has settled down for some hours of reading and study, having assembled the briefs in a multi-party case, to find that briefs thought to be the appellant's were really briefs of the appellees. I have received countless briefs with white covers and the notation on the brief cover, "Please note—this a red brief!" My advice is—don't do it!

In stating the issues in your brief, take a leaf from the manner in which judges write their opinions. Most opinions will lead off with a statement of the issue that the court has determined to resolve. That statement almost always eschews general, vague, and uninformative concepts in favor of a concise, fact-related declaration of what must be decided. Contrast:

Whether Congress's new definition of an alien's residency qualifies to vest diversity jurisdiction in this court?

With:

[Does] the amendment to the diversity jurisdiction statute defining a permanent resident alien as a citizen for diversity purposes give[] a federal court subject matter jurisdiction over a case brought by a permanent resident alien against two defendants, one of whom is a nonresident alien.

See Singh v. Daimler-Benz AG, 9 F.3d 303 (3d Cir. 1993). I, along with most judges, would much prefer the second statement of the issue, which gives specific content to the question on appeal.

Do not combine your statement of the case and your statement of facts. Tell us briefly the history of the case and how the case reached us. Leave out extraneous motions and orders that have no bearing on the appeal, e.g., motions to extend time for answer or motions and orders for discovery.

Similarly, the statement of facts should recite only those facts necessary to the appeal. While it undoubtedly might pique some judge's interest as to whether the appellant has blue eyes, blond hair, and has a batting average of over .300, if the issue before the court is whether an appeal will lie from a state court action, removed to federal court, and then remanded to the state court, I would suggest you delete the particulars of the appellant's physical characteristics. And, oh, yes—don't argue facts or evidence to us where the court made findings of fact, unless, of course, you are challenging the fact findings as being clearly erroneous or challenging the sufficiency of evidence.

Having made these suggestions, and being confident that your arguments are concise, succinct, well written, and will not exceed the maximum allowed (50 pages), let me offer the following additional hints:

Hints for Success

1. Don't try to beat the page limit game by utilizing smaller typeface or by writing your brief in footnote-size type. The judges are old hands at this game and have no compunctions about having the clerk of the court reject your brief—all 25 copies.

2. The Federal Rules of Appellate Procedure now require a summary of argument. This is one of the more valuable parts of your brief. I invariably consult the summary of argument, both after I have prepared myself for oral argument and just before I hear the argument itself. If a judge has 40 cases to hear, the summary of argument is tremendously helpful. It brings up the facts of the case (e.g., after school hours prayer club, declared unconstitutional) and brings the issues on appeal back to mind without the need to read through the entire brief once again. A

summary, of course, should be just that, a summary, that is, no more than 1 to 1 and 1/2 pages, and not a full exposition.

3. If you are an appellee, be certain that you answer all of the arguments raised by the appellant. If the appellant raises issues A, B, C, and D, and you answer only issues A, B, and C, it leaves the judges in a quandary: "Is there no answer to Issue D?" "Is Issue D so frivolous as to not warrant an answer?" "How do we go about ruling on Issue D without knowing the appellee's position?" "Do we ourselves then conduct independent research—research that is normally the appellee's job?"

In a recent case, the appellant had been convicted for selling a videotape depicting his rape of a 15-year old girl. The appellant argued that because the statutory period during which he could have been prosecuted for the rape had already elapsed, his sentence could not be increased. The government failed to respond to that contention. The appellant's legal position was without merit, but I was more than irritated upon discovering that I, and not the government lawyer, had to do counsel's job of researching the case law so as to resolve the argument and reach a responsible decision.

4. Do not mischaracterize the cases you cite by referring to statements in the cited cases as "holdings." Holdings are precise; statements and discussions, theorizations, and the like, are not of the same dignity and may temporarily mislead the judge by the manner of recitation in your brief.

5. The single, easiest way to make a good brief better is by the judicious use of parentheticals following case citations. There is nothing more frustrating than a brief that spends 15 pages discussing every detail of every case tangentially related to the real question at issue. If brevity were not important, we would not have called briefs "briefs" in the first place.

6. Check slip opinions and electronic citations—even after your brief has been submitted. The court is always issuing new pronouncements, and you will want to be sure that the panel that is hearing your appeal is armed with the court's most recent precedent. You will not want the panel to be forced to stumble on such a case itself and interpret it without the benefit of your analysis.

7. Always give us, as circuit judges, Supreme Court law or the law of the circuit in which your appeal is filed. We are bound by both the Supreme Court and our own circuit precedents. We are not bound by the law of sister circuits, although that law may be persuasive. Above all, do not ignore case law that is unfavorable to your position. Distinguish it if you can. If you cannot and if the court is not bound by the precedent, explain why it should not be followed. Rest assured if you do not refer to the unfavorable cases, the court will find them. You will then have to explain your lack of recognition.

8. Do not write law review articles. Write succinct, clearly understood arguments. And please keep footnotes to a minimum.

9. Try to track the argument of the appellant if you are the appellee. If the appellant's brief is structured A, B, and C, follow that structure in your response. Do not start your response with Issue B followed by Issue A and then followed by Issue C. It makes it difficult for the judge to follow, and when you make life difficult for judges it can only result in judicial unhappiness.

10. Do not ignore the record. If there are questions and answers that support your argument, quote the "Q and A" from the record. You can judge for yourself which of the following two arguments is the most effective:

The defendant conceded that he stabbed the victim.

or

Q: On the night of January 16, were you with the victim?

A: Yes.

Q: On that night about 9 P.M. did you, using a switchblade knife, stab the victim in the arm and then in his chest?

A: Yes I did—I did. I don't know why I did it—but I did!

11. Use the same identification for each party. Fed. R. App. P. 28(d) requires that you do so. Preferably, use each party's name or title, and use that same identification throughout your brief. Why confuse the court by your literary forays in calling the plaintiff at various times, "the plaintiff"—"the land owner"—"the mortgagor"—"the landlord"—"the movant"—"the appellant"—"the respondent," when it is the same individual to whom you are referring?

12. When you conclude your argument, tell us what you want. Do you want an affirmance, a reversal, a remand, an evidentiary hearing, or a stay? If there are alternative holdings that you find acceptable—"We urge you to reverse for a new trial, but at the least to remand for further findings of fact"—let us know that by stating it in your conclusion.

13. When you argue before us, remember that we are not a jury. We neither expect nor desire jury arguments. We expect appellate arguments grounded in the applicable law. We also expect you to adhere to and obey the traffic lights on the rostrum. Yellow lights generally inform you that you have a certain percentage of your time left to argue. Make the most of it by zeroing in on your main arguments before the red lights go on.

14. Face up to an adverse question. If the record reveals unquestionable error, you may not do well in trying to convince us otherwise. Perhaps you should argue or segue into a harmless error argument.

15. Only the appellant may file a reply brief. If new matter is raised by the appellee, e.g., a jurisdictional argument, be sure to reply to it. Sometimes the court will suggest the filing of supplemental memorandum. If so, try to comply with the court's timing requests. We prefer

deciding cases while the arguments are still fresh in our minds. If we suggest 48 hours for simultaneous supplemental briefs discussing a new case or furnishing particulars from the record, don't start angling for a two-week submission.

A good deal of what I have written may be familiar and "old hat" to you. However, there are three precepts that bear constant repetition.

The first is: Prepare—prepare—prepare. Abstract and know the record so that you can find the answer to any question a judge may ask. Know the cases that you and your adversary have cited. If possible, have your partners or associates or lawyer friends grill your position at a mock moot court. This is a practice used more and more by the counsel appearing before us. Indeed, the U.S. Solicitor General's office has adopted this practice for its Supreme Court appearances.

The second is: Your job is to educate and teach us. If you cannot do either, you are not prepared to discharge your appellate function.

The third is: So long as we are the decision-makers, it always helps to keep us happy. What keeps us happy? By and large, we are the happiest when your brief conforms to the rules, when your arguments bear on the issues, when you refrain from ad hominem remarks about your adversary and his brief, and when your argument is cogent and clear so that we can understand your position.

If you do all this, does that mean you will always prevail on appeal? Unfortunately, it does not. It does mean that your appeal will always appeal to an appellate judge, that you will always be a welcome figure when you enter the courtroom, and that you will always be a favorite in our court.

PART III

Language of the Appeal

Why Can't Lawyers Write?

Christopher T. Lutz

Lawyers write badly. Everyone knows that; we hear it all the time. There is a whole industry devoted to telling lawyers how poorly they write and how easy it should be to do better. Articles and speeches by writing specialists are predictable. There will be ten minutes, or three paragraphs, of scorn for examples of ludicrous legal writing. The rest of the lesson will combine a stern Calvinist lecture and a self-help seminar: Follow these rules, work hard, and you will surely improve. Even if your verbosity is terminal, a quick trip to the woodshed with Strunk and White will make it right.

By now, you may want to flip to something else. "Not another writing article," you say. "I don't need the aggravation. I don't need the insults. It won't help."

But wait. This is not another self-improvement lesson. Begin by getting some perspective. It is not just lawyers who write poorly. *People* write poorly. Lawyers are not even the worst offenders. If you want to read really wretched writing, look at something by someone in the soft sciences. Almost any journal article in sociology, psychology, or social work will do. The first time you encounter a two-page paragraph, full of Germanic sentences, words like "cathexis" and phrases like "cognitive dissonance," you will know real agony. It makes a phrase like "the hereinbefore cited case" seem eloquent.

Are Lawyers Different?

What makes lawyers different is not the muddiness of their prose. It is the attention given to their writing. The word "legalese" is ubiquitous.

Christopher T. Lutz is a partner in the Washington, D.C., law firm of Steptoe & Johnson, L.L.P., and is a former editor-in-chief of LITIGATION.

In the public mind, lawyers *are* the world's worst writers, regardless of the facts.

The profession's response is likewise unique. Probably no group has been more relentlessly hounded by calls for better writing. Articles, speeches, courses, even this publication have tried to improve things. Compare this with any other line of work. Have you ever heard of a writing seminar for sociologists?

The difficulty is that it has not really worked. Some believe that trial advocacy courses have improved performance in court. Maybe. But no one claims the general level of lawyer writing has gone up. Anyone who reads briefs knows better. Has it been a mistake to try to teach lawyers to write?

The problem stems from confusing the desirable with the possible. There are many litigators who, because of attitude, ability, or circumstance, will not write well. Knowing who they are and why explains the limited impact of writing education on lawyers. It also suggests how things might be improved.

Consider, for example, the mental process involved in writing. Confused writing is often caused by confused thinking. Some lawyers—not many—just do not have the mental candlepower to understand grammar, composition, and style, but that is not common. The real problem is not the absence of any thinking. It is instead a lack of clear thinking.

If an issue is not well thought out, or a point of law not understood, its written expression will be a clotted mess. Unwieldy sentences will curve behind, over, and around a point but never really hit it. Surplus adjectives and adverbs will pile ceiling high. Steroid-like, the writing puffs up naturally puny substance.

Despite what writing teachers say, this is not always bad. Make no mistake about it. For lawyers, confused writing is often an essential protective device. Good, clear writing mercilessly exposes its author's message. If a skillful, honest author must write a brief peddling a bad line of reasoning, there can only be two results: Either the document will be short, because there is nothing to it, or it will make no sense.

Junior lawyers, particularly associates at big firms, understand this problem. A partner promises a valuable, irascible client the moon, and then some: "You want to argue that refusal to quash a deposition subpoena is a final, appealable order? No problem. That tips are gifts and not income? You bet. That citizens of different counties in the same state are diverse? Leave it to us." The senior lawyer then summons the junior, outlines the argument, and tells him to "make it work."

Of course, nothing can make it work, particularly if the unsound position is gracefully expressed. The only hope is subterfuge. Clouds of words. Smoke screens thick with dependent clauses. If that fails, there is the written equivalent of shouting: overwhelming adjectives and adverbs—extremely, very, absurd, ridiculous, baseless. Personal slurs and insults also come in handy. And, when a position's logic has no force, there are always lawyers' most common adverbial crutches: the words clearly, plainly, obviously, and patently.

In such desperate circumstances, writing primers are useless. They are also useless for nonthinkers and bad thinkers. So, when evaluating whether legal writing can be improved, begin with the proposition that the dumb, the confused, and the oppressed are beyond hope.

The *process* for writing legal papers also affects their quality. This is the big case era. While huge lawsuits are bonanzas for a few firms, they cost big money, clog the courts, and move like glaciers. They also float on oceans of boring prose.

The problem is joint brief writing. One firm among the twelve representing the defendants is assigned to write the first draft of a motion to dismiss. Four weeks later, a fifty-page effort lands on eleven desks. Fifteen or twenty sets of eyes pore over each page. Comments, interlineations, and suggestions rain down on the poor draftsman. Ten days later, another draft goes the rounds. This continues without forseeable end until the brief is accepted by everyone or, more likely, until a filing deadline cuts the process off.

The dynamics of committee editing are inevitable. If the first draft is plodding and dull, no one will pump life or verve into it. That is a limb out on which few lawyers will venture. The reviewing firms have only limited interests: risks for their client; the substance of certain arguments; and, sometimes, the technical rules of grammar, spelling, and punctuation. No one will care much about style or force.

But suppose the first draft *did* have punch and flair. Well, as surely as night follows day, the punch will be muffled, and the flair suppressed. Committee editing displays lawyers' conservatism in fullest flower. Distinctive language is homogenized for a whole string of reasons: "That's a little offbeat"; "I'm not comfortable with that phrase"; "What will the judge think?"; "That's a bit extreme (or blunt or crisp or harsh)"; "Too strong"; and so on.

Such comments come from a single source: timidity. A haze of caution settles quickly over committee drafting, blurring everything. At the end of the line, what the committee of law firms ends up with is this: a longer version of the brief that has not a comma or colon out of place; that spells every word right; that scrupulously adheres to the rules of grammar circa 1922 ("which" and "that" are precisely differentiated, infinitives are uncloven, and few prepositions live at sentence ends); but that is about as plain and dull as English can be. Its style will usually resemble the narrative portion of recipes, dictionary entries, or directions for assembling a child's toy.

Writing courses cannot do a thing about this. Committee drafting will be with us forever, and committees can't write. Good writing is the product of one person. It has a distinctive voice. There is behind it a thinking, breathing human being. That single person gives his writing sharp edges; such jaggedness gives writing shape and force. But, if you rub fifteen separate conceptions of style against one another, the sharp edges will break off. The writing will be smoothed to a flat, placid, uninteresting surface.

There is another tendency that compromises writing. Lawyers are not always selective. They dread losing and finding that an omitted contention might have won the day. This leads to diffuse, overly inclusive arguments. It also produces anticipatory contentions, especially in written submissions: Lawyers not only state their own case, they answer rejoinders their opponents have not yet made. Sometimes they even deal with anticipated responses to these unstated rejoinders.

It is impossible to overstate how much inclusiveness is ingrained in litigators. From the day they begin practice, they are taught there is a greater ill than losing—namely, forgetting something. You do not want to forget the statute of limitations. You do not want to neglect a notice of appeal. And you surely do not want to leave out any conceivable argument. This approach is essential for some things—limitations periods or appeal notices—but, unchecked by common sense, it becomes a fetish.

Nowhere is inclusiveness more a mania than in the editing of legal prose. I would wager a large sum of money that over half the written comments on draft briefs or memos come in these forms:

> "What about _____ ?"
> "Have you thought about _____ ?"
> "We need more on case *A* (or argument *B*)."
> "What if they say *X*?"

Of course, there are times when such comments are essential. A slow or inexperienced lawyer may really have missed something big. But when that happens, the written comments will be much stronger, with rows of exclamation points and harsh underlining. Usually, however, editorial comments aim not at getting the best arguments in, but at including them all.

The effect of such editing is pernicious. Briefs are longer. They become exhausting to read. Distracting cross-references—"as noted"; "as shown supra"—proliferate. Footnotes grow and begin to devour pages from the bottom. Case citations in the text spread like mold, their scattered patches breaking up otherwise readable discussions. And, above all, the main concepts, the essential arguments, are lost in the white noise of add-ons, inclusions, and extra thoughts.

In a way, the construction of such legal prose is like the design process for an Air Force bomber. A brief or memo may begin in a trim, efficient form. It is crisp and does what it needs to do. Then suggestions come in, and the brief is asked to do more. Footnotes and citations are slung at the bottom of pages. Clauses and qualifiers are patched into well-designed sentences. New sections are jammed into the existing framework. In the end, the brief, which might have flown or even soared in its original form, lumbers down the runway, laden with extra thoughts and words, and struggles aloft, with successful completion of its mission much in doubt.

Saying Everything

It is wrong to expect writing seminars to correct this, or to criticize them for not doing so. For many, inclusiveness, completeness—some may call it attention to detail—is what it means to be a lawyer. Many litigators believe they are paid to think of, and say, everything. It is a quality that degrades lawyers' writing, but educational efforts can no more change it than Arthur Murray could teach a goldfish to tap dance. Further progress is a matter of species evolution, not training.

The pressures of litigation also reduce the quality of legal prose. Good writing is a lapidary art. Words and phrases must be polished time and again. Work must be set aside, looked at later, and edited over and over in small steps. With repeated effort, awkward phrases are smoothed and inelegant constructions chipped away.

All this takes time. Good writing cannot be rushed. Diamond cutters do not often race the clock. They are never asked, at noon, to produce forty cut stones for delivery at 5:00 P.M.

Time, however, is exactly what lawyer-writers do not have. Litigation is crises and deadlines. It is not just that courts and the march of events impose intractable time limits. In the era of the law as big business, most firms relish having almost—sometimes actually—more work than they can humanly handle. Gone are the days, if ever they existed, of reflection on legal points. Nowadays, an efficiently managed firm is thought to be one where almost everybody barely has enough time to do his work. Care, style, and editing suffer.

Some may protest that time and reflection, a tweedy, languorous approach to writing, are needed only for literature. After all, newspapers are written to deadlines.

That is partly true but ignores what most journalists are: reporters. They recount what they have seen, heard, or read; and they usually need not bother with arguments, citations, and similar paraphernalia of brief writing. Of course there are reporters who produce powerful columns quickly, but they are writers of real talent.

For most of us, it is just wrong to think that rushing will not degrade writing. It is an iron law: The quality of prose is directly proportional to the time taken to write it. When your writing is rushed, you will rely more on clichés and crutches. "With respect to" is one of the first weeds to sprout when time is short. "Clearly" emerges soon afterward.

Rushing has other drawbacks. Any writer sometimes has blocks. If there is a filing deadline, however, and you cannot think of the right word or phrase, you must grab something to fill the gap. The inapt construction you pull out will then repeat monotonously, because you will not have time to think of an alternative. Worse yet, you may not be able to think through the next step in your argument. But you must push on. The result is papering over the gap in logic with the kind of verbal baloney so common in so many pleadings. For the reader, it is like a movie going out of focus. He has read a brief for some pages and then comes to four pages of fuzz—a place where some poor lawyer at one in the morning did not have time to be clearer.

For those who criticize legal writing, the message is this: Have some sympathy. If you read a filing you do not like, remember how it may have been written. An exhausted associate, fortified by cups of coffee, stale sandwiches, and dreams of partnership, labored over the brief for twenty consecutive hours. He last lifted his pen from his yellow pad late at night. His bleary eyes were proofreading just hours before filing. Under the circumstances, it is a wonder the thing makes any sense at all.

For those who teach legal writing, there is an equally clear lesson. It is a mistake to peddle standard writing bromides to lawyers. *The Elements of Style* is a wonderful book, the finest of its kind. But think about our friend the weary associate. What will he say when, perhaps enrolled in a seminar, he reads this:

> Writing is, for most, laborious and slow. The mind travels faster than the pen; consequently, writing becomes a question of learning to make occasional wing shots, bringing down the bird of thought as it flashes by. A writer is a gunner, sometimes waiting in his blind for something to come in, sometimes roaming the countryside hoping to scare something up. Like other gunners, he must cultivate patience; he may have to work many covers to bring down one partridge.

Strunk & White, *The Elements of Style* 69 (3rd ed. 1979).

Having been ordered repeatedly to find and obliterate whole flocks in a matter of hours, the associate may doubt the complete relevance of Strunk and White to the modern litigator.

Cost Pressures

The time available for writing is pressured by something else. While lawyers increasingly want their hours up, clients increasingly press firms to keep bills down. This tug and pull is unending.

The push to cut legal costs is no help to good writing. At $125 per hour, a short memorandum can be dashed off for $300 or $400. But really polishing it may cost over $1,000. Many clients—especially small or midsized companies in cases with modest sums at stake—do not want to pay the difference. If you have to tell them that $1,000 of the bill bought them elegant prose, you may have a rocky relationship. So, even if your workload gives you time for editing, a client who wants you to spend less money, and therefore less time, may not.

But, even infinite time to write would not be a panacea: Hard work can get you only so far. Athletics teaches this lesson unmistakably. Every child who is a sports fan at some point believes that stardom is just a matter of determination. Run and practice enough, and you can do anything. But most also learn otherwise. It is one of life's first disappointments.

My own disillusionment came at about the age of 13, while reading about baseball spring training. A team's sometime star first baseman had stumbled into camp, overweight, hung over, and dressed in street clothes. His teammates snickered as he lined up for a mile run—a test of physical fitness. He finished in under five minutes, the best on the team, and then was violently ill. While no world record, five minutes was, I knew, faster than I would ever run the distance. No amount of work could take me where talent alone—even masked by a winter's dissipation—had gotten the baseball player.

In this way, writing is like an athletic event. Work and classes can only do so much. Past some point, writing ability is a gift.

Of course writing courses can help. Diligently pursued and applied, unrestrained by all the other problems mentioned here, they can strain sediment out of muddy prose. But courses and seminars can never make writing sing.

It is therefore foolish to criticize any lawyer's writing in comparison to that of Learned Hand, Cardozo, or Justice Robert Jackson, as many writing advice-mongers do. It is worse yet to counsel close study of Dickens, Shakespeare, Hemingway, or Twain. Telling a lawyer to write like Cardozo is like giving a Little Leaguer a film of Babe Ruth and telling him to hit 60 home runs in the big leagues.

What you write about also affects how you write. Have you ever noticed that articles on legal writing always seem to get examples of good prose from tort suits, constitutional litigation, or simple contract cases? (The same is true, by the way, of articles on brilliant trial summations or searing cross-examinations.) At the same time, specimens of bad writing—big paragraphs, odd phrases, and wordy sentences—usually come from more technical suits, such as tax or regulatory litigation.

There is a reason for this. Writing (and trial practice) teachers have stacked the deck. It is easier to write pungently about people, emotions, and everyday events than about crop security interests, automobile repossession, or freight rate regulation. Careful editing and thoughtful composition can improve prose on the dreariest subject, but there is a limit. Some matters are just plain dull or inescapably complex. Others have developed terms and phrases that hurt the ear but have particular meanings. "Income in respect of a decedent" makes teeth grind, but in tax law there is no choice. Unleash Oliver Wendell Holmes on Subchapter L of the Internal Revenue Code, and the result would not be the majestic cadences of *The Common Law*.

There is another situation in which lawyers must write poorly. Almost all writing, if rigorously analyzed, has ambiguities. But sometimes absolute precision or inclusiveness is needed. The drafting of proposed statutes or model codes is one example. Writing interrogatories or document requests that cannot be evaded is another. Such things demand complex, repetitive, almost unreadable prose. In *Plain Words*, a barely remembered classic on written English, Sir Ernest Gowers has a chapter on just this problem. Speaking of officials who must write regulations, he says:

> It is . . . the duty of a draftsman of these authoritative texts to try to imagine every possible combination of circumstances to which his words might apply and every conceivable misinterpretation that might be put on them, and to take precautions accordingly. He must avoid all graces, not be afraid of repetitions, or even of identifying them by *aforesaids*, he must limit by definition words with a penumbra dangerously large, and amplify with a string of near-synonyms words with a penumbra dangerously small; he must eschew all pronouns when their antecedents might possibly be open to dispute, and generally avoid every potential grammatical ambiguity. All the time he must keep his eye on the rules of legal interpretation and [on] the caselaw . . . and choose his phraseology to fit them. . . . No one can expect pretty writing from anyone thus burdened.

Gowers, *Plain Words* 7 (London, 1948).

Such imperatives still confront practicing lawyers. All the writing maxims in the world cannot change that.

Attitude also affects prose. There are lawyers who do not bother about writing because they do not think it makes much difference. They rightly believe that polished prose costs time, money, and effort; and they think such investments are not justified.

Such litigators come in many shades. Some are pure fatalists. They think what you do in litigation usually does not make much difference. Just serve your case up somehow or the other to the court, meet all the basic requirements, and there will be a result. It will either be a win or a loss. Lawyers with such beliefs are usually found in cases with small stakes or almost certain outcomes: modest personal injury matters; appointed criminal work; and the like. Not much affects much in those cases; elegant writing is especially far down the list.

Slightly different are semifatalistic litigators. They, too, put little stock in writing, but they do so for a reason. Mostly they rely on the judge and the facts. They take the view that the judge is there to untangle what happened or help the jury do so. Besides, the facts are the facts, and they control the outcome more than tight sentence structure.

Finally, there are those—not really fatalists—who do not bother with fine writing because they need not. Successful plaintiffs' personal injury lawyers (many of whom *can* write), for example, depend more heavily on courtroom dramatics than gripping topic sentences. They rely on sound and sight, and they appeal mostly to the jury, not the judge. Some of them believe time spent editing is usually not time well spent.

The galling thing for writing instructors is that many of these lawyers are right. In some cases and some areas of practice, it does not matter whether you can write. Writing teachers may cringe, but fine prose is not always a necessity; is often a luxury; and is sometimes a waste of time.

Far removed from those who care little about writing are those who involve themselves in it too much. Everyone has strengths and weaknesses. No one can do everything. These are basics, but the legal profession often loses sight of them. Though litigators are increasingly grouping themselves into tinier and tinier substantive specialties, skill specialization is almost unheard of. As a result, the lead lawyer in most lawsuits reviews almost everything for substance and style. He or she edits, comments, and makes wholesale changes.

There is a problem with this. Great litigators are not necessarily great writers. Trial skill has nothing to do with writing skill. The aptitudes they draw on are far apart. It is asking a lot to expect one lawyer to combine the spontaneous, emotive, theatrical abilities of the courtroom with the reflective, analytical talents of the drafting table. A few can do it, but not many. Thus, despite all the attention devoted to writing, very often the wrong people are doing it.

A final deterrent to good writing—lawyers' views of themselves—is serious and stubborn. Every profession has a tinge of self-importance. Each sees itself as a group of enlightened souls, scholar-priests, bound together by common experience and arcane knowledge. Such pomposity waxes and wanes, depending on the profession and the person. Unfortunately, some lawyers have a bad case of professional insufferability, and their writing shows it.

Describing the phenomenon is difficult. The lawyers I have in mind seem to believe that talking or writing like a lawyer means doing something unique. That is, they seem to think it means talking or writing like no other group in the world. It is like having a foreign accent. Even in a crowd, you can tell a lawyer when he opens his mouth or puts pen to paper.

Unfortunately, the patois chosen by many lawyers is something out of a sixteenth-century guild hall. Awkward constructions, musty words (herein, therein, divers), and Latinisms (*vel non, arguendo,* contra) speckle the page. The subjunctive voice and conditional tense dominate. Overly formal constructions (This Honorable Court) and a mock heroic tone are used. A pose of humble politeness (defendants respectfully submit) is adopted. The writing and speech of such lawyers are those of people who are staying for a time in the modern era, but who, on the whole, would be more comfortable making small talk at the coronation of Henry the Eighth.

Writing instruction takes dead aim at such archaisms. They are big targets and fun to ridicule. Alternate modern constructions are easy to propose. It all seems so obvious.

But composition courses go wrong in suggesting that, if you just tell a lawyer to stop writing like Sir Thomas More, he will. Things are not that simple. Even a lawyer who can speak perfectly acceptable standard English will lapse into something else when he is playing his role as an lawyer. For many, jettisoning the ancient formality would mean eliminating what they think defines them as lawyers. A bad habit that is a matter of personal identity is much harder to erase than a mere bad habit.

Everyone can make his own judgment about how many lawyers run afoul of particular writing problems. Each of us does sometimes, and some are permanently immune to writing improvement. The conclusion, however, is not to give up hope. It is, instead, to make changes.

The first step is to lower the general goal. Recognize that some lawyers do not need to write and would waste time and money if they tried to do so. All lawyers will sometimes write badly, and few will write with the compactness and power of Hand or Cardozo.

A second step is adopting different methods. Advice that takes time to apply, or requires care or thought, will be ignored in the rush of events, deadlines, and judicial impatience. Better would be strict rules of automatic application. Here is an example: Ban certain words and phrases. Prohibit them completely. No exceptions. Absolutely eliminate things like:

> instant (when used instead of "this")
> divers (the nonscuba variety)
> *arguendo*
> *vel non*
> the herein family
> wherein
> therein
> with respect to
> aforementioned
> wherefore
> herewith

The list could go on and on. Just banning this small group would scrape a lot of sludge from briefs and memos.

How could such a ban be enforced? Even severe penalties might not be equal to the challenge, but modern technology may have an answer. Most lawyers use word processors. Most word processors have spelling checkers. At minimum, offending words could be depicted as misspelled. Even better, and probably not difficult, would be programming the computer to type nothing. Thus, if "instant" were used before "case," or "*vel non*" were used anywhere, there would be only a blank. With more sophisticated systems, a buzzer, warning siren, and flashing red light would go off when a bad word was typed. Compliance would be automatic and complete.

Besides such inescapable measures, efforts at writing improvement should concentrate on fundamental issues. Attitudes need to change more than rules of composition need to be memorized. Lawyers must be convinced that there is no purpose, or value, in sounding archaic. This is a tall order. It will take an emotional, almost psychological, pitch to teach many lawyers that there is nothing wrong with sounding like a citizen of the second half of the twentieth century. You are no less a lawyer for being understandable.

There is a way to enforce a simpler, more contemporary writing style. Whenever you write a brief, give it to someone who knows nothing about the case—a nonlawyer is perfect—and have him read it aloud. It will be an education. The "hereinbefores" that seemed so lawyerly will sound awkward and cumbersome. The "supras" and "infras" that seemed so helpful will be distractions. If your reader can say the sentences in a meaningful way—with emphasis on the right words and the basic message coming through—then you have done a good job. If not, if there are stammers and restarts, go back to the drawing board. If you get bored or lost while listening, major surgery is needed. And if the reader takes breaks, gets hoarse, and drops from fatigue, pull out your machete and start hacking text.

There is, of course, a drawback to reading briefs aloud. It takes time. Its curative effect will not touch lawyers in a hurry. But if there is time, do it.

There are other changes the profession should adopt. Some are obvious antidotes to equally obvious writing problems: Committee drafting should be banned or sharply curtailed. Besides its harmful effects, it really does waste enormous amounts of money. At the same time, writing should be done by good writers. Stop spending money teaching the unteachable. Let those who know how to write do it.

These are pipe dreams. Lawyers will never give up a chance to have their say on a joint brief, partly because they rarely will trust any other lawyer to do the job. Besides, the money "wasted" in committee editing largely goes to lawyers themselves. Skill specialization is also not likely; it is just too alien to the traditions of the profession.

But there is a final step that can help and is feasible: Trade research for writing. Stunning amounts of time are wasted on dredging up case citations. Even more time is wasted on citation-related enterprises that add not a penny of value to most projects: Shepardizing; cite checking; blue booking; and the like.

Most of this is unnecessary. Almost all the time, the law you need falls into three categories: (1) It is obvious and universally accepted; (2) It is for or against you in your jurisdiction; (3) It is unclear and goes both ways elsewhere. In the first case, you do not need a citation. In the second, you need no more than two or three citations from your own jurisdiction, and none from elsewhere. Even in the third instance, you need not list a lot of cases, just the best ones. A judge will likely decide a new matter on the basis of logic and reason, and not by piling up everyone else's decisions, weighing them, and awarding the case to the party with the heaviest stack.

The time freed from string cites can be spent making a brief or memo better. That is where the emphasis ought to be. Polishing the writing, focusing the argument, and crisply explaining the equities are what it is all about. That is far more productive than finding two Idaho cases on contract interpretation for a lawsuit in a New York state court.

Writing Instead of Citing

There will be resistance even to this means of writing improvement. Given the choice between editing and finding cases, many lawyers would prefer to fill up a three-inch footnote. It is not just that research is easier, though it is. A computer, after all, can do a solid job of the unimaginative task of case finding. There is also a sense of security in research. It is a black-and-white world. Either you find a case or you miss it. Either you use "cf" correctly or you do not. In comparison, writing and editing—more subjective and standardless—are risky things. This leads lawyers to take refuge in the library. While many lawyers really have too little time to write well, others waste much of it piling up research.

Troubles with legal writing will, of course, be with us always. Human nature rarely changes, but some improvement is possible. By targeting courses and seminars on the right people and right occasions, and by changing tactics, those who can improve will. Those who cannot, or need not, will be able to pursue their profession in a more restful, less anxious, but no more literate way.

The Ba Theory of Persuasive Writing

Miriam Kass

Persuasion is making someone feel your idea is right.

Feel.

Know from the gut and the heart, not just the brain. The idea should feel like an old shoe, a threadbare teddy, the shredded satin edging of a cherished baby blanket—the Ba you used to curl up with, to rub on your cheek, to clutch as you sucked your tender puckered thumb. Persuasion is making someone feel your idea is fundamentally, yea, primordially, right.

This is the Ba Theory of persuasive writing, based on the observation that we spend our lives trying to feel good (winning trials, drinking Scotch, running to keep fit, and so forth), that we experienced some of our best feelings in the nursery, and that most of us would like to recapture that early contentment if we could do it without feeling foolish. (If you are the macho type, pretend you are reading this for a friend.) The Ba Theory says, make the reader curl up contentedly with your ideas by getting rid of bad writing habits that make the reader grouchy, then enrich your writing to make your idea feel good.

The big bad habit is writing so your idea is hard to follow. Struggle is distracting, frustrating, and tiring. It makes the reader want to run away and hide. Your ideas, through your words, should flow into the reader's mind without resistance or self-consciousness.

Think of the reader's mind as a small container. Do not fill it with dead words, bloated sentences, or other garbage that makes reading feel like eating bony fish or fat meat. Garbage hogs the space and wastes the mind's energies cleaning house. Adopt the marketing strategy of Mark Twain:

Miriam Kass, a former editor-in-chief of LITIGATION, *was a litigator for 17 years and is now a mediator in Houston, Texas.*

I never write "metropolis" for seven cents when I can get the same price for "city."

Do not use a long word when a short one will do. Short words are not only easier to read, they are also more likely to be of Anglo-Saxon, rather than Latin, origin and to have a dependable salt-of-the-earth quality.

We will use this sample sentence to illustrate several points:

Through the utilization of budgetary manipulations, a conspiracy with regard to the lease transaction was implemented by Defendants whereby expenses received treatment as capital investments.

Here is one way to trim it:

Defendants conspired to budget the lease expenses as capital investments.

Most of the big words cut out of the sample sentence are of Latin origin, sometimes through French. Is the idea to revert to the English language before the Norman Conquest? No, English is rich because it is so inclusive. There is no denying the beauty of English used to its fullest. If you are Shakespeare or Faulkner, stop reading this, and go for it in your own style. But if you are an ordinary person trying to persuade ordinary people, read on, and be prepared, not for memorizing rules, but for developing a sense of what writing feels good and why.

Imagine yourself surveying a battlefield. Bodies are everywhere, some alive, some dead, some salvageable with proper treatment. Your job is triage. You must bypass the corpses, get them out of the picture, and devote yourself to life. Every word is a body. Ask yourself about each, "Is it alive?" If it is barely alive, ask if it is worth saving.

Dead Words

Does the "very" in "It was a very hot day" make the day feel hotter? Hmmm. How about those high-falutin' transitions:

It may be recalled that. . . .
In this regard, it is interesting to point out the fact that. . . .

To Michelangelo, every piece of marble had a form hidden in it. He had only to chisel through to reveal a Pietà or a Moses. So it is with verbs hidden in and weighted down by noun forms like these:

negotiation
administration
documentation
utilization
transmittal

"Mr. Jones had the company's authorization" is correct, but "The company authorized Mr. Jones" is better. "They made a determination of" is correct, but "They determined" is better. Notice how many such words are in the sample sentence.

Whether a word is dead depends mainly on what it is doing in a sentence. Some words are dead because they are redundant. If every word cost you a dollar, which ones would you use? Surely not the italicized words in these phrases:

ask *the question whether*
advance planning
consensus *of opinion*

Some dead words are prepositions leading other dead words or phrases. Look at the sample sentence and see how many nouns with good verbs hidden in them are used as objects of prepositions. Prepositions should alert you to search for corpses, which also abound in these kinds of fancy phrases lawyers use when they could use one word:

in the event of (if)
in order to (to)
for the purpose of (for)
for the reason that (because)
at this point in time (now)
with regard to (about)

Have you ever noticed what new awareness does for you on any subject? Say you decide to have your yard landscaped. Suddenly you "see" colors and shapes of leaves, heights of bushes, effects of monkey grass along the sidewalk. Awareness works the same for everything from cars to gender roles. Something must first make you notice. Then you will see more and more refinements. So it is for writing.

How many times have you been told to avoid passive construction? Passive construction bloats sentences with dead words, especially those marbled verbs and excess prepositions. See how much garbage the sample sentence's passivity creates.

Passive construction backs ideas timidly into the reader's mind. Passivity is not merely a writing problem. It is a responsibility problem. Will the real subject of the sample sentence please stand up? The word "by" in a passive sentence often precedes and announces the real subject. "Defendants," not the "conspiracy," were the bad actors in the sample sentence. Put them where they belong and see how fast editing goes.

A sentence often feels passive when its verb is a form of "to be." Being is a passive thing to do. Being is nice for philosophers to speculate about, but it does not exactly sit up and sing. "The day was hot and humid" is not as active as "The day steamed." Instead of telling what, make the reader feel how. The following sentence combines a passive verb ("exists") in the main clause with another weak form, a conditional verb ("would preclude"), in a dependent clause:

> There exists no issue of material fact which would preclude the granting of this summary judgment.

Make the same point actively in fewer than half the words:

> No material fact issue prevents summary judgment.

Do not use conditional forms like "would" and "could" unless you really mean to speak conditionally, as in, "Mr. Jones would pay his debts, but he has no money."

Sometimes you will purposely weaken a point. "Intentionally untruthful testimony" is a lie. If there is a reason not to come out and say "lie," fine. Otherwise, be courageous and say what you mean. And when you do use a strong word, do not take the wind out of it with a timid modifier:

> somewhat terrified
> a bit malicious
> rather dishonest

The result is absurd, like being slightly pregnant.

Think about what it is like to start watching a movie that is half over. You may get the general idea, but you have to guess what happened before you came in. Then you can hang around and see the first part to find out if you guessed right. Trying to figure out what you should already know wastes mental energy, which should be spent understanding an idea.

There is an order that ordinarily makes sense for storytelling:

> Once upon a time, there was a boy. He was a mean boy. He played a dirty trick on his brother. He told their mother his brother had a ride home from school when he didn't. So his brother waited outside the school for his mother, who never came.

The story is easy to follow because each sentence supplies the information necessary to understand the next. The sample sentence does it backwards. It starts describing the conspiracy before it tells that there is a conspiracy and tells that there is a conspiracy before it tells who is responsible. The reader's mind wastes energy holding unrelated facts until it gets the basic who and what that make it all fit. This is fine if the purpose is to hide the ball, to create tension or suspense, but not if the purpose is to make the reader relax and curl up with your idea.

Short Sentences

Although it is easier to keep your ideas straight with short sentences than with long ones, logical unfolding is not necessarily related to the length of a sentence. The first four sentences in the mean boy story also unfold logically as one sentence:

> The mean boy played a dirty trick on his brother by telling their mother the brother had a ride home from school when he did not.

It is easier to write short sentences and turn them into a longer one than to write a long, convoluted sentence and break it into short ones in logical sequence. Whenever you write a long sentence, however, be sure you have not so separated the subject and the verb that the reader forgets who before learning what.

Although construction, not length, determines whether a sentence is easy to read, a good rule of thumb is to average about twenty words to a sentence. Some long sentences, well constructed, are interesting. Some very short ones are as powerful as karate chops.

Varying sentence length purposely for effect goes beyond avoiding bad habits. It goes to stage two of the Ba Theory. Having assured that your reader will not develop a tummy ache or be seized with an impulse to run and hide, you can concentrate on rockabye good feelings to make the reader want to snuggle closer to your idea.

Serve with Spice

Legal writing tends to be bland. You have an edge if you can serve your idea with spice. Remember the old metaphors and similes from freshman English? They not only surprise, they clarify, by casting ideas in concrete and familiar forms. They tell little stories that are fun.

See how the simile conveys the impact of a transaction that dictated the parties' positions in a future plan of reorganization:

> In short, the parties to the PSA transaction were like actors given their lines to be recited on cue. When faced with a formal reorganization plan, they were bound to perform the roles assigned to them in the PSA transaction.

And notice how you can ridicule the attempt to stretch a case too far: Compare the parties to "Cinderella's stepsisters, pinching and straining to claim a glass slipper that does not fit." The stepsister simile evokes all the connotations of the Cinderella story—not only that the slipper did not fit the stepsisters but that they knew it was not theirs. Besides being ugly and clumsy, they were cynical, deceptive, and comical.

An analogy is sometimes a most powerful argument:

> The Union's argument that the [stock purchase program] equals a plan of reorganization not only lacks support, it lacks logic: They say restructuring of debtor's equity is an essential element of a plan; therefore, all restructuring of equity must signify a plan. The fallacy: All apple pies contain apples; therefore, all apples must be in apple pies.

In addition to the apple pie analogy, the paragraph makes its point by parallelism. Parallelism may also be used within sentences or paragraphs and often provides rhythm and repetition like this:

> The DC 10-30 lease transaction has nothing in common with the PSA transaction and the *Braniff* decision. It conditions nothing on a plan of reorganization. It dictates no voting for a future plan. It requires no release of claims against any party. It alters no priority. It evades no disclosures. It leaves inviolate those "hurdles erected in Chapter 11" to be scaled in a future reorganization plan.

Parallelism makes a sentence or paragraph easier to understand by exploiting the mind's natural comfort in order and predictability. It emphasizes similar relationships.

The DC 10-30 paragraph combines parallelism with contrast by negation. By saying what the proposed transaction does not do, it highlights what the transaction does do. It outlines the picture, clarifying what is in and what is out.

In another example of parallel construction, Bill Pannill of Houston, Texas (another former editor-in-chief of LITIGATION), combined simile, parallelism, and negation by contrast to emphasize the hypertechnicality of the court's decision in a will case:

> Making a will is not playing a game or assembling a puzzle. It is not running an obstacle course. It is the final solemn act of a lifetime. It is an act of supreme importance to the dying.

The paragraph also persuades by shifting from the abstract to the human. The following sentence humanizes still further by painting a picture:

> The decision of the Court in this case is wrong. It is wrong as a matter of statutory interpretation and application. It is wrong as a matter of justice. It is also wrong because the respondent has been deprived of her right to an appellate ruling on her Point No. 3 in the Court of Appeals. If a woman can walk into a bank carrying a will prepared by a lawyer, sign the will in a ceremony attended by her lawyer and two other witnesses, have two witnesses subscribe under her signature and yet fail to make a will, the law does not make sense.

Nothing feels better than to be on the side of justice and morality. But justice and morality have meaning only for people. Humanize your position to dramatize its significance.

Saying point blank that something is right or wrong can be persuasive, but the statement must be well supported or it will ring dogmatic.

Irony, another powerful technique, must be used with care or it will sound sophomoric. When it is directed toward the opponent rather than the argument, it may appear mean or petty. The analogy is to cross-examination in trial, where you must damage a witness's credibility before you go in for the kill, or the jury may identify with the witness instead of you.

To be persuasive, you must establish your own credibility. Trial lawyers know that once a witness's credibility is undermined, it is hard to salvage. The same rule applies to writers. Cite cases incorrectly, and you will deprive yourself, not only of case support, but of credibility. Grammar or spelling errors may also undermine your credibility.

If a cited case is helpful to you, but its language is not well focused for your purposes, paraphrase with more helpful words. But stretch the point beyond reasonable recognition, and you impeach your credibility for all other cases you discuss or cite.

Admitting or giving away a point you have probably lost anyway may enhance credibility, as you know from this kind of jury argument:

> Yes, Mr. Brimble did drink too much before he drove that night. He knows he has a drinking problem. He is not proud of it, and he is not asking you to excuse it. But the fact that he passed out at the stop sign did not give Beulah Bistro the right to ram the back of his pickup.

'Fessing up also works in writing:

> True, Dr. Pangloss did not introduce evidence that Mr. Rambo intended to waive his right to notice. Dr. Pangloss does not rely on the waiver defense. He does rely on estoppel.

To find a good giveaway, make a list starting with your strongest points and graduating to your weakest. Then consider whether you have a point so weak you may gain more by giving it away than by asserting it.

Your strongest-to-weakest list should also dictate the order in which you present your ideas. Use your strongest shots to bias the reader's evaluation of successively weaker points.

Journalists call writing from most to least important the "inverted pyramid." Editors, who may have to cut the story under deadline pressure, can begin at the end and cut paragraph after paragraph, yet leave a story that stands on its own. Especially in a long writing, where the reader's lapsing attention may in effect cut your story, get your best licks in at the beginning.

Now take that principle a step further. You remember your first day of school, first boss, first teacher, first trial. Because your reader is likely to remember best what you say first, begin your writing by summarizing your position in its most compelling light. Transcend technicalities and say exactly what you want your reader to conclude.

The language quoted below is from a response to an appeal challenging Continental Airlines' authority to expand its operation by leasing two aircraft. In a preliminary statement, counsel touted Continental's success under Chapter 11 and stressed that the airline industry is extremely competitive and that Continental has obtained its financial results, not by shrinking from the competition, but by challenging it vigorously in the marketplace.

The Institutional Creditors . . . want to treat Continental's bankruptcy like the liquidation of the corner grocery store. Their constricted approach misses the point of Chapter 11 not merely to keep the debtor from dying, but to restore it to health and vigor.

Do Not Appear Defensive

The preliminary statement sets the mood for an offensive argument. The challenge of responding to a writing—to an appellant's brief, for example—is not to appear defensive. To avoid sounding defensive, do not repeat your opponent's position followed by your response. Repetition reinforces. Assert your idea positively, negating your opponent's by implication.

Do not be controlled by your opponent's overall organization. A logical order for your opponent may make sense for you, too, or it may put you on the defensive when you need not be. It may be better to stress a different order of importance, so that you need not respond dutifully to each point raised against you. Better yet, develop an argument that will subsume several of your opponent's points and cast them in a light favorable to you.

Headings and subheadings also help to focus the issues on your terms. Depending on the nature, complexity, and length of your writing, use them to assert your points in positive words. Headings should be short and easy to read. Like newspaper headlines, they oversimplify. Use that fact to your advantage. In a brief, headings and subheadings together form an assertive outline and table of contents. Repeating an idea in a table of contents, headings, and text creates familiarity and comfort. It reinforces.

Headings and subheadings do double duty. In addition to pointing the reader in the right direction, they require white space, and white space is restful. Reading is, after all, a visually aesthetic experience. The eyes see patterns on paper before the brain recognizes meaning.

A gray page is deadly. Paragraph indentations on a page promise a breath of air after submersion in an idea. White space lets you relax your focus as though you were gazing at the horizon. Leave good size margins and extra space between sections of your writing. Center quotes or lists.

The eye seeks variety, though not busyness. Underlinings, italics, and all capital letters vary the appearance of writing. They are refreshing in small doses but tiring in many single-spaced lines.

Change the scenery and rest the mind with pictures, plats, graphs, flowcharts, lists, or diagrams. Consider not only what already is, but what could be, in visual form. For example, a complex real estate transaction is clarified by a picture showing the flow of deeds and lien documents.

Footnotes interrupt the flow of argument, especially in the middle of a sentence or paragraph. Use them only if they are worth the interruption, and try to put them where there is a natural break or at the end of your writing.

The end of this writing has come, though there is no end of guidelines for persuasive writing, each with its elaborations and exceptions. Do not try to memorize rules. Instead, recall that the reader is a human being who wants first not to have an unpleasant reading experience and second to have a pleasant one. Writing your way into the nursery is hard labor, but better hard writing than hard reading.

The Language of Appellate Advocacy

Bryan A. Garner

Never has a case been argued in which some aspect of language did not play a crucial role. At a minimum, lawyers' uses of language make their arguments more or less persuasive. But lawyers and judges are often called on to muster greater linguistic sophistication: to interpret the Constitution or statutes, to construe private legal documents, or to explain the precise import of precedents. The effective appellate lawyer must be more than a legal technician; he must also be a rhetorician, a semanticist, and a stylist.

Chief Baron Pollock surely included each of these three when he called judges "philologists of the highest order." *Ex parte Davis* (1857) 5 W.R. 522, 523. Even when Pollock wrote those words he must have been stating an ideal, not the reality. But if the ideal is a true one, it must apply equally to lawyers, who regularly philologize to the philologists.

Skeptics should read *United States v. James*, 478 U.S. 597 (1986), a case that called upon rhetorical and semantic, as well as stylistic, skills. The case arose from two separate incidents at flood-control projects used as water-sports facilities. Government employees at the facilities had, without adequate warning, opened the floodgates to drain off water while water-skiers and fishermen were nearby. Several people were haplessly sucked through the gates, and two were killed. The trial judge in one case said it went "beyond gross negligence" and "constitutes a classic classroom example of death and injuries resulting from conscious governmental indifference to the safety of the public."

The question in *James* was whether a statutory exemption from liability for "any damage from or by floods or flood waters at any place" would immunize the government from suit. The question whether

---

Bryan A. Garner is the president of LawProse, Inc., a Dallas-based firm of legal-writing consultants. He is the author of A Dictionary of Modern Legal Usage *(OUP 1987) and* The Elements of Legal Style *(OUP 1991).*

"damage at any place" refers to the loss of human life implicates rhetorical concerns—why was the statute so phrased?—and semantic ones—at what level of abstraction is "damage" to be read? Making the distinction between "damage" and "damages"—which the dissenters in the Supreme Court did, but the majority failed to do—requires at least an instinctive understanding of semantics.

Alas, the Court held that Congress, by using the phrase "damage at any place," intended to immunize the government even from gross negligence—or worse—that results in human death. Congress, it seems, intended to lump loss of life, among other things, into the phrase "damage at any place." Whether members of Congress resented this imputation of callousness one can only guess.

Before turning to semantics and style, let us consider rhetoric. Many lawyers may resist thinking of themselves as rhetoricians. The word "rhetoric" calls up negative images of word-mongering and verbal distortion, as in Disraeli's reference to Gladstone as a "sophistical rhetorician, inebriated with the exuberance of his own verbosity." But I refer to rhetoric in the older sense: "the art of adapting discourse, in harmony with its subject and occasion, to the requirements of a reader or hearer." J. F. Genung, *The Working Principles of Rhetoric* 1 (1901). In deciding what the issues will be, for example, and in stating those issues for the court, an appellate advocate employs just such rhetorical skills. This is the type of rhetoric that helps win an appeal; the other type—that attributed to Gladstone—will doom you to failure.

Though every case is unique, certain rhetorical approaches determine success or failure for the advocate. The rhetorician knows, for example, not to argue that the court's failure to overturn the ruling below will result in a grave injustice. Every appellant believes that, and generic arguments carry no power. Better to show why and how injustice will result, without ever resorting to the abstract statement.

The most important analytical step in the appellate process—in fact in most aspects of litigation—is framing the issues. "First settle what your case is before you argue it," wrote Lord Chief Justice Wright. *Trial of the Seven Bishops,* 12 Howell's State Trials 193, 342 (1688). A number of rhetorical considerations enter this process. It is usually unwise, for example, to heap a dozen or more issues into your brief, hoping that the court will find an appealing one. This all too common method relegates the lawyer to little better than an issue-spotter, and burdens the court deciding the issue. The seasoned, confident lawyer argues with sophistication. He does not pray that his fiftieth point of error will be that final straw that breaks the back of the lower court's judgment. "One has to try to strike the jugular," wrote Holmes, "and let the rest go." O. W. Holmes, *Speeches* 77 (1913). (Criminal cases, of course, are different: A lawyer is more obliged to raise every issue that might arguably be meritorious.)

Second, use the alembic of your mind to distill the essence of the issues. Formulate your thoughts so you express them crisply. If your arguments are shrouded in nebulous terminology, the court will very likely suspect that they are either ill-formed or wrong. As Sir Frederick Pollock observed, "[A] doctrine capable of being stated only in obscure and involved terms is open to reasonable suspicion of being either crude or erroneous." 2 *Holmes-Pollock Letters* 38 (1941).

Even substantive issues implicate rhetoric. You must thoroughly analyze what it is you ask the court to do. Too many lawyers become confused by questions from the court about whether, for example, simple reversal is possible without a remand to determine a remaining issue. You cannot mold your message to an appellate audience without knowing all its dimensions, including such basics as the applicable standard of review and the case law on such standards.

The tone of advocacy is another important element of rhetoric. More and more lawyers take the most combative tone possible, thereby giving new meaning to the antique legal phrase *"brutum fulmen."* Every position of an opponent is "utterly fallacious," "a logical absurdity," "completely without support in law or in fact," or the like. Advocates who adopt this approach seem to want every case to be a knockout; they launch roundhouse punches in every argument. Judges are quickly wearied by rhetoric like this. The world is more complicated than the proponents of such arguments suggest. Most cases have some merit on both sides; not every opposing argument need be ground down to absurdity. Judges faced by a bellicose advocate are more likely to suspect something amiss in his case than to believe he is rightly (much less righteously) indignant. Heed Laurence Sterne's observation in *Tristram Shandy:* "Heat is in proportion to the want of knowledge."

One final point about rhetoric. What I have been describing is a part of a larger trend toward overstatement. Overstating the facts or the law damages your credibility as an officer of the court; if you fudge here or there, you are bound to be found out. Conscientiously avoid overstatements of any kind, lest you undermine not only your immediate client's cause, but also your own credibility and therefore the chances for future clients.

The lawyer as semanticist has a different orientation from the rhetorician. Rather than seeking to persuade, the semanticist seeks primarily to understand and remain clearheaded. This linguistic sensitivity helps the lawyer avoid arguing at length about words without knowing that verbal confusion is the basis of the dispute. The phenomenon is common. Though any practitioner might confirm Lord Mansfield's observation that "most of the disputes in the world arise from words," many seem unable to get behind the words in seeking solutions.

Words can be slippery, and the semanticist knows it. Wesley Newcomb Hohfeld used a semantic approach in showing that "property" in one sentence could refer to the rights in a thing, and then in the next sentence to the thing itself. And Holmes, a consummate judicial semanticist, observed: "The law talks about rights, and duties, and malice, and intent, and negligence, and so forth, and nothing is easier, or, I may say, more common in legal reasoning, than to take these words in their moral sense, at some stage of the argument, and so to drop into fallacy." "The Path of the Law," in *Collected Legal Papers* 167, 171 (1952).

Semantic shifts of this kind plague the law. If you can sort them out in a given case, you do your client and the court a great service. You might, for example, need to show a court the two quite different meanings of "conclusive evidence," where application of the term will win or lose the case. Unfortunately, legal lexicography has been in shambles for the past century, and so no existing dictionary will help you in handling this (or myriad other) linguistic difficulties. But the adept lawyer-semanticist knows that the phrase may mean: (1) "irrebuttable evidence that must, as a matter of law, be taken to establish some fact in issue"; or (2) "evidence that, though not irrebuttable, so preponderates as to oblige a jury to come to a certain conclusion." Both senses have strong historical support, although the latter probably began as a loose usage. The difference can be significant. Yet how easy it is to argue about "conclusive evidence" without ever knowing the ambiguity of the phrase.

The semanticist may also help the court with what appear to be simple English words, such as "intent" or "malice." When it comes to words like these, we are all likely to be lulled into thinking, "Well, everyone knows what that means!" But, as one of the founders of modern semantics, I. A. Richards, warned: "The really serious misunderstandings (from the lost point to the quarrel) concern those other words we all think we do really know—the familiar, friendly, incessantly useful key words [that occur] in every third sentence. In general the more useful a word is the more dangerous it can be." I. A. Richards & C. Gibson, *Learning Basic English* 88 (1945). As a result, semantic vigilance is essential to deal skillfully and knowledgeably with the innumerable tricky words that occur in law. Particularly is it essential in the intellectual world of the appellate court.

Such vigilance is not directed just to the key words in one's own argument or in precedents. The appellate advocate must be equally vigilant about his opponent's use of key words and phrases. Remember, "a word's job—what it is doing at a place in a passage—is not settled simply by its dictionary sense or senses; it is settled by what the occasion and the rest of the passage hands it to do then and there." Richards & Gibson, *Learning Basic English* 88 (1945). Do not let your opponent use broad legal words to perform unorthodox jobs. The judges deciding the case will benefit from your semantic keenness.

The lawyer-semanticist realizes that, because words have more than one meaning and meanings change, root senses of a term ordinarily provide little insight into its current meaning. Learned Hand cautioned against making a fortress of a dictionary. It may seem odd for a lexicographer to reinforce the point, but dictionaries are easily abused. Etymologies, for example, are generally of no use to courts in understanding the modern senses of legal words. Although it may not hurt to observe that *perjury* is "oath-breaking," we shed little if any light by asking whether those in a conspiracy "breathed together." Yet advocates sometimes rely on such arguments.

Semantic discipline does not just steer you away from fallacy. By sensitizing you to the uses of emotive language, it enhances your ability to persuade. In spite of the truism that jury arguments make lousy oral arguments on appeal, judges are not impervious to common human feelings, even if the effects are subliminal. In tailoring the emotive vocabulary for your side of a case, think about how your description of the parties might affect a dispassionate tribunal. Take, as an example, an appeal from a jury verdict awarding damages to a widow in a wrongful death case. If you represent the appellee, you want to call the decedent "Bobby Whitfield" and the defendant "XYZ Corporation." But if you represent the appellant, you will want the court to hear the case on a more abstract level: "appellant" and "appellee," or "plaintiff" and "defendant," will do nicely.

Exceptions occasionally arise, as when Archibald Cox argued the Nixon tapes case before Judge John Sirica. When Cox referred to the possibility that the tapes might "implicate respondent," everyone in the courtroom had a vivid picture of that certain respondent. But that was an exceptional case.

There are subtler, and more important, uses of emotive language than what you call the parties. The facts of most cases can be faithfully presented in a number of ways. But your side's characterization will naturally be slanted, and you should premeditate your slant. For example, if you seek to enforce a guaranty against a savings and loan association whose former chairman of the board signed the guaranty, you might make frequent (though seemingly incidental) references to honoring one's obligations, or failing to do so; and you may, depending on the facts, be able to use charged verbs such as "renege" and "dishonor."

If you represent the thrift, on the other hand, and you contend that the former chairman defrauded the association in signing the guaranty, your vocabulary should portray the association as a victim. You want to distance your client from the malfeasances of its former chairman.

These observations may seem self-evident. They should be, but experience suggests they are not: All the time, advocates slip into a faceless, soporific argument in which the facts come across as lifeless data. If your opponent errs in this way, you have a much greater chance of capturing the judge's imagination and sympathy with a vivid, forceful depiction of the issues.

If you doubt the effect of emotive language on appellate judges, then note how they themselves use it. When affirming a capital conviction, appellate judges ordinarily set out at length—and, increasingly often, in gory detail—the crimes committed by the defendant. Rarely, however, do you get more than a glimpse of the crime in an opinion explaining a reversal. Usually, you must turn to the dissenting opinion to learn just how heinous the offense was.

Beyond rhetorical and semantic prowess—or perhaps because of it—appellate lawyers ought to be stylists. One commentator has listed several advantages of a good legal style: "[I]t develops analytical thought; it creates the necessary clarity; it subordinates the parts to the whole; it gives a sense of direction by which the necessary ground may be covered; and it brings the law and the facts into relation with each other." Fallon, "The Relation Between Analysis and Style in American Legal Prose" 28 *Neb. L. Rev.* 80, 92 (1949). My sole quarrel with that statement is that it suggests that style is the cause, rather than the effect, of careful analysis, clarity, and concinnous arrangement.

Despite the truism that words are a lawyer's stock-in-trade, the skill with which lawyers wield their words does not seem to be increasing. In the judicial ranks, we encounter fewer impenetrable opinions than two generations ago, yet it is hard to point to a literary equal of Holmes, Cardozo, or Jackson among contemporary judges. These extremes aside, however, lawyers today are generally no more fastidious in using language that they ever have been.

Here are three reasons why lawyers should nurture an interest in—if not a romance with—the English language. First, expression is substance. "It is not," as the novelist Martin Amis has written, "that . . . you get your content and soup it up with style; style is absolutely embedded in the way you perceive." Still, many lawyers seem to believe that style is merely the sometimes unnecessary spit and polish of writing.

Why, after all, be concerned with the distinction between that and which? Why fret over whether to call an indictment duplicitous or multiplicitous when questioning its efficacy? The answer is that these niceties affect meaning. In criminal law, duplicitous means one thing (charging two separate crimes in the same count), and multiplicitous means quite another (charging one crime in two or more counts). It simply will not do to use both words where only one fits, or to use the wrong word. Further, the legal writer must be sensitive to the lay meaning of duplicitous—namely deceitful.

Even lesser questions, such as the placement of a comma, can also affect meaning. Indeed, sometimes "men's lives may depend upon a comma." *United States v. Palmer*, 16 U.S. (3 Wheat.) 610, 636 (1818). Assume, however, a situation in which the placement of a comma is purely discretionary. The basic meaning would be the same with or without it. Should one give this a moment's thought? Of course! Even if the substance of the sentence remains unaffected, a discriminating reader will draw inferences and will perceive differences in tone. For example, a sensitive reader sees the difference that a comma makes here:

> He beat his dog with a steel rod.
> He beat his dog, with a steel rod.

If you read the two versions carefully, you will notice that the comma in the second sentence conveys a tone of disgust and condemnation absent in the first. One thinks of Oscar Wilde's perfectionist statement: "All morning I worked on the proof of one of my poems, and I took out a comma; in the afternoon I put it back." Lawyers do not have the leisure to consider their punctuation at such length, but we would all be better off inching closer to Wilde's approach.

Where punctuation is merely wrong, and the meaning is unaffected, the discriminating reader draws other types of inferences—usually unfavorable ones—about the writer. Any writer wants to avoid these, for they commonly extend beyond the writer's grammatical knowledge to his level of education and carefulness in general. Well-crafted writing lends credibility to what is being said. It is worth repeating: We cannot divorce style from substance.

The second reason for seeking to develop an effective writing style is that lawyers must convince, not just communicate. It is said that communication is the end of language. Perhaps. But there are higher purposes as well. We might justify all manner of clumsy, flat prose if communication were the ultimate, or only, criterion. For example:

> Your Honor, for the aforesaid and above-referenced reasons, plaintiff respectfully submits to this Honorable Court that, he should prevail in the motion submitted simultaneously herewith.

The sentence may communicate, but it is unlikely to persuade.

In law, we should set for ourselves a higher standard than merely communicating. One aspect of that higher linguistic standard is a heightened sensitivity to context. In a conversation at home, you have more latitude in grammar and word choice than you do in a letter to a client. And you have still less latitude in a brief that you submit to an appellate court. With your family, it is usually enough to get your point across, however rough-hewn your expression. In appellate briefs, though, you want to make your point so compellingly that the judges will not just understand it, but agree with it. The context is more formal, the language more formal. (That is not, to be sure, an invitation to use legalese—almost always out of place before an appellate tribunal.) Precision, clarity, and succinctness move to the fore. Like it or not, grammar and diction are professional accoutrements that you cannot neglect or abuse with impunity.

Finally, recognize that the English language is our greatest legacy. It is a legacy not just in the sense that we have inherited it from the great writers and orators of the past, to whom it links us, but also in the sense that we will pass it on to succeeding generations. The English language provides us with an unparalleled word-hoard. It is a living organism that constantly evolves because of the ways in which people use it every day. Whether or not pop grammarians are right in bewailing the "deterioration" of the language, there are, in any given context, unquestionably better and worse uses of language. Whenever we strive for the most appropriate uses of language, we do our fellow speakers of English, and certainly the legal profession as a whole, a great favor.

The task of effective legal writing is not just reveling in the glories of the English language. It can be something as mundane as proofreading. *The New York Times* once quoted me as saying that briefs in the Fifth Circuit "were on the whole rather appalling" when I clerked there. Friends asked whether that was not an exaggeration. I had to say it was not. Many of the briefs seemed to have been dictated but never revised, much less proofread. Apart from the lack of thorough research and analysis, the briefs too often lacked even the most superficial indication of care.

As a result, my fellow clerks and I began collecting an all-too-lengthy list of "howlers"—statements in briefs that were unintentionally humorous. It was one thing to discover an unpersuasive contention such as, "The defense objects to the characterization that the defendant is a scumbag who imported large amounts of cocaine into the country." It was quite another to see slips of the pen, or slips of the word processor, such as these:

- The ALJ failed to acknowledge the presents of the testimony of the claimant's wife.
- The expert testified that on wet grass verses dry grass the turning circle was bigger.
- When he was being questioned regarding the fact the monitoring procedures regarding Title III tape recordings had no president.
- The court cut the defendant off by sustaining non-existent objections from the prosuctors.
- On discussion now turns on the most damaging evidence in the entire record that the District court failed to give any evidence to in describing the question of retaliatory discharge for engaging in the protected activity.
- Only the musician can control the content of a liver performance.

These are only a few of the typographical horrors that appeared. I had always assumed, as a law student, that an argument before a federal court of appeals would be an occasion for utter meticulousness and professionalism. Instead, many lawyers filed what seemed to be a first draft. Too often, it was the prosuctors against the scumbags; and the typographical errors usually reflected the degree of substantive concern.

In the end, care and hard work, are the keys. Few of us can pretend to be a Charles Alan Wright, turning out masterly briefs only a short time before the deadline, or writing a law-review article in 45 minutes. *See* R. Price, *With Nixon* 248–49 (1977). To be effective, most of us need to begin the research and writing long before the due date, and to revise the draft several times in the light of our colleagues' comments and criticisms.

The writing process varies from person to person. Some draw inspiration from long walks in the morning, others from cups of coffee late into the night. But when the writing has properly begun, one thing is certain: You have begun to think about the problem and its complications as never before.

How much better your written thoughts are when you become accustomed to examining legal issues—as well as your own prose—from different linguistic vantages. When you acquire that ability, you are considerably closer to virtuosity. And, as an advocate, to victory.

The Art of Brief Writing: What a Judge Wants to Read

Albert Tate, Jr.

An appellate advocate wants a brief and argument to contribute to the success of the client's cause. My primary theme, however, is how the appellate brief can help the court, not the client. A court only uses briefs that help it make decisions. If counsel regards the appellate brief as more than a perfunctory, functionless tool, he or she therefore must prepare it primarily for the court. The judges may then rely on it as they prepare the decision. Win or lose, this always benefits the client, because *the client's* counsel has contributed to the decision-making.

To help the judge, the brief need not be eloquent or even persuasive about the client's cause. It is sufficient that it furnish ready access to the record, the authorities, and the reasoning by which the lawyer's client is to prevail. If the client is to lose, the brief and oral argument should at least enable the judges to understand the authorities and reasoning that support the client's position. (Perhaps 50 percent of the briefs filed with our courts are so one-sided or superficial as to be essentially discarded after an initial skimming. From the point of view of both client and court, it is as if no brief at all had been filed.)

Before suggesting in more detail how briefs may perform this function most effectively, I should perhaps consider the appellate judge for whom the briefs are prepared.

As counsel writes the brief, he or she should visualize what the judge is trying to do in deciding the case and how the judge will use the brief. Counsel should keep in mind what the judge's approach may be to the problem, what will hold interest, and what may be disregarded as irrelevant or useless. The brief is not written to be fed into an impersonal,

---

Albert Tate, Jr., now deceased, was an associate justice of the Supreme Court of Louisiana and served as chairman of the Committee on Appellate Advocacy of the Appellate Judges' Conference, American Bar Association.

computerized justice machine, but to be read and studied and weighed by fellow human beings.

The present-day appellate judge performs in a milieu of ever-increasing appellate volume. In the 1980s the law explosion tripled the number of cases many appellate courts decided each year. In my own court, for instance, each of the seven judges participated in deciding nearly 2,000 appeals or supervisory writs each year.

Yet the appellate judge today is essentially the same sort of person as his or her predecessor of two (or ten) decades ago. The same central perception of function and duty is shared: in each case he or she accepts personal responsibility for the duty of seeing that individual justice is done, within the framework of the law.

The result that seems "just" for the present case must be a principled one that will afford just results in similar conflicts of interest. The brief, then, is addressed to a human judge, not an abstract legal technician. This judge has an initial human concern that the litigants receive common-sense justice, but also realizes that the discipline of legal doctrine governs the determination of the cause.

In writing for this judge, counsel must also keep in mind that the volume of cases exposes several hundred appeals a year. Consequently, the judge knows much law and has seen many approaches to appellate advocacy. He or she quickly recognizes sham and superfluous arguments. Each appeal in a burgeoning caseload competes for interest and limited time. Considering all this, the appellate advocate will do well to concentrate on the strengths of the case, as concisely and lucidly as possible, to attract the judge's interest in and reliance upon the brief.

In this era of high volume, the brief serves a function that is increasingly important: to obtain oral argument or, at least, an articulated opinion deciding the appeal.

Perhaps 80 percent of appeals present issues clearly destined for appellate rejection. They may involve the contested but correct application of settled law, or an attack upon a factual finding of the trier not clearly erroneous. They may even involve frivolous contentions or ones the appellate court has consistently rejected in the past. Since an articulated and published opinion will add nothing to the law or the parties' understanding of why the appeal resulted in an affirmance, some appellate courts have devised summary proceedings to eliminate full-scale consideration of such appeals and to provide for their disposition without opinion or oral argument. This helps to preserve more time to hear, study, and prepare opinions in appeals involving more substantial or uncertain issues.

In the summary instances, the appellant's brief is the primary basis upon which the screening is made. To assure a hearing beyond the brief, let alone to prevail, the appellant must strongly demonstrate the possibility of individual unfairness or of a truly arguable question of law, or its application, in need of articulated resolution. The appellee's brief, of course, should demonstrate the lack of merit to these contentions, if indeed there is none.

Although my suggestions primarily concern preparing a brief to help the court in deciding a case by an articulated opinion, after oral argument, the same considerations apply even more strongly where the appeal may be decided without oral argument or by summary affirmance or reversal.

I should not overemphasize the skills of advocacy in determining the result in the bulk of litigation. Although appellate advocates frequently disagree, most appellate judges feel that they might ultimately have blundered upon the correct result without the assistance of counsel. Litigation should be decided on the basis of the law and the facts, not on the technical skills of counsel. Most appeals are decided by the pleadings and evidence in the trial court and the law in the books, and not on the basis of appellate advocacy. This of course is as it should be.

On the whole, the effective appellate advocate's contribution will be to sharpen and hasten the decisional process, while assuring full consideration of the client's position. Also, by the choice of issues and authorities, counsel may add important dimensions and perspectives to the rationale and future usefulness of the decision.

Generally speaking, the form and organization of a brief should serve two purposes. First, it should be so complete within itself that in writing the opinion the judge need not refer to extrinsic sources, except to confirm the accuracy of the presentation. Second, the brief should allow the court to understand it and obtain access to the record or authorities cited without spending any unnecessary effort.

Court rules about the form of the brief typically provide for (1) a "preliminary statement," which states in one or two sentences the general nature of the action and the procedural history of the case; (2) a "statement of the issues"—a succinct listing of the questions presented for decision; (3) a "statement of facts"—a concise narrative summary of the material facts in the context of which the litigation arises; (4) the "argument"—points of law or fact, discussed under appropriate point headings, with analysis of the legal problems on argument of law, and with presentation of the accurately cited evidence on argument of fact; and (5) the "conclusion"—a succinct, summarized reiteration of why the judgment should be reversed or affirmed, sometimes including a suggested decree. Whether the rule of court so provides or not, this format presents for ready comprehension by the judge the essential issues of law in their factual context.

The "preliminary statement" and the "conclusion" are self-explanatory. Before I note what I find helpful to the client's cause and to the court in a brief's statement of the issues, statement of the facts, and argument, I have some general observations applicable to the brief as a whole.

Recognizing the mass of reading and research competing for the judge's time and attention, appellate counsel should revise to be concise and lucid. From the mass of materials available, he or she should repeatedly select and discard. *Select* essential issues, facts, and authorities; *discard* and winnow others ruthlessly, along with excess words and repetitious argument.

Counsel's worry, of course, is that what is discarded as superfluous might, if left, somehow catch the court's eye. Hence, the lawyer errs unwisely on the side of inclusion. Unless there is particular reason to believe otherwise, however, a safe rule is to assume that appellate judges will have the same good sense as counsel in concluding that the discarded issue or fact is indeed noncontributory. Part of the craft of counseling is the ability to balance the *possible* contribution of the issue or fact against the undoubted loss of impact and persuasion of a brief that wastes the court's time on side trails that lead nowhere.

Need I add that accuracy and candor should guide counsel's selection of the issues and statements of factual argument and of the arguable import of the authority relied upon? Inaccuracy in statement or misleading argument will obviously destroy the court's confidence in the brief.

For readability and easy comprehension, the brief should be coherently organized, with appropriate headings and subheadings to facilitate ready reference to topics of special interest. Short sentences and relatively short paragraphs allow immediate understanding. Italics should be sparingly used, exclamation points practically never, and capitalized boldface type not at all. Rather, the emphasis should result from the content and arrangement of the thoughts. From reading several thousand briefs a year, a judge has learned that what is shouted and exclaimed could usually be whispered, if it needs mouthing at all.

Counsel should accurately note page numbers for facts in the record and have someone proofread for accuracy of doctrinal and decisional citations, including page numbers of quotations; case citations must be shepardized to assure their current viability. Inaccurate citations will waste the court's time and subconsciously undermine confidence in the reliability of counsel's argument as well.

The brief is a companion of the judge from before the oral argument until after the rehearing is denied, and it will be referred to or reread as often as necessary. The judge to whom the decision is assigned will continually consult the effective appellate brief—issue by issue and fact by fact—in research and as the proposed opinion is drafted. Primarily on the basis of the briefs, each judge of the panel will decide to sign the proposed opinion or instead to dissent, concur, or suggest changes in it.

Even before the opinion is assigned and circulated, the participating judges all use primarily the briefs to prepare for oral argument and to reach a tentative conclusion for the opinion-assignment conference immediately following argument. After the opinion is issued, they again consult the briefs in deciding whether to grant a rehearing. At all stages, each participating judge relies largely upon the briefs when deciding whether to engage in independent research of the record or the law.

At the outset, the statement of the issues acquaints the court with the essence of the case. It should provide a concise statement of the controlling questions for decision. The statement of the issues is not the same as a statement of counsel's contentions; it is rather an attempt to state fairly to the court the crux of the case in terms of the precise legal issue to be decided and of the ultimate facts that gave rise to this issue. Ideally, the question should be stated so that the opponent must accept it. When the opposing parties frame an issue differently, the party who misstates what the court concludes to be the real issue loses much credibility.

The questions should be stated in the briefest and most general terms, without names, amounts, or details. The conciseness of what is expected is indicated by some court rules that provide that this statement should not ordinarily exceed fifteen printed lines and never more than a page. Of course, the statement of a central issue includes every subsidiary issue fairly comprised within it, which then may be developed more fully in subheadings of the argument proper.

In my experience, counsel often overlook the importance of the statement of the central issues and sometimes prepare it as an afterthought after having written the argument. The judge's initial reaction to the seriousness and merit of the appeal is often based upon this indication of what issues counsel considers to be vital to the case; in the light of this statement, and of the statement of facts, the judge tends unconsciously to screen the appeal as substantial or not, even though this impression may yield to later study. When the questions at issue are effectively stated, the judge is able to decide and to read and understand more quickly the argument that follows in the brief.

The questions should be few in number. Rare is the appeal with many reversible errors; when a great number of questions are presented as serious issues, the judge's expectation that most or all of them are insubstantial is rarely disappointed. It has sometimes seemed to me that a large number of insubstantial issues raised might have been abandoned, and the argument section more tightly concentrated on the arguable issues, if counsel had attempted to articulate concisely the precise questions he wished the court to decide *before* writing the brief. I have never been able to understand the motives of counsel who raise a great number of issues. They must realize the court will decide adversely to them. The few arguable issues raised by them tend to be regarded as nonmeritorious by association. It is like shooting with a blunderbuss crammed with eggshell; it will annoy and distract without affecting the outcome.

Selecting and characterizing the issues may determine the course of the appeal. Llewellyn once described an unsuccessful appeal, stated in terms of the duty of an "agent," and suggested that a contrary result would have been reached if the issue had been instead characterized as the duty owed by a "broker." In my own experience, an appeal—stated and briefed in terms of a subrogation issue—was nearly lost, until our court, after much study, discovered that the issue was one of indemnity. The issues stated should be selected not only in view of the facts and the state of the law, but also in the light of what will appeal to the particular reviewing court.

The most helpful statement of an issue is in terms of its facts, not as an abstract question of law. The statement should show the precise point of substantive law and its applicability to the facts at hand. Thus, "Was plaintiff guilty of contributory negligence?" does vaguely indicate the general issue; but how much more helpful to the court's concentration and understanding of the issue is: "Plaintiff's car struck the rear of a vehicle operated by the defendant, who had made an emergency stop without signaling. Where plaintiff admits that he could not have stopped his car within an assured clear distance ahead, is he chargeable with contributory negligence so as to bar his recovery?"

An overly argumentative statement of the issues turns me off. Self-evident, overtly self-serving, or overgeneralized statements are not helpful and may be misleading (and thus prejudicial to the court's appreciation of counsel's sincerity). Thus, the issue in a tax case, if stated as "Whether a man is taxable on income which his son receives?" is not indicative of the true issue. "Whether the owner of coupon bonds should include in his gross income the amount of coupons which he detached and gave to his son several months before maturity?" I should note that, if fairly stated, a formulation of the issue is not out of order when it subtly suggests the response desired by the litigant; as, for instance, in the tax collector's reformulation of the above issue to suggest the taxpayer's evasion of tax on income from property still owned by him: "The taxpayer owned coupon bonds. Several months prior to maturity of the interest coupons he detached them and gave them to his son, retaining the bonds themselves. Is he relieved of income tax with respect to such interest coupons?"

The statement of the facts is regarded by many advocates and judges as the most important part of the brief. In the first place, regardless of how much the judge knows about the legal issues beforehand, the facts are not known until this statement is read. Second, law and legal principles are designed to produce fair and socially useful results when applied to *facts*. This fundamental aim of law lurks always in the mind of the judge. If the application of the given legal principle produces a result deemed unfair by the judge, he or she will wish to study carefully whether indeed the given principle was intended to apply to the particular facts.

This initial statement of facts should not be confused with any argument about the facts to be advanced in the subsequent section of the brief. By this initial statement, counsel attempts to state accurately and with reasonable fairness the material facts, without failing to disclose those that are contested. The attempt is to summarize, without too much unnecessary detail, only those facts that are most cogent and persuasive, without omitting unfavorable circumstances, so that the court may understand the basic factual background of the legal issues. Accurate reference to the transcript or appendix should be provided to allow the court immediately to verify counsel's facts as stated. Counsel's selection, arrangement, and emphasis of these facts, if without sacrifice of accuracy, may readily suggest to the court how the legal issues presented should be decided.

John W. Davis and Frederick B. Wiener are numbered among America's greatest appellate advocates. Davis said:

> [I]t cannot be too often emphasized that in an appellate court the statement of the facts is not merely a part of the argument, it is more often than not the argument itself.... The court wants above all things to learn what are the facts which give rise to the call upon its energies; for in many, probably in most, cases when the facts are clear there is no great trouble about the law.

Davis, "The Argument of an Appeal," 28 *A.B.A. J.* 895, 896 (1940). Wiener has said:

> The real importance of facts is that courts want to do substantial justice and that they are sensitive to the "equities." Consequently the objective of the advocate must be so to write his statement that the court will want to decide the case his way after reading just that portion of the brief.

Wiener, "Essentials of an Effective Appellate Brief," 17 *Geo. Wash. L. Rev.* 143, 145 (1949). *See also* to the same effect, K. Llewellyn, *The Common Law Tradition: Deciding Appeals* 238 (1960).

Judicial writers agree on the importance of the statement of facts, among them Justice Robert H. Jackson:

> It may sound paradoxical, but most contentions of law are won or lost on the facts. The facts often incline a judge to one side or the other.

Jackson, "Advocacy Before the Supreme Court," 37 *A.B.A. J.* 801, 803 (1951).

Chief Judge Irving R. Kaufman of the Federal Second Circuit has said:

> Let the narrative of facts tell a compelling story. The facts are, almost without exception, the heart of the case on appeal.... The facts generate the force that impels the judge's will in your direction.

"Appellate Advocacy in the Federal Courts," Address before Association of the Bar of the City of New York (April 21, 1977).

The Argument

In the argument section of the brief, counsel is a partisan advocate urging the court to adopt his or her analysis of the legal authorities and view of the facts. Here, the points of law will be treated consecutively. Headings and subheadings should indicate to the court the thrust of the argument on each point (e.g., "Appellant had notice of the defect and therefore is not a holder in due course"), followed by counsel analyzing and arguing the legal and factual data in support of each heading. If there are numerous points, a final summary may provide for the court a ready synthesizing review of the arguments covered.

From the court's point of view, the principle of "select and discard" should here apply also. Only truly arguable points should be selected and relied upon; unessential or diversionary points rarely affect the result, and normally should be discarded.

Generally, a point that goes to the very heart of the case should be argued first. An experienced judge will usually select the strongest issue for study first. But the judge initially may not know what counsel's strongest issue is, unless counsel, based on knowledge of the facts and legal research, so directs the court.

When the judge has decided on affirmance or reversal, he or she usually addresses the appellant's strongest premise first in drafting the opinion. If the judge accepts the premise and decides to reverse, often it is not necessary to research or address other points relied upon by the appellant. As a psychological matter, appellant's counsel should force the court early to face head-on the strongest argument; otherwise, the judicial impression of its forcefulness may be lessened, if its study is not reached until after the judge has half-decided on affirmance, having rejected counsel's previous arguments.

In many instances, of course, counsel cannot argue the strongest point first because of logical priority. Then the arguments must be set forth in a logical step-by-step progression, relying upon placement, emphasis, and the "Statement of the Issues" to indicate the greater importance the points. Also, the appellee's order of argument is normally directed by sequential response to the points raised by the appellant; if, however, the appellant has minimized some overriding argument in favor of affirmance, the appellee should likewise emphasize early the forcefulness of the strongest argument. An appellee may safely ignore an illogical sequence of insubstantial arguments, although he or she should explain why it's done, and why the appellant's arguments lack merit, rather than ignore them.

The type of argument must of course vary with the type of case and the type of issue. However, counsel should prepare it, as he or she selected its points and the issues of the appeal, with some knowledge of the tribunal to which the brief is submitted. For example, a Louisiana intermediate court decides many workmen's compensation cases each year; detailed jurisprudential and statutory argument may unnecessarily burden a brief to that court, whereas it might enlighten the Supreme Court of Louisiana, which in this legal area only occasionally issues full-scale opinions. Similarly, there is no point in urging that a court overrule a prior decision if you know that court never overrules decisions. The same court may not be as reluctant to "distinguish" the same prior decision, with identical practical consequences. Some courts, or some panels of a court, are more oriented to technical issues of law or to innovative arguments than are others.

About citations: a lawyer should include as few as practical, mainly those of the leading or more recent cases. Also, where possible, citation should be made to decisions of the court that hears the appeal; the judges are more likely to be familiar with them and accept them without additional verifying research. If counsel intends to rely heavily on a particular decision, it is well to make the effort to summarize its facts, and to show that the cited case is applicable to the *facts* of the present case. Quotations from the case, if used at all, should be restricted to the relevant sentences. Opposing authorities should be distinguished, not ignored, lest the court feel that counsel cannot answer them.

Blind citation of precedent without functional analysis is of minimal assistance. As Justice Rutledge observed:

> What judges want to know is why this case, or line of cases, should apply to these facts rather than that other line on which the opponent relies with equal certitude, if not certainty. Too often the *why* is left out.

Rutledge, "The Appellate Brief," 28 *A.B.A. J.* 251, 253 (1942).

Also, it is useful and often persuasive to find counsel's position supported by an authoritative treatise or illuminated by law review commentaries and ALR annotations.

Arguments over facts are rarely persuasive if founded solely upon long excerpts of questions and answers from the transcript. The most useful and persuasive technique, if accurately done, is a concise summary of the factual evidence on the issue, including that opposed to counsel's position, with accurate reference to the pages in the transcript that verify these statements. Key phrases or statements, rather than entire dialogues, may be quoted to give flavor and force, if not done out of context. The strongest factual arguments emphasize the commonsense fairness of the client's position, or call into play the undoubted application of settled law. But it is important that, in so arguing, counsel does not distort or ignore contrary facts, however much he or she evades their forcefulness by explaining their context or supposed lack of weight.

For appropriate cases, such as where the court is essentially concerned with weighing policy values in the selection or creation of a rule with future consequences, I personally would like to see more nondecisional authority. Social statistics of which we may take judicial notice, for instance, sometimes afford data by which to evaluate the practical implications of a proposed interpretation. Thus, in deciding whether a personal injury lawyer violated ethical canons by an occasional advance of small loans to an impoverished client when the latter was beset by financial emergencies, we found to be of some aid the Bureau of Census reports concerning the population's poverty level. *Louisiana State Bar Association v. Edwins*, 329 So. 2d 437, 447 (La. 1976). In criminal cases the standard of fairness, or a better interpretation of our own procedural law, may often be formulated with the aid of studies and recommendations founded on both scholarship and practical experience, such as the American Bar Association Standards for Criminal Justice, the American Law Institute Model Code of Pre-Arraignment Procedure, or the National Conference of Commissioners on Uniform State Laws' Model Code of Criminal Procedure.

I have already mentioned the importance of headings and subheadings to clarity and immediate understanding. I should add that charts or tables may inform the judge at a glance of what he or she could similarly understand only with minutes of reading and of puzzling out words and figures. Complex machines or locales, such as unusual intersections, may likewise be quickly demonstrated or understood by a diagram, where it might take hours for counsel to write (and minutes for the court to read with understanding) words purporting to convey the same information.

Before concluding, I should note several publications that treat with much greater detail, with practical illustrations of effective and ineffective technique, effective appellate briefing: G. Rossman, ed., *Advocacy and the King's English* (1960); E. D. Re, *Brief Writing and Oral Argument* (4th ed., 1977); and F. B. Wiener, *Effective Appellate Advocacy* (1950). *See also* F. B. Wiener, "Essentials of an Effective Appellate Brief," 17 *Geo. Wash. L. Rev.* 143 (1949).

In summary, the truly effective appellate brief, from the point of view of the court, is one quite similar to a superior law clerk's memorandum. It contains discussion and analysis and summary of all factual considerations and legal rationales necessary for the decision. Once the contents are verified, through the ready means furnished by accurate citation to the record and published material, the judge should be able to dictate his or her opinion from the brief, including liberal paraphrasing or plagiarizing of its concise and accurate wording. In serving through the brief as a valued research assistant to the court, counsel has certainly aided the administration of appellate justice, whether the client wins or loses.

I have emphasized my concept of the appellate brief as chiefly a vehicle to enable the judge to understand quickly the issues and facts, disputed or not, of the appeal, and for him or her most readily to grasp the argument of counsel, its strengths and weaknesses. I do not, however, imply that the brief's usefulness is negated by its advocacy. By selection, emphasis, and articulation, counsel properly attempts to persuade the court of the correctness of his client's position, although (if counsel wishes the brief to be useful to and used by the court) he or she must do so accurately and with candor about the factual and legal data applicable to the issues of the case. The more clear, concise, complete, and coherent the brief is as furnished for the court's use, the more certainly will the brief afford the court access not only to the legal materials furnished by it for decision, but also to counsel's persuasiveness in the contention that the law and the facts demand that his or her client prevail.

How to Write a Good Appellate Brief

Andrew L. Frey and Roy T. Englert, Jr.

In theory, every law school graduate should know something about how to write an effective appellate brief. After all, first-year legal writing classes in law school often concentrate on that skill. Moot court competitions do too. Compared to other kinds of legal work, appellate briefs seem tidy and self-contained, with a predictable structure. So they are what law schools teach.

Once in practice, regardless of law school background, trial lawyers sometimes seem to believe that no special talent or training is needed to write a good brief on appeal. The idea appears to be that what works before a jury or is acceptable to a busy trial judge should be more than adequate for an appellate court.

Despite what law students should learn and despite what lawyers think they know, appeal after appeal is lost, or at least made harder to win, because of ineffective briefs. Why? In part, because many lawyers write appellate briefs infrequently. When they do have to brief an appeal, they fail to appreciate that the job is different from much other lawyering. It poses special problems, but presents special opportunities, for advocacy.

The most common mistake made by trial lawyers is to think that they should do the same thing in the appellate court that they did in trial court. They write their jury speech and call it a brief. At best, they address the appellate judges as they would address the trial judge. At worst, they treat the appellate judges like jurors.

Such advocates bog down in irrelevant detail and empty rhetoric. Ninth Circuit Judge Alex Kozinski's comments about oral argument apply even more forcefully to the brief: "When a lawyer resorts to a jury

---

Andrew L. Frey and Roy T. Englert, Jr., are partners in the Washington, D.C., firm of Mayer, Brown & Platt.

argument on appeal, you can see the judges sit back and give a big sigh of relief.... [W]e know, and you know we know, that your case doesn't amount to a hill of beans, so we can go back there in the conference room and flush it with an unpublished disposition."

Even those who understand that a court of appeals is different from a trial court often fail to seize the opportunities for advocacy that an appellate brief offers. They may recall their early law school lessons, but they do not know and do not take (or do not have) the time to study the more sophisticated lessons that actual experience in appellate practice can bring. Their written product is formulaic. It fails to take advantage of the flexibility that an appellate brief writer has in packaging arguments to meet the needs of a particular case.

Packaging Arguments

Here is what we mean by effective packaging: Several years ago, the Supreme Court considered a case that turned on the interpretation of two complex, interrelated statutes. One statute involved regulation by the FDA, and the other involved patent law. Conventional law school wisdom would have called for the brief to begin with a statement of the events giving rise to the controversy, followed by a description of the proceedings below. The winning brief did not do that. Instead, it opened with a four-page description of the statutory scheme. Not one sentence on those four pages was argumentative or even disputable. The passage alerted the Court to the statutory elements that the brief writers knew were most significant and helpful to their side. It gave the Court a framework to understand everything else the brief said—from the statement of facts through the conclusion of the argument.

Ultimately, the Court ruled in favor of the side that had taken the unconventional approach, saying that it found "'the structure of the [statute] taken as a whole'" to be dispositive. The critical information the Court needed to rule as it did was in those first four pages. Of course, this technique is not right for every appeal (although it probably makes sense more often than not in cases turning solely on statutory construction). But it is one way an advocate can achieve maximum effectiveness while staying within the rules.

Note that we have referred to "staying within the rules." That is important. The rules are the first thing any lawyer must consider before putting pen to paper—or fingers to keyboard.

A surprising number of prominent litigators fail to read, understand, and follow the rules that govern appeals. A noted constitutional lawyer got egg on his face when the D.C. Circuit rejected one of his briefs because it "evaded" the court's page limits by having too many long footnotes. The Seventh Circuit frequently writes tart opinions about such behavior.

Judges can express their disapproval of noncompliant counsel in even more emphatic ways. Many years before he became a Supreme

Court Justice, John Marshall Harlan briefed an appeal to the Second Circuit. His brief was too long, but the clerk's office did not reject it. When Harlan's senior colleague, Emory Buckner, stood up to present oral argument on the appointed day, Judge Learned Hand demanded to know who wrote the brief. Buckner said that he himself had merely "put [his] name on it"; he complimented his junior colleague as the author.

Learned Hand Throws a Brief

Some compliment: After huffing that the brief was too long and saying he would not read it, Hand *threw* it over the bench. It landed on counsel table with a thud. The youthful lawyer (and future justice) sitting there was left with a queasy stomach and a sinking feeling. If you want to avoid being pelted with your own handiwork, consult and follow the rules.

A lawyer writing a brief in the United States Supreme Court need consult only one set of formal rules: the Rules of the Supreme Court of the United States, which became effective in their current form on October 2, 1995. Those rules are clearly written and easily understood, as far as they go. Experienced Supreme Court litigators know, however, that certain Supreme Court practices do not appear anywhere in the rules.

For example: If a brief writer has cited materials in the brief and wants them readily available to the justices, but those materials cannot be included in the joint appendix (perhaps because they are not part of the record), the clerk usually will allow copies of the materials to be "lodged" with his office. (The materials must, of course, be served on opposing counsel.) The *Oxford Companion to the Supreme Court of the United States* (1992) mentions this technique, but only in the book's discussion of the solicitor general—as if the procedure was somehow available only to the government. In fact, it can be used by any litigant who knows to ask the clerk's office for permission to use it.

Because this useful technique (and several others) are not in the rules, a Supreme Court brief writer ordinarily should consult the leading treatise on the nuts and bolts of Supreme Court practice. Popularly known for decades as "Stern and Gressman," the book *Supreme Court Practice* came out in late 1993 in a seventh edition, written by Robert L. Stern, Eugene Gressman, Stephen M. Shapiro, and Kenneth S. Geller.

The lawyer writing a brief for a federal court of appeals must consult two sets of rules. One is the FRAP. Lawyers quickly learn that is not a Boston native's term for a milk shake, but is instead an acronym for the Federal Rules of Appellate Procedure, which apply in all federal courts of appeals.

But the FRAP is not enough. A brief writer also must study the "local rules" of the court to which the appeal is being taken. Each court of appeals has authority to supplement or modify the FRAP; idiosyncratic rules abound, setting traps for unwary advocates. For example, the

FRAP sets page limits for reply briefs, but the D.C. Circuit regulates brief length by the number of *words*. The same court also has special procedures and unusual timetables for obtaining leave to file an amicus brief.

State appellate courts also usually have detailed rules. There is so much variation from state to state that it is useless to generalize, other than to repeat the basic point: Find, read, and follow the rules.

One rules-related question comes up more than any other: When a case is complicated and adequate briefing will push up against the page limits, how, within the rules, can you squeeze the text you need into the allotted number of pages? Almost all appellate courts specify in their rules the maximum number of pages and the minimum size of margins. But there is considerable variation in the degree to which courts regulate type styles and sizes. Many courts will allow proportional spacing (easy to do on modern word processors) or submission of printed briefs, without imposing a page-limit penalty. These techniques, if permitted by local court rules, enable you to expand the content of a brief by 20 percent or more while still producing an attractive, readable product.

Not all courts will countenance clever format shuffling, however. When a court does have rules governing the format of a brief, obey them or be prepared to face the music. A few years ago, a petitioner seeking review of an NLRB decision in the Seventh Circuit was denied permission to file a 70-page brief. It then resubmitted the same brief "stuff [ed] . . . into 50 pages" by "a variety of typographical techniques" prohibited by the Circuit's rules, such as 1-1/2 spacing and type smaller than the required 11 points. "[T]he lawyers, caught with their hands in the cookie jar, . . . apologized and promised not to play the same trick . . . again." But apologies were not enough. The court forcefully expressed its disapproval of the lawyers' conduct and imposed a $1,000 penalty. You probably don't want something like that to happen to you.

Unsubstantiated rumor has it that some United States circuit judges have requisitioned special rulers that printers use to measure type sizes and margins, illustrating an amateur detective's zeal for catching lawyers who try to squeeze too much material into their briefs. Whether or not that is true, one judge has written for public consumption his reaction to a brief that chisels on the type size: "It tells the judges that the lawyer is the type of sleazeball who is willing to cheat on a small procedural rule and therefore probably will lie about the record or forget to cite controlling authority." Encountering *that* attitude could be worse for you than a $1,000 fine.

Let us pause for a moment and consider the standard advice for how to meet page limits without disobeying or evading the rules. It is a humorless, spartan maxim: Write short briefs; be so economical and terse that no squeezing is needed. As is often the case with standard advice, these admonitions have much truth to them, but they are not uniformly correct.

Some cases *do* warrant short briefs. The first case that one of us argued in the Supreme Court was a relatively simple Fourth Amendment matter; the total number of pages in the petitioner's brief, respondent's brief, and reply brief *combined* was less than the 50 pages the rules allowed for a single party's opening brief. But that is unusual. Other cases *do* warrant the full number of pages allotted by the rules, or (with the permission of the court) even more.

"Write short" is not a panacea. Relatively extended treatment may be necessary because the case involves an especially complex issue or because a number of issues must be presented. In some cases, a court could follow any one of several routes to the same conclusion, and the advocate must present each logical path, not knowing which the court will take. When appellate judges lament—as they frequently do—the unnecessary length of some of the briefs they see, they may not appreciate fully that a lawyer cannot, as a judge can, simply settle on a single true path to the desired result.

Our own advice on how to meet page limits is not merely to be brief. Instead, first write lean prose that makes the necessary points and avoids excessive repetition. Then, if the brief is too long, take advantage of whatever latitude the rules provide (but no more) to vary margins, typefaces, line endings, and so on. Then edit the prose to make it leaner still.

Judges may always grumble about the length of briefs, but, if you stay within the rules and write briefs that tell them what they need to know in economical prose, they usually will come around. After flinging John Marshall Harlan's brief at him, Learned Hand eventually voted in favor of Harlan's client. Hand even called Harlan in to tell him it was "a very good brief."

So much for format and length. What about substance? Usually the first non-boilerplate item in an appellate brief will be something called the "Questions Presented" or the "Issues Presented" or the "Statement of Issues." This section can be critical. It is difficult to underestimate the importance of clear, effective framing of the issues: In advocacy, as in life, first impressions last. Unfortunately, many briefs state the issues in a way that either impairs the author's credibility or confuses the court's understanding of what the appeal is about.

Advocacy has a role in drafting the questions presented, but it is a mistake—and a common one—to slant the formulation of the issue too obviously in your own favor. Consider an extreme example: Suppose your case presents a question of whether exigent circumstances entitled police officers to enter your client's dwelling without a warrant; the police say they acted to prevent the destruction of drugs that could be used as evidence. In such a case, you should not present a question such as "Whether the Fourth Amendment has been suspended as a result of the 'War on Drugs.'" You may, if the situation warrants, want to suggest to the court that the search was unreasonable and that excessive zeal in the "War on Drugs" explains the government's behavior (and the trial court's ruling condoning that behavior)—but save the point for the argument section. If you start out so contentiously in the question presented, the court will conclude that you are unwilling—or unable—to ever be balanced. It will cast a skeptical eye on everything else you say and assume that it is all slanted. Your credibility—a key element of a brief—will be gone.

You can preserve your credibility by formulating the issues on appeal even-handedly. But there is another challenge: You must also make the questions comprehensible. If the judges cannot understand what the case is about from this initial substantive exposure to your writing—a statement they expect to be clear—they may have far less patience with the parts of your brief that may legitimately be complex.

A good brief writer can formulate clear, neutral-sounding questions but frame them in a way that tends (subtly, of course) to suggest the answer the writer seeks. The question should not present your argument, but it should express a clear point of view about the case.

An example from one of our cases may demonstrate the distinction. It was an antitrust case. Our opening brief (for the appellants) stated five issues presented and did so in less than half a page. We slightly loaded one of them with what we thought were helpful facts:

> Whether defendant can be labeled a "monopolist" under Section 2 of the Sherman Act because it owned the only bowling center in a small area, even though uncontradicted evidence showed that defendant lacked power to exclude competition or control price.

Our adversaries took a different approach. They heavily loaded their issues presented and took five pages of their brief to state them. The first issue presented, according to our adversaries, was:

> Was the finding of the jury that [defendant] possessed monopoly power in the Antelope Valley of California ("the relevant market") supported by substantial evidence when there was evidence (a) that over time [defendant's] share of the relevant market increased and, ultimately culminated in [defendant] achieving a 100% share of such market; (b) that two competitors of [defendant] withdrew from, and no competitors entered, the relevant market; (c) that the prices charged by [defendant] for bowling services in the relevant market were higher than those charged by [defendant] in markets where it faced competition; and (d) that because of the limited availability of bowling center and equipment financing, potential competitors confronted a significant barrier to entering the relevant market?

Sometimes these things are a matter of taste. Lawyers might differ over which of these formulations is preferable, and the decision in a case is unlikely to turn on such phrasing variations. We cannot help thinking, however, that judges tire quickly of laboriously reading such detailed Questions Presented and would prefer to see the minutiae elsewhere.

Remember, the Questions Presented section is likely a judge's first exposure to your side of the case. It is a place to provide a concise overall view of what is at stake. It is not a place to bury a judge in detail. If judges must wade through facts, the significance of which is not immediately apparent, they may have a hard time grasping what your arguments are about.

Another key to successful appellate litigation (at least for the appellant or petitioner) is to limit the number of questions presented. Here again, there are no universal rules: Two questions presented are *sometimes* too many and five are *sometimes* too few. But it is fair to say that judges are more likely to give full attention to fewer issues than to many. An appellate lawyer must resist the temptation (and the pressure from client or trial counsel) to include many issues in the hope that, somehow, lightning will strike one of them. And it is never good advocacy to present two or more questions that simply rephrase what is really a single legal issue.

Sometimes, a succinct introductory sentence or two, or even a succinct paragraph, placed before the questions presented will aid understanding of a complex case. Most courts permit this device, although relatively few advocates use it. Here is an example:

> Prior to 1983, the tax code prohibited the compounding of interest on tax deficiencies or on tax overpayments. In section 344 of the Tax Equity and Fiscal Responsibility Act of 1982 (TEFRA), Congress repealed that prohibition and provided for the compounding of all such interest. Section 344(c) of TEFRA directed that these changes would apply to "interest accruing after December 31, 1982." The question presented is whether section 344(c) authorized the compounding of appellant's tax-deficiency interest, which had completely ceased accruing on February 1, 1982.

Elegant prose? Perhaps not. But imagine how much more inelegant it would have been to cram a single sentence with enough subordinate clauses to embrace all of these ideas. The case was technical, as were the issues. The statement of the question presented broke out the main ideas into separate sentences so that the judges could understand more easily what they were being asked to decide.

No Argumentative Statements

We now come to one of the few absolute—but, unfortunately, often violated—rules of brief writing: The Statement of Facts should *never* be argumentative in tone. The Statement of Facts is for telling the court what the case is about. The *argument* portion of the brief is for contention about the significance of those facts. Nothing impairs a brief writer's credibility more than an emotional, sarcastic, plaintive, or visibly one-sided Statement of Facts.

In other words, in the Statement of Facts, understated advocacy works best. A judge will be more prepared to believe that your client should win if your statement seems objective than if it editorializes. A judge will be more inclined to accept the fairness of your statement if it acknowledges the other side's strongest points and introduces—but does not argue—the facts or concepts you will later use to counter the other side. Remember, judges are lawyers, too, who are accustomed to careful analysis of facts and authorities. If your statement presents your case in a fair but favorable light, you do not need to carry every argument all the way to its logical conclusion at that point. You certainly need not drown the reader in rhetoric.

A closely related blunder is committed by many appellants challenging adverse jury verdicts. They fail to recognize that the evidence will be reviewed on appeal in the light most favorable to the verdict—that is, most favorable to the other side. It may be appropriate to describe both parties' evidence, but you should never present only the version favorable to you when that version has been rejected by the factfinder.

Of course, it is essential in the Statement of Facts to describe the record accurately. An answering brief that can show that you have distorted the record, or quoted material out of context, or otherwise arguably misled the court, can be devastating. The resulting loss of credibility will—you may be sure of this—undermine the reception that every other part of your brief receives.

This does not mean, however, that advocacy plays no role in drafting the Statement of Facts. Quite the opposite. Although the *tone* must at all times remain neutral and dispassionate, artful selection, emphasis, and organization of facts can go far to shape a reader's perception of the case.

The trick for the *appellant* is to make the reader feel that the statement presents a fair description of what happened—an account of the material facts leavened with a recognition of the presumption of correctness that fortifies the factfinder's resolution of factual disputes—yet, at the same time, have the reader come away with the feeling that the outcome of the trial court proceedings was none too sensible or fair.

Conversely, if you are the *appellee*, you will try to suggest that the appellant has distorted the facts, which, when correctly described, make the trial court outcome seem fair, reasonable, and almost inevitable.

One final point regarding the content of the fact statement: Every lawyer should know, though not all honor, the rule that you are limited to stating the facts contained in the case record (even though you may believe that the record is not what "really" happened). What is less often appreciated is that the statement need not be confined to the historical facts—who did what, and when. In addition, it can introduce relevant statutes, cases, and arguments to the court, as long as it presents them in a descriptive rather than an argumentative manner. It can also set forth—though carefully—what might be called "legislative facts," even though those "facts" are not part of the trial record, if they are background facts of the kind that a responsible judge would consider in determining the appropriate legal rule. Such a submission—a "Brandeis brief"—has an honorable place in American law; it is proper as long as the line between legislative and adjudicative facts is scrupulously honored.

How long should the statement be? Recall what Lincoln said about how long a horse's legs should be: long enough to reach the ground. A statement should be long enough to tell the judges or justices what they need to know, and no longer. Sometimes that will mean four pages of a 50-page brief, and sometimes 20 or 25.

In a case involving a plain legal issue, a short factual account may suffice, followed by a more elaborate legal analysis. In a fact-intensive case, on the other hand—a challenge to an administrative agency rate-making decision, for example—the statement may need to be much more elaborate. It may have to set forth in some detail the relevant statutory scheme and the structure of the particular regulated industry, followed by an account of the course of agency proceedings. In such a situation, it may then be possible, building on the factual foundation that the statement has laid, to have a comparatively short legal discussion.

In general, a reader is unlikely to grow too impatient with a statement that usefully sets forth relevant facts, even at some length. However, if the statement seems to be loaded with irrelevant detail—either because it actually is full of irrelevancies or because it is so poorly organized that the reader cannot grasp the relevance of what is being said—then it is likely to receive an unsympathetic reading.

One final point on this topic: The Statement of Facts is the place to introduce the parties and to explain any shorthand you will use to refer to them, plus the acronyms that you intend to use in the brief. Such shorthand references can help keep the writing lively, which is an important goal. Rule 28(d) of FRAP specifically advises counsel to "keep to a minimum references to parties by such designations as 'appellant' and 'appellee.'" That advice is but one example of a larger point.

Avoid Dense Prose

A mostly excellent brief filed in the Supreme Court a few years ago flirted with loss of its audience in the dense prose of the very first substantive sentence of the brief:

> The issue presented in this case—which arises under the Federal Service Labor-Management Relations Statute, 5 U.S.C. § 7101, *et seq.* ("Federal Labor Statute")—is whether the most basic policies

of that Act should play any role in a major area of its administration, *viz.*, in determining whether a union acting as the exclusive collective bargaining representative of federal sector employees—having been selected by those employees through the secret ballot electoral processes provided by federal law—is entitled to the disclosure of personnel records of bargaining unit employees when such disclosure is "necessary for the full and proper" performance of that representative's collective bargaining functions.

The writer of that sentence asked it to do too much. The sentence introduces too many concepts without a pause. By contrast, one of the authors a few years ago had a rare opportunity to use lively prose to make his point, which was that an Arkansas highway tax unconstitutionally discriminated against interstate commerce by exempting trucks carrying agricultural products (which were by no coincidence predominantly local), while fully taxing those carrying equally heavy shipments of other commodities (which came predominantly from out of state):

> There is an old riddle: Which weighs more, a ton of feathers or a ton of bricks? While many find the question deceptive at first, the correct answer, that a ton is a ton regardless of what is being weighed, becomes irrefutably clear once explained. But in enacting and now defending the NR Exemption, the State has managed to get the answer wrong—a ton of soybeans or chicken feed is treated as though it weighs less than a ton of baked beans or dog food.

The reader is sure to understand the point and may even have gotten a smile out of the arduous task of reading a brief.

Another point that frequently crops up with fact-intensive legal issues (for example, the sufficiency of the evidence to support the verdict) is whether it is best to recite all the relevant facts in the statement or save them for the argument. There is no general rule, but be aware of this: It is permissible to mention such facts briefly in the statement and then explore them fully in the argument. Often such treatment will reduce repetition and enhance the comprehensibility of your presentation. The section is called the Statement of Facts, but that does not mean all the facts you rely on must be there.

Turning to a point of general application, you should be especially careful how you refer to the court or agency below. If you are the appellant or the petitioner, you are, of course, asking the appellate court to reverse that court or agency. The appellate court knows that. It knows you disagree with the outcome thus far. It will reverse in an appropriate case. But its initial inclination, almost always, will be sympathetic to the fellow judge who had to sit through the trial or to the agency that had to sift through the entire record now being selectively quoted on appeal.

Criticism of the lower tribunal therefore should be stated carefully and objectively (for example, "the trial court did not address the 'waiver' issue" or "the agency's entire response to this argument was as follows"). Although this advice may seem obvious, lawyers do the contrary often enough that Judge Kozinski has been led to write, in a passage dripping with sarcasm: "Chances are I'll be seeing that [lower court] judge soon at one of those secret conferences where judges go off together and gossip about the lawyers. I find that you can always get a good chuckle out of the district judge by copying the page where he is described as 'a disgrace to the robe he wears' or as 'mean-spirited, vindictive, biased and lacking in judicial temperament' and sticking it under his nose right as he is sipping his hot soup."

Should the brief include a summary of the argument? FRAP does not require a summary of argument. Supreme Court Rule 24.1(h) does, as do the local rules of many—but not all—of the federal courts of appeals. Even when the rules do not require a summary, it usually is a good idea to write one except in the simplest cases. And it is *always* essential to good appellate advocacy that *somewhere* in the brief—if not in a summary, then near the beginning of the argument itself or even somewhere in the statement—counsel provide an overview of the position they will be arguing. Without this, it often becomes impossible (or possible only after an amount of effort that exceeds what the judges are able to spend) to understand a litigant's exact position. If judges do not understand a litigant's position, they may well substitute a position that is easy to understand—but is *not* what the party meant and is easy to rebut.

The Summary Follows the Argument

Experienced brief writers know that the summary of argument is usually written after the argument itself. The summary ordinarily should have the same structure as the argument. In our experience, the structure of the argument tends to evolve over the course of drafting and editing. Writing out a summary before writing the argument may serve the same useful function as preparing an organizing outline, but a summary written in advance rarely will be phrased and organized as well as one written after thinking through all the ideas that come up during drafting.

Often, you may wish to begin with some background or table-setting that will not be repeated in the argument section and therefore is not, strictly speaking, a "summary" of any part of the argument. In such instances, it is perfectly legitimate to combine the summary of argument with an introduction, as long as the combination of "introduction and summary of argument" is so labeled and does not cause the section to be too long (more than four or five pages).

Supreme Court Rule 24.1(h) cautions that "[a] mere repetition of the headings under which the argument is arranged is not [a] sufficient" summary of argument. The same caution surely holds true in every court that requires a summary. But it is equally important to remember that the argument headings themselves *will* also serve a summarizing function. Some readers of appellate briefs do skip over the table of contents and table of authorities when they first pick up a brief, but many do not, and virtually all return to the table of contents at some point when they try to understand the structure of a brief. Thus, you should pay attention to the argument headings so that when they are plucked out from the text and stand on their own, they will comprehensively, comprehensibly, and (within limits) persuasively state the party's position.

Ironically, the most critical section of the brief—the argument itself—is least subject to general rules or advice. There are two primary determinants of the quality of the argument section of a brief: (1) the quality of the arguments available and (2) the analytical and writing skills of the lawyers involved. Nevertheless, some aspects of writing an argument are specific to the appellate process.

Organization Above All

First, never forget the importance of organization. It is vital to organize, not only the writing, but also the theory of the case. Appellate judges know that they are setting precedents. They therefore worry about whether the theory they adopt in one case will or will not apply appropriately to slightly different sets of facts. Appellate lawyers should assist the judges by having—and expressing—clear theories with reasonably clear limits.

Unfortunately, many appellate briefs are organized in ways that do not advance an overall theory. One common but particularly unsatisfactory form of appellate brief (whatever its merit in a trial court) is to quote snippets from one precedent after another without fitting those precedents into an overall pattern. Such filings are long on cut-and-paste, but short on logic or explanation. Likewise, it is tempting (but equally ineffective) to use a brief to take a series of potshots at the opinion below (in an appellant's brief) or the adversary's brief (in an appellee's brief or a reply brief), never bothering to devise an overall theory of the *correct* approach to the case. And it bears repeating that *ad hominem* criticisms of adversaries or the decisionmakers below—as opposed to their legal positions—are counterproductive.

It also is desirable to explain the client's position in a way that makes sense from a policy (or commonsense) perspective. Judges are concerned about both the institutional and the real-world consequences of the rules they adopt. Relatively few cases that reach appellate courts are controlled so squarely by precedent that the judges have no wiggle room. Accordingly, even if favorable precedent is available and you intend to rely heavily on it, write the argument in a way that gives the judges confidence that they *should* follow that precedent. That is far better than baldly telling them that they must follow it—and daring them to disagree.

But be careful about policy forays. You cannot just make up the law. Most appellate judges are offended by briefs that are merely naked policy arguments and that pay no attention to such familiar judicial guideposts as case law, statutory language, and (for most judges) legislative history.

Statutory language can be especially important. More than once we have edited draft briefs that contained dozens of pages of material before ever quoting the actual language of the statute being construed. That is *always* a mistake in a true statutory construction case—one in which the court is called on to determine the meaning of statutory language, rather than construe precedents that have infused meaning into broad statutory generalities (such as those of the Sherman Act).

If statutory language makes your position difficult, do not hide the statute at the back of your brief. The court will see such placement as a tacit admission that the statute cannot be construed your way. The judges may think you want the court to ignore the statute. If the statutory language *is* favorable, you have done your client even more of a disservice by not beginning with that and telling the judges that Congress has made all necessary policy choices. Judge Kozinski, in his advice on how to *lose* an appeal, has written: "[S]tart out by discussing policy.... [I]nstead of talking about what Congress did, talk about what it *should* have done."

An important tactical question that often confronts the drafter of an appellant's opening brief is the extent to which the brief should provide responses, then and there, to arguments the other side may make in its brief. Should the rejoinders be saved for the reply brief instead? Remember, anticipating arguments entails some risk, especially if opposing counsel are weak; you may put ideas into their heads that they would not otherwise discover or articulate coherently. In general, however, an appellate brief that tries to hide from the adversary's best arguments is less effective than one that confronts them. And, when the point has already been made by the trial court or argued by your adversary at earlier stages of the proceeding, you cannot expect to hide. You will almost surely want to address such hard points in the opening brief, stating the issue in your terms rather than letting your opponent set the agenda.

Content is not everything, of course. Writing also matters in an appellate brief and in the argument section especially. The point is not that judges consciously grade style or decide appeals based on which brief they think is better written. Rather, it is that judges must understand and remember your position before they can agree with it—and a stylish brief usually is more understandable and memorable.

Appellate judges are busy people. Judge Kozinski estimates that he must read 3,500 pages of briefs a month. There is not always sufficient time for a judge to untangle convoluted sentences or dense prose. In addition, typographical and grammatical errors can distract from more important matters. And, if it is possible to write the brief in a lively fashion—without making the writing style itself a distraction—the reader is likelier to comprehend and remember it.

Here again, heated rhetoric and overstatement are harmful. Perhaps the most common flaw in appellate briefs is writing in emphatic, unequivocal, and conclusory terms. Such briefs, overconfident, even cocky, in tone and uninformative in content, are likely to obscure what the judges must really decide and what analytical steps are needed to reach a sound decision—especially if the weakness in the argument has been glossed over in an effort to make the position seem stronger than it is. This is not only unhelpful to the court, but injurious to the advocate's own cause. It is far better to confront the issues coolly, honestly, and logically, guiding the reader lucidly down a path that leads to victory.

Tone matters too. In one highly publicized criminal case, appellate counsel did a masterful job of identifying the issues and mustering legal and factual support for his client's position. He did so, however, in a self-righteous tone, overstating accusations of prosecutorial misconduct, belittling the trial judge, and portraying his client as the victim of a person who, the jury had found, was herself the victim of the client's serious criminal conduct.

The Perils of Overstatement

The lawyer, who is prominently affiliated with an elite East Coast institution, should have been careful to adopt a respectful tone toward the Midwestern state judges he was addressing. We read the briefs before the case was argued. We concluded that, if the judges thought the issue otherwise close, human nature probably would make them *want* to rule against the defendant because of his lawyer's imperious tone. We are not mind readers, but we do know that the defendant lost on appeal by a 2–1 vote.

The brief of an appellee or respondent—the "bottomside" brief, in the jargon of appellate practice—has certain special features. The bottomside brief writer has the disadvantage of not being able to introduce the judges to the case and the issues; they will read the topside brief first. But there are advantages too. The party filing second has a target to shoot at: the appellant's brief. And, except in cases involving cross-appeals, the bottomside writer has prevailed below on all of the issues before the appellate court; that litigant has the advantages that flow from having already had one decisionmaker agree with its position. The bottomside party wins if the decision below was right on the merits *or* if the appellate issues were not preserved below.

The first item on the checklist of the writer of the bottomside brief should be to ask: Was each of the arguments now being raised on appeal properly preserved below? Were alleged instructional errors properly objected to? Were the grounds now advanced for overturning evidentiary rulings the same ones offered in timely objections at trial? In a related vein, is the legal theory urged on appeal the same one presented to the trial court and, if not, is there an advantage to be gained from the change?

Appellate rules usually give the bottomside brief writer the option of dispensing with several of the features required in the topside brief. There is rarely a need to repeat or correct the predictable recitations of the basis for jurisdiction and the nature of the rulings below. On the other hand, it is usually worthwhile in a bottomside brief to reformulate the questions presented and write a competing statement of the case.

Some appellees seem to feel compelled to go further and to tell the court at the outset that the other side has misstated the questions presented and tendered a slanted version of the facts. That can be a bad idea. The court often will know from reading your questions presented and your statement that you believe the other side's version is either inaccurate or incomplete; you waste space and possibly goodwill by adding another sentence with an accusatory tone. However, if you can demonstrate flat out distortion, and it concerns something important, do so.

The other major difference between a bottomside and a topside brief is that the writer of a bottomside brief already knows exactly what arguments are being made on behalf of reversal. It is therefore appropriate and—because the appellee gets no reply—necessary to take on those arguments. This does not mean, however, that the brief should consist simply of a point-by-point refutation of each of the appellant's arguments. The aim of a bottomside brief is not just to debate the other side. There also must be an affirmative and coherent statement of the reasons why the decision being appealed is correct.

Having prevailed below can also have its burdensome features. Sometimes, to put it bluntly, the decision below is bad. It may be difficult to defend in whole or in part. The topside brief will have mercilessly laid bare its central defects. The bottomside brief writer then must offer *other* ways to reach the same result. Occasionally, it may be wise to abandon the lower tribunal's reasoning and substitute a different and better rationale. In essence, the appellee ends up defending, not the opinion that was written, but the opinion that should have been written.

Most times, however, it is prudent to defend the lower court's approach and offer, in addition, either something explicitly called an "alternative" approach or an embellishment on the decision below. Of course, there are times when defending the rationale of the decision below will be the only way to secure an affirmance. In cases coming from administrative agencies, for example, the appellate court is not allowed to adopt a rationale that was not the basis of the agency's decision; similarly, a court reviewing a jury verdict may not affirm on a basis never presented to the jury.

A Better Rationale

The decision in *TXO Production Corp. v. Alliance Resources Corp.*, 509 U.S. 443 (1993), represents a triumph of the tactic of presenting a new and better rationale on appeal. The highest court of West Virginia had upheld an award of punitive damages that was many times the compensatory damages; the award was therefore greatly out of proportion to the actual harm suffered by the plaintiff. The state court had opined that the case implicated no federal constitutional limit on the size of the punitive damages on the dubious ground that the defendant had been "really mean." The Supreme Court's grant of certiorari suggested likely dissatisfaction with the West Virginia court's rationale.

Then respondent's counsel went to work, scouring the record and discovering a theory that, although it might have been barely hinted at before the jury, seemed more likely to persuade the nine justices in Washington: The *potential* gain to the defendant from its alleged misdeeds much more closely approximated the punitive damages award than the amount that the plaintiff *actually* lost. Because counsel advanced this theory in the bottomside brief (and argument) and showed to the satisfaction of the necessary number of Justices that it had been preserved below, the West Virginia court's judgment (but not its reasoning) was upheld.

Finally, what about reply briefs? They are optional, but it is the rare case—if any case at all—in which it makes sense to forgo the opportunity to file one. One of us once argued on behalf of the government a Supreme Court criminal case in which the petitioner simply did not bother to file a reply brief. The Court decided the case 5–4 in the government's favor, with the unusual coalition of Justices Brennan, Marshall, Scalia, and Kennedy dissenting. It would be easy to believe that the government's sterling written and oral advocacy assured the result no matter what the other side did, but one must wonder whether an effective reply might have swayed one of the justices who formed the tenuous majority. It is a mystery why counsel passed up the chance to have the last word in such a close case.

The reply brief must be (relatively) short, (relatively) punchy, and selective. Sometimes it will follow the same structure as the opening brief, but sometimes it will not. What it *must* do, to be effective, is identify from the start one or more overall themes in the argument or arguments with the best chance of winning and explain to the court where the appellee's brief, which it just read, went fundamentally astray.

The function of a reply brief is to respond to an adversary's arguments. The court can look back to your opening brief as a reminder of the overall structure of your argument and to answer nagging questions. It is therefore usually unnecessary to retrace all the steps of your logic in the reply brief, and it is far more acceptable in a reply than in an opening brief to concentrate on sharply focused (but polite) debate. Sometimes, however, your adversary may have confused things so much that re-emphasizing the structure of your arguments will be the most useful thing to do in reply.

If you must put a rhetorical flourish somewhere in your briefs—and sometimes that may be useful—the beginning or end of the reply brief is the place to put it. Rhetoric turns appellate judges off when they see it as a substitute for analysis. By the time they read your reply brief, however, the judges should know that you are prepared to analyze—and have analyzed—the issues fully. Having, in a way, paid your dues, you have more leeway for a catchy phrase or metaphor at the beginning of the reply brief. This may help dramatize the central defect in the adversary's brief, which the judge will have just read; such a phrase at the end of the reply brief may be the last word the judges read before they put down their papers.

Do not strive to write a pithy ending for its own sake, however. LITIGATION gives its authors and editors a style sheet that advises: "Formal conclusions are not worth the trouble. Start at the beginning, go to the end, then stop." The same goes for reply briefs.

Anatomy of the Written Argument

Gary L. Sasso

Brief writing has become the appellate advocate's most important skill. If trends continue, it will soon be the only skill that matters. Appeals today increasingly are decided on the briefs. In the Eleventh Circuit, nearly 50 percent of all cases are decided without oral argument. When oral argument *is* scheduled, particularly in federal courts, counsel often get just 15 minutes—enough time to stand up, clear your throat, answer a few questions, and sit down. Oral argument will be used to nail down points already developed in the briefs and to address the court's particular concerns. The basic case must be made—and will often be won—through the written briefs.

Although appellate judges rely heavily on briefs, they nevertheless have little time to devote to them before deciding the case. It may not be enough that a crucial point is made *somewhere* in your brief or that a key argument will gradually come into focus after repeated reading, careful analysis, and lengthy meditation on your scholarly discussion. Points must be apparent quickly. A brief that is ineffectively organized and analytically obscure—or one that is unnecessarily subtle and complex—may jeopardize an appeal that should be won.

Problems of this kind are common. They occur most often with the argument portion of the brief, the very section that must explain why the court should rule one way or the other. This happens because lawyers chronically assume that others—including judges—have the same understanding of an issue, or a whole case, that the participants have attained only after weeks or months of study. If you start out thinking that an appeals court knows, or even cares, as much about your case as you, you are already on the wrong track.

Gary L. Sasso is a partner with Carlton, Fields in Tampa, Florida, and is a former associate editor of LITIGATION.

The argument section of a brief must be organized and reasoned on a very different assumption. You must assume that the court neither knows about, nor is especially sympathetic to, your legal position. That may sometimes—rarely—be an inaccurate assumption, but if it is, it will do no harm.

Once you have the correct view of your judicial audience, you can take the first step in structuring the argument section of your brief: Make your affirmative case at the outset. Remember, the operative assumption is that panel members know *nothing* about your case. They will be lost or unconvinced if you start by refuting arguments made by the other party or adverse positions taken by the court below.

This is a common trap. Counsel for the appellant often begin and end their argument by attacking the lower court's rulings. Likewise, appellees typically devote their argument to refuting the appellant's contentions. The problem with that is that it does not show the court that you should win; it proves only that opposing counsel or the lower court may not have adequately explained why you should lose.

Appeals are not debates. They are not decided on the basis of who refuted the most points and subpoints. Appellate courts want to identify the right way to analyze the issues before them. But finding fault with arguments or picking at misstatements made by the other side or by the lower court is not the same as providing the correct solution to the legal issue on appeal. That—and not mere fault-finding—is what the appellate court wants.

The party that gives the court a cogent explanation of how the issues should be analyzed has a substantial advantage. Before you engage in fencing with your opponent or the court, you must provide an overall picture into which the fencing fits. This is because, in most appeals, there is more involved than who is right in the tripartite contest between the parties and the court. Appellate judges read the briefs for guidance on how an issue can sensibly be resolved, not only for the parties in the immediate case, but for others facing the same problem. Until the court is satisfied about this, it will be uncertain how to decide the case. It will read with impatience your naysaying about the failings of opposing counsel or the court below.

Setting forth your affirmative case may not require very much. If you have a simple case, all the better. The sooner the court understands this, the sooner it will be inclined to rule in your client's favor. But be careful: Just because *you* think your affirmative case is self-evident, do not assume the court will. You have a perspective, and a grounding in the case, that the court will not share. You must explain your view to the court.

Once you have explained to the court why your client deserves to prevail under applicable legal principles, then attack arguments to the contrary. Now you can do so from a position of strength. The court will have the benefit of the frame of reference you have provided as it considers arguments made by your opponent. It will more likely be receptive to your refutations and may think of others on its own. By helping the court do its job, you stand a better chance that it will make your position its own.

You may be tempted to disregard these principles in particular cases. You may be so troubled or offended by your opponent's outrageous arguments that you will feel a special need to meet them from the start. You may be aiming for some kind of dramatic effect. Resist these temptations. Do not engage the other side on its own turf until you have demonstrated to the court that you know your own. As for dramatic effect, appellate judges are, for the most part, unmoved by drama. They read briefs to gain information, not exhilaration or entertainment.

In constructing your affirmative case, be sure to start at the beginning—not the chronological beginning, but the logical beginning. Every argument has a predicate. You must identify it and establish it before moving on. This is a rule that is usually honored in the breach. Countless briefs just jump into the middle of a legal analysis. They start arguing a point of view before laying the groundwork. Such a brief will do little to persuade someone who does not subscribe to that point of view from the start.

Your objective in constructing an affirmative case should be to start with a proposition that the court—whatever its bent—*must* accept; then reason logically, step by step, to your conclusion. If you do this well, you will arrive at your destination with the court right beside you. Your conclusion will make sense, not just because you say so, but because the court will have reasoned along with you. In a way, the technique is one familiar to cross-examiners. You nibble toward your destination with a series of points or questions that can only be answered yes. The main constraint on this approach is the page limit on your brief and the realization that judges do not have all day to read.

But what exactly *is* the "predicate" of a legal argument? For some arguments, it comes from statutory or constitutional language. (This is obviously more true of statutory issues; constitutional disputes often depend as much on decades of judicial gloss as on the bare language of constitutional provisions.) You are almost always on safe ground starting with statutory language. However hostile the court may be, it simply *must* accept that a statute says what it says. This first step may include discussion of an entire statutory scheme, selected components of the scheme, the narrow provision at issue, or all of these.

After laying the predicate of statutory language, begin to argue your case by emphasizing, grouping, or excerpting the language that makes your point. At this stage, relying still on the statutory language, you try to show what the legislature meant to achieve.

Identifying the aims of legislation is a vital part of any argument based on a statute. Statutory language is notoriously ambiguous. Clever lawyers can single out, juxtapose, or just outright construe statutory terms to reach, within reasonable limits, any number of results. Courts understand how this is done. What makes one construction more persuasive than another is its harmony with legislative aims. Every statute, and each of its provisions, is enacted to serve a purpose. You must identify that purpose, and whenever possible demonstrate that it will be served best by the construction you propose. If you do that, then your construction of the law will be more than just a demonstration of your facility with the English language.

The next step in a statutory argument is developing support, if you can, from the legislative history for your construction of the statutory language and your interpretation of the legislature's objectives. If the statute is implemented by a regulatory agency, buttress your construction by interpretations or applications of the statute by the agency.

All of this may seem elementary, and it is. But it is basic knowledge apparently forgotten in brief after brief. The fact is that there are simple, sensible ways to put together most arguments. Though you ignore them at your peril, they are neglected every day.

Of course all rules—even ones as basic as these—have exceptions. You must be adaptable. Occasionally, for example, judicial decisions may supply the best predicate for a statutory argument. This may happen if the statutory language seems unfavorable to you but has been given a helpful (for you) judicial construction. It may also occur when a truly controlling decision has established a vital part of what you must show. The holdings of these cases will constitute the predicate of your argument—they will be a starting point that the appellate court must accept. When relying on case law in such circumstances, however, you must explain the basis for the courts' conclusions in order to satisfy the reader that you have properly represented the cases.

If the appeal involves common law questions, then your predicate will be the common law principle that you seek to apply. This will be taken, of course, from judicial decisions. To establish that the principle can properly be applied on your client's behalf, you must develop the rationale of that principle and show that it will be satisfied by a ruling in your favor.

Such a matching of policy to the case is critical, but it is often omitted. Appellate judges want to know why. They will not be satisfied if you simply state a precept, cite some cases, and say you win.

The reason for this insistent inquisition is easy to explain: Courts want to know *why* you should win. We all know that decisions can be found to support virtually any result. Appellate briefs typically recount— and often just pile up—the cases that support the results urged by the respective parties. Often such briefs fail to give the appellate court a clue why it should follow one line of cases rather than another. The decisive factor will often be the policy behind the principle. In fact, that policy may well provide the basis for reconciling seemingly conflicting cases. It is therefore vital to identify and establish the policy behind the rule. Without doing this, you cannot show that the application you advocate makes the most sense.

Occasionally, you may have the opportunity (or misfortune) to argue an issue of "first impression"—supposedly an issue that has never been directly and authoritatively addressed. In such matters, having a proper predicate is especially important. The truth is that no issues are truly novel. Ironically, the more "novel" an issue may seem, the more basic and familiar will be the predicates for its resolution. Any issue reduces ultimately to a few basic principles that have found expression somewhere in the law—things such as the integrity of the family or the inviolability of freely negotiated contracts. Such basic precepts—firmly and indisputably established—are the predicates you must use when briefing an issue of "first impression." Your job is to make the novel proposition seem familiar or, at most, a natural extension of something that is.

By starting with your affirmative case and clearly establishing the predicates for your argument, you will necessarily have developed a structure—an organization with a point of view—for your brief. If you rely on judicial authority, you must fit the cases into that structure; do not permit them to dictate it. Judicial decisions are useful, normally indispensable, tools; there must be authority for what you argue legally. But appellate briefs that merely collect cases and regurgitate their holdings provide little assistance to the court, and—even worse—squander an invaluable opportunity to persuade.

Appellate opinions are rarely written like briefs. They are never written with your case in mind. You cannot just cite them or quote them. Because they are often hastily written, many opinions are cryptic, incompletely reasoned, or logically unsatisfying. Some have gaps in research. And, apart from those fresh off the press, they are written without the benefit of all the authority that may be at your disposal. Your brief must do more than merely catalog and digest this imperfect material.

The best briefs, the most persuasive ones—the briefs that assist the court the most—are those that fit cases into a logical, cogent analysis of the issue on appeal. Such an analysis will emerge only *after* you have read the case law, but it will rarely be found in any given opinion.

At times, you may be able to develop your analysis from one or two decisions. Usually, however, just summarizing those opinions will not be enough. You must adapt the analysis in the decisions to the particular issue in your case. Consider how the reasoning of those decisions might be tightened by organizing the discussion differently, or by giving greater emphasis to certain points. Then, by quoting selectively from those decisions, restructure them in your brief to gain the maximum effect from them. Be sure, however, to do so fairly. Although you enjoy considerable license as an advocate in making an argument, if you compromise your own credibility, you will severely compromise your client's case.

Often you will not have one or two key cases that do the job. You may have to canvass a wide range of authority—bits, pieces, and snippets of the law that may seem in disarray. In that case, do this: Read the cases and other authorities and then put them aside. Ask yourself what, in general, was the key concern of the courts that ruled in your direction and, on the other hand, what troubled the courts that leaned the other way. Do not get bogged down in details; distill the main themes. Then scrutinize the facts of your case. Study the issue in your case as though *you* had to decide it. Only then will you perceive how the law may be explained, sensibly and concisely.

Do this by structuring your discussion of the case law according to how you—and not necessarily a given opinion or two—conclude that the legal issue must be analyzed. Your analysis will be informed by what the cases say or hold, and will draw support from them. Whenever possible, such an analysis should be constructed largely from well-chosen but short quotes from the decisions. Throughout, remember that your analysis, and the passages you quote, must be organized to address directly the issue in your case and to guide the court on how to resolve it. Your analysis must provide the court with a framework for reading other cases, a hypothesis that other cases will prove.

Finally, although you must fully explain the analysis you develop, do not make the court trudge through every dreary yard of your thought process. Briefs should not read like law review articles or meandering essays. Your discussion must move from point to point, logically and effortlessly, as though prescribed by natural law. It must sound authoritative, not exploratory or exotic. Although your brief may not mimic the judicial opinions that buttress your argument, your analysis must have sufficient authenticity as a statement of the law so that the appellate court can adopt it as its own opinion. Your objective, after all, is to *show* the court how it can rule in your client's behalf.

Strategy of the Brief

Girvan Peck

A brief should be designed and written so that it will, by itself and without the aid of oral argument, persuade the judges and clerks for whom it is written. Since the brief constitutes the only complete argument the advocate will make to the court, the writer cannot afford to draft it merely as a source of information, like a reference work or a law review article, and then rely on the oral argument to carry the burden of the persuasion. The brief itself should do the job.

How, in general, does the brief writer approach the task of persuasion? More than 2,000 years ago, Aristotle identified the three major elements of rhetoric, or persuasion, as follows:

Ethos, the element in which the speaker establishes his own character and credentials, and hence his believability;

Pathos, the element in which the speaker appeals to his listeners' emotions, so that they are disposed to decide in his favor;

Logos, the final element, in which the speaker provides the logical reasons why his side of the issue should prevail.

All three elements should be abundantly established in a brief.

The writer of a brief establishes character and credentials, or the element of *ethos*, primarily by being accurate and honest in what is said. He or she builds confidence on the part of the judges by making each statement trustworthy. The writer remembers that the case need not be perfect, but only better than the opponent's, and accordingly does not risk forfeiting the trust of the judges with exaggerations or evasions at any point.

The brief writer establishes the second requisite element, *pathos*, by painting a sympathetic picture of the client and the client's cause.

Girvan Peck, now deceased, was a solo practitioner in San Francisco. This chapter was adapted from Writing Persuasive Briefs, *published by Little, Brown & Co. in 1984 shortly after Mr. Peck's death.*

Throughout the brief, by a statement of facts and by the approach to the argument, he or she demonstrates to the court the individual equities and the overall policies of the law that favor the position. The aim is to induce the judges to want to decide for his or her client if there is any legally justifiable way to do so.

Lastly, the brief writer supplies the judges and their clerks with the element of *logos*—the most logical and precedential reasons to support a favorable decision. Collectively, these appear as the argument of the brief. Together they furnish the raw materials for an opinion, if one is called for, or in any case the reasoned basis for a decision. These remain the essential elements in the art of persuasion.

Persuasion is and remains an art, and lawyers may differ on its finer points. But judges and most effective advocates will agree on the fundamentals, which are much as the teachings of the ancients described them.

Persuasion begins with sensitivity. The writer or speaker seeks to understand the audience: who they are, what they want, what they need. If this can be done, the next step is to shape a convincing brief. But if the audience is not understood, the lawyer is communicating in a vacuum.

Advocates may differ from automobile salesmen, but they can learn from them. The good salesman has no doubt about the first step. When a potential customer walks in, the salesman approaches, introduces himself or herself, and immediately starts to size up the prospect. He or she notes at once how the customer dresses and talks, and whether the customer is looking at the engine or the upholstery or the price sticker. A word here, a question there, and the salesman has a profile. A few more words, a few more questions, and the salesman can guess what the customer really wants and what he or she actually will buy. The salesman's antennae are sensitive because a livelihood depends on keeping them so.

A persuasive advocate will be no less sensitive. The advocate will find out all about the individual judges who will decide the case: what decisions they have made before on similar issues; what they may have written in opinions or public statements; what has been their education, prior professional experience, their religious and political affiliations, their hobbies and interests; what other lawyers who know them have to say about them. This information he or she will bear in mind when writing the brief. It may not affect the logical progression of the argument, but it may influence what is highlighted or emphasized. Certainly it will shape the ultimate decision on how to appeal to the court's sense of equity and justice. The court, after all, consists of individuals. If the advocate is to persuade them, he or she must persuade them as individuals.

In considering the audience, the advocate will be careful not to ignore the clerks or staff lawyers on whose labors the judges to a growing extent rely. Some, like the clerks permitted to each justice of the Supreme Court of the United States, are largely young and bright; others, like those allotted to each federal circuit judge, or assigned to each federal district judge, or the ones assigned to state court appellate judges, may be permanent staff members, and may or may not be as intellectually distinguished. Some clerks have strong political persuasions to left or right, which may or may not be the same as those of the judges themselves; some have a marked desire to change the law in one direction or another, which may not be shared at all by the judge they assist. Their predilections may be difficult or impossible to discover, as compared to the judges' own, but reasonable assumptions may be made, and they may affect the tone and content of the brief. It may, for example, be a safe assumption that a young law school graduate will be less concerned with precedent than the judge to whom the memorandum is sent; if so, an ingenious but novel argument may be justified. Then again, when the issue in a case is between subordinates and their supervisors, the clerk may relate to one, where the judge will more readily identify with the other; if so, the brief should be careful not to offend the sensibilities of either.

Whatever the advocate can guess about the readers individually, the characteristics of the judges as a group should be known. They share a specialized vocation, and therefore have much in common.

Dealing with Judges

Judges are professional buyers of ideas. They are professionally skeptical, because they listen to salesmen every day. Nevertheless, they will pay attention to a good presentation, not only because they are required to make a decision one way or another, but also because they depend on the advocates of both sides for essential facts and ideas. They are proud of their high calling, but they also have great respect for the other members of the bar. They never stop hoping that each advocate who appears before them will merit their respect and earn their admiration.

Judges wield great power in individual cases, but their powers, nevertheless, are sharply limited. Accordingly, judges urge lawyers to recognize both their powers and the limits of those powers. A trial judge will be impatient if an advocate fails to focus on the authorities from higher courts in his or her jurisdiction, for there is no choice but to obey them. Appellate judges wearily reject the advocate's attempt to retry a case merely because it was lost below, for they have no power to do so. At the same time, judges sitting on courts of last resort are particularly sensitive to the broad impact of any opinion they may write. Accordingly, they invite the advocate to address not merely his or her own case but also the merits of the rule of law they are asked to affirm or modify.

When the brief writer has thought through what is known about the judges on the court, and found out about them individually, and what can be safely assumed about their clerks or staff lawyers, he or she will have a good sense of what must be done to persuade the readership.

The advocate may never have met them or seen them, but he or she will still be acquainted with how they think and what facts and authorities and arguments will be most convincing. With this in mind an approach can be planned. It may or may not persuade them, but at least it will be in their language.

The goal of the judge is not merely to reach a decision supported by a rule of law, but to dispense justice to the parties. Accordingly, the judge will be uncomfortable with an argument based on precedent alone, unless it is clear where the equities lie. Often the judge is not required to follow the precedents cited in such an argument; there are overlapping rules of law and conflicting precedents that could also serve as the basis for decision.

Accordingly, a judge searches for those rules that will do justice and equity. Here, too, he or she looks to counsel for guidance. The judge can read the authorities, but wants the advocate, with a fuller understanding of the parties and their dispute, to tell him or her which options will bring about a just result.

The judge's clerk or staff lawyer who first reads the briefs and then writes a memorandum to the judge may also be expected to care about the apparent equities. Perhaps it cannot be safely said that the clerk is more concerned with individual justice and less concerned with the structure of the law than the judge who must live with the decision, but at least there is no reason to believe the opposite. The clerk will learn the equities with interest, and presumably they will affect the memoranda prepared.

If the just and equitable result is disclosed to the judge and his staff through the process of briefing and oral argument, they will try to find a way to reach that result. As Judge Gurfein of the Second Circuit has written:

> It is still the mystery of the appellate process that a result is reached in an opinion on thoroughly logical and precedential grounds while it was first approached as the right and fair thing to do.

The key word here is "first." The judges and their staffs will first form an impression of where the equities are from scanning the briefs. Analysis of the authorities and the hearing of the oral argument follow later, and still later the opinion is written, all against the background of the judges' and clerks' first impressions of the case. Under these circumstances it is not entirely surprising or mysterious that judges will so often find logical and precedential grounds to reach the result that they have already decided is "the right and fair thing to do."

Argue the Equities

For the advocate the lesson is unmistakable. Since judges will normally read or scan the briefs first, then hear oral argument, and then analyze the issues and decide, the brief writer has an invaluable opportunity. In the brief itself, and right from the beginning of it, the writer should give the judges and their clerks the impression that the client's position is just and fair. From then on the brief and oral argument need only show the way to rationalize the result they already desire to reach. If done successfully, the opponent's arguments will bear the incomparably greater burden of showing the judges and their staffs that there is no acceptable way for them to reach the result they want.

The question, then, is not whether the brief writer should point out the justice in his client's position, but how. What will appeal to the judges as "right and fair," and when and how can such equitable considerations be effectively expressed?

In part, the circumstances that appeal to judges and their clerks are those that would appeal to anyone. The advocate depicts the client as a sympathetic individual, or a responsible and forward-looking company, or an even-handed agency of the government. The advocate's client's opponent, unfortunately, lacks these characteristics, as the evidence all too clearly shows. The dispute itself is one-sided. For the plaintiff, a great wrong has been committed, which cries out for redress, while for the defendant there is no wrong, and it is regrettable that the court's time and energy should be lavished on such a storm in a teacup.

Such, simplistically stated, are the equities for the individual parties, but the advocate also must be concerned with the effects of the decision on nonparties. Appellate judges, and particularly judges in courts of last resort, are acutely aware that hard cases can make bad law. The precedents they set, thinking to do justice in one case, may come back to haunt them in a series of others. Accordingly, they must consider the equities as applied to the categories and classes of parties affected. They must adopt rules of law they can live with. As Chief Justice Vanderbilt of New Jersey wrote:

> Counsel should hesitate to rest his case on mere technicalities, however strongly they may be embedded in earlier decisions. He should never feel safe unless he can and does demonstrate the reasonableness and utility of the rule he is advocating.

To put it another way, the advocate must deal with the policy of the law, and the social policies that the law affects, whenever he or she appeals to judges who have the power to influence these policies.

The experienced advocate starts to evaluate the equities of the case from the moment he or she is retained, because they will shape his or her strategy. At the same time, the advocate starts to persuade himself or herself of the justice of the client's position, because it must be expressed at every turn. This is not to say that in the advocate's heart of hearts he or she is totally convinced that the client should win. The advocate is not the judge. But, like any good salesman, the advocate knows each appealing feature of the case and each weakness of the opponent's case, and will be wholly convinced that these features deserve the consideration of the court.

When it comes to writing a brief, the advocate uses the appealing features of the case as an equitable setting for argument. He or she does not so much push them to the forefront as allow them to show through. All that is needed is some legitimate reason to refer to them or suggest them. Accordingly, whenever the equities have some bearing on the issues before the court—directly or as relevant background that could influence the decision—the advocate will permit them to shape the argument, statement of facts, and choice of words, so that the judges will glimpse the point of view. The advocate is convinced that they should understand what is right and fair from the client's perspective.

As an illustration of the advocate's way of thinking about a case, let us imagine that the brief writer is concerned with a motion to suppress in a robbery case.

For the prosecution, the motion is one of those regrettable (though perhaps inevitable) impediments to the cause of justice. The defendant is clearly guilty of the crime charged, and a conviction is a foregone conclusion if the motion is defeated. In this instance, the police officers had reason to suspect what the search might discover and, once it was made, their suspicions were amply justified. Accordingly, the brief for the prosecution stresses the facts showing guilt and measures the reasonableness of the search by the salutary results achieved.

For the defense, the underlying considerations are wholly different. What is at stake is a constitutional principle far transcending in importance the outcome of any one criminal case. It is not the defendant's guilt or innocence but the conduct of the police that the motion puts in issue. Accordingly, the defense brief stresses the intent of the policemen when they made the challenged search, and any arbitrary or outrageous incidents of the search. The brief seeks to isolate the search itself from irrelevant issues of guilt or innocence, which will never be reached if the motion is granted.

As a different illustration of the advocate's technique, let us suppose an antitrust case. A merchant opens a discount store but major suppliers refuse to sell to the store, whereupon the merchant sues for treble damages. The issues on the merits are whether the manufacturers and distributors have conspired to fix prices and effect a boycott, and whether the discounter has been damaged as a result. The equities, however, are broader.

For the plaintiff and his lawyer, the merchant is a small businessman trying to compete in a world of giants. The merchant tries to retail goods at low prices for the benefit of the public; the suppliers try to stop the merchant to keep their prices high. The inference of conspiracy is obvious, because the suppliers would surely want the benefit of the high volume. The inference of damage is clear, because the merchant has been forced to do without the prestige merchandise wanted. The policy of the antitrust laws must now be vindicated. Big companies must be taught that they cannot use their combined power to stop the discount store.

The mind-set of the defense lawyers is diametrically opposite. Their clients sell quality merchandise bearing famous brand names, and accordingly want their goods showcased through major stores, which provide trained salespeople and full services. Each defendant has reached the separate business judgment that a discount store would be undesirable for its business purposes, and each has a right to make that choice independently. The defendants' freedom to trade as they wish is to be protected. That freedom should not be infringed by the unreasonable demands of the discounter. The antitrust laws were not intended to confer on discount stores any special privilege to force unwilling suppliers to sell to them, and they should not now be so construed.

Each side thus develops a set of equitable considerations to give a different emphasis and color to the evidentiary facts. Neither side is misstating, but each is looking at the case itself from a wholly different point of reference. Each has a different perspective to offer to the court.

Once adopted by the parties, such equitable considerations will appear again and again in the briefs. In motions on the merits in the trial court—for preliminary injunction, summary judgment, judgment notwithstanding the verdict—the briefs will touch on or at least suggest the equities. Again, they will appear in briefs on appeal dealing with the merits, as when the issue concerns the sufficiency of the evidence, the adequacy of key instructions, or the correctness of major evidentiary rulings.

At each of these points the advocate's brief will project an equitable setting for the case. The advocate may or may not set aside a separate section to argue it, for it may not be directly relevant, but he or she will make sure that the court sees the case the way he or she sees it. The advocate will ask the judges to adopt, for the moment, the partisan viewpoint of the client, confident in the knowledge that the adversary will do likewise, and that only in this way can the court truly understand the bedrock issues, and the fundamental impact of the decision it is asked to make.

When judges read a brief, they do not need to be told that a dispute is in progress, or that each party is outraged with the position of the other, or that counsel may have developed personal quarrels of their own in the course of the litigation. All of this they have seen all too often. What the judges need is a reliable basis for a decision. They are grateful to the advocate who provides them one, and who declines to feud with an opponent or to snipe at judges who have ruled against him or her.

The seasoned advocate accordingly reins in any emotions, so that he or she can concentrate on the factual, legal, and equitable issues. The advocate knows that an argument in court is not an occasion for anger, like a squabble among bad-tempered relatives. The advocate recognizes that this is not a debate, where points are gained for clever dialectics. The purpose is to show the judges that the advocate's side of the question before the court is the meritorious side. If that is done, the advocate wins.

Understanding the rules of the game, the advocate will recognize that it is bad tactics to downgrade the adversary. It is not the lawyers' arguments that are on trial, but the issues. If the adversary is belittled by the advocate, it suggests that the opposing argument was poorly made, and could have been much stronger. But if the adversary's skills are praised, it suggests that the opposing argument is as strong as it can be: The weakness is not in the argument, but in the case.

At the same time, the advocate will be convinced, as a good salesman is, that he or she has something important and valuable to sell. The adversary may be respected, but unfortunately the product is less desirable, for a series of reasons that are stressed in a point-by-point comparison. The judges are sophisticated buyers who need only to be alerted to the merits of the product for sale; happily, it offers them exactly what they need, and their decision should be simple.

Such attitudes make for effective advocacy. There are others, however, that create unpersuasive briefs. Some of them are all too common.

Some brief writers fail to recognize that judges have the power to make decisions and advocates do not. The brief writer may be learned and may know the case, but if he or she lectures the judges, they will resent it. If judges are told they "must" reach a certain decision or conclusion, or that they "cannot" reach another, they might well regard the lawyer's imperative as a challenge to do otherwise. They will accept the commands of legislatures and higher courts, but they are not prepared to obey the directives of counsel. The function of advocates is to advocate. The function of the judges is to decide.

Some brief writers are unwise enough to disparage the trial judge, or judges of other courts. They should remind themselves that the judges they are writing for will not throw stones at their brother judges, and they are not likely to appreciate advocates doing so. If the brief writer will imagine speaking directly to the court, which has decided against the client or position, and then phrase any comments accordingly, he or she will instinctively avoid the contemptuous or disrespectful or sarcastic epithet.

A writer will not refer to an adverse decision as "outrageous" or "pernicious" or "irrational." Instead, a respectful alternative will be found: The court has been "misled" or "led astray" by counsel's argument; it has "failed to appreciate" or has "apparently overlooked" the key facts or the pertinent cases; it has acted under a "mistaken impression" of the evidence or an "outmoded view" of the law; therefore its decision is "out of harmony" with controlling precedent and is, unfortunately, "unsound," "incorrect," "in error," or "erroneous." With phrases like this what needs to be said is said with courtesy.

Accusations of impropriety directed at opposing counsel are less of an affront to the court, but judges grow weary of them. They are normally irrelevant to the issues and, therefore, a waste of the court's time. If they are bitter, they are also unpleasant, as the spectacle of cats fighting in a back alley is unpleasant. Even though they are not so extreme that they violate court rules or rules of ethics, they leave a bad taste in the mouth.

Just as an experienced cross-examiner will approach an attractive witness with courtesy, taking care not to alienate the jury, so will the brief writer approach the opponent's argument. For all anyone knows, the judges or their clerks may find it appealing. Accordingly, the writer will at first describe it in terms that merely imply its weakness: The opponent "attempts" or "suggests" an argument, "advances" or "urges" or "insists upon" a position. There is no suggestion of bad faith; the advocate avoids adjectives like "absurd" or "ridiculous" or "nonsensical."

Next, point out that the adversary has been "unable" to find facts or law to support the argument, and accordingly "must rely" on inapposite authorities. The implication is that the adversary is doing the best possible but no such authorities exist.

Meanwhile, the brief writer continues that the opponent "seeks to avoid" or is "forced to ignore" the authorities against him or her; the opponent cannot, however, do so successfully, for they are so clearly pertinent. As a result the opponent's argument, while "apparently logical" and "superficially appealing," must fail, for it is "without support" and "fatally flawed" and, in fact, "untenable." Throughout such a passage the opposing counsel is accorded respect as an able and worthy advocate. It cannot be helped if the cards are so heavily stacked against him or her.

Even when opposing counsel is flagrantly inaccurate or misleading, the brief writer will do well to let the facts speak the loudest. Epithets like "deliberately false" or "concealed from the court" are fighting words that ruffle not only the opponent's feathers, but also the court's. They call for proof of intent, which may be hard to find, and which may not be worth the effort. The advocate will usually disrupt the argument less, and be more persuasive, if he or she understates the conclusion by writing that the opponent has "misconstrued" or "neglected" or "no doubt overlooked" some obvious fact or case, while citing chapter and verse to the court. The judges will draw their own conclusions without difficulty.

If the advocate avoids wrangling with the opponent, he or she will earn the respect of the judges. At the same time, they will keep focused on the issues, so that the advocate can proceed with persuasion.

The brief writer must expect that this product will be tested by experts. The opponent will seek to find each flaw or crack, each chink in the armor, and then try to pull the argument apart. The judge who reads the brief will do much the same, but for a different purpose. The judge will want to know if the brief presents a reliable basis for decision. The judge and the clerk will test it section by section against the opponent's brief—first the issues presented, then the statement of facts, then the argument itself—to see which side has the better of each issue.

Knowing that the brief must withstand multiple attacks, the author will try to make it impregnable, by asserting only what can be supported or proven, unless the proposition is so obvious it needs no support. If the author makes an assertion of fact, cites to the relevant evidence and perhaps quotes from it will be included; if he or she states a proposition of law, cites or summaries or quotes from a pertinent authority will be listed. Step by step and point by point, the brief writer will nail down each plank of the argument.

When writing, the advocate will be careful never to overstate, or to claim more than can be proven, or the opponent will pounce upon the reply. Instead, a conclusion will be expressed conservatively, and often with deliberate understatement, so that the judge will be wholly convinced of it as far as it goes. As one carefully documented assertion succeeds another, the advocate will build an impression of reliability, which in time will take on a cumulative force of its own. That is to say, the judge will begin to trust the author.

The reverse, of course, is the exaggeration, the careless or perhaps deliberate overstatement. Judges have repeatedly warned in their writings that they are no fools, and that they are experienced in sniffing out the sham argument or overblown statement of fact. They know what is mere implication or inference. They know the difference between a dictum and a holding. They resent overstatements when they find them, and when they do they cannot help but mistrust the brief as a whole.

The real danger for the brief writer is not that he or she will deliberately exaggerate, but that the advocate's zeal gets the better of him or her. The writer may distort the truth as a child does, saying not what is verifiably true but what it wished were true, and therefore imagined to be true. Anything to the contrary is simply blotted from the mind.

The brief writer's safeguard against these temptations is to read and reread each assertion skeptically, as the judges and the opponent certainly will. The advocate must test each statement with the questions a judge would ask: Where is the evidence for this? Is this proved? Does the case really stand for that proposition? Does this necessarily follow?

If the answers are not clear and positive, the assertions must be scaled down until they conform to the supporting facts or authorities. When this is done, frequently the limited version is not weaker but stronger. It still says all that needs to be said, but now it is beyond attack. For example, the brief writer may find on reading a draft that the following sentence is written:

> On September 13, Oppenheimer advised O'Reilly that the shipment would be delivered not later than the end of the month.

Unfortunately, as is now realized, the evidence at trial is not clear enough to justify this flat statement. What the evidence shows is a reasonable and probable inference that Oppenheimer so advised O'Reilly. Very well, the writer decides, let the facts speak for themselves. Accordingly, the revision is as follows:

> On September 13, according to O'Reilly, Oppenheimer advised him that the shipment would be delivered "in about two weeks"; O'Reilly therefore marked it on his calendar as probable by the end of the month (Tr. 572). Oppenheimer testified he could not recall any such telephone call (Tr. 849). He conceded, however, that the schedules of his own production and shipping departments (Exs. 143, 144), were, as he put it, "compatible with such a delivery date" (Tr. 894) and that O'Reilly was calling him about the shipment "almost daily" (Tr. 863). Thus the inference is fully justified that Oppenheimer did assure O'Reilly the shipment would arrive about the end of September, and not six weeks later.

This revised statement conforms to the evidence. It is not vulnerable to attack, and it may be stronger in its impact than the original.

Let us now suppose a different case, where, during revising and editing, the advocate has written the following sentence:

> None of respondent's cases holds that such a determination by the agency is beyond review in this court.

On reexamining the opponent's cases, however, the brief writer finds that one of them does include a statement to that effect, although it is only dictum, and the facts of the case are distinguishable. On reconsideration the advocate rewrites the assertion as follows:

> Respondent has cited only one case in which a court has stated that such a determination was beyond the review of the courts, but the facts were very different and the statement was dictum. Apart from this case there is no authority to support respondent's position.

The strength of the revised version is that the writer has now dealt with the adverse dictum rather than seeming to avoid it. Now the assertion cannot be attacked as overbroad, because it has been hand-tailored to fit the authorities themselves.

Throughout, the brief writer will do well to keep in mind that the case need not be perfect, but only better than the opponent's. Inevitably, there will be some contrary evidence or case authority. The skilled advocate will seek to overbalance the contrary evidence, or show why it is unimportant, but will not misstate it; he or she will try to distinguish the contrary cases, but will not fail to discuss them. The advocate knows that if unsupportable factual summaries or untenable legal conclusions are asserted, the trust he or she is trying to build is jeopardized and there goes the persuasiveness of the whole argument. A brief writer would far rather concede a point than risk the integrity of the position as a whole.

If the brief writer is to be persuasive, there is no choice but to be selective. At hand is a mass of detailed fact and an almost infinite body of law, but the judges cannot be expected to consider more than a fraction of it. The advocate must choose what is important and discard the rest.

The judges themselves urge this to be done. As Justice Tate of the Louisiana Supreme Court wrote:

> From the mass of materials available [the advocate] should repeatedly select and discard—*select* essential issues, facts and authors; *discard* and winnow others ruthlessly, along with excess words and repetitious argument.

Even if the judges had more time to read briefs than they do, the able brief writer would use only the best of the raw materials and discard the remainder. Selectivity is the first principle. A brief writer highlights the essence of the testimony and the exhibits and picks out the definitive decisions and clearest and most memorable passages from judicial opinions. What is secondary or repetitious or cumulative is excluded because it will only detract from the force of the presentation.

The principle is clear enough, but applying it is more difficult. How does the advocate go about making this choice? There are no hard and fast answers, for it all depends upon the individual case, but there are at least a few questions that may be helpful in testing the value of available points and authorities.

Padded Propositions

One question the brief writer may keep in mind is whether any part of the presentation is so obvious that it need not be stated at all. Many briefs are padded with propositions of law so simple, assertions of fact so apparent, that no one would question them, and yet there they are, complete with accompanying citations to authorities or to the record, as if they needed to be proved in the first place. These should be deleted, or at most merely mentioned in passing. The way for the writer to test them is to take them out, and then see if anything of substance is lost. Relevance is not the test, but utility: Does the obvious statement add anything to the argument?

Another useful question is whether any part of the writer's brief is unnecessarily repetitive or cumulative. Again, relevance is not the test.

Added value, or utility, is. The writer, let us say, has five sound and relevant cases to support a point of law. The question is: Why use more than one? If the writer asks the question whenever tempted to use string citations, usually a better alternative will be chosen:

1. Use one case, which is complete, up to date, and authoritative;
2. Use an older but leading case, together with a recent holding to bring it up to date;
3. Use a leading case, together with another very close on its facts;
4. Use a leading case, together with another for its apt and telling quotation. Only when the repetition is itself significant will an advocate use the whole group, as, for example, where a single principle has been applied to a variety of comparable fact patterns. If so, the brief writer should show the significance of such applications with parenthetical phrases after each case, which will flag for the judge the reason each decision is independently significant.

Perhaps the writer has available the testimony of three witnesses and passages from two exhibits, all of which tend to prove the same fact. How much should be quoted, how much should be paraphrased, how much should be cited? Here, as in choosing legal authorities, the advocate should weigh the persuasive value of each source, and then, having picked the best, ask if any further source would add anything. The advocate may decide to quote the witness whose phraseology is sharp and clear, and merely note that the others testified to the same effect, with citations to the record.

On the other hand, it may be decided that a contemporaneous memorandum is the most convincing, and that the later testimony of witnesses can be attacked as self-serving; if so, even a reference to the testimony may be omitted. If one of the witnesses is an adverse party, and therefore that witness's testimony is an admission or concession, the writer may weigh it most heavily of all and perhaps briefly describe the rest and then, as a climax, triumphantly quote the adversary.

Whenever a quotation is used, it is especially important to be concise. The writer should be sharply selective, but at the same time scrupulously fair. Quotations are often too long. The writer may insert an entire paragraph when the essence of it appears in a single sentence or perhaps even a phrase or a word. Words should not be taken out of context, and sometimes the full quotation is necessary to convince the reader. But whenever possible, the writer will pare the quote down to what makes it distinctive and important. He or she will also try not to repeat, as by stating the substance of the quotation in a paraphrase and then adding the quote itself. This may be redundant. It may be more forceful to omit the paraphrase and to allow the quotation itself to state the thought.

The main point is that in brief writing, as in any art, the author makes a point most tellingly with quality, not quantity. In this sense, less is more. A brief that contains nothing but directly relevant points, and nothing but apt authorities and pat quotations, can hold the judge's attention from beginning to end. If so, it has the best chance to persuade.

A persuasive brief, in a word, is one that is sensitive to its reader's characteristics, needs, and limitations. Its author has realized that his or her job is not to lecture the court, or to engage in a battle of dialectics, but to appeal to a human judge.

If a brief is to be appealing, it must deal not only with the precise application of authority to fact, but also with the reasons why a line of authority may soundly be applied. It must concern itself not only with the narrowly relevant, but with those broader considerations that bear upon ultimate justice in the present case and similar cases.

If a brief is to be trustworthy, it must be accurate and reliable throughout, not only for what it states, but for its completeness. It must meet the important facts and authorities cited by the opposition. From time to time it must make concessions, for the advocate's case is not perfect and need not be.

If a brief is to be emphatic, it must set forth the predigested essence of the facts, the equities, and the law and logic of the case, not only to save the judge's time and energy, but also to stress what is important. It must be selective and succinct, or the essentials will be lost.

If a brief is to be persuasive, it must offer, in the end, a course of action the judge can follow with confidence. The judge must be able to rest with it, satisfied in the main with its result. It may not be perfect, for nothing is perfect, but the judge must believe that it is, in essence, the soundest of the alternatives available to him or her.

Building a Brief

John E. Nelson III

The how-to literature on appellate advocacy stresses and repeats common themes: Know the record, do thorough research, proofread carefully. Such admonitions should be heeded, but they leave much to be desired as practical guides to action. At what point does the record move from unknown to known? What is *thorough* legal research? Experience will teach a lawyer how to measure performance against these standards, but learning by experience alone can be painful. Some of that pain can be avoided by following a few unfamiliar guides to efficient, persuasive, and intellectually honest brief writing.

This article offers eight such maxims. If they are observed, lawyers should be able to spend less time pursuing unprofitable research leads, sitting listlessly over a draft brief, or discovering, too near a filing deadline, ideas that would have supplied force and coherence.

1. *Get something done.* This is not an exhortation to work hard; diligent effort is a given. Instead, it is an invitation to work smart.

Writing an appellate brief involves three basic steps: (1) analysis of the record; (2) discovery and application of the law; and (3) written explication of the desired result. Neither memorizing every minute detail in the case, nor exhaustively accumulating citations and cases—nor the two together—guarantees a successful brief. Brief writing demands a balanced approach to all three tasks.

Begin with a medium-depth analysis of the record. This will lay a foundation for intelligent research—for research focused on the issues most likely to decide the case. Such focus is critical, because, in doing legal research, you must be disciplined. For those familiar and comfortable with books, there is a temptation to remain mired in the safe and

---

John E. Nelson III is of counsel to the firm of Holtzman & Urquhart in Houston, Texas. A different version of this article appeared in Instruments of Appellate Advocacy (4th ed. 1987).

stable world of legal research. This process, though soothing (and eminently billable), only postpones the terror of actual composition. A stack of notes and photocopies looks impressive. It creates the largely false impression that something has been done. By contrast, a blank legal pad or empty word-processor screen shames and intimidates.

So, rather than postponing the agony, begin to write at the first feasible point. After your first exploratory pass through the record and the library, put the principal ideas in the case on paper. Draft an outline based on them, and try to write the entries in that outline in the crispest, closest-to-final language that you can.

Such writing, even at a preliminary stage, can have salutary effects. It is easy to keep an argument or concept in your head and not notice its flaws and fuzzy edges. It floats like a cloud in your mind. You know its general shape, but never have to measure its exact dimensions. Writing changes that. The very attempt to articulate an unclear concept will suggest facts to be checked and ideas to be pursued.

After your first exercise in outlining, repeat the process. Go back to the record, establish precise fact sequences, demonstrate preservation of error, and add details that align your case with or distinguish it from the legal authorities discovered during research. Return to the library to verify your theories, to understand opposing positions, and to identify legal policies that may be affected by the ruling you seek. Finally, return to your outline; flesh it out and correct any conceptual errors exposed by the second phase of factual and legal research.

Ordinarily, repeating this cycle three or four times will produce a near-final draft brief. Yet to come, of course, are inevitable and time-consuming quality control steps: style polishing, cite checking, proofreading. But this "trialectical" approach has several advantages over its chief rival, the study-and-stack method. First, it builds morale. *Something*, no matter how rough, emerges from the daunting mass of raw record and research material. Second, the usual approach—unbroken periods of factual or legal research—may make concepts go stale. Periodically looking at all the aspects of a project improves your focus. It reduces the feeling of having a mountain of ideas, citations, obstacles, and facts somewhere in your head or in a stack of paper where they resolutely resist extraction. Third, going through repeat versions of a brief helps accustom a writer to editing his or her own work and to having it edited. A writer who begins with the knowledge that many drafts are part of the process will have less emotional commitment to the text than does the writer who tries to write a perfect, first-and-only draft. Finally, the process is more fun; it provides variety. Writing becomes a break from the library, which in turn is a break from study of the record, which in turn is a diversion from the mind- and body-cramping task of composition.

Caution and courage must be part of the process, too. Both minimize the temptation to be satisfied with preliminary drafts. The writer-advocate must relentlessly criticize and change work. When possible, he or she must submit it to competent critics for their review. Courage is also required when discarding a large chunk of manuscript as wrong or hopelessly inarticulate. The method I suggest provides no immunity from such a prospect, but, because it is evolutionary and contains its own ongoing verification process, there is less risk of wholesale discards.

2. *Tell the story.* Every case, murder or tax, negligence or antitrust, records the unique history of a human transaction. Perhaps it is the sort of transaction that only a student of a particular discipline will appreciate, but it contains drama nonetheless. By plan or accident, the actors did what they did. They responded to their own ideas or the acts of others. Legal rules may have shaped the actors' plans; their actions and reactions will have legal consequences. In urging the application of particular rules, do not forget the story that calls them forth.

Visualizing every case in this way will help sustain the attention of writer and reader alike. It is far better than treating the argument as a sterile exercise in the manipulation of testimony, documents, and citations. It also lends coherence to the brief.

For the respondent, telling the story of the case may amount to summarizing the themes developed in closing argument at trial, but it should not merely repeat those themes. On appeal, the focus shifts from establishing what happened to determining the legal authority for, and the wisdom and social utility of, the outcome; more is needed than a jury argument. For the petitioner, telling the story of the case is an opportunity to show the court where the process went awry and to demonstrate—and not merely complain—that the legal interpretation of the facts established at trial was wrong.

Of course, briefs are not fairy tales. You cannot begin by saying, "Once upon a time. . . ." Still, viewing the case as a process acted out by *people,* directly or through constructs such as corporations or government agencies, will help correct the temptation to assemble a brief from a set of standard parts. By telling the story, you can make your case unique and make it come alive. By presenting the law and the facts as parts of a small drama, you can pose more vividly for the court one of humankind's oldest questions: Was it fair?

3. *Keep it simple.* Watching a talented athlete or dancer inspires awe; difficult physical feats are performed with apparent ease. The same should be true of a skilled brief writer. The reader should not marvel at the writer's virtuosity, but at the clarity of the position advanced. Too often, those skilled with words try in their written work to show the court how hard they have worked, how brilliantly they have thought, or how elegantly they have written. Doing this loses sight of the ultimate goal: to persuade.

Built on precedent, the law is a conservative profession, even when placed in the service of liberal or radical goals. It seeks the simple and avoids the unfamiliar. This means that demonstrating at length the novelty or difficulty of your position will rarely help. Life and the laws that govern it are complex enough; judges are likely to prefer a simple solution to a complex problem instead of one that compounds the complexity.

Of course, achieving simplicity usually provides all the challenge that even the most skillful writer could want. Simple expression rarely reflects simple thinking. Usually the reverse is true: Those who can explain a concept simply usually understand it thoroughly, while those with imperfect understanding stumble around in windy, turgid generalities. And simplicity has its own rewards: When the text makes it easy for a judge to appreciate a difficult proposition, he will thank the advocate for the favor, sometimes in the form of a favorable ruling.

Although there are many writing manuals explaining how to achieve simplicity, some of the most elementary maxims *are* worth repeating. Use ordinary language, assembled in a manner and sequence as ordinary as accuracy will permit. Complexity may appeal to grammar theorists, but a simple declarative sentence, activated by a transitive verb, conveys the most information. If qualifying phrases are necessary, begin the sentence with the qualifier, and build the independent clause as if it were a simple declarative sentence.

Avoid ostentatious displays of your vocabulary. For many of us, words are fun, but thesaural pyrotechnics in a brief force a choice between bad and worse. Either a judge *will* understand a word, in which case he may try to compete with the writer, or he will *not* understand, in which case he will be annoyed, both by the inconvenience of having to consult the dictionary and by the subtle arrogance implied in the author's successful deployment of an unfamiliar word.

4. *Indulge yourself elsewhere.* Many lawyers use appellate briefs to express personal convictions or to exhibit personal oddities. Such peculiarities may appear in the form of idiosyncratic theories or bizarre writing styles. Neither lawyer nor client can afford such luxuries. An opportunity for a subtle witticism may present itself; but perhaps not. One thing is sure: The lawyer who constantly searches for emotional or stylistic release has lost sight of the objective. Though it may be emotionally unsatisfying, a simple, straightforward exposition of the client's position is the most direct route to the desired result. The most successful brief writers make their personal preferences, in style or substance, secondary to their message. If maximizing your client's chances of winning is not enough for you, write poetry or horror novels on the side— or await appointment to the bench.

5. *Move toward the goal.* In Euclidean geometry, the shortest distance between two points is a straight line. A similar axiom applies to appellate briefs. In everything you do, get straight to the goal; avoid digressions and excursions. Try to minimize separations between the subject

and verb. Attention in sentences to sequence, either logical or chronological, helps the reader follow the argument; modifiers or qualifiers of any kind interrupt this flow. If, because of intellectual honesty or substantive complexity, secondary ideas *must* be developed, relegate them to footnotes. But the presumption should always be against the use of such devices; where possible, reorder an argument to eliminate the parenthetical comment, or any secondary idea at all.

6. *Make every sentence count*. On the surface, this instruction appears to be a platitude, but it is not. Many sentences contain rhetorical flourishes, highly abstract contentions, or untestable propositions that cannot be objectively verified ("the most egregious mockery of justice since the *Dred Scott* decision"). These statements are empty; they lack content. They count for nothing. Legal briefs, and every sentence in them, must be different; they should rest on verifiable legal propositions or facts in the record below. Stress the message; the clearer the picture, the less necessary the frame.

As a brief writer develops skill and experience, he or she will discover that each case has a theme or themes against which the text of the brief can be checked. Each clause, each sentence in the brief, should illuminate that theme. Any sentence failing this test should be modified or eliminated. Asking, sentence by sentence, "How does this help?" will curb a tendency to include superfluous material.

7. *Leave yourself time*. Time for what? The answer is this: time for a host of unforeseen but almost inevitable problems. The library will be closed unexpectedly; the computer system will go down for a day and a half; your composition will be interrupted by illness in the family. No brief should be assembled without a timetable; no timetable should be drafted without leaving room at each stage for unexpected events. Try to anticipate each stage of production, including word processing, duplicating, binding, and mailing or delivery. Find out what resources are at your disposal and what the capabilities of your support system are. Do not tolerate indifferent service, but do not expect miracles either. Throughout, remember that writing is not the whole job. Logistics and production details are essential and must be accounted for.

Include one or more "dead days" in the timetable. Total immersion in a problem may make you an expert, but it robs perspective. Frequently, after several days of hard labor on a brief, followed by a day or two of attention to something else (or, where the luxury is available, absolute rest), a writer can identify passages that would have been gibberish to most readers. Remember, no matter how skilled, judges and law clerks will not understand the facts and law in your case as well as you. They will not have immersed themselves in the materials as the advocates have. Scheduled breaks will help you know less; they will reduce the surplus expertise that may prevent you from carefully evaluating your own writing.

8. *Don't trust technology.* This is a special note to those who have mastered the use of the dictaphone or the word-processing functions of a personal computer. Like many who have not converted from quill to keyboard, I harbor a Luddite fear of unfamiliar technology. However, in reviewing writing samples submitted directly from personal computers, I have noticed a symptom that I believe is attributable to word-processor brief writing: poor organization. Even the most sophisticated word processors display no more than two to four conventional pages of text at a time. This leads to a kind of tunnel vision when composing or editing on-screen without frequent printouts of hard copy. This in turn results in a loose, haphazard narrative style. The result is a loss of linear idea development and persuasiveness.

When applied to brief writing, word-processing technology should be confined to its most efficient use: speedy editing and reordering of portions of text. (Similarly, though the dictaphone can preserve a fleeting thought, its use should also be restricted. It is ill-suited to extended composition.) Except for minor revisions like spelling and punctuation, compose the text, print it out, revise the hard copy, and enter the revisions in the system. Skipping the hard copy step may save time, but it frequently sacrifices crisp reasoning and tight organization.

Michelangelo is said to have claimed that each of his sculptures already lived in the mass of stone he chose to work. His task, he said, was to chip away the excess material and reveal the hidden creation. The maxims in this article were developed that way, by extracting rules from the mass of briefing problems encountered in teaching and practice. Use them to help you find your message in the mass of facts and ideas in your case, and to reveal that message in its pure, persuasive form.

PART IV

Oral Argument

Time for Oral Argument

David W. Peck

Courts have become impatient with oral argument. Some routinely begin the call of their calendars with a reminder to counsel that they are familiar with the briefs and the pertinent parts of the record—a not too subtle invitation to avoid repetition and to deal briefly with the facts.

If a lawyer decides to argue a case on which the adversary has "submitted," a court might well remind the lawyer that there has been a submission. This reminder is probably meant to embarrass him or her into also submitting without argument. The implication is that it is somehow unfair for only one side to argue. At the very least, the court might imply that it is puzzled why only one side finds it necessary to explain its brief. Still other courts have a specific hierarchy of appeals in which certain classes of cases are afforded less time for argument.

The most direct way in which appellate courts have curtailed oral argument is by eliminating it entirely. The Federal Court of Appeals for the Fifth Circuit is notorious for deciding approximately half of its cases—those on its summary calendar—without any oral argument. And, other courts refuse to hear argument on specific applications, motions, or types of appeals.

The question whether oral argument should be curtailed is thus academic. It has been curtailed and will continue to be curtailed although that is hardly the most desirable approach to appellate procedure. The issue is why courts have found it necessary to perform such radical surgery on oral argument and how appellate counsel can handle these restrictions.

When lawyers and judges discuss the limitations on the time allowed for oral argument, the lawyers usually complain about the limitations

---

David W. Peck, now deceased, was a presiding justice of the Appellate Division, First Department, of the New York State Supreme Court and a partner in the New York City firm of Sullivan & Cromwell.

and the judges complain about the quality of the arguments they do hear. The suggestion is that judges might hear more arguments if the arguments were more helpful.

Judges' dissatisfaction with the quality of so many oral arguments certainly contributes to their disposition to curtail oral argument. However, the sheer number of cases compared to the judicial time available is the principal reason for limiting oral presentations.

A comparison of the British and American systems illustrates the problems faced by American appellate courts. Critics of American oral argument frequently point with admiration to the British practice of allowing extended oral argument. But these critics often ignore the different conditions that result in much lighter court loads in Britain.

Aside from having a less litigious nature, the British do not use contingent fees and discourage litigation by taxing lawyer's fees against the losing party. In the American system, litigation is virtually a free ride except for one's own lawyer's fees, and, through contingent fee arrangements, fees may often be avoided if the litigation is unsuccessful. Similarly, for many of the same reasons, there is a far lower percentage of appeals in Britain than in the United States. In short, it is the vast difference in caseloads that enables British appellate courts to take their time in hearing and considering appeals.

There is also a big difference in caseloads among the states of the United States and correspondingly a difference in the allowance of time for oral argument. A court will be more relaxed and indulgent about oral argument if not pressed by the volume of cases on its docket. It is the courts with heavy calendars, fighting for time, that have to make efficiency and economy dictates of their practice. It is their calendars that fix their attitudes toward oral argument.

In addition to the caseload, a court's practice of reading or not reading the briefs in advance of argument determines the time allowed for oral argument. Individual judges or whole courts increasingly read briefs before argument and regard oral argument as an opportunity to pose questions on bothersome points rather than an occasion for hearing counsel cover the case as they might like. The impetus for this practice is the twofold belief that oral argument can best be controlled and directed with a prior knowledge of the case and that oral argument is more meaningful and helpful with such knowledge.

It is unquestionably valuable for a judge to be familiar with a case when argument is heard. It will provide an opportunity, otherwise unavailable, to put questions to counsel that the briefs may prompt. A judge should not be discouraged from reading the briefs even if a majority of other judges does not. It is quite evident, however, from the standpoint of both court and counsel, that it is better if all members of a court are prepared for argument. Courts should, and generally do, let it be known if their practice is to read the briefs in advance of argument, but then in all fairness they should live up to their representation. All of the judges should be reasonably equally informed and ready for a "hot court" argument.

How uniform the practice is within a court depends on the preference of individual judges for how they like to come to grips with a case. Most appellate judges prefer to do it with the eyes and get the case from the briefs. Many, however, prefer to get their introduction and grasp from oral argument. A rare few seem able to read and listen at the same time.

Whether time in oral argument is really saved by the reading of briefs beforehand is debatable. Whether development of the argument by questions from the bench is more expeditious than if it is left primarily to counsel is questionable. But there is no doubt that reading the briefs in advance affects the course of the argument. The questions from the bench are more to the point and are apt to start at once with the court indicating where it wants the argument addressed.

It also affects counsels' preparation and organization of the argument if they know that the briefs will have been read before the argument and that they can go to the heart of the matter at once. What puts counsel into a quandary is not knowing the degree of a court's familiarity with the case before starting to speak. The problem is compounded when there is a substantial difference among the members of the court in the attention they have given the case before argument and consequently in each judge's need for education. It is embarrassing for an appellant's counsel to be reminded by a judge that the court has read the briefs and that a detailed statement of the facts is unnecessary. But it would be even more embarrassing if the truth were known and only half the judges had read the briefs.

Less experienced appellate lawyers may prefer to speak their piece and not be thrown off by the court's taking over the argument. Experienced counsel, however, should welcome the opportunity to meet the court on the grounds that give the judges concern. This is a better use of the time of counsel and the court than a fuller formal argument. It is nevertheless a disappointment to counsel to have an argument so preempted by the court that there is no chance to present an orderly argument. The best protection against this, and the lawyer's best chance to be of service to the court as well, is to recognize what is important and get to it straight off. As John W. Davis said some years ago in probably the finest lecture on appellate advocacy: "Go for the jugular."

If oral argument is to be effective—particularly in these days of impatient appellate courts and curtailed arguments—lawyers should realize that oral arguments are an art wholly apart from brief writing. Too many lawyers believe that when their briefs are written their oral arguments are prepared; that the oral presentation should cover the same ground in the same way, only in a condensed form. To believe that is to miss the opportunity to make an effective oral argument.

Oral argument requires its own preparation for its own purpose. It is a rare argument where the time allowed permits a lawyer to cover all the grounds urged in the briefs. To attempt such coverage almost inevitably leads to cutting off an argument in midstream when the little red light on the podium or the presiding judge announces that time is up. Even an argument that managed to touch all the bases in the briefs will probably be so cursory as to lack impact. Briefing is meant to present a full and rounded argument in an orderly fashion for judges and clerks to study, one hopes with adequate time. (But bear in mind there is still pressure on judicial time in dealing with briefs, so make them as brief as possible for needed coverage.) Oral argument is to let the court see and grasp the guts of a case.

Whatever introductory remarks are required, oral argument—which must be geared to the time allowed—should get to the heart of the case quickly. The first guide to oral argument is a determination of the order of importance of the points involved. If there are several points in a case, it is unlikely that all can be covered in oral argument.

Unless there is a compelling reason, such as one's being introductory to another, points should be covered in the order of importance. It is better to cover one point sufficiently to make it clear and convincing than to try to hit many and probably lose the impact of every point. The points that cannot be covered can be mentioned and the court can be referred to the briefs. The dominant consideration throughout, from the first preparation to the final delivery of the oral argument, is to achieve maximum effectiveness, to make the best use of the time allowed. That time should fix the frame and scope of the argument. The plan of argument should be counsel's thoroughly considered judgment of how much can be fitted effectively into the time allowed and hence what matter and manner of coverage will make the best use of the time.

Not only must the oral argument be plotted with a conscious awareness of time and the relative importance of various points, but counsel should be aware of time throughout the argument. Rarely can an argument be made just as planned. Questions from the court will interrupt and consume time, and those questions will often alter the order and direction of argument. Several considerations should be kept in mind in answering questions from the bench. First, the question must be answered, not put off or postponed. Second, if a question can be answered by making a point that is planned, it is probably advisable to make the point then and mentally tick it off as covered. Third, if the time necessarily used up in answering questions means that the remainder of the argument cannot be made as planned, the argument should be revamped on the spot so that the vital points are still made.

Courts should be more considerate than they are of counsels' requirements in making adequate arguments and they should have more confidence than they do in counsels' ability to make arguments as they should be made. Lawyers must earn that respect, however, and demonstrate that they can and will make the most valuable use of their own and judges' time in addressing oral argument to the court.

Preparing for Oral Argument

Steven F. Molo and Paul P. Biebel, Jr.

Reputation and experience mean little if you walk into court unprepared. A prominent government lawyer once learned this the hard way when arguing as an amicus curiae before the United States Supreme Court. One of the justices asked about a significant case decided years earlier. The lawyer hesitated for a moment and then responded that the Court should overrule the earlier case. He could not understand why his colleagues at counsel's table broke into nervous whispers. After he sat down, he learned that he had urged the Court to overturn a 50-year-old precedent supporting his position.

Here is one approach to preparation for oral argument that is designed to prevent that sort of problem. It is based on our experience in handling a variety of appeals for a large government law office.

Bob Hanley said that during the last 30 days before a trial, he entered into a state of complete and total misery. Hanley, "The Last Thirty Days," 10 *Litigation*, No. 2 at 8 (Winter 1984). Notification that oral argument has been set often induces the same state.

Unlike the trial lawyer, the appellate lawyer does not have to orchestrate the testimony, exhibits, and arguments that must flow smoothly by a judge or jury. An appeal involves fewer human elements. But the appellate lawyer's job is just as tough.

The appellate advocate must take that trial and all its human elements, along with the two or three preceding years of litigation, and reduce the entire case to a coherent argument that will convince an appellate panel, in 30 minutes or less, that the result in the trial court was right or wrong. The appellate lawyer *is* the case for those 30 min-

---

Steven F. Molo is a senior litigation partner in the Chicago office of Winston & Strawn. Paul P. Biebel, Jr., is a judge of the Circuit Court of Cook County, Illinois. Previously, Biebel served as first assistant attorney general of Illinois, and Molo served as an assistant attorney general of Illinois.

utes. He stands alone in the batter's box when the court throws a fastball, change-up, or curve. There are no walks or base hits; it's either a home run or a strikeout.

But he was not always alone while preparing for argument. He honed his arguments with the other lawyers who helped write the brief. They tried to anticipate every counterargument the other side might raise and every bizarre hypothetical question a judge might ask.

He tested his theories on anyone in the office who would listen and he consulted outside experts to make sure all the bases were covered. He subjected himself to the unflinching eye of a videotape camera and the critiques of his colleagues. He bored his wife, alienated his friends, and drove himself to the brink of insanity trying to reduce his case to its simplest terms.

So how does it all come together? The team approach works best, particularly if the case is complex or the advocate inexperienced. Yet, even the most seasoned appellate lawyer with the simplest case can benefit from the assistance and insights of a legal Sancho Panza.

Working with a team has several advantages. First, it saves time by allowing you to delegate some tasks. Indexing the record, compiling photocopies of the important authorities, reviewing advance sheets, and going over the local appellate rules are necessary tasks, but the first-chair lawyer might not have time to do them all alone.

Second, the team approach gives you more knowledge to draw on. Working with people who are familiar with the case and the issues it presents can provide valuable insights and assure that you are not ducking the tough questions.

Finally, the team approach gives you perspective. Discussing your case with newcomers to the facts and the legal issues involved promotes clarity and simplicity.

So who should comprise your team? Of course, you will need the help of the lawyers who worked on the brief. If you did not handle the case in the lower court, rely on the lawyers who did. As elementary as this sounds, in some large government offices an appellate lawyer might talk to the trial team only when preparing the brief, if at all. Remember, the case was once as much a part of your predecessor as it is now a part of you.

The Illinois Attorney General's office consults with law professors and specialists in preparing for important arguments. It also has enlisted the help of former members of the Solicitor General's office and other experienced appellate lawyers. These people are eager to help in significant matters. If your case is simpler, rely on anyone in the office who has expertise in the area or experience with a similar issue.

Even if you are a sole practitioner, your secretary or spouse can help you with your phrasing and logic. Nonlawyers often have the uncanny ability to see through the legal haze and ask the really tough questions about the practical effect of your positions. But do not rely on laymen alone; it is also a good idea to involve some lawyers who have had no prior exposure to the case.

Study the Court

Once you have selected your team, where do you start? First, get to know the battleground. Before you dig into the issues, take some time to learn about the court and the judges who will hear the appeal.

If you have not argued in the court before, become familiar with the court's rules. They vary significantly. For example, the rules in the Fifth Circuit are quite different from those in the Seventh Circuit. Learn the procedures for submitting new authority, supplementing the record, reserving time for rebuttal, requesting more time for argument, and checking in the day of argument. In short, be prepared for any procedural matter that might arise between the day the oral argument is set and the time the court renders an opinion.

Each of the federal circuits publishes a practitioner's handbook that sets forth the Federal Rules of Appellate Procedure, the local circuit rules, and the court's internal operating procedures. For Supreme Court advocacy, there is no better guide than R. Stern, E. Gressman, S. Shapiro, & K. Geller, *Supreme Court Practice* (7th ed. 1993). Most state appellate courts publish their own rules. These sources often include both the rules and comments on oral argument.

The court's scheduling procedures may affect your approach. Some courts, like the United States Supreme Court, sit *en banc* and schedule arguments for intermittent five- or ten-day periods during which the court hears argument all day. If your case is before a court that schedules arguments that way, you might do well to spend a bit more time detailing the facts before you start your legal argument. Even if the court has read your brief and is familiar with the law, a thorough explanation of the case can help the judges to distinguish it from the other appeals on the calendar.

See if you can find out which judges will sit on the panel that will hear your appeal. Then learn something about the way those judges approach oral argument: Do they usually read the brief beforehand? Which judges ask the most questions? Find out how the judges have decided similar issues. Will Justice Freemarket apply his economic analysis to your contract case? Will Judge Hardliner think that your client had a reasonable expectation of privacy in the bank satchels filled with the money he stole?

Talking to lawyers who regularly practice before the court is a good way to learn about how the judges think. LEXIS is another window to particular judges' views. It is also helpful to observe another argument before the same panel.

Now to the substance of your argument. Remember that the brief and the oral argument serve different purposes. The brief gives the court the authorities and analysis supporting the result you seek. It also distinguishes the record excerpts, statutes, and cases cited by your opponent.

Oral argument gives you a chance to talk to the decision-makers. It is your opportunity to give life to the cold facts and authorities in your brief and to allay any doubts the judges have about your position.

Do not plan to argue every point in your brief. You simply will not have time. Besides, arguing too many points minimizes the impact of the ones that really count. But how do you know which points really count? You do not know. If you have not been an appellate judge you are fooling yourself if you think you know. Even a former appellate judge can sometimes be surprised by what his or her former colleagues seize on to reach a particular decision.

There are some things you can do, though, to keep on track. Decide what the case is really about. Reduce it to its simplest terms. Noted Chicago appellate lawyer Bill Harte calls this finding the "essence of the case."

Determine what you want the court to do and how that result will affect the law. What is the least the court must do to give you what you want? Can the holding you seek really be limited to the facts of your case? Will the result you seek conflict with precedent or with the decisions of other courts?

Isolate the most important reason for deciding in your favor. If the appeal were limited to one narrow issue, what would that be? Look at the big picture. If the appeal is discretionary rather than of right, ask yourself why the court decided to hear the case.

Consider these questions before rereading the brief. Think about the ultimate equities without immersing yourself in legal authorities or the record.

It helps to imagine how you would argue the appeal in ten minutes, then five minutes, then two minutes. What would you tell the court if you had only one minute to present your case? Imagine that your brief were limited to a one-page letter to the court. What would you write?

This will not always work. In *Illinois v. Gates*, the Illinois Attorney's office had what we thought was a straightforward Fourth Amendment issue in an appeal before the Supreme Court. We wanted the Court to simplify the *Aquillar-Spinelli* test for reliability of anonymous informants used to obtain search warrants.

But, the Court had other ideas about the case and wound up ordering additional briefing and argument on whether there should be a good-faith exception to the exclusionary rule. So, sometimes there is no way short of clairvoyance to anticipate what will be important to the court. Nonetheless, mortal appellate lawyers should do what they can to identify the important issues and focus their arguments accordingly.

Develop a theme. Keep it simple. It can be a sentence or phrase that sums up your case and that will recur throughout the argument. Like the theme of a successful summation or opening statement at trial, this is the glue that holds the whole argument together. A good theme makes for a smooth transition from point to point and provides a bridge back to your argument after you have responded to a bizarre hypothetical or confusing question.

A lawyer in the Illinois Attorney General's office handled an appeal concerning the use of documents that had been subject to a magistrate's protective orders. We were never a party to the suit in which the orders were entered, but we wanted to use the documents to expose a fraud that, we alleged, the appellant had perpetrated on another court in another case. The protective orders had been dissolved and reinstated several times in a series of inconsistent rulings that left the record in a procedural shambles.

The appellant charged that we had violated the protective orders when we obtained the documents from another lawyer. We said that we got the documents before any protective order had been issued, and that we were not bound by the orders in any event, because we were never a party to that lawsuit.

The appellant's lawyer began his argument by stating, "Let me first say what this case is not about." He then launched into an attack against the Illinois Attorney General's office, the district court, and the proceedings in which we wanted to use the documents.

Rather than telling the court why he was there, he began with a negative statement that failed to capture the essence of his case. He made a confusing appeal even more confusing and he never really told the court why it should decide in his favor. There was no cohesiveness. He lacked a theme.

Our lawyer did not dwell on the erratic procedural history or respond directly to the appellant's charges of misconduct on the part of the office. Instead, he focused the court's attention on the big picture. His theme was that the appellant "should not be allowed to use the Federal Rules of Civil Procedure to conceal a fraud that it perpetrated on another court."

It worked. Each time the argument came to an exchange on the rationale for the irrational orders, our lawyer brought the argument back to where he wanted it by returning to his theme.

Of course, incanting a theme should never substitute for answering a question from the bench. But a well-thought-out theme lets you redirect the court's attention to your main point after you answer a question that sidetracks you. This is particularly important when your case is complex or your opponent has led the court astray by strewing your path with red herrings.

Once you have found your theme, review the brief and decide which points *not* to argue. You have decided the case is about commercial speech, so why waste the little time you have talking about res judicata, unless the court asks about it? You think the admission of the co-conspirator's hearsay statements will be the most likely basis for reversing the judgment on the jury verdict, so why squander half your time arguing that your opponent's closing argument was improper?

Integrate your remaining points into a single argument drawn together by your theme. Think about how the argument should flow. Do not yet concern yourself with the fine points. Rather, establish the framework that you will fill in later.

Lead with your strongest punch. A well-known Chicago litigator once argued a complex commercial matter before the Illinois Supreme Court. His brief gave many reasons the lower court's decision should be reversed. But he began his argument with one of the weaker points. The first question he drew within two minutes was, "Counsel, do you have something more substantial to say to us today?"

To avoid that embarrassment, leave the less important points in your brief out of your oral argument. Then rank the remaining points and cover them in order of decreasing importance.

As you decide what to include in your argument, remember that credibility is your most valuable but most fragile asset. In a case before the Illinois Appellate Court, a lawyer argued that his client's 30-year sentence for murder was excessive. He marshaled the mitigating circumstances and cited the appropriate rules of law, but he neglected to mention that the defendant had spent 11 years in prison on a previous murder conviction and was paroled only three months before he committed the second murder.

Whatever credibility the appellant's lawyer started out with was demolished when his opponent pointed out, in his opening remarks, the critical but previously unmentioned facts. As difficult as it sometimes may be, it is essential to maintain some degree of objectivity as you decide what you will argue to the court.

If your case involves multiple parties or an amicus curiae, you may have to decide whether to divide oral argument. This decision is best made after you have an idea of how your argument should flow. You will know then whether the issues can be painlessly divided between counsel. If, before preliminarily structuring your argument, you commit to dividing your time, you may discover during your preparation that your argument does not lend itself to division.

You will then be a likely victim of one of the three problems that commonly befall lawyers who divide argument time:

- The court questions lawyer A about the issues lawyer B will address.
- The court's questions take lawyer A past his allotted time, and lawyer B makes a hurried, incomplete argument or never speaks.
- Lawyer A's thoughtful, well-prepared argument is cut short so that lawyer B can begin his abrasive, ill-prepared lecture to the court.

Do not divide your time, if possible.

If you must divide the argument, allocate discrete issues for each lawyer to address. Repetition bores the court and wastes your team's limited time. The less your issues overlap, the less likely it is that you will intentionally or inadvertently make your co-counsel's argument.

Now you are ready to get down to the business of learning the record and authorities. This may be drudgery, but it is essential. Even if you did not represent your client in the lower court, you must become the leading expert on the case.

Reread the cases and statutes cited in the briefs and prepare abstracts of the important ones. You should do this yourself, particularly if you were not the principal draftsman of your brief. This exercise forces you to become familiar with the pertinent authorities and to recognize the distinctions between your case and those that you and your opponent cite.

Arrange your abstracts and photocopies of the important authorities in an indexed, three-ring notebook. This will be a ready source of the relevant authorities for quick reference during your preparation and argument.

Use *Shepards*, advance sheets, session laws, and LEXIS to find any new statutes or cases on point. Do this during your initial review of the authorities, but check again periodically right up until the day before argument.

Years ago, a lawyer from the Illinois Attorney General's office had an argument before the Supreme Court. The justices questioned him about another case that the Court had decided the day before. Fortunately, the second-chair lawyer had heard about the decision on the news, and he got a copy of the opinion from the clerk's office the morning of argument.

You must know the entire procedural history of the case right up until your appeal. A lawyer once had an appeal before the Illinois Appellate Court in a case that had been before the court previously on an interlocutory appeal. During oral argument, he unwittingly attempted to reargue a point that was decided against his client the first time the case was up on appeal.

After several minutes, one of the justices stopped him midsentence and asked if the court was not bound to follow its earlier decision, referring to the opinion on the interlocutory appeal. To the amusement of everyone in the courtroom, the uninformed advocate replied, "But Your Honor, that case is distinguishable on its facts."

Soliloquies Sound Stilted

Take notes on the important parts of the record and prepare an index. Use whatever format works best for you, but remember that an index is of value only if it provides a handy guide to the entire record.

You have selected a theme, sketched a framework, and reviewed the record and the authorities. Now you are ready to commit your argument to paper.

Working with the brief, your indexed record, and your notebook of authorities, prepare the first draft of your argument. Include all the details; worry about paring down your argument later.

Do not write a speech. If you have a full-blown text to read, you will be more interested in delivering your soliloquy than in answering the judges' questions. Also, a prepared address almost always sounds stilted.

Besides, it is unlikely that you will get through the text as you prepared it. Questions may make you lose your place and keep you from reaching important points. Lawyers with prepared texts also tend to give the off-putting nonanswer, "I'll get to that point in a minute," in response to a straightforward question.

So, how do you get your argument down on paper? Outline. Think in terms of the headlines rather than the whole story. You may have to jump from one section to another depending on the questions the judges ask, and the more elementary your notes are, the easier this will be.

At the same time, carefully craft and write out a handful of key statements as you would like to say them to the court and integrate them into your outline. Because you will not be able to recite a whole prepared text, you should have a few sentences or phrases that capture your main points. Work on strong, affirmative phrasing in the active voice.

Some lawyers still feel the need to sound "lawyerly." Fancy, polysyllabic language obfuscates rather than elucidates.

Remember Strunk and White's admonition, "Omit needless words." Do not tell the court that "an incorrect standard was erroneously applied by the trier of fact when it considered and admitted the out-of-court statements offered for the truth of the matter asserted therein." Say, "The trial court applied the wrong standard in admitting the hearsay statements."

Decide which points might need subtler phrasing. If you are prepared to concede a point, be sure not to give away your whole case. Sometimes a concession can enhance your credibility by making you appear reasonable. Yet the way you concede the point must be carefully planned.

A few years ago, we opposed a constitutional challenge to a state statute with a severability clause providing that, should a court find sections, words, or phrases of the act invalid, the remainder would nonetheless remain in effect. The trial court held that both of the operative sections of the act violated the due process clause.

Objectively, the constitutionality of each section was somewhat dubious. But we were not prepared to concede that. Addressing severability in our opening argument could have come across as such a concession.

We decided not to raise severability in our opening argument unless questioned about it but to address the issue on rebuttal if the court questioned our opponent on the point. Although you can never really plan your rebuttal, sometimes you can anticipate that an issue will be best addressed at that stage of the argument.

The strategy worked. During opening argument, our lawyer focused on the reasons for upholding both sections that the trial court had struck down. The question of severability arose during the appellee's argument, and our lawyer responded in rebuttal.

Coping in this way with a point that otherwise might have been perceived as concession had several advantages. First, it allowed us in our first pitch to tell the court what we really wanted it to do—to uphold the entire statute. Second, it gave our lawyer a chance to listen to the court's questions about severability during his opponent's argument. Third, it provided our lawyer with an opportunity to address the court's concerns and rebut his opponent's analysis. Finally, arguing severability in rebuttal made the lawyer appear reasonable by tacitly conceding that there was another outcome we were willing to accept: The court could uphold one section of the act and find the other unconstitutional.

With your written outline to work from, you are ready to practice your argument. Prepare a version that uses about one-half to two-thirds of your allotted time if given without interruption. Run through this version alone to get your phrasing down. Then present it to someone else and have him critique your argument's clarity, organization, style, and persuasiveness. Again, people who are unfamiliar with the case are often the best judges. If your argument is clear and persuasive to them, it should be clear and persuasive to the court. If you have access to videotape, now is a good time to use it.

Once you have your argument down and have satisfied yourself that it is intelligible and in basic working order, it is time to test it under fire. You are ready to present your argument to the lawyers most familiar with the case and the issues and have them bombard you with legal, factual, and hypothetical questions.

Do not worry about how long it takes to get through your argument the first few times you practice it with these people. The idea is to think on your feet and to deal with the tough questions.

Have your team members ask questions to disrupt your presentation and throw you off balance. Nothing is more disquieting than being asked about a point you intend to address last when you are only 30 seconds into your recitation of the facts. But that happens sometimes, and you should learn to roll with the punches while you are still sparring for the big match.

Learn to use questions to your advantage. John W. Davis's famous article "The Argument of an Appeal," 26 *A.B.A. J.*, 895 (1940), says that the advocate should "rejoice when the court asks questions." Davis says that questions show that the court is interested in what you are saying, and they give you a chance to respond to the court's concerns.

Questions have another advantage. As you take note of the questions that come up during your practice arguments, you should be able to anticipate at least some of the major questions that the court will ask.

Some issues are so significant that the court *must* ask you about them. Work the main points of your outline into the answers to these questions.

This serves two purposes. First, it tells the court that you know your case, have thought about the important questions, and have logical (although not necessarily acceptable) answers. Second, it lets you make the most of your limited time by moving through your outline with the aid of, not despite, the court's questions.

The Illinois Attorney General's office had a case in the United States Court of Appeals for the Seventh Circuit involving a constitutional challenge to an Illinois law that resembled an Indiana law the court had struck down the year before. The difference between the two statutes was the heart of the case. Our lawyer had intended to spend a great deal of time distinguishing the earlier case. During argument, he began addressing the various reasons supporting the statute's constitutionality without mentioning the earlier case. When the court asked him about the case, he detailed the distinctions, answering the court's question and covering a major part of his outline at the same time.

As you practice with your team, anticipating questions and formulating answers, you refine continually. The entire process of preparation for oral argument is one of synthesis and clarification. It is helpful to put pen to paper to work over the rough spots even after you have gone through your argument with the people most familiar with the case and the issues.

Using flowcharts or graphs while you prepare sometimes simplifies complicated points. Several years ago, a lawyer had a Fourth Amendment case in the Supreme Court. In his brief, the respondent contended that the decision of the Illinois state court was based on an adequate and independent state ground and, therefore, that the Court lacked jurisdiction to hear the case.

The law governing that issue was confusing, and several opinions had discussed the issue without enunciating clear guidelines. Also, two justices seemed to have a special interest in the issue at the time, so it appeared likely that the issue would come up at oral argument.

Our lawyer feared that if the court got into a long dialogue on the procedural point, he might never reach his argument on the Fourth Amendment issue. He needed a quick but complete answer to a complex question.

He used a flowchart during his preparation to reduce the issue to its simplest terms. At the top, it said: "OK Counsel, don't we lack jurisdiction to hear this case since the decision below rests on adequate and independent state grounds?" Beneath that, it read: "There are three ways that this case is properly before the Court, Your Honor; count 'em." Each of the three grounds for jurisdiction was then summarized with the supporting law and facts diagrammed beneath it.

The lawyer was able to think through the issue by mapping out the problem and its solution on a 2-by-3-foot sheet of butcher paper. With this preparation, he was ready to give a satisfactory response to the first question the Court asked him, and he promptly moved on to the rest of his argument.

Except in the most extraordinary cases, charts and graphs should not be used during oral argument. Because your time is limited, you should avoid any distractions that might prevent you from making all your points. But charts and graphs can be a great aid in understanding the relationships between various facts or issues when you are preparing.

Once you feel confident in your ability to answer the hardest questions and get through your main points within your allotted time, you are ready to prepare your argument notebook.

There is no hard-and-fast format for your notebook. The only requirement is that it be arranged and tabbed so that it is easy to use at the podium. Unlike your authorities notebook, which contains all the statutory and case authority that you digested to formulate your argument, your argument notebook should contain no more than you think you will need during the argument.

The most important entry in your argument notebook will be your final outline. Like the notebook itself, the outline should be in whatever format allows for quick reference. Key words and phrases generally work best.

Jot down important record references or case names next to the major points. This way, the outline will be a handy guide to the record and authorities. It will let you find the citations you need without flipping through your notebook or fumbling with the other materials on the podium.

You may wish to use a different color ink to distinguish record references from the key words or phrases of your argument. Most people use some form of highlighting, underlining, or asterisks to call attention to the main points.

If you can, confine the outline to two $8\text{-}1/2$-by-11-inch facing pages in your argument notebook. With your outline containing key case names and record references in front of you, you may not need to turn a page during argument.

Along with your final outline, the argument notebook should include a brief index of the most important record entries. This will be more detailed than the notes on your outline but less detailed than the record index that you used in outlining your argument. You may want an index to the major cases as well. Presumably, you will know the cases well enough not to need this, but it can be a comforting security blanket for the inexperienced lawyer.

Some people list alphabetically the ten or fifteen most important cases, with a one- or two-sentence summary of the holding and facts of each. Other lawyers group the cases according to the points they support. In any event, this list should not be more than a page or two to which you can turn if you get stumped during your argument.

Include photocopies of important statutory language, jury instructions, record excerpts, or anything else you are likely to refer to during argument. This section should be kept to a minimum, but it makes sense to have a copy of a contested statute or jury instruction at your fingertips if it is the basis of the appeal.

Finally, include brief outlines of the points that you do not intend to argue but that you covered in your brief. Despite your best efforts to anticipate the points that will most interest the court, the judges may want to hear about res judicata, even though you decided that the case is about commercial speech. Be ready just in case.

If you have the time, it helps to run through one last practice argument after you have compiled your argument notebook. This final practice session will let you decide whether you are comfortable with the format of your notebook and whether you need to add or drop anything.

Leave yourself time to mull over the case as you prepare. We have set out some specific steps that can help you get ready. Yet preparation for oral argument means more than just completing a checklist of tasks. It includes random reflection, often at odd times, on the problems of your case. The essence of the case may come to you over early morning coffee or during your evening commute home.

At this point, you have done about all you can do, except for last-minute reviews of your notes and case abstracts. Your preparation has produced several tangible assets to aid you in court: your argument notebook with its outline and notes, your authorities notebook with its photocopies and abstracts, and your indexed record. But, the most important thing your preparation has given you is intangible. It is the confidence you now have in your case and in your ability to present it succinctly and persuasively.

Appellate Advocacy, Modern Style

Murray I. Gurfein

Some appellate courts are hot; some are cold. Some advocates like them hot and some like them cold. On a cold court the judges generally have not read the briefs and the relevant parts of the appendix before argument. The worst bench—and this must be the rare exception—is one on which at least one but not all the judges have studied the appeal before argument. A court should not blow hot and cold because that is unfair to the advocate who is sidetracked by giving answers that the other judges already know. The good advocate will be ready for all the vagaries of individual judicial idiosyncrasies.

Even Jupiter may nod on occasion. Taft once related that he said to Holmes, "But do you think it was right or fair to leave *that* fact out of consideration?" Holmes replied, "I'm sorry; I didn't read that far in the record."

Oral argument today is not the structured, cohesive oration it once was. There are as many variations among courts as there are among panels and even individual judges. Some judges shoot the first question before the advocate has cleared his throat. Others hold their fire until the argument is well under way. And still others ask no questions at all. The maxim for the advocate must be *Semper Paratus*. The lawyer must be prepared to be told that the panel needs no oral recitation of the facts, to have the argument taken over completely by questions from the bench, or to find that the delivery of an entire argument is without a single question.

This does not mean that felicity and clarity of speech are no longer required. The worst vice for appellate lawyers is to be inarticulate. Remember that by the time judges get to an appellate bench they are, on the whole, no longer young. And while not deaf, they tend to be some-

---

Murray I. Gurfein, now deceased, was a member of the U.S. Court of Appeals for the Second Circuit.

what hard of hearing and without benefit of lip-reading courses. When there is a microphone in the courtroom, speak directly into it, but do not shout. Adjust it to your mouth level before you begin and do not move your head from side to side. And just as judges groan when the lawyer hems and haws, so they despair when the lawyer simply talks too fast, when words come too trippingly off the tongue. The worst offenders in this regard seem to be young lawyers who are so bright that they cannot restrain their train of thought to a reasonable speed limit. You are not trying to hear yourself think. You are trying to get the judges to understand what you are saying and to think along with you. Therefore, do not exceed a proper intellectual cruising speed.

Since you cannot foretell how thick and fast the questions will come, it is well to prepare for a full-scale uninterrupted argument. Fritz Wiener, in his excellent book *Briefing and Arguing Federal Appeals* (BNA, 1961), advises practicing the argument aloud to hone the rough edges and acquire a sense of timing. This is still a good idea. It helps a lawyer to recover after a series of questions, picking up the argument at a place that provides a chance to finish the main points.

Practice will also help to improve the manner of presentation. I would emphasize measured speech, clearly articulated, spoken in a confident but unpatronizing manner. An appellate advocate is a salesman. Skill in advocacy is shown by how well the wares are "sold." Assurance and belief in the cause are important ingredients. And even dress may play a part. While I doubt that many of us still own what used to be called a "Court of Appeals suit"—striped trousers and morning coat—I would hardly recommend as proper apparel dungarees or T-shirts.

As important as expository preparation is, an advocate must be prepared for a dialogue with the court. It is the advocate's only chance to insinuate himself or herself into the voting conference. A good answer to a hard question may make the difference in the decision. This means that in appellate advocacy, as in trial preparation, it is important not only to scout the other side but to give adequate weight to the strongest counterarguments. An overconfident team is often a losing team.

Search out the difficulties in your case. They cannot be wished away. Appellate judges generally are people of first-rate legal minds. Do not underestimate either their learning or acuity. Assume they will go for the jugular. If the hard point is not raised at argument, be assured that they will find it before an opinion is filed.

This could lead to the generalization that there is no generalization for planning an oral argument. It depends on the subject of the appeal. But some generalizations are still in order. In some respects an appellate argument is an obstacle race for the appellant's counsel. To be particularly pitied is the lawyer who did not try the case below and comes to the appellate bar with fresh ideas and a veritable key that should give a reversal.

In gambler's parlance, the cards are stacked against this lawyer. In federal civil cases he or she will run into the obstacle that the finding of the trial court must be sustained unless it is "clearly erroneous." And the verdict of a jury is quite sacrosanct. If the lawyer turns to attack the charge to the jury and no objection was made below, "plain error" must be shown. In criminal cases, the nemesis is "harmless error." Even when there has been a constitutional violation, the defendant will not prevail on appeal if the appellate court thinks the error was "harmless beyond a reasonable doubt." Another impediment is that motions addressed to the indictment even for constitutional deficiency may not have been timely made before trial.

Appellate judges are, by and large, self-limiting toward the scope of their review and self-deprecating in matching skills with trial judges. One must approach quite gingerly, yet firmly, the proposition that a respected trial judge has "abused his discretion." This pejorative word, probably grounded originally on the opportunity of the trial judge to measure the credibility of witnesses, now carries a distinct weight of its own on the balancing scale.

The appellee's lawyer, including a prosecutor, will be wise to stress these "technicalities," for they will, more often than not, bring him a relatively easy affirmance. The appellant's lawyer, on the other hand, cannot afford to disregard these obstacles. They will surely prove his or her undoing.

Unless there is a paramount error of law that can be relied on as the sole point, the appellant must often take the hard road of attempting to show that a crucial finding was "clearly erroneous," that a ruling constituted "plain error," or that the judge "abused his discretion."

The success or failure of such an attempt may well turn on whether the advocate can convince the court that the client may be innocent or that it is grossly unfair to mulct the client in damages under the circumstances of the case, or that the dismissal of the complaint was a denial of justice. If appellant's counsel can find some legitimate way to convince the court of the intrinsic unfairness of the judgment below, he or she should press the point with cultivated vigor. For, while it is the fashion to deprecate decisions that are "result-oriented," Holmes was probably exaggerating when he told Learned Hand that "we do not do justice; we simply apply the law." It is still the mystery of the appellate process that a result is reached in an opinion on thoroughly logical and precedential grounds while it was first approached as the right and fair thing to do. If there is any legitimate way to argue the equities, it should be done, though not in the style of a jury summation. As Karl Llewellyn put it, "The very reason that appellate courts exist is that there is doubt that skilled men do not agree about the outcome."

It is here that the doctrine of stare decisis becomes a roadblock. In federal courts of appeal where the judges sit in panels of three, the vote of two judges can effectively make "the law of the circuit," which binds as many as fifteen other judges. Succeeding panels are bound by the decision of the panel that first got the question the week before. Reading the advance sheets to see whether your issue has been written about is essential. There is nothing more devastating than a pronouncement from the bench that it is bound by a case that came down last month, when counsel has not read the opinion and is not prepared to distinguish it.

Some lawyers try to argue that the decision of a particular panel is aberrant or simply wrong. Unless the advocate can distinguish the decision on the facts, it will be found that the entire court is bound to follow it. Here a skill in dialectic is a useful tool. It is sometimes said of one of my colleagues that he can find a distinguishing feature for any precedent because of his scholarship and dialectic skill.

Despite the importance of precedent, however, it is generally a poor advocate who cites a number of cases in oral argument and compounds the error by reading quotations. The judges read the briefs and that is where the citation of authority to support the points belongs.

There is an exception, of course, when one or possibly two cases may be the key to the decision. In that event the advocate faces the difficult choice of directly distinguishing or asserting the authority of the particular decision or lying in wait for what may be the inevitable question from the bench. Some great advocates prefer the latter technique. I recall that when United States Attorney George Z. Medalie was preparing to argue the McGovern contempt case in the Second Circuit in 1933, each of us noted that the basic issue would turn on whether McGovern had been given adequate notice and opportunity to defend. As a neophyte assistant, I suggested that he open his argument with a direct statement of the facts showing that the prosecution had afforded adequate due process. "No," said Medalie. "The point is so vital that they are bound to ask about it. It will be more effective if I give our position in answer to a question." That is precisely what happened. Judge Learned Hand asked, "What about due process?" Medalie responded, "If Your Honor will look at page so-and-so of the appendix you will see how far we went." The judges looked at the reference. Judge Hand slammed the book shut, and we had won the appeal.

There will be occasions when a judge will imply that the answer given is not good enough. Here the advocate must stand ground with dignity and assurance but without overt antagonism. There are other judges on the panel who may remain convinced, and there is always hope of leading the questioning judge to a better appreciation of your point of view. If you have thought your case through in advance, you may have devised a pithy comment to cover the circumstance. And, sometimes it is easy to summon a countervailing approach to that urged by your questioner. For example, if the matter deals with statutory interpretation you will find ample authority for strict construction, for liberal construction, for a literal reading, or for a reading that makes more sense in context. Preparation will enable you to remind the court that decision by maxim or by canons of interpretation is likely to be no more acceptable than in-depth analysis of the coverage of the statute. On the other hand, if you are on the other side, be ready with maxim and canon to bolster your argument that the court is not at liberty to stray too far afield.

The advocate should also be prepared to identify apparent trends in Supreme Court doctrine. He or she must be prepared to argue either that the most recent case goes no further than its facts or that it spells a new era of jurisprudential thinking. Either approach is legitimate, and the court will be grateful for the reasoned help in solving the problem. I say "reasoned help," for the mere assertion of a position without more can only serve to irritate. Courts do not accept *ex cathedra* judgments from lawyers. In short, it is not safe to assume that a recent decision of the Supreme Court establishes "new" doctrine as the wave of the future. Judge-made law proceeds, as it always has, on a case-by-case basis.

This raises the question of how to argue a hard case that may make bad law—a variation of the problem of the guilty defendant who has been convicted by an allegedly unfair process.

The federal courts of appeal are reviewing courts of first instance as well as courts of last resort in most cases, given the limited number of cases that reach the Supreme Court by certiorari. As courts of first instance review, they have a responsibility to the litigants that, for the most part, is limited to reversal only for egregious error. On the other hand, the responsibility for fashioning the general law of the circuit will sometimes aid a particularly unworthy litigant or, perhaps as often, deprive an objectively worthy litigant of success because of the need to preserve uniformity of decision or to avoid recognizing a doctrine that would not be in the broader interests of the law.

This is where the able advocate recognizes the common problem of appellate judges and tries to help them to move along "his or her way." A sharp appellate advocate will not falter at recognizing the equivocal position nor ignore discussing it. Perhaps some cases in point are the application of an exclusionary rule, a doctrine of suppression of evidence, or dotting the i's and crossing the t's in a wiretapping order and its implementation. A defense lawyer should measure the boundaries of rational interpretation or precedential compulsion and try to explain why the challenged conduct was beyond the extreme limit. The prosecutor should not rely on a literal reading alone but should muster arguments of policy with adequate reference (without boring detail) to cases in his or her favor that suggest controlling precedent.

If the trend of the authorities is against you, you must try to show why, on the facts, a distinguishing decision will not disrupt the trend unwisely. Sometimes you can do this by stressing that the result in your case is so far different from the ordinary that it deserves special treatment. Perhaps you can argue that, contrary to the outcome in the cases cited, the result in your case is harsh and unwarranted.

This approach is particularly significant in criminal appeals involving business crimes where intent, smothered in swaddling clothes, shows its head only on intermittent occasions or is wholly circumstantial in proof. Judges, we may assume, are unanimously against sin, but there may be room for doubt that a particular business conduct bears the stamp of illegitimacy, or that the practices of the appellants so far deviate from the morals of the marketplace as to be held criminal. In those cases, since the appellant is faced with a jury verdict against him, he should bolster his argument on the insufficiency of the evidence with an attack, where legitimately possible, on the instructions to the jury and the reception or exclusion of evidence. Sometimes the whole turns out to be greater than the sum of its parts.

The prosecutor of course should not assume the role of an avenging angel, though a few well-chosen words on the evil of the practices found criminal are in order. It should be stressed that the salient facts point to criminal intent, not with the calm, dispassionate approach of a law professor, but without the undignified exhortation of a soapbox orator. Above all, the lawyer must be prepared to answer the harder questions that a good appellant's argument will prompt the court to ask. In those cases, rehearsal with a colleague who knows the record well enough to ask the hard questions is useful.

An important appellate argument demands as much random reflection as the concentrated thought given to it while the clock is running. The opening gambit may come to the lawyer on a quiet walk or while sleeping lightly. The synthesis of the argument, sometimes its reduction to simplicity, may not come except through thinking that is not trammeled by a time clock. I heard John W. Davis on several occasions come to a point in his argument where he would say, "After all, Your Honor, this is quite a simple case" and then follow with a pithy sentence going to the essence. I have a sneaking suspicion that sometimes the *tour de force* did not come to him while he was sitting at his desk.

While every lawyer likes to be associated with an extraordinary case, the appellee generally has nothing to gain by noting that the case is one of first impression, for he or she has the judgment below. The appellant, on the other hand, may whet the appetite of the court for an intellectual challenge if the importance of the case is stressed as one of first impression. The lawyer may do this, however, only if able to distinguish earlier case law or if the statute has not been interpreted before.

On the civil side, subject-matter jurisdiction of the federal court, and recently "standing," are often issues upon which the appeal will turn. It should be routine for the advocate to check jurisdiction, standing, and appealability in any case where such questions may fairly arise. Familiarity with the case law is essential.

The oldest advice is still the best. Know your case thoroughly and deal openly and fairly with the court. We once had before us a lawyer for an appellant in a criminal case whom we had never seen before. The presiding judge asked him, "Did you come here *pro hac vice?*" to which he responded, "No, I came by taxicab." The moral, I suppose, is if you cannot penetrate a Latin fog do not be ashamed to ask what it means.

The Don'ts of Oral Argument

Roger J. Miner

Effective appellate advocacy requires good oral argument as well as a good brief. The object of both is persuasion, which is accomplished by imparting factual and legal information to the court. An often-told story concerns a British judge who purportedly said to a barrister during the course of oral argument, "I have been listening to you for half an hour and am none the wiser." The barrister supposedly replied: "I know that, my Lord, but I had hoped you would be better informed."

I use this story in support of my thesis that an appellate court cannot be persuaded without well-organized and properly presented information.

Many books and articles have been written about appellate argument. *See, for example,* S. Wasby, *The Functions and Importance of Appellate Oral Argument: Some Views of Lawyers and Federal Judges,* 65 Judicature 340 (1982). *See, generally* R. Stern, E. Gressman, S. Shapiro, & K. Geller, *Supreme Court Practice* 577, n. 1 (7th ed. 1993). John W. Davis, one of the most famous appellate advocates, wrote an article giving ten commandments for those who would argue appeals. Davis, "The Argument of an Appeal," 26 *A.B.A. J.* 895 (1940), reprinted in Committees on Federal Courts & Continuing Educ., N.Y. State Bar Ass'n, Federal Court Practice 287 (1983). Davis said, in that article, that no one would listen to the discourse of a fisherman if he could hear from the fish.

Indeed, some well-known "fish" have made known their views on the subject. Justice Jackson (Jackson, "Some Suggestions for Effective Case Presentations," 37 *A.B.A. J.* 801 (1951), reprinted in *The Supreme Court and Its Justices* 254 (J. Choper, ed., 1987)); Justice Rehnquist (Rehnquist, *The Supreme Court* 276–282 (1987)); Judge Kaufman (Kaufman, "Appellate

---

Roger J. Miner is a judge of the U.S. Court of Appeals for the Second Circuit and an adjunct professor at New York Law School.

Advocacy in the Federal Courts," 79 F.R.D. 166 (1977)); and Judge Re (Re, *Brief Writing and Oral Argument* (5th ed. 1983)), just to name a few, have written extensively about appellate argument. Much of what these judges have written has been confirmed by my own experience. I now have developed my own list of 25 specific "don'ts" for oral argument. In the hope that they will be of some use, I herewith present them to you, in no particular order of importance.

1. Don't pass up the opportunity to argue. I guess that we in the Second Circuit are the last to allow oral argument to anyone who requests it, including pro se litigants. It amazes me that people decline to argue in our court. No matter how often we say that oral argument is important, lawyers continue to ignore us. Believe me, it is important! It can win your case.
2. Don't try to argue more than two or three points. In our court, the average time allowed for argument is 15 minutes. You cannot possibly make more than a few good legal points in such a limited period of time. Remember that the argument should include the history of the case, the holding below, the challenges on appeal, a brief statement of the facts, and responses to the judges' questions, as well as the legal points you want to emphasize. With all this, it should be clear that you should make only your best arguments on the law and leave the rest to the brief.
3. Don't ask us to overrule the Supreme Court. We are very reluctant to do that. A lawyer who once appeared before us was discussing an obscure point of admiralty law. The point had been settled in a Supreme Court decision some years before, but the lawyer insisted that the Supreme Court was wrong. I am afraid he got short shrift from us.
4. Don't spend a lot of time explaining our own recent decisions to us. You may presume that we are familiar with what we have written, at least recently. Our collective institutional memory sometimes needs refreshing, but extended explication is unnecessary. A convoluted discussion of precedent in the court in which you are arguing is a waste of everyone's time.
5. Don't read your oral argument. It still seems strange to me that so many lawyers breach this rule. Although notes and outlines are helpful, a full textual reading turns us off. I often have been tempted to ask a reader to hand up a copy of the warmed-up version of the brief he or she has been reading. A lawyer once read to us at such a rapid-fire rate that we asked no questions for fear he would lose his place. Justice Rehnquist calls such a lawyer "Casey Jones," because of his similarity to the engineer on an express train.
6. Don't permit co-counsel to pass up notes or to tug on your clothing. This is something of a pet peeve of mine. I find it very dis-

tracting. Certainly, the lawyer who is arguing is distracted. When the note is received, argument stops or slows down. Then there is a shift in subject matter or emphasis. Most frequently, the note comes up after a question that counsel has had trouble answering. The response provided by co-counsel usually is as unsatisfactory as the original answer.

7. Don't try to "wing" it. If you do not know the answer to a question, offer to furnish a response in writing after oral argument. I have seen much grief come to those who responded with a guess. You can really paint yourself into a corner with a wrong answer. It simply is not necessary to create that kind of trouble for yourself.

8. Don't say, "I'll get to that," in response to a question. Many lawyers who answer that way never fulfill their promises. Although this is a well-known rule, it is broken more frequently than one would expect. Once, a leading New York City lawyer, arguing an important corporate takeover case, responded to one of my questions by saying, "I'll get to that, Your Honor." He never did.

9. Don't quote extensively from the record or from a case or statute. Extensive quotation is a great waste of time. We can read for ourselves. Paraphrase whenever possible. Quote only when it is absolutely essential to your argument.

10. Don't answer a question with a question. Sometimes a judge's inquiry needs clarification, and you shouldn't hesitate to ask for it. Otherwise, questions, even rhetorical ones, should be avoided. One of my senior colleagues put a question to a young lawyer during oral argument and received this reply: "Why do you ask that, Your Honor?" That sort of reply is not well-received. Of course, it is far better than the following reply received by a judge in the Eighth Circuit: "You wouldn't want to know that, Your Honor."

11. Don't give a page number of the brief or of the record in response to a judge's inquiry. Such a response prompts the judge to root around in the papers and become distracted from the argument. Answer the question to the best of your ability and then refer to the appropriate page if necessary.

12. Don't cite any cases in your brief that you are unable to discuss on both the facts and the law. During my days at the bar, I was always careful to reread every case cited in my brief just before oral argument. A judge easily loses confidence in your presentation when you are unable to discuss a case cited as authority for some proposition you are urging on the court.

13. Don't come to oral argument without shepardizing the citations in the brief and checking for current authority just before your presentation. One case we decided went off on a Supreme Court decision handed down between the filing of the brief and oral

argument. Counsel adversely affected by the decision was unable to discuss it with us, much to his detriment. A brief trip to LEXIS or Westlaw before his appearance could have saved him this embarrassment.

14. Don't engage in prolonged discussion of basic legal principles. You may assume that judges generally are familiar with the notion that guilt in a criminal case must be proved beyond a reasonable doubt. If you can pick up the legal discussion somewhere at the point of intermediate legal difficulty, I am sure we will be able to grasp it.

15. Don't underestimate the importance of the facts. A lawyer arguing an appeal should be able to respond to any question a judge may have about the facts. If the lawyer did not present the case in the trial court, he or she must become familiar with every part of the record. The facts are every bit as important as the law, frequently more so, and I am very much put off by a lawyer who has not mastered them.

16. Don't get caught in the crossfire. Sometimes two judges will use a lawyer as a foil while they argue with each other. This is a very interesting phenomenon and one with which I was somewhat unfamiliar until becoming an appellate judge. One judge asks, "Isn't it true that. . . ?" After the lawyer answers, the other judge says, "Yes, but isn't it also true that. . . ?" Don't be deterred from holding to your position while the judges attempt to use you to persuade each other.

17. Don't undertake an emotional appeal to the court. I am surprised by the number of lawyers who try to boost their cases with a visceral approach. Of course, judges get just as emotional as anybody else, but a lawyer who asks whether we would like our grandmothers to be victimized by the kind of conduct demonstrated in the case at bar is marked as a sure loser. Once during the course of a very bad argument, a lawyer screamed, "I have a most unfortunate client!" All three of us nodded in agreement.

18. Don't discuss your pleasure at being in our court or disparage yourself or try to flatter the judges. This is unnecessary and wasteful. One lawyer started his argument by explaining that it was his first time in our court, although he had argued many appeals in state courts and in other circuits. He went on to describe the great honor that had befallen him by being retained to argue before us. He had been assigned only ten minutes for his argument, and he used up most of it with this type of persiflage. Moreover, as Justice Jackson said, there is no need to flatter judges; they have a high enough regard for themselves.

19. Don't use your rebuttal time unless it is absolutely necessary. It probably is a good idea to reserve some time for rebuttal when

you represent an appellant. Many lawyers, however, do not use the time to rebut the respondent's arguments. They merely repeat what they already have said. The same deficiency is characteristic of many reply briefs. Repetition always should be avoided.

20. Don't divide the oral argument. When more than one lawyer argues for one side, trouble often ensues. The custom in such a situation is for one lawyer to argue one or more points and for the other lawyer on the same side to argue the other points. Unfortunately, the court often fails to honor the division. The result is utter confusion, with lawyers being questioned on points with which they are unfamiliar. The representation of separate clients and separate interests, of course, presents a different situation.

21. Don't present an unstructured argument. Some lawyers appear for argument with no idea how they intend to present their cases. I suppose they hope we will take up their time with questions. When no questions are forthcoming, they flounder around with no beginning, middle, or end to their arguments. While one lawyer was engaged in such an exercise, one of my senior colleagues passed me a note that said, "Isn't this god-awful?"

22. Don't speak in a monotone. You cannot catch the attention of judges with soporific speech. Although you should avoid purely emotional appeals, you must demonstrate some passion for your cause, and this usually is accomplished by modulations of speech. Effective use of voice can be most helpful in an oral presentation.

23. Don't allow distracting mannerisms to interfere with your oral argument. Playing with a pencil, sticking your hands in front of your face, pacing up and down in front of the podium, and tapping a pen on the microphone are just some of the things that draw our attention from the argument. Avoid these distractions.

24. Don't be unprepared. When I was a young lawyer, I learned that Justice Frankfurter would ask questions about Roman law during oral argument. I lived in fear that some judge would ask me about Roman law during the argument of one of my cases. While it generally is not necessary to have such arcane information at your fingertips, there is no substitute for thorough preparation for oral argument. Many large law firms conduct moot arguments in-house. A law professor at the University of Minnesota Law School told me that she is retained from time to time to assist lawyers in preparing for oral argument. Some of the best oral arguments are given in law school moot court competitions. The reason, of course, is the frequent rehearsals. Practice, indeed, makes perfect!

25. Don't forget the tenth commandment of John W. Davis, who argued in the Supreme Court more often than any other lawyer of his generation: "When you are finished, sit down." One of the most discouraging things seen by an appellate judge is a lawyer who has finished his argument but insists on saying a few more words to fill his remaining time allotment. Sometimes those extra words merely are superfluous and annoying to the judges, and sometimes they actually are detrimental to the speaker's case.

Appellate Oral Argument

Gary L. Sasso

Some lawyers say you can't win appeals in oral argument, but they think you can *lose* them there. I think that is half right. Close cases especially can be won *or* lost in oral argument. There are many reasons. Appellate judges are busy, and they are fallible. The time they can spend on an appeal before they vote is a tiny fraction of the years of litigation history that make a case what it is. An appellate court must depend upon lawyers to supply what it needs to know to decide the case, but counsel have few chances to do that. The briefs are crucial, of course, but many judges read briefs quickly, sometimes 15 minutes here or there, amidst their other duties. And a few judges do not read the briefs at all; they ask their law clerks to do the reading and prepare bench memos summarizing the parties' contentions.

An appellate court's only direct contact with counsel is oral argument. This is the sole occasion when the panel can talk to a lawyer, and it is usually the first time that the panel devotes its undivided attention, as a group, to your case. So it is that several years of litigation, scores of depositions, warehouses of documents, hundreds of thousands of dollars of expense, and millions of dollars in controversy may depend on how you use 20 minutes at the lectern. It deserves thought.

Too often, lawyers fail to take full advantage of this chance to inform and persuade the court. Worse, by mishandling argument, a lawyer may make a good case look bad. The problem stems from a failure (or refusal) to grasp certain fundamentals. Most lawyers have heard these fundamentals; they may claim that they observe them. But, in actual practice, counsel either do not take them to heart, or they wrongly feel justified in making exceptions that swallow the rules.

Gary L. Sasso is a partner with Carlton Fields in Tampa, Florida, and is a former associate editor of LITIGATION.

Before considering these principles, there is a yet more basic matter: You cannot—absolutely cannot—be effective in oral argument unless you establish and maintain *credibility* with the court. This is not a gimmick. Credibility does not mean merely sounding sincere, although that will follow from doing everything else you need to do. Credibility comes from having command of the issues, the facts, and the law. It comes from clear reasoning. And it comes from your honesty and integrity in dealing with the court. In other words, it means demonstrating, in all you do, that you are worth listening to and that you can be believed. The principles that follow all contribute to that.

1. Keep it simple. This maxim has been stated so often that it may seem numbingly obvious. But the same might be said of "Thou shalt not kill." Each is repeated a lot because each means a lot. Violating either rule can lead to disaster.

Chances are, whatever you *expect* to argue, the court will make you keep it simple by using up your time asking questions. Those inquiries will concern a few central issues. But you don't want to get to simplicity by accident. To be most effective, you need to *plan* a limited, incisive argument. If you begin complex, the court will leave you stammering, searching vainly for a way to argue what the court does not want to hear.

In handling an appeal, "keeping it simple" means limiting the appeal, as counsel for the appellant, to one to three grounds, and, as counsel for either side, selecting one to three points about those grounds to emphasize in argument.

If you represent the appellant, you should have made hard judgments, long before argument, when selecting the grounds for the appeal. Frustrated by an adverse outcome and peeved by many unhappy rulings, large and small, trial counsel often want to appeal on six or eight grounds. Bad idea. Appellate courts are skeptical of scattershot appeals. Appellate courts loathe appeals that (l) take issue with a trial judge's exercise of discretion in gray areas, or that (2) attack rulings that probably had no impact on the outcome. Appellate courts cannot and will not second-guess trial judges on such points. Almost always, appeals that raise too many issues spend too much effort on points that fall into one of these two categories.

What is worse, pursuing weak grounds on appeal limits the attention you can give, and that the court will give, to the few grounds that really matter. Equally important, asserting weak grounds will impair your credibility; it will cast doubt on your good judgment and on your understanding of the difference between trial and appellate courts. Resist the temptation to make all possible arguments. Your client is paying you to exercise judgment. Do this by selecting the strongest grounds for appeal. And decide *not* to argue some points.

Whichever side you represent, you must tighten the focus even more when selecting points to be emphasized in oral argument. You will not have time to say everything that could be said about even two or three grounds for appeal. You may not even have time to address such grounds adequately. Take your best shot; focus your time and attention on the pivotal point or points. Then tell the court that you will rest on your brief on the remaining points, and offer to answer questions on those issues.

2. Do not reargue your brief. Resist the temptation to base the text and structure of oral argument on the contents of your brief. It usually is unwise to organize your argument exactly the way you organized your brief.

This is so because briefs and oral argument have different functions and conventions. Writing and talking are different activities. What works in one does not in the other.

The written brief will discuss the record and the law in considerable detail. Although you should prepare the statement of facts, the discussion of the law, and the written argument in ways that substantiate your basic analysis, a brief must incorporate material that you need not repeat, and cannot repeat, in the short time allotted for oral argument. Remember, we do not talk like we write—and judges do not listen like they read, flipping back and forth through parts or pages, or even sentences, of the brief.

A brief and oral argument have different starting points. Your brief will constitute the court's first exposure to the case, or to your side of it. By the time you argue the case, however, the court probably will have read your brief, or at least will be familiar with it. In fact, your own perspective on the case may have evolved since the time you filed your initial brief.

In preparing for oral argument you should of course carefully review the briefs. (More on that later.) But then put them aside; with the written argument fresh in your mind, ask yourself what the case is really about. Do not cheat by looking back at the briefs. Simply *think* about the case.

Once you have that clear idea of the essence of the case, independent of your earlier written exposition, address it head-on in your argument. Feel free to characterize or analyze the issues differently from the way you did in your brief (without injecting entirely new issues, of course).

Briefs begin with a detailed statement of the case. Oral argument should not. Begin your oral argument with a concise (one or two sentence) statement of the issues. Then tell the court how you believe the issues must be resolved. Next, state the key facts—not all the facts—that should dictate the outcome. This should take no more than a minute—the oral equivalent of a paragraph. (You will have a chance to discuss significant details later during your argument.) You should include in this early part of your argument only those facts that provide a necessary predicate to your analysis.

Having set the stage for your analysis, discuss why your client should prevail. This is the heart of your argument; it should consume most of your time. Begin with a concise statement of the controlling legal principles. Do not ramble, and do not make things complicated. By this time, you should have sufficient command of the case to reduce the controlling principles to clear, simple statements that are compelling and supportable. Do not digress to discuss authorities in any detail unless the entire appeal turns on a key case.

Next, if possible, state the policy served by these principles or the practical basis for them. This should take no more than two or three sentences. Then apply the controlling principles to the central facts in your case. You should have these facts at your fingertips; each should be reduced to a sentence or two.

If your case involves an issue of statutory construction, you will need to organize the argument somewhat differently. Start with a short description of the issue and of the factual setting in which the issue arises. If particular canons of statutory construction may be dispositive, start with them. If not, begin by characterizing the statutory provision involved, asserting your interpretation. Then concisely discuss the exact language of that provision and the language of other relevant provisions, demonstrating how the text of the statute supports your construction. Discuss any applicable legislative history. Next, summarize any judicial interpretations. Finally, apply the statutory language and purpose to your case. You will have done all this in detail in your brief, of course. In oral argument, the discussion must be reduced to simple, distinct points that flow logically from one to the next.

The object of your analysis is to help the court forge a rule of law—a decision with possibly wide-ranging implications—to decide your case. This will amount to the court's "holding" in your case, and the court understandably will be interested in it. Your framework for analyzing the issues and the holding that emerges must be good policy, not only in your case but in others like it.

At all times, you should move logically and briskly through your argument, keeping the points you want to make and the crucial facts you want to emphasize distinctly in mind. Regardless of the case, you should be able to state the key elements of your argument in two or three minutes. You should be able to list these elements in bullet-point form on the front of one page, and you should be able to recount the holding you seek in a sentence or two. If you cannot do this, work harder at really understanding your case.

3. Explain why you are right. In planning and making your argument, you must develop an explanation of why your client should win, *regardless* of what your adversary argues. You must show the court why you are right, not just why the other side is wrong. The two are not the same.

It surely is possible that your opponent will stumble. He may overlook important arguments or facts in his favor, or he may make weak arguments that you can destroy. But beating your opponent—hammering at these fault lines—is not enough. An appeal is not a debate to be won on points. Regardless of the respective lawyer's skill, the court wants to reach the *right* result—an outcome that will make good law and good sense. If you focus your efforts on attacking your adversary's argument, you may stint on helping the court determine the right way to analyze the case.

Remember, even if you leave the other side's bad arguments sprawled in the dust, the *court* may think of its own reasons why you should lose. So you must give the court a sound framework for deciding the case that will guide the panel after it retires to chambers. It helps to think about how you would justify what you want if the other side had never submitted a brief or entered an appearance.

This means that if you represent the appellant, you should first make *your* case; save your refutation of the appellee's arguments until rebuttal, unless the court's questions require you to do that earlier.

As counsel for appellee, you must take special care not to be yanked onto the other side's turf. If you do, you will spend all of your time on the defensive—and you will have, in a sense, accepted the appellant's approach. You will have dignified it by attacking it. There may of course be times when you should begin by addressing points that came up during your opponent's argument. But, in so doing, explain your own perspective and framework for the case.

Say, for example, that in making a particular point, opposing counsel has overlooked a central principle that governs the case. Then tell the court what that principle is and how it controls the outcome. If you have done your homework well, you should be able to address all the arguments your adversary makes, but within your framework for the case.

Do not, however, feel obliged to refute *everything* your adversary says. You must make judgments about what is important and what is not. Once again, your objective is to hammer home the right way—*your* way—of analyzing the issues. Do not let your adversary take you (and the court) down rabbit trails that will lead away from this central objective.

4. Answer questions promptly and responsively. I have heard even experienced counsel complain about "interruptions" during oral argument by the court. The court's questions should *never* be regarded as interruptions. You are thinking the wrong way if you fail to see questions as the principal reason for oral argument. Appellate briefs usually are thorough. What oral argument adds is a chance for the court to ask lawyers about questions it has after reading the briefs. If oral argument were merely a time for restating the contents of the briefs, it might inflate lawyers' egos, but it would be largely useless to the court.

Questions by the court must be taken as important opportunities to learn what may be troubling the judges. Many judges prepare questions before argument starts. Each question is asked for a reason.

Address the court's questions directly and immediately. In *all* cases, begin your response with "yes," "no," "it depends," or "I don't know." *Then* provide any necessary explanation. *Never* say, "I will get to that shortly," or "I need to provide some background before I answer the question." The panel may allow this, but the judges will not like it. If a judge asks a question at a particular point in the argument, it is because the judge wants the answer *then*, not later.

It is equally unacceptable to answer a question circuitously, with a long-winded answer, rather than by starting with "yes," "no," or the like. *You* may believe that you are answering the question directly, but the court surely will not. The court will perceive that it has hit a nerve. It may conclude that your long-winded response is an effort to be fuzzy about a topic on which a simple, pointed response would be unfavorable to your client. At best, the court will lose patience with you.

In fact, if your adversary sidesteps a question, or answers it evasively, you should seize the opportunity during *your* argument to answer the question squarely. That way, you show the court that *you* have command of the case, that *you* have nothing to hide, and that *you* understand what the court expects from lawyers during argument.

If you have prepared well, you will anticipate all the court's important questions. You will be able to use these questions as points of departure to explain your framework. Ideally, you will be able to make every point you need to make by developing your responses to the court's questions.

By the same token, if you have prepared well, you will be able to recognize when a question has little to do with the central issues. Sometimes, after all, an inquiry may emerge from judicial misunderstanding. Answer such questions anyway, but do not belabor the point. Return as gracefully as you can to the matters at hand.

5. Be flexible. Partly because the court's questions are so important, you must be flexible going into argument. Several years ago, Lawrence G. Wallace, a deputy solicitor general, began an argument before the United States Supreme Court by giving an elaborate outline of what he intended to cover. "Mr. Wallace," then Associate Justice Rehnquist asked dryly, "will you be entertaining questions?"

If the court starts by asking about an issue you wanted to cover last, be prepared, on the spot, to reorganize your argument; cover the last point first. You may not have time to take up the issue "in turn." Remember also that if you address the point at any length in responding to questions, the court may not have the patience to hear more about the same point later merely because it is there on your outline.

If your argument is as simple and cogent as it should be, you ought to be able to reshuffle its parts, like reorganizing flash cards. Only the transitions will change. This approach may be new to you; you may balk. But such flexibility is crucial if you are to have any chance of making an argument that the *court* wants to hear—as opposed to one that *you* are determined to make.

The court understands that its questions take time to answer. It knows that its questions may affect the organization of your thoughts. But the court wants dialogue, not speeches. If you have prepared (as you should) to make a few key points, you will get them across in response to some question or other. And if you understand how each is significant to the rest of your analysis, you can explain that effectively, too.

6. Be honest with the court. In responding to the court's questions, you may be called upon to address difficult matters of law or fact that you did not develop in your brief. Such questions may make you squirm. Answer them anyway, like all others, honestly and concisely. It is permissible to use your skills as an advocate to put your weak points in the best light, but *never* trifle with the court. Apart from ethical considerations, you will wreck your credibility and seriously compromise your client's interests if you are evasive or untruthful.

Sometimes the court may ask you hypothetical questions. Such inquiries test the limits of the rule of law that you advocate. These are different from questions about the record or the case law. You are free to tell the court that "we take no position" on a hypothetical question, but it may be imprudent to do so. You *may* irritate the court or lose credibility, and you *will* leave unaddressed the concerns that prompted the question. Generally you will be better served by thinking through the implications of your position enough to be able to address hypothetical questions directly and succinctly. This may include making concessions when necessary, while making clear that your client must still prevail in the different, *non*-hypothetical circumstances of your case.

7. Maintain a tone of "respectful equality." You must show the appellate panel deference in presenting your case and in responding to questions. Still, you should not confuse respect with timidity or obsequiousness. Maintain a tone of "respectful equality." In your demeanor and in the force and conviction of your argument, show the court that you are an intellectual peer, but at the same time treat judges courteously. Do not raise your voice, make faces, or show impatience at questions from the bench—and *never* interrupt a judge before he or she completes a question or finishes making an observation. But do not be intimidated into conceding an argument that you believe you should win.

Remember that when you and the panel reach an impasse, the panel will win (absent review by a higher tribunal). You thus may sometimes be called upon to decide during argument that you should move on. It may become apparent that what you are arguing is going nowhere. If this occurs, do not show disgust or despair. Simply move on to grounds that may meet with more success.

8. Prepare with the end in mind. Finally, you should prepare for oral argument with a view to what will actually happen at argument. Many lawyers prepare by planning what they will say uninterrupted by the court. By now, it should be clear that oral argument involves much more than that. You are not the only player. You must anticipate what the other players—the court and opposing counsel—may do.

Begin by reviewing all the briefs. Make notes of problems that you must resolve by the time of argument, and then resolve them. Become completely familiar with all your weaknesses.

Next review the full text of the principal cases cited by the parties. With the benefit of the briefs and the passage of time, you will likely gain new insight into the issues. Having taken this step, update your research to catch developments in the law and in the later histories of the cases you cited.

Review the record, cover to cover. You must know key passages and pleadings for the argument. Tab these pages and include citations to them in your notes. You can also note pages in your brief that cite those portions of the record. During argument, you should be able to direct the court's attention to important parts of the record.

At this point, put all your materials aside and simply think about the case. Jot down the key issues, and rough out an outline of your analysis. Then think about the case some more. The aim is to come to grips with what the case is really about—to develop a simple analysis that cuts through the fog. You must work until you identify straightforward, compelling reasons why your client should win. Keep revising until your argument is forceful, simple, and tight.

Do *not* write out your argument. Many lawyers do. If you are wedded to this practice, so be it. But if you have not developed the habit (or superstition), do not start; and, if you have, break it if you can. Scripting your argument will reduce your flexibility. Even during preparation, you will feel obliged to "edit" your script instead of trashing your simple outline and starting afresh when warranted. During argument, the script will do you even less good. If you rely on it much, it may hamper your ability to adapt. At best, writing your argument will waste time. Faced with persistent questions, you almost never will have a chance to deliver the argument as written.

Do not be too concerned about stumbling around somewhat in argument if you operate without a script. Almost everyone does. Remember, *what* you say is more important to the court than *how* you say it. An effective oral argument has less to do with eloquence than it does with clear thinking and getting to the point. We no longer live in the era of Daniel Webster and his florid oratory.

Having developed a basic idea of what your argument will be, broaden your preparation by reviewing all cases of any significance cited by the parties. You may want to annotate your brief with a one-phrase description of the holding or key facts of each such case. Be prepared to distinguish bad cases that the court may ask you about.

Next, list all difficult questions that the court may ask. Put yourself in the court's shoes for this exercise. Keep in mind that the court will be concerned about jurisdictional issues and the procedural posture of the case. It may want to determine the narrowest possible ground on which to dispose of the case. Do not ignore these matters simply because the *parties* have not devoted much attention to them or because you do not intend to raise them in argument. You may not have a choice. Ultimately, you must satisfy the court; you must be prepared to address *its* concerns.

Prepare a one- or two-line response to each question, jotting down in your notes a phrase or two. This will take some thought. You should not write out responses word for word. That will be less helpful preparation than key words or phrases. You will not have time to find these answers and to read them during argument. The point is to think through your potential responses *before* argument so that you can respond quickly and concisely, and to make a list that you can use to refresh your memory the day before argument. This will help you avoid long, rambling, non-responsive answers.

Anticipate Opposition Arguments

Anticipate the arguments your adversary will make, and prepare short, direct responses to them. Identify the crux of your opponent's case, and decide how to meet it. Again, in argument you will not have the time to dispute unimportant, incidental arguments or assertions. Do not succumb to that distraction.

Rehearse your argument two to three times, *without memorizing it*. You will present the argument somewhat differently each time, but that is perfectly acceptable—in fact, it is desirable. Rehearsing the argument will help you develop deft transitions, and it will "groove" the argument in your brain. Rehearsing the argument also will give you some sense of how long it will take to make the points you must make. You almost always will have to trim down the argument as a result of this exercise. In fact, even once it is trimmed, assume that actual delivery will take 40 percent longer than your best rehearsal.

A compromise security blanket is to memorize your opening line (usually a statement of the issues). This will have a calming effect as you first stand at the podium; it will help get you off to a good start. But from that point on, look the judges in the eye and *talk*—not declaim or recite—to them.

For important cases, or for your first few appeals, ask colleagues to put you through a moot court. This can be tremendously helpful. Moot court members will see problems—even gestures or fidgeting—you may not know you have. Allow at least one day between moot court and the actual argument to give yourself enough time to research or think through issues that come up for the first time in the practice session—and perhaps to recover your self-confidence.

Having prepared your argument, condense your outline to one or two pages if possible. Set forth only the key points, key facts, and key citations that you may need at argument. Use words or phrases rather than full sentences. This will be far more helpful when you are on your feet than a full-text script attractively bound and tabbed in a three-ring notebook.

Be sure to review your court's procedural rules before argument. Check the rules *and* any internal operating procedures published or made available by the court in which you will appear.

Make a checklist of all materials that you want to bring to court, and list last-minute chores that you need to complete before argument. These details are easy to forget amid the interruptions and distractions that inevitably occur before argument.

Finally, when and if you can, find out which judges will sit on your panel. If you have time (some courts will not tell you the panel's makeup until the day of the argument), review the key cases cited by the parties to determine whether any of your panel members participated in those decisions. This can help you avoid embarrassment if a panel member brings up a case during argument.

You may hear or believe that oral argument is an art. To a degree, that is true, but it is irrelevant. Whatever your experience or inborn skill, the fundamentals count. Observe them, and you will improve your artistry.

Questions, Answers, and Prepared Remarks

Stephen M. Shapiro

Nearly 50 years ago, John W. Davis aptly commented that there would be scant occasion to listen to lawyers if appellate judges would divulge the secrets of oral argument. "[S]upposing fishes had the gift of speech, who would listen to a fisherman's weary discourse on flycasting?" "The Argument of an Appeal," 26 *A.B.A. J.* 895 (1940). More than two generations later, the fish have begun not only to speak, but also to give detailed advice to struggling flycasters. Appellate judges have furnished the bar with speeches, articles, and even books containing practical tips and insights. Consider, for example, the advice of the justices of the Supreme Court of the United States.

In a television program commemorating the constitutional bicentennial ("This Honorable Court," WETA, 1988), several of the justices provided a behind-the-bench view of oral argument. Justice Scalia, one of the Court's most active questioners during oral argument, said he "was quite surprised at how much difference it makes." The Justice noted that the argument is both a colloquy between the Court and counsel and among the members of the Court: "It isn't just an interchange between counsel and each of the individual justices. What is going on is also to some extent an exchange of information among the justices themselves. You hear the questions of the others and see how their minds are working, and that stimulates your own thinking. I use it," he added, "to give counsel his or her best shot at meeting my major difficulty with that side of the case. 'Here's what's preventing me from going along with you. If you can explain why that's wrong, you have me.'"

Stephen M. Shapiro, formerly deputy solicitor general of the United States, is a partner at Mayer, Brown & Platt in Chicago. He is a co-author of R. Stern, E. Gressman, S. Shapiro & K. Geller, Supreme Court Practice *(7th ed. 1993).*

In the same program, Justice White remarked that oral argument operates in effect as a preliminary conference for deciding the case: "All of us on the bench [are] working on the case, trying to decide it.... They think we are there just to learn about the case. Well, we are learning, but we are trying to decide it, too." In other words, "[I]t is then that all of the justices are working on the case together, having read the briefs and anticipating that they will have to vote very soon, and attempting to clarify their own thinking and perhaps that of their colleagues. Consequently, we treat lawyers as a resource rather than as orators who should be heard out according to their own desires." B. White, "The Work of the Supreme Court: A Nuts and Bolts Description," 54 *N.Y. State Bar J.* 346, 383 (1982).

How does a lawyer make a positive impression in this conference environment? Chief Justice Rehnquist offers an answer in his book, *The Supreme Court* 281 (1987). He describes the "All American oral advocate" in the following terms: "She will realize that there is an element of drama in oral argument.... But she also realizes that her spoken lines must have substantive legal meaning.... She has a theme and a plan for her argument, but is quite willing to pause and listen carefully to questions.... She avoids table pounding and other hortatory mannerisms, but she realizes equally well that an oral argument on behalf of one's client requires controlled enthusiasm and not an impression of *fin de siecle* ennui." Thus, the difference between live argument and a written brief "may perhaps be summarized by the difference between a preview of a movie and the movie itself. The preview consists solely of scenes from the movie, but the preview selects dramatic or interesting scenes that are apt to catch the interest of the viewer and make him or her want to see the entire movie." W. Rehnquist, "Oral Advocacy: A Disappearing Art," 35 *Mercer L. Rev.* 1015, 1024–1025 (1984).

Chief Justice Rehnquist's predecessor, Warren E. Burger, stressed the need for thorough preparation in presenting appellate arguments: "Oral arguments, which help the justices get quickly to the core—the jugular—of the legal issues call for a high degree of skill and careful preparation. The Supreme Court is no place for inexperienced or ill-prepared advocates; such advocates provide little help to the Court; they do a disservice to their clients—and to themselves." At the same time, Chief Justice Burger warned against attempting to read to the Court from a rigid "set argument." He urged counsel "to tell us about the case in your own words." "Foreword, Conference on Supreme Court Advocacy," 33 *Cath. U. L. Rev.* 525, 527 (1984).

These comments from the bench place the oral argument process in a clear light. Like their colleagues in most appellate courts, the justices of the Supreme Court view the argument not as an occasion for speeches or a game of 20 questions, but rather as an initial conference convened to decide the case. Counsel is invited into the conference for two purposes:

to serve as a resource providing information needed to clarify the thinking of the justices, and to bring an organizing theme, emphasis, and note of drama needed to marshal the information in a meaningful way.

Preparing Flexible Arguments

That, of course, is a tall order for any lawyer. It is hard enough to make an oral presentation that is legally sound and also dramatic and interesting. It is still more difficult to get to the heart of the case while providing spontaneous answers to tough questions posed by a "hot" appellate bench. To accomplish both goals simultaneously—and in a half hour or less—is a daunting task.

And yet it is a task that cannot be shirked. Who has not witnessed the embarrassing futility of the appellate lawyer who merely plays the part of a speechmaker or off-the-cuff commentator? The lawyer bent on delivering a carefully drafted speech is quickly disconcerted by interruptions and questions that reduce the speech to a shambles. The spontaneous commentator, despite quiz-show ingenuity, thrusts and parries with the bench but fails to guide the discussion to any discernible goal. The rough-and-tumble conference environment of modern appellate courts requires a flexible oral argument, in which answers to questions and prepared remarks blend into a single stream of discussion that produces an overriding understanding of how to decide the case properly.

A flexible argument suitable to the conference environment of modern appellate courts requires special preparation. To begin with, the prepared argument must have an accordion-like capacity. It must expand or contract to accommodate unpredictable amounts of questioning. Lawyers with 30 minutes of allotted time often prepare an argument that occupies ten minutes and an alternative argument that occupies 20. One of these alternative formats can be chosen depending on whether questioning is light or heavy. An adjustable argument can also be fashioned by outlining the presentation and then bracketing points and subpoints that are expendable if questioning becomes intense.

Bear in mind that the first few minutes of argument are the most likely to include a peaceful interlude for presentation of affirmative points. It is therefore essential to plan the opening of the argument to set forth the most compelling grounds for a favorable decision, without elaborate recitations of facts or procedural history. These opening remarks must, of course, focus on the most convincing reasons that can be advanced in favor of a party's position. They must be simple enough to be explained in a few sentences and understood through the oral medium. In the words of Chief Justice Burger—and many others—go for "the jugular."

Going for the jugular means not only going for the most important reasons for victory but also stripping the case down to its essentials. Give the judges the few dispositive ideas they must take with them into the voting conference.

Practice your exposition of these points on your colleagues and friends to confirm that it makes good common sense and is intuitively appealing.

A brief description of the points to be elaborated in the course of the argument is helpful at the outset, but this should not be carried too far. One lawyer who ambitiously described the many subjects he hoped to canvass during his argument met with the following humorous query from the chief justice: "Will you be entertaining questions?"

The points in a flexible argument must be not only expandable and contractable, but also interchangeable. During the heat of argument, the court inevitably will disrupt the flow of your outline by asking questions about subjects you hoped to reserve for later treatment. Questions that emerge out of order must be dealt with as they arise to avoid antagonizing the questioner. This requires you to become so familiar with each issue in the case that you can take it up on the spur of the moment despite the prearranged structure of the argument. The best means for acquiring this flexibility is practice. Moot court sessions and freewheeling discussions with colleagues will equip you to take up issues outside of their preconceived order. But do not totally jettison your argument plan. If the coherence and optimal arrangement of points can be preserved, try to do so.

Perhaps the most important step in preparing a flexible presentation is anticipating questions and devising responses that interlink with affirmative arguments. Advance scouting of questions lays the intellectual groundwork for a weaving together of planned remarks and responses to questions. This helps avoid awkward moments in which counsel gropes for the lost thread of the argument after sharp questioning from the bench.

In trying to predict questions from the bench, keep foremost in mind the familiar commonsense concerns of the court:

- What is the case about? (What holding do you want? What rule do you want the court to adopt to justify that holding? Is there any other rule that would satisfy you?)
- How would your rule work? (What are the practical consequences of the rule? How would it change current practices? Can it be administered?)
- What will the rule mean in future cases? (How far does your rule go? Where does it meet a limiting principle? Will lower courts have trouble applying it?)
- Can the court do that? (Is there a legally respectable argument for the rule based on traditional principles of interpretation? Is it consistent with what the court has said before? Does it conform to governing statutory or constitutional language and history?)
- Why should we do that? (What values and interests would be advanced by adoption of the proposed rule? Would opposing values and interests be fairly accommodated?)

After anticipating questions in these categories, try to develop simple and commonsense replies that are convincing on an intuitive level even to a layman. Many lawyers find it helpful to jot down the questions and answers and use them as aids throughout the period of argument preparation.

The briefs and opinions below should be reviewed with care to spot difficult questions. Take off your advocate's hat and formulate questions that relentlessly expose the weaknesses in your position.

In particular, use your best imaginative efforts to anticipate hypothetical questions—questions about future cases presenting similar problems that the appellate court will want to consider when drafting its opinion. Appellate judges may besiege counsel with hypothetical questions, some of them long, complex, and not easily grasped. They often require a lawyer to range a great distance from the facts before the court. Even if you do not anticipate the very questions that ultimately arise, the mental process of grappling with a host of hypothetical questions before argument will improve your ability to respond spontaneously to such inquiries.

A key component of preparation for questions from the bench is the familiar process of studying the record below, the cited authorities, the legislative history, and the scholarly commentary. This part of argument preparation is time-consuming and tedious. But it serves you well by permitting quick and accurate communication of information called for by the court, thereby enhancing your usefulness and elevating your credibility in the fast-moving conference environment.

Once affirmative arguments are identified and outlined, questions have been anticipated, and transitions between prepared remarks and answers to questions have been considered, you must practice the argument to improve its clarity and impact. Rehearsals permit you to cut out fuzzy detail, long-winded explanations, lengthy quotations, and detailed case discussion, and provide good practice in shifting smoothly between prepared comments and responses to questions. They also permit you to prune your argument to meet time limits.

Practice the argument both in the solitude of your office and before a moot court panel. Many lawyers argue to a moot court several times. First let the panel hear your argument without interruption to assess its strength and clarity. Then rehearse with your panel without time limitation to make sure that you can present affirmative points while responding to all questions that emerge. Finally, practice the argument subject to the time constraints of the actual argument.

In preparing for argument, bear in mind the differences between the presentation of the appellant and the appellee. The appellee, in addition to presenting prepared remarks and answering questions, must respond in short measure to points made by opposing counsel and to questions discussed in the preceding colloquy with the bench. Even the appellee, however, must have a prepared outline of essential affirmative reasons for ruling in his favor. It is not enough merely to rebut the points made by opposing counsel.

All Kinds of Questions

During the argument itself, the key to efficient integration of prepared comments with answers to questions is making snap judgments about individual questions and the appropriate scope of your response. Questions from the bench come in all forms and varieties: They range from the difficult to the obvious, from the subtle to the whimsical. Some of them are good springboards for affirmative arguments; others are sideshows that call for accurate, but brief, answers and a prompt transition to more important subjects. Here are some examples:

Questions that go to the heart of the case. As noted by Justice Scalia, some appellate judges ask questions that go to the central issue in the case and that are critical to their votes. The answers to such questions not only may determine the vote of the questioner, but also may sway the judgment of others on the panel who share the same point of view. If the questioning judge has an erroneous view of the record, the governing law, or your submission, this kind of question affords a golden opportunity to set the matter straight. First provide a direct response to the question. Then weave in more general affirmative points from the outline of prepared remarks.

Background questions. Many questions during argument simply require a clarification of a record fact or some finding or conclusion in the courts below. Other questions manifest curiosity about matters such as the background of the litigation or the votes of the judges below. These questions require an accurate answer, but it is inefficient to dwell on them. Move along without delay.

Fencing or debating questions. Appellate judges sometimes engage in extended debates with counsel that may or may not relate to the central issues in the case. You cannot, of course, cut off such debates, even if the issue seems tangential. By the same token, however, you need to avoid becoming bogged down in intellectually stimulating digressions while precious argument time ticks away. Give the best possible answer and find a tactful way to get back to the main points.

Humorous questions or observations. Enjoy the remark and get back to business. While appellate judges may offer a humorous observation or question, lawyers ordinarily should refrain from introducing jocular comments of their own. As often as not, attempts at humor fall flat, and in most instances are a waste of limited argument time.

Irrelevant questions. It is not unusual to hear a question that sounds irrelevant. But it is not for counsel to call it that. Never display irritation over a question that seems beside the point. Give a polite answer and suppress any annoyance.

Hostile questions. Assume from the beginning that some of the judges will present hostile or unfriendly questions. Do not be unnerved or disappointed. Tough questioning usually is an effort to test the soundness of a position, not necessarily a rejection of it. A hostile tone also may be a sign of frustration that the questioner is in the minority. Keep in mind that while one judge may be dissatisfied with a position or answer, a majority may be leaning the other way. Give a polite but firm response to the hostile questioner and interject affirmative contentions. Avoid a "cross-examination" environment, in which you concede negative matters but neglect to weave in positive considerations.

Friendly questions. Not all questions are hostile or unfriendly. A sympathetic judge may intervene with a friendly question or even a restatement of your position, which is designed to place the case in a favorable light. Ordinarily, such helpful reformulations should be acknowledged and accepted. On occasion, however, a judge may ask a question that is not quite accurate in its friendly implications. The best response is to accept the help but politely point out the mistake. For example: "I would agree with Your Honor's approach, but I think the main support in this situation comes from. . . ." It is not advisable merely to accept the help if it rests on a mistaken premise; the other judges will identify the fallacy and embarrass you for failing to do so.

Vital to your efforts to participate constructively in the conference environment and avoid unnecessary friction are a few simple rules of courtroom etiquette. The cardinal rule in dealing with all questions from the bench is this: Give a direct, nonevasive response. Inexperienced lawyers annoy appellate judges by evading questions—responding, for example, by saying "that presents a different case" or "that really isn't what this case is about." The court is well aware that its questions call for analysis of a point different from the point counsel is pressing. Yet, it expects a straightforward answer.

In many instances, the questioning judge will ask for a yes or no answer. When that can be given—and it ordinarily can—you should do so. Explanation and elaboration can follow. When it is impossible to answer yes or no, briefly explain why and allow the judge to rephrase the question, or simply state: "The answer is yes, but my answer requires this qualification: _____."

All answers must be concise and clear. Ordinarily, it will be difficult to include more than one or two sentences in a response. A hot panel will interpose a different question if you drone on too long. But, never let eagerness to get back to a planned speech result in a back-of-the-hand answer. If the court has raised an important point and is willing to hear an extended response, counsel should not hesitate to provide it. An effort should be made to weave in affirmative points from your planned remarks as the answer unfolds.

Another potent source of annoyance is any attempt to postpone an answer. You cannot say "I have not yet come to that point in my argument." Interrupt your planned sequence and provide the answer. In some instances it is possible to give a concise answer on the spot, and then assure the court that you will elaborate after laying a bit of groundwork. When returning to the question later in the argument, be sure to link your elaboration to the earlier inquiry.

Listen Carefully

Confusion and irritation also result from failures by lawyers to listen carefully to questions from the bench. The object is not to blurt out a response to the question before it is finished, in the manner of a high school quiz show. Make sure that you understand exactly what the court is asking. If the question is unclear, the judge will recast it. Appellate judges are justifiably annoyed by lawyers who waste argument time by responding to questions that the court has *not* asked.

Many questions are difficult ones that put the arguing lawyer on the spot. It is futile to try to dodge these questions. They must be answered to the best of one's ability. It is permissible to say "I have not considered that variant of our situation," but you should then proceed to describe what factors are pertinent and give the best analysis of the proper outcome.

Judges frequently ask lawyers to make concessions during the course of the oral argument. Be careful in responding to these questions, because concessions made in open court can be used against you in deciding the case on the merits. Still, you cannot run away from concessions that must be made, and some concessions can actually improve a lawyer's credibility. This is particularly true of factual matters. For example, if a judge asks: "Isn't it true that your client testified _____?" an answer must be given in the affirmative if that is the case. In dealing with a question calling for a concession, *it is essential first to answer the question*, and only then explain why the conceded matter is not damaging. If a judge is disturbed that you are not making a concession that you must make, simply say "I do acknowledge Your Honor's point. The record shows _____ . That, however, is not dispositive here because. . . ."

Even greater care must be used in dealing with questions calling for a concession of law. For example, an appellate judge may ask: "Wouldn't you agree that the result would be different if the facts were _____?" If you are willing to stand on the distinction between your case and the variation described by the judge, you should answer in the affirmative. On the other hand, if it is not clear that the distinction is a dispositive one, or if your case is not greatly different from the hypothetical case, it is best not to concede the point at all. It is permissible to respond, "I wouldn't concede that this variation would produce a different result.

Your Honor has, of course, described a far less favorable case for applying the principle we rely on, but it would still control because...."

Because appellate courts must anticipate the future consequences of their decisions in the wide variety of cases arising throughout their jurisdiction, they are naturally concerned with the breadth of legal principles they announce. Be ready therefore for the question: "How far do you carry that principle? Would you apply it in the following instance: _____?" Hypothetical questions such as this are a central feature of modern oral argument and, as previously noted, require substantial preparation and analysis in advance. Bear in mind that every principle has a breaking point; stated otherwise, every principle meets a contrary principle at some point. Be wary of presenting arguments that sound radical because principles are extended too far. In distinguishing a hypothetical situation, remember also that it is not enough merely to say, "That is a different case." The judges know that. They want to understand where to draw the line and why.

Perhaps the most difficult problem of diplomacy faced by appellate counsel is the judge with a bulldog instinct for the weaknesses in your case and a disposition to wring concessions out of you without affording any opportunity to place the case in a positive light. Often, another judge will divert this colloquy by posing a different question that permits you to shift back to a more fruitful line of argument. In the absence of such relief, however, you must give the best answer firmly and politely, and attempt to steer the argument back on course by weaving in affirmative points. If it is necessary to disagree at the end of a colloquy, counsel should do so courteously: "With great deference, Your Honor, we see the issue in a very different light. In our view _____."

An effective way to add spontaneity and interest to a reply or rebuttal argument is to return to important questions asked of opposing counsel, who provided wrong or inadequate information or failed to face up to the difficulties implicit in his position. For example: "Justice _____ asked Mr. _____ whether _____. He answered _____. In fact, however, this court's decision in _____ forecloses that contention and makes clear _____." The argument should never turn into a flyspeck, point-by-point rebuttal, as opposed to a presentation of affirmative points, but a few well-selected responses of this kind will ensure that questions are adequately answered in areas of special interest to the court.

Appellate judges school lawyers in many ways. In addition to their extrajudicial commentary, they teach unforgettable lessons to all who attend oral arguments. Those who listen to a number of oral arguments not only gain an improved appreciation of the fine points from the performance of outstanding advocates, but also witness the harmful consequences of certain errors that are repeated with distressing frequency. The following mistakes spawn judicial annoyance, distraction, and simple boredom:

- Leading off the argument with a dubious or unnecessarily provocative contention that generates friction at the outset
- Sticking inflexibly to a prepared speech when the court expresses interest in other areas, or—worse yet—reading from a text with eyes glued to the typed page
- Failing to come to grips with the plain language of governing statutory, constitutional, or contractual provisions, or of controlling judicial precedent
- Attempting to cover all of the points raised in the briefs rather than only a few of the most important
- Racing through the argument at a rapid speed while judges struggle to absorb the points delivered
- Using overstatement or exaggeration in describing record facts
- Using an emotional jury argument or high-flown oratory
- Bellowing at the judges in a stentorian tone of voice or, conversely, mumbling and muttering
- Inflicting long delays while groping for page references, cases, or notes
- Wandering around or slouching over the lectern, rocking back and forth before the lectern, using awkward gesticulations, pointing at the judges, jiggling keys, or delaying proceedings while drinking water at the podium
- Using dry, monotonous speech, without any variation in pitch, pace, or volume
- Displaying lack of respect toward the bench, including flippancy or overfamiliarity
- Reading at great length from legislative history, opinions, statutes, regulations, or the trial record
- Using distracting physical exhibits
- Mischaracterizing the court's institutional role. For example, arguing in a constitutional case that "this court requires . . ." as opposed to arguing that "the Constitution, as construed by this court, requires . . ."
- Arguing to a particular judge that "Your Honor has held in the *Jones* case that. . . ." It is the court that has so held, in an opinion written by a particular judge

Perhaps the most harmful errors of all are made by counsel while responding to questions. Some of these mistakes are matters of substance; others are matters of style. All of them can throw a bath of cold water on your presentation. Besides the problems mentioned earlier, such blunders include:

- Giving long-winded, multiple-paragraph answers to straightforward questions, or relying on complex and incomprehensible factual descriptions in responding to questions

- Bluffing about knowledge of a case, statute, or trial transcript
- Indulging in repeated conferences with, or reviewing lengthy notes from, lawyers at counsel table prior to answering questions
- Disclaiming essential knowledge of the record with the lame excuse, "I didn't try the case, Your Honor."
- Giving fearful or timorous responses to overbearing questions, or displaying disappointment when questioning is hostile
- Attempting to answer questions by propounding other questions back to the court

It is little wonder that appellate judges, burdened with ever-increasing caseloads, are exasperated by the commission of these unnecessary blunders in case after case. By avoiding them, you will make yourself a welcome and effective participant in the conference environment of the modern appellate argument.

Moot Courts: Scrimmage for the Appellate Lawyer

Charles G. Cole

Looking over the podium at the panel, I could see that each judge had a list of questions and a stack of well-thumbed briefs. I remember introducing myself and explaining the question presented by the appeal. Then the barrage of questions began.

It was relentless: inquiries about the cases, about policy issues, about the record, and even about facts outside the record. Each of my answers became the starting point for yet another question. All of the soft spots in my case were exposed. What I thought were strengths were hammered repeatedly. But, at the end, I walked up to the panel members, shook their hands, and thanked them profusely. It had been humbling at times, but it was a great moot court.

My experience had done exactly what moot court is supposed to do: rehearse arguments, identify weaknesses, sharpen reflexes, and deepen knowledge of the case. Most lawyers encounter a moot court for the first—and, unfortunately, sometimes the last—time in law school. There, it is an academic exercise, on an imagined question. But real lawyers also do moot courts, and good lawyers take them seriously. In fact, an appellate advocate who does not participate in a moot court before oral argument is like an actor who skips a dress rehearsal or a quarterback who sits out the preseason.

Like other forms of practice, moot courts increase proficiency. The oral presentation becomes smoother, references to the record quicker and more assured, answers to questions more effective and natural. A moot court forces an advocate, not just to prepare his argument, but to *hear* it. That is often critical. It is not enough just to write or outline a pre-

---

Charles G. Cole is a partner in the Washington, D.C., law firm of Steptoe & Johnson, L.L.P.

sentation. Often, arguments that seemed weighty in the briefs sound sterile or ineffective when presented aloud. By listening to the argument as it is delivered, a lawyer can identify the themes that are effective in oral argument and those that are best left to written exposition.

But moot courts are more than just rehearsals. A good moot court simulates the give-and-take of a real oral argument. It is a laboratory for testing themes and expressions against the reactions of a group of uninvolved judges. It therefore does more than just add polish to a set argument. It is an opportunity for changing the argument and finding the most powerful means to persuade.

A well-designed moot court helps an appellate advocate in the same way a shadow jury assists a trial lawyer. The responses of a representative group of lawyers unfamiliar with the case can help predict the actual panel's reactions. If the moot court judges are confused by the briefs, it is likely that the panel will be, too. If the stand-in judges are swayed by particular arguments or facts, those arguments or facts will likely move the real court. If the moot court has questions about things not in the record, the panel may be similarly curious. It is a wonderful opportunity to test different theories and approaches, with no associated risks.

A good moot court will also help project your adversary's moves. Preparing for an oral argument without an opponent is like clapping with one hand. For the appellant—who usually submits the last written word in the appeal—the absence of any response in the days or weeks before the oral argument can be unsettling; it is always uninformative. An appellant wants to make the oral argument different from the written presentation, but needs to know if it is on target. This is difficult because he or she does not know how the appellee will respond to the reply brief. Probing questions and comments from a moot court panel will often supply that information.

Help for the Appellee

An appellee's needs are different, but can also be met by the moot court. An appellee often cannot wait to spring the carefully crafted, perhaps devastating, responses to the appellant's reply brief. But, at the actual argument, it will not be as easy as a simple ambush. The appellee will also need to respond to the appellant's immediately preceding oral presentation. Unanticipated, that oral argument can take the starch out of the appellee's rejoinders.

The moot court can help with this. The judges (or even a designated opponent) can be expected to extract the best arguments from the appellant's reply brief *and* launch them at the appellee during the practice session. This provides an opportunity to develop answers for *both* the appellant's reply brief *and* the anticipated oral argument.

Of course, any effort in litigation can be improved by advice from experienced lawyers uninvolved in the case. But it is often impractical, and sometimes not even helpful, to get such views until the positions and supporting evidence of both parties have been laid out in the briefs. The fact is that a moot court comes at just the right time, when the appellate case is ripe for independent assessment.

Moot courts have a final, and perhaps less obvious, virtue. They compel preparation. Busy litigators with many other competing cases, scores of depositions, and unending phone calls have difficulty finding blocks of quiet time to prepare for an oral argument. It is not a routine occurrence, but may still be pushed to the bottom of the stack. A moot court, scheduled in advance of the argument, gives you little choice: You must focus early.

For all these reasons, many organizations that repeatedly handle appeals usually insist on moot courts before argument. The appellate sections of the Justice Department and the Solicitor General's Office routinely arrange moot courts for their lawyers. And, the National Association of Attorneys General regularly provides moot courts for many representatives of state governments who argue in the U.S. Supreme Court.

Despite the advantages, it is not true that just any moot court will help. As means of preparation, all moot courts definitely are *not* created equal. Following a few basic rules will make a big difference.

1. *Select a representative panel.* The quality of a moot court depends on two things: the panel and the advocate's preparation. You must give careful thought to who will be your stand-in judges. The time it takes to persuade the right lawyers to serve is always time well spent.

Usually, the lawyers who can most easily be persuaded to take part are those who have worked on the case. They feel they have something at stake. They know the case well, have experience with the applicable law, and may even be familiar with the briefs. In fact, some of the most eager moot court designates are lawyers who have helped write the briefs. These folks are more willing to prepare but need less time to do it.

Avoid Case Veterans

Stay away from such well-informed case veterans when assembling your panel. Eager as they are, they may have the least to contribute as moot court judges. Lawyers who have worked on the case will know too much about the history of the litigation, about the terms of art used in the industry, and about the intricacies of pertinent case law. They cannot replicate the informed—but not immersed—responses of the actual appellate panel. They will not become confused in the same way a real appellate panel would. They will not ask the same questions. Their inquiries will be too sophisticated; none will come out of left field, like some appellate questioning.

Lawyers who have worked on the case will focus on the small cracks in logic that caused problems in drafting the briefs, but they may miss larger problems with the argument that will concern an appellate panel. More than that, lawyers who have served as advocates may have difficulty seeing the case as an adversary would and will therefore not provide the most effective preview of an opponent's approach.

Still, lawyers who have worked on the case *can* play a useful role. They should be the moot court audience—listening, taking notes, and suggesting how to handle difficult problems. Such listeners will have enough knowledge of the case law and the facts to propose responses to the panel's more difficult questions. Lawyers who have been in the case are best deployed not as judges but as participants in a post-argument postmortem.

For judges, I look for intelligent, articulate lawyers whose knowledge of the subject matter of the case is roughly that of a real appellate panel. Most federal and state appellate panels are composed of generalists, and so lawyers who are generalists often make good moot court judges.

Specialists often turn out to be less-than-satisfactory moot court judges. Too often, a lawyer who is expert in a particular area of law will become interested in questioning on a relatively narrow point. This is especially true if the lawyer specializes in the substance of the appeal. Such a technical catechism may purify the advocate's presentation, but the larger themes of the argument may not be fully presented, attacked, or even mentioned. To prevent a moot court from becoming snarled in such technical filigree, schedule discussions with experts separately.

Specialization is not completely bad, however. The actual appellate panel may well have one judge who has a specialized understanding of the applicable area of law. It may even include one who is very familiar with many of the cited cases. To simulate that possibility, it makes sense to include one moot court judge with a good—though perhaps not comprehensive—understanding of the legal principles involved in the case, but not familiarity with the facts.

Once you decide the kind of judges you want, how many should you get? The size of a moot court panel is usually determined by available resources rather than by rule. My ideal, however, is a three-judge panel. This replicates most arguments in the federal courts of appeals. It is large enough to provide different perspectives and to produce some interaction between panel members, but not so large as to create competition for time between the panel members and the advocate. Sufficient airtime can be a big problem. When a panel is larger than three, its members may interrupt one another so much that the thread of the analysis is lost. In addition, articulate panel members can become frustrated when they have little opportunity to question or comment. If you are deluged by articulate, intelligent, generalist moot court volunteers, organize two separate events. That is far better than staging one super-panel.

2. *Do not schedule the moot court just before the oral argument.* Immediately after selecting the panel, set an early date for the moot court. Ideally, the moot court should occur at least two or three days prior to the actual argument. Allowing some breathing room between the moot court and the argument is useful for a number of reasons.

First, as noted, an early moot court date forces early preparation. It can be just as embarrassing to be unprepared before your colleagues as before a panel of unfamiliar judges. An early moot court date also forces you to clear away calendar conflicts and other distractions that prevent study and preparation.

Second, a moot court may suggest projects to undertake before the real argument. The panel may ask for additional facts, which can be confirmed only through additional review of the record. Sometimes, the panel's inquiries may suggest specific lines of authority that should be researched. Most likely, the advocate will need time to rework a presentation in light of the panel's questions and comments. Whatever the case, there are few things worse than having a moot court spotlight a troublesome gap, and then not having time to fill it in.

Finally, remember that a good moot court may greatly disturb an advocate's sense of superiority over the subject matter. Scores of penetrating questions may put big holes in the argument, and leave the presentation in tatters. In these circumstances, time for reflection, study, and confidence building may be needed. In fact, if the moot court has been particularly devastating, an advocate may want to present a revamped argument to a second moot court. Such rescue operations, however, take time. If the moot court takes place just before the argument, a lawyer may be left with shattered self-confidence but no time to pick up the pieces.

3. *Prepare as though the moot court were the argument.* The only sensible way to prepare for a moot court is as though it were the real thing. Intensive review of the record and case law should take place *before* the moot court, not after. If a written outline will be used in court, it should be prepared in advance and used at the moot court.

Only with serious preparation can a moot court yield its full benefits. Only then will it provide a full rehearsal and test a presentation. Without such advance preparation, a moot court will not improve a lawyer's understanding of a case; it will simply restore that understanding to where it was when the briefs were written.

Preparing completely also eliminates a form of self-deluding rationalization that can follow an imperfect moot court. A lawyer, having decided to wing it at the moot court, is eaten alive by the stand-in judges. Responses, though, are not humility or hard work. Instead, the lawyer may think that the performance "wasn't bad for someone who didn't spend much time preparing." That kind of attitude can be corrosive. Think of it this way: Unless you prepare fully for the moot court, you will not be able to tell whether your troubles come from lack of preparation or from fundamental flaws in your approach.

Even relatively ministerial aspects of preparation for oral argument are more valuable if completed before the moot court. If you intend to use a tabbed version of the record for easy access to particular pages, have it ready for the moot court. That will help you determine whether the right pages have been tabbed and whether the transcript can be handled fluidly under fire. Similarly, if you rely on a notebook of copied cases, it should be ready for the moot court to help you determine whether your indexing of the cases is adequate. Obviously, any visual aids planned for the courtroom should be tested in the moot court. The principle is simple. If there is *anything* you expect to use or do for the real argument, and it can be tested in a moot court, get it ready.

4. *Stay in character.* The best way to conduct a moot court is to simulate the conditions at an actual argument. This means that the appellate advocate will deliver the presentation, the judges will ask their questions, and the advocate will answer them, all without anyone stepping out of the assigned role.

A good moot court panel will always ask a few questions that leave the advocate without a ready answer. If that happens, avoid the temptation to indulge in an apology, explanation, or joke. That will interrupt the flow of the argument and, worse, will provide the advocate a deceptively easy way out of the predicament. You should instead confront the embarrassment created by a difficult question during the moot court—just as you would have to at the real argument—and search for the most plausible answer. That is far better than postponing the reckoning by stepping out of character and bantering about how hard the question is. This Johnny Carson approach to a moot court argument—witty asides that let the panel know that the lawyer knows his answer was bad—should be avoided.

Judges should stay in their roles, too. They can help the most by asking tough questions and by saving their comments for the conclusion of the presentation. If the judges do not take the proceedings seriously, the lawyer won't either.

Realism is further enhanced by limiting argument time in a moot court just as it would be in a real argument. At a minimum, this will indicate whether the prepared argument fits within the usually meager period allowed. You do not really know what can—and cannot—be done in 15 or 20 minutes until you have been forced to do it.

In some instances, however, you may not want to adhere precisely to a particular time period. Depending on the intensity of the moot court's questioning, you may not be able to rehearse all of the argument. Conversely, if you give your whole presentation in a limited time, you may miss some valuable panel questions. It may therefore make sense to ask someone to announce aloud the moment when the allotted time has ended, but to continue your presentation until you, the panel, or the subject matter is exhausted.

Finally, the physical environment for the moot court should be similar to the courtroom. The advocate should stand at a podium, with no more surrounding table space than will be available in court. This dry run will prevent the awkwardness that comes from bringing to the courtroom more notebooks, binders, and yellow pads than the podium can hold.

5. *Allow time for a critique.* After the formal argument is over, the panel members and others present will be brimming with comments. Often there will be criticisms and suggestions that did not emerge in the give-and-take of the argument. There may even be ideas on the overall structure and content of the argument. Post-argument discussion of these points can—and probably should—last as long as the argument itself, or longer.

It is useful to collect these comments in orderly fashion, perhaps organizing them according to the argument's main contentions. It also makes sense for the lawyer to identify the portions of the argument that gave the most trouble and to ask the panel for advice on those points.

6. *Record the event.* An effective panel will keep you off-balance most of the time. By the end, it will be hard to remember all the questions that produced weak answers and all of the suggestions from the panel. Just keeping up with the questions may occupy all of your available mental resources.

For this reason alone, it is useful to record the moot court. You might ask a lawyer who participated in the briefing of the case to serve as scribe, writing down the panel's questions and a rough outline of your answers. This will provide some notes on problem areas that emerge. For those with resources and time, videotaping may be even more useful. This allows you to see mannerisms and gestures that—unknown to you—detracted from the argument.

7. *Invite your client.* Good appellate court judges often use oral argument to pose questions that cannot be answered by reading the briefs. They may inquire, for example, about the procedural history of the litigation, the future intentions of the parties, or the practices of the particular industry. Good moot court judges will ask the same kinds of questions.

Why not invite your client to help find answers to these inquiries? A client present at the moot court has an opportunity to hear and respond to such questions, often drawing on knowledge the lawyer does not have. Of course, such questions could be relayed to the client after the moot court, but there is no substitute for timely participation; answers are best provided when the questions are fresh.

Clients frequently enjoy participating in this process. By commenting at the moot court, they can shape the oral argument. And clients can profit in other ways by hearing their positions advocated, attacked, and defended. The fresh perspective of the panel and the live presentation of the argument may give a client a more realistic view of the strength of the case and of particular arguments—information that can be extremely valuable to both client and lawyer at subsequent stages of the litigation.

There is another benefit for you in having your client attend. Any lawyer always faces the possibility of loss and the associated task of explaining such an outcome. A lawyer whose client has seen firsthand the kind of difficulties the case presents may have an easier time with such an explanation. More than that, if he wins, the lawyer will get the full measure of admiration deserved.

It is often said that every appeal produces four oral arguments: the argument you prepare in advance; the argument you make in court; the argument you wish you had made; and the argument you tell your friends you made. A moot court experience condenses the first three of these phases into a single event; it tests the planned argument against the reality of a panel and provides an opportunity for retrospective fine-tuning. The only thing it leaves unrehearsed—and few lawyers need practice on this point—is the after-the-fact war story of how well the argument went.

Brush Up Your Aristotle

Robert F. Hanley

Demosthenes of Athens was the greatest orator of ancient Greece. His eloquence, says Professor Epiphanius Wilson, was of unique power.

According to Professor Wilson, "It is the intellectual grasp, the trenchant vehemence, the face and vigor of the orator that affect us." Demosthenes scorned mere ornaments of rhetorical finish. "Yet his language has all the living glow, all the purity, all the transparency that belongs to the best age of attic Greek. . . ."

How did he do it? Can he light the fires of today's advocates?

Demosthenes' oratory was simple and unadorned. He used it in a lifelong struggle against Philip II of Macedonia (hence the term "philippic"). Demosthenes justifiably feared that Philip intended to extinguish Greek liberty.

By his words, Demosthenes drew the Thebans into a confederacy against Philip. The Thebans at the time were the best soldiers in the world, but, according to Plutarch, they

> had before their eyes the terrors of war and their losses in the Phocean troubles were still recent; but such was the force and power of the orator [Demosthenes] fanning up . . . their courage and firing their emulation that casting away every thought of prudence, fear or obligation in a sort of divine possession, they chose the path of honor, to which his words invited them, and this success, thus accomplished by an orator, was thought to be so glorious and of such consequence that Philip immediately sent heralds to entreat and petition for a peace. . . .

Robert F. Hanley, who died in 1991, was a partner in Morrison & Forester in Denver, Colorado; adjunct professor, advanced trial advocacy, University of Colorado Law School; and a chairman of the ABA Section of Litigation.

Nice result.

What Demosthenes was to Greek advocacy, Marcus Tullius Cicero was to Roman advocacy.

Plutarch tells us: "For Cicero, it may be said, was the one man, above all others, who made the Romans feel how great a charm eloquence lends to what is good."

These were powerful advocates.

In a school for trial lawyers, Cicero's *De Oratore* and Demosthenes' *Orations* should be required reading.

The students' heads should be filled with excellent advocacy—from the classics to the trials of Edward Bennett Williams—and with the literature of trials—from Aristophanes, Tacitus, and Shakespeare's *Julius Caesar, Henry V,* and *Richard II* to Wordsworth's *Character of the Happy Warrior*. The students would read great speeches, too: Henry George's "The Curse of Poverty," Abraham Lincoln's "A House Divided," and Adlai Stevenson's "There Are No Gibraltars."

They would discover power through simplicity, grace, and unadorned sincerity.

Then, when they are panting to learn how to duplicate these masterpieces, they should be hit with a good solid dose of Aristotle's *Rhetoric* and Quintilian's *Institutes of Oratory*.

These were geniuses who knew how to make language work. There were few writers of rhetoric before them. There were few teachers. What they had was a magnificently sensitive power of observation. They learned by raw observation of human behavior what makes arguments tell—how to persuade, how to change the minds of biased listeners.

Lane Cooper, in his book *The Rhetoric of Aristotle* (1932), says that Aristotle's treatise on rhetoric is one of the world's best and wisest books. It is a book to be chewed and digested. It is the greatest of all books on the philosophy and technique of persuasion. The work is "a textbook of human feeling; a storehouse of taste; an example of condensed and accurate, but uniformly clear and candid, reasoning."

Aristotle created the art of rhetoric, and no work on the subject since is comparable. It stands apart and above.

Aristotle's *Rhetoric* is essential reading for anyone who would persuade others. Aristotle's *Rhetoric* taught Cicero and Quintilian, and its basic precepts serve as anchors to every good book ever written on persuasion. It is amazing how modern, how relevant, how robust, how untrite his treatise on the art of persuasion remains today. Read Aristotle, and learn how to frame an argument.

Aristotle stresses the importance of knowing one's audience. The advocate must be a psychologist. He must understand human nature, and he must know how his listeners think, their habits, desires, and emotions.

Today, we use jury surveys to tell us to whom we are talking. Gerry Spence says he uses his belly. Aristotle used his powers of observation.

Observing his audience, he decided what kind of argument would be most persuasive. He watched his listeners, and he knew what sort of emotional appeal they would accept. Aristotle tells us what kinds of words, phrases, and organization of ideas will move which audiences. His emphasis is on the nature of the person to be persuaded. He teaches us how to use a combination of logic, empathy, and emotion.

His concept of ethos is worth careful study. Aristotle uses "ethos" to mean the manifest character of a person, group, or culture. The ethos of the speaker must be good, for the audience will not side with an advocate they do not trust. If there is one characteristic common to successful advocates, it is the ability to project sincerity.

Aristotle teaches that a persuasive speech not only convinces through argument; it must evince the right character (ethos) of the speaker and bring the audience into the right state of feeling. The speech should show the speaker to be a person of intelligence, virtue, and goodwill. Such a speaker wins the confidence of his audience.

A successful advocate must also be able to tell and act out a story, to organize its pieces so his listeners can put it together for themselves. In life, people make decisions first and then find the arguments to rationalize them, though rarely is this sequence consciously appreciated. Few people argue matters out, either in their heads or with their friends, and make their decisions based on the results of the debate. Human beings may be a rational species, but, more often than not, the reason proceeds from the emotion, not vice versa. These basic insights come booming forth from Aristotle's text. He points out the necessity of a theme that will win the mind of the listener. If the theme is convincing, the arguments will fall into place.

A trial lawyer could profitably spend time studying Aristotle's concept of the enthymeme. He tells us that enthymemes are the essential instruments of persuasion.

An enthymeme is a kind of syllogism with two parts rather than three. In an enthymeme the minor premise is taken for granted instead of being expressed. If this sounds theoretical, it is not. It is the way to explain a powerful mode of communication. An example will show how it works.

Aristotle did not use full-blown syllogisms. He would not say:

All men are mortal;
Socrates is a man;
Socrates is mortal.

Instead, he would employ the enthymeme:

Socrates is a man;
he is mortal.

The point is, it is an effective way to argue. Syllogisms are for professors. They have a tone of condescension. Persuasive speakers use enthymemes. The audience does not have the time or patience to follow syllogisms.

An enthymeme is a great deal more than a truncated syllogism. It is a powerful form of argument. You begin with an easily accepted truth, and you proceed to an inevitable conclusion. St. Paul and Lincoln were among the post-Aristotelian rhetoricians who built speeches of unbelievable power using enthymemes as their foundations.

Take Lincoln's Gettysburg Address. It is an emotional powerhouse. Yet it depends for its effect largely on unstated but indisputable assumptions, not on explicit hard sell.

Aristotle teaches us the same technique. Be quiet; use examples whose lessons are inescapable, but let the listeners discover the conclusions for themselves.

For today's trial lawyer, the moral is the value of the implicit. A prosecutor should not say, "You should be outraged at the conduct of the defendant." Instead, he should simply tell the story of what the defendant did, and let the jurors discover the outrage for themselves.

Irving Younger tells us that, in cross-examining the defendant's mother, you should not ask, "As the defendant's mother, Madam, you would cheat for, you would steal for, you would lie for your son, wouldn't you?" Just ask the witness quietly, "Madam, you are the defendant's mother?" Then sit down. The implicit message is inescapable, and it will sound all the louder if left unsaid. Lead the jurors to the conclusion you want them to embrace, then let them believe they found it themselves.

Aristotle points out that rhetoric is an art that students can acquire. The essence of persuasion lies in the arguments or proofs. Proofs are so much more important than the emotional appeals that many poor speakers stress. But emotions also have a place in Aristotle's rhetoric.

Aristotle recognized that most audiences are untrained in rigorous thinking and unable to follow long, involved arguments. So, the listeners' emotions are what we in the twentieth century might call battery rechargers. The emotions invigorate the listener's minds and keep their interest alive.

Happiness is an important word to Aristotle. He points out that all men aim at happiness and that upon it all effective exhortation, persuasion, and dissuasion turn. The advocate must be familiar with the popular conception and the main constituents of happiness. Happiness is prosperity joined with virtue. It is a self-sufficient existence. It is the pleasant life with security, a thriving estate with the ability to use and preserve it. It involves the possession of internal goods of the soul and the health of the body, as well as external goods.

Aristotle sets out the constituents of happiness, including good birth, children, wealth, reputation, homes, health, beauty, strength, size, a good old age, friends, good looks, and virtue. Recognize that those are the qualities your audience yearns for. Show them how the acceptance of your argument is consistent with the constituents of their happiness.

Aristotle also talks about anger and how to arouse it against an opponent. He treats love, friendship, and hatred, as well. We learn about fear and confidence, shame and shamelessness, benevolence and the lack of benevolence, pity, indignation, envy, emulation, and contempt.

He analyzes the character of age and talks about how the advocate should take the age of his audience into consideration.

If you represent a defendant or a respondent, you might do well to read Aristotle on refutation. He tells us that we can refute an argument either by a counterargument or by an objection. Objections can be raised in four ways: by attacking your opponent's premise, by bringing forward a premise like it, by bringing one contrary to it, or by citing a previous decision. He gives examples of each method.

Having previously dealt with the sources of persuasion—like working on the emotions of the audience, giving the audience the right impression of the speaker's character, and convincing the audience with proof—Aristotle, in the third book of his *Rhetoric*, moves on to style: how the speaker expresses himself. The book deals with choice of words, syntax, and delivery.

His treatment of delivery has a modern ring. He explains that the whole point is to make an impression on an audience. Good style is, above all, clear. Clarity is achieved through the use of nouns and verbs that are in current use. Naturalness is endearing, artifice a turn-off.

Today how often we hear young lawyers in court using big words and complex sentences, as we watch the jury squirm. People grow suspicious of a pretentious speaker, "and think he has designs upon them. . . . In style, the illusion (of spontaneity) is successful if we take our individual words from the current stock. . . ."

The advocate should, we are told, use rare words, compound words, and coined words sparingly. But he or she should sprinkle them into the argument among the commonplace words. Review Lincoln's Gettysburg Address and find the "fourscore and seven years ago" and "our fathers brought forth" scattered among words used in everyday conversation. Lincoln's use of the lofty phrases mixed with currently used words gives a freshness to his speech—a novelty. It is absorbing.

Aristotle suggests use of metaphors because they lend clarity, charm, and distinction to speech, but they must fit comfortably, without stretching. Their relevance must be immediately apparent.

Aristotle cites four faults of style: the misuse of compound words, the overuse of strange words, mistakes in the use of epithets, and the use of bad metaphors and similes. These faults expose the speaker as a charlatan, as insincere—the purveyor of artifice. Epithets should be used as sauce for the meat. Inappropriate language injects absurdity and bad taste into an argument.

Aristotle turns to propriety and says that our language "will be appropriate if it expresses emotion and character and if it is in proportion with the subject." By "proportion" he means that weighty matters should not be treated lightly, nor trivial matters solemnly. Ornamental epithets should not be attached to commonplace nouns or the effect becomes comic.

When your subject is wanton outrage, your language should convey anger. If you are speaking of filth, you should use language of aversion and reluctance. If you are speaking of praiseworthy deeds, use the language of adoration, and so on for the other emotions. The choice of words will make people believe in your case. Aristotle gives us a secret that fine advocates know about how jurors react:

> In their souls they infer, illegitimately, that you are telling the truth, because they, in a like situation, would be moved in the same way as you are. Even when the facts are not as the speaker says, the audience thinks he is right.

I have just touched the surface. Lane Cooper's translation of Aristotle's *Rhetoric* is only 241 pages long. There is an important lesson for the advocate on every page.

In a four-hour plane ride, you can build a base of persuasive technique that will serve you for a lifetime in court. Another four- to six-hour investment in Quintilian's *Institutes of Oratory* will reinforce that foundation.

Marcus Fabius Quintilianus, known as Quintilian, lived from 35 to 100 A.D. He was a Roman born in the region that is now Spain. His *Instituto Oratoria (Institutes of Oratory)* is the most thorough textbook in the art of oratory that has come down to us from ancient times.

Quintilian's work shows the influence of Cicero and touches on all aspects of Roman education and public speaking, including the organization of a speech, the use of argument, stylistic devices, memorization, and the art of delivery. He also stresses the importance of good character in a speaker. He stresses knowledge of philosophy and a thorough familiarity with literature.

There is a Loeb Classics edition of Quintilian's *Institutes* in four small, attractive red volumes, which will not only ornament your library but also provide you with a firm foundation for effective advocacy. If you get bored with Quintilian's discourses on elementary education, grammar, language, analogy, spelling, pronunciation, and composition, you can jump to Book III, Chapter 9, and read his fascinating treatment of forensic oratory.

First, he says, you must state what you are going to prove; then you work your way logically to the conclusion. You must consider the nature of your case, the question at issue, and the argument for and against the proposition you wish to assert. Then you must consider what points are to be made and what points must be refuted. You must consider how the facts are to be stated. The statement of facts is designed to prepare the way for the proofs. Finally, you must consider how best to win the judge to take your view.

You must consider all of the facts of the case before you can decide what kind of an impression you wish to make on the judge. Do you wish to mollify or increase his severity? Should you excite or relax his interest in the case? Do you wish to render him susceptible to influence or the reverse?

You should consider your entire case before you begin to frame your argument. Then you should put it together in the order in which you will deliver it.

Although charming and of interest to historians, much of the *Institutes* can be skimmed. The delectable morsels will readily appear. In Book IV, Chapter 2, Quintilian treats the subject of studying the temper of the judge, the use of pathos, ethos, and emotional appeal. This chapter is a must.

He tells us that an extremely important and difficult task is to stir the emotions of the judge and to mold and transform them to the attitude that we want him to take. We can substitute "jury" for "judge" without doing violence to Quintilian's text.

There is scope for an appeal to the emotions in every portion of an argument, and few are those orators "who can sweep the judge with them, lead him to adopt that attitude of mind that they desire, and compel him to weep with them or share their anger. . . . It is this form of eloquence that is the queen of all."

We are reminded that proofs may induce the judges to regard our case as superior to that of our opponent, "but the appeal to the emotions will do more, for it will make them *wish* our case to be the better."

What they wish, they will believe. This passage is too delectable to paraphrase:

> For as soon as they (the judges) begin to be angry, to feel favorably disposed, to hate or to pity, they begin to take a personal interest in the case, and just as lovers are incapable of forming a reasoned judgment on the beauty of the object of their affections, because passion forestalls the sense of sight, so the judge, when overcome by his emotions, abandons all attempt to enquire into the validity of the arguments and is swept along with the tide of passion and yields himself unquestioning to the torrent.

The orator must devote all of his power to moving the judge (or jury) emotionally "for it is in its power over the emotions that the life and soul of oratory is to be found."

One way the successful advocate evokes an emotional response to the argument is through ethos—goodness, moral character. The advocate excites pleasure and affection in the audience by the revelation of his or her character and presents himself or herself as decent, ingratiating, and courteous.

To evoke hatred, we might pass silent censure on the conduct we seek to condemn. We establish our goodness and silently condemn the conduct that is so far below that countenanced by persons of our unmistakable character. We should also remember that it is far more effective to make our antagonist unpopular than to use abuse. The former course makes the audience dislike the speaker's antagonist; the latter course makes the audience dislike the speaker.

It is essential that the advocate possess the virtues, or lead the judges to believe he or she possesses the virtues, that would have them apply as standards by which to judge the opponent.

When seeking to persuade a jury that a person is evil, an advocate should be calm and mild with no trace of pride. It is enough to speak pleasantly using good, tough color words—quietly.

Quintilian also discusses the use of strong emotional appeals when we try to evoke anger, fear, hatred.

Quintilian points out that, to stir the emotions of others, it is necessary to feel those emotions oneself. Without feeling the emotion, an advocate runs the risk of showing transparently counterfeit grief, anger, or indignation. A great speaker's mind is stirred to power by the depth and sincerity of feelings. Empathy is essential. You must feel the feeling you wish to produce in the minds of the jurors.

> Will he grieve who can find no trace of grief in the words with which I seek to move him to grief? Will he be angry, if the orator who seeks to kindle his anger shows no sign of laboring under the emotion that he demands from his audience? Will he shed tears if the pleader's eyes are dry? It is likely impossible.

We must be moved ourselves before we can move others. We reach the emotional state we seek to evoke through our imagination—a power we can acquire if we try. We must turn a form of daydreaming or mild hallucination to some profit.

When you prosecute a murderer, you imagine what must have occurred and you see the murderer bursting from the hiding place as the victim trembles, cries for help, begs for mercy, tries to run. You see the blow delivered and the stricken body fall, hear the groans, the death rattle. Your emotions are stirred.

When we wish to awaken pity, we must believe that the ills we complain of have actually happened to us. We must empathize with the person on whose behalf we complain. We must feel suffering before we can put it across to a jury. We must feel the suffering as if it were our own.

Quintilian treats us to a delightful discussion of laughter and the importance of getting the judge to laugh, to divert attention from the facts, or to refresh and revive the judge when bored. He counsels us to use humor to dispel hatred or anger.

Those of us who have watched John Shepherd of St. Louis or Murray Sams of Miami in action have seen what a useful talent it is to be able to provoke a burst of laughter from the jury every now and then.

The successful use of humor requires timing, acute observation, charm, and a range of expression. Wit often works best in the counterpunch.

Murray Sams's use of humor during rebuttal in answer to the opponent's metaphors is a joy to observe. So are the jocular counterthrusts of Anthony Scrivener, Desmond Fennell, and other talented English barristers.

Quintilian tells us to practice being clever in our everyday encounters. He says that you can learn to be funny, but it takes practice.

Quintilian suggests that the deadpan delivery works best, for there are no jests so insipid as those that parade their intention to be witty. I suppose that is why most of us find Woody Allen or Jack Benny so much funnier than Bob Hope.

Quintilian concludes with a modest aspiration that still serves today: "If the knowledge of these principles proves to be of small practical utility to the young student, it should at least produce what I value more—the will to do well."

PART V

The Supreme Court

An Invitation to State Courts

William J. Brennan, Jr.

When asked what decisions over the last 30 years most importantly changed the face of our federal constitutional jurisprudence, most would point to *Brown v. Board of Education* 349 U.S. 294 (1955), for its triumphs of banning racial segregation, or to *Baker v. Carr* 369 U.S. 186 (1962), for recognizing the principle of one person, one vote. Surely these were great triumphs for our nation and our Constitution. But, I suggest that just as significant for the preservation and furtherance of our ideals fostering the protection of the individual from the vast powers of the state were the decisions, most handed down in the short space of seven years between 1962 and 1969, that bound the states to almost all of the restraints of the Bill of Rights.

For, while the framers of the Constitution went far to prevent despotism by diffusing power among three branches of government and leaving much power in the states, even this was not thought to be enough protection against oppression. Thus, the Bill of Rights, every one of which limits the power of government over the individual, was quickly added. But, almost a century and a half was to pass before their extension against the states.

The vehicle for this dramatic development was, of course, the Fourteenth Amendment. This nation has been transformed by the standards, promises, and power of the Fourteenth Amendment, which assures that the citizens of all our states are also and no less citizens of our United States, and that our federal constitutional liberties protect each of us against encroachment by governmental action at any level of our federal system, from our state governments no less than from our national one.

William J. Brennan, Jr., now deceased, was an associate justice of the Supreme Court of the United States.

It is true that before the Civil War not the federal government but the states were perceived as protectors of, rather than threats to, the civil and political rights of the individual. The framers who wrote the Constitution did not create a paper tiger. What they wrought was a set of relationships between the individual and government that counted on the states to do their part to advance human liberty.

Only after the Civil War did people realize that the states were not playing the role of protectors. Then demand arose for the national protection of individual rights against abuses of state powers. The war had exposed a serious flaw in the assumption that the states could be trusted to nurture individual rights. In fact, the primary impetus to adopting the Fourteenth Amendment was the fear that the former Confederate states would deny newly freed persons the protection of life, liberty, and property formerly provided by the states.

The 1960s series of decisions transformed the basic structure of constitutional safeguards for individual political and civil liberties in the nation and profoundly altered the character of our federal system. The agenda of our Court also was altered radically by them. I do not believe it overstates the case to say that most Americans have now come to know of the Bill of Rights as the source of their liberties. Even in casual parlance, people speak of "taking the Fifth" or of their "First Amendment rights."

So, although we certainly have not yet achieved equal justice for all members of our society, Congress and the judiciary did much during the 1960s to close the gap between the promise and the social and political reality envisioned by the framers of the Fourteenth Amendment.

But recently there has been some unease abroad in the land about whether the Supreme Court is treating the great rights as inferior to the ever-increasing demands of governmental authority. For several years now, it is said, there has been an unmistakable trend in the Court to read the guarantees of individual liberty restrictively, which means that the contents of the federal rights that must be respected by the states are likewise diminished.

Some of us on the Court have expressed concern about this trend, as the following dissent from summary dispositions of criminal cases without briefing or oral argument illustrates:

> [T]his [practice poses] disturbing questions concerning the Court's conception of its role.... [For] we must not forget that a central purpose of our written Constitution, and more specifically of its unique creation of a life-tenured federal judiciary, was to ensure that certain rights are firmly secured against possible oppression by the Federal or State Governments.... Yet the Court's recent history indicates that, at least with respect to its summary dispositions [of criminal cases], it has been primarily concerned with vindicating the will of

> the majority and less interested in its role as a protector of the individual's constitutional rights. . . . [T]he Court has decided in summary fashion [numerous] cases . . . concerning the constitutional rights of persons accused or convicted of crimes. All . . . were decided on the petition of the warden or prosecutor, and in all he was successful in obtaining reversal of a decision upholding a claim of constitutional right. [We are] not saying that none of these cases should have been decided summarily. But [we are] saying that this pattern of results, and in particular the fact that . . . the Court has been unwilling in even a single criminal case to employ its discretionary power of summary disposition in order to uphold a claim of constitutional right, is quite striking. It may well be true that there have been times when the Court overused its power of summary disposition to protect the citizen against government overreaching. Nevertheless, the Court must be ever mindful of its primary role as the protector of the citizen and not the warden or the prosecutor. The Framers surely feared the latter more than the former.

Florida v. Meyers, 466 U.S. 380, 385–387 (1984) (*per curiam*) (Stevens, J., dissenting).

And another respected commentator has observed:

> A generation of Americans has come to maturity under a legal system in which the Supreme Court has provided sustained and effective protection for individual rights. Unfortunately, the Supreme Court is now failing to provide that check. Individual freedom is the exception, not the rule. When the Supreme Court abdicates its role as protector of the individual, the fragile institutional structure which keeps us free is placed at risk. Moreover, when, as [has] happened repeatedly . . . the individuals whom the Court has elected to sacrifice to the government are the poorest and weakest in the society, the Court's greatest asset—its capacity for moral leadership—is mortally wounded.

American Civil Liberties Union Annual Report (1983).

This trend is not visible solely in the enfeebled protection of individual rights under the federal bill and the Fourteenth Amendment. The venerable remedy of habeas corpus has been sharply limited in the name of federalism; the Equal Protection Clause has been denied its full reach; and a series of decisions shaping the doctrines of justiciability, jurisdiction, and remedy increasingly bars the federal courthouse door in the absence of showings probably impossible to make.

For a decade now, I have felt certain that the Court's contraction of federal rights and remedies on grounds of federalism should be interpreted as a plain invitation to state courts to step into the breach. Of course, in the 1960s, the enthusiasm that accompanied the Court's application of the Bill of Rights to the states was a disincentive for the growth of state constitutional rights. Busy interpreting the onslaught of federal constitutional rulings in state criminal cases, the state courts fell silent on the subject of their own constitutions. Now, the diminution of federal scrutiny and protection—out of purported deference to the states—mandates the assumption of a more responsible state court role. And state courts have taken seriously their obligation as equal guardians of civil rights and liberties.

Between 1970 and 1984, state courts, increasingly reluctant to follow the federal lead, handed down more than 250 published opinions holding that the constitutional minimums set by the United States Supreme Court were insufficient to satisfy the more stringent requirements of state constitutional law. Collins, "Reliance on State Constitutions" in *Developments in State Constitutional Law* 2 (B. McGraw ed. 1985).

When the United States Supreme Court cut back the reach of First Amendment protections, the California Supreme Court responded by interpreting its state constitution to protect freedom of speech in shopping centers and malls. *Robins v. Prune Yard Shopping Ctr.*, 592 P.2d 341 (Cal. 1979). The Washington, Pennsylvania, and Massachusetts courts responded in kind when confronted with similar questions involving freedom of expression. Under the federal Constitution, if one is stopped by a police officer for a simple traffic violation, the motorist may be subject to a full body search and a search of his vehicle. *United States v. Robinson*, 414 U.S. 218 (1973); *Gustafson v. Florida*, 424 U.S. 260 (1973). Such police conduct offends state constitutional provisions in Hawaii and California, unless the officer has articulable reasons to suspect other illegal conduct. *State v. Kaluna*, 520 P.2d 51 (Haw. 1974); *People v. Brisendine*, 531 P.2d 1099 (Cal. 1975). Truly, the state courts have responded with marvelous enthusiasm to many not-so-subtle invitations to fill the constitutional gaps left by the decisions of the Supreme Court.

It may be that the institutional position of the Supreme Court may cause it to "under-enforce" constitutional rules. The national court must remain highly sensitive to concerns of state and local autonomy, obviously less of a problem for state courts, which are local, accountable decision-makers. It must further be remembered that the federal bill was enacted to place limits on the federal government, while state bills are widely perceived as granting affirmative rights to citizens.

In addition, the Supreme Court formulates a national standard which, some suggest, must represent the common denominator to allow for diversity and local experimentation. In the Warren era, federalism was unsuccessfully invoked to support the view of the antiincorporationists—that the rights granted in federal courts need not apply with the same breadth or scope in the state courts. Dissenting justices "extolled the virtues of allowing the States to serve as 'laboratories'" and objected to incorporation as "press[ing] the States into a procrustean federal mold." *Crist v. Bretz*, 437 U.S. 28, 39–40 (1978) (Burger, C.J., dissenting).

Justice Harlan and others felt that the phenomenon of incorporation complicated the federal situation, creating a kind of "constitutional schizophrenia," as the Court attempted to recognize diversity and faithfully to enforce the Bill of Rights. *Williams v. Florida*, 399 U.S. 78, 136 (1970). To make room for such diversity, Justice Harlan felt that the Bill of Rights should not apply to the states exactly as it applied to the federal government.

But the Court has held that the Fourteenth Amendment fully applied the provisions of the Bill of Rights to the states, thereby creating a federal floor of protection, and that the Constitution and the Fourteenth Amendment allow diversity only above and beyond this federal constitutional floor. Experimentation that endangers the continued existence of our national rights and liberties cannot be permitted; a call for that brand of diversity is antithetical to the requirements of the Fourteenth Amendment. While state experimentation may flourish in the space above this floor, we have made a national commitment to this minimum level of protection by enacting the Fourteenth Amendment. This reconciliation of local autonomy and guaranteed individual rights is the only one consistent with our constitutional structure. And the growing dialogue between the Supreme Court and the state courts on the topic of fundamental rights enables all courts to discern more rapidly the "evolving standards of decency that mark the progress of our maturing society." *Trop v. Dulles*, 356 U.S. 86, 111 (1958) (Warren, C.J.).

This rebirth of interest in state constitutional law should be greeted with enthusiasm by all those who support our federal system, liberals and conservatives alike. Developing and protecting individual rights pursuant to state constitutions is no threat to enforcing national standards; state courts may not provide a level of protection less than that offered by the federal constitution. Nor should these developments be greeted with dismay by conservatives; the state laboratories are once again open for business.

As state courts assume a leadership role in the protection of individual rights and liberties, the true colors of purported federalists will be revealed. Commentators have highlighted a substantial irony; it is observed that "the same Court that has made federalism the centerpiece of its constitutional philosophy now regularly upsets state court decisions protecting individual rights." R. Collins, "Plain Statements: The Supreme Court's New Requirement," 70 *A.B.A. J.*, March 1984, at 92. When state courts have acted to expand individual rights, the Court has shown little propensity to leap to the defense of diversity. In fact, in several cases, the Court has demonstrated a new solicitude for uniformity.

The Court, for example, has reminded the residents of Florida that when their state court's decisions rest only on state constitutional grounds, citizens have the power "to amend state law to insure rational law enforcement." *Florida v. Casal*, 103 S. Ct. 3100, 3101–102 (1983) (Burger,

C.J., concurring). Some state courts and commentators have taken umbrage at the suggestion that proceeding in lockstep with the Supreme Court is the only way to avoid irrational law enforcement. As one state court judge reminded us recently, the United States Supreme Court is not "the sole repository of judicial wisdom and rationality." *State v. Jackson,* 762 P.2d 255, 264 (Mont. 1983) (Shea, J., dissenting). One wonders if ringing endorsements of state independence will be transformed into assertions of the importance of federal uniformity in law enforcement.

State experimentation cannot be excoriated simply because the experiments provide more rather than less protection for civil liberties and individual rights. While the Fourteenth Amendment does not permit a state to fall below a common national standard, above this level our federalism permits diversity. As tempting as it may be to harmonize results under state and national constitutions, our federalism permits state courts to provide greater protection to individual civil rights and liberties if they wish to do so. The Supreme Court has no conceivable justification for interfering in a case plainly decided on independent and adequate state grounds.

Finally, those who regard judicial review as inconsistent with our democratic system—a view I do not share—should find constitutional interpretation by the state judiciary far less objectionable than activist intervention by their federal counterparts. State court judges, after all, are often more immediately subject to majoritarian pressures than are federal judges. Federal judges are guaranteed a salary and lifetime tenure; in contrast, state judges often are elected or, at the least, must succeed in retention elections. The relatively greater degree of political accountability of state courts militates in favor of continued absolute deference to their interpretations of their own constitutions. Moreover, state constitutions are often relatively easy to amend; in many states, the process is open to citizen initiative. Prudential considerations requiring a cautious use of the power of judicial review, though not insignificant, should not burden elected state judges as much as they do tenured federal judges.

Some critics fear that the Supreme Court will become increasingly hostile to state courts' protection of individual rights and will meddle in those cases, refusing to find that a decision is based on independent and adequate state grounds. I am not so pessimistic. Despite the tendency of the Court in recent years to give gratuitous advice to state citizens to amend their constitutions, I believe that the Court has set appropriate ground rules for federalism with its decision in *Michigan v. Long,* 463 U.S. 1032 (1983), 103 S. Ct. 3469 (1983). If a state court makes clear that its judgment rests on its analysis of state law, the United States Supreme Court will honor that statement and will not review the state court decision.

As long as the Court adheres strictly to this rule, state courts may shield state constitutional law from federal interference and ensure that its growth is not stunted by national decision makers. I join Justice Mosk of the California Supreme Court in his most apt observation: "I detect a phoenix-like resurrection of federalism, or, if you prefer, states' rights, evidenced by state courts' reliance upon provisions of state constitutions." Mosk, "The State Courts in American Law" in *The Third Century* 216 (B. Schwartz ed. 1976).

This said, I must conclude on a warning note. Federal courts remain an indispensable safeguard of individual rights against governmental abuse. The revitalization of state constitutional law is no excuse for the weakening of federal protections and prohibitions. Slashing away at federal rights and remedies undermines our federal system. The strength of our system is that it provides a double source of protection for the rights of our citizens.

Federalism is not served when the federal half of that protection is crippled. Federalism does not require that one level of government take a back seat to the other when the question involved is one of individual civil and political rights; federalism is not an excuse for one court system to abdicate responsibility to another. Indeed, federal courts have been delegated a special responsibility for the definition and enforcement of the guarantees of the Bill of Rights and the Fourteenth Amendment. Our founders and framers, and here I include the framers of the Fourteenth Amendment, took it as an article of faith that this nation prized the independence of its judiciary and that an independent judiciary could be counted on to enforce the individual rights and liberties of our citizens against infringement by governmental power. As James Madison said, "The independent tribunals of justice will consider themselves in a peculiar manner the guardian of those rights." 1 *Annals of Cong.*, 439 (1834 ed.).

In that seven-year stretch of the 1960s when the Supreme Court finally began to seek achievement of the noble purpose of the Fourteenth Amendment, it took giant steps in the direction of equality under the law for all races and all citizens. While the full breadth and depth of the promise of the Fourteenth Amendment have not been fulfilled, the promise itself remains—a vibrant symbol of the hopes and possibilities of this nation and a forceful challenge to those who have become complacent. Our entire Constitution is a national treasure; a document of heady ideals and eloquent, elegant language; a political landmark for individual rights. But one thing the old parchment is not is a china doll that has to be protected from the regular world by a good layer of cotton wool. It is a tough old soldier that has collected quite a few respectable dents in the line of duty in the past two centuries, and it will most certainly collect a few more.

But it will survive intact. As a nation, we shall adhere to our commitment to its ideal of justice, equal and practical, for the poor, for the members of minority groups, for the criminally accused: for all, in short, who do not partake of the abundance of American life.

Certiorari Petitions in the Supreme Court

A. Raymond Randolph

Litigants in their zeal may promise to take their cases all the way to the Supreme Court of the United States if necessary, but no amount of resolve can ensure that the Court will grant them a hearing. With few exceptions, entree to the High Court is by invitation only, an invitation extended by the discretionary writ of certiorari.

Lawyers handling petitions for writs of certiorari are engaged in one of the more unusual aspects of Supreme Court litigation. One thing they share in common is that the courts below, federal or state, have ruled against their clients. To be effective at the certiorari stage, however, they must recognize that their opposition is no longer merely the prevailing party in the lower court, but the other certiorari petitions vying for the Court's attention during the term. Above all else, the certiorari practice in the Supreme Court is a contest of cases.

This much is apparent from the fact that although there are nearly 5,500 new case filings in the Supreme Court each term, the Court manages to hear only about 140 cases on the merits. Since the Judiciary Act of 1925, 43 Stat. 936, the certiorari process has enabled the Court to control its docket and to decide only the most important cases in the nation by first determining which cases are worthy of review. In any given term, only a tiny fraction of all petitions for writs of certiorari qualifies.

Despite these odds, certiorari petitions continue to pour into the Court. Many lawyers may be unaware of the small chance they have of persuading the Court to hear their case or of the standards the Court applies in deciding whether to grant review. Others may simply decide that they must seize their last opportunity to redeem a rejected position

---

A. Raymond Randolph is a circuit judge, U.S. Court of Appeals for the District of Columbia Circuit. This chapter was written in 1978 and updated in 1992.

they have spent considerable time and expense supporting. Indigent petitioners, whose rate of success in having certiorari granted is less than 1 percent, doubtless act on the belief that they have everything to gain and nothing to lose by seeking Supreme Court review.

Whatever the reasons, hundreds of meritless certiorari petitions are filed each term. Of course, no lawyer can transform a frivolous case into one of national importance. By effective advocacy in a certiorari petition, however, counsel can prevent a possibly meritorious petition from being buried in the avalanche of worthless ones.

In preparing a certiorari petition, counsel must recognize that the goal is to convince the Court to hear the case on the merits. This sounds simple enough, but year after year petitioners—and respondents—continue to address the Court as if it were merely another appellate tribunal sitting to review whatever errors might have been committed below. Petitioners spend all their time seeking to demonstrate that the decision below is wrong; respondents counter by vigorously asserting that the lower court correctly ruled in their favor; and the Supreme Court denies certiorari for reasons neither side has discussed.

When the Court grants a petition for a writ of certiorari, it does not do so to pass on evidence or to give a defeated party another hearing. While it is usually necessary to argue in the certiorari petition that the lower court erred (most cases reviewed on certiorari are reversed), this will not be sufficient. Correcting errors in appellate court decisions is not the Supreme Court's main concern. The case, as presented to the Court in the petition, must be shown to have significance beyond the private interests of the parties. It must appear to be one of the 140 or so most significant cases that will reach the Court that term. "A petition for a writ of certiorari," Rule 10 of the Supreme Court's rules says, "will be granted only when there are special and important reasons therefor."

It is, of course, counsel's responsibility to demonstrate that there are such "special and important reasons." His only opportunity to do so will be in the certiorari petition itself; the Court does not hear oral argument on whether to grant certiorari. Because petitioner's counsel may speak to the Court only through written presentation, counsel must be aware of the process the Court follows in passing on certiorari petitions, a process the justices have developed informally and one that will not be found in any statutes or formal rules.

After a petition has been filed and the respondent has filed a brief in opposition, the clerk of the court distributes copies of the pleadings to each of the nine justices. Only one justice handles certiorari petitions exclusively within his own chambers. The remaining eight justices belong to a "pool": the petitions are divided among them at random by the chief justice, with a particular chambers having responsibility for each eighth petition. A law clerk from that chambers writes a memorandum on the petition and the memorandum is distributed to the eight justices in the pool. Each justice then decides individually whether a case warrants plenary review.

The next step in the process is the justices' conference, held every Friday morning while the Court is in session. Forty years ago it was the "settled practice" that individual consideration of each petition by a justice would be "followed by collective discussion at each conference and individual votes on each. . . ." Robertson and Kirkham, *Jurisdiction of the Supreme Court of the United States* 596 (Wolfson and Kurland ed. 1951). This is no longer the practice. A certiorari petition will be considered at conference only if at least one justice so requests.

If no justice places a petition on the conference list, it will not be discussed collectively or formally voted upon. Instead, the petition will be treated as denied, and the clerk of the court will prepare an order to that effect. If a petition does make it to the conference, the justices will discuss it among themselves and then vote. As has been the Court's historic practice, certiorari will be granted only if at least four of the nine justices agree to hear the case.

The Court has adopted these internal procedures in order to cope with the high volume of petitions that are filed. The Court's main business is, and always has been, deciding cases on the merits, and it has sought to prevent having the time needed for that crucial task used up in passing on certiorari petitions. As a result, each justice may devote on the average only a few minutes to each petition. While wading through the certiorari petitions and memoranda from law clerks that reach their desks, the justices will be able to decide very rapidly that particular cases are not "certworthy." Only those that are culled from the pile will be given more careful scrutiny. There is a clear lesson in all this: Lawyers should make their points early in the petition and in such a way that the reader's interest is immediately aroused.

The basic structure of the petition is governed by Rule 14 of the Court's rules. The petition should be divided into seven main sections, with the following headings: Question Presented; Opinions Below; Jurisdiction; Statute, Regulation or Constitutional Provision Involved; Statement; Reasons for Granting the Writ; and Conclusion.

The question or questions presented must be stated on the first page following the cover. This is a crucial portion of the petition, far more so than many lawyers may realize. The "question presented" shapes the case in the Supreme Court. It informs the Court for the first time in the petition what the case is about and what counsel suggests the Court ought to decide. If certiorari is granted, the Court will generally consider on the merits only those issues raised by the question presented or fairly comprehended within it. *Adickes v. S.H. Kress & Co.*, 398 U.S. 144, 147 n.2 (1970).

The question presented may itself reveal that the case is not worthy of Supreme Court review. It is doubtless true, although there are no studies on the point, that the justices decide against voting for certiorari in a great percentage of cases without reading much more of the petition. It therefore will not do for counsel to state the issue in vague or general terms, such as "whether the search in this case complied with the Fourth Amendment to the Constitution" or "whether a defendant in a criminal case is entitled to a speedy trial under the Sixth Amendment to the Constitution." It is also a mistake to adopt the shotgun approach, stating every possible issue involved in the case in the hope that one will hit the mark. That not only diverts attention from a meritorious issue but also invites a denial of certiorari because there is too much clutter in the case.

To make the petition stand out, the question presented should be limited to one or two precise issues; it should focus on the case at hand and at the same time demonstrate that the case has importance beyond the interests of the parties. It should, in short, get the justices interested in the case. This is no easy chore, and if counsel is unable honestly to distill such a question presented from a particular case, he or she should think twice before hitting the certiorari trail.

In the "Opinions Below" section, which follows the listing of the parties, the table of contents, and the table of authorities, counsel must provide "[a] reference to the official and unofficial reports of the opinions delivered in the case by other courts or administrative agencies" (Rule 14.1(d)). The reference should also include a citation to pages in the petition's appendix where these opinions are reprinted (*see* Rule 14.1(k)).

The "Jurisdiction" section must include the date of entry of the judgment or decree below and a citation to the statute petitioner is invoking to support the Supreme Court's jurisdiction. Petitioner must also give "[t]he date of any order respecting a rehearing, and the date and terms of any order granting an extension of time within which to petition for certiorari" (Rule 14.1(e)(ii)). Counsel should be careful not to confuse the entry of the judgment of the court with the issuance of its opinion. In some courts, the clerk may enter a separate judgment; this must be appended to the certiorari petition if the date is different from the date of the opinion (Rule 14.1(k)(iv)). The date upon which the judgment was entered is important because the time for petitioning for certiorari begins running from that date.

Counsel must next provide a statement of the case. This should not repeat what was said in the appellate brief. The facts should be condensed as accurately as possible, and the relevant portions of the opinions below should be summarized. If petitioner is seeking review of the judgment of a state court, Rule 14.1(h) sets forth additional material that must be included to assure the Court that a federal question is properly presented. If the case is coming from a federal court of appeals, counsel must show "the basis for federal jurisdiction in the court of first instance" (Rule 14.1(i)).

In most cases, lengthy quotations from the lower court's opinion should be avoided, particularly if the quotations make a convincing case against one's client. If the Court needs to refer to the language used in the opinion it can easily do so by turning to the appendix of the petition, which must contain reprints of the opinions below (*see* Rule 14.1(k)(i) & (ii)). Counsel should also be careful to state the case in such a way that the respondent cannot reasonably claim that the Court has been given a distorted picture. Otherwise, even if the Court believes that the question presented warrants review, it may deny certiorari because it has doubts about the existence of facts upon which the question rests.

In preparing the statement of the case, petitioner's counsel should keep three objectives in mind. First, counsel should give the Court a clear and succinct idea of what the case involves and how the courts below dealt with the question presented in the petition. Second, he or she should avoid getting into a squabble over the facts with opposing counsel. If there is an unavoidable disagreement about the evidence, petitioner may be able to blunt respondent's criticism of the statement of the case by giving both sides of the factual controversy. Finally, counsel must demonstrate to the Court that if it grants certiorari, the facts are that it will be required to decide the question presented and that a decision in petitioner's favor on the question will result in a reversal or a significant modification of the judgment below.

Under Rule 14.1(j), the statement of the case must be followed by a section containing the reasons why the Court should grant the writ. Counsel would be well-advised to begin this critical portion of the petition with a paragraph or two stating why the case is important. In light of the manner in which the justices review certiorari petitions, first impressions are all important. The opening paragraph should summarize what follows and avoid holding in suspense a reader who will be rapidly reviewing the papers and quickly coming to a judgment about the petition. In seeking to persuade the Court to hear the case, counsel should also describe early on the consequences of allowing the opinion below to stand. He or she should explain why these consequences are unacceptable and what harm can be avoided by Supreme Court review.

Rule 10 of the Supreme Court's rules recites, in general terms, the reasons that tend to make a case "certworthy." One of the reasons most frequently invoked is that, with respect to the federal question raised in the petition, there is a conflict of decisions. Whether such a conflict will persuade the Supreme Court to grant certiorari depends, in the first place, on the courts involved.

The Supreme Court, for example, will not give much weight to conflicts between decisions of different panels of the same federal court of appeals; these can be resolved by en banc review in the court of appeals. Similarly, the Supreme Court will not be impressed by a conflict between a federal district court opinion in one circuit and the opinion of a court of appeals in another; supervising district courts is the function of courts of appeals.

However, if the conflict is between decisions of different federal courts of appeals or between the Supreme Court and the appellate court below, state or federal, the certiorari petition stands a better chance of being granted. From the beginning, one of the primary functions of the Supreme Court has been, as John Rutledge said during the Constitutional Convention, to secure "uniformity of judgments."

The term "conflict" in this context has a particular meaning. The opinions of the courts on the issue must be irreconcilable. There is no true conflict if the opinions are sufficiently open-ended that they may be reasonably construed to resolve the apparent inconsistency. The conflict must arise out of the holdings of the courts; mere dicta is not enough. Factual differences between the cases must be insufficient to explain the disagreement among the courts on the law.

Even if counsel is able to demonstrate that a square conflict exists on the question presented in the petition, there is no assurance that the Court will hear the case. The Court may still deny certiorari if it believes the conflict may be resolved by future decisions of the courts of appeals, or if the Court sees some benefit from allowing the issue to percolate in the lower courts for a while longer, or if the conflict is over an issue that is insignificant or unlikely to recur. In arguing that the Supreme Court should grant review, counsel should give reasons why prompt action by the Court is needed to settle the conflict.

If a real conflict does not exist, counsel should not strain to create one. The Court will not be misled and petitioner's attempt to stretch the decisions may itself doom the petition. Counsel is far better off arguing—if he or she can reasonably do so—that although there is no actual conflict, the courts are in disagreement about the legal principles involved or have used inconsistent reasoning to reach their decisions. Only the Supreme Court, petitioner would contend, can clear up the uncertainty that exists and put an end to the resulting litigation that burdens litigants and the lower courts.

For petitions that do not rest on the existence of a true conflict, the critical factor will be the importance of the case. This obviously is a quite general standard. If a federal statute or regulation has been held unconstitutional, the case has obvious significance, but private counsel rarely will be in a position to invoke this as a reason for Supreme Court review. Factors that bear on the importance of the issue presented include the number of persons affected, the amount of money involved, and the number of other cases that will be influenced.

In arguing why the case is important despite the absence of a conflict, counsel should attempt to answer a question that will be on the Court's mind: If the issue presented is so significant and if it has been decided incorrectly by the court below, as petitioner maintains, should not the

Court wait until a conflict develops before deciding the issue? The burden on counsel will be to show that, in addition to the harm to petitioner from allowing the decision below to stand, other adverse consequences will follow.

To have some idea of what the Court might consider important, counsel should keep track of the cases in which petitions have been recently granted. If the question presented in the petition is related to a case the Court has already decided to hear, counsel may be able to come in on the coat-tails of the other case. As an alternative to requesting full plenary review, counsel can suggest that action on the petition be deferred pending the Court's disposition of the related case. If the related case is decided favorably, the Court may then grant certiorari, summarily reverse or vacate the judgment, and remand the case for reconsideration by the lower court.

Prior Supreme Court decisions may also furnish a basis for arguing that the question presented warrants review. If the question raised in the petition bears some relationship to a case decided earlier by the Court on writ of certiorari, counsel may invoke the Court's decision as a precedent supporting the argument that the issue is important enough to command the Court's attention.

Counsel should also follow closely the Court's denials of certiorari. The issue presented in one petition is often similar to that presented in other petitions the Court has denied. Counsel can assume that this filing will meet the same fate unless he or she is able to distinguish this case from those the Court has declined to review or to point to intervening developments, such as new legislation, regulations, or court decisions that render the issue more significant than it has been.

It is not easy to know exactly what will move the justices to vote for certiorari on any particular occasion. The writ is discretionary. When the Court denies certiorari, it issues only an order. After it grants certiorari, the opinion on the merits rarely gives any detailed explanation of why the Court decided to review the case. As Justice Harlan wrote, "Frequently the question whether a case is 'certworthy' is more a matter of 'feel' than of precisely ascertainable rules." "Manning the Dikes," 13 *Record of N.Y.C.B.A.* 541, 549 (1958). This of course makes it far more difficult for petitioner's counsel to step back from the case, as should be done, and evaluate it from the position of the decision makers. Only by following the Court closely can counsel begin to develop the type of understanding of the Court that will enable counsel to decide which is the most effective way to frame the petition or, indeed, whether it is even worthwhile to file one.

It is frequently said that one of the cardinal rules for preparing a certiorari petition is to keep it brief. Without question the justices prefer short petitions, if only because this lightens their workload and that of their law clerks. One tends to doubt, however, whether many otherwise "certworthy" cases have been denied review because the petitions were too long, although Rule 14.5 of the Court's rules states that a petition may be rejected on this basis alone.

From a petitioner's viewpoint, there are two dangers in filing a lengthy certiorari petition. The first is simply that the longer the petition is, the less likely it will be that the reader will get through all of it. Second, the longer the petition the greater the chance that petitioner's important points will become obscured. If the petition is short, crisp, and to the point, there is a much greater likelihood that the reader—whether justice or law clerk—will not have reached a judgment about certiorari until he or she has absorbed all, or at least a large proportion, of what petitioner's counsel has to say. For that reason, and because of Rule 14.5, petitioner's counsel must make every attempt to be brief.

It would take an entire volume to write about these matters and other requirements a petitioner must meet, such as jurisdiction, filing fees, time limits, form of the petition and appendices, and so forth. Fortunately, such a volume has been written: Stern and Gressman's *Supreme Court Practice* provides a wealth of information on jurisdiction, practice, and procedures regarding the Court. It deserves careful review by any practitioner facing the prospect of filing a petition for a writ of certiorari in the Supreme Court of the United States.

Petitioning for Certiorari in the Big Case

Charles G. Cole

Exxon Corp. v. United States, 474 U.S. 1105 (1986), was the classic Big Case. It lasted more than eight years and involved complex questions of federal energy law. The judgment entered against Exxon amounted to more than $2 billion. Five certiorari petitions, on behalf of 15 parties and supported by several amici, were filed in the United States Supreme Court.

Yet, the Supreme Court disposed of the case in a single, crisp sentence: "The petitions for certiorari are denied."

Exxon illustrated what most observers of the Court have known for some time—big cases don't necessarily become Supreme Court cases.

There are several reasons for this: some obvious, others more subtle. First, the chances of obtaining a grant of certiorari from the Supreme Court are, in general, exceedingly slim. The Court hears an argument in only about 4 percent of the cases on its paid docket.

Ironically, the chances of obtaining certiorari in a big case are no better, and perhaps worse. Big cases often have many interconnected issues. The Court may be reluctant to review one issue because that may require accepting others and create the risk that the Court will divide into several pluralities.

Second, big cases have big records. The Justices are scrupulous students of the record, but they cannot scrutinize extensive records in more than a handful of cases each Term.

Last, the attributes that make a case seem big to the litigants will not necessarily impress the Supreme Court. The number of parties, the dollars at stake, or the complexity or duration of the litigation will rarely affect the Court's decision whether to grant certiorari.

Charles G. Cole is a partner in the Washington, D.C., law firm of Steptoe & Johnson L.L.P. He was a law clerk to Justice White during the 1977 term.

Instead, the Supreme Court has its own notion of a big case. The Court considers the nationwide impact of resolving the legal issue presented in the petition—not the size of the litigation in which the issue arises. The Court is concerned primarily with precedential impact. It wants to know how many other cases will be determined by the result in this one and whether doctrine will be affected. It evaluates these questions with an eye to the economic and social consequences for the nation as a whole.

In short, the Court often chooses small cases that present big issues over big cases with many smaller issues.

Of course, some big cases do have big issues that compel a grant of certiorari. For example, in *Sony Corp. v. Universal City Studios,* 464 U.S. 417 (1984), the Supreme Court was asked to decide whether companies that sell home video cassette recorders to the public were responsible for copyright infringement. The eight-year-long litigation involved many corporate parties and hundreds of millions of dollars in potential royalties. The outcome of the case would affect the future of an important young industry, as well as the at-home activity of millions of Americans. *Sony* was a litigant's big case that also had every element of a big case from the Supreme Court's perspective.

But most cases—even big cases—do not. Usually a lawyer must work to persuade the Court that his case presents an issue whose resolution will affect many other cases and have practical consequences for the nation as a whole.

The first task is to identify the issue most likely to engage the Court.

The issue most intensively litigated in the lower courts often is not the most "certworthy" issue. Some secondary issues, such as a question of procedure or damages, may have greater appeal. Since the petitioner's overriding objective is to obtain a grant of certiorari, he must search for the best issue to hook the Court's attention.

The classic hook is an issue that has created a conflict between the lower courts. In fact, the Supreme Court identifies a conflict among the lower courts as the reason for granting certiorari in about one-third of its argued cases. Since the Court rarely explains its other reasons for granting certiorari, the conflicts rationale may be the easiest to identify, analyze, and invoke.

The Court's view of the role of conflicts in granting petitions for certiorari has changed dramatically over the last several decades. In preparing a petition using the conflicts rationale, it is important to understand the Court's current view.

At one time, the Court appeared to believe that it was obliged to ensure uniformity on matters of federal law. Under this theory, inconsistency on matters of federal law between two federal courts was itself an evil requiring prompt correction. Thus, a 1951 treatise on the Supreme Court declared that when two circuits reach decisions in direct conflict on a question of law, "the Supreme Court grants certiorari as of course, and irrespective of the importance of the question of law involved." R. Robertson & F. Kirkham, *Jurisdiction of the Supreme Court of the United States* § 322, at 629 (R. Wolfson and P. Kurland, 2d ed. 1951).

Recently, many Justices have been following a different theory—what might be called the percolation theory of conflicts jurisdiction. Under this theory, a conflict is allowed to percolate in the lower courts until all theories and factual situations have been explored, and it is apparent that no consensus can be reached. When the conflict is widespread and recurring, the issue has "perked" and is ready for Supreme Court review.

Under the percolation theory, a conflict in the interpretation of federal law is not alone an adequate reason to grant review. Thus, many petitions presenting conflicts are routinely denied review. Through his dissents from the denial of certiorari during the 1991 term, Justice White identified 17 occasions when the Court refused to resolve a conflict during that Term. Apparently conflicts among the lower courts are no longer viewed as evils sufficient in themselves to require prompt correction, but only as evidence that particular issues may be difficult and ripe for review.

In view of this change in approach, what must the petitioner show to obtain a grant of certiorari based on the conflicts rationale?

First, that the conflict is a "true" conflict; second, that the conflict is recurring; and third, that it is important. Each of these criteria deserves attention in framing the question presented and in outlining the petition.

A true conflict is what Professor Felix Frankfurter called a "head-on collision" between two courts. Two decisions conflicting in dicta or even in principle are not enough. It must be clear that the *holdings* of two courts are in conflict—that Court A, if presented with the same facts as Court B, would decide that case differently. If there is any ambiguity in the doctrine of Court A that would permit it to reach the same result as Court B, the cases do not present a true conflict. The same is true if factual differences between the two cases justify different results. In these circumstances, the Justices' law clerks—who typically prepare the preliminary legal analysis of the petition—are apt to conclude that there is a "false" conflict.

A false conflict also may arise when the two decisions alleged to conflict are widely separated in time. The court from which review is sought may have considered recent developments in judicial doctrine, in the relevant body of statutes, or in the economy. The Supreme Court may conclude that the earlier court would have reached the same result had it been able to consider those developments. Thus, the reasoning goes, the alleged conflict is false.

A true conflict can exist between two federal circuits, between the highest courts of two states, or between a federal circuit and the highest court of a state. Generally, when a conflict involves only a federal circuit and a federal district court or intermediate state courts, the Supreme Court is not interested. Instead, the Court is prepared to let the issue percolate through the next level of review.

The petitioner cannot create a true conflict if none exists. But he can be artful in demonstrating the conflict. Here some long-range planning can help. While the case is before the court of appeals, the litigant can create a record showing that the court of appeals was fully informed of the contrary views of its sister circuits but nevertheless refused to follow them. That will prepare the way for arguing that the conflict is a head-on collision.

Of course, precedents from other circuits are often included in appellate briefs to persuade the panel to adopt the litigant's position. But it is especially important to make the record for a certiorari petition after an adverse decision from the court of appeals. Then the litigant bound for the Supreme Court should file a petition for a rehearing, calling attention to the conflict between that decision and decisions in other circuits. Although this is unlikely to change the minds of any members of the original panel, it may cause the panel or another judge to acknowledge the conflict. Even if this does not happen, the petitioner still will be able to tell the Supreme Court that the court below was advised of the contrary position of another appellate court and refused to change its mind.

A word of warning. If the cases do not present a true conflict, do not try to manufacture one. Law clerks love to detect and highlight false conflicts in the memoranda they prepare for the Justices. Once the clerks uncover the false conflict, everyone is likely to lose interest in the petition. If the decisions below do not collide head-on, the litigant is better off designating the disagreements as conflicts "in principle" or as evidence of "confusion" in the lower courts.

Even if the petition demonstrates a true conflict, there is no guarantee of a grant. During the 1991 Term, for example, at least 70 percent of the cases in which the Court identified a conflict involved conflicts of three or more courts; 60 percent involved conflicts of four or more courts. For many Justices, once is not enough; the petition must show a recurring conflict.

The percolation theory suggests why. The lower courts may develop a consensus position as the issue percolates; if one court is out of step, it may be encouraged to fall back in line. In that way, the conflict may get resolved.

Alternatively, the lower courts may develop many different, competing legal theories from which the Supreme Court can choose. Also, the larger number of cases will allow the Court to see how the issue affects a wide variety of factual situations.

Finally, recurring, conflicting opinions show a lively interest in the issue. Usually they are also a sign that no other institution—such as Congress or an administrative agency—is able to resolve the problem quickly.

The key to demonstrating a recurring conflict is to dig through the library for every case in which the issue has been decided. Once the petitioner demonstrates a true conflict among federal circuit courts or the highest state courts, other state cases and federal district court cases may be given weight. Such lesser authorities show the recurring nature of the issue and also may provide additional legal theories or factual situations.

Recent cases that have not yet been published are extremely important. Typically, the most certworthy conflicts are those that have developed rapidly and recently because of new statutory, doctrinal, or economic developments. Decisions too recent to be published may signify such an emerging controversy. Of course, a case that has not been published at the direction of the deciding court is not as helpful because it lacks precedential impact.

The effort to demonstrate a recurring conflict presents one of the few occasions in which a lawyer will strengthen his position by presenting cases that support the opposition's legal position. This is because the petitioner aims primarily to show that the issue has arisen frequently, not that most courts have favored his position. Adverse precedent, even that not cited by the opponent below, helps because it is further proof of the conflict.

In attempting to demonstrate a recurring conflict, little is gained from mischaracterizing cases with only a marginal relationship to the conflict. The respondent or the law clerks will distinguish cases that are not really in conflict, and the petition will lose credibility. If these related cases are helpful in demonstrating that the problem is widespread and confusing—and such slightly off-point cases often are—then the best approach is to describe them as reflecting additional confusion on a related issue.

The Justices Want More

Also, in demonstrating a recurring conflict, the petitioner should avoid arguing that the decision he seeks to appeal conflicts with an earlier decision of the same court. This argument almost always backfires. The Supreme Court is likely to reason either that the court below was not aware of its prior decision—in which case the decision below is a "sport" unlikely to recur—or that the court below *was* aware of its prior decision—in which case the court below must have viewed the two decisions as harmonious. If the analysis the petitioner has invited shows that the earlier, supposedly conflicting decision remains good law in the circuit and the decision below simply represents an exception or a different application of the same legal standard, then the law in that circuit may be viewed as roughly consistent with the law in other circuits. In short, by stressing an internal circuit conflict, the litigant highlights a means of resolving the apparent intercircuit conflict.

Even if a petition has demonstrated a true and recurring conflict, the Justices may want something more. The petitioner also should show that the conflict is sufficiently important to warrant Supreme Court resolution. "Importance" as used in this context is hard to define, but it is best explained in practical, rather than doctrinal, terms. Who is affected by the conflict? In what way? How often? Can the person live with the conflict?

At one end of the spectrum of importance are conflicts about non-constitutional issues of procedure or evidence in the federal courts. Perhaps, because there is great procedural diversity in our federal system and because individual judges have wide discretion on evidentiary matters, those issues often do not seem important enough for a grant of certiorari. Clearly, conflicts on such issues may percolate for a long time before the Supreme Court resolves them.

At the opposite end of the spectrum of importance are conflicts concerning rules of conduct for individuals or entities that must operate in more than one state. An example from the 1984 term is *Pattern Makers' League of North America, AFL-CIO v. NLRB*, 473 U.S. 95 (1985), in which the Court upheld the NLRB's view that a union could not prevent its members from resigning from the union during a strike. The Court's opinion noted that "very few" unions had rules preventing resignations. *Id.* at n.12. Yet the petitioning union did have such a provision in its national charter. The Seventh Circuit had held that a union could not restrict its members' right to resign, while the Ninth Circuit had held that it could. Thus, a national union's restriction on resignation might be unlawful in the Seventh Circuit, enforceable in the Ninth, and uncertain in the rest. The Court agreed to review the case even though the conflict consisted of only two decisions.

In the middle of the spectrum—where most of the cases lie—are cases raising issues about the appropriate secondary consequences of prohibited conduct. These cases typically address the rights of action or remedies for violations of federal civil and criminal statutes, not the conduct permitted or prohibited by those statutes. Such issues might include standing to sue under a federal statute or the applicable statute of limitations. In this middle range of cases, above all, a showing of the importance of the issue presented can affect the Court's decision about whether to grant certiorari.

How does a lawyer show the importance of the question presented? First, quantify the problem. Tell how many similar cases are pending in the federal or state courts or how many incipient cases are moving through the pipeline of an administrative agency. Government reports are often good sources for such information. These include annual reports, budget statements, or rulemaking notices.

Private associations can help, too. Trade journals or other publications of industry trade associations are one source. Another is information collected by trade associations but not published. The petitioner should consider putting a notice in an industry newsletter asking litigants or companies with similar problems to contact the trade association or the law firm drafting the certiorari petition.

If quantitative data are not available, the petition should discuss the practical consequences of the conflict for the petitioner. What economic opportunities has the litigant declined because of uncertainty about applicable law? Have there been additional litigation costs and delays because of the confusion created by the conflict? An accurate, detailed account of the quandary faced by the petitioner can often be as persuasive as numerical data.

Remember that the argument should focus on the problem created by the conflict—not simply on the undesirable effects of the adverse ruling below. Viewed individually, any one of the conflicting legal rules followed by the courts below may be workable, yet the uncertainty over the right rule may be hamstringing an industry or creating unnecessary litigation.

If a big case does not present a conflict, other strategies must be examined. For example, Supreme Court Rule 10—which sets forth the criteria used by the Court in deciding whether to grant certiorari—refers to a category of cases in which "a state court or a United States court of appeals has decided an important question of federal law which has not been, but should be, settled by this Court...." This category permits the Court to initiate doctrinal advances (or halt them) in the absence of a conflict. Often the best sign that the Court is willing to consider such a case is a footnote in a recent opinion noting that a particular issue is unresolved.

Supreme Court Rule 10 also refers to cases involving the flip side of that situation, where the court below "has decided an important federal question in a way that conflicts with relevant decisions of this Court." In reality, the Supreme Court rarely grants certiorari simply because a court has erred in applying a well-established Supreme Court opinion. The Supreme Court does not sit to correct individual errors. If there is already a clear opinion on point, the Supreme Court does not need to use its valuable time to restate the law.

More often, this category might be invoked if the court below has followed one strand of Supreme Court precedent and a different line of precedent seems more appropriate. Indeed, in most cases where the petitioner asserts that the decision below conflicts with Supreme Court precedent, the Court grants certiorari if it concludes that the issue presented involves a factual configuration that it has not addressed and that therefore requires clarification.

Whether a litigant proceeds on the basis of a "conflicts" strategy or another theory for seeking certiorari, the critical factor may well be the Justices' perception of the national importance of the issue. In every big case the petitioner should consider getting help from other sources to illustrate national importance.

First, the petitioner may seek support from amici curiae at the certiorari stage. Amici may be able to draw on their own experience to identify practical consequences of the decision below that are not apparent from the record. *See generally* Shapiro, "Amicus Briefs in the Supreme Court," 10 *Litigation*, No. 3 at 21, 23 (Spring 1984). Of course, an amicus brief is most effective if the amicus' position is not obviously compelled by self-interest. Thus, a brief from a regulated industry may carry great weight if it supports a regulation. Similarly, an amicus brief that argues for the prompt resolution of an issue but does not take a position on the merits could have substantial impact.

A second means of confirming the importance of a big case is to enlist the support of the Office of the Solicitor General in the U.S. Department of Justice. The solicitor general has tremendous credibility with the Court, both because he represents the United States and because of his restraint in requesting a grant of certiorari. Even if the United States is not a party, the solicitor general may file an amicus brief recommending a grant of certiorari. Moreover, after the petition and opposition have been considered by the Court, the Court frequently asks the solicitor general for his views. The solicitor general's answer can be decisive.

In seeking the solicitor general's support, remember that the solicitor general, like any other lawyer, perceives that his primary obligation is to his client, in this case the United States, and in particular the Executive Branch. The solicitor general's office is not interested in correcting federal decisions simply because they are wrong, but it may respond to cogent arguments that the interests of the United States lie in reversal. Moreover, although the Office of the Solicitor General cannot be "lobbied" in the traditional sense, the clients of the solicitor general can be. It is proper to seek support from the agencies or departments potentially interested in the case. The agencies then can talk to the solicitor general, who has an obligation to listen to his client's views and, where appropriate, to follow them.

The structure of a certiorari petition in a big case should not be substantially different from that of any other petition. *See* Baker, "A Practical Guide to Certiorari," 33 *Cath. U. L. Rev.* 611 (1984). In drafting a petition in a big case, keep these guiding principles in mind.

First, resist the temptation to present a long series of questions reflecting the complexity of the litigation. All that will do is suggest to the Court that the petitioner does not have a great deal of confidence in the certworthiness of any one of the questions.

Second, do not quarrel with the court below over the facts. Any opinion deciding a case with a big record is bound to contain what are arguably factual errors. These factual disputes should not be highlighted and perhaps should not be mentioned at all. If it appears that the controversy turns on an assessment of the facts, the Court will be reluctant to take the case. The better approach is to emphasize that, even on the facts claimed by the respondent, the court below committed an error of law.

Sometimes, though, understanding a complex scientific or regulatory background is essential to appreciating the key legal issue. When this is true, provide the background information in clear terms at the outset of the petition. For example, in cases involving regulated industries, it is often useful to begin the statement of the case with a brief, neutral explanation of the governing statute so that the reader, often a law clerk with no prior experience in the regulatory scheme, can appreciate the significance of the facts presented in the litigation.

Last, avoid the "uniqueness" trap. Particularly in a big case, the petitioner may be tempted to assert that the factual background or litigation history makes the lawsuit the "first in history" or "one of a kind." From the Supreme Court's perspective, this makes the petition less, rather than more, enticing. A unique case will probably never recur. A decision on unique facts will not, in any event, have much precedential impact. Here again, unless the case is of extraordinary intrinsic importance, it is wiser to stress the ways in which the big case is similar to, rather than different from, other cases.

Finally, a word of encouragement. Small cases, too, can create good law. Even though the odds may seem daunting and your case may appear to be a small one, its issue may be certworthy. And once the Supreme Court has granted certiorari, any case becomes a Big Case.

Opposing Certiorari in the U.S. Supreme Court

Timothy S. Bishop

For its recipient, a certiorari petition can be an anticlimax. After years of successful litigation, you and your client deserve a break, but do not get one. Ninety-odd days after you celebrate a hard-fought victory in a federal court of appeals or state supreme court, you receive an impressively printed petition for writ of certiorari to the United States Supreme Court. After reporting on the petition to your client, who hoped to have heard the last of the case, you reassemble your appellate team and ponder what to do.

The odds are in your favor. The Supreme Court denies the vast majority of requests for review: 1,945 of the 2,130 so-called paid (i.e., nonindigent) certiorari petitions or appeals acted on during the Court's 1995 term were turned down. An even higher proportion of the 4,500 in forma pauperis (IFP) cases were unsuccessful. 61 U.S.L.W. 3100 (Aug. 6, 1996). In fact, during the tenure of Chief Justice Rehnquist, as the number of lower court decisions has increased, the number of cases set for argument in the Supreme Court has declined. The drop has not been trivial: down from 167 in the 1987 term to 116 in the 1992 term and 90 in the 1995 term. Many of the cases accepted for argument, moreover, are those in which the federal government has sought or supported review; or they involve constitutional, civil rights, or criminal matters. Few are civil business cases like yours. *See* Bator, "What Is Wrong with the Supreme Court?," 51 *U. Pitt. L. Rev.* 673, 681–84 (1990).

So, the odds are with you. But that almost increases the pressure. Your client will not be happy if lightning strikes. It will not want to incur the expense of another round of briefing and oral argument just to

---

Timothy S. Bishop is an appellate litigator with Mayer, Brown & Platt in Chicago and an adjunct professor at Northwestern University Law School. He was a law clerk to Supreme Court Justice William J. Brennan, Jr.

put at risk a favorable judgment. And what is worse than a lawyer who fumbles a virtual sure thing?

What should you do to maximize the chance that no four justices—enough to grant certiorari—see yours as that rare case deserving the Court's plenary attention?

Start with what the other side must do—that is, with what you want to prevent. A petitioner for certiorari bears a heavy burden to persuade the Court to select its case for review out of the many thousands of petitions filed. Understanding the nature of that burden is crucial to writing a successful brief urging denial of certiorari (called a "brief in opposition").

The major peculiarity of petitioning for certiorari is that the merits of a case are not the main thing. They are not a reliable indicator of whether the Court will grant the writ. True, in the cases it hears, the Court often determines that the judgment below was incorrect. The Court reversed or vacated (at least in part) 57 (68 percent) of the 84 cases reviewed on writ of certiorari and decided with a full opinion during the 1995 term. "The Supreme Court, 1995 Term," 110 *Harv. L. Rev.* 372 (1996). But, at the petition stage, there is no straightforward relationship between the merits and whatever review will be granted. The reason for this—and it is an awkward concept for many lawyers—is that the Supreme Court does not regard its principal job to be the correction of errors.

What is Not Cert Worthy?

Instead of seeking merely to correct erroneous decisions, the Court is looking, Chief Justice Rehnquist has written, for cases "involving unsettled questions of federal constitutional or statutory law of general interest." Rehnquist, *The Supreme Court: How it Was, How it Is* 269 (1987). Selecting these is inevitably "rather subjective" and involves "intuition" as well as "legal judgment." *Id.* at 265. Indeed, Justice Harlan thought "the question whether a case is 'certworthy'" to be "more a matter of 'feel' than of precisely ascertainable rules." Harlan, "Manning the Dikes," 13 *Rec. of the N.Y.C. Bar Ass'n* 541, 549 (1958).

Intuition plays a role, but it is a patterned kind of intuition: Most cases in which certiorari is granted fall into one of three well-established categories (discussed at length and in all their variations in the Supreme Court practitioner's bible, Stern, Gressman, Shapiro and Geller, *Supreme Court Practice* §§ 4.3–4.15 (7th ed. 1993)). These categories are (1) cases raising a federal law question on which a conflict has developed among the federal circuit or state supreme courts; (2) cases in which the lower court reached a decision in conflict with governing Supreme Court precedent; and (3) cases squarely presenting an important issue of federal law with significant practical consequences. *See* Rule 10.

Therefore, although the correctness of the judgment below is certainly of some importance—even where there is a clear circuit conflict, the justices may prefer to take a case to reverse rather than affirm—it is rarely controlling. A petitioner for certiorari—your opponent—must thus do more than show the Court that the decision below was wrong. An effective petition for certiorari must also demonstrate that one or more of the established factors making for "certworthiness" are present. As a corollary, the job of the brief in opposition is to show not only that the decision below was correct, but (more important), either that certworthiness factors are absent or (if some are present) that the case is not worth the Court's attention.

To talk about the content of a brief in opposition, however, is to get ahead of the game. The first question to ask after studying the petition is whether the Court will really need any further persuasion to deny certiorari—or whether the petitioner has already done that job for you. In short, do you need to file anything at all?

It remains true today, as Justice Harlan complained four decades ago, that "a great many petitions for certiorari reflect a fundamental misconception as to the role of the Supreme Court" and stand no chance of being granted. Harlan, *supra* at 549. Some petitions from state courts fail to identify any federal issue, even though they bristle with a multiplicity of questions presented (itself a sign of a poor petition). Others argue only that the decision below was wrong, or leave no doubt that the issues raised are of little consequence beyond the particular case. Petitioners routinely fail to show that the questions presented arise out of a conflict in the courts of appeals or state supreme courts; have previously been settled by the Supreme Court in a way that is contrary to the decision below; or involve issues of general importance that are ripe for Supreme Court review.

Chief Justice Rehnquist estimates that "between one and two thousand" of the petitions filed each year are so "patently without merit" that "no one of the nine [justices] would have the least interest in granting them." Rehnquist, *supra* at 264. Justice Brennan has been even harsher. He opined that about 90 percent of IFP and 60 percent of paid petitions are so "utterly without merit" as to require a "minimum of time and effort" to determine that denial was the proper disposition; he, himself, often decided that a case was not certworthy by doing nothing more than reading the questions presented. Brennan, "The National Court of Appeals: Another Dissent," 40 *U. Chi. L. Rev.* 473, 476–78 (1973).

If you believe that the petition for certiorari in your case will receive this dismissive treatment, compare notes with lawyers who are farther removed from the case and who have had the opportunity to develop a "feel" for certworthiness. Have an experienced Supreme Court practitioner, a past law clerk, or an alum of the solicitor general's office read the opinion below and the petition. If there is general agreement that the petition is obviously meritless, talk to your client about whether the time and expense of preparing and printing a brief in opposition is warranted.

Should You File Anyway?

No rule requires that the respondent file a brief in opposition (except in capital cases, see Rule 15.1). If the petition in your case is so plainly meritless that the Court will not need the assistance of a brief in opposition, you may wish to waive your response. The solicitor general and state attorneys general often do this.

One way to waive is simply to allow the period for response to elapse without filing a brief. A much more helpful and courteous course is to write a letter to the clerk (be sure to serve it on opposing counsel). It should say something such as "because this case clearly does not warrant review by the Supreme Court, respondent does not intend to respond to the petition for certiorari unless requested to do so by the Court." Such a letter tells the clerk that respondent received service and identifies respondent's counsel of record. *See* Rule 9.

The clerk prefers a respondent to file its waiver letter as soon as possible after receipt of the petition. That is because the clerk may circulate the petition to the justices immediately after receiving the waiver letter, instead of waiting until the time for response expires. Rule 15.5. This may be an important factor if you want to move rapidly to enforce a judgment in your favor—especially when a Court recess looms. For example, when a petition is filed close to the long summer recess, quickly filing a waiver can reward you with a June denial of certiorari and avoid the long wait until the first October order list.

Waiving response displays the proper disdain for a frivolous petition. And it is not the risk one might imagine: A respondent can be sure of an opportunity to file a brief in opposition if the justices surprisingly do find something of interest in the case. A summary of the Court's current procedures for handling certiorari petitions shows why, but it also shows that a waiver must be approached with care.

Once a week throughout the year, the clerk circulates papers to the justices for paid cases in which a brief in opposition or waiver letter has been received or the time for response has expired. *See* Rule 15.5. There is another weekly circulation of IFP cases. The circulated cases are divided among the law clerks to the eight justices who currently combine their clerks' efforts at the petition stage into what is called the "cert pool." A single law clerk from the cert pool is assigned to each case and writes a memorandum, known as a "pool memo," to guide the justices who participate in this arrangement. The pool memo discusses the certworthiness of the petition and makes a recommendation as to its disposition. (Justice Stevens is the only justice who currently does not participate in the pool. His clerks read all the petitions themselves.)

The cert pool ensures that each set of certiorari-stage submissions receives more detailed attention than would occur if clerks or justices in every chambers had to read the papers in each of the more than 100 cases circulated each week. The pool clerk has time to study cases alleged by petitioner to be in conflict and even to do research independent of the briefs. On the debit side, the pool arrangement means that the most careful attention to the petition (and to your brief in opposition, if you file one) comes from a single law clerk, who will recommend to the justices in the pool whether to grant the writ.

After the pool memos are distributed to participating chambers, clerks annotate the memos, paying special attention to anything in the case that might interest their own justice. The justices then review the annotated memos themselves prior to conference. Pool memos have become an important element in the Court's review of certiorari petitions. The chief justice has said that "with a large majority of the petitions" he does not "go any further than the pool memo." Rehnquist, *supra* at 264–65. The justices are most likely to go beyond the pool memo to read the briefs where the certiorari decision appears close or where the pool memo has recommended a grant.

On the basis of the pool memo, their clerks' annotations, and (where necessary) their own review of the briefs, the justices decide whether a petition should be discussed and voted on at conference. The chief justice compiles a list of cases he believes should be set for a conference discussion—called the "discuss list"—and circulates it to other members of the Court, any one of whom may add a case to the list. Any case not appearing on the discuss list is "dead listed" for denial without a conference vote. Only 15 percent to 30 percent of circulated petitions appear on the discuss list. See Rehnquist, *supra* at 265–66; Caldeira & Wright, "The Discuss List: Agenda Building in the Supreme Court," 24 *Law & Soc. Rev.* 807, 808 (1990).

What Is the "Discuss List"?

The Court's current handling of the "discuss list" has great importance for a respondent considering whether to waive its brief in opposition. At present, the Court does not include any petition on the "discuss list" until a response has been filed. Thus, if the pool memo writer (or, after reading the pool memo, one of the justices) believes that, despite a waiver of a brief in opposition, the petition should be included on a discuss list for a conference vote, he or she will ask the clerk to "call for a response."

A request for a response obviously must be taken seriously. It is not necessarily bad news, however. It does not mean that a grant is imminent, or even that it is under consideration. After all, the origin of the request will usually be some concern of a single law clerk or, less often, a single justice. It may be perfectly clear to most justices that there is nothing to the petition. Even the requester may only want some clarification. In fact, a response sometimes may be sought because the petition is so unclear that the law clerk writing the pool memo simply cannot understand the case. In such circumstances, the Court may need the respondent's help to identify the issues and determine a proper disposition.

You will know neither the source of the request for a response nor the reason for it. Such a request can therefore be unnerving. If you were careful in deciding to waive a brief in opposition, there is little reason to fear that you have prejudiced your case by waiver itself. Chances are that the Court is looking for clarification rather than weighing a grant.

There is a modest danger to waiver. If you waived in a case that was not frivolous, there may be a remote risk of prejudice. The pool memo writer or even some justices may already have developed a bent towards a grant, based on reading the petition alone, that you will now have to counteract. This possibility cautions care in your initial determination whether to waive and counsels filing a brief in opposition when in doubt.

If you don't waive, what does drafting a brief in opposition involve? The brief is limited to 30 printed pages and is due 30 days after receipt of the petition or of the Court's request for a response. Rule 15.

Your brief in opposition should be low key, befitting the trivial issue the petitioner has tried to foist on the Court. A tone of bemusement, of a patient adult dealing with a confused child, is about right. You will rarely need the full 30 pages (although a long brief showing in nauseating detail why a petition is uncertworthy may sometimes be effective to deaden any spark of interest in the case). "A brief in opposition should be briefly stated and in plain terms" (Rule 15.2), and focused on the precise problem at hand. This is not the place for an extended disquisition on the governing legal principles. As E. Barrett Prettyman, Jr., has warned, if the justices and their clerks finish reading your brief "more impressed with the importance of the case than they were when they finished the petition," you have made a mistake. Prettyman, "Opposing Certiorari in the United States Supreme Court," 61 *Va. L. Rev.* 197, 198 (1975).

Take pains to deter any would-be amici. You don't need their help right now. Their participation at this stage would only suggest that the petition raises an issue with broad impact, and would be self-defeating. Amicus support for a respondent—the opponent of certiorari—has been shown actually to increase the likelihood of a grant. Caldeira & Wright, *supra* at 824, 828.

The parts that may be included in a brief in opposition are, in order: (1) questions presented, which may either track the petitioner's formulation or, more usefully, restate the issues for clarity and in less loaded language; (2) a Rule 29.6 statement of a corporate respondent's parent and non-wholly-owned subsidiaries; (3) tables of contents and authorities; (4) a formal description of the opinions below; (5) a jurisdictional statement; (6) any statutes or other relevant provisions not set out in the petition; (7) a statement of facts; (8) an argument section, often headed

"Reasons for Denying the Petition"; and (9) a formal conclusion requesting denial of the writ. Some of these sections may be omitted if the respondent has nothing to add to the petition. Rules 15.3, 24.2.

If you are lucky, you may not need to do more than explain why the Court lacks jurisdiction. There is nothing more to say if there is a decisive jurisdictional defect. In particular, check whether the petition was timely filed; in civil cases, this is a jurisdictional requirement, and no excuses are accepted. *See* Rule 13.2. An untimely petition is not always caught by the clerk, who may assume that a petition filed more than 90 days after entry of judgment is proper because a petition for rehearing was filed in the lower court. *See* Rule 13.3.

Are Any Issues Moot?

In addition to the timeliness of the petition, consider whether the issues presented have become moot. In a case coming from a state court, examine too whether the judgment rests on an independent and adequate state law ground—one over which the Supreme Court lacks jurisdiction. A substantial number of petitions are filed each year that raise only state law issues or seek review of a decision based in the alternative on a state law ground. They can be knocked out quickly.

In most cases, more will be required—starting with a factual statement. In rare cases, when you are satisfied with petitioner's treatment of the facts, you can omit the statement from the brief in opposition. *See* Rule 24.2. Even if the petitioner's statement is faulty, some recommend keeping the brief in opposition short by simply referring the Court to a satisfactory summary of the facts in an opinion below. Baker, "A Practical Guide to Certiorari," 33 *Cath. U.L. Rev.* 611, 627 (1984).

Almost always, however, something can be made of the facts. Perhaps they are complex (the Court prefers factually straightforward cases); your statement should convey that. Perhaps the petition is interlocutory and key facts remain unresolved so that the Court's decision on the merits might not affect the outcome of the litigation. Perhaps you can emphasize facts that distinguish your case from others said to be in conflict. Perhaps a full account of the facts will show that the case is unusual and the issues are not of general importance. In any event, you almost certainly will want to present the facts to the Court with your own nuances and free of the petitioner's inevitable slant.

Certainly, if there is *any* factual misstatement in the petition, correct it in your brief in opposition. If you try to bring the misrepresentation to the Court's attention at the merits stage, you may find that the point is deemed waived. Rule 15.2 says that "Counsel . . . have an obligation . . . to point out in the brief in opposition and not later, any perceived misstatement made in the petition."

Infrequently, facts outside the record may show lack of certworthiness. You may have found statistics that demonstrate the practical insignificance of the question presented. The petitioner may have made statements to the press that contradict its submissions to the Court about the importance of the issue. Refer to these in the argument section of your brief rather than in the statement of facts—but exercise this option with discretion.

The heart of the brief in opposition is the "Reasons for Denying the Petition" section—the argument. A demonstration that the decision below was absolutely right is one, though subsidiary, reason why the Court may not wish to review the case. The brief in opposition should therefore include a concise defense of the judgment below, either under a separate heading (usually at the end, befitting its secondary status) or possibly incorporated into your explanation that certworthiness is absent. If the opinion below is the work of a respected jurist or strong appellate panel, it doesn't hurt subtly to remind the Court of its provenance. If you were less fortunate, do not limit yourself to defending the decision below on its own terms. If the lower court's reasoning is indefensible, argue that the judgment is nevertheless correct on other grounds. Remember also to point out any absurd consequences that would follow from the rule urged by petitioner.

But, for reasons mentioned before, your focus usually should *not* be the merits of the underlying decision. A more compelling reason for the Court to deny review is that there is some barrier to reaching the merits at all. The issues raised in the petition may be beside the point because the lower court gave alternate grounds of decision that are sufficient to support its judgment. If so, point that out early in the brief in opposition. If the lower court did not pass on the merits of the question presented because petitioner did not raise (or failed to preserve) the issue, make that point early too. A crisp procedural defect of this sort is worth pages of argument defending the correctness of the decision below, and you must raise it in the brief in opposition or risk waiving it. *See* Rule 15.2.

The main job of a brief in opposition is to show that the petition fails to satisfy the criteria for certworthiness. Where possible, directly refute any claim that the questions presented have split the federal circuits or state supreme courts; are issues of great practical importance; or have already been addressed by the Supreme Court and decided contrary to the judgment below.

Are the Conflicts Real?

Frequently, you will be able to show that the petitioner is wrong to say that one or more of these certworthiness criteria is present. One study concluded that although about 60 percent of petitions for certiorari allege a split in the courts as to the question presented, the conflict is real in only *6 percent* of those cases. Caldeira & Wright, *supra* at 820. Ask whether the alleged conflict is a "square" one—would the other court have decided your case differently? Maybe the different outcomes are attributable to different facts and not legal disagreement. Often cases alleged to be in conflict are actually distinguishable on the facts or the law. Sometimes only dicta are inconsistent.

Even where there is a square conflict, it must be at a sufficiently authoritative level of the legal system to warrant review. Some petitioners rely on conflicts among federal district court decisions, but the Court very rarely intervenes in such situations because the courts of appeals can iron out inconsistencies.

A claim that the question presented is "important" enough for Supreme Court review is likewise susceptible to disproof. You can point out in the brief in opposition that the issue has never (or only rarely) arisen in the courts; that the lower courts are consistent in their approach to the question; or that the facts of the case are unusual. Sometimes, by citing past denials of certiorari on precisely the same issue, you can remind the Court that it has previously found the questions presented unworthy of review.

Do not despair if there is a clear split among the circuits or state supreme courts or the petition raises a question of obvious practical importance. Even in such cases, review is discretionary, and it is often denied. In fact, Justice White has complained that the Court is failing to maintain federal law in a "satisfactory, uniform condition" because it "regularly" denies certiorari despite a conflict. *Beaulieu v. United States*, 497 U.S. 1038, 1039 (1990). This occurred in 56 cases during the 1989 term, according to Justice White, who also noted that the Court refused review in 11 cases that term that he believed sufficiently important for the Court's attention.

There are various ways a respondent may take advantage of this tendency. One way to deal with a real conflict is to minimize its importance; argue that any disagreement concerns a narrow issue or is otherwise so insignificant that the Court need not use it to fill one of the spots on its limited docket.

Another method of avoiding certiorari is to suggest that the Court's intervention would be untimely. Certiorari in your case may seem unnecessary, for example, because a conflict has only recently developed. If so, you can argue that it may still be corrected without the Court's intervention. Conversely, you might point out that the conflict is old and has proven tolerable.

Is It the Right Time to Decide?

Other timeliness considerations abound. The Court may decline to review a case in apparent conflict with one of its own decisions if the case seems unlikely to spawn recurring problems or does not provide an occasion to reconsider a particularly dubious decision. The Court often bypasses even federal constitutional or statutory questions of large consequence until they have "percolated" in the lower courts long enough to define the problem and air competing views. Impending legislative attention to an important issue may also lead the Court to take a wait-and-see approach. *See generally* H. Perry, *Deciding to Decide: Agenda Setting in the United States Supreme Court* 216–70 (1991).

Where a petition accurately identifies a conflict or an important issue, you also may want to argue that your particular case is not a good vehicle for settling the problem. In potentially certworthy cases, demonstrate (if you can) that the case is factually or procedurally murky; the Court has a distinct preference for "clean" cases. If the petition mischaracterizes the facts, say so; the Court wants to deal with settled facts, not ongoing factual disputes. Point out ambiguities in the opinions below that may complicate the Court's job. If the case is an interlocutory appeal, emphasize that fact, and point out that the issue presented may take on a different aspect as the case proceeds in the trial court. *See* Stern, Gressman, *et al., supra* § 4.18. Remember, the presumption is against a grant, and the Court is looking for reasons to deny the petition.

Studies have shown that the filing of amicus briefs in support of a petition increases the likelihood that the petition will be granted. *See* Caldeira & Wright, *supra* at 826. Amicus briefs urging a grant need not be filed at the same time as the petition. Rather, they may be "submitted within the time allowed for filing a brief in opposition." Rule 37.2. A savvy petitioner will therefore ask amici to file their briefs the day your opposition is due. This prevents you from responding to amici in your brief.

If an amicus brief makes a point that requires response, you may file a supplemental memorandum to address this "intervening matter not available at the time of [your] last filing." Rule 15.8. Such a supplemental brief may not exceed 10 printed pages. Generally, it should be much shorter, so as not to suggest the amicus brief is important. To be of any use, your memorandum usually must be prepared quickly. You should determine from the clerk when the petition for certiorari will be set for conference; and ensure that your supplemental brief arrives in ample time to be circulated to the justices before the conference vote is taken. If you can get your brief on file before the papers in the case are circulated to the justices (Rule 15.5), so much the better. If printing the brief would cause too much delay, the clerk may grant permission to file initially in typescript. A printed brief can be substituted a few days later.

Your suit may involve only private parties, but if the issue raised in the petition is of consequence to the federal government and appears potentially certworthy, the Court may postpone action until it has heard from the solicitor general. If three justices vote for this at the conference, the Court will issue an invitation to the solicitor general to file a brief "expressing the views of the United States." This is quite common, for example, where a plausible petition raises a question about the implementation of a federal program (such as Medicaid) or the interpretation of a statute enforceable by the United States (such as the antitrust laws).

If it serves your interest, it is sometimes possible to forestall a call for the SG's views by persuading the Court that the government's position—at least on the merits—already is well known. To do this, summarize the government's views in your brief in opposition and lodge with the clerk any supporting documentation, such as government briefs filed in the lower court or in other cases, government reports, or congressional testimony. *See* L. Caplan, *The Tenth Justice* 21–22 (1987).

The solicitor general's view on whether a case merits review carries great weight with the Court. *See* R. Salokar, *The Solicitor General* 27 (1992) (reporting that the Court grants 88 percent of petitions where the SG has filed an amicus brief in support of petitioner and denies 60 percent of petitions when the SG supports the respondent). In addition, when drafting an invited certiorari brief, the SG likely will develop a merits position that will persist in any later filings. Therefore, if the Court has issued an invitation, the respondent should work hard to convince the SG that the petition is not certworthy and that the merits favor respondent. This may be done by letter or sometimes through a meeting with the solicitor general's staff assigned to the case.

It is equally important to contact the agency with primary responsibility for subject matter of the case (including the responsible division of the Justice Department). The agency's position will be influential with the SG, and agency staff may produce the first draft of the government's brief. *See* R. Salokar, *supra* at 78–80; E. Griswold, Ould Fields, New Corne 260 (1992). Think too about contacting other government agencies that may support your position with the SG, especially if the primary agency is against you, urging the SG to recommend a grant.

The Court does not always heed the solicitor general's invited views. If the SG comes down against you, you should file a Rule 15.8 supplemental memorandum responding to the government's brief. The guidelines for responding to petitioner's amici, discussed above, apply equally here, including the need for speed in getting your memorandum on file.

Having the petition granted is not the only bad outcome you want to ward off by filing a brief in opposition. Besides the petitions the Court grants to decide on the merits after full briefing, another 50 to 80 cases a term are disposed of summarily on the basis of the submissions at the petition stage. Sometimes the Court will summarily reverse, but, in most of its summary decisions, the Court *grants* the petition, *vacates* the judgment below, and then *remands* the case for reconsideration in the light of a recent Supreme Court decision. This disposition is referred to as a "GVR." A GVR is certainly not equivalent to a reversal on the merits—after remand the lower courts often adhere to their earlier views—but it does put your judgment at risk and can rekindle the litigation.

If three justices believe that the Court's resolution of a case awaiting argument or decision may settle (or affect) the issues raised in a petition, their votes suffice to "hold" the petition—delay acting upon it—until that case is decided. *Watson v. Butler*, 483 U.S. 1037, 1037–1038 (1987) (Brennan & Marshall, JJ., dissenting). If the anticipated decision materially changes the law applied by the lower court in the "held" case, the Court will then dispose of the petition by GVR. *See* Hellman, "Granted, Vacated, and Remanded," 67 *Judicature* 389 (1984). A petition may also be held so it can be discussed in conference along with other petitions raising similar issues. If one of the petitions is granted, the others will then be held pending the outcome of the granted case. The Court does not announce that it is holding a petition. However, you will know that your case is being held if it is not disposed of on the order list following the conference at which it was considered.

Granted, Vacated, Remanded

The Court often holds cases and then hands down GVRs; it prefers to let the lower courts determine the impact of any new precedent. *See Henry v. City of Rock Hill*, 376 U.S. 776 (1964). For example, it GVR'd no fewer than ten cases for reconsideration in light of its reassessment of RICO's "pattern" requirement in *H.J. Inc. v. Northwestern Bell Telephone Co.*, 492 U.S. 229 (1989).

Sometimes a petition will signal the potential relevance of a pending decision or similarities with other petitions, but you cannot rely upon this. If there are similar cases pending, it is likely that the justices and their clerks will be aware of them, even if the petition in your case has not drawn the connection. The only sure means of tracking down such connections is to search the Court's docket (which is detailed in *U.S. Law Week*) to identify petitions or cases set for argument that might cause your case to be held. You should deal with the supposed relationship explicitly in your brief in opposition; explain why your case is different from, and cannot conceivably be affected by, the outcome in other pending matters.

If you discover that there are a lot of similar petitions pending in circumstances that suggest one will be granted and the others held, discuss another option with your client. Rather than letting others who may have different interests control the Supreme Court litigation, consider filing a brief urging the Court to hear *your* case to affirm on the merits. And, if you nonetheless still want to argue that the petition should be denied, remember that if it is instead held, you can file an amicus brief in the granted case.

Opposing certiorari is an unusual process, with its own rules for success. With more than 7,000 petitions filed annually, most litigators will at some point need to master its peculiarities. For the respondent, the costs of misunderstanding the Supreme Court's case selection principles can be high. The good news is that this is one area in which the Supreme Court is not especially secretive. The grounds for a denial of certiorari are well understood. The road map is there. Follow it.

Amicus Briefs in the Supreme Court

Stephen M. Shapiro

Despite the heavy caseload of the Supreme Court, I have little doubt that the Court welcomes amicus curiae briefs of high quality. Amicus briefs provide data and perspective to the justices that assist them in deciding complex cases. Justice Black observed that "[m]ost cases before this Court involve matters that affect far more people than the immediate record parties" (Revised Rules of the Supreme Court, July 1, 1954, 346 U.S. 947). Wise disposition of cases like these frequently requires information beyond the grasp of the litigants. The paradox has been that only certain types of associations appear very often as friends of the court. Business groups, for example, file fewer amicus briefs than the issues warrant.

The Supreme Court's frequent requests to the solicitor general to file an amicus brief attest to their importance. In fact, even without a request, the solicitor general files about 50 amicus briefs each term. The opinions of the Court often refer to them.

The government is by no means alone in filing amicus briefs. For decades, public interest groups, usually of a liberal political outlook, have made their views known to the Court through amicus briefs. Today, organizations such as the American Civil Liberties Union, the NAACP Legal Defense & Education Fund, and the AFL-CIO advocate their positions in nearly every Supreme Court case that impinges on their goals. To a somewhat lesser extent, conservative public interest groups, such as the Mountain States Legal Foundation, also file amicus briefs in Supreme Court cases.

Stephen M. Shapiro, formerly deputy solicitor general of the United States, is a partner at Mayer, Brown & Platt in Chicago. He is co-author of R. Stern, E. Gressman, S. Shapiro & K. Geller, Supreme Court Practice *(7th ed. 1993).*

In the 1981 Term, 231 amicus curiae briefs were filed in the Supreme Court by parties other than governmental litigants. K. O'Connor & L. Epstein, "Court Rules and Workload: A Case Study of Rules Governing Amicus Curiae Participation," 8 *Just. Sys. J.* 35, 40–41 (1983). The numbers were roughly the same over the prior five terms. Amicus curiae briefs are now filed in two-thirds of the civil cases argued before the Supreme Court each year, and multiple filings are common. K. O'Connor & L. Epstein, "Amicus Curiae Participation in U.S. Supreme Court Litigation: An Appraisal of Hakman's 'Folklore,'" 16 *Law & Soc'y Review* 311, 317 (1982).

Amicus curiae briefs were cited or referred to in approximately 18 percent of the opinions rendered by the Court or by individual justices from 1974 to 1984. In the 1995 Term, 32 percent of the cases decided by the Court referred to amicus curiae briefs. To obtain additional information about the Supreme Court's use of amicus curiae briefs, I have spoken with former law clerks from the chambers of many justices. The picture that emerges is as follows.

The justices handle amicus curiae briefs on the merits of cases in different ways. Some of them take all the briefs, including the amicus briefs, and study them before argument. Some justices ask the clerks to pick out the most significant amicus briefs. Other justices ask the clerks to circle passages in amicus briefs of the greatest importance to the analysis of the issues. Still others require the clerks to summarize important points made in amicus briefs either orally or in a bench memorandum. The clerks themselves reported that they examined each amicus curiae brief that was filed.

The clerks agreed that a good amicus brief gets attention. In fact, if the parties prepare poor briefs, the amicus brief can virtually replace the briefs filed by the parties. Even in cases where the parties file effective briefs, amicus briefs nonetheless can influence the Court because they provide additional information.

Briefs That Fail

On the other hand, the clerks agreed that many amicus curiae briefs are a waste of time and money. The Court is flooded each term with short amicus curiae briefs that say little more than "me too"—the amicus agrees with one side in the controversy. Other amicus briefs repeat the analysis of one of the parties with slightly varied wording. Still other amicus groups file documents so one-sided that they fail to meet the countervailing arguments, and thus they fail to assist the Court in comparing and evaluating competing claims. In addition, some amicus briefs insist on discussing issues that are far removed from the issues before the Court, and thus they contribute nothing to the analysis of the case. Finally, some amicus groups plague the Court with filings that are little more than political or economic editorials, and thus they fail to acknowledge and analyze the relevant statutory or constitutional principles, or even the decisions of the Supreme Court itself. Any of these deficiencies will take the amicus brief out of serious consideration.

The law clerks said that to be effective, an amicus brief must bring something new and interesting to the case. This might be better research, an explanation of the connection between the particular case and other pending cases, an improved discussion of industry practices or economic conditions, a more penetrating analysis of the regulatory landscape, or a convincing demonstration of the impact of the case on segments of society apart from the immediate parties. It also can be helpful to discuss the appropriate breadth of the Court's decision in light of such considerations. In considering what will be most useful, remember that the justices labor in a state of relative isolation and have only a small amount of time for research in any particular case. An amicus brief must try to overcome that isolation by providing the information they need to declare legal rules of nationwide applicability.

The law clerks with whom I spoke said that some organizations develop positive reputations and, as a result, the Court relies on their briefs more than those of other organizations. This is particularly true of the solicitor general's office. But it is also true of other well-established organizations, such as the American Bar Association. The Court knows it will get high quality and objective analysis from them. On the other hand, some organizations regularly file briefs of little value.

There is an important lesson here. Each brief filed in the Supreme Court that bears the name of an amicus curiae organization should be of the highest quality, because it will affect the reception that your next several briefs receive.

There is a perennial debate about whether an amicus curiae should retain a lawyer who is well known and respected by the justices and include that lawyer's name on the brief. The law clerks told me that inclusion of such a name, while not affecting anybody's judgment about the issues, is at least a foot in the door. There is curiosity about what such a person has to say. And generating interest is an important facet of effective amicus participation.

Ordinarily, an amicus curiae only makes its views known by a written brief. While the solicitor general often obtains the Court's permission to argue orally as amicus curiae, private amici almost never receive that luxury. That is true even if the parties are willing to cede some portion of their time. This places a premium on effective and lucid written argument.

Fortunately, those undertaking to draft an amicus brief in the Supreme Court have the advantage of the good counsel of Robert L. Stern, who has written two books on this subject. *See* R. Stern, *Appellate Practice in the United States*, ch. 10 (2nd ed. 1989). *See also* R. Stern & E. Gressman, *Supreme Court Practice*, ch. 13 (1978). I would like to offer only a few additional suggestions. Most of these suggestions reflect the practice of the solicitor general, who in all probability is the most frequent and the most successful filer of amicus briefs in the Supreme Court.

1. *Length.* Brevity is an important virtue in an amicus curiae brief. Yet, the goal of brevity should not override the more important goal of helpfulness. The Court expects to receive a developed legal analysis with appropriate research, not just a bare-bones statement of position. The justices are accustomed to receiving amicus briefs that vary from 20 to 30 pages, with a limit of 30 pages. The solicitor general's amicus briefs are typically in the range of 25 to 30 pages. This does not mean, of course, that the brief writer should use all available pages. On rare occasions, an amicus curiae asks for and obtains an extension of the 30-page limit. In my experience, such requests are rarely justified. In most instances, an extended presentation only impairs the effectiveness of an amicus curiae brief.

2. *Motion for leave to file and statement of interest.* If the parties have granted permission to file a brief amicus curiae, that must be recited at the outset of the brief and the letters of consent must be filed with the clerk. If the parties have withheld consent, that should also be recited. The amicus curiae must then precede its brief with a motion for leave to file.

The motion must concisely state the nature of the interest of the amicus organization and explain why its analysis of the issues will help the Court. Ordinarily, an amicus asserts that it has a special perspective on the issues in the case and summarizes the information it can supply. This includes information concerning the effect of the litigation beyond the immediate parties. But remember, whether or not you file a motion, the amicus brief must include a separate statement of interest. This comes before the statement of facts, summary of argument, argument, and conclusion. If the motion has fully described the interest of the amicus curiae, the statement of interest can be short.

3. *Questions presented.* Although the rules do not require an amicus curiae to set forth the questions presented, the amicus may do so. Rephrase the questions if they are awkwardly or obscurely stated by the parties. But, be wary of attempting to smuggle in new and unrelated questions that the Court has not agreed to decide. *See United Parcel Service, Inc. v. Mitchell,* 451 U.S. 56, 60 n.2 (1981); *Bell v. Wolfish,* 441 U.S. 520, 531–532 n.13 (1979); *Knetsch v. United States,* 364 U.S. 361, 370 (1960). This is not to suggest that you must rely on the same rationale as the party you support. You may certainly improve on the analysis and research presented to the Court. But refrain from reformulating the underlying questions for decision.

4. *Statement of facts.* If the party you support has stated the relevant facts well, incorporate that statement by reference, or omit a statement

of facts altogether. In many cases, however, the parties state the facts poorly. Sometimes they do not even set forth all the facts that are essential to resolve the legal issues. If that has happened, include a short statement of the facts. Support your factual propositions by reference to the lower court opinions in the case, which appear in the appendix to the petition for certiorari, and which are cited as "Pet. App. _____." Other materials from the record reproduced in the joint appendix filed in the Supreme Court may be cited as "J.A. _____" (for Joint Appendix).

5. *Style.* As in other Supreme Court briefs, an amicus brief should be simple, unadorned by rhetorical devices, and undefaced by overstatement or exaggeration. Make the sentences and paragraphs relatively short. Draft the brief with active, not passive, verbs. The goal is ready comprehension. If the reader cannot comprehend the brief on the train on the way to work, it is too complicated. Boil it down. Resist any impulse to resort to purple prose. Likewise, resist the frequent use of adjectives, adverbs, or expressions like "obviously," "plainly," and their kin. Never succumb to the temptation to heap scorn on opposing counsel. Keep a moderate tone in an amicus brief.

6. *Organization.* Careful organization of an amicus curiae brief promotes comprehension. It also gives the impression of a logical, orderly analysis. Precede the main sections of the argument with argumentative headings numbered with Roman numerals. Use the argumentative headings to tell the Court what the section is all about in a short sentence. Introduce subordinate points with argumentative headings in smaller print. Set them off with capital letters rather than Roman numerals.

7. *Citations.* The cardinal rule is to rely on Supreme Court decisions. Collect lower court cases and analyze the trend. But do not make an argument hinge on a lower court opinion, no matter how eminent the author. If you find the reasoning of a lower court opinion persuasive, incorporate it and elaborate on it in the argument. Remember that the authority of a lower court decision will not, by itself, impress the justices.

8. *Statutory analysis.* Many cases before the Supreme Court require construction of federal statutes. The Supreme Court does not grant review to resolve issues of state law. It uniformly accepts the construction placed on state law by the highest state court. In a diversity of citizenship case, it almost always relies on the views of the lower federal courts, which have greater familiarity with local rules of decision. There is little or no point, therefore, in attempting to persuade the Supreme Court that the lower court has misconstrued state legislation or common law rules.

The Court has repeatedly held that the starting point for construing a federal statute must be the literal language of the statute itself. E.g., *Ernst & Ernst v. Hochfelder*, 425 U.S. 185, 197 (1976). Next, the amicus brief should present arguments based on the statutory scheme to the extent that structure illuminates the issues. Then it is appropriate to examine the legislative history. Do not omit this step, since—despite the qualms of some justices—the Court itself relies on legislative history in many decisions. Unfortunately, many briefs filed by parties do not analyze the legislative history. An amicus brief can serve a valuable function by filling that gap. Finally, the brief should analyze the issues in terms of statutory policy and general public policy.

9. *Practical consequences.* An amicus brief should not solely discuss statutes and cases. Common-sense reasoning, addressed to real consequences, has great importance to the Court. An amicus brief can show the effect of the decision on an industry and the public at large. In particular, an amicus brief can provide substantial assistance to the Court by demonstrating the effect of an affirmance or reversal on various segments of society other than the immediate parties. The amicus brief that puts technical legal reasoning into a pragmatic context will receive the most attention.

10. *Nonrecord materials.* Avoid the impression that you present policy arguments ex cathedra. Refer the Court to authoritative academic works, including economic studies. For example, in antitrust cases, the solicitor general's office commonly refers to leading economic studies to supplement its legal analysis. No one would think of arguing an antitrust case today with reference to nothing but statutes and judicial opinions. The same is true of other cases that raise economic issues.

Occasionally, a valuable article will not be published at the time of briefing. In that instance, lodge ten copies of the article with the clerk, with a cover letter explaining that the unpublished article is referred to in the amicus curiae brief and is being lodged for the convenience of the Court. Serve copies on the parties.

In presenting such information, the amicus brief is, of course, transcending the record. That is acceptable if handled forthrightly. Robert Stern has said:

> If the presentation by the amicus is to be given weight by the court, the nonrecord facts relied upon should have the ring of truth on their face. They should not relate to the facts of the particular case as between the parties, but should resemble the "legislative facts" having "relevance to legal reasoning and the law-making process" . . . In general, an amicus brief should lose credibility with the court (with or without an opposing presentation) if it goes too far in setting forth nonrecord material as indisputably true. The good sense of the court should enable it to recognize when this occurs. A good lawyer should be aware of this danger of overstatement and avoid it.

R. Stern, *Appellate Practice in the United States* 307 (2d ed. 1989). Such matters frequently present close questions of judgment. For example, if an amicus organization wishes to tell the Court how many suits of a particular kind its members have been exposed to, it is obviously speaking outside the record. The Court can be referred to no authoritative writing to substantiate the proposition. Still, the information may have great relevance to the Court's analysis of a policy issue. Inform the Court that the statistics have been gathered by the amicus organization from internal sources for the Court's information. It may be appropriate to make a summary of the underlying records available to counsel and the Court for examination. Serve them on the parties and lodge them in the clerk's office.

The amicus brief may not, however, attempt to supplement the record in the case before the Court by adding evidence that the parties should have provided concerning their own situations. Nor may amici attempt to assume the role of class members once the case reaches the Supreme Court. As the Court explained in *Sony Corp. v. Universal City Studios*, 464 U.S. 417, 435 n.16 (1984):

> [We] reject respondent's attempt to cast this action as comparable to a class action because of the positions taken by amici with copyright interests and their attempt to treat the statements made by amici as evidence in this case. The stated desires of amici concerning the outcome of this or any litigation are no substitute for a class action, are not evidence in the case, and do not influence our decision; we examine an amicus curiae brief solely for whatever aid it provides in analyzing the legal questions before us.

Stated otherwise, materials outside the record are appropriately referred to in an amicus brief only in analyzing general legal and policy issues. They are not substitutes for record evidence.

11. *Objectivity.* The amicus brief, although forcefully supporting one side of the controversy, will not be effective unless it gives the impression of considering, comprehending, and carefully analyzing the interests and claims on both sides. Most of the cases that reach the Supreme Court are close cases, which frequently result in a vote of five-to-four or six-to-three, or even plurality opinions. An amicus brief that does not weigh competing interests will not help the Court in a close case.

Beyond this, convey the impression that the amicus curiae is indeed a friend of the Court concerned with the development of the law and not just a partisan. Emphasize the correct articulation of legal rules of general applicability, not just the correct resolution of the particular case before the Court. The amicus brief should project a moderate tone. The brief should offer information and expertise about legal and policy issues, not myopic concern over a particular result in the case before the Court.

12. *Coordination.* If possible, coordinate at an early point with the party the amicus wishes to support. This will permit the amicus to receive copies of essential court papers and the record. It will help avoid duplica-

tion in argument. Send a draft of the amicus brief to the party well before the filing date. The party the amicus supports may correct factual misconceptions and other embarrassing errors before the brief is filed.

13. *A unified front.* Several different amici from related industries may plan to file briefs in the Supreme Court in a single case. Consider a single brief in which all amici join. Not only can you pool research and analysis, you can share the cost. You also avoid burdening the justices with repetitious briefs. Repetition only scatters the Court's attention.

14. *Certiorari.* Amicus briefs can influence the Court at the certiorari stage, but only file them in truly "certworthy" cases. Every year, the clerks and justices process more than 7,000 new filings and they may miss an important case. An amicus brief can help a petition for certiorari that might otherwise be overlooked. In filing such a brief, emphasize the considerations that the Supreme Court will focus on in granting certiorari. Those are, mainly, conflicts among the circuits, conflicts with Supreme Court decisions, the recurring nature of the legal issue, and the practical importance of the case to a substantial number of people.

Never file an amicus brief *opposing* certiorari. That merely highlights the importance of the case and thus conveys an impression exactly the opposite of the impression the amicus organization wishes to convey.

15. *Procedural rules.* Amicus curiae briefs are almost never rejected if they comply with the Supreme Court's rules. They are rejected, however, for failure to comply with the time requirements in Supreme Court Rule 37. Amicus briefs at the certiorari stage must be filed when the brief in opposition is due. Amicus briefs on the merits must be filed by the date the brief of the party supported is due.

The cover of the amicus brief must disclose whether the brief supports the petitioner or the respondent. You must list a member of the Supreme Court bar as counsel of record. You may not add names of additional amici or counsel after the brief has been filed. Nor may the brief be corrected after it is filed. If an error or omission is found, the only recourse is to ask the clerk's permission to file corrected copies.

An amicus curiae must bear in mind that it does not have the same procedural rights as parties to the litigation. Thus an amicus curiae may not obtain extensions of time for filing any document. Do not ask the parties to seek an extension to accommodate the schedule of the amicus. An amicus curiae may not file supplemental or reply briefs. An amicus curiae is entitled to file only one brief at the certiorari stage and one brief on the merits.

This catalogue of procedural problems is by no means complete. Carefully review and comply with the relevant rules of the Supreme Court. Also review the treatises. Beyond this, when drafting a brief amicus curiae, have ready at hand a copy of a brief filed recently in the Supreme Court to illustrate the correct format and arrangement of an amicus brief.

16. *Minimizing costs.* If an amicus curiae plans to use outside counsel to prepare a draft brief, it may save a substantial amount of money by furnishing all of the relevant research and arguments it has available. Most amicus organizations have continuing concern with legal issues and maintain libraries of briefs, memoranda, law review articles, economic studies, and the like. The amicus should furnish relevant materials to the lawyer who drafts the brief.

In addition, it is possible to make repeated use of certain portions of amicus briefs. For example, in analyzing the exclusionary rule developed by the courts under the Fourth Amendment, the solicitor general has made repeated use of a cost-benefit analysis that originally appeared several years ago. That analysis is updated and modified as necessary in many Fourth Amendment cases. If previously formulated arguments are used judiciously, costs can be minimized without giving the appearance of a canned presentation.

Money can also be saved when it comes to producing amicus briefs in the booklet format required by the Court. It is now possible to use a printer with computerized typesetting equipment that is compatible with the word-processing equipment in a law office. All editorial revisions can be incorporated in the draft on the word processor. When the brief is in final form, it can be transmitted by telephone to the printer's computer and page proofs obtained within hours. Alternatively, and even more conveniently, word processing systems can produce camera-ready pages that comply with the Court's rules and that have to be sent to the printer only for photocopying and binding. Either method avoids the expense and delay in using traditional hot lead typesetting. With a word processor, you can produce a brief for half what it would cost with manual typesetting.

Supreme Court Advocacy: Random Thoughts in a Day of Time Restrictions

E. Barrett Prettyman, Jr.

I have previously ventured, however timorously, to give advice in law review journals about petitioning the Supreme Court of the United States for writs of certiorari, and about opposing such petitions when they are filed by one's adversaries. But I have curbed until now any tendency to counsel others about oral argument before our highest court. There are two reasons.

First, the subject has been brilliantly covered by a number of others, including John W. Davis and Justice Jackson. An ex-solicitor general has written an article on advocacy before the Supreme Court, and a former member of the solicitor general's staff has written a book that includes several sections on the same subject. R. Stern, E. Gressman, S. Shapiro & K. Geller, in their *Supreme Court Practice* (7th ed. 1993), p. 569 n.1, list 21 judges who have counseled lawyers in print about arguing before appellate courts, including the United States Supreme Court. At first glance, this would not appear to be territory worth retrampling.

Second, oral argument is quite a different matter from petitions and briefs that are within the lawyer's exclusive control. In written submissions, what the lawyer chooses to say, says, and chooses to leave out never faces judicial scrutiny. Advice about written submissions, therefore, goes directly to the substance and content of the lawyer's argument and stands an appreciable chance of proving helpful. Oral argument—particularly before the Supreme Court—is another matter. A lawyer frequently has very little choice over what he or she talks about, no matter how well prepared. The Justices can and frequently do take over the course of the discussion. Questions, the assertion of personalities, and

---

E. Barrett Prettyman, Jr., a member of the Washington, D.C., firm of Hogan & Hartson, was law clerk to three Supreme Court justices and practices regularly before the Supreme Court.

conflicting legal viewpoints often combine to turn an advocate's well-rehearsed arguments into a shambles.

Despite all this, still more advice on Supreme Court advocacy may be in order. Most of the articles referred to above were written at a time when lawyers were granted an hour on each side to argue all or many of the cases heard by the Court. Today, the overriding fact of life in oral argument before the Supreme Court is that in every case (except those few granted special dispensation by the Court), the advocate is strictly limited to 30 minutes, including his answers to questions. This means that much of the prior advice about a coherent development of one's argument—stating the nature and history of the case, the facts and the applicable rules of law—may no longer apply in a practical sense, particularly when the Court is in a questioning mood.

Moreover, advocates before the Court are still making mistakes—often very bad ones. In fact, some arguments are so dreadfully dull that even a justice sitting on his or her first cases would have trouble finding something of interest in them. This being so, some additional words of caution are perhaps in order.

In his famous article "The Argument of an Appeal," 26 *A.B.A. J.* 895 (1940), Davis listed ten rules for the advocate to follow. I would add seven more in light of the exigencies that face the lawyer before today's Court.

1. *If you are the petitioner, prepare two arguments.* The first should be about ten minutes, and the second about 20, in length. The first argument presupposes that you are going to be bombarded with questions from the bench. If you are, you obviously must attempt to weave your main points into the answers to those questions. But the questions may be quite foreign to the main points you are seeking to make. Therefore, you should have notes that remind you of what it is you really want to get across in the brief time allowed.

The ten-minute argument will make you face up to something you should be deciding anyway, regardless of how long you are allowed to argue: What, in your judgment, is the main point that is most likely to win this case for you? Whatever questions are asked, whatever direction the discussion goes, you should make absolutely certain this one overriding point in your favor is driven home to the Court at some time while you are on your feet.

In your brief, there may be any number of reasons for not placing your best point at the outset of your argument. For example, if you are making a constitutional argument, ordinarily it would not appear in fifth place in your brief on the theory that four other arguments are stronger. It would go first because otherwise the Court's reaction would be the same as anyone else's. If a violation of constitutional proportions were really involved, it would not be brought to the Court's attention so late in the game.

But, in a half hour's oral argument, you are not allowed the luxury of placing various points in sensible order. For one thing, if there are many questions you may have time to argue only *one* point before you sit down. For another, it may quickly become apparent that the justices are interested in only one or two points, regardless of the ones you think should be capturing their attention. That is the reason you must "go for the jugular" in oral argument, as Davis and others have so often emphasized.

But what is the jugular? In *Hughes Tool Co. v. Trans World Airlines*, 409 U.S. 363 (1973), the Supreme Court reversed a judgment against petitioners in excess of $145 million on the ground that the challenged transactions were under the CAB's control and surveillance and thus immunized from antitrust attack. That point was number four in our brief for the petitioners and was not the first point made in oral argument. I say this not defensively, but merely to point out that even those presumably familiar with the Court cannot always judge just which argument has the best chance of prevailing. Certainly, it is even a far more difficult task for those not used to the Court and who are approaching it for the first time. In any event, one must make the effort, and thus the ten-minute argument.

The reason for the 20-minute argument, of course, is that you may not be asked many questions, and yet you will want to reserve at least ten minutes for rebuttal. You should know within a few minutes after you have risen whether you will be forced to present your ten-minute argument or whether you will be graced with the chance to give the longer version. Either way, the time flies like a sail in high wind, and your opportunity to convince at least five persons to adopt your position slips all too quickly away.

In addition to the two arguments—one of which you actually plan to deliver—do not forget to map out notes, separately tabbed at the end of your notebook, covering points that you do not intend to bring up yourself but with which the justices may confront you. These should relate not only to your own position but to your opponent's.

I have repeatedly referred to notes. I do not agree with those who give blanket advice against standing up without notes, because on several occasions I have witnessed brilliant arguments when the podium was totally bereft of a scrap of paper. But I simply do not have the mind that allows people such as Charles Alan Wright or Anthony Amsterdam to do this; I need the crutch, if you will, of some written notes that will draw me back to sanity after a sharp exchange with the Court. I suspect that most persons reading this article will need the same crutch, whether they realize it or not.

When you prepare your two arguments, I agree wholeheartedly with those who advocate that you practice before a "moot court" of your partners or associates before the actual presentation to the Court. You should first give the argument you intend to make—not from a written speech, but from key words or phrases that remind you of what you want to say. This should be done without interruption so that you can be judged on the quality and persuasiveness of your basic approach. Next, you should go through the exercise again, this time allowing your compatriots to interrupt you at will with pertinent, tough questions, as well as with impertinent and wide-of-the-mark ones. The point is not only to prepare you but to dislodge you, upset you, throw you off balance, because this is precisely what may happen when you get to your feet in the real world of the courthouse.

I always put my notes on the right-hand pages of my notebook, and even though these notes are themselves cryptic and truncated, I underline in red certain key words or quotes (kept to an absolute minimum). On the left-hand sheet facing each page of notes are the detailed citations to the record and to the key cases that support every statement I am making.

A number of advocates favor the use of tabs in the record to allow them to locate immediately any key sections of interest to the Court. This is satisfactory if the record is relatively small but becomes virtually unmanageable if the record is immense, and it often is in the complex cases before the Supreme Court. I favor an index of key words and phrases that I prepare myself. The index appears entirely on one page, if possible. Next to each word or phrase is the place in the record or the case citation relevant to the subject in question.

Thus, you have two ways of getting at the record or relevant cases very quickly. If you are asked about the very point you are discussing, the necessary references will appear on the left-hand page facing you, and you need not turn to any other source. If you are asked about a subject you are not then discussing, you can turn to the index in your notebook, catch the key word or phrase that brings that subject matter to mind, and again give the record or case citation without having to pick up and thumb through one or more volumes sitting at counsel table.

It goes without saying that if you are going to prepare a ten-minute argument and a 20-minute argument, not only must you restrict the points you wish to make to the one or two that you believe to be of crucial importance—no matter how many were discussed in your brief—but you also must stay totally away from obvious propositions of law, recitations of cases, string citations, virtually all quotations, and the like.

2. *Make a judgment about the intent and usefulness of each question asked.* I have read time and again that the questions from each justice should be considered a golden opportunity because they reveal what is truly bothering him or her, and that the advocate should therefore solemnly address and fully answer each and every one of them. Of course you must answer questions—then and there. But not necessarily with the same degree of depth or precision. My own experience is that questions

from the bench are asked for a number of different reasons, not all of them of equal value or importance.

There is, indeed, the question that reveals what is truly troubling a justice or one that really needs to be answered to help decide the case. Such a question most often seems to come from those Justices who very rarely ask questions. A second type of question is one that just happens to spring to the mind of the justice and may or may not have very much to do with the case. The justice is simply inquisitive or curious; something occurred to him or her and so was asked.

A third type of question comes from the justice who loves the battle of the courtroom, the jousting between lawyer and judge, the testing of wills and knowledge. This type is having fun with you, enjoying himself or herself. And the better you are, the more enjoyment for the judge. This type of questioning can be most misleading in the sense that it very seldom reveals what that justice really feels about the case.

And finally, there is the question asked for the very simple reason that the justice is bored. After all, sitting there day after day, week after week, year after year, listening to argument after argument is boring sometimes. So much of it has been heard before. The same cases are referred to again and again. The justice has been told as if for the first time that due process does not allow the police to beat a confession out of a suspect, or that price fixing is a per se violation of the antitrust laws. One can hardly blame him or her for breaking the monotony occasionally with a question, serious or silly, that simply helps him or her get through the day.

The point is that the advocate must decide on the spot which of these four types of questions is being asked. If the question is of the first variety—one that a justice really needs answered—you may want to devote your entire argument to the answer, weaving central points all through the reply. On the other hand, if the question really is not relevant or is being asked for one of the other reasons cited, the lawyer must have the good sense to answer that question, with great respect, in an abbreviated fashion that will allow getting on to more important matters. I have seen this done both very well and very badly.

One otherwise distinguished practitioner, I recall, used to throw a withering glance in the direction of the justice who had asked what the lawyer deemed to be a frivolous question, pause as if to say, "I cannot believe you seriously intended to say what you just did," and then give an abrupt and cursory answer before returning to the main argument. This is obviously counterproductive since it makes the questioning justice feel like a fool—a very dangerous business indeed when every vote counts.

On the other hand, it is just as bad a mistake to take a question you very well know is totally beside the point and treat it at great length simply because a justice happened to ask it. Since you can never tell a justice that the question is irrelevant, the only guideline I can give is that counsel should answer such a question directly and courteously, but as quickly as possible. I must warn you, if you are a first-timer, that this is easier said than done in the case where the justice is not aware of his or her question's irrelevance and fully intends to cling to your neck like a bulldog until an answer is gotten from you that satisfies. I have seen as much as five precious minutes wasted in this kind of encounter.

3. *Assume that the justices have at least a working knowledge of the case.* There has been a debate for years over which presumption you should make: that the Court knows nothing about the case when you take to the podium, or that each member has religiously reviewed the briefs and relevant parts of the record. My own view is that, for two reasons, your presumption should be somewhere in between. First, several justices have recently said that all members of the Court review the briefs at least to some extent before argument. Second, it is almost never possible to tell the *whole* story in ten, twenty, or even thirty minutes. Therefore, your recitation of the facts and your argument itself should presume that each justice has a general knowledge of what you are about. This allows for greater concentration on the points you hope will win the case.

4. *Be tougher with your own case than anyone else could, should, or would.* Obviously, when first preparing your case, either in written or oral form, you must dream up and explore every possible argument that can be made on behalf of your client. The next step is to eliminate those arguments that will not stand up and to give as much support as possible to those that appear to have merit. In my experience, too many lawyers stop there. I have mentioned above the usefulness of "moot court" sessions with associates, where they presumably attack you with all of the weak points in your case. The able advocate, however, should not be satisfied with that. You should take the hardest look of all at what the case is really about. One method—a kind of extension of Davis's first rule—is to assume that you are a judge who for some reason (presumably legitimate) wants to hold against you. What possible grounds could be found for doing so? What possible facts could be relied upon? What possible theories could be used to destroy your own carefully laid plans for success? I am constantly amazed, during Supreme Court arguments, to hear a lawyer virtually struck dumb by questions from the bench that anyone with any knowledge of the case should have anticipated. It is as if the lawyer has become so imbued with the spirit of the cause that he or she is totally blinded to the legitimate concerns that someone else might have in adopting the position.

In this regard, many writers have advocated making concessions so as to impress the Court with one's fairness and faithfulness to the record. This is all very well when the concession does not in effect concede the outcome of the case, but there are a number of examples in which advocates have given everything away, apparently without realizing it at the time. *See, e.g., Regional Rail Reorganization Act Cases,* 419 U.S. 102, 132–3 (1974); *Williams v. Georgia,* 349 U.S. 375, 381–2 (1955). The trick is to make a concession only to those points which you have carefully considered in advance and to which you have a counterargument. Thus: "It is quite true that there is evidence in the record that could lead a jury to believe that X made those statements to Y, but I would remind the Court that the law in New York requires. . . ."

The most dangerous mistake is to make a concession you have not thought out in advance and the natural repercussions of which you do not fully appreciate because of the tensions of the moment.

5. *Use your rebuttal time.* I know there are differences of opinion about rebuttal, with some judges and lawyers taking the position that you should not even make one except in the unusual case. My own view is that while rebuttals are more often than not mishandled—with lawyers attempting to answer virtually every point raised by their adversaries and cramming far too many facts, figures, and arguments into a few moments' time—the carefully made rebuttal can be extremely helpful in leaving the Court with its focus not on the last words of your adversary but on the striking point that you believe to be most in your favor. The rebuttal should never be prepared in advance. You should make notes during the respondent's (or appellee's) argument, and then, just before he or she sits down, strike for discussion everything except the one or two points which are most helpful to your cause.

In a recent Supreme Court case, a lawyer representing a state felt called upon to defend the state's highest court for its delay in hearing an appeal from a trial judge's prior restraint on the press. He pointed out, quite accurately, that so many lawyers from around the state were scheduled to make arguments and had to make plans well in advance, it was virtually impossible for the state supreme court to expedite a matter involving a prior restraint. But this point, while sensitive to the problems of the state supreme court, was precisely the one opposing counsel had wanted to drive home. It was helpful during rebuttal to draw the Court's attention to the fact that what had in effect been conceded by the state—that it was a practical impossibility to obtain an immediate review of a prior restraint on the press—was equally true in most other states and in some federal courts, so that these orders, even if blatantly unconstitutional, could work their harm for prolonged periods.

6. *Be prepared to discuss subjects never before raised.* Some subjects, even if never before mentioned by any lawyer or court in the case, the advocate must be prepared to discuss. That is because the appellate court may raise them *sua sponte* and, unless satisfied, may dismiss the case. The subjects are: the jurisdiction of the courts below and of the appellate court; the standing of the parties; mootness; the standard of review for *each* point raised on appeal; whether there is a true case or controversy; how

the issues on appeal were raised and preserved below; whether the alleged errors were harmless; and, if the appeal is from a state court, whether there is an adequate state law ground for the judgment.

7. *Be interesting.* By this, I obviously am not referring to theatrics or banging the podium or waving your arms or wandering back and forth, first in and then out of earshot of the microphone. What I am getting at is that too many of the arguments before the Court are simply dull. They are given in a kind of singsong voice, with very little intonation, as if the arguer himself is barely interested in his cause. Even several of the people who have argued a number of times before the Court are guilty of mumbling or failing to change the tone of their voices by more than a few decibels.

Obviously, I cannot advise anyone to have personality. You either have it or you do not. But the fact is that to convince a court of your viewpoint—which is what advocacy is all about—you have to catch the Court's attention in the first place. If the justices are writing, talking, or even thinking of other things, you might just as well have submitted your case on your briefs. So the answer is that, without flourish or bombast, without shouting or embarrassing mannerisms, you must make some effort to speak directly to each justice, to catch his eye on occasion, to change the tone of your voice according to the nature or importance of the words you are speaking, to be interesting and agile even while you retain your own respect and proffer respect to the Court.

Justice Jackson said that "the most persuasive quality in the advocate is professional sincerity." I agree, but would add that it should be a joy for the Court to hear you, not just its duty. Certainly, it was always a joy for the justices to hear Davis and then–Solicitor General Jackson, whether or not they were on the losing end of their causes.

Two examples of differing but effective styles appear in Richard Kluger's book *Simple Justice: The History of Brown v. Board of Education* (Random House, 1975). In the first, John W. Davis argued to the Court on behalf of the state of South Carolina:

> ... Who is going to disturb that situation? If they were to be reassorted or commingled, who knows how that would best be done?
>
> If it is done on the mathematical basis, with 30 children as a maximum ... you would have 27 Negro children and three whites in one schoolroom. Would that make the children any happier? Would they learn any more quickly? Would their lives be more serene?
>
> Children of that age are not the most considerate animals in the world, as we all know. Would the terrible psychological disaster being wrought, according to some of these witnesses, to the colored child be removed if he had three white children sitting somewhere in the same schoolroom?

> Would white children be prevented from getting a distorted idea of racial relations if they sat with 27 Negro children? I have posed that question because it is the very one that cannot be denied.
> You say that is racism. Well, it is not racism. Recognize that for 60 centuries and more, humanity has been discussing questions of race and race tension, not racism. . . . [T]wenty-nine states have miscegenation statutes now in force which they believe are of beneficial protection to both races. Disraeli said, "No man," said he, "will treat with indifference the principle of race. It is the key of history."

The second example was the counterargument of the late Thurgood Marshall, not then a justice:

> . . . I got the feeling on hearing the discussion yesterday that when you put a white child in a school with a whole lot of colored children, the child would fall apart or something. Everybody knows that is not true.
> These same kids in Virginia and South Carolina—and I have seen them do it—they play in the streets together, they play on their farms together, they go down the road together, they separate to go to school, they come out of school and play ball together. They have to be separated in school.
> There is some magic to it. You can have them voting together, you can have them not restricted because of law in the houses they live in. You can have them going to the same state university and the same college, but if they go to elementary and high school, the world will fall apart. . . .

The styles could not have been more different, but both arguments were interesting, logical, imaginative, and arresting.

More Do's and Don'ts

There are a few other points that have been made time and again in speeches and articles about the do's and don'ts of oral argument, particularly as they relate to the Supreme Court of the United States. A few bear repeating for the simple reason that they are so often ignored:

- It is a good idea for your notebook to contain brief abstracts of all cases both for and against you, particularly where a great many cases have been cited on both sides. The fact is that, unless you have one of those miracle memories, cases and their facts and holdings can become confused in your mind in the give-and-take of oral argument. You should prepare these abstracts yourself so that a brief glance at them can remind you of the information you need to know.

- I am opposed to putting a time schedule next to your notes, as proposed by some writers. The purpose is to clue you in as to where you ought to be, timewise, at each section of your argument. The schedule starts at minute zero and is keyed to a watch that you take with you to the podium. The trouble is that in most instances the argument will not proceed according to your notes. You will be flipping back and forth between point three and point one, or perhaps ignoring point one altogether. Any time schedule in your notes will simply confuse you once you have skipped a section or flipped back and forth from point to point.
- I agree with those who have recommended against the use of such confusing appellations as "plaintiff in error." But do not hesitate to use "petitioner," "respondent," "appellant," or "appellee" if those designations come easily to hand. Remember that the Court has heard many arguments before yours, and your simple reference to "Mr. Jones" or to the "State Insurance Company" may not, particularly at the outset of the argument, inform the justices even that these are parties to the case, much less which side they are on.
- I thoroughly agree with what has been said so many times about reading. Do not read your argument. Do not read from other cases. Do not read anything at all unless it is necessary and brief. A particular statutory provision may be so essential that it must be read and perhaps sections of it reread. The main point, however, is that you should not put everyone to sleep by pure recitation of lengthy quotations. A general rule of thumb is that quoting anything over two sentences should make your wary.
- Under no circumstances attack other judges, the litigants, or opposing counsel, even when you feel justified in doing so. As far as other judges are concerned, their best friends or greatest admirers might be on the bench in front of you. As to a personal attack upon the parties or counsel, it is a demeaning practice and one that does not sit well with the Court. Far too often I have heard a lawyer complain that his opposing counsel has distorted the record, misled the Court, manufactured facts not of record, and so forth. If opposing counsel has in fact been in error, the presumption on your part should be that he or she misspoke or that the lapse was inadvertent, even if you think you have reason to believe otherwise. Two officers of the Court do not attack each other. As for litigants, they are not there to speak for themselves, the Supreme Court podium is not the proper place to attack them, and it is simply bad advocacy to be anything but courteous in regard to them, just as you would always be courteous to the Court.

The point of all of this is to convince. And the balance may lie very close indeed, for even cases that are decided unanimously may have caused a great deal of difficulty for each individual justice. As my father related in his own discourse on this same subject (E. Barrett Prettyman, "Some Observations Concerning Appellate Advocacy," 39 *Va. L. Rev.* 285, 297 (1953)), one judge when worried about a particular outcome suggested to his colleagues that they return the appellant's filing fee and tell him to take the case somewhere else.

The trouble with the Supreme Court is that there is nowhere else to go.

PART VI

Special Problems of the Criminal Case

What to Do Till the Plumber Comes

Jill Wine-Banks and Carl S. Nadler

Sometimes there is no way out.

You know all the reasons against it. Criminal law is a genuine specialization. The criminal jungle is not just in the streets. It is in the station houses and courts as well. One false step, and a simple case becomes a nightmare. Statements are made, objections waived, procedural protections vanish—all because a civil lawyer becomes involved in a criminal case. And the prospect of trying to save such a case on appeal by making the claim of very real incompetent representation at trial is not a happy one.

So you know what to tell your client: Call a criminal lawyer, or let me call one for you.

Only sometimes there is no way out.

It is 10 P.M., Friday. Your best client is on the telephone. She is very upset. The police have arrested her son. The only criminal lawyer she knows is out of town until Monday. She wants your help, and you cannot refuse. But you practice civil law. You have never handled a criminal case in your life. You do not even know where the jail is.

What do you do?

First, you find out everything your client knows about the arrest. What is her son's name? When, where, and why was he arrested? Where was he taken? Then arrange to meet your client at the police station as soon as possible.

Next, call the son. If the police deny that he is at the station, ask to speak to the highest ranking officer present. Get the officers' names and identification numbers. *See* Wolfson & Cutrone, "The Attorney-Client Relationship" in IICLE, *Illinois Criminal Practice 1–13* (1980). If the son is

---

Jill Wine-Banks is Director of Business Development for Motorola, Inc. in Arlington Heights, Illinois. Carl S. Nadler is a partner with Jenner & Block in Washington, D.C.

there but the police will not bring him to the telephone, give them your name and number so that he can call you. If the son does not know your name, tell the police that you are his mother's lawyer, she has asked you to represent him, and you plan to do so if he wants it.

The accused has a statutory right in many states to make a reasonable number of phone calls. Applicable statutes are listed in *ALI, A Model Code of Pre-Arraignment Procedure*. Appendix V, at 633 (Proposed Official Draft 1975). The right to call a lawyer, moreover, is constitutionally protected. *See Miranda v. Arizona*, 384 U.S. 436 (1966). And telling the police you are the mother's lawyer and have been asked to represent the son can be important. A confession may be invalid if it is given after the police deny a minor access to a lawyer retained by his mother, even if the minor did not ask to see a lawyer. *People v. Nemke*, 23 Ill.2d 591, 179 N.E.2d 825 (1962).

When you reach the son, tell him that his mother called you and asked you to get involved in the case. Tell him that if he agrees, you will come to the police station immediately to represent him.

He may want to talk to you about the case right then on the telephone. Do not let him. Never discuss the facts of the case with your client on the telephone. The police may be listening on the line or they may overhear your client speaking.

Although you should not let your new client tell you anything on the phone, there is some advice you should give him in this initial call. First, advise him to say nothing. Not a word to the police, government lawyers, cellmates, reporters, or anyone else. Tell him as clearly and as firmly as you can, and in as many ways as you can think of, that he must refuse to say anything until you have arrived. It is not enough to advise him not to make a "statement." He may interpret "statement" to mean only a formal, written confession. *See* A. Amsterdam, B. Segal & M. Miller, *Trial Manual for the Defense of Criminal Cases*, 2–21 (2d ed. 1971). (This is a particularly useful book with a number of sound suggestions.) Tell him not to answer any questions, to refuse interrogation, and not even to talk to the friendly guard or to cellmates.

This advice is critical. If your client makes a statement, the prosecutor may use it as direct evidence of his guilt, or to impeach his testimony at trial. Even if the police have not given him proper *Miranda* warnings, or if they interrogate him after he has said he wants his lawyer present but before you arrive, any statement he gives may be admissible to impeach his testimony at trial. *Harris v. New York*, 401 U.S. 222 (1971). But if you convince him to say nothing, his silence cannot be used against him. *Doyle v. Ohio*, 426 U.S. 610 (1976).

There is a second piece of advice you should give your client in the first phone call: Tell him to refuse to participate in lineups or other identification procedures until you arrive, but not to resist such a procedure physically. Advise him to refuse any physical examination, inspection of his body, or other test, including a lie detector, until you arrive. Again, tell him not to resist physically.

The legal standards police must meet to conduct these tests vary significantly. Procedures that invade the body, such as blood sampling, stomach pumping, or the surgical extraction of evidence, may require the police to: (1) use reasonable methods; (2) have probable cause to believe evidence will be discovered; and (3) obtain a search warrant or have emergency circumstances justifying their failure to obtain one. *See Schmerber v. California*, 384 U.S. 757 (1966) (blood sampling) and *Rochin v. California*, 342 U.S. 165 (1952) (stomach pumping). A good general source book is 2 W. Lafave, *Search & Seizure* (1978).

On the other hand, to conduct nonintrusive procedures such as fingerprinting, the police need only legal custody of the defendant.

The standards required for other tests, such as taking hair samples, swabbing or scraping parts of the body, or obtaining urine samples, vary widely. Some jurisdictions only require police to have lawful custody to perform these tests. Others may require probable cause or a warrant.

Whatever the standard, all of these rights will be waived if your client consents to the test. It is up to you to make him understand that he must refuse to take any tests.

Next, tell your client to remain calm if news reporters try to photograph or interview him. Tell him not to duck, hide his face, or make faces. If the newspapers or television show him that way, it could give prospective jurors a bad impression and make him look bad in his own community.

Finally, before ending this first phone call with your new client, ask him if he has been mistreated in any way, and if he knows of police plans to move him to another location.

Your next call should be to the police officer responsible for your client's case. Find out all of the charges that have been filed or are being considered. Ask the officer if bail has been set or, if not, what he thinks it will be. Find out if the police plan to move your client and, if so, to what location. Tell the officer that you have instructed your client to refuse interrogation, lineups, identification procedures, and physical tests until you have arrived. Be sure you get the officer's name and identification number. Keep careful notes of what you tell the police and what they tell you.

Before you leave for the police station, get copies of the statutes your client is charged with violating and the rules of criminal procedure as well. Take them with you. Also, before leaving for the police station, determine whether the mother can post bail or whether you need a bail bondsman. If you do, look in the Yellow Pages, call the bail bondsman, and make the necessary arrangements before leaving for the station.

When you arrive at the station, identify yourself at the desk. At the station, you can often obtain complaint or arrest papers that will identify the charges against your client. Do not skip this step. These documents may show some defect in the charges or procedures that led to your client's arrest.

The next step is meeting your new client. The first interview with a criminal defendant is a delicate matter. Unless you already know him, a detailed interview is probably inappropriate. Having his mother present may keep him from being entirely candid with you about the facts. Worse, her presence may waive the protection of the attorney-client privilege. So it may be better to wait until you have gained your new client's confidence before asking for detailed responses about the charges. Nevertheless, you must cover some important points at your first meeting with the son:

- Learn the most basic facts of the events. In particular, determine if there are places you must see or objects you must preserve immediately.
- Ask about the circumstances of the arrest. Was a search made? Was anything found? Did the police have a search or arrest warrant? Were others arrested with your client?
- Were there witnesses to the alleged crime? If there were, you must locate them before they move or become impossible to locate.
- What has happened since the arrest? Has your client been abused? Was he advised of his rights? When? Have the police interrogated him or conducted identification procedures or tests? If so, what are the results?
- Finally, get the facts you will need to have your client released on bail. You may wish to put these facts in an affidavit for your client to sign which then can be attached to any necessary pretrial release motions.

You should normally defer any decision about defense strategy pending a full investigation. *See* Sullivan & Warren, *White Collar Crime, National Law Journal,* June 20, 1983, at 22, col. 1. There is at least one exception to this rule. It is when your client admits his guilt, or the government has clear evidence of it, the other participants are represented by separate counsel, and the prosecution needs a participant-witness in their case. Then full investigation may be less important than speed in contacting the prosecutor's office. The first participant to offer the government his cooperation will probably receive the best deal. If you choose to negotiate, keep a few rules in mind:

- Before contacting the prosecutor, do enough investigation so that you can give the prosecutor an accurate summary of your client's expected testimony. If your version of the facts varies from what the prosecutor already knows, the prosecutor may not want to deal.
- Negotiate with the prosecutor, not the police. The police are often unable to make binding agreements. The Federal Rules of Evidence, moreover, provide a privilege for statements made by a

defendant in plea negotiations with the prosecutor. This privilege does not extend to negotiations with the police. FED. R. EVID. 410(4).
- You—not your client—should do the negotiating. Your client will have a natural tendency to minimize his involvement in the alleged criminal activity when talking to a prosecutor. Even after giving you an accurate account of his involvement, he may be less candid with the prosecutor, and a misstatement may be fatal to the negotiations. If the prosecutor insists on interviewing your client, prepare your client for the interview as you would for his trial testimony, to prevent misstatements or understatements.
- Finally, in deciding whether your client should cooperate with the government, you must consider his safety after testifying. You may wish to discuss witness protection or relocation with the prosecutors.

Back to the station house. You told your client to refuse any identification procedures until you arrived. Now you are there, and the police want to proceed with a lineup. What do you do?

The police may not let you attend the lineup. Your client has a Sixth Amendment right to assistance of counsel at a lineup only after adversary criminal proceedings have been instituted. *Moore v. Illinois*, 434 U.S. 220 (1977). If your client is in federal custody, he may not have a right to your presence at a lineup shortly after his arrest. *See Kirby v. Illinois*, 406 U.S. 682 (1972).

Several states, however, require counsel at all pretrial identification procedures. *See generally* F. Miller, R. Dawson, C. Dix & R. Parnas, *Criminal Justice Administration* 524–25 (1982). So check the state law before going to the police station to determine whether your client has a right to your presence at the lineup.

If you are permitted to attend the lineup, your role is generally limited to observing the procedure to ensure that the police conduct it fairly. ALI, *A Model Code of Prearraignment Procedure*, 428–33 (*Proposed Official Draft 1975*). Your client has protection under the due process clause against lineups that are "unnecessarily suggestive and conducive to irreparable mistaken identification. . . ." *Stovall v. Denno*, 388 U.S. 293, 302 (1967). So at the lineup, do everything you can to prevent suggestive procedures and to preserve your client's rights. You should tell the officer in charge about any problems you see. If they are not corrected, make a careful record.

Watch for:

- The date, time, and lighting conditions of the lineup, and the distance of your client from the person who is identifying possible subjects in the lineup.
- How many individuals are in the lineup and their appearance as compared with your client. If possible, get the names, addresses, mug shot numbers, and photos of everyone in the lineup.

- How many witnesses view the lineup and what is said between the witnesses and the police.
- The names and description of the police officers who are present.

If you cannot attend the lineup, tell your client to observe these things.

Having talked with your client and attended whatever tests or procedures are necessary, you are ready to leave. Before you do, repeat every one of the warnings you gave your client in your initial telephone conversation with him. Speak to the investigating officer and ask him to tell you what he knows about the case. He may say nothing, but it is worth asking. After talking to the officer, tell him again that your client is not to be interrogated or tested in your absence. Finally, see if the complaining witness or other eyewitnesses to the alleged crime are still present at the police station. If they are, try to interview them.

One task remains. Your client's main concern is likely to be getting out of jail immediately and staying out pending trial. Getting him out of jail should be a major concern of yours as well. The sooner your client is released, the less chance there is that he will make a damaging statement to the police. The quicker he is out of jail, the more opportunity he will have to help his defense by finding witnesses and other evidence, and by just talking to you without the constraints of the jailhouse.

In almost every jurisdiction, an accused has a right to pretrial release on bail or other conditions in noncapital cases. R. Cipes, *Criminal Defense Techniques* § 1.02[1], at 1–25 (1983). Traditionally, pretrial release in this country has been conditioned on the defendant's deposit of monetary bail with the court. In the last two decades, however, legislatures and courts have placed greater emphasis on alternate conditions of release.

The best example of this change is the Federal Bail Reform Act of 1966, 18 U.S.C. § 3146 (1976). The Bail Reform Act provides that in setting bail, the judicial officer shall consider: (1) the nature and circumstances of the offense charged; (2) the weight of evidence against the accused; and (3) the accused's family ties, employment, financial resources, character, mental condition, length of residence in the community, record of convictions, and record of appearances or failure to appear on previous court proceedings. These factors tell you the information you will need from your client so you can make a persuasive argument for his release without bail.

In noncapital cases, the Bail Reform Act provides that a defendant should ordinarily be released pending trial on his own recognizance or on his execution of an unsecured bond. 18 U.S.C. § 3146(a). The court may impose additional conditions of release only after a finding that the conditions are necessary to secure the defendant's appearance. After making such a finding, however, the court may impose various conditions, ranging from release into someone's custody to a traditional cash bond.

You must determine at which point your jurisdiction sets these conditions of release. In federal proceedings, a defendant's conditions of release are established at his first appearance before a judicial officer. This is usually the arraignment. But state procedures vary. In some states, the court issuing the warrant will endorse on the warrant the amount of bail required. In others, the police are authorized to release a defendant on bail according to an approved schedule keyed to the nature of the charge.

If your client is not released through one of these methods, bail will be set at an "initial appearance" before a judicial officer. Almost all states have statutes requiring that the defendant's initial appearance occur "without unnecessary delay," "immediately," or within a specified time, usually 24 to 48 hours. *See ALI, A Model Code of Pre-Arraignment Procedure*. Appendix I, at 626–27 (*Proposed Official Draft 1975*).

The actual timing of the initial appearance, however, will depend on when a judicial officer is first available to set bail after your client's arrest. Some jurisdictions have night court or bail commissioner systems to ensure that conditions of release can be established promptly even for defendants arrested at night or on the weekend. Defendants in other jurisdictions are not so fortunate. In about half our cities, no weekend court is conducted to set bail. If you live in one of these cities, you may have trouble finding a judicial officer before Monday morning.

But no matter what the procedure, if your client cannot establish acceptable conditions of release at his initial appearance, he may appeal the bail decision or challenge the conditions of release through habeas corpus.

You have now taken your client through the first stages of his case, including his pretrial release. You have significantly helped him in all the proceedings that will follow. Finally you can return home to what is left of your weekend.

On Monday, thinking back over the spectacular job you did on the weekend, you may be tempted to handle the entire case yourself.

Resist.

Remember that effective criminal practice requires experience. Bring in a lawyer with that experience.

Heading Off an Indictment

Andrew J. Levander

"Another opening, another show" would be an appropriate theme song for many criminal defense lawyers. Most defense counsel thrive on trial work; they revel in the art and drama of the courtroom.

No doubt, as far as professional experiences go, there are few things as exhilarating as a crisp cross-examination or a scintillating summation before a packed courtroom in a criminal jury trial. During a break in a criminal trial in New Orleans, an experienced practitioner from Chicago told me: "Cross-examination is my life."

The courtroom also seems to furnish defense lawyers with a kind of bonding experience. In my observation, criminal lawyers uniquely appreciate, if not exult in, the successes of their comrades-at-arms (albeit, perhaps, with varying degrees of wistful jealousy). Certainly, the courtroom is the primary source of our war stories and folklore. In fact, if autobiographies like *Gunning for Justice* and *My Life in Court* are any gauge of the defense bar's collective psyche, trials are the only aspect of criminal defense work worth talking about.

I too enjoy the thrill of trial work. Often, though, defense counsel's first duty and primary task is to avoid trial. Particularly in the area of white collar defense work, the indictment of your client is a disaster, even if he is later acquitted. Politicians, executives, licensed professionals, fiduciaries, and others simply cannot withstand the opprobrium of indictment, much less the scrutiny, tension, and stress that they and their families must endure during a public criminal trial.

Ask Washington lawyer Robert Altman, former automobile magnate John DeLorean, former national security advisor Thomas Reed, or former Arthur Andersen partner Warren Essner whether acquittal at

---

Andrew J. Levander is a partner in Shereff, Friedman, Hoffman & Goodman, L.L.P., in New York City.

trial restored their careers. I do not denigrate the skill of the trial lawyers who represented them; to the contrary, their results speak for themselves. Nor do I suggest that the lawyers in those cases did not ably attempt to head off the indictment at the pass. But the fact remains that a publicized indictment and trial almost inevitably sully a person's reputation and close off career paths, despite a jury's verdict of not guilty.

So the skillful criminal lawyer's repertoire necessarily includes the art of disposing of criminal matters before indictment and trial. This less publicized role of defense counsel involves a variety of strategies and techniques quite different from courtroom skills. If you are going to represent defendants in criminal cases, you should be familiar with the techniques that have been used to convince prosecutors not to indict.

First, some words of caution: Sometimes the prosecutor will indict regardless of the defense lawyer's skills. And each case is unique, requiring careful evaluation of all the facts and circumstances and difficult judgment calls that are subject to second-guessing. Even the same case may require different approaches at different times.

Equally important, different lawyers would handle the same case in very different ways, and each approach may well be sound. During my days as a federal prosecutor, I was repeatedly impressed by the effectiveness of strikingly dissimilar approaches taken by different defense counsel in the same white collar case. In short, the strategies discussed in this article are neither exhaustive nor fail-safe.

The sooner a lawyer gets started, the better. Unfortunately, the timing is usually beyond his control. Whenever you are retained, though, the first step should be an in-depth investigation of your client's situation.

Ordinarily, the investigation begins with *thorough debriefings* of the client. Although some defense counsel believe that, at least in some cases, it is better not to know the full story from the client, the lawyer is usually best prepared to serve his client if he knows all the facts, good and bad.

Despite lawyers' best efforts to explain that to their clients, and despite the attorney-client privilege, clients are often reluctant to confide in their lawyers. Perhaps because of embarrassment, fear, or mistrust, most clients tend initially to sugarcoat or even dissemble the events under investigation. A client may also labor under the misapprehension that the lawyer will not work as hard if he thinks his client is less than angelic.

Through hard work and patience, these barriers can usually be overcome. It is necessary to remind a client often about the attorney-client privilege and to resort to homilies such as, "A doctor cannot treat a patient properly if the patient won't tell him the symptoms." Or, as a partner of mine tells his clients, "You can tell me now, when I can help you, or you will tell me later, when I may not be able to help you." With enough encouragement, most clients will tell you most of the facts. Almost always this process takes time and persistence.

At the same time, counsel should consider what other sources of information are available. If a case involves documents, the lawyer should review them carefully. That is necessary for trial anyway, and the earlier you digest the "hard" evidence, the better informed your early and often critical decisions will be. You may also need to hire an expert, like an accountant, to help evaluate the documents. To preserve the privilege, it is essential that the lawyer and not the client retain the expert. *See United States v. Kovel,* 296 F.2d 918, 922 (2d Cir. 1961).

In some cases, you may also be able to interview other witnesses. But be careful not to disclose the fact of the government's investigation to witnesses who are not already aware of it. As Whitewater and the municipal corruption investigations in New York have vividly demonstrated, the publicity surrounding an investigation can be as ruinous to your client's reputation (and health) as an indictment or conviction. If the fact of the investigation is not already public, you may decide to skip certain interviews altogether, rather than risk potentially disastrous leaks to the press. In addition, since defense counsel's interviews are discoverable, consider whether an interview would risk tipping your hand for the prosecutor.

If you decide to conduct interviews—for example, with your client's key employees or associates who are already aware of the investigation, or with potential alibi or other defense witnesses—bring someone with you, such as a paralegal or a private investigator. In some cases, you may decide not to participate at all, and instead rely entirely on a trusted investigator.

You may wish to avoid a face-to-face interview if the defense of the case rests on demonstrating that the witness is lying or that he despises your client. In still other cases, only the lawyer will be able to interview the witness, such as the chief executive officer of a major company.

Generally, it is better to conduct interviews without your client. Occasionally, though, a witness, such as a spouse, may refuse to talk to you in the absence of your client. If the witness is inclined to help your client, say that, to best serve your client's interests, you need to understand exactly what happened. It is also good practice, if the witness is a corporate officer or employee, to tell him that you represent your particular client and not the witness.

Other lawyers in the same case may also be a source of information. Defense counsels' willingness to share facts depends on *their* professional relationship as well as their clients' relationship. Generally, the lawyers should communicate, rather than allowing their clients to talk about the case.

Discussions among counsel are ordinarily covered by the joint-defense and work-product privileges, while conversations among clients are not privileged. To avoid any incriminating statements or claims of obstruction, instruct the client not to discuss the investigation with anyone.

Even counsel for witnesses adverse to your client may be willing to talk to you. Sure, a lawyer for a hostile witness is not going to give you devastating impeachment material. But most witnesses are reluctant to testify, and the other lawyer may decide to give you a summary of the witness's testimony to encourage your client to plead guilty. Also, even if a witness's testimony would hurt your client, the witness may still be sympathetic enough to let you interview him or to provide information through his counsel.

The prosecutor, too, may provide important information. Most prosecutors will at least disclose the general nature of the investigation and tell you whether your client is a subject or a target. If the government lawyers are confident of their case, they may tell you much more than that before they indict.

Also, when the government wants a quick guilty plea or your client's cooperation, you can often get the prosecutor to talk. When I was on the other side of the fence, I regularly invited defense counsel to review documentary evidence or to listen to tape recordings early in the investigation. That kind of disclosure depends largely on the chemistry between the lawyers. So, while keeping in mind that the prosecutor is not your client's friend, it may be important to tone down the adversarial nature of your initial dealings with him.

As you seek information from the government, you begin to form impressions of the prosecutor and of where the investigation is likely to go. Is the government intent on making a case, and, if so, against whom? Is your client a major target or a peripheral figure? At what stage is the investigation? Will the prosecutor listen to your presentation fairly and with an open mind? Especially if you have not dealt with the particular government lawyer handling the case, it is certainly worth getting your colleagues' views of the person who will largely determine your client's fate.

Armed with as much information as possible about the prosecutor, the investigation, and the client, you must devise the best strategy for avoiding indictment.

If your client is an important target and the violations are serious and obvious, there may be few alternatives. In some cases, there may be no choice but to wait out the investigation in the hope that the prosecutor will be unable to make a case or that, with a change in government personnel or priorities, the case will slip between the cracks. If, as usual, this tactic fails and the client is about to be indicted, the only options are plea bargaining, limited motion practice, or trial.

In most cases, though, defense counsel should not simply await the indictment. Rather, develop a plan of attack to beat the charges before they are brought. Although this is an uphill battle, it is usually worth fighting.

First consider whether your client is a candidate for immunity. If he played only a minor role in the events under investigation, the government will probably grant immunity. Even if the client's role was significant, sympathetic circumstances such as old age or poor health may commend the exercise of prosecutorial discretion.

Perhaps even more important to the prosecutor is the impact of your client's potential testimony on the investigation. "Who can your guy give up?" or "Can your guy testify against Mr. X?" are questions frequently heard in the prosecutor's office.

More than once, a prosecutor has granted immunity to a former lover or a longtime subordinate of the main target despite that person's involvement in serious offenses over a long period of time. According to published reports, the key witness against former Undersecretary of Defense and LTV Chairman Paul Thayer was his girlfriend, Sandra Ryno. Ryno was granted immunity despite her participation in an insider trading scheme, her apparent participation in the initial stages of a cover-up before the SEC, and her personal profits from the fraud of more than $150,000. Thayer was sentenced to four years in prison.

Timing is critical in the immunity game. It is sound courthouse wisdom that the first one in gets the best deal.

The municipal corruption scandal some years ago in New York City vividly illustrates this point. Ordinarily, a federal prosecutor relishes the opportunity to go after a corrupt lawyer. In the early stages of the New York City investigation, though, the U.S. attorney's office granted immunity to a lawyer who had paid cash to one or more city officials, but who was in a position to testify against a powerful politician.

When I was a prosecutor, a lawyer who represented a middle-level conspirator in a securities fraud case came to my office to volunteer a "proffer"—a hypothetical recitation of his client's testimony. After he made a detailed proffer (without names) regarding the fraud, I consulted all relevant agencies to confirm that the government was unaware of the scheme.

Satisfied that serious crimes might otherwise go unpunished, I reluctantly recommended immunity in exchange for cooperation and complete restitution. The very day after the immunity agreement was signed, the victims of the scheme came to my office to report the crime. To this day, the defense counsel in that case reminds me of his good timing whenever we see each other.

Although early requests for immunity are usually more successful, sometimes a prosecutor will be compelled to give immunity late in an investigation because of lack of evidence or other problems with the case. If, after exhausting all other leads, a prosecutor needs a critical piece of proof or feels uncomfortable with a largely circumstantial case, he may immunize someone he would otherwise indict. Occasionally, even a murderer or a drug dealer is the beneficiary of this circumstance. Although luck may play a part in who gets immunity, a defense lawyer serves his client well by keeping track of the investigation as it unfolds, so that he can go for immunity, if circumstances warrant it, at the most propitious moment.

Of course, before attempting to arrange immunity, a lawyer must consult with his client. Sometimes a client will not want to cooperate—the price tag may be unacceptable—even if immunity is available. Fear, business realities, or loyalties to family or friends may outweigh immediate self-interest.

The lawyer must carefully explain all the consequences of and alternatives to the decision to go for immunity. In particular, it is the defense lawyer's obligation to explore with his client any possibility of violent retaliation; the practical impact on the client's life, including loss of livelihood; and the likelihood that the client will be prosecuted, convicted, and sent to jail if he does not cooperate. Ultimately, of course, it is the client's decision whether to seek immunity and to cooperate if immunity is offered.

It is especially important that the client understand that immunity ordinarily results in the disclosure of all criminal problems, not just the facts of the particular violations under investigation. So, if the client has other skeletons in the closet, cooperation may be out of the question, even though his role in the events being investigated was minor.

The Importance of Candor

Emphasize that in talking with the prosecutor your client must be completely candid and accurate, and that any attempts to cover up can only lead to disaster. Partial cooperation will result in damaging admissions and preclude an effective defense. Prosecutors are understandably hard on "cooperators" who fail to tell the whole truth, and judges are notoriously unsympathetic to defendants who blow their immunity agreement by lying to the prosecutor or the grand jury.

If, after full consultation, the client elects to seek immunity, do everything you can to get it for him. Since timing may be critical, a prompt visit to the prosecutor's office is in order.

In almost all cases, the prosecutor will want at least an oral proffer spelling out the testimony your client will give. You should agree to make a proffer only after the prosecutor agrees to treat it as a hypothetical recitation that he will not use directly against your client if you do not get together on an immunity agreement. In my experience, all prosecutors accept such limited-use proffers. But be sure to make your agreement explicit.

Generally, the fewer details that the proffer divulges, the better. If immunity is not granted, too many details could provide the prosecutor with leads that he can follow up without violating the letter of your limited-use agreement. The resulting turn in the investigation could lead the government right back to your client.

Also, a witness's recollection of events often varies upon retelling, and you do not want to be in the position of having to explain discrepancies between your proffer and your client's actual statements to the prosecutor. For similar reasons, written proffers are to be avoided.

But it is equally dangerous to say too little. If the grant of immunity is based on a proffer that omits material facts of your client's involvement in the events under investigation or of his other crimes, the immunity agreement may be voided. Or the prosecutor may insist on a guilty plea to the crimes that were not disclosed. In either event, you will lose your credibility with both the prosecutor's office and your client, and your client will lose much more than credibility.

In some cases, the prosecutor will request a proffer that comes right from the client's mouth. That poses tremendous risks.

With your client present to tell his own story and to answer the prosecutor's questions, the prosecutor learns about your defense case and, if you do not get together on an immunity agreement, he can use what he learns to shape the investigation and to avoid surprises at trial. Your client will also undoubtedly make damaging admissions in the course of the proffer.

By getting the prosecutor to agree in writing to the limited use of the proffer, defense counsel can control some of these risks. Nevertheless, a proffer by the client inevitably locks in his story and divulges leads, wrinkles, and avenues for cross-examination that the prosecutor can often use to demolish the defense case and, with it, your client's future if you do not get the immunity you wanted.

So, if the prosecutor insists that the proffer come directly from your client, carefully weigh the risks against the likelihood of obtaining immunity. Particularly if you suspect that the prosecutor is not acting in good faith or is unlikely to be sympathetic to your client, you should usually decline to bring your client in to make his own proffer. Some defense lawyers flatly refuse to submit their clients for in-person proffers under any circumstance, and most prosecutors will not insist on a direct proffer.

If the prosecutor is willing to grant immunity, the next question is what form of immunity best serves your client's interests. Federal and most state prosecutors can provide either transactional or testimonial immunity.

Transactional immunity offers complete protection against any criminal liability relating to the specified transactions. But transactional immunity covers only the events described in the immunity agreement.

Because transactional immunity is generally governed by contract, it binds only the government authority that enters into the agreement. So a transactional immunity agreement with one federal prosecutor does not preclude the local prosecutor or even a federal prosecutor in another district from indicting your client.

Although the prosecutor granting immunity can usually convince the prosecutor in the other jurisdiction to honor the immunity agreement, it is imprudent to rely on their good relations. Turf battles among law enforcement authorities are neither rare nor gentlemanly. To protect your client, arrange for immunity agreements with each authority investigating the case.

Testimonial or statutory immunity, which in the federal system requires both a court order and approval from the Department of Justice, bars any direct or indirect use of the immunized testimony. *See* 18 U.S.C. §§ 6001 *et seq.* Technically, though, a prosecutor remains free to indict so long as he can demonstrate that his proof is wholly independent of the immunized testimony. *See Kastigar v. United States*, 406 U.S. 441 (1972). Because "taint" or *Kastigar* hearings are so burdensome and because they require pretrial disclosure of the government's entire case, as a practical matter testimonial immunity ordinarily precludes prosecution of your client.

Particularly when only one prosecutor's office is investigating or likely to investigate a matter, transactional immunity is generally your best bet. Some clients nonetheless prefer testimonial immunity because they can tell their associates that they did not voluntarily cooperate but did do so only under compulsion of court order. Also, unlike transactional immunity, testimonial immunity is binding on all federal, state, and local prosecutors. But testimonial immunity cannot bind foreign prosecutors. *See Zicarelli v. New Jersey*, 406 U.S. 472 (1972).

Testimonial immunity may also have one other advantage. Experienced defense lawyers know that, despite their repeated admonitions to tell the truth and their client's insistence that they *are* telling the truth, some clients still lie. In the case of transactional immunity, such falsehoods breach the agreement and subject the client to prosecution for all offenses, including the underlying crimes plus perjury.

In contrast, a mendacious witness who testifies pursuant to a grant of testimonial immunity probably cannot be charged with the underlying crimes, although he can be prosecuted for perjury, false statements to a grand jury, and obstruction of justice. This distinction may be small comfort, though, for the client who opts for testimonial immunity and gets caught lying. Under federal law, perjury is punishable by up to five years in jail and a $10,000 fine.

Suppose immunity is not a viable alternative. Say your client is the prime target of the investigation. Or your client is a highly visible figure, a politician, a lawyer, or chairman of the board. What then?

First, you can resort to familiar damage-control measures: Prepare potential witnesses (keeping in mind that, if they are not your clients, your preparation sessions will be discoverable) or advise them to retain counsel and to have their counsel prepare them; make sure that all witnesses are advised by counsel of their rights, including the right to remain silent; review all documents before your client produces them and take vigorous good-faith positions on the attorney-client and other applicable privileges; and take steps to limit the scope of any subpoenas served on your client.

A target of an investigation may also go to court to protect his rights. Lawyers have had mixed success recently in challenging grand jury subpoenas *duces tecum* on Fifth Amendment grounds. In rarer circumstances, Fourth Amendment claims of unlawful searches and seizures may be litigated prior to indictment. *See* Fed. R. Crim. P. 41.

Other issues that may be litigated at the preindictment stage involve the attorney-client and spousal privileges, grand jury abuses, and violations of the rules governing parallel criminal and civil investigations. When the investigation concerns foreign banking records or other documents maintained abroad, potential defendants often succeed in invoking bank secrecy and foreign blocking statutes in litigation both here and in foreign countries to bar, limit, or delay production of incriminating records.

If successful, preindictment litigation may result in suppression of evidence or may even derail an investigation. And, whether or not it is successful, litigation at this stage may compel the government to make helpful disclosures about its activities. The government may also decide to abandon certain aspects of the investigation because of the delay and expense involved in litigating complicated issues. Especially if the statute of limitations is about to expire, the prosecution will be unable to await an appellate ruling on a complicated privilege or treaty question.

Balance the Psychological Impact

Against the possibility of winning usually limited victories through preindictment litigation, balance the psychological impact it is likely to have on the prosecutor. When faced with a series of witnesses invoking the Fifth Amendment and fighting document production, he will inevitably conclude that somebody has something to hide. If he already appears to be dead set on putting your client in the slammer, you have little to lose by throwing up every barrier you can get your hands on. But if you still hope to convince the prosecutor that there has been no crime or that whatever technical violation there has been does not warrant criminal sanctions, you cannot simultaneously engage the government in guerilla warfare.

Before you decide which way to play it, consider the nonconfrontational alternatives.

At some point in the investigation, many defense lawyers make a pitch to get the prosecutor not to indict. Although anyone who regularly throws strikes in this league is an all-star, the game is very often worth a try. If nothing else, in the course of the dialogue, the prosecutor may reveal the government's theories or its evidence. Also, even if your presentation does not convince the prosecutor to abandon the investigation, you may lay the groundwork for a favorable plea bargain. And, in some cases, prosecutors do change their minds.

The presentation should be orderly and low-key. There is no advantage to yelling at the person in charge of the investigation, and a rambling presentation is as ineffective as a rambling opening or summation. Even if histrionics are your style, save them for the courtroom.

Think through in advance what your pitch should be. What issues are really worth discussing with the prosecutor? What are the investigators' concerns? Why shouldn't the government go forward with its case? Keep in mind that, in the prosecutor's office, the target is presumed guilty until proven innocent, no matter what the judge charges a jury.

It is often effective to let the prosecutor know right off that you have considered his position, that you realize that the government has invested considerable time and effort in the investigation, but that you are confident he will fairly consider what you have to say. Most prosecutors are responsible people with a sense of fair play and some degree of rationality. Many are inexperienced. Appeal to the prosecutor's better instincts, but avoid talking down to him, even if you are 20 years his senior. And be careful not to overstate or overplay your hand. Any inaccuracies will undermine your credibility with an already skeptical audience.

What you say will, of course, vary from case to case. The most effective presentations generally focus on two or three major points.

Reasons to sympathize with the client, including poor health and old age, are favorite themes—so much so that, during my years as a prosecutor, I began to wonder why every potential defendant has a dying relative and is either old and decrepit or a young, naive victim of some older Svengali. Aside from reacting to such arguments with a certain degree of cynicism, prosecutors often respond that those considerations are appropriate for the sentencing judge. Nonetheless, personal circumstances that favor your client should not be ignored. Remarkably, most prosecutors are human.

You may also be able to argue that criminal sanctions are unnecessary. Defense counsel often contend that the client has suffered enough—through restitution, loss of license or business, other professional sanctions, public opprobrium, and the like—and will not repeat the mistake. It is sometimes appropriate to suggest that criminal sanctions would be disproportionate to the alleged misconduct.

In a close case, it may be possible to convince a prosecutor that civil sanctions, such as an SEC injunction, are sufficient, and that a criminal prosecution would destroy the career of a generally upstanding citizen. Although these points are worth making, they rarely save the day.

Another common tactic is to emphasize the weaknesses in the government's case. Nobody likes to lose. More than that, with the government's scarce resources, a responsible prosecutor may agree to drop a marginal case, particularly if your client is not a bad guy or a recidivist. But to be persuasive, you must be able to point to major flaws in the government's case. Mere aspersions against the informant, for example, are unlikely to have any impact on the prosecutor unless the case is a one-on-one swearing contest and there is independent evidence to corroborate your client's version.

Also, the prosecutor may be sensitive to claims of serious government misconduct. Depending on the nature of the problem, he may choose to drop the case rather than to expose the government's dirty deeds.

After the arrest in New York of an assistant U.S. attorney on charges of stealing drugs and money from the prosecutor's safe, the government dismissed cases that the same assistant U.S. attorney had been handling. Likewise, prosecutors occasionally abandon cases in which law enforcement agents have committed egregious Fourth or Fifth Amendment violations.

Sometimes, defense counsel try to convince the prosecutor that he lacks jurisdiction or that the incident in question is really "civil" in nature and not a crime. These arguments, bordering on the metaphysical, are most likely to be effective in technical cases involving tax, securities, or similar matters, or in any case where intent is a critical issue. Sometimes it is possible to argue that what is at issue is a controversial technique, such as a tax "straddle," the illegality of which has not been clearly established, and that the target acted on the advice of counsel or other experts.

Besides just making oral presentations, experienced defense counsel often give the prosecutor a brief presenting the applicable law and marshalling the relevant facts. Of course, a written submission has its risks. The prosecutor may go after additional proof, revise his instructions to the grand jury, or restructure the charges to get around the problems that the defendant's lawyer has raised. Still, a good brief submitted to a fair-minded prosecutor sometimes heads off the indictment. So, at least when the indictment would be devastating to the client and the prosecutor has an open mind, submitting a brief is often a good idea.

Sometimes defense lawyers go one step further: They give the prosecutor a preview of their client's case. In essence, the defense tries its case in the prosecutor's office to avoid an indictment and the publicity that comes with it.

The risks of this tactic are great. If the prosecutor is not persuaded to drop the case, the government can redirect or extend its investigation, revise the charges, pursue new leads, and prepare a response to the defense, including a rebuttal case. In short, the defense gives up the element of surprise.

Since the "testimony" of the target is ordinarily the centerpiece of this kind of presentation, this approach also locks in the defense, supplies the prosecutor with damaging admissions, and gives him a unique opportunity to prepare the most devastating cross-examination possible. No wonder many defense counsel *never* take this approach. Certainly in most cases, it is far too risky.

There are special situations, though, in which defense counsel should consider rolling the dice and bringing the client in to talk to the prosecutor. Too often, prosecutors forget that their target is a human being with feelings, hardships, and a reasonable explanation for his behavior. An effective face-to-face interview can restore the human element, which, in some cases, might tip the balance in your client's favor.

Recently, a prosecutor told me that she had decided to drop an investigation because the target turned out to be so much more impressive and credible than her informant. Although hardly commonplace, reactions like these are not unique.

In the difficult calculation of whether to expose the defense case before the indictment, a critical factor is the prosecutor. Is he fair minded? Will he listen, or is an indictment inevitable?

Have a chat with the prosecutor about the possibility of laying your cards on the table. Although few people admit to having closed minds, the nuances you pick up and the impressions you form at a face-to-face meeting are invaluable guides. A prosecutor's general reputation among defense lawyers is another useful barometer. Let's face it: There are some law enforcement officials who probably cannot be trusted to come to a reasoned conclusion under any circumstance. In a particularly important case, you might also consider making a presentation to a panel of prosecutors.

An equally important factor is your best objective evaluation of your client and his story. Does the defense seem probable? Is there any corroboration for your client's version of what happened? Will your client be a credible witness and make a good impression? Unfortunately some people appear to be lying even when they are telling the truth.

Give your presentation a dry run in front of a colleague who is not closely familiar with the case. If your colleague does not believe the defendant, neither will a cynical, mistrusting prosecutor.

Some defense lawyers give their clients a lie detector test before taking them to the prosecutor's office. Although the results of these tests are usually inadmissible as evidence in court, a test administered by a reputable operator is useful for several reasons.

First, a favorable polygraph report increases the likelihood that your client will be credible and that you will have confidence in his presentation. Second, a lie detector examination is a useful form of corroboration in the prosecutor's office, even if it is not admissible in court, and a positive result may be decisive in a close case, particularly if it comes down to your client's word against that of an informant or other witness. Third, when the client has passed a reliable private examination, his lawyer should be eager to allow a government operator to conduct a second polygraph examination—something that prosecutors often request in any event. And recent decisions have increased the likelihood that a polygraph examination may be admissible in a criminal trial.

Lie detector or no lie detector, in deciding whether to submit your client for an interview with the prosecutor, the fundamental question is whether the presentation is likely to persuade him to stop the investigation. If the government's evidence is unambiguous, not even Abraham Lincoln could talk his way out of an indictment. It makes sense to try your defense in the prosecutor's office only if the case is a close one. Also, the presentation is most likely to be effective if the case turns on your client's knowledge, intent, or some other credibility issue.

Say your client, a licensed stockbroker, is about to be indicted on insider trading charges because of his suspicious pattern of securities transactions and his close relationship with someone who had access to confidential information. If your client can credibly deny receiving confidential information and also offer another believable explanation for his investment pattern—particularly one that someone else can corroborate—the risk of bringing him in to talk to the prosecutor may well be worth taking.

Once you decide to make a presentation, you need to consider when and how to do it.

It is usually inadvisable to make a full-scale presentation to the prosecutor early in the investigation. He will ordinarily not be in a position to make a final judgment, and he will be able to steer his investigation around any obstacles you present. Later in the investigation, you can get a better read on the prosecutor's strengths, attitude, and goals, and you can better judge whether a presentation might be effective.

By delaying the presentation, you run the risk that the prosecutor will so harden his position over the course of a lengthy investigation that no presentation, however brilliant, will shake his resolve to indict. In my view, though, it is unlikely that a prosecutor would reach a different conclusion following a thorough investigation after a presentation. And you can always approach the prosecutor early on to plant seeds of doubt and to let him know that, later in the investigation, you would be willing to consider bringing your client in to discuss the case.

As usual, though, there are no absolute rules. If you believe that an investigation is really off the mark and the allegations are frivolous, you may wish to put your ace on the table early in the game. But you will rarely have that good a hand.

Before the actual presentation, establish the ground rules, put them in writing, and arrange for both lawyers and the client to sign. The prosecutor ordinarily agrees not to use anything the client says as part of his direct case. Defense counsel in turn should be prepared to let the prosecutor use the presentation for leads. The prosecutor should also be free to take notes at the meeting, but not to tape-record it, mainly because recording equipment increases the tension and formality of an already stressful event.

The difficult question is whether to permit the prosecutor to use the client's statements on cross-examination or in the government's rebuttal case if the client is indicted and he testifies at trial. Although this issue is worth negotiating, I would not let it become a sticking point.

Presumably, you have decided to try your case before the prosecutor only after satisfying yourself that your client is telling the truth and is not likely to change his testimony. The statements your client makes to the prosecutor will only become significant at trial if he changes his story. And, by refusing to allow his statements to be used for cross-examination, you may subliminally communicate a lack of confidence in your client's story.

In preparing the presentation, take the same pains that you would in preparing a client to testify at trial. Several preparation sessions may be required.

Aside from thoroughly going over the facts and any documents, brief your client on the prosecutor's concerns and attitude and take him through all the tough questions that the prosecutor might ask. Make the client understand that he must be completely accurate and forthright in his answers and that, if he does not comprehend what he is being asked, he should get the investigators to repeat or explain their questions. Although repeated conferences between lawyer and client during the presentation will make a bad impression, I always instruct my client to consult with me privately if he feels the need.

Get Some Feedback

In the prosecutor's office, I ask for a break whenever my client seems tired or starts to flounder. Try to get some feedback from the investigators early in the meeting. If you sense that the prosecutor and the law enforcement agents utterly disbelieve your client, cut your losses and call it a day. If the conversation has become a one-way street, do not let them exploit the opportunity for discovery they otherwise would not get.

You may want to present other evidence to the prosecutor as well. I would be inclined to bring in any powerful corroborating or exculpatory proof you have. Do not waste the prosecutor's time with character witnesses or other incidental matters. But consider whether to save one or two little surprises for the courtroom in case the presentation fails.

Occasionally, the prosecutor will encourage the target to testify before the grand jury. More often, your client will want to tell the grand jury everything in order to clear his name now.

Resist these temptations. A defendant's testimony before the grand jury is given under oath, subject to the penalties of perjury, and can be used in the government's direct case. Besides, in the federal system, counsel is not allowed into the grand jury room. Even in those states where counsel may be present during a client's testimony, the prosecutor almost always controls the proceedings. So, if the presentation in the prosecutor's office has not convinced him to drop the investigation, an appearance before the grand jury is usually a suicide mission.

If the prosecutor decides to indict despite your presentation, consider a preindictment appeal. In most jurisdictions, counsel can arrange to meet with at least a supervisory level prosecutor, if not with the chief prosecutor. Beyond that, in certain federal cases, including tax and RICO prosecutions, you can appeal to the Department of Justice. Usually, the national office is more conservative about bringing prosecutions than are the local United States lawyers. To maintain good relations with the prosecutor handling the case, politely ask him to arrange the appeal, rather than just going above his head.

Experienced defense lawyers recognize that a preindictment appeal is rarely productive, and usually not worth pursuing. If you appeal every time a prosecutor decides to indict your client, you will quickly lose all credibility with the senior authorities. But, by picking your shots, your few most deserving cases will get more serious attention. Investigations involving serious legal problems, circumstantial proof, or government misconduct are usually the best candidates for review. The chief prosecutor is simply too busy to review credibility determinations or other run-of-the-mill prosecutorial decisions of the staff.

And, of course, when all these strategies fail, strap your six-guns back on and get ready for the showdown at your old favorite corral—the courtroom.

The Grand Jury: An Overview

James M. Kramon

It is by now commonplace to hear it said that grand juries no longer serve their historic function of protecting citizens against arbitrary or even malicious prosecutions. Indeed, while it is clear from the history of grand juries, both in England and in the United States, that the right to be tried for serious offenses only after presentment of a bill of indictment was conceived of as a basic form of protection for the accused, somewhere between Blackstone and Holmes the conception of the grand jury changed radically.

Today no one casually familiar with the work of grand juries would seriously defend their existence on protective grounds. The grand jury is, as every lawyer with any prosecutorial experience knows, an instrument of the prosecution, and because it emerged in the Anglo-American criminal law system clothed in a different garb, it is a particularly insidious instrument.

So that my position will be clear, I state at the outset that I am offended by the preservation of the fiction of the protective grand jury and by the unbridled power the grand jury system confers upon prosecutors, some of whom have sound judgment and some of whom do not. For my own part, I would abolish grand juries.

A salient aspect of grand jury proceedings is that they are almost totally ex parte and unreviewed. Counsel for witnesses, who may be potential unindicted co-conspirators or even defendants, are not permitted to enter the grand jury room. In fact, under federal and many state procedural rules, the presence of anyone other than the grand jurors, the

---

James M. Kramon is a member of the Baltimore firm of Kramon and Graham.

reporter, if any, the prosecutor or prosecutors and the witness, renders the hearing unlawful.

Since the grand jury does not generally have its business reviewed, it is not in any meaningful way bound by limitations on the subject matter of its inquiry. The scope of admissible evidence is broad—to say the least—and, even in the unusual case where the evidence presented comes up for review, hearsay, multiple hearsay, not-the-best evidence, tainted evidence, and other forms of evidence the admission of which would clearly be precluded in any other judicial proceeding suffices to satisfy the government's burden.

The great bulk of indictments returned are based solely upon hearsay since the only witness who presents himself is the government agent or police officer who has investigated the offense. Since that person is clearly present to persuade the grand jury to indict, most presentations do not include facts that would, in the mind of someone not disposed to indict, raise a question as to the existence of probable cause.

Unfettered Discretion

Even the burden of proof, to the extent that there is one, is largely established by the prosecutor since he alone is available to reinterpret for the grand jury the meaning of the probable cause requirement. In essence, then, the prosecutor runs the grand jury in his almost unfettered discretion, deciding what to investigate, how to investigate it, what evidence to produce, what procedures to use, and what standard must be met for it to act.

"Special" grand juries are from time to time empaneled expressly to investigate particular offenses or categories of offenses such as "racketeering," "organized crime," or "narcotics," but the great bulk of grand juries in federal and state courts are general grand juries with a mandate to investigate all offenses indictable in the courts by which they are empaneled. Occasionally certain functions with respect to reviewing public agencies and issuing reports are assigned to grand juries in some state court systems; however, these represent a very minor portion of total grand jury efforts.

While the formalities of empaneling grand juries vary somewhat, certain similarities transcend all such procedures. At the outset, grand jurors are selected in the same general fashion as petit jurors, usually from voter lists, from which the clerk of the empaneling court composes the grand jury. In the absence of motions or requests by the government to strike particular individuals, usually after they have found their way onto a grand jury panel, the procedure will necessarily take place without any equivalent of peremptory strikes or strikes for cause.

At its first session a judge or lesser judicial officer will advise the grand jury of the offenses it is to investigate and, in the case of a special grand jury, of the limited role it will enjoy.

Grand juries are empaneled for particular terms, such as 12 months, but they may be extended for a variety of reasons with the consent of the court.

The primary function of a grand jury is to determine whether there is probable cause to believe that crimes have been committed and that particular individuals have committed them. The proof necessary to meet the elusive probable cause standard is not entirely clear. Upon its empanelment each grand jury is advised about what constitutes probable cause.

The advice is first given by the grand jury judge, then explicated by either a senior prosecutor or the prosecutor who will be in charge of the grand jury. As problems arise over the interpretation of probable cause, it is the person who is seeking to use the grand jury to obtain an indictment who interprets the meaning of that standard. There is general agreement among persons who have worked with grand juries that probable cause is at best not very much cause and at worst none whatsoever.

In one not-so-funny experiment, a federal grand jury was asked to indict an individual upon a proffer by a special agent of the Secret Service that contained no evidence whatsoever. In effect, the special agent told the grand jury that he was fairly convinced the individual had committed the offense for which he was being presented or, the agent suggested, some other similar offense at some time. The indictment received the requisite number of votes and the foreman affixed his signature to it in the normal course of business.

The probable cause requirement may, however, be utilized in certain artful ways by skillful defense counsel. For example, it is well established that probable cause must be found for each element of an offense charged. If one dissects a statutory or common-law crime to isolate its constituent elements, it may appear unlikely that any evidence tending to show the existence of one element, or more, was presented to the grand jury.

Useful Procedure

In such a case, the prosecution may be required by appropriate motion to proffer to the court the evidence that was presented regarding the element or elements, failing which the indictment would be dismissed. While dismissal is unlikely, the procedure is particularly useful where the requisite proof of a particular element of an offense is in question. In such cases it may be utilized to determine at an early stage what the court interprets to be the requirements for proving the offense, since the court must necessarily define the elements to interpret the proffer meaningfully.

The court's definition, if it is more restrictive than the government would like it to be, may afterward be used to limit the range of proof upon which a conviction could be sustained at trial. In effect, such a motion is a useful adjunct to normal discovery motions or those to require a bill of particulars.

Once the grand jury is empaneled, its scope of inquiry defined for it and the burden of proof necessary to indict set out, it begins its business of hearing evidence. Whether transcripts of its hearings are prepared is determined largely by custom. In some federal districts and states all grand jury proceedings are transcribed; in others, none are. In some, the prosecutor may choose to have certain proceedings, but not others, transcribed.

One common form of differentiation is to transcribe the testimony of outside witnesses, especially before special grand juries, but not that of government agents or employees. In all instances, the prosecutor reserves the right to speak "off the record" and does so simply by indicating to the court reporter that his remarks are not to be transcribed.

A Big Obstacle

Obviously, the unavailability of grand jury transcripts has presented a substantial obstacle when alleged infirmities in the proceeding are sought to be challenged. While there is little definitive authority, many lawyers familiar with grand jury procedures feel that judicial requirements of plenary, or at least nonselective, grand jury transcription are on the horizon.

In districts or states where grand jury proceedings are transcribed as a matter of course, or in instances where a proceeding is transcribed at the behest of the prosecutor, review of grand jury proceedings before trial will, when required by a defense motion, frequently be conducted in camera. When a witness who testifies at trial against a defendant has previously testified before a grand jury and that testimony has been transcribed, it will be provided to defense counsel pursuant to the federal Jencks Act, 18 U.S.C. § 3500 (requiring the production of the testimony of a government witness after the conclusion of his direct testimony at trial) or an analogous state statute.

As noted, the decision concerning what evidence is presented to a grand jury is strictly within the prosecutor's control. He may present all of the evidence about a violation being scrutinized or only some of it. He may present the inculpatory evidence without presenting the exculpatory evidence. He may permit a witness who wishes to testify to do so or he may not. Although grand juries do occasionally "ask" for certain evidence, experience teaches that aside from very infrequent "runaway" grand juries, most such requests coincide nicely with the prosecutor's objectives.

Many prosecutors, mindful of the responsibility that attends their ability to exercise unfettered discretion, devise rules for their own personal conduct before the grand jury. For example, a number of prosecutors will not, simply because they deem it offensive to use the power of the grand jury in that fashion, require parents to testify against their children or children against their parents or brothers and sisters against one another.

Many prosecutors will invite a potential defendant to testify if he or she wishes to do so and will also present the same opportunity to a third-party witness who believes he can provide exculpatory information. As a matter of prosecutorial ethics, the Standards of the American Bar Association require a prosecutor to decline to call a witness before a grand jury if the purpose is simply to cause him to invoke his constitutional privilege not to testify about matters that may tend to incriminate him.

Some prosecutors go beyond this and advise each potential "target" defendant of his status as such when it becomes clear; they also advise him that he will be entitled to appear before the grand jury if he wishes, but will not be required to do so. A number of prosecutors tell witnesses who may be in precarious positions that they are in need of counsel and that their attendance will be postponed until they obtain a lawyer.

Since the requirements respecting admonitions to vulnerable witnesses are less stringent before grand juries than in other forums (in general, *Miranda* warnings need to be given only to a "putative" defendant), these self-imposed standards are particularly commendable. In my own experience I have found that one hallmark of a responsible and fair-minded prosecutor is the extent to which he goes beyond the requirements of law in an effort to use the grand jury in a manner consistent with generally accepted standards of fair play and decency.

Take Counsel Along

Every witness before a federal or state grand jury is entitled to counsel and in some courts there are provisions for the appointment of counsel for an indigent witness. As a general rule, even if a witness's appearance before a grand jury is purely a formality, he is very foolish to attend without counsel. Although counsel is not permitted to enter the room, a witness is permitted to leave after as many questions as he wishes—even after every question—to confer with his counsel about the appropriate answer.

Representing witnesses before the grand jury requires considerably more than customary legal skill. First, counsel must be aware of the manner in which the grand jury is being used, the scope of its inquiry, and the way in which his client fits into the matter under investigation. He must determine whether his client is vulnerable to prosecution—not in the mind of the fairest, most evenhanded person, but in the mind of a prosecutor and a grand jury, most of whose members will have become more than a little cynical as their term progresses. If the witness is vulnerable, counsel must understand the nature of that vulnerability and the options available for dealing with it.

Sometimes the prosecutor may be prepared to make certain commitments to a grand jury witness. Such a commitment may take the form of a limited or total immunity from prosecution and may range from a statutory, self-actualizing immunity from all offenses about which a witness will speak to the most limited of use and, perhaps, derivative use immunities. To judge how to proceed in such circumstances, counsel for a grand jury witness must know exactly what kind of immunity is being considered, how complete that immunity will be with respect to his client's situation, and what choices the lawyer may present his client at each juncture in the proceeding.

Obviously, there are some occasions when a lawyer will advise his client that he as his lawyer should tell the prosecutor his client will invoke his privilege not to testify about a matter that may tend to incriminate him. This should be done in writing to preserve a record. If the client is nevertheless called, he should state his name and invoke the privilege in response to the very first substantive question. No knowledgeable lawyer would ever advise his client to invoke selectively a privilege against self-incrimination before the grand jury. The risks of unintended waiver always outweigh any possible benefits of such a choice.

On other occasions a lawyer will advise his client, quite properly, to go beyond the questions asked and provide particular information to the grand jury even if it is not specifically sought. One might do this, for example, in representing a federal grand jury witness who has been immunized pursuant to the federal witness immunity statute, 18 U.S.C. § 6002, upheld in *Kastigar v. United States,* 406 U.S. 441 (1972). Since use immunity encompasses in most instances derivative use immunity as well, defense counsel will wish to foreclose other avenues by which the government could, if it chose, establish a case against his client by independent evidence.

Where immunity is pursued, counsel should also be aware of the doctrine of *Murphy v. Waterfront Commission,* 378 U.S. 52 (1964), that immunity in state proceedings presumptively carries over to federal proceedings absent a clear showing of independent source. The *Murphy* doctrine is a two-edged sword. On the one hand it renders largely futile an effort to withhold information over a proffered immunity on the basis that there is a residual fear of prosecution by the other sovereign. On the other, it accommodates the interest of an immunized witness by erecting a substantial hurdle in the path of a prosecution by the nonimmunizing sovereign. There is at least one possible exception to this, where the immunity conferring sovereign is cooperating with the other, but in that situation the possibilities of the latter sovereign proving independent source are so small as to make it especially attractive not to assert the self-incrimination privilege before the former.

Write It Down

Whenever counsel elects to permit his client to testify pursuant to some form of offer of immunity that is not conferred in a recorded judicial proceeding in the presence of counsel, he should commemorate the conferral of immunity in an explicit letter, hand-delivered to the prosecutor himself in advance of any relevant grand jury session.

The privileges available to witnesses before grand juries are essentially the same as those available in judicial proceedings generally. While the available privileges differ among states and between the federal government and various states, all assertions of privilege take the two generally acknowledged forms of vicarious and personal assertions of privilege. Into the vicarious class fall privileges such as those of husband-wife, attorney-client, physician-patient, accountant-client, and priest-penitent. A grand jury witness who invokes one of these privileges will be doing so on behalf of the absent privilege-holder. The other form of privilege is the personal privilege against self-incrimination. In that instance, of course, the witness invokes the privilege for himself.

It is difficult to say anything general about privileges other than that most lawyers experienced in grand jury work agree that, when in doubt, a privilege should be invoked. There is little to be gained and much to be lost by voluntarily providing information that might otherwise be withheld from a grand jury. Almost surely if an indictment is sought against the witness or a third person, it will be returned with or without the possibly withheld evidence and, when that occurs, the only party to the ensuing case that will benefit from the statements before the grand jury is the state. Almost never does a witness before a grand jury vindicate himself or someone else.

In complex cases the acquisition of massive documentation by grand juries has presented problems. The grand jury is no doubt entitled to demand and receive copious quantities of original documents if they are available. On the other hand, copies are often received in lieu of originals, particularly from cooperating witnesses. Any counsel representing a client from whom voluminous documents are subpoenaed should devise some agreeable procedure for maintaining a complete record of his client's documents.

If the documents to be supplied are too voluminous to copy, some agreement with the prosecutor should be reached about access to them. If not, a duplicate set should be prepared so that the lawyer will have one available to him at all times. Where counsel is familiar with grand jury procedures and with how to deal with prosecutors, a mutually satisfactory arrangement is generally possible. Occasionally, however, courts have had to pass specific orders controlling how documents will be delivered, copied, and stored.

Where the necessity for producing testimony or documents is disputed, the generally accepted method for bringing the matter before the court is a motion to quash the subpoena, which should be filed sufficiently in advance of the return date. Since the procedure is usually somewhat rushed, it is customary to deliver a copy of the motion directly to the grand jury judge. In appropriate instances the motion to quash should be accompanied by a motion to seal. In all instances it should include an explanation of the basis for the motion, a brief statement of the authorities relied upon and, if the disposition of the motion requires the court to notice facts, a proffer, perhaps supported by one or more affidavits. In courts that require it, a hearing should specifically be requested.

Obviously grand juries acquire substantial information that would be useful in a variety of contexts other than the criminal cases growing out of their indictments. As a result, procedures have evolved by which government agencies in particular may obtain access to information acquired by a grand jury and use it in other proceedings. All of these procedures have the common element of required judicial approval.

In federal practice Rule 6(e) of the Federal Rules of Criminal Procedure is construed to provide, upon order of court, for the transfer of information gathered by a grand jury. In some instances, such an order may be sought to transfer information from one grand jury to its successor. In others, such as criminal investigations in which information having civil tax implications is found, the information may be ordered to be made available to an entirely different arm of the government. In state grand jury practice, information is at times made available to professional licensing associations and other state regulatory agencies.

Counsel for a client who has provided information to a grand jury, and who has a reason for not wanting that information transferred, will generally be given the opportunity to address the court before a determination is made about a request to transfer. Very few courts will ever approve a transfer of information other than to a government agency that has demonstrated a proper purpose for having the information. Even in those instances, a compelling showing of a reason not to transfer the information may be successful. In all instances, the matter is largely discretionary, and any hope of overturning the decision of the deciding judge, who is usually the supervising grand jury judge, is very small.

Delegated to Prosecutor

In recent years, as increasingly complex cases have been presented to grand juries, a trend has developed toward delegating the functions of the grand jury to the prosecutor and his investigative agents and assistants. In many situations the subpoena power is delegated to the prosecutor, who then issues and serves the subpoenas and subpoenas *duces tecum* in the name of the grand jury. Prior approval of the grand jury for each subpoena may or may not be sought.

Where the case is particularly complex, the delegation may go one step further: The prosecutor may ask the grand jury's permission to forgo bringing before it all of the evidence acquired. For example, in a case where extremely copious documentation is sought, the prosecutor may designate certain government agents or accountants to review the evidence for the grand jury and to summarize their findings for it at some future time. As this procedure progresses, additional steps are omitted so that it is not uncommon for the documents never to appear in the grand jury room or for any real summarization of them to take place.

Occasionally an overzealous prosecutor may overstep the wide limits of permissible delegation and, for example, require evidence to be delivered to him pursuant to a subpoena *duces tecum* on a day when the grand jury is not even in the courthouse. If defense counsel can find such a clear violation of the prosecutor's authority, it may sustain a motion to dismiss the indictment. Where a dismissal even with the certainty of reindictment might yield a tactical benefit, it is well worth defense counsel's time to review the technical aspects of the grand jury proceedings, including days of convening, presence of a quorum, and concurrences of the requisite number of grand jurors in the true bill vote.

Most lawyers who have had experience with grand juries believe that there is a trend toward greater scrutiny of their conduct, largely because of increasing concerns about their legitimacy. This trend is reflected in one way by the nascent concept that the presentation of different evidence to different members of the grand jury is a denial of due process, since that procedure fails to ensure that any particular member of the grand jury has considered all of the evidence upon which the ultimate indictment is based and, therefore, undermines the requirement of a quorum and a certain number of concurrences.

Perhaps the most delicate of all grand-jury-related lawyering is the bargaining that takes place between defense counsel and prosecutors outside of the grand jury room. Here the first rule is for defense counsel to learn exactly what the prosecutor thinks his client has done and is able to say to the grand jury if he chooses to speak.

Next, counsel must learn the prosecutor's objective—whether he wishes to have the client indicted, to make him an unindicted co-conspirator, or simply to use him as a witness. Even if the last is the prosecutor's objective, there is still much for counsel to do.

For many clients the way in which their testimony is to be used in subsequent trials is of particular concern, since their relationships with other people may be very much affected by this and since the publicity that may attend their testimony in court may be nearly as damaging as the use of their name in an indictment. Therefore, whatever the prosecutor's objective, it must be understood and the client advised in accordance with that understanding. If there is doubt about the objective, either the doubt must be resolved or the client advised to invoke all available privileges and to resist questioning in every lawful way.

The sparring between the prosecutor and counsel for a grand jury witness who is vulnerable to prosecution is a sophisticated form of cat-

and-mouse. On the one hand, the prosecutor does not usually wish to tell counsel for such a witness exactly what he knows and what he suspects. On the other hand, counsel for the witness does not under any circumstance want to highlight the area of vulnerability by raising questions concerning it unless and until he can be certain that the exposure of his client's knowledge is in the interest of his client.

Only One Course

If it is clear that one's client is a target of a grand jury investigation and that the prosecutor will, under no circumstances, abandon his intention to seek the indictment of that client, then there is but one undisputed course of action to follow: Absolutely no information whatsoever should be provided to the grand jury (or to the prosecutor in any other fashion).

Counsel in this instance should write to the prosecutor, advising him that he represents the individual, that if called before the grand jury his client will invoke his constitutional privilege not to testify about matters that may tend to incriminate him, and that he expects the prosecutor, having been so advised, not to call that individual to testify. If the witness's subpoena is a subpoena *duces tecum,* an alternative method for delivery of the requested items, assuming that they are nonprivileged, should be sought.

If the possibilities are less clear, however, and if counsel believes the prosecutor can be persuaded to entertain various alternatives for his client, then head-on dealing becomes essential. The negotiation usually takes the following form: Counsel for the witness will ask the prosecutor how he envisions the role of his client in the matter under investigation. In doing this, he will seek to elicit some reasonably clear understanding of the prosecutor's objectives regarding his client.

Some prosecutors will candidly tell counsel for a grand jury witness that the possibilities are "witness or defendant." In other situations a full knowledge of the possibilities may require a number of carefully conducted sessions and, in a few situations, the prosecutor himself may be uncertain of all the possibilities. If the possibilities include that of nonindictment, counsel should also determine whether his client may still become an unindicted co-conspirator or be placed in a position where the testimony he will be required to give may badly damage him in civil or collateral matters.

Once it is clear that the client may escape indictment, defense counsel must obviously determine how that can be accomplished. The prosecutor will generally inform defense counsel that if, arguendo, certain information were forthcoming from his client, he would be assured of not being indicted in the investigation. The assurance might take the form of a letter of immunity, a statutorily authorized judicial conferral of immunity, or some other vehicle.

Hypothetical Disclosure

Whichever is the case, the prosecutor will want to know, before he agrees to immunity, that the witness will say the things he hopes he will say. At this point defense counsel should offer to make "hypothetical disclosure," a disclosure in which counsel for a witness, with the witness not present, presents in generalities what his client would, if an agreement were reached, agree to testify.

Usually by the time a hypothetical disclosure takes place, defense counsel already knows that a particular scenario will bring about the desired results. Astute defense counsel will, in the same manner as is often done in plea bargaining, tailor his client's knowledge to the prosecution's needs.

As the prosecutor becomes more definite in his undertaking, the hypothetical disclosure becomes more specific. Later, when the agreement is ultimately reached and made concrete, the actual interrogation of the client may also take place outside the presence of the grand jury.

In those instances where the immunity is one that flows from the use of the grand jury and the discussions are to take place outside its presence, it is particularly important to make certain that all discussions are expressly agreed to be pursuant to the mechanism by which immunity is to be conferred and that judicial approval for that procedure is, if necessary, obtained.

For a variety of reasons, both sides often prefer to work outside the grand jury room where counsel for a witness (who may now be doing all he can to assist the government's investigation) may be present and where the prosecutor may explore certain avenues without the risk of commemorating what may turn out to be exculpatory testimony.

Of all of the difficulties besetting modern grand juries, the problem of secrecy is perhaps the greatest. Grand jury investigations, especially those with political or public interest overtones, rarely can be conducted with total secrecy. As a result, many persons often are unfairly embarrassed simply by having their names associated with a process suggestive of wrongdoing.

Witnesses Often Talk

As a general rule the prosecutor, all persons under his supervision, the reporter, and the grand jurors themselves are subject to strict rules forbidding them to divulge information that comes to them in the grand jury sessions. Witnesses, however, are not generally burdened by such limitations, and they frequently discuss quite openly their testimony and their general feelings about the matter. Furthermore, in any major grand jury investigation there is always a good deal of collateral investigating outside the grand jury, and in most instances the line between the two becomes somewhat blurred.

Experienced counsel almost always advise clients who appear before a grand jury not to discuss their testimony because the risk of such conduct far outweighs any potential benefit. Prosecutors become quite unhappy when their grand jury proceedings are publicized and, if they learn the source of such publicity, they may respond unfavorably to it. There is also a quality inherent in the entire criminal process that often makes persons find themselves wishing they were able to put words they have spoken back into their mouths. If the witness has testified in a certain fashion, he may by speaking publicly, perhaps not wholly consistently with his testimony, be raising a suggestion of perjurious testimony that otherwise would never have been present. Perhaps the best reason for not discussing one's testimony before a grand jury is that a great many witnesses who are called before grand juries are vulnerable as a result of their association with the matter under investigation and the less attention such a person draws to himself the better off he may be.

Whatever its shortcomings, the grand jury system survives as one of the chief investigative tools of prosecutors in all state and federal courts. The implications of its use are many and varied as are the procedures available to counsel who must deal with it. There are very few aspects of the practice of law where the risks of incomplete knowledge or ill-considered action are greater.

Representing a Grand Jury Witness

William L. Osterhoudt

Recently, while reviewing with a client her options in responding to a federal grand jury subpoena, I was reminded of an episode of the old television series "L.A. Law." In that episode a prosecutor threatened a criminal defense lawyer who had bested him in court with a spurious money-laundering prosecution for having taken a legitimate fee from her client. Spurning her lawyer's advice, the gallant defense lawyer went voluntarily before the grand jury, which she held spellbound as she castigated the prosecutor and extolled the Constitution. Just before a commercial, the prosecutor limped from the room, and the grand jurors warmly embraced the virtuous defender.

This charming story was, and alas remains, a fairy tale. In reality, a grand jury might well have indicted the lawyer for perjury and obstruction of justice along with money laundering, leaving the prosecutor gloating as his victim faced the expense and trauma of a criminal trial.

Some people harbor romantic notions of the grand jury as a fair, independent tribunal. The fact is, however, that the modern grand jury is firmly under the government's control. The prosecutor decides what cases to present, who to call as witnesses, who should receive immunity, and who should be targeted for prosecution. The prosecutor draws up the charge and presents it to the grand jury, which routinely votes to return an indictment.

In such a world, every person subpoenaed to appear before a grand jury—without exception—needs competent representation. Such representation has two aspects: protecting the witness against later prosecution on the basis of his testimony, and ensuring that the witness's rights and privileges are respected throughout the grand jury experience.

William L. Osterhoudt practices law in San Francisco.

When a client receives a grand jury subpoena, you must determine what the government wants. A federal grand jury subpoena may call only for testimony. It may require production of specified documents. It may also require that the witness engage in conduct that is considered nontestimonial—such as providing handwriting samples. What a lawyer does will depend on the type of subpoena served.

Start with documentary subpoenas. They fall into two categories: those that require testimony from the witness and those that do not. Where the government wants only your client's documents, the subpoena will call for their production on a particular date before the grand jury and will state that furnishing them to a specified federal agent will make an actual appearance unnecessary. When the government also wants to question the witness about the documents, the subpoena will require the witness to testify and to bring the documents with him.

Whenever a client must actually appear to testify, even if the primary aim of the subpoena seems to be documents, a lawyer faces special problems. *Any* testimony requires care. The issues involved will come up in a few pages. The immediate topic is exclusively nontestimonial subpoenas.

Documents Only

When a subpoena demands the production of documents, a lawyer's options are limited by Supreme Court decisions on the Fifth Amendment. It is a large and controversial body of law, but certain basic principles stand out. First, there is *no* Fifth Amendment privilege covering the contents of documents belonging to a corporation, partnership, labor organization, or other associational entity. This rule applies even to corporations owned and controlled by a single person. The government can acquire all such documents without granting immunity.

Second, so-called "private papers"—those that do not belong to any associational entity—fare little better. Even an individual's personal documents are subject to Fifth Amendment protection only if they were originally created under government compulsion. It is thus not enough that the subpoenaed documents may bury your client in the penitentiary forever. Unless the government compelled creation of the documents, you generally cannot rely on the Fifth Amendment.

There is a glimmer of Fifth Amendment hope, however. In *United States v. Doe*, 465 U.S. 605 (1984), the Supreme Court concluded that where the very act of handing over documents may incriminate the witness—by helping establish the existence and authenticity of the documents under his control, for example—the witness can invoke the Fifth Amendment. Unfortunately, that reliance often doesn't help much. The government can respond to such a claim by seeking a limited grant of immunity to compel production. "*Doe* immunity," as it is sometimes called, precludes later use of the act of production to prove the witness's connection with the documents.

Whether the limited *Doe* privilege applies depends on the facts. If your client is, or may become, a target, and her control or authentication of the documents could become an issue in a future prosecution, you should advise her to claim the *Doe* privilege. This effort may seem futile. But, although the government seems to give up little by conferring *Doe* immunity, prosecutors are often reluctant to do so, preferring long legal battles over the privilege's scope.

The only other significant limitations on the government's power to compel document production are found in the Fourth Amendment—which imposes a reasonableness test on such demands—and Fed. R. Crim. P. 17(c)—which permits a motion to quash if compliance would be "burdensome or oppressive." These limitations have been much litigated, and the case law must be reviewed carefully.

Such study, though essential, will yield few victories. The government ordinarily will have little difficulty meeting the reasonableness test: Document demands, unlike subpoenas for testimony, *are* subject to a relevancy challenge, but the government can turn this challenge aside with a modest (and usually in camera) showing that the materials sought are rationally related to the subject matter of the inquiry. It is true that subpoenas virtually limitless in scope or burden can be attacked, but the remedy will be a winnowing of the overbroad demand, either by the court or by the prosecutor. You can safely assume that any documents you do *not* want to turn over will have to be produced after the dust settles.

The conclusion to draw from this short visit to the world of documentary subpoenas is depressingly simple: Your client probably will have to comply substantially with the government's demand.

When compliance is necessary, you must obey the letter of the subpoena, a task that requires careful study of the demand and a firm grasp of the case. A lawyer must avoid the trap of unintentionally withholding required documents; that could lead straight to later allegations of obstruction of justice. All documents produced to the government must be numbered and copied. Remember that the response to a documentary demand may someday define or limit the client's participation—as a witness or defendant—in a criminal trial.

Sometimes a grand jury subpoena will demand that a person do certain things that may produce incriminating evidence. Though the most common are demands for handwriting specimens, fingerprints, or voice prints, the possibilities are limited only by the prosecutor's ingenuity. The Supreme Court has upheld a subpoena requiring the witness—a potential defendant—to sign a "consent directive" to foreign banks telling them to release on demand any records that each bank might have on him. The directive even contained a clause announcing that it was to be "construed as consent" to release documents for purposes of any nation's bank secrecy laws. *Doe v. United States*, 487 U.S. 201 (1988).

This *Doe* case again exemplifies the Supreme Court's limited view of the Fifth Amendment. Handwriting exemplars, voice samples, and blood specimens are not seen as compelled "testimony" because they convey no factual assertion by the witness about the matter under investigation. The bank consent directive is closer to the line, but, technically, it did not assert that the witness actually had foreign bank accounts; instead, the directive simply facilitated the release of records for the bank accounts, if any did exist.

All this means that your client usually must comply with demands for nontestimonial production of evidence. In such cases, a lawyer must be present at all contacts between her client and the authorities extracting compliance. Counsel's presence will at least deter the government from talking with the client. It will also help ensure that the prosecutor obtains no more from the witness than he is entitled to.

Though production of documents or handwriting samples can be important, the main event in most grand jury representations is dealing with a testimonial subpoena. There is more risk, but also more room for creative lawyering.

The first, obvious step is to interview the client thoroughly. You must learn as much as possible about your client's view of the events being investigated. If the case was referred by another lawyer, the witness may already have been interviewed at least once. Get such statements and review them; they may have been taken when the witness's memory was keener. In addition, maintain a respectful skepticism about the client's version of events, and try to develop additional information.

One interview area merits special emphasis. The government may have spoken with the client before she went to a lawyer. The agents who serve subpoenas often will have a pleasant chat with the unwary and often unsettled recipient. This is not just civility; it is a calculated attempt to obtain useful statements and possibly damaging admissions. The witness may think nothing significant occurred during her brief conversation with the agents. That may be true, but a defense lawyer cannot just accept that assurance. He must determine exactly what was said. Statements made to government representatives in a criminal case *never* lack significance.

Once you have scrutinized the subpoena and interviewed the client, it is time to talk with the prosecutor. You want to learn as much as possible about the investigation and your client's connection with it. Such a talk is not a one-way street, however. Throughout these contacts, recognize that the prosecutor also wants to talk with you. Just as you want to know your client's status and the *timetable* for the investigation, the prosecutor wants to know how hard you intend to resist the investigation; whether you will turn subpoenaed documents over early and without troublesome objection; and whether you will allow the witness to testify without delay or only with unwelcome objections. Such issues can offer opportunities for compromise; a cordial, honest relationship with government counsel cannot hurt. But you must be cautious. You are very much adversaries. Despite an appearance of cordiality, you and the prosecutor are trying to get as much as possible from each other without giving up much.

First, and most important, is to learn the precise nature of the government's interest in the witness. Is the client a "target," a "subject," or just a "witness"? These terms pretty much mean what they seem to mean. Thus, a target is someone the government intends to indict using its power over the grand jury.

A prosecutor knows that a person identified as a target, if actually compelled to appear before the grand jury, will surely invoke his privilege against self-incrimination. Because the government knows it will not get testimony from such a witness, the witness's grand jury appearance will likely be excused. The Constitution does not forbid the government from calling a target before the grand jury to force him to invoke the privilege, but prosecutors rarely insist on this empty exercise.

What if the prosecutor says the client is not a target, but is a "subject," of the investigation? The *U.S. Attorney's Manual* and other Justice Department pronouncements draw a distinction, mostly technical, between targets and subjects. Whereas a target is someone the government *expects* to indict, a subject is a person the prosecutor thinks *may* be indicted, but against whom sufficient evidence may not exist. In most cases, however, this distinction is one only of degree and has no practical significance.

Because a decision to indict has not been finally made, there is a slightly greater chance that a subject will actually be called before the grand jury. You must treat your subject-client as if he were a target. If the only thing between your client and an indictment is more evidence, the last thing you want to do is provide the missing link. A subject who testifies can rarely do anything but harm himself, by creating a trail of testimony that may return to haunt him, possibly in the form of a perjury indictment.

The normal course for a lawyer with a target or subject-client is thus obvious: Tell the prosecutor that the witness does not wish to appear, and the appearance will probably be excused. If the appearance is not excused, the witness should, with counsel's guidance, assert the Fifth Amendment. This should end the client's involvement with the grand jury, unless he is downgraded to a mere witness or he is granted immunity.

Unfortunately, the choice is not always that simple, because the prosecutor's advice on your client's status will not always be explicit. This is not necessarily because the prosecutor lacks candor—although that is possible. More likely, the government really does not know how to categorize the witness; it knows only that it wants to question him. Frequently, the prosecutor will tell you something like this:

Well, your client is certainly not a target or anything like that. Of course, we're really just beginning. Frankly, I'm surprised he even went to a lawyer. We just want to ask him some questions. As far as I know, he's just a witness. It won't take long at all. If you just send him in for a brief chat with us first, it will speed matters up. You are welcome, too, if you want to come. As far as I know he's got nothing to worry about, and should have no concerns about cooperating with us. There may be a few areas where he can help us.

These soothing words offer no protection. In such a situation, there are a number of things to do. First, keep asking questions. No matter what the prosecutor seems to be saying, your client is close enough to the fire to feel the heat of a subpoena. You must determine everything you can about what is burning. Prosecutors are reluctant to discuss their investigations, repeatedly pointing to the grand jury secrecy provisions of Fed. R. Crim. P. 6(e). Still, persistent inquiry may yield useful information. There are also information sources besides the prosecutor. Talk to lawyers representing other witnesses or targets. It is a mistake simply to accept the prosecutor's bland assertion that the witness has nothing to worry about.

The next thing to do is to slow down. Prosecutors are nearly always in a hurry—or at least they like to appear that way. There may be reasons for their haste, such as a ticking limitations clock. Other times, the prosecutor just wants to look busy and vigilant. Whatever the prosecutor's motives, speed is usually your enemy in grand jury work, and time may be a valuable ally. The prosecutor's haste may simply be an effort to push you along—to your disadvantage.

Therefore, if the proposed date of your client's grand jury appearance is upon you when you are retained, ask the prosecutor for a postponement to digest what you have learned. Most prosecutors, still hoping for voluntary cooperation, will accommodate a reasonable continuance request unless the dwindling term of the grand jury or limitations deadlines dictate otherwise. If the prosecutor refuses unreasonably, file a motion to quash the subpoena with the judge supervising the grand jury.

The most important way to protect your client is to insist on immunity as a price for testimony. Some lawyers believe that unless a person is in specific, identifiable jeopardy of prosecution, she should not offend the government, or appear to confess weakness, by demanding immunity. I think that is wrong. For me, if any rule approaches an absolute, it is this: Before allowing a client to testify, I insist that she be granted immunity. If the government is unwilling to do that, I advise the witness to invoke the Fifth Amendment and tell the prosecutor I have done so.

Why this dogmatic approach? Mostly because no one can predict the future. Despite the prosecutor's assurances that a client is not a target, there might be danger later. Information obtained during the investigation—matters the prosecutor didn't know when he talked with you—

may implicate your client. Regardless of the actual facts, the government may believe that this information is true. This point bears emphasis. Law-abiding people believe that their innocence will protect them. This confidence is unjustified. Even innocent people may look guilty to the government. Prosecutors sometimes make mistakes, and most witnesses are not sufficiently detached (or informed) to decide whether conduct has straddled or crossed the line into criminality.

It is worth repeating: There is no way to foresee the future course of an investigation. A client may testify about his company's billing practices as part of what begins as an investigation into possible fraudulent claims on the government. A year later he may find that the inquiry has come to center on alleged bribery of public officials. When such sharp changes are possible, the prosecutor cannot be held to his assurance that the witness is "not presently a target" of the investigation.

If a witness's status changes, he may find himself indicted for perjury as well as for the items under investigation. Such indictments are a big handicap: The defendant begins the case accused of lying about the facts underlying the principal charge. The Michael Deaver case is illustrative, as is the experience of Alger Hiss, who was indicted, convicted of, and imprisoned for perjury even though the statute of limitations had long run out on the espionage accusations against him. Had people like these refrained from testifying, charges might well have never been brought.

Prosecutors Understand

Such disasters are unnecessary. A lawyer must try to protect his client from future prosecution. Prosecutors know this. They are lawyers too; most of them would not dream of allowing a client to appear unprotected before a grand jury. A concern that the government will think a person guilty for demanding immunity is usually groundless and always irrelevant. The prosecutor may huff and puff about how unnecessary such protection is, but huffing and puffing is all it is.

A useful strategy in getting immunity for a nontarget witness is to ask the prosecutor this: If the witness is neither a target nor a subject, why *not* grant him immunity?

If the prosecutor is being candid in saying the witness has nothing to fear, there is no good answer to this question—at least none that should satisfy a witness's lawyer. Tactically, prosecutors prefer that their trial witnesses testify without any favors or inducements, such as immunity at the grand jury stage. This makes the witness less vulnerable to cross-examination. But that should not dissuade a witness from demanding necessary protection. The paperwork burden even for formal immunity is slight. Of course, if it is early, and the prosecutor does not yet know where the investigation will lead, immunity may not yet be in the cards. But learning even that is valuable; it means your client is not as safe as the prosecutor's words suggest.

If you get immunity, what form should it take? The federal immunity statute, 18 U.S.C. § 6002, confers only "use plus fruits" immunity and not the broader "transactional" immunity recognized by many states. *See Kastigar v. United States*, 406 U.S. 441 (1972). Use immunity—which leaves a witness subject to prosecution for the matter under investigation—may seem inadequate. In practice, however, the government rarely prosecutes those to whom it has extended use immunity. This is because, where it does, the prosecution bears the substantial burden of showing that the case is untainted by prior immunized testimony.

Should such immunity be formal, or will informal letter immunity suffice? Formal immunity has the advantage of clarity; its protection is exactly that defined in the immunity statute. But, if it tracks the statute, informal letter immunity is often satisfactory. An undertaking by letter not to use the testimony or its fruits will bind the prosecution. Of course, if the client is in jeopardy of prosecution in other federal districts or jurisdictions—which would *not* be bound by letter immunity—the prudent course is to insist on formal statutory immunity.

All rules have exceptions. There will be instances—not many—in which a lawyer will decide to allow a witness to testify without immunity. Some people—public officials or law enforcement officers—may face professional ruin if they invoke the Fifth Amendment. In addition, a witness may be in the midst of a personal crisis so extreme that the best course is to testify. In the aftermath of the Peoples Temple tragedy in 1979, the government convened a grand jury to investigate the death of Congressman Leo Ryan. Survivors of the mass suicide, many of whom had lost their entire families in the carnage, were subpoenaed. Though the government did not label them targets (ultimately only one person was indicted), it would not commit to immunity early in such a sensitive investigation. Under these circumstances, several lawyers, including me, allowed their clients to testify. The survivors' tragedies were so extreme that I thought the danger of extending the ordeal outweighed the insubstantial danger of indictment. Even then, other lawyers in the case disagreed.

Though such limited exceptions exist, there *is* one unbreakable rule. If the witness is a target, he *must* claim the privilege. Targets do not talk their way out of indictments.

Once you learn all you can about the investigation and your client's place in it, and once you have an immunity grant in your pocket, you begin preparing for your client's grand jury appearance.

The prosecutor will likely suggest that you and your client meet him before the appearance. A preview of the grand jury session can have advantages. Chief among them is that, unlike during the grand jury appearance itself, you—the witness's counsel—will be present. The meeting will help prepare the witness and will probably shorten and simplify the actual appearance. In rare cases, in which the government finds the witness less helpful than expected, it may even eliminate the need for an appearance altogether.

A preappearance meeting can have risks, however. The client will tend to say more in freewheeling chat than she would in the formal atmosphere of the grand jury room. She may show she knows more than the government thought. Worse, the meeting may show she was involved in previously unknown ways in the matters under investigation. For this reason, it is absolutely essential—if you go to the meeting—that it be expressly covered by the immunity you have negotiated.

If you participate in the interview, prepare the witness to respond carefully, directly, and succinctly. Make certain that she takes advantage of your presence, stopping for private consultation with you whenever a question or subject matter raises problems. Caution the client not to respond if you have objected to a question and advised her not to answer. In short, preparation for an interview with the prosecutor is little different from preparation for a civil deposition.

By contrast, preparing a witness for a grand jury appearance *will* differ from deposition preparation. The main reason is that counsel cannot attend the grand jury proceeding. This places a greater burden on the witness, and so more careful and detailed preparation is required.

Review the known areas of inquiry and anticipated questions with the client. Tell her to answer simply and directly, without embellishment or speculation. Stress the need to understand the questions fully before answering. This is especially important in the grand jury room because, without opposing counsel there to object, the prosecutor may lapse into compound or ambiguous questions. He may try to lead the witness into a desired answer. It is up to the witness, and the witness alone, not to blunder into unintended or misleading answers and to seek clarification of ambiguities.

Be sure to cover your role. Although not in the grand jury room, counsel is almost always just outside. Therefore, if the witness is uncertain about the meaning or propriety of a question, she should ask to be excused to consult with the lawyer. There is nothing wrong with such a request, and it will almost always be granted, although the prosecutor may try to discourage the interruption.

You must emphasize the need to be truthful. Immunity does not protect against a prosecution for perjury. The need to be truthful does not, however, require the witness to be loquacious or to volunteer unrequested information. She simply must respond honestly to questions.

The lawyer should try to demystify the grand jury, which can be intimidating. The witness must be told what to expect and be assured of your comforting presence and availability just outside. The basic limitations on the prosecutor's power should be emphasized: There is no jail cell at the other end of the room—a witness who displeases the inquisitor will not immediately be locked up. Even a recalcitrant witness, one who flatly refuses to testify, is entitled to a contempt hearing before a district judge.

The witness should be cautioned against angry or intemperate responses, even if the prosecutor provokes her. Outbursts of temper or annoyance will only complicate and prolong the ordeal, and they will not penalize the prosecutor in any way. A witness confronted with a bullying prosecutor should ask to be excused and bring the problem to her lawyer's attention. The lawyer can then raise the problem directly with the prosecutor and, if necessary, take it to court.

The witness should be told that he will be debriefed immediately after the appearance. It is important for the witness to recall as much of his testimony as possible; reminding him of this beforehand may help his memory. It may also help for the witness to aid his recall by making notes of questions as they are asked.

Regardless of whether the witness and his lawyer previously have met the prosecutor, a lawyer should, just before the client's appearance, confer with the Assistant U.S. Attorney conducting the inquiry. This will be an opportunity to resolve any remaining problems. It will also remind the prosecutor that the witness's lawyer, though barred from the grand jury room, is present and alert.

If your preparation has been thorough, there should be few surprises and no serious problems during your client's appearance. A few general observations regarding counsel's role during testimony are in order, however.

Although a witness may leave the room to consult his lawyer, prosecutors occasionally become impatient with witnesses who do this repeatedly. The prosecutor cannot do anything about such requests, except in cases of blatant abuse. Acting in good faith, the witness can ask the foreman of the grand jury for leave to consult with his lawyer as often as necessary.

This right is valuable, and it should be exercised fully. Witnesses can engage in private, privileged conversations with counsel before answering any pending question, and lawyers can formulate appropriate objections. In most jurisdictions, the witness may even write down the questions to facilitate such consideration. The extent of these consultations depends on the circumstances. Where the subject matter is complex or the situation tense, the witness may need to leave after practically every question.

The role an lawyer *can* play during a grand jury session should be underscored. Normally there is much emphasis on how a lawyer *cannot* go into the grand jury room. That is surely undesirable, but in fact a witness who has the resolve to leave when necessary can get plenty of advice. What a lawyer can do on the outside is more than he would be able to do if he were in the grand jury room but had his status reduced to that of the now-famous "potted plant."

Despite a lawyer's preappearance work, there may be cases when the Fifth Amendment must be claimed before the grand jury. A witness who might face this should be instructed on when and how to assert the privilege. As a general rule, absent immunity, the privilege should be claimed in response to all questions other than those concerning the witness's name and address. The witness should not pick and choose among questions. This usually disastrous approach inevitably leads to waiver problems, and can result in the complete loss of the privilege with no compensating immunity. If any doubt exists, the witness should consult with counsel about invoking the privilege after every question, if need be.

The mechanics of actually claiming the privilege may seem simple, but witnesses often stumble. The best practice is for the lawyer to write out an invocation of the privilege on a piece of paper, which the client can take into the grand jury room. But do not worry much about your client's reading ability. Courts have held that no magic words are needed to invoke the privilege; a witness who is able to mumble "Take the Fifth" will undoubtedly be protected.

Often a prosecutor tries to intimidate the witness, or make him adopt the government's preferred phraseology, by asking, "Are you telling the grand jury that a truthful answer would incriminate you?" This is meant to embarrass the witness, who is already uncomfortable relying on the Fifth Amendment, and to cast him in a generally bad light. Such a characterization of the privilege is also incorrect legally; merely answering the prosecutor's loaded question is incriminating. There is an easy solution to such nonsense and game playing: Instruct the witness not to respond, but to assert the privilege in the form you advise.

Grand jury witnesses have other rights besides the privilege against self-incrimination. For example, even if immunized, a grand jury witness is entitled to the Fifth Amendment guarantee of due process. He can object to questions that are abusive and oppressive. He can also object to improper questions that are compound, incomprehensible, or argumentative. The witness has a right to be treated fairly and need not suffer badgering or harassment.

The witness may also refuse to answer questions that invade a recognized testimonial privilege. Questions that intrude upon the relationship between the witness and her lawyer or that call for confidential lawyer-client communications fall into this category, as do those that invade the marital privilege or involve spousal communications.

Associational questions may violate the First Amendment. It is important to be clear about what that means. Of course, many crimes involve an association of individuals allegedly engaged in unlawful conduct; the First Amendment does not bar the investigation and prosecution of such crimes. But gratuitous efforts to learn about a witness's personal associates, particularly in a political or journalistic context, violate the amendment, and justify an objection. *Bursey v. United States,* 466 F.2d 1059 (9th Cir. 1972).

Objections of All Kinds

Though a witness cannot object that a question is based on illegally seized evidence, *United States v. Calandra,* 414 U.S. 338 (1974), he can object if he believes the question is derived from illegal electronic surveillance. The federal wiretap statute, 18 U.S.C. §§ 2510, *et seq.,* has been construed to give the witness standing to challenge the legality of such surveillance before the grand jury. *Gelbard v. United States,* 408 U.S. 41 (1972).

These objections, like invocation of the Fifth Amendment self-incrimination privilege, should be drafted by counsel and read by the client to the grand jury. This means that the witness must be advised in general terms of the kinds of objections that may come up. She must be instructed to consult with counsel if she suspects that one or more might apply.

One area on which all witnesses, especially those before a grand jury, need advice is failure to recall. The witness must understand that no one expects perfect memory. It is proper for a witness to respond that he has no recollection of an event when that is the case. "I do not remember" is *not,* however, a proper substitute for a truthful answer when the witness *does* remember but would prefer not to answer. "I do not recall" is itself a statement that may, if knowingly false, subject the witness to a prosecution for perjury.

Clients sometimes hold dear certain values that the law governing witnesses simply does not recognize. There is, for example, no privilege to withhold testimony against a parent, child, or sibling. There is no right to avoid giving adverse testimony about a common law spouse and no recognition of relationships that fall outside traditional marriage. Nonetheless, witnesses sometimes feel so strongly about such issues that they refuse to testify.

There may be many reasons of principle for recalcitrance. I once had an anarchist client who passionately believed that the Constitution forbade the government, or the grand jury, from requiring him to take the oath. His argument was destined to fail, but it was an intellectually respectable claim based on his firm view of Fifth Amendment history. Faced with his rather fierce resolve, the government decided it could do without his testimony.

Cases like that are rare. In this age of the whistle-blower, when people are applauded and financially rewarded for informing on friends and associates, there is usually little sympathy for those who are reluctant to become government witnesses. Therefore, if there are topics on which a witness finds it ethically or emotionally impossible to testify, his lawyer should identify them before the appearance so that the lawyer can prepare the witness, advise him of the consequences of refusal, and raise an appropriate objection.

A lawyer should never encourage a witness to be recalcitrant, but it is sometimes necessary to protect a witness who is so disposed. You must understand 28 U.S.C. § 1826, which permits a court to hold a witness in civil contempt and impose coercive sanctions if he refuses to testify "without just cause." In federal court, recalcitrant witnesses facing civil contempt are entitled to the benefit of Fed. R. Crim. P. 42(b), which generally provides at least five days' notice to prepare for a contempt hearing.

The customary sanction for unjustified refusal to answer is commitment to jail until the witness is willing to answer, or for the remaining life of the grand jury or 18 months, whichever is shorter. The court is not required to jail the witness. Effort should be made to demonstrate that confinement would be undesirable. Physicians and psychiatrists may be used to show this, and creative alternatives to incarceration (such as community service, work furlough, or even house arrest) should be explored. It may also be possible to reach an agreement with the prosecutor that will limit questioning in a way acceptable to the government and the witness.

After your client finishes his grand jury testimony, debrief him immediately and thoroughly. Debriefing is likely to be the only detailed record you will ever have of the appearance. Such a record may be important for a number of reasons. An investigation may change direction and focus on your client. Information from other sources may cast doubt on the accuracy of some of your client's testimony. There may be attempts to call your client to testify again before the grand jury or at trial. An accurate record may be essential to an appropriate response.

Detailed Debriefing

Debriefing requires a careful, probing interview. The client was probably nervous; he will forget large chunks of his testimony unless prompted. The more meticulous your preparations for the appearance, the more effective the postappearance debriefing will be, because the client will know in advance the importance of later review. If there was a preappearance conference with the prosecutor, your notes of that interview provide a convenient starting point from which to reconstruct the grand jury questioning. Although the witness may be drained from the ordeal of testifying, counsel must press the interview immediately, before the client's memory fades.

Sometimes a question comes up about whether a lawyer should share the fruits of a debriefing session with lawyers for other witnesses. The answer depends on whether such sharing will benefit the client. Knowing what other witnesses were asked and what they said can help put the client's testimony in perspective. It may provide valuable insights into the investigation. Remember, however, that the future is unknown. Sharing information may end up hurting your client if witnesses' interests later diverge. It could also constitute a waiver of the attorney-client privilege absent an appropriate joint defense agreement. Finally, sharing information could create serious problems if the government suspects a conspiracy to obstruct justice.

A word about the grand jury secrecy provisions of Fed. R. Crim. P. 6(e): They do not apply to a grand jury witness. Still, prosecutors sometimes caution witnesses against revealing the substance of testimony given before that body. Such warnings may just be prosecutorial bullying and should not deter any disclosure that is determined to be in the witness's interest. Lawyers should be alert, however, to the possibility that obstruction of justice charges are in the works. Advise the witness to avoid unnecessary discussion of his testimony, particularly with others involved in the investigation.

Occasionally, the government recalls a witness for a second appearance before the grand jury. This should concern a defense lawyer, even if his client had immunity. Does the renewed demand mean that the government suspects the witness of lying or obstructing justice? Is the prosecutor trying to lead the witness into a perjury trap by eliciting testimony he suspects to be false? Or is there an innocent reason for requiring further testimony, such as something the prosecutor forgot to ask during the initial appearance?

Try to get the answers to these questions from the prosecutor. This is usually not as difficult as you might think. Successive grand jury appearances are uncommon; some explanation is usually provided. If there is no explanation, move to quash the second subpoena, and argue that it is a form of grand jury abuse. Although such a motion may be unsuccessful, it will occupy the prosecutor and may cause the court to question the government's motives. Faced with this, the prosecutor is likely to talk about the reasons for a new subpoena.

If you suspect the government doubts your client's previous testimony, try to identify the problem areas and clear them up. As long as the prosecutor is proceeding in good faith—and your client told the truth—a resolution should be possible without the need for a second appearance. If you suspect that the prosecutor is not acting in good faith, ask the court for relief. It is generally seen as an abuse of the grand jury process for the government to call a witness not for the substance of his testimony but to set up a perjury prosecution. *See generally* Gershman, "The Perjury Trap," 129 *U. Pa. L. Rev.* 624 (1981).

If the client must appear before the grand jury a second time, the lawyer should request a transcript of the first appearance. There is no general right to this, but some cases hold that if repeated appearances are demanded, due process requires that the witness be provided with her prior testimony. *Bursey v. United States*, 466 F.2d 1059 (9th Cir. 1972).

Otherwise, through innocent failure of recollection, the witness may subject herself to a perjury prosecution.

Representation of a grand jury witness may be simple and direct, or complex and frustrating. Witnesses have relatively few rights against an inquisitive government, and they need help. Success will rarely be dramatic. If a witness has been protected from future prosecution and has had his rights fully respected, his lawyer has done well.

Getting Immunity and Using Privileges

Andrew R. Rogoff

An FBI agent appears one day at your client's business. The client, who ordinarily barges into your office when he gets a speeding ticket, does not consider calling you. Instead, filled with misguided bravado or fear, he tells the agent he has nothing to hide. He then concocts a tall tale in response to the agent's questions. A few days later, the agent returns with a grand jury subpoena. Now the client calls you.

Many lawyers, regardless of specialty or geographic location, have had a client in this situation. The client has real problems. He may actually have committed a crime that prompted the agent's visit. He has also lied to the FBI—probably another crime. 18 U.S.C. §§ 1001, 1505.

Despite these handicaps, the client might avoid prosecution by becoming a government witness. Even if he cannot escape prosecution altogether, he may be convicted of, or plead guilty to, reduced charges and then become a prosecution witness. Either way, his testimony, ultimately given under a grant of immunity, may be a bargaining chip to secure a compromise between the prosecutor, who needs to snag a bigger fish, and your client, who wants to remain free.

Immunity issues arise most often in the federal system, or in complex criminal prosecutions at the state level. Prosecutors usually need not grant immunity in cases involving run-of-the-mill street violence in which an arrest occurs soon after the crime. Such matters proceed to trial on the testimony of victims and witnesses.

White collar, organized-crime, or conspiracy cases are different. The government may be unable to prosecute these cases if key witnesses were part of the conspiracy for which the defendant is on trial. Such former conspirators may have been involved in complex transactions

---

Andrew R. Rogoff is a member of Pepper, Hamilton & Scheetz in Philadelphia. The author acknowledges the assistance of Diana Vondra Carris, an associate with the firm, in updating this chapter.

with many people over a long period. Unless the government offers testimony from insiders, the prosecution will fail. The problem for the prosecutor, of course, is that few insiders can testify without incriminating themselves.

Recognizing these prosecutorial problems, what can you do for a client who wants to avoid conviction? What about one who does not want to testify at all? If you understand the government's resource problems, appreciate how immunized testimony is obtained, and know how to block a grand jury subpoena, you can limit your client's criminal exposure and, occasionally, even keep him out of the witness chair.

Immunity litigation usually begins with service of a grand jury subpoena. Your client rushes to your office, seeking help. After he describes his past escapades, he probably provides your first, and perhaps your only, defense to the subpoena: the Fifth Amendment.

Corporate/Personal Documents

Before rushing out to do Fifth Amendment battle, check to see who—or what—was served with the subpoena and what the subpoena demands—testimony or documents. These distinctions are significant because, although individuals enjoy Fifth Amendment protections, corporations and other collective entities do not.

For example, if your client received a subpoena for documents, he may invoke the Fifth Amendment privilege to avoid production when the existence of the documents, their authenticity, or his possession of them is incriminating. *United States v. Doe*, 465 U.S. 605, 612–13 (1984). The same holds true when your client receives a subpoena for his business records if he runs a sole proprietorship. *Id.*

If, however, your client is subpoenaed as a corporate custodian or agent, he has no right to invoke the Fifth Amendment because corporations have no such privilege. *Braswell v. United States*, 487 U.S. 99 (1988). This is true even if your client is the corporation's only shareholder. *United States v. Stone*, 976 F.2d 909, 912 (4th Cir. 1992), *cert. denied*, 507 U.S. 1029 (1993). Indeed, even if your client was subpoenaed personally (not in a representative capacity) to produce corporate documents, he does not have a valid Fifth Amendment right to avoid compliance. *In re Grand Jury Witnesses*, 92 F.3d 710 (8th Cir. 1996).

Be aware, however, that state law may be different. Some states do extend the privilege against self-incrimination to a corporate records custodian. *See, e.g., Massachusetts v. Doe*, 544 N.E.2d 860, 861–62 (Mass. 1989).

Now take the time to analyze your client's role in the grand jury investigation. Federal prosecutors and investigators generally categorize recipients of a grand jury subpoena as "targets," "subjects," or "witnesses," according to their perceived culpability. A "target" is defined as "a person as to whom the prosecutor or the grand jury has substantial evidence linking him/her to the commission of a crime, and who, in the judgment of the prosecutor, is a putative defendant." *Department of Justice Manual* § 9-11.150 (1996) ("DOJ Manual"). A "subject" is defined as "a person whose conduct is within the scope of the grand jury's investigation." *Id.* Although the DOJ Manual does not define the term, a witness is a person subpoenaed to testify before the grand jury who is neither a subject nor a target.

The government's characterization of your client's culpability will affect the treatment he will receive from the prosecutor. For instance, although the grand jury may subpoena and interrogate a subject or a target, DOJ guidelines prohibit prosecutors from compelling a target to appear before a grand jury without the approval of the grand jury and the U.S. attorney or assistant attorney general. DOJ Manual § 9-11.151.

Determining the government's characterization of your client is not always easy. Although prosecutors often notify targets and subjects of their status, they need not do so. Additionally, prosecutors do not always use the classifications consistently, and, in any event, your client's status may change as the investigation proceeds and evidence develops.

Assuming that your client's proposed testimony presents a genuine risk of criminal liability—and that he does have Fifth Amendment rights—you can and should ask the prosecutor to withdraw the subpoena on this basis. This is imperative if your client is the target of the grand jury investigation, because DOJ policies frown upon calling the target before the grand jury to make him assert his Fifth Amendment right. DOJ Manual at § 9-11.154.

If you cannot convince the prosecutor that the Fifth Amendment applies, you should move to quash the subpoena. The motion goes to the judge supervising the grand jury that issued the subpoena. A hearing on this issue may occur in camera, if necessary, so that the witness can explain the claim of privilege in confidence to the judge.

If the court rules that your client has properly asserted his Fifth Amendment privilege such that he may validly refuse to testify, the government's lawyer has three choices: (1) forgo your client's grand jury testimony and simply prosecute him, (2) compel his testimony by a grant of immunity from prosecution, or (3) leave him alone. (By the way, if the court rules against your Fifth Amendment claim, your client may insist that you find another way to challenge the subpoena. More on that later.)

Since this article is not meant as advice on how to get your client prosecuted, I will not dwell on it long. You should know, however, how prosecution or a guilty plea affects the obligation to testify. Convictions can wipe out Fifth Amendment protections, and your client may have to testify. Plea agreements, on the other hand, may allow your client to admit guilt to a lesser charge while requiring that he provide testimony in return for a promise of nonprosecution on other counts. Such agreements, almost always put in writing in the federal system, can be complex when, for example, a defendant pleads guilty to one of the underlying crimes that expose him to prosecution under RICO. You must be sure the agreement gives you all the protection you need.

If you are lucky, prosecution of your client may not be the government's chief goal. Or, you may convince the prosecutor that your client is more useful as a witness than as a defendant or a convict. The government may then immunize your client and compel his testimony.

Immunity

Prosecutors prefer not to grant immunity. An immunized witness is a courtroom liability, an inviting target for cross-examination on the deal he struck with the government. Therefore, if you demand immunity, the prosecutor will scrutinize her case to determine if your client's testimony is essential. If the government cannot prosecute its target without your client's cooperation, it will immunize the client or prosecute him. If, however, your client happens to be the principal target, forget about immunity.

Department of Justice guidelines require the prosecutor to consider a variety of factors before offering immunity, including the value of your client's testimony, your client's relative culpability and criminal record, and the possibility of successfully prosecuting him before granting immunity. *See DOJ Manual* at § 9-23.210. Such considerations can lead to immunity for many kinds of miscreants. Thus, the small army of contractors who bribed government officials, or even the contract murderer whose hits were orchestrated by an organized-crime superior, might be candidates for immunity.

Although your client probably wants to avoid prosecution *and* testifying, you cannot prevent a determined prosecutor from immunizing your client and compelling his testimony unless your client possesses some other recognized testimonial privilege. Unfortunately, such instances are rare. Accordingly, most immunized witnesses have only two choices: testify or risk contempt. Most testify.

If you are seeking immunity, you must know what the concept means. There are two kinds of immunity: transactional immunity and use immunity.

Transactional immunity protects a witness from prosecution for any matter about which he testifies under the grant of immunity. If, for example, your client bribes government officials to obtain contracts, transactional immunity can shield him from prosecution for the bribes he paid. Transactional immunity is powerful protection, but it is rarely granted to people who then get off scot-free. Instead, transactional immunity is usually part of a plea agreement or a by-product of a successful prosecution: A defendant may be convicted of—or plead guilty to—one or a few of many charged offenses; he then agrees—or is compelled—to testify against others on their roles in the conspiracy. In such a situation, the government may approve transactional immunity as to those additional crimes.

Use immunity confers more limited protection. It is employed more often when the witness is not first indicted. With use immunity, the government may not rely on the immunized witness's testimony or any leads derived from that testimony in a later prosecution of the witness. 18 U.S.C. § 6002. Use immunity defeats a claimed privilege against self-incrimination because the law regards a witness who testifies under a grant of use immunity as the equivalent of someone not compelled to testify. *Kastigar v. United States*, 406 U.S. 441 (1972).

Immunity is no license to lie. Immunized testimony still may be used to prosecute the witness for perjury and related offenses. In addition, because use immunity affords limited protection, the government may occasionally prosecute a witness for the crimes underlying his testimony. That is not common, however. Unless your client commits perjury, use immunity is usually equivalent to transactional immunity. There is a good reason for this. As we will see, in the rare case where the government prosecutes a witness after she testifies under use immunity, it shoulders the substantial burden of proving that the immunized testimony is not being used in any way.

If the government has decided to grant your client immunity, a federal prosecutor must choose either "formal" or "informal" immunity. Formal (or statutory) immunity, the rarer of the two options, is more cumbersome—requiring approval within the Justice Department bureaucracy—and, more important, does not offer the prosecutor the advantages of informal immunity.

The statutory scheme that governs formal immunity, 18 U.S.C. §§ 6001–6005, authorizes a federal court to grant use immunity after an application from the U.S. attorney. Such immunity may be granted for testimony in federal court, before a grand jury or agency, and in congressional proceedings. To obtain congressional immunity (as obtained by John Dean with regard to Watergate and Oliver North during the Iran-Contra investigation), two-thirds of the committee or a majority of the House involved must approve the application. In administrative proceedings, a government agency may grant immunity with the Attorney General's approval.

To immunize a witness formally in a criminal proceeding, the government applies *ex parte* to the court. The prosecutor simply alleges that the testimony sought is in the public interest and that the witness is likely to invoke the Fifth Amendment. In a step that is usually ministerial, and is often taken without notice to you or your client, the court will confer—perhaps a better term is impose—immunity.

Generally, statutory immunity covers only the proceedings for which immunity was specifically granted. *Pillsbury Co. v. Conboy*, 459 U.S. 248, 263–64 (1983) (witness who received use immunity for grand jury testimony properly asserted Fifth Amendment privilege at later proceeding where not given fresh grant of immunity). Therefore, if your client receives formal immunity, be sure that the court's order extends to any prep sessions and later trial appearances. If the court order is not clearly worded, you may have to get a separate, informal immunity agreement covering these situations.

Most immunity agreements are not formal. They come only in the form of a letter agreement from the prosecutor addressed to you. Although a few courts have frowned on informal immunity, *see, e.g., United States v. Biaggi,* 675 F. Supp. 790, 804 (S.D.N.Y. 1987), these agreements are commonplace and enforceable. An immunity contract usually emerges from negotiations you have with the prosecutor after your client receives a subpoena. The letter or letters can cover interviews, prep sessions, and testimony.

A prosecutor may require some convincing that it is in the interest of justice to immunize your client. Although a prosecutor may grant immunity blindly, without "sampling" your client's testimony, this occurs only in rare cases in which the prosecutor already knows what your client is going to say, but needs his testimony anyway. *See* Larry D. Thompson and Phyllis B. Sumner, "Structuring Informal Immunity: Problems of Scope and Enforcement," 8 *Crim. Justice* 17, 18 (Spring 1993) (hereinafter "Thompson"). In the vast majority of cases, however, before agreeing to immunize a witness the prosecutor will try to pin down the substance of the witness's testimony by obtaining a proffer and/or conducting an "off-the-record" interview.

A prosecutor may request that defense counsel make a proffer of the witness's anticipated testimony. Proffers are usually given in one of two forms: (1) the hypothetical proffer, in which counsel "suggests" the occurrence of specific events but does not attribute the information to the witness, or (2) the subject-matter proffer in which counsel notifies the prosecutor of the various topics upon which the witness is prepared to testify. *Id.* at 18–19; *see also* Roger C. Spaeder, "The Challenge of Negotiating Immunity: What You Must Know Before You Seek Immunity For Your Client," 7 *Crim. Justice* 8, 12 (Summer 1992) (hereinafter "Spaeder").

In making a proffer on behalf of a client, you should: obtain an agreement that the proffer does not waive the attorney-client privilege, make the proffer orally and without your client's presence, and attempt to obtain a grant of informal immunity to prevent the prosecutor's use of the proffer. Thompson at 19.

Off-the-Record Interview

In addition to, or instead of, the proffer, a federal prosecutor interested in discussing immunity may offer the witness a "free ticket" to visit the U.S. attorney's office. This visit will be used to interview your client, supposedly off-the-record. The invitation—which usually comes after discussions between the prosecutor and the defense lawyer—will read something like this:

> During our earlier conversations, you stated that your client is interested in meeting with the investigating agents and me for purposes of an "off-the-record" proffer or discussion. We are interested in pursuing this matter, and will consider such a proffer or discussion in formulating an appropriate resolution of this case.
>
> So that there are no misunderstandings, this letter will clarify the ground rules. First, no statements made by you or your client during the off-the-record proffer or discussion will be used against your client in any criminal case. Second, the government may make derivative use of and may pursue any information provided by you or your client. Third, in the event that your client is a witness at trial and offers testimony materially different from any statement made or other information provided off-the-record, the attorney for the government may cross-examine your client concerning any statements made or other information previously provided. This provision is necessary to ensure that your client does not abuse this offer, does not make materially false statements to a government agency, and does not commit perjury.

As a careful reading of the letter shows, such interviews are scarcely "off-the-record." The prosecutor's letter offers little real protection. Despite the risk, the free-ticket discussion may be necessary to obtain immunity, with the government using the threat of prosecution as the stick for the carrot of immunity. You can and should try to negotiate more favorable terms for your client, including a broad immunity agreement in connection with the meeting. Whether you get it will depend on the strength of the prosecutor's case, the importance of your client's testimony, and the status of the investigation.

After the prosecutor decides to immunize your client and use him as a witness, she will send an offer of informal immunity (sometimes called letter immunity). The offer could, depending upon your negotiations, read as follows:

> Based on your representation that your client will cooperate with the Government in its investigation of alleged unlawful activities by [the target individual or company] if he is granted immunity, the Government hereby grants immunity to your client on the following terms and conditions:
>
> 1. No testimony or other information provided by your client in this matter, pursuant to this agreement, or any information directly or indirectly derived from such testimony or other information, will be used against your client in any criminal case, except in a prosecution for perjury or giving a false statement.

2. Your client must testify truthfully and completely before the Federal Grand Jury conducting this investigation, and at any later hearing or trial, when called upon to do so by the Government. Your client must furnish any documents in his custody or possession or under his control that are relevant to the investigation. He must also make himself available for interviews by lawyers and law enforcement officers of the Government upon request and reasonable notice.

3. Notwithstanding this grant of immunity, your client can and will be prosecuted under federal perjury statutes for any materially false statement made under oath.

4. This agreement is in lieu of a formal immunity. It does not and shall not be construed to impose any duty or limitation on the Government beyond that which would be imposed by a formal immunity order.

5. This agreement is limited to those statements made by your client concerning acts committed as of the date of this letter and does not limit in any way the right or ability of the Government to investigate or prosecute crimes occurring hereafter.

Certain aspects of letter immunity deserve emphasis. Although something like the text set forth is likely to emerge, it is not inevitable. Almost anything is negotiable. It all depends on what the client knows, what he has done, and what the prosecutor needs.

Note that the grant of letter immunity affords the prosecutor advantages not available under the narrow terms of the immunity statute. It enables the government, before a jury, to bolster your client's testimony by pointing out the horrible events that will befall him if he lies. By contrast, statutory immunity usually comes in a spare, form-book order. District judges do not become involved in negotiating the more elaborate terms found in letter agreements.

Although some prosecutors claim that the biggest problem with a grant of informal immunity is that the courts may interpret it more broadly than the government intended, your concern is just the opposite. You must guard against finding later that you have less than you thought. To avoid any problem, specify in the agreement the type and scope of immunity granted, the prosecutors or districts bound by the agreement, and the proceedings to which the agreement applies. *See* Thompson at 21. Additionally, don't use terms like "full cooperation" or "full and complete testimony," which could leave the later determination of your client's compliance up to the judgment of the prosecutor. *Id.*; *see also* Spaeder at 10. An immunity agreement is a contract just like any other contract. If your client breaches the terms, the government's obligation to perform evaporates, and it can use your client's testimony to prosecute him.

Another important point: although statutory immunity protects against prosecution in other districts and by state and local governments, informal immunity agreements usually will bind only federal prosecutors in the particular district from which the letter was issued. If your client's conduct subjects him to prosecution in more than one federal jurisdiction, or in a state or local jurisdiction, you must argue for additional protection (and you may have to go to each jurisdiction separately) or move to quash the subpoena until your client receives a formal statutory immunity order. Likewise, state prosecutors' grant of formal or informal immunity does not bind their federal counterparts.

State immunity is too vast and varied a topic to treat here, but a few highlights can alert you to the lurking complications. For example, although the federal statute provides only use immunity, immunity statutes of about half of the states provide transactional immunity. 2 S. Beale & W. Bryson, *Grand Jury Law and Practice,* Ch. 9 (Supp. 1989). Indeed, some states have found use immunity to be insufficient to protect the broader privilege against self-incrimination defined by their state constitutions and, therefore, permit only transactional immunity. *See, e.g., State v. Thrift,* 440 S.E.2d 341 (S.C. 1994); *State v. Gonzalez,* 853 P.2d 526 (Alaska 1993). As in the federal system, almost all states require a prosecutor to apply for a court order before immunity can be granted and testimony compelled (although informal immunity agreements are common and are generally upheld). In addition, most states give courts discretion to refuse an immunity order when, for example, the court finds that compelling the testimony would be unjust or contrary to the public interest, or would subject the witness to prosecution in another jurisdiction. A few states, including New York, Florida, and Oklahoma, grant automatic transactional immunity to grand jury witnesses. N.Y. Crim. Proc. Law § 190.40 (McKinney 1993); Fla. Stat. Ann. § 914.04 (West 1996); Okla. Const. art. II, § 27 (West 1996). Finally, a few jurisdictions forbid using a grant of immunity to compel grand jury testimony from targets or prospective defendants. *See* A. Amsterdam, *Trial Manual for the Defense of Criminal Cases* § 161 (1984).

What if immunity is not what you want? No matter what the prosecution has to offer, some witnesses do not want to testify. Some have good reasons. Immunized testimony may be used in noncriminal proceedings. If your client receives immunity in an insider-trading prosecution, for example, his testimony may provide the foundation for a costly civil lawsuit against him. Lawyers have been disbarred based on testimony given under a grant of immunity.

Other witnesses have practical reasons to remain silent that are no less compelling. Some develop cold feet about testifying. Fear can be a powerful motivator, as can loyalty or friendship. Potential witnesses not only may refuse to testify, but they may lie. Regardless of whether your client received use, transactional, formal, or informal immunity, the prosecutor offered him no protection from charges of perjury or contempt. Getting immunity and then lying is a mistake.

Refusing to testify after a court grants immunity can also lead to civil and criminal sanctions, as a former Whitewater business associate of President and Mrs. Clinton recently learned. *In re Grand Jury Subpoena (McDougal),* 97 F.3d 1090 (8th Cir. 1996). And there is another risk: If the client violates an informal immunity agreement, the prosecutor might consider her in breach and prosecute the previously ignored crimes.

To avoid these results, you should—before your client refuses to testify—move to quash the subpoena if you can invoke an appropriate privilege or detect some irregularity in the subpoena or underlying proceeding. Remember, however, that because the grant of immunity can defeat the privilege afforded by the Fifth Amendment, fear of self-incrimination is no help. You must find other privileges that can provide greater protection.

Attorney-Client Privilege

If your client consulted a lawyer in connection with the transaction at issue or is himself a lawyer, he may be able to avoid testifying by asserting the attorney-client privilege. You should know, however, that federal courts have narrowed the attorney-client privilege in recent years, precluding protection for fee arrangements and client identity. The courts have reasoned that such information falls outside the scope of the attorney-client privilege because it does not relate to the "substance of legal advice rendered by the attorney" or because such information is not confidential.

Client identity and fee information may nonetheless find shelter in the attorney-client privilege if disclosure would reveal client confidences essential to obtaining legal advice, or if such disclosure would have the effect of significantly incriminating the client. *See In re Grand Jury Proceeding (GJ90-2),* 946 F.2d 746, 748–49 (11th Cir. 1991).

Remember also the crime/fraud doctrine, which provides another important exception to the attorney-client privilege. Here, otherwise privileged client confidences lose any protection if they were communicated in furtherance of a crime or fraud. For a more detailed treatment of this privilege and others, *see* Capra, "The Federal Law of Privileges," 16 LITIGATION, No. 1, at 32 (Fall 1989), and Max D. Stern & David A. Hoffman, "Privileged Informers: The Attorney Subpoena Problem and a Proposal for Reform," 136 *U. Pa. L. Rev.* 1783 (1988).

Other grounds for moving to quash a grand jury subpoena include the adverse spousal testimony privilege and the confidential marital communications privilege. The adverse spousal testimony privilege protects spouses from being compelled to testify against each other while they are married. The privilege is, however, limited in that it may be raised only by the witness-spouse. Additionally, one court has held that the privilege may be raised only if the nontestifying spouse is the target of the grand jury investigation. *See In re Snoonian,* 502 F.2d 110 (1st Cir. 1974).

The confidential marital communications privilege protects confidential communications made during the marriage. It may be asserted by either spouse, and may even be asserted after a divorce as long as the pertinent communication occurred during the marriage. Once again, be aware that the protections vary from state to state.

If you happen to represent a member of Congress or one of her aides, you may try to quash federal grand jury subpoenas based on the Speech and Debate Clause of the Constitution. *See* U.S. Const. art. I, § 6, cl. 1. This privilege protects any material that has been discussed in a congressional session or that constitutes an integral part of Congress's deliberative legislative process. *Gravel v. United States,* 408 U.S. 606 (1972).

Suppose there is no available privilege and your client does not want to testify, even with immunity. What can you do? Not much. The law provides few additional safe harbors. One is Rule 17(c) of the Federal Rules of Criminal Procedure, which permits any person—including even an immunized witness—to move to quash his grand jury subpoena if "compliance would be unreasonable or oppressive." In *In re Grand Jury Proceedings (Schofield),* 486 F.2d 85 (3d Cir. 1973), the Third Circuit said a subpoena might be "unreasonable or oppressive" for a number of reasons. These include (1) overbreadth; (2) requests for irrelevant information; (3) lack of authority to conduct the investigation; (4) improper issuance of the subpoena; (5) improper purpose of the subpoena, as when it is designed solely to gather evidence for a pending civil case; (6) lack of good faith (e.g., a subpoena issued solely to harass); and (7) to compel an appearance in the U.S. attorney's office for interrogation outside the grand jury.

Illegal Surveillance

Grand jury witnesses may also move to quash their subpoenas if the investigation resulted from, or has been tainted by, illegal electronic surveillance. If a motion to quash is unsuccessful, a witness can raise the defense of illegal electronic surveillance at a contempt hearing. *See Gelbard v. United States,* 408 U.S. 41, 51–52 (1972).

This may seem like a long list of additional grounds for challenging a subpoena. So it is, but the opportunities it affords are mostly theoretical. Subpoenas are rarely quashed on nonprivilege grounds.

Suppose all challenges have failed. Your client has had to testify under immunity. Showing no gratitude, the government now indicts him. An accused in this position should demand a hearing under *Kastigar v. United States,* 406 U.S. 441 (1972). At such a proceeding, the government must demonstrate that its evidence was derived from independent sources and was not based either directly or indirectly on immunized grand jury testimony. This is a heavy burden.

As a matter of Justice Department policy, the attorney general personally must authorize the prosecution of a previously immunized witness for offenses "either first disclosed in or closely related to" the substance of his compelled testimony. A prosecutor who believes that future prosecution of the immunized witness is possible must keep meticulous notes of witness testimony, and document all access to these materials. He must have equally clear records of the sources of evidence he will use in the prosecution.

Suppose you lost the *Kastigar* hearing or you represent an accused kingpin for whom immunity was never an issue. The testimony of an unindicted co-conspirator could help acquit your client. If only you could immunize the witness and force him to testify, acquittal would be certain.

It is a nice idea, but it probably won't work. Immunity, an invaluable tool for prosecutors, is normally unavailable to an accused. The decision to grant immunity lies solely within the discretion of the Executive Branch. *United States v. Warfield*, 97 F.3d 1014, 1020 (8th Cir. 1996). Thus, courts generally hold that they lack the authority to grant immunity to defense witnesses and cannot compel prosecutors to do so.

Recently, however, several courts have recognized an exception to this rule. They have expressed a willingness to exercise their inherent equitable power to compel the government to immunize a defense witness when the government has deliberately distorted the fact-finding process by refusing to grant immunity. *See, e.g., United States v. Ballistrea*, 101 F.3d 827, 837 (2d Cir. 1996) (court should order government to grant immunity to defense witness where: (1) government has engaged in discriminating use of immunity to gain tactical advantage, (2) witness's testimony is material, exculpatory, and not cumulative, and (3) testimony is unobtainable from other source); *United States v. Young*, 86 F.3d 944, 947 (9th Cir. 1996) (exception to general rule that criminal defendant may not compel government to grant immunity to witness, is established by showing: (1) testimony is relevant and (2) government distorted fact-finding process by denying immunity); *United States v. Abbas*, 74 F.3d 506, 511–12 (4th Cir.) (recognizing that despite general rule that district court lacks power to grant immunity or to force government to grant immunity, district court can compel prosecution to grant immunity to defense witness when: (1) defendant shows prosecutorial misconduct or overreaching, and (2) proffered testimony would be "material, exculpatory and unavailable from other sources"), *cert. denied*, 116 S. Ct. 1868 (1996).

In determining whether the government has deliberately distorted the fact-finding process, courts consider all of the relevant circumstances, including the exculpatory value of the proposed witness's testimony, any reasons the government may have for refusing to grant immunity (including anticipated or pending criminal proceedings against the witness), and the grant of immunity or a favorable plea bargain to prosecution witnesses. Such exceptions are rarely granted. Nonetheless you should demand that the prosecutor request immunity for your client (or for a favorable defense witness), or you should file a motion seeking it.

If all else fails, your final point of attack is the immunized testimony others have offered against your client. Remember that a co-conspirator's immunized testimony must be viewed with suspicion. Hammer him on cross-examination about the sweetheart deal he received—a deal, of course, that you desperately wanted for your client—and explain to the jury that the government seeks to convict an innocent person on the word of an admitted criminal.

Basic Strategy in Federal Criminal Defense Litigation

George J. Cotsirilos and Robert M. Stephenson

In your reception area sits a person staring starkly at the wall. His face is ash gray and drawn, perhaps reflecting recent sleepless nights. His appearance is surprising. He is an executive vice president at a major bank, a person of means with a lovely family, who lives on a tree-lined street in an affluent suburb.

This peaceful existence was shattered a week ago, when a federal grand jury returned a 20-count indictment charging him with violation of the federal bank fraud statute and the Racketeer Influenced and Corrupt Organizations chapter of the Organized Crime Control Act. If convicted, he faces a substantial mandatory jail sentence, a significant mandatory fine and restitution order, and a period of supervised release upon service of the mandatory incarceration period. In addition, he risks a ruined reputation and a broken home.

Scenes like this, where human liberty is at stake, are familiar to the criminal defense lawyer. Criminal defense work is the most romantic in the law. Our democratic processes are dedicated to protecting individual freedoms and dignity. Indeed, the Sixth Amendment of the United States Constitution mandates the role of the criminal defense lawyer by providing the criminally accused the right to counsel. Thus, there is no nobler undertaking than representing defendants threatened with the loss of their liberty. With this task comes a heavy burden—the obligation to provide effective assistance. Here are some ways to do that.

The first client interview is the most important meeting you will ever have with the client. Gain the confidence and trust of the distraught client; deal with the psychological trauma he is experiencing. Always allow sufficient time for the interview. First impressions leave an indelible mark. A

George J. Cotsirilos and Robert M. Stephenson are members of Cotsirilos, Stephenson, Tighe & Streicker, Ltd., in Chicago.

crisply conducted interview, with no opportunity for the client to express his thoughts, spells doom for your later relationship. At the outset what you say is less important than having understanding and a listening ear.

If possible, your work should have begun before this interview. If the client already has been indicted, obtain a copy of the indictment. Become thoroughly familiar with the factual allegations of each count and the statutes involved. In addition, contact the prosecutor who is assigned to the case. Explain that you may be representing a defendant in the case and that background information would help with your first client meeting. In most instances, the prosecutor will cooperate. If the prosecutor does not yet know much about the case, ask for permission to speak to the investigating agent.

If the client has not been indicted before your first meeting, you should still speak with the government. Discover the scope of the investigation and your client's role in it. If the case involves multiple defendants or subjects, talk with the lawyers representing them. They may provide you with a reservoir of knowledge about the case. This kind of preparation enhances a client's confidence in his lawyer.

Suicidal Impulses

Often when the client arrives for the first interview, he is frightened and bewildered. He sees his life crumbling into oblivion and may even have suicidal impulses. Your first task is to ease the client's tension. If you do not already know the client, introduce yourself and describe the nature of your practice. Discuss the lawyer's role in the case. Assure the client that you represent him, that his interests are paramount, that you owe him total loyalty, and that you will do everything within the bounds of propriety to protect his rights.

Explain the attorney-client privilege and the work product doctrine in layman's terms. It is important for the client to understand that communications between lawyer and client are confidential and are protected from disclosure except in very rare circumstances. Encourage the client to talk freely. Impress upon him the importance of his participation throughout the case. He should talk with you about the case and also about any problems that confront him or his family. In turn, tell the client you are willing to deal with whatever arises.

Then ask the client whether there are any problems he wants to discuss with you such as the jeopardy of professional licenses, related civil actions, and bond in the event of a conviction. Explain to the client that your representation is complete and genuine.

Next, review the indictment generally. If the client is not yet under indictment, discuss the subject matter and scope of the investigation. Let the client know that you have prepared beforehand. Tell him about your discussions with the prosecutor or the investigating agent. The client is entitled to know the obstacles that confront him.

Probe the client's background—his employment history, education, family, military record, and past contacts with authorities. Listen to him. Here is your first opportunity to know whether you have succeeded in gaining his trust and confidence.

Complete Candor

Only then are you ready to focus on the client's version of the specific charges in the indictment or the investigation. This is also the time to respond to any additional problems, personal or otherwise, that the client has raised. Emphasize the need for complete candor. Compare yourself to a doctor treating a patient. Without the correct information, you cannot diagnose the disease or recommend treatment. Avoid extensive note-taking during this stage of the interview. Nothing is served at this time by placing things in concrete. Recollections change as they are refreshed.

In some cases it may not be wise to discuss the client's version of the events at the initial interview. It may be best to await the results of your independent investigation. Then, after thoroughly reviewing your information with the client, you can ask about the client's version. If you believe that the client does not have total confidence in you, or has a faulty or confused memory, then defer discussion of the client's version until a later date.

You must discuss the client's fee arrangement at the initial interview. To avoid any misunderstandings, make certain that you have a written fee agreement. Meticulously record your hours, describing the actual work performed for each hour. At the end of each month, give the client a monthly status report describing the work done and the status of the amount owed to you. He is entitled to no less. Conversely, the monthly notice to the client provides the client with an opportunity to question the bill and services rendered. Failure to object to monthly status reports helps provide a basis to establish the reasonableness of the fees.

Before the initial interview ends, tell the client not to speak to anyone else about the case. If he is contacted by anyone, he should politely decline comment and say that he is following your advice. A questioner who persists should be referred to you, and the client should advise you immediately of the contact.

Avoid appraising the case at the initial interview. Early predictions are rarely correct and often return to haunt the predictor. However, a client who has an unrealistic view of his problem should be brought back to reality. If possible, tell the client generally about his chances of success, or in the event of failure, the likely punishment. As investigation and preparation proceed, the lawyer can be more specific in assessing the case.

When the initial interview ends, tell the client that you will begin work on his case immediately and that you will keep him informed about your progress. Encourage him to communicate with you again when he feels the urge. When the client leaves your office, he should feel at least a little better than the distraught person who first sought your help.

Once you begin your defense of a criminal case, a vigorous motion practice is essential. Study the indictment and the manner in which the grand jury investigation was conducted. Instead of assuming that things have been done properly, scrutinize every move of the prosecutor and investigating agent and every paragraph of the indictment.

Some objections must be made before trial or else they will be waived. *See* Fed. R. Crim. P. 12(b). Many of these pretrial motions also help to define the issues at trial. A motion for a bill of particulars, a motion to suppress unconstitutionally seized evidence, a motion to exclude evidence, such as evidence of prior convictions, or a motion for severance based on improper or prejudicial joinder each limits the boundaries of admissible proof against the client. A favorable ruling on one of these motions may deprive a prosecutor of a key element to his case.

These motions may also force the prosecution to disclose information that otherwise would have remained hidden in the normal discovery available in criminal litigation. *See* Fed. R. Crim. P. 16. Finally, pretrial motions may place before the court mitigating circumstances that serve to explain the client's conduct, even if they do not constitute a legal defense.

For example, in a bid-rigging conspiracy case brought under the federal antitrust and mail fraud laws, the defendant moved for leave to present state-of-mind evidence to show that he had acted as he did because he feared economic reprisals from a dominating labor union. Although the trial court ultimately rejected the proffer because it was not evidence of a legal defense, the information proved very helpful when the court had to decide how to sentence the defendant.

The other virtue of filing legitimate pretrial motions, even if they are denied, is that they prolong the proceedings. Buying time often increases the likelihood of a favorable turn of events in a criminal case. Exculpatory evidence may turn up; recollections may change; prosecutorial misconduct may surface. At the very least, a vigorous use of properly available motions creates obstacles to the prosecution that may improve your bargaining position for a more acceptable disposition of the charge. Remember: Delay never serves the prosecution. More than likely, it will benefit the defense.

Thorough Investigation

Most criminal cases ultimately turn on the facts rather than the law. A successful defense depends on a thorough investigation. Your efforts should exceed the prosecutor's rather than pale by comparison. Employ independent investigators for much of this work. Good ones always are available and often come from the ranks of former government agents. The investigator's fee will be less than you would have to charge the client for this work, and your time will be freed for other tasks. Because of their expertise, training, and contacts, good investigators have access to people and information that are difficult for lawyers to uncover. Finally, investigators can testify to establish a key point of the defense or to impeach a prosecution witness.

The nature of the case dictates the type of investigator. In a tax case, hire a former intelligence agent from the Internal Revenue Service or a reputable accounting firm. Other financial crime cases may require a former FBI agent or a postal inspector who is familiar with the kind of business involved in the case.

Do everything possible to preserve work-product protection for the investigator's activities. You, not the client, should hire him. Draft an employment agreement, carefully stating that the investigator acts as your agent. Require him to surrender his work to you upon request, and make him notify you first before responding to any subpoena. Instruct the investigator not to tape interviews or to memorialize them verbatim in any form. Instead, the investigator should discuss with you his impressions of the information derived from the interviews.

Finally, always keep the lines of communication open with the prosecutor. Any information you receive as a result of these communications is part of a thorough defense investigation. Immunity or some other favorable disposition may become possible. Always be ready to listen. To close this avenue of investigation only hurts the client. Also work closely with other defense counsel. If there are common defenses, the attorney-client privilege protects communications among counsel and their respective clients. Of course, if the defenses are antagonistic, you must go it alone. Even then, do not sever all lines of communication. There is validity to the timeworn phrase, "United we stand, divided we fall."

After completing your investigation, meet with the client to review the results, including your discussions with the prosecutor; to discuss the client's version of the events; and to evaluate his position. Based on this meeting, you will decide either to prepare for trial or to recommend withdrawing the not guilty plea. If this meeting occurs before the client has been indicted, the client must decide whether to seek immunity.

When you review the case with the client, be frank and open. Do not paint any false pictures, but do not be a false prophet of doom. The final decision about how to proceed rests with the client, but he will seek your advice. Give it. The client hired you for that purpose.

If an indictment has been returned, the number one priority is keeping the client out of jail or minimizing the amount of his jail time. If that result can be attained only through trying the case, then prepare for trial. However, if the prosecution is willing to accept a guilty plea in return for a favorable disposition, consider the offer seriously. It would be intolerable for the client to reject the offer and then be sentenced to substantial jail time after a protracted trial.

If prison is an inevitable result, with or without a trial, the next priority is to obtain the least restrictive sentence available, such as a sentence to a work release program. Sometimes trying the case is the only way to achieve this goal. At the very least, a trial may bring out mitigating factors to convince the court that the conduct charged in the indictment is not as heinous as it first appeared. Most often, however (especially under the Federal Sentencing Guidelines), a negotiated plea is the only vehicle to reduce the incarceration period.

It is vital to know the sentencing habits of the judge. Before some judges, it is very dangerous to plead guilty without either some limit on the potential maximum period of prison or an agreement on the exact sentence to be imposed. Finally, if your client is the object of a grand jury probe but has not yet been indicted, the first priority is to avoid indictment. Explore the possibility of obtaining immunity, either by court order or by letter agreement, in exchange for your client's cooperation with the grand jury.

If your client decides to go to trial and you expect it to be a protracted one, make certain the client understands the costs—especially if there is little hope of success. Make certain the client knows all the consequences of a guilty plea. Explore the possibilities that the client may lose his professional license or face private civil-damages suits. These consequences may be as important as the risk of jail, and the client may prefer to "go the course."

If the client decides to go to trial, begin your preparation immediately. Some key commandments apply in every case.

- Know the documentary exhibits. Generally, the prosecutor will give you copies of the prosecution exhibits prior to trial. Study them. Commit them to memory. Prepare an exhibit list for those exhibits as well as for your exhibits.
- Review the prior statements of the prosecution's witnesses. In our district, the prosecutor generally discloses those statements before trial. To a great extent, your cross-examination of these witnesses will be shaped by the witnesses' prior statements and other valuable impeachment material.
- Prepare an outline of your closing argument before the trial. Although this outline will change to match the evidence, your investigation should enable you to develop a theory of defense that will shape the argument. If it does not, you are not ready for trial.
- Outline your cross-examination of the prosecution witnesses. Elicit only information that supports the defense theory and forget about everything else. Many a defense lawyer has proved the

prosecution's case during his cross-examinations. Do not join that long gray line of barristers.
- Plan as though the defendant will testify, but try the case on the assumption that the defendant will not testify. Too often, the defendant is his own worst witness. If the defendant is nervous, arrogant, or timid, or there is some other reason he will not be a good witness, keep him off the stand. Build your defense around disinterested witnesses and cross-examination of the prosecution's witnesses. At times, properly instructed juries do acquit without hearing from the defendant. Conversely, a jury that has doubt about guilt will convict after hearing from a defendant whose testimony is basically weak or who is badly impeached.
- Prepare the defendant before he testifies. This preparation should begin as early as possible, even during the investigative stages. Go through mock cross-examinations with the client; ask him the hard questions. Continue this process until that fateful day when you decide that the client must testify. Then, Godspeed!

Unfortunately, despite your best efforts, the trier of fact may convict your client. This does not end your work. Indeed, the services that you render the client at the time of sentencing may be the most meaningful of all.

Most districts have qualified probation offices that submit presentencing reports. Do not rely on such a report. Prepare a written sentencing brochure introducing the client to the judge and relating the client's family and employment history. Tell the judge about the client's military record, his philanthropic efforts, and the state of his health. Submit character references from people who know the client best. Have the client's children or spouse write on his behalf.

Since the enactment of the Federal Sentencing Guidelines, defendant-prepared sentencing submissions have less effect on the ultimate sentence. However, the defendant in white collar crime cases usually has a wealth of material that will help persuade the court to give a more lenient sentence even under the Federal Sentencing Guidelines. Too often, lawyers forget that our primary task is to make it as difficult as possible for the court to sentence the client to jail.

Dealing with the Prosecutor

Howard Wilson

Fashioning an effective criminal defense requires going back to first principles. According to the Supreme Court, one of the most basic principles governing a U.S. attorney is that his office's interest in a criminal prosecution "is not that it shall win a case, but that justice shall be done." *Berger v. United States*, 295 U.S. 78 (1935). More than 35 years after *Berger*, the United States Attorney for the Southern District of New York issued a written code elaborating that standard. He instructed his staff not to pursue a case unless convinced of the guilt of the accused and the rightness of the prosecutor's position.

Such precepts evoke skepticism among criminal defense lawyers, but I believe most prosecutors try to follow them. They try to make fair, accurate judgments about the truth in a case. In doing this, prosecutors must think of more than just getting an indictment. They must also consider whether the available evidence can persuade a jury of the defendant's guilt beyond a reasonable doubt, and not just whether it establishes probable cause.

What is the point of reciting these fundamentals? The answer is that such basics should form a framework for defense counsel dealing with a prosecutor. In my view, if the facts warrant, the first step in your defense is an appeal to the decency and fairness of the individual prosecutor. You must urge her to make the right decision.

Some may scoff at this advice. They reject prosecutors' supposedly high standards as platitudes. I think such cynics do their clients a disservice. A prosecutor is not the same as an adversary in a civil case. He is

---

Howard Wilson is a partner in the law firm of Rosenman & Colin in New York City, specializing in white collar criminal defense. He was chief of the criminal division in the U.S. Attorney's Office for the Southern District of New York from 1985 to 1988 and was chief assistant to the New York State Special Nursing Home Prosecutor from 1975 to 1976.

not obliged to make the most of his client's legal and factual position, regardless of the equities. Of course, not all prosecutors are as sensitive to their obligations as they should be. But most are, and the fact that all *should* be is the start of a defense strategy.

The first step is to analyze the facts. Do you have a case of simple innocence, where the prosecutor can be persuaded that he is making a mistake by pursuing your client? Is it a case where the prosecutor lacks the evidence to believe he can win? Does the prosecutor need your client's help? If you are unlucky, is it a case where the prosecutor knows enough that he probably cannot be dissuaded from bringing a criminal charge?

Answers depend on the facts, but the facts are hard to get. The best place to start is with your client, but even that presents problems. As all criminal practitioners know, a client may choose to be less than candid. Some clients think you will fight harder for them if you are not told the truth—especially if it is unpleasant. Others are simply distrustful and reluctant to bare their souls.

Apart from concerns about client candor, there are criminal defense lawyers who, almost as a matter of principle, refrain from asking their clients directly about the facts. They do this because they believe that they will have more flexibility if not personally encumbered by incriminating statements or unhelpful information. Such lawyers focus their fact gathering on what the prosecutor can learn or has learned from witnesses and documents. They do not press their clients about all aspects of the case.

I disagree. The preferred course is to learn as much as possible from the client (and others). Truly sound judgments and tactics require complete knowledge. If you have not questioned your client thoroughly, you may face a major surprise later and be unable to do anything about it.

At a minimum, the client must be asked the names of people who know the facts, and what they know or might have heard or seen. This will start you on the way to knowing what the prosecutor does (or could) know and what you can do about it. A review of the pertinent documents—if you can get them—will help fill out the situation. Conversations with others involved in the supposed criminal scheme—or, if they are represented, their lawyers—may provide further help.

All the time the prosecutor is conducting an investigation, you must constantly probe and ask questions to learn any new facts that have emerged. There are myriad ways to do this. The lawyers for those involved as subjects, targets, or witnesses can be helpful. If you decide to conduct interviews with, or even simply telephone, witnesses, be aware that your notes might become discoverable by the prosecutor and used if the witness testifies. You should try to ensure that the work product privilege will apply to those materials by avoiding a verbatim record of the conversation and fitting the information you receive into an overall analysis of the defense. If such witness interviews result in recollections helpful to your client, consider locking in the testimony by securing a written statement or affidavit.

While you are monitoring the investigation, instruct your client not to talk with witnesses. At best, such conversations are not careful or detailed and serve no useful defense purpose. You also will never know precisely what was said. Worse, they are not privileged, and are thus discoverable. Such conversations can also make the prosecutor suspicious of your client's conduct. In aggravated cases, the prosecutor may take such a dim view of these conversations that he will seek charges of obstruction of justice.

Another source for some of the facts is the prosecutor himself. In some cases, you should delay contacting the prosecutor. You may have been retained by someone who fears an investigation, even though he has not received a subpoena or a visit from the FBI. You may not want to alert the prosecutor to your client's identity or involvement—or to the fact that he has hired a criminal defense lawyer. Especially if the investigation appears dormant, or your client is not an object of any questioning, it may be best to avoid an early contact.

Talk to the Prosecutor

In most situations, however, there is no reason to avoid the prosecutor. Prosecutors deal all the time with innocent people who happen to have defense lawyers. In fact, if appropriate, you may choose to explain why you were retained. In any event, if you know that questions are being asked about your client, or he has received a grand jury subpoena, do not hesitate. Pick up the phone and call.

Usually, a meeting with the prosecutor will improve your understanding of the facts and the problems you face. Some prosecutors will freely discuss their case. They may outline the powerful evidence they have accumulated, and they may even let you listen to tape recordings they have made of your client. Such an "open file" approach is enlightening, but it is often bad news. Sometimes prosecutors really do have your client dead to rights. They may tell you so right from the start, especially if they hope to gain a quick plea or to secure your client's cooperation against others.

Other prosecutors may be reluctant to talk at all, especially early in an investigation. When you ask for a meeting, some just say no. Such prosecutors see a discussion with you as a waste of time. They may see you as a danger—someone who is trying to learn facts that they do not want you to know. They see no legitimate reason for any conversation at this early stage—unless you want to discuss a guilty plea or to cooperate in the investigation.

Most prosecutors fall between these extremes; they will tell you something—but not everything—about your client's status. In the federal system, a prosecutor should be willing to advise you whether your client is a target (a person whom the prosecutor then believes should be or will be charged with a crime); or a subject (someone the prosecutor does not yet think should or will be charged but whom he has nevertheless focused on as a possible target); or exclusively a witness.

These categories establish the general boundaries within which you must operate. Reluctance by the prosecutor to categorize your client should send up red flags. The prosecutor's caution may mean that she thinks something is suspicious about your client's conduct, but does not yet know where the investigation will take her. A lawyer should press the prosecutor hard for as explicit an answer as possible. If you do not get a clear response, act as if your client is a target.

How to read, and react to, the facts developed in an early meeting with the prosecutor can be a challenge. The prosecutor rarely knows all the facts until late in an investigation. Sometimes, he never learns all of them. What he thinks he knows may be just plain wrong. You may have information from elsewhere that shows the prosecutor's initial evaluation is a mistake—perhaps to your advantage. For example, the prosecutor may believe your client is merely a witness to a fraud at his company perpetrated by others, but you may have learned that the stolen money knowingly went into the client's pocket too. In such a case, you want to find a way for the client to remain a witness, and yet not speak to the prosecutor at all—or not until immunity has been obtained.

In many cases, you must realize that there is not just one set of facts that will determine what you may accomplish. There are the facts you are told by your client and others. There are the facts as the prosecutor sees them. And there are the facts as you believe them to be, or as a jury will most likely determine them. The "facts" in each of these categories may be different. You must keep them straight and use the variations to your client's advantage.

You begin with a realistic evaluation of what you can achieve. You may hope that your client can avoid prosecution because:

(1) He is innocent and you can persuade the prosecutor that he is; or
(2) The prosecutor *believes* the client should not be a target or subject and is at most a witness; or
(3) There is insufficient evidence of the client's guilt to permit a criminal case to go forward; or
(4) The client should obtain immunity because of the help he can provide the government; or
(5) There are mitigating factors that should convince the prosecutor not to pursue an indictment. (E.g., the client is 80 and not well or is the sole support of ten children.)

Finally, of course, you may conclude that none of these options is available, because a prosecution will surely result from the investigation and your client cannot avoid being named a defendant.

If, after careful assessment, you believe you can avoid prosecution, try to meet with the prosecutor to achieve that goal. Even where there is no chance to avoid prosecution, you may still gain from talking with the prosecutor. Such benefits can include:

(1) A favorable plea bargain;
(2) A limit on the nature or number of charges;
(3) Information about the prosecutor's witnesses, theories, and documents;
(4) Learning about your adversary—his strengths and weaknesses;
(5) Establishing a professional and cordial relationship—or a hostile and antagonistic one—that may be useful in your defense.

A word of warning concerning discussions with prosecutors: Make sure that *you* are careful and cautious. The open door to the prosecutor's office may allow him to learn more about your case and your tactics than you want. A conversation is a two-way street. As a prosecutor, I invariably learned helpful facts in meetings with defense counsel.

Before engaging in such conversations—or setting strategy generally—you must try to understand the individual prosecutor assigned to your case. You cannot do any dealing unless you know with whom you are dealing.

Prosecutorial Personalities

Prosecutors come in all sorts of personalities and temperaments. They mirror the variety of the legal profession—at least its litigation side. Some are tough and aggressive. Others are easygoing, open, and friendly. Some relish confrontations, while others prefer professional and congenial relations. Some are career prosecutors and plan to spend years in the job; they are less likely to care if they are seen as self-important and unfriendly. Others expect to be prosecutors for a brief time—three to five years—and are relatively young. They want to join the criminal defense bar in the future and may try to avoid hostility and needless arguments with future colleagues.

Different prosecutors often have different goals. Some will want a quick resolution; they will not be much concerned with the number of counts or the years your client may spend in jail. Others want to maximize punishment. Some prosecutors are afraid to lose any cases and will bring only strong ones. Others see each case as a challenge and are more willing to proceed with a thin prosecution.

Almost all prosecutors see themselves as "good guys"—as being on the right side of the case. They perceive themselves as guardians of justice, of society's moral values and laws. They have no real client—only a sense that they should do the right thing for the public. Not surprisingly, this attitude can at times breed arrogance and inflexibility. Defense counsel must learn to expect and deal with it.

The message is obvious: You must get to know the prosecutor to achieve the best results. Your own meetings with him will tell you a lot. You can also get information from other defense lawyers. Each prosecutor has great discretion; knowing what makes the prosecutor tick and establishing an appropriate relationship can be helpful.

In learning about the prosecutor, remember you may need to deal with others in addition to the government lawyer directly in charge of the case. If you are not satisfied with the results of your meetings with the prosecutor in charge, you have recourse to supervisory prosecutors. Defense lawyers sometimes fear that going over the head of the prosecutor will alienate him and disadvantage the client. Though that can happen, it should not deter you. Be candid when you intend to seek such a review; make it clear that you really have no choice if you are to represent your client.

The more critical calculation, however, is whether it makes sense to go to the supervisory level. Appeals of decisions normally committed to the line prosecutor's discretion when the facts and law fully support him will not be productive. In fact, a defense lawyer may lose credibility if he seeks review of every decision.

Still, where the facts and circumstances are favorable, and you believe there is a good argument that the line prosecutor is wrong, go forward. If the matters at stake are things like a demonstration of your client's innocence; the unfairness of going forward with a weak case; the wisdom of immunity for your client; or a guilty plea to limit your client's exposure, an appeal is often warranted.

Just as you should know the line prosecutor, you must also try to understand his superiors' roles before you meet them. A supervisory prosecutor's job is to correct mistakes and ensure that sound law enforcement decisions are made. As more experienced lawyers, supervisors are better able to evaluate the strengths and strategies in an investigation. Though a supervisor will tend to support his subordinate's position, he may have different attitudes and concerns. For example, a senior prosecutor is more likely to consider the normally limited resources of the prosecutor's office—and thus be more sympathetic to your efforts to avoid a trial.

Finally, do not ignore the possibility of appealing decisions to the head of the office—the United States attorney or the district attorney. Though the chief prosecutor, too, is wary about undercutting subordinates' decisions, if the issues are crucial or the prosecution particularly important (e.g., big complex cases, or cases involving significant people or events), you should ask to see the chief prosecutor. He is generally more experienced and more sensitive to broader public needs and the effective operation of his office than many of his subordinates. In the federal system, although the U.S. attorney will almost always be the final arbiter, appeals to the Department of Justice are possible. This is particularly true in RICO and tax cases, where the U.S. attorney must obtain Washington's approval before he can proceed.

Once you have set your goals and understand the prosecutors, what do you do? You must fashion a position based on reason that persuades the prosecutor that your client can advance one of the prosecutor's objectives. There are many such objectives: They include not indicting the innocent; not bringing a losing case; or helping catch the more important players in the criminal scheme.

Doing this will not be easy. Negotiations with a prosecutor can be an uphill fight. A prosecutor is often wary and cautious. He knows about his public obligations, but he has also heard the defense war stories. Prosecutors are well aware that some defense counsel like to joke about having just met their first innocent client, or their first such client in years. They have heard the old saying that a criminal trial has nothing to do with the search for the truth. Be prepared for the prosecutor to see you as a hired gun simply trying to get the best deal possible for a guilty client. Resistance will be a prosecutor's first instinct.

Despite this, your best approach in the preindictment stage is to be reasonable and friendly. Build your arguments to meet what you perceive to be the prosecutor's attitude, objectives, and personality. Even if skeptical, a prosecutor will usually listen and try to make a reasoned judgment.

Threats and accusations rarely will succeed. Prosecutors may not always be aggressive, but they are seldom intimidated. It surely will not help if you alienate the prosecutor—a certain result if you threaten him or impugn his motives or brains. Even if you have concluded that the prosecutor is a jerk, or worse, it won't help your client to say so. Rather than feeling threatened by such treatment, prosecutors revel in describing their encounters with tough-guy defense lawyers.

After an indictment, there are some who believe it is tactically wise to take on the prosecutor, both in personal dealings and in court. Such tactics work on occasion, but they are generally not productive and often harmful.

Judges may occasionally be receptive to arguments aimed at the mistakes of young, inexperienced prosecutors, but they more often dismiss claims of prosecutorial bad acts and conclude that defense counsel have no credibility. Juries, too, generally see prosecutors as honest public servants. They may reject the prosecution case as inadequate, but they will rarely believe the prosecutor has made it up. Ad hominem arguments often reinforce the strength of the prosecution case by making the prosecutor's credibility, which is high, a factor before the jury. Finally, angering the prosecutor through personal attacks can disadvantage defense counsel. Any nonmandatory professional courtesies that you might otherwise have gotten—advance information on witnesses or early production of their prior statements, for example—will not occur if you accuse the prosecutor of foul deeds.

In all conversations with the prosecutor, there is a principle you can count on: A prosecutor wants to win the case. There is little point in a long, expensive investigation, indictment, and trial if, at the end, there is an acquittal. Some prosecutors worry more than others about a loss, particularly when the case is important. Therefore, where a prosecution presents obvious and difficult proof problems, a defense lawyer can try to scare a prosecutor off. Failing that, he may negotiate a better plea for his client by working on the prosecutor's fear of possible defeat.

Pointing out the possibility of loss may work well in highly publicized cases, where well-known people are under investigation. A lot is probably riding on the prosecution, and everyone is watching. In pointing out the risk of a big loss, however, pay attention to personality. Some prosecutors will try to meet your challenge, insisting that the criteria for a decision are the same in all cases. They may go forward simply to demonstrate that they are fair and fearless. Other prosecutors may feel the pressure more acutely. They may worry about the public's perception of effective law enforcement, or their own futures, if they lose.

Efforts to persuade a prosecutor to accept your position are usually more fruitful early in an investigation. The longer an inquiry proceeds, the greater its momentum. Agents and prosecutors become committed to cases on which they have labored for years. The prosecutor may have developed a fixed view of the facts—and your client's culpability—as a result of extended efforts. He does not want to admit to himself (or explain to others) that his efforts were wrong or pointless. Start early.

Even if you cannot eliminate prosecution, an early start may nevertheless enable you to negotiate a better plea bargain. Prosecutors are less likely to limit your client's exposure if you barge into their offices to negotiate on the eve of trial. The new federal sentencing guidelines make the number of counts and the identity of the judge before whom you plead less important than before, but most plea bargain negotiations will still proceed more favorably for the defendant if the prosecutor has not been working feverishly to prepare for trial or complete the investigation.

Negotiating Safely

Early negotiations with the prosecutor raise recurrent problems. How do you discuss facts with the prosecutor without harming your effort to avoid prosecution? If you seek immunity for your client, what form does it take and how do you get it? When should you reject the prosecutor's efforts to discuss the case?

First, how do you talk about the facts? Suppose your client has told you he did no wrong. You have reviewed the facts and have evidence that suggests he is innocent. You have concluded that, at a trial, you have a decent or better chance of an acquittal. You recognize, however, that a trial is risky. Furthermore, you know the prosecutor is skeptical, has some evidence of your client's guilt, and will gain a tactical advantage if you give him a preview of the defense case.

What do you do? Your inclination is to try to persuade the prosecutor of your client's innocence—or at least convince him he should not go forward because the evidence won't persuade a jury of guilt beyond a reasonable doubt.

Many grizzled criminal defense veterans would say all this is bad thinking. They would say such tactics have a slim prospect of success. Such lawyers argue that the prosecutor already knows the reasons not to go forward and that you are simply harming your client by disclosing your case and strategy.

You have decided otherwise. Having talked to the prosecutor preliminarily, you believe he is open-minded. In addition, even if you win at trial, an indictment by itself could destroy your client's business and reputation. It is worth the risk to try to head it off.

The first step is to discuss the facts with the prosecutor. Before doing so, you must have an agreement that your statements will not be viewed as admissions by your client or directly used against him. You can do this two ways. You can enter into an "off-the-record" understanding; this means the words you speak will never be used in the courtroom, through a witness, in cross-examination, or otherwise. You can also employ the fiction that you are speaking hypothetically.

Such understandings generally are not written. You want, if possible, to create an air of trust and informality in the process of persuading the prosecutor not to go forward. Drafting an elaborate document at this stage can interfere with that effort. Regardless of the form of your understanding, however, remember this: You cannot prevent the prosecutor from using the facts you provide to develop new evidence or new tactics and strategies. That is the fundamental risk you take in talking to the government.

Your presentation must be accurate and candid. As elsewhere in litigation, preparation is the key. Argue clearly and take into account the strengths *and* weaknesses of your position. Do not come on too strong or be self-righteous. Remember, the prosecutor surely has concluded that there are incriminating facts. He may know things you do not. Be careful about arguing too much that prosecution witnesses are liars, particularly if they have pled guilty, though you can point out factors that undercut their credibility.

The use of a lie detector examination—one showing your client is truthful—can be effective. Everyone knows that such results are not admissible evidence, but they can help corroborate your position with the prosecutor and can be decisive where the prosecutor is uncertain. Be sure to use a reputable polygraph expert, and be aware that if you play a polygraph trump card, the prosecutor may seek to have your client tested by his own expert or agent.

Even after intense exposure to your persuasive powers, the prosecutor may still be skeptical. She may want to talk with your client directly before she makes a final decision. In fact, the prosecutor may have asked—or you may have agreed—to have the client at the first meeting. Such a conversation is particularly risky. You cannot control the situation tightly; more may be disclosed to the prosecutor than you want. Nonetheless, a prosecutor may not be convinced unless she hears from your client. And your client may be more effective than you alone.

When your client comes to the table, an unwritten understanding is insufficient. You must have a document clearly recording the basis of the meeting. Such a proffer agreement typically bars the use of your client's statements as direct evidence against him at trial. However, there will usually be no restrictions on the use of information by the prosecutor to develop leads. In addition, under most such agreements, the client's statements can be used in cross-examination if there is a trial and your client takes the stand. If you prepare properly and believe you know all the facts, this should be a small risk: The client's statements to the prosecutor should occur only after the most thorough checking of the facts. Later contradictions should be rare. Nevertheless, because that risk cannot be eliminated entirely, you should take a stab at securing an agreement that there will be no cross-examination use.

When is a client proffer worth the risk? There are, to say the least, no easy answers. Decisions depend on a careful weighing of the facts, your client's presence, and the prosecutor's attitude. But a proffer *can* work.

High-Risk Tactics

In one case, for example, the government decided after a long investigation to prosecute an important securities industry executive for filing false documents regarding stock ownership. There was evidence of wrongdoing, but the facts were complex. There was some indication that the putative defendant had not known that what he was doing was wrong. The defense lawyer took the biggest possible risk: He offered a full, on-the-record interview—under oath and with a transcript. The lawyer thought this was the most forceful way to show that the prosecutors were about to err. The facts that emerged during that deposition, and the executive's demeanor, led the prosecutors to close the case. This approach worked, but the lawyer courted genuine danger by rejecting the protection of a proffer agreement, thereby permitting full use of the client's testimony if the prosecution had proceeded.

Another example illustrates this danger: In the Wedtech investigation, Congressman Mario Biaggi decided to give an on-the-record deposition, but he failed to convince the prosecutors of his innocence. Instead, the deposition provided the prosecutors with more evidence and admissions, which were introduced by the government at Biaggi's trial. Even worse, Biaggi was convicted of perjury for testimony in the deposition that he hoped would be a ticket out of prosecution.

As the Biaggi case illustrates, it is rarely wise to forgo the protection of the proffer agreement. Grand gestures, like that of the executive I mentioned, should be made only where you believe you need something extra to convince the prosecutor of your client's innocence. In that event, you must thoroughly prepare your client so that his testimony is as complete and compelling as if he were on trial.

The alternative to your client's appearing in person to plead his case is a written proffer. This is seldom as effective as a good in-person presentation. It is, however, easier to control and presents fewer risks. Written proffers may be particularly useful if you are focusing on specific weaknesses in the prosecutor's case—clearly defined factual or legal errors. There is still risk, however: A written presentation can be a road map to your case for the prosecutor. Draft it with extreme care and present it subject to the same ground rules that would govern a face-to-face meeting.

Now for a really tough question: Should you ever refuse an invitation from the prosecutor to talk with your client when you claim the client is innocent or the prosecution's case is weak? Maybe. If you suspect the prosecutor is leaning against an indictment, or simply does not have the evidence to justify one, you may want to avoid giving her anything new. The decision will turn largely on the facts the client will recount and how they can be interpreted. A refusal to talk does not mean an indictment is inevitable, although the prosecutor may well assume from a refusal that the witness has something to hide. As before, there are no certain rules. You must simply make your best call.

Doing a Deal

Unfortunately, few criminal defense lawyers have only innocent clients. Often you will not be able to claim with a straight face that your client is blameless, or that the prosecutor's case is too weak to proceed. Instead, you will seek a pass for your client in exchange for his cooperation with the government. Doing this requires tough negotiation, conducted with skill and tenacity. The variables are endless. What does the prosecutor know about your client? How much evidence of his wrongdoing does he have? How badly does the prosecutor need the evidence your client can provide? How culpable is your client? When do you act—early in the investigation, or later, after things have developed?

The prosecutor's need for evidence and his desire to move quickly (instead of spending months piecing together the facts from those with limited direct knowledge) are the usual grounds for a negotiation. If you see an opening, act promptly. Too much delay or too much negotiation may result in a missed opportunity. Another witness may take your client's position.

Here is an example of the value of quick action. In a corruption investigation, an experienced defense lawyer made an early visit to the prosecutors. He thought that they did not then know the identity of his client. He also knew that his client had made payoffs to a public official and that such testimony would rapidly advance the prosecutor's investigation. During the meeting, the lawyer withheld the identity of his client. But he insisted on complete immunity in return for his client's cooperation. At the same time that he provided facts damaging to his client but helpful to the prosecutors, he also included positive facts—for example, that the payoffs were stopped voluntarily before the investigation had started. The lawyer correctly evaluated that the combination of what he had to offer and when he offered it would be productive. His client got immunity. Delay might have provided a different result.

Haste is not always the answer, however, especially if what the government first offers is unappealing. In the same corruption case, another lawyer monitored the investigation for a time. This lawyer represented an important witness who had refused to cooperate with the government as long as a guilty plea was required. He did this because the government's case against him appeared weak and an indictment unlikely. By withstanding the early pressure to make a deal, the lawyer was later able to obtain immunity in return for his client's testimony—and without a guilty plea—when the prosecutor concluded that he needed more evidence.

What prosecutors generally want from a cooperating witness is a guilty plea in which the witness admits to wrongdoing with others. The credibility of a witness is much greater if he has himself pleaded guilty, admits he has done wrong, and faces jail time. Immunity is less desirable to a prosecutor because it creates a more vulnerable witness. Whether you can get it turns on the facts.

The process and the risks involved in getting immunity are like those involved in a proffer of your client's innocence. A lawyer will normally advise the prosecutor of the scope of his client's helpful testimony. The prosecutor will ordinarily verify the promised facts with the client in person after he has agreed that such testimony—if it is solid—warrants immunity. If all works as hoped, the client gets what he wants. However, if the prosecutor decides not to grant immunity—because the testimony is not sufficiently helpful or he has doubt about the client's candor and reliability—the client has problems. The prosecutor has learned valuable facts and information. To guard against this outcome, a defense lawyer should always seek to limit the details provided. In addition, you should obtain an agreement that mirrors the written proffer agreement discussed above for use when you are seeking to prove innocence.

Immunity comes in two forms—use and transactional. "Use" immunity usually arises out of invocation of the federal immunity statute, 18 U.S.C. § 6001 *et seq.* Transactional immunity in the federal system often comes in a written cooperation agreement. Each form offers different protections and therefore different risks of later problems for the client. As a practical matter, there is little significant difference between the two forms of immunity. Your client will rarely be pursued by other prosecutors if he is truthful and candid, regardless of the kind of immunity. In any event, you rarely have much choice. Normally, the prosecutor will *tell* you what he wants to do; the procedures in each office tend to be nonnegotiable.

There are times when immunity is granted without negotiation or a proffer—in other words, it is forced on you. Your client has decided that he does not want to help the prosecutor. He may have a host of personal reasons for such a decision—loyalty, fear, loss of livelihood. There may also be times when your client has information that prosecutors would find helpful, but providing it would mean endless hours as a witness. This is particularly so where the case is complex, and counsel for the other defendants are likely to be tough. As a result, the client may prefer the risk of jail to the certain and unattractive consequences of becoming a prosecution witness. In such circumstances, even though you and your client want to play hardball, the prosecutor can still subpoena your client to appear before the grand jury, force statutory immunity on him, and obtain his testimony.

Whether you seek immunity or a closed investigation, remember the basic materials from which you fashion your case. Appeal to the prosecutor's sense of decency and fairness and urge him to make a just decision. Some may say that is foolish, but the cynical view provides few options. You must of course be careful—not revealing too much and remaining clearheaded about risks to the client—but part of the leverage you will have with a prosecutor lies in what some wrongly regard as platitudes.

Criminal Discovery: Leveling the Playing Field

Jeffrey E. Stone and Corey B. Rubenstein

Every great criminal defense lawyer must be willing to gamble, but it often seems like a losing bet. Statistics show that the odds are stacked against the criminal defendant: The government wins far more than it loses. Even before the first court appearance, the prosecutor holds almost all the cards—greater resources, grand jury power and secrecy, undercover operations, and the ability to tempt prospective witnesses with promises of immunity or reduced sentences. Perhaps most important, the government decides when and if it wants to play the game at all: If the government does not like the odds, it simply chooses not to play. And when the prosecution decides to deal an indictment, the stakes are frequently high—especially given the trend toward longer, more definite sentences.

But despite the odds, an indictment is still not a conviction. Every good card player knows what Francis Bacon said more than 400 years ago: "Knowledge is power." Learning what cards are in the dealer's hand can be, and often is, the difference between winning and losing. The defense lawyer thus has two important tasks in preparing a case: First, learn what the government knows. Second, learn something that the government doesn't know.

By and large, those jobs are easier today than they were years ago. Although the breadth of criminal discovery does not even approach what is available in a civil case, a criminal trial by ambush is, or at least should be, a thing of the past. Whether practicing in federal or state court, you have a number of formal and not-so-formal ways to discover what evidence the government has against your client, and, if you are lucky, you'll find some evidence that actually exonerates him. What is

Jeffrey E. Stone and Corey B. Rubenstein are with the Chicago firm of McDermott, Will & Emery.

more, mandatory disclosure—under the rules of procedure or as required by case law—is only the tip of the iceberg. With a little ingenuity—and some time and resources—you can obtain a wealth of information from sources outside the "rules."

The place to start, though, is with those rules. Just as the blackjack dealer must deal his second card face up, so there are certain things that the prosecutor must reveal to the defendant. Obtaining that basic information and material should be the foundation for discovery in every criminal case.

Of course, some prosecutors may voluntarily give you more than they are required to provide. In theory, at least, the prosecutor is not just your adversary but is also an agent of truth and justice. In pursuit of truth and justice, some prosecutors have an "open file" policy or a variant of such a policy. Embrace it when proffered, but don't count on it. Frequently, you must fight tooth and nail just to obtain the evidence to which you are entitled.

The heart of the federal government's discovery obligations is neatly outlined in Rule 16 of the Federal Rules of Criminal Procedure. Upon your written request to the government, you get: (1) any statement your client was foolish enough to make, presumably before you were hired; (2) his criminal record, presumably obtained before you represented him; (3) documents or physical exhibits to be used by the government at trial; (4) reports of examinations or tests; and (5) expert witness summaries. State prosecutors often have similar discovery obligations under provisions of state law.

Obtain Your Client's "Statements"

The most significant discovery under such rules will probably be in the first category. In fact, your client's statements will set the tone for the rest of the defense. Has your client already nailed his coffin shut? Do you have any leverage in negotiating a plea agreement? If you go to trial, can your client take the stand? What affirmative defenses have already been discarded by your client's indiscretion?

In addition to transcripts of your client's grand jury testimony and station-house statements actually written or signed by him, you are entitled to see the substance of any oral communications your client knowingly made to any government agent. Be sure to demand all such statements—but don't stop there. If a conspiracy is alleged, request copies of statements made in furtherance of the conspiracy by co-conspirators. If your client is a corporation, demand all statements of corporate agents, especially those who had authority to bind the corporation.

This rule also covers any of the defendant's letters or notes that are relevant to the case. Courts usually apply a liberal standard in determining whether something constitutes a "statement" of the defendant. Be adamant and wide-ranging in your quest to obtain anything that is arguably a statement of your client's.

The second category of Rule 16 discovery is the defendant's criminal record. The results of this discovery are obviously important in determining whether your client can testify at trial: The longer the criminal record, the more devastating the cross-examination by the government.

The government will usually satisfy its obligation simply by turning over your client's F.B.I. "rap sheet." Read it carefully, paying particular attention to the idiosyncracies and nomenclature of your particular jurisdiction. For example, in Illinois, the initials "SOL" after an arrest do not express an opinion about how much luck the defendant might have in fighting the charges, but rather indicate "Stricken on Leave [to Reinstate]," meaning that the government dropped the case. In the same state, a notation of "BFW" (Bond Forfeiture Warrant) indicates bond jumping, a bad sign for any future bond or detention hearing. Learning such a system of nomenclature is not difficult, but will require some inquiries by the novice.

The third discovery entitlement under Rule 16 affords defense counsel an opportunity to preview the government's case in chief by seeing its trial exhibits. Although busy prosecutors and busier trial judges might pressure you to stipulate to the foundation for the physical evidence included in such exhibits, think twice before you do. At a minimum, never stipulate to the introduction of such evidence before seeing it yourself.

This entitlement also permits you to examine documents and other property belonging to your client that is now in the government's possession. In cases where a search warrant has been executed, look at everything taken by the government. Those documents that make the prosecutor's "smoking gun" less inculpatory will be buried amidst thousands of others. Those materials that give you the basis of your defense will be camouflaged by cartons of worthless trash. Don't expect the prosecutor to give you your best evidence on a silver platter. Take the time to ferret it out.

Rule 16 also gives some warning about what the government's experts will say about the defendant's guilt. Not only are you entitled to see the reports of any physical or mental examinations and scientific tests (such as handwriting or fingerprint analyses), but you can also obtain a summary of any expert testimony that will be offered. Furthermore, the testifying experts' qualifications should be disclosed on request. This will enable defense counsel to get a head start on cross-examination by checking the potentially vulnerable professional backgrounds of these often critical witnesses.

A Truckload of Evidence

Rule 16 will thus provide you with a roomful of discovery. But what you get from the government is not the only consideration; when you get it may prove just as important. For example, suppose that during plea negotiations with the prosecutor you argue that your client, an alleged rapist, acted with consent. Shortly after you stake out that position, the prosecutor tells you that she has one more packet of evidence subject to disclosure under the applicable rules. To your surprise and horror, she shows you pictures of the victim's bruises that she intends to introduce when the victim testifies. Your credibility, your bargaining power—indeed, your defense—disappear.

Obviously, the earlier you obtain discovery materials, the better off you are. Most trial judges will order discovery to be provided some time before trial. Moreover, there is some authority that the government must comply with your requests as soon as reasonably possible. But the question is essentially one of discretion, and untimely disclosures will be judged under a standard of prejudice. From a practice perspective, push for full disclosure at the first possible instance.

So far, Rule 16 has been something of a one-way street moving in your direction. You have obtained a truckload of evidence—presumably in plenty of time to review and analyze it before trial—and have turned nothing over yourself. But there's a catch: After the government complies with your requests, it's the defendant's turn. As might be expected, you have the reciprocal obligation to turn over your physical exhibits, expert witness summaries, and reports of examinations and tests that you intend to use at trial.

Because the defendant's duty to disclose arises only if the defendant submits discovery requests of his own, defense counsel must decide if the game is worth the candle before taking advantage of the rule. In virtually every case, however, the decision is an easy one: Get what you can and give back what you must. The government has already put its case together, has been investigating the matter for months or years, and has had an army of investigators and experts at its disposal. Your job is to counterpunch. In order to assess the government's case—and to evaluate your available defense options—you must see what the government has. It's as simple as that.

Rule 16-type discovery, at a minimum, is also required in most state criminal cases. In fact, a number of states have more comprehensive discovery schemes. For example, California has a bright-line rule requiring the prosecution to make certain enumerated disclosures at least 30 days before trial, whether or not the defendant requests such information. California Penal Code 1054 *et seq.* In Florida, criminal defendants are entitled to additional disclosure not required under Rule 16, such as documents relating to electronic surveillance and the names of all individuals who were present when the defendant gave any statement to the police. Florida Rules of Criminal Procedure 3.220. A criminal defendant in the New York State courts has access to all statements made by his co-defendants. New York Criminal Procedure Law 240.20. Be aware of your particular jurisdiction's quirky rules so that you can make your Rule 16-type discovery requests sufficiently broad.

Although Rule 16-type discovery provides an abundance of information, something is conspicuously absent: impeachment material. To fill this void, a number of jurisdictions require the prosecution to produce any prior statements made by its witnesses. In the federal system, this requirement is found in the Jencks Act, 18 U.S.C. 3500 (also codified as Rule 26.2 of the Federal Rules of Criminal Procedure). A large number of states have enacted similar provisions for the disclosure of witness statements, such as Illinois Supreme Court Rule 412(a) and Colorado Rule of Criminal Procedure 16(1)(a)(III).

Under a literal reading of the Jencks Act, the defendant is entitled to obtain all statements related to a witness's testimony, but only after the witness testifies. As with Rule 16, the defendant must ask for the disclosure, and the government is entitled to reciprocal discovery. Unlike Rule 16 reciprocity, however, a defendant's obligations under the Jencks Act exist whether or not he made any such requests of the prosecutor. Therefore, defense counsel should make a Jencks request for every government witness.

A "statement" covered by the Jencks Act includes (1) anything written, signed, or adopted by the witness, (2) a substantially verbatim account of any oral statement made by the witness, and (3) a transcript of any grand jury testimony given by the witness. The first and last categories are well defined and self-explanatory; the second category, however, may raise some issues. For example, in many cases, the government may take the position that an agent's interview notes with a witness are not a "substantially verbatim" transcript, and therefore are outside the scope of Jencks. In fact, because most federal agents understand the Jencks Act as well as you do, they are sure to keep their notes rough enough to avoid being "substantially verbatim"—at least when the witness is not the subject of the investigation.

But do not allow your request for Jencks material to be so crudely circumscribed. Under *Giglio v. United States*, 405 U.S. 150 (1972), the government has another obligation that is constitutionally required: It must disclose any evidence that is sufficiently impeaching of a witness's credibility. Any written memorandum, even if not "substantially verbatim" and thus outside Jencks, can still be *Giglio* material and therefore discoverable. The lesson? Be certain to ask for all material required under Jencks, as well as all material that might be impeaching under *Giglio*.

Unlike Rule 16, which generally requires disclosure to be made sometime before trial, Jencks material must only be disclosed during trial and not until after the witness has testified on direct examination. For practical reasons, however, most judges will grant a motion for earlier disclosure of the statements—usually at least a day or two before the jury is sworn. If the prosecutor will not voluntarily provide early disclosure, move for it. Make the heart of your argument the burden that this will place on you, your client, and the process: "Judge, the government intends to call 13 witnesses to explain how the defendant allegedly defrauded thousands of people by way of a pyramid scheme. If I don't get their statements at least a week or two before trial, I'll be forced to ask the court for a lengthy continuance after each witness testifies."

If your judicial economy argument fails to win earlier disclosure, make your Jencks requests after the completion of each direct examination at trial. Then move for a continuance to review the material. Of course, if the judge has already denied your pretrial request, your plea may fall on deaf ears, so be prepared for the court to give you only enough time to skim the statement. A mere five minutes to review an uncomplicated, 12-page statement has been held sufficient under the act. *Washington v. United States,* 499 A.2d 95 (D.C. 1985).

You can also use the Jencks Act at pretrial proceedings, such as suppression and detention hearings. Be sure to ask for prior statements of any witness who testifies at any stage of the case. In addition to giving you impeachment material to use at those preliminary proceedings, the witnesses' prior statements could be valuable evidence at the trial itself.

Even if evidence is not covered by Rule 16 or the Jencks Act, the prosecutor must disclose to the defendant all additional evidence tending to show his innocence. The Supreme Court established this constitutional requirement in *Brady v. Maryland,* 373 U.S. 83 (1963), believing that a prosecutor's attempt to bury exculpatory evidence is inconsistent with due process.

Evidence falls under *Brady* only if there is a reasonable probability that its admission will lead to the defendant's acquittal. Naturally, the defendant and the prosecutor are likely to differ on whether evidence is *Brady* material. So how does this definition shake out in practice?

Neutral, irrelevant, speculative, inculpatory, and inadmissible evidence is not *Brady* material. For example, the prosecutor does not have to share the fact that the defendant passed a lie detector test because the defense could not use that fact at trial (even though it might provide negotiating leverage with the prosecutor's office, or ammunition to use to provide media pressure against the filing of charges). But *Brady* encompasses more than just obviously exculpatory evidence; it requires disclosure of more than just your client's negative DNA results or another person's confession to the same crime. Indeed, *Brady* material can be as subtle as the absence of the license plate number of the defendant's car from a list of cars canvassed at the scene of the crime.

Similarly, under *Giglio,* mere impeachment evidence can be *Brady* material, even though such evidence may not be directly "exculpatory." For instance, the fact that a government witness is contemplating a civil suit against the defendant will probably not constitute Jencks material, but it should nevertheless be discoverable under *Brady* and/or *Giglio*.

Likewise, evidence that a government witness has struck a deal with the prosecutor should fall within the parameters of *Brady/Giglio* discovery.

If you become embroiled in a *Brady/Giglio* dispute—perhaps by way of a motion to preclude or to strike testimony because of an alleged violation—remember that the court is likely to ask two questions in determining whether the material at issue must be disclosed. First, how strongly does the evidence impeach the witness? Second, how important to the government's case is the witness whose impeachment is at issue? Evidence showing that the government's star witness is heavily biased against the defendant is almost certainly discoverable; evidence that an eyewitness to a peripheral or unimportant event wears glasses may not be. In arguing the issue, be sure to emphasize the importance of the witness and the value of the impeachment material.

Although you technically do not need to make a formal request for disclosure under *Brady*, there are good reasons to do so anyway. First, it may be important to put a request on the record so you can later argue (when you discover that the prosecutor failed to disclose certain material) that the prosecutor was given notice that such evidence was exculpatory. Second, it may provide the basis for an argument that the government acted deliberately (and therefore more egregiously) in failing to meet its constitutional obligations.

Be specific, exhaustive, and creative when you make your requests. In a murder/manslaughter case, ask for any statements by the victim's neighbors regarding any tendency of the victim toward aggression. You might get lucky and get something like, "The guy had it coming—I've seen him beat up his wife."

The timing for disclosure under *Brady* is similar to that under Rule 16: It will largely depend on when the prosecution wants to give it to you or whether the court will back your effort to get it sooner. The formal standard is one of prejudice, that is, whether the evidence is still of substantial use to the accused when it is finally disclosed.

The Subpoena, an Essential Tool

If the evidence is truly late, make lemonade out of the lemons. Ask the trial court for payback—the deposition of related government witnesses, the preclusion of related prosecution evidence or testimony, an instruction to the jury about the late disclosure, or, if appropriate, the dismissal of any related charges.

The subpoena power provides another discovery tool available to every defense lawyer in every criminal case. In federal court, this power arises under Rule 17 of the Federal Rules of Criminal Procedure. Although not intended as a discovery device (its true intent is to compel the attendance of witnesses at trial, with or without documents), the rule can nevertheless be used for pretrial discovery of documentary evidence by way of a "Motion for Early Return." Indeed, because it is the only formal method to compel the production of documents by third parties, this tool is often one of the more important available procedures.

The motion for early return of a trial subpoena can be used only to obtain "evidentiary" materials, that is, Rule 17 does not cover documents that would be inadmissible hearsay. Nor does it cover mere impeachment materials. In addition to showing the evidentiary nature of the documents, defense counsel must show good cause to get the early production. That standard can be met by showing that the documents are not available from some other source, that they are needed to prepare for trial, that production will avoid an unreasonable delay during trial, and that the motion is not a mere fishing expedition.

Even if the court refuses to grant your motion for an early return, the subpoena *duces tecum* remains a very powerful discovery tool. For example, you might convince the recipient of such a subpoena that if she speaks with you and shows you the requested documents before trial, you might not need to call her to testify. With that incentive, she might agree to meet with you, or at least to let you see or copy the documents in advance.

Several additional discovery devices can supplement the more basic techniques. One of the more common supplemental tools is the "Motion to Preserve Evidence."

Even if evidence may ultimately be discoverable under *Brady*, the Jencks Act, or Rule 16, it will be of little use if the government destroys it before trial. Indeed, while destruction of evidence can possibly be used itself as evidence at trial, or can provide the basis for a favorable jury instruction, notice to the government may well be a prerequisite to such strategy. When in doubt, move to preserve evidence. If blood was found at the scene of a suspected murder and your client is the suspected murderer, bring a motion to preserve a sample of the blood. Otherwise, you may be stuck with the government expert's conclusions about the results of the DNA testing. If you think that the court will not grant such a motion for some reason, then simply write a letter to the prosecution demanding preservation of the evidence pending discovery. Although a letter demand does not have the same bite as a court order, it will enable you to argue later that the government destroyed the evidence in bad faith and should therefore be punished to your client's advantage.

A Rule 15 deposition can also be used to preserve evidence in a federal prosecution. Although the rule ostensibly applies only to preserve the testimony of otherwise "unavailable witnesses," it can be used as a discovery tool. But there are significant limitations. The procedure is supposed to be limited to a party's own prospective witnesses and applies only where the deposition is needed to prevent injustice. Under its literal terms, then, the rule seems to provide only for the depositions of potential fugitives, deportees, or terminally ill witnesses who would exclaim the defendant's innocence at trial. The clever defense lawyer will look for ways to fit prospective witnesses and testimony into that mold whenever possible, however, in order to squeeze every drop of potential discovery from the rule.

Depose Witnesses If You Can

A number of states go well beyond Rule 15, and specifically provide for discovery depositions in criminal cases. In fact, Florida law goes so far as to require the prosecutor to give the defendant a list of witnesses that the defendant might want to depose. Florida Rules of Criminal Procedure 3.220. Again, there is no substitute for intimate familiarity with the applicable discovery rules and aggressive use of the devices available in a given jurisdiction.

If you cannot depose a witness yourself, the next best thing may be to read the witness's grand jury testimony. Unfortunately, under Rule 6(e) of the Federal Rules of Criminal Procedure, the defendant usually cannot get this "secret" testimony unless it also qualifies as Jencks or *Brady* material. But like virtually every rule, this one has exceptions. If defense counsel can show a "particularized need" for the testimony, for example, then the court might require its production. When in doubt, ask. If you do not want to reveal your theory of defense at an early stage of the prosecution, bring an ex-parte motion explaining why the grand jury testimony is particularly necessary to your defense. Although this is a long shot, there is a handsome payoff for success.

Defense counsel can often supplement basic discovery requests by reading the affidavits offered in support of the government's requests for search warrants. Ordinarily, such affidavits are public court records obtainable by the defendant (or anyone else). The information in those affidavits might very well be your first clue about the government's theory of the case and the evidence behind it. Most important, the affidavit may have been written by an agent who will testify at trial and who can be impeached with his written words.

Sometimes such affidavits are sealed on the government's request to protect an ongoing investigation or a confidential informant, or to preserve the general secrecy of law enforcement techniques. Don't let that deter your efforts to obtain them. A number of courts have found a constitutional or common law right of public access to affidavits supporting search warrants. *See, e.g., Baltimore Sun Company v. Goetz,* 886 F.2d 60 (4th Cir. 1989); *Lawmaster v. United States,* 993 F.2d 773 (10th Cir. 1993); *Search Warrant for Secretarial Area Outside Office of Gunn,* 855 F.2d 569 (8th Cir. 1988). Under this case law, the defendant will get access to the affidavits if his need for disclosure outweighs the government's interest in maintaining the seal. Especially when the investigation is complete and has resulted in an indictment, the government's interest in maintaining secrecy should give way to the defendant's need for the information.

If the government supplemented its traditional investigatory techniques with some form of electronic surveillance, the defendant might have yet another source of discovery. Under Title III of the Omnibus Crime Control Act (18 U.S.C. §§ 2510–2521), the government cannot engage in wiretapping or certain other types of electronic surveillance without a court order. The application submitted to obtain such an order will probably include much of the same type of information given in an affidavit supporting a search warrant request. For example, it will probably refer to the government's version of the alleged offense and the suspected perpetrators of that offense. Ordinarily, the court will allow the defendant to see the application in order to assess any possible suppression claims. But the information contained in such documents may well have value beyond a motion to suppress.

For example, if you can make a prima facie showing that the government's application contains falsehoods, then the court might also allow you to cross-examine some government witnesses as part of a suppression hearing. *Franks v. Delaware*, 438 U.S. 154 (1978). Even if the suppression motion is not ultimately granted, you will have gained some valuable discovery in the meantime.

A few other discovery tools are seldom used very effectively, but deserve some mention. Rule 7(f) of the Federal Rules of Criminal Procedure allows the court, upon the defendant's motion, to direct the prosecution to supplement the indictment with a bill of particulars. Most states have parallel or similar provisions. In both federal and state court, the ostensible purpose of a bill of particulars is not to provide discovery, but to clarify unusually vague or incomplete indictments. At least one court has held that a bill may legitimately be used for other purposes as well, such as ascertaining names of co-conspirators to be called by the government at trial. *United States v. Hughes*, 817 F.2d 268 (5th Cir. 1987).

Exchange Witness Lists

Rule 12.1 of the Federal Rules of Criminal Procedure is likewise a less obvious, but possibly significant, source of discovery for the defense. Although the primary purpose of the rule is to require the defendant to disclose his intent to raise an alibi defense, the rule also requires the government to disclose the names of all witnesses it will call to rebut that defense. Rule 12.1, therefore, gives a defendant a relatively painless way to test an alibi defense before presenting it to the jury. If the government discloses no rebuttal witnesses—or only very weak ones—then you will have gained some confidence in your chosen strategy.

Finally, in preparing formal discovery requests you should consider suggesting, or even moving for, a pretrial exchange of witness lists. An "open file" prosecutor might well agree to such an exchange. Of course, you should only make this motion or request if you are prepared to disclose your witnesses (that is, if you have a good idea of who your witnesses will be) and if it is strategically sound to exchange information (that is, if you are not relying on the element of surprise). Most federal courts will not grant such a motion, but the results in state court may be more favorable. In fact, a number of states allow for some kind of pretrial discovery of witnesses, even absent a reciprocal duty of the defendant.

Formal discovery should be only the beginning of your trial preparation. The government does not rely exclusively (or even significantly) on formal discovery techniques to prepare its case, and neither should you. Given enough resources, you can and should enhance your defense by doing your own investigation.

In a number of contexts, especially white collar cases, hire a private investigator. Choose that investigator carefully. Certainly an investigator's experience, creativity, and aggressiveness will be key factors in your evaluation. But don't forget that your investigator may well have to testify at trial. Look at her resume, her demeanor, her past trial experience. Evaluate her credibility. Think about how she will come across on the stand.

Sometimes former federal agents make very good defense witnesses; often they will be more qualified and more experienced than the government's own case agent. Indeed, the defense testimony of a former federal agent might itself be enough to create a reasonable doubt. Consider tapping into the network of former federal agents as you recruit your investigative team.

Whether or not you hire a private investigator, there is no substitute for pounding the pavement yourself. You should personally interview each witness, not only to learn what the witness has to say, but to establish a rapport and to encourage the witness to remember something positive about your client. Even if a witness refuses to talk with you, you can use that fact at trial: "Mr. Witness, isn't it correct that you met with Mr. Prosecutor five times to talk about this case and that you spent at least two hours rehearsing your testimony during each of those meetings? Isn't it also true that you refused to talk to me even though I called you four times and came to your home twice?" In an effort to bolster such a line of questioning, consider sending a letter, or multiple letters, to a reluctant witness formalizing your request for an interview.

If the witness is a "flipper" whose identity is being kept secret or who has been placed in a witness protection program, then the government may think that it has stymied you. Don't be fooled—you can turn this stonewalling to your advantage. First, send the prosecutor a formal written request to speak with the witness. You have nothing to lose. At worst, the prosecutor will refuse or ignore your request, giving you ammunition to use in attacking the government's "overzealous" prosecution. Make a motion under *Brady* and *Giglio* to learn how much money the government is spending to protect, house, wine, and dine the flipper. Such information can make juicy impeachment material. And, of course, move to discover the informant's identity well in advance of trial.

You can also use the federal Freedom of Information Act (FOIA) and its state counterparts as a discovery device. Just like any other citizen, you are entitled to see nonexempt government records. Although you are unlikely to hit a home run with such requests (law enforcement files, rap sheets, and the like are usually exempt from disclosure), you may get important background information, which might narrow your investigation and in turn lead to more significant evidence. Needless to say, because the bureaucracy grinds slowly, your FOIA requests must be made early if they are to be of any value.

If the government intends to rely on expert testimony to convict your client, supplement your Rule 16 discovery by obtaining and reading everything the expert has said or written on the relevant subject. An exhaustive on-line literature search, combined with an Internet search, is a good place to start.

Consider discovery in other cases as a possible way to help you prepare your case. For example, if your client is also a defendant in a parallel civil case—such as a drug forfeiture action, a civil tax fraud case, or a personal injury case—you can use the civil discovery rules to unearth evidence relevant to the criminal prosecution. Be prepared for a government motion to stay all civil discovery pending a completion of the criminal prosecution or a decision not to prosecute, however. The government will argue that civil discovery will disrupt the criminal investigation, and its motion will most likely be granted unless you can show that a stay of the proceedings would unduly prejudice your client in the civil case.

Finally, if you are in a multiple defendant prosecution, consider entering into a joint defense agreement with the other defendants to pool your resources, to exchange information and documents, and to coordinate both formal and informal discovery. The agreement does not have to be reduced to writing. As long as the defendants agree to share information and have some common defense interests, their communications with one another and with one another's lawyers will remain privileged.

You may never learn the prosecutor's hole card until she's forced to turn it over. But if you use the rules—and your imagination—to get all the discovery you can, you will at least be able to play the game with some sense of parity. And if the prosecutor has a card or two up her sleeve, you will have a few of your own. If you're diligent, good, and lucky, you might just be able to turn them into the winning hand.

Joint Defense Agreements

Michael G. Scheininger and Ray M. Aragon

The day of trial. You are more prepared than you have ever been. You have examined the case from every angle, gathered every bit of information you could beg, borrow, or . . . well, almost. You know your client's story inside out.

Amazingly, you also know the stories of his co-defendants, even the one (and there always is one) who made an early plea and will testify for the prosecution. You negotiated joint defense agreements with counsel for each of the co-defendants early in the investigation. Thanks to that, you know all the defense evidence. If ever a conspiracy defendant had a chance, your guy is it.

"Are there any final matters before we pick a jury?" asks the judge. You shake your head confidently. Let the games begin.

The prosecutor pops up: "Your Honor, the United States moves to disqualify Joe Counsel due to a conflict of interest."

Disqualify *me*? For a conflict of *interest*? *Why*?

The prosecutor continues: "Mr. Counsel is party to a joint defense agreement with counsel for Thomas Turncoate, the government's primary witness. Mr. Counsel has information about Mr. Turncoate and other critical witnesses. He has promised not to use this sensitive information at trial. He cannot now claim to represent only his client's interests."

The government says I know *too much*? How is that bad? And why does the government care?

The Honorable N.C. Mentis peers over the bench. "Well, Mr. Counsel, do you oppose the motion? Do you have information useful to your client that you have agreed not to disclose?"

Michael G. Scheininger and Ray M. Aragon are partners of McKenna & Cuneo, L.L.P., Washington, D.C. Mr. Scheininger is chair of the firm's white collar criminal defense group, and Mr. Aragon is a member of the firm's litigation group.

"Yes, Your Honor," you finally blurt out. "I mean, yes, I do oppose the motion and I do have some privileged information about some of the government's witnesses. But that's not a conflict!"

The judge shakes his head. "You have information helpful to your client, yet you won't use it because of your commitments to someone else. That sounds like a conflict to me." He shakes his head again. "I'll have to think about this." He calls a recess. Your client begins tugging frantically at your sleeve.

How did this happen? Sure, you have some goodies you promised not to use—that's how you got them! You learned where all the bodies were buried so that you could step around them at trial. In exchange, you promised not to dig them up before the jury. Isn't that what a joint defense agreement is all about? And is your malpractice insurance paid up?

Joint defense agreements were once the subject of handshake deals between counsel and neglect by the courts. No longer; they are coming of age. Government enforcement efforts increasingly focus on corporate and white collar misconduct. Major prosecutions are more likely than ever before to involve many defendants with separate counsel. As a result, agreements to share but maintain the confidentiality of vital defense information have become a staple of white collar litigation.

On the civil side, massive multiparty actions often involve teams of plaintiffs and defendants with an interest in sharing information. As civil litigators have become attuned to the benefits of sharing critical information without risking waiver, the use of joint defense agreements in civil litigation also has increased. Indeed, sometimes parties are essentially *ordered* to cooperate as a joint defense group when courts require them to jointly submit briefs or discovery requests, or to appoint "defense liaison counsel." In such a case, a joint defense agreement may be necessary to protect such mandatory cooperation.

Attention and Diversity

The new focus on confidentiality agreements has engendered several reactions. First, lawyers do more to protect sensitive information. No longer satisfied with a handshake, counsel are employing ever more elaborate agreements to protect their clients and themselves. Many insist on putting the whole thing on paper. But how best to protect "joint defense" information has become a subject of disagreement. Some lawyers insist on broad one-paragraph agreements, others swear by detailed contracts, and still others, suspicious of written agreements or following local custom, make only oral agreements.

Second, protection of such information, formerly only an occasional issue of contention between prosecutors and defense lawyers (and a nonissue in civil cases), has become a battleground. Prosecutors do not like joint defense agreements for the same reason defense lawyers favor them: They can limit the pressure the government can bring to bear on an individual defendant, and they give individual defendants an overall view of multiparty cases. Divide and conquer efforts by prosecutors may be less likely to succeed, as well-informed defendants are less likely to be the object of attention in a rousing game of Prisoner's Dilemma.

In recent years, the government has made efforts to limit such agreements or tried to discourage their use. The government has even attempted, as the opening vignette illustrates, to disqualify lawyers who are parties to confidentiality agreements, or demanded that counsel state whether they are parties to such agreements and identify all shared information.

Taken together, these events add up to ongoing scrutiny of joint defense agreements and prosecution efforts to limit them. However, the very boundaries of joint defense agreements remain unclear, and after years of sporadic litigation, uncertainties persist. For example:

1. To paper or not to paper? No one knows for sure whether written joint defense agreements are more likely to be upheld than a handshake, or even whether written agreements could expose a criminal defendant to a conspiracy charge;
2. The boundaries of the joint defense/common interest privilege are murkier than those of the Milky Way; and
3. For all their love of nomenclature, lawyers cannot even agree on what to call the privilege or the agreements applying it.

Depending on who you ask, you will also learn that:

4. Joint defense agreements are (or are not) defense-led conspiracies to undermine the integrity of the legal system; and
5. Prosecution efforts to undermine joint defense agreements are (or are not) unwarranted intrusions into the lawyer-client relationship and violations of fundamental constitutional rights.

In the spirit of Dr. Livingstone, we stand at the edge of the jungle, ready to strike off into the undergrowth. Our mission: to discuss the nature of the joint defense privilege, the use of joint defense agreements, and the advantages and risks to be considered by counsel in making them. Today's journey is worthwhile because the issues involved may be considered and decided by the courts (in someone else's case, you hope) tomorrow.

Our saga begins in 1871 (the year Henry Stanley in fact found Dr. Livingstone on the shores of Lake Tanganyika). The joint defense privilege was first recognized by a U.S. court in *Chahoon v. Commonwealth*, 62 Va. (21 Gratt.) 822 (1871). In *Chahoon*, three conspiracy defendants met, each except Chahoon with counsel, to plan a defense. At trial, co-defendant Sanxay testified about Chahoon's statements at the meeting. Chahoon called Sanxay's lawyer in rebuttal. Sanxay's lawyer, invoking the attorney-client privilege, declined to testify. *Id.* at 836.

The Virginia Supreme Court found the refusal to testify justified:

> The parties were jointly indicted for a conspiracy. . . . They had the same defen[s]e to make, the act of one in furtherance of the conspiracy, being the act of all, and the counsel of each was in effect the counsel of all. . . . They had a right, all the accused and their counsel, to consult together about the case and the defen[s]e, and it follows as a necessary consequence, that all the information, derived by any of the counsel from such consultation, is privileged, and the privilege belongs to each and all of the clients, and cannot be released without the consent of all of them. Otherwise what would such right of consultation be worth?

Id. at 841–42.

Chahoon was followed by decades of near-silence on the subject. Few cases discussed the joint defense privilege until the mid-1960s, when a pair of Ninth Circuit opinions, *Continental Oil Co. v. United States*, 330 F.2d 347 (9th Cir. 1964) and *Hunydee v. United States*, 355 F.2d 183 (9th Cir. 1965), put the privilege prominently on the criminal defense map.

In *Continental Oil*, employees of the Continental and Standard Oil companies testified before a grand jury and were thereafter debriefed by counsel. Counsel for each oil company exchanged memoranda of the interviews "in confidence in order to apprise each other as to the nature and scope of the [grand jury] inquiry." 330 F.2d at 348. The Ninth Circuit found the right to exchange information confidentially "a vital and important part of the client's right to representation by counsel," and that disclosure of the memoranda "would tend in substantial measure to destroy the privilege." *Id.* at 350. In support, the court relied on *Chahoon* and *Schmitt v. Emery*, 2 N.W.2d 413, 417 (Minn. 1942). Significantly, the *Continental Oil* court found the asserted privilege fundamental to a defendant's right of representation.

Hunydee, decided the following year, clarified that the joint defense privilege extended to communications between litigants with some common interests, even if their interests were largely adverse. 355 F.2d at 184–85.

Hunydee involved a husband and wife who met jointly with counsel to plan their defense to charges of income tax evasion. The trial court permitted the wife and her lawyer to testify about the husband's statement at the joint meeting that he would "plead guilty and take the blame." *Id.* at 184.

The Ninth Circuit held that such testimony could not be compelled; it specifically concluded that whether the defendants had actually agreed to develop a joint defense was not dispositive of the issue of privilege:

> [W]here two or more persons who are subject to possible indictment in connection with the same transactions make confidential statements to their attorneys, these statements, even though they

are exchanged between attorneys, should be privileged to the extent that they concern common issues and are intended to facilitate representation in possible subsequent proceedings.

Id. at 185. In short, exchange of confidential information about "common issues" to facilitate representation of the exchanging parties is protected. This statement (with various and sundry qualifications, such as the extension of the privilege to civil and prelitigation situations, and intercircuit variations on how much common interest there must be for there to be an agreement) accurately states the basic law on the privilege today.

Several twists in the privilege have been straightened out in the years since *Continental Oil* and *Hunydee*. It is now possible to define the privilege in general terms, at least on the federal level: The joint defense privilege extends the boundaries of the attorney-client and work-product privileges to protect communications exchanged among litigants (and potential litigants) when the communications were made to further a common legal interest. The parties must have some common interests for the privilege to apply, but need not be allies in all respects or even have predominantly shared interests.

The privilege may attach at any point in the litigation or even before litigation begins. It encompasses otherwise privileged discussions, legal analyses, witness interviews, and other work product. As with other privileges, the party claiming the privilege has the burden of proving its existence.

The joint defense privilege does not expand the scope of the attorney-client privilege or the work-product doctrine. It is not an independent privilege; rather, it is a doctrine of "nonwaiver," protecting the confidentiality of information exchanged in furtherance of common interests in circumstances in which it might otherwise be waived.

The privilege is available without regard to the nature of the proceedings; joint defense material has been protected in criminal, civil, and administrative actions. Communications between counsel who are parties to the agreement are protected, as are communications from one defendant to a co-defendant's counsel or to that counsel's agents.

Get the Lawyers Involved

The involvement of lawyers in the communication may be essential, or at any rate is highly important in the determination of whether the material was intended to be confidential. Telephone calls between joint defendants in the absence of a formal agreement and without knowledge of counsel have been held not privileged. *United States v. Gotti*, 771 F. Supp. 535, 545 (E.D.N.Y. 1991); *see also United States v. Bay State Ambulance & Hosp. Rental Serv.*, 874 F.2d 20, 29 (1st Cir. 1989). Conversely, statements made by a litigant to the agents of other lawyers in the case are privileged, if they are made at the direction of that litigant's counsel in furtherance of common interests. *United States v. McPartlin*, 595 F.2d 1321, 1335–37 (7th Cir. 1979). In cases where parties have effectively been ordered to participate in a joint defense group through imposition of complex litigation rules, the court itself can be asked in a proposed case management order to recognize the joint defense privilege and the protection that is due joint defense activities.

The practical justification for the joint defense privilege is simple: Parties with common interests often have different lawyers but want to share information without waiving lawyer-client or work-product protection. This arises often in multidefendant criminal cases, in which the government is investigating a number of targets for allegedly cooperating in illegal activity. The defendants usually have adverse interests in at least one sense: Each wants, above all, to protect his own skin, even at the cost of his compatriots' hides being nailed to the barn door. On the civil side, multiple defendants also have a conflict among themselves when it comes time to apportion liability. These conflicts necessitate separate counsel. But the parties may also have helpful information they can share without damaging themselves. In such a situation, pooling defense strategies can benefit all the defendants.

The advantages of a joint defense agreement—increased knowledge and an informed evaluation of what is available to the litigation opponent—can be crucial. These benefits are worth reviewing.

In a criminal case, more complete information on the strength of the government's case can limit the prosecutor's plea-bargaining leverage and contribute to a favorable disposition. Your client is less likely to be the defendant unaware of what the prosecutor knows and frightened by dark warnings that "the train is about to leave the station." Defense counsel can make a more informed appraisal on when to hold 'em and when to fold 'em, rather than basing decisions on hunches, instinct, and the client's anxiety level.

In a civil action, more complete knowledge of the evidence in a case can promote more meaningful settlement discussions or, at the very least, early recognition that the case cannot be settled and is likely to go to trial. Just as in the criminal arena, an informed lawyer can more easily determine which battles should be fought and which consigned to St. Jude.

A second benefit: A joint defense arrangement facilitates a coordinated defense strategy. If each defendant knows what the evidence will be, he can try to develop defenses to protect himself without damaging other defendants. There will be less risk of each client promoting his own defense without regard to the cost (evidentiary or monetary) imposed on others. Legal and factual memoranda can be shared among defendants, thus facilitating a thorough analysis of the case and coordination of potential defenses.

Third, a joint defense agreement lets defendants share resources, thereby combining the experience and knowledge of the members of the defense group while reducing the staggering cost of defending a large case. In particularly important (or huge) cases, cooperative litigation may allow members of a defense group to specialize, with different firms handling various aspects of discovery and trial. A joint defense agreement will also allow the parties to share out-of-pocket costs such as experts, consultants, and computer databases.

Consider a typical case in which a company and its officers are being investigated by the government. In such a setting, a joint defense agreement offers big advantages. The company is spared the ordeal of preparing a case without the assistance of the target employees, whose knowledge is likely to be critical. With a joint defense agreement, such employees can, to some extent, be kept in the fold. The individuals, in turn, benefit from having access to much of the company's defense effort. This is a valuable advantage to an individual defendant in this day of multitarget criminal investigations aimed at reforming entire companies or industries. A person caught in the maelstrom may, through a joint defense agreement, have access to a defense that even wealthy individuals could not afford. Both the company and the individuals benefit. Of course, the prosecutor loses: There is less leverage to wring pleas or settlements out of defendants who do not know what waits behind the government door. Similar logic supports the use of joint defense agreements in multidefendant civil actions and investigations.

At trial, knowledge of the evidence available to your opponent helps in formulating defense strategy, dealing with opposition witnesses, and, in a criminal case, making that most painful of decisions—whether your client should take the stand.

Such advantages explain why joint defense agreements can be essential to a fair defense. The right to separate, conflict-free counsel may mean little if defense lawyers and their clients cannot communicate without having the communications made subject to discovery. The interests of defendants may be handicapped, perhaps unconstitutionally, if they cannot share relevant information with co-defendants. As the Seventh Circuit stated in *McPartlin*: "Uninhibited communication among joint parties and their counsel about matters of common concern is often important to the protection of their interests. In criminal cases it can be necessary to a fair opportunity to defend." 595 F.2d at 1336 (citation omitted).

While the practical reasons for a joint defense *agreement* are obvious, the legal rationale for a joint defense *privilege* to protect communications under the agreement is less certain. Most courts consider the joint defense privilege to be an extension of the attorney-client privilege. *Waller v. Financial Corp. of Am.*, 828 F.2d 579, 583 n.7 (9th Cir. 1987). Some scholars claim that the term is a misnomer: The "joint defense privilege" is not limited to defendants nor is there a requirement that litigation exist before the privilege applies. In *Continental Oil*, the Ninth Circuit applied the privilege to preindictment activities, and in *Schachar v. American Academy of Ophthalmology, Inc.*, 106 F.R.D. 187, 191–92 (N.D. Ill. 1985), exchanges of information among co-plaintiffs were protected. The privilege has even been extended to information shared by plaintiffs with a joint interest in an administrative claim. *See In re Grand Jury Subpoenas*, 902 F.2d 244, 248–49 (4th Cir. 1990).

The joint defense privilege may not even be a privilege at all: It adds no protection to otherwise unprivileged materials, but rather protects lawyer-client communications and shared lawyer work-product from being waived. As a result, it also has been referred to as the "common interest rule" and the "pooled-information privilege." *See United States v. Schwimmer*, 892 F.2d 237, 243 (2d Cir. 1989); *see also* Susan K. Rushing, Note, "Separating the Joint-Defense Doctrine from the Attorney-Client Privilege," 68 *Tex. L. Rev.* 1273, 1273 n.4 (1990).

While the joint defense and attorney-client privileges are not the same, their purposes are similar—to assist counsel in providing legal advice to their clients. Whether the case is a criminal investigation or a complex multiparty civil action, enlisting co-parties with common interests to share relevant information is an excellent way to gather the most information.

An articulate justification for the joint defense privilege occurs in an opinion that does not mention the privilege at all. In *United States v. Kovel*, 296 F.2d 918 (2d Cir. 1961), Judge Friendly discussed the now-settled question whether the attorney-client privilege extended to an accountant assisting a lawyer in the representation of a client. Finding such communications were privileged, Judge Friendly said:

> [I]f the lawyer has directed the client, either in the specific case or generally, to tell his story in the first instance to an accountant engaged by the lawyer, who is then to interpret it so that the lawyer may better give legal advice, communications by the client reasonably related to that purpose ought fall within the privilege. . . . What is vital to the privilege is that the communication be made in confidence for the purpose of obtaining legal advice from the lawyer.

Id. at 922 (emphasis omitted).

If a client can tell his story to an accountant to assist his lawyer in providing the best legal advice, he also ought to be able to tell the story to another lawyer, who is the agent of his lawyer for the purposes of the statement. As the court stated in *In re Grand Jury Subpoena Duces Tecum*, 406 F. Supp. 381 (S.D.N.Y. 1975):

> The layman's course through litigation must at least be evened by the assurance that he may, without penalty, invest his confidence and confidences in a professional counsellor. That assurance is no less important or appropriate where a cooperative program of

joint defense is helpful or, *a fortiori,* necessary to form and inform the representation of clients whose attorneys are each separately retained.

Id. at 388 (citation omitted).

Do not be blinded by the brilliant advantages of joint defense agreements. They have disadvantages too.

At the top of the list is false confidence. A quickly executed joint defense agreement may give you a misleadingly warm feeling. It may make you think you have access to everything important happening in the case. Depend on this: You never will. In the pantheon of human endeavor, joint cooperation agreements have a place close to the children's game of doctor: I'll show you mine if you show me yours—but you go first. After some initial suspense, someone finally does but holds something back, just in case.

Your client's co-defendants are in it for themselves. They *are* withholding something. It may be a little—a tiny pearl to be used in cross-examination to deflect suspicion—or it may be a lot—that someone formerly near and dear to your client is selling him down the river. A joint defense agreement does not *require* disclosure; it merely permits disclosure of whatever the parties choose to disclose. Thus, a rule: There will be surprises, unpleasant ones, at trial. Plan for them.

An example is *FDIC v. Cheng,* No. 3:90-CV-0353-H, 1992 WL 420877 (N.D. Tex. Dec. 2, 1992), which concerned an alleged illegal bond trading scheme. One defendant, Levin, was represented by counsel provided by his employer, Shearson Lehman Brothers, Inc. Levin also had private counsel. Levin signed a joint defense agreement with Shearson and the other defendant traders, but he also secretly negotiated a settlement with the government through his private counsel. Levin's joint defense comrades learned of his two years of cooperation with the government only during his deposition.

The jilted co-defendants moved to disqualify the government's counsel and Levin's own lawyer and to dismiss the case. They argued Levin had fraudulently joined the agreement, disclosed privileged information, and undermined the remaining defendants' trial strategy. Levin denied he disclosed privileged information, maintaining that he had simply outmaneuvered his co-defendants. 1992 WL 420877, at *2.

The court, while concerned with "the degree of deception" practiced by Levin's counsel, was not persuaded that the remaining defendants had been "substantially prejudiced" and determined that any breaches of the agreement should be addressed at trial. *Id.* at *3–*5. Levin got his deal and his lawyer; his co-defendants got partial motion costs. *Id.* at *6. Dicta suggest interdefendant *esprit de corps* did not survive the motions.

Learn the lesson taught to Mr. Levin's co-defendants before it is painful for you: Keep your eyes open when you enter into a joint defense agreement. Such an agreement is a litigation tool, both useful and dangerous. It can help or hurt.

A second danger is that damaging breaches of the agreement can happen without anyone's knowing. If detected, the conduct may be impossible to trace to the source and likely will evoke little court sympathy. If a breach is identified, there may be little that can be done before trial, even if it threatens extensive damage to a coordinated defense or ends hopes of a negotiated disposition.

The *Cheng* court held that breaches of a joint defense agreement could be countered through suppression of privileged information at trial; that does nothing, however, to offset the pretrial damage to victimized defendants in the interim. *Id.* at *3. The lesson is simple: If you snooze (or get stabbed in the back), you lose. That may seem a harsh maxim, but other cases agree with it. For example, in *United States v. Melvin*, 650 F.2d 641 (5th Cir. 1981), the district court dismissed a criminal indictment after a defendant who was cooperating with the government (and who was not formally represented) attended a meeting of defendants and their counsel with a "wire," permitting authorities to eavesdrop. *Id.* at 642–43. Thereafter, the cooperating defendant continued to meet with defense counsel and to debrief the government.

The Fifth Circuit reversed the trial court's dismissal of the indictment, following *United States v. Morrison*, 449 U.S. 361 (1981), in holding that no rule requires dismissal as a sanction for government intrusion into the lawyer-client relationship. In *Morrison*, the Supreme Court stated its "approach" to Sixth Amendment violations had been to

> identify and then neutralize the taint by tailoring relief appropriate in the circumstances to assure the defendant the effective assistance of counsel and a fair trial. The premise of our prior cases is that the constitutional infringement identified has had or threatens some adverse effect upon the effectiveness of counsel's representation or has produced some other prejudice to the defense. Absent such impact on the criminal proceeding, however, there is no basis for imposing a remedy. . . .

Id. at 365.

Thus, the Fifth Circuit held there was no "breach" remedy available to complainants absent a showing of prejudice. In an aside, it observed that even if there were prejudice, the remedy is simply suppression of the information. 650 F.2d at 643–44. To elaborate on the rule: If you snooze, you lose, and the court won't do much about it.

A third danger of joint defense agreements is that they can create potential or actual conflicts of interest between the lawyer and his client. Remember the melodrama with which we began: A lawyer who is party to a joint defense agreement cannot use information gained through the agreement to further the interests of his client at trial, even if the information is helpful or exonerating.

This mix of loyalties comes into sharpest focus in the multiple-defendant trial in which the lawyer, a party to the joint defense agreement, must cross-examine other defendants who are themselves parties to the agreement. The cross-examining lawyer will not be able to impeach with incriminating or inconsistent information acquired through the agreement.

Some defense counsel might say "So what?" and rationalize as follows: But for the joint defense agreement, the information would not be shared at all. My client would be worse off in that case. It's better to have information I cannot use than to have nothing at all. It's a small price to pay, and no rational client would disagree. Besides, who would complain?

This once rhetorical question has been explored in several recent criminal cases, in which the government has tried to disqualify counsel who were parties to joint defense agreements. An intriguing (and, to defense counsel, offensive) example is *United States v. Anderson,* 790 F. Supp. 231 (W.D. Wash. 1992). In that case, Anderson, an employee of VSI-Chatsworth, entered into a joint defense agreement with other employees, including some who expected to testify at his trial. *Id.* at 231. Upon learning of the agreement, the government moved to disqualify Anderson's lawyer.

Moving to Disqualify

In two sets of motions, the government argued that Anderson's counsel might have to cross-examine VSI-Chatsworth employees who were sources of joint defense information, and that this limitation would prevent Anderson's lawyer from conducting a full examination. The government also claimed the joint defense agreement was effectively an obstruction of justice, permitting the defendants to engage in an ongoing criminal conspiracy. *United States v. Anderson,* No. 91-109R, slip op. at 3 n.1 (W.D. Wash., Sept. 3, 1991) (order and opinion describing government's claims). The government relied on *Wheat v. United States,* 486 U.S. 153 (1988), in which the Supreme Court determined that the Sixth Amendment presumption in favor of counsel of choice can be overridden by the Court's interest in conflict-free criminal trials. *Id.* at 163. The *Anderson* prosecutor also raised as a conflict the payment of Anderson's legal fees by a corporate parent of VSI. 790 F. Supp. at 232.

The district court denied the motion. It determined that Anderson "knowingly and intelligently waived his right to counsel with undivided loyalties." *Id.* The government persisted with a second, similar motion. In response, the court appointed a special master to determine whether a conflict existed, concluded there was none, and permitted the trial to go forward. *Id.* at 232–33.

Anderson teaches mixed lessons. Because the district court found both an intelligent waiver of potential conflicts and no actual conflict, it never had to state its view of the conflict issue in general. In addition, the motive and the standing of the government to move to disqualify opposing counsel remain uncertain. Was the prosecutor altruistically concerned about Anderson's constitutional rights, distressed that a defendant would be victimized by a conflict-ridden lawyer? Was he guarding against the risk that Anderson himself might later attack a conviction with conflict arguments? Or was he merely playing the chutzpanik, the one who cries "help, help" while beating you up?

Anderson is not an aberration. It is far from the only case in which the government has tried to disqualify counsel who join joint defense agreements. In *United States v. McDade*, No. 92-249, 1992 U.S. Dist. LEXIS 11447 (E.D. Pa., July 30, 1992), the court declined to disqualify a law firm that had a joint defense agreement with (and had briefly represented) a defendant who agreed to testify against the firm's current client, Congressman Joseph McDade. The government claimed the law firm could not represent McDade competently while honoring its joint defense responsibilities.

The court recognized the irony, saying "it would appear something of a perverse paradox for me to drive a cold chisel in between client and counsel under the constitutional rubric of affording him effective counsel." *Id.* at *6–*7. As to cross-examination of the former client, "logic suggests that not only could that lawyer not cross-examine on those confidential matters, but no lawyer could. . . . [B]y forgoing the right to cross-examine on those otherwise unearthed pieces of evidence, the defense, in effect, forgoes nothing." *Id.* at *8. The court also noted that the joint defendant did not want privileged material disclosed, but had also disclaimed interest in disqualifying his former counsel. *Id.* at *9.

And there is more: In *United States v. Bicoastal Corp.*, No. 92-CR-261, 1992 WL 693384 (N.D.N.Y., Sept. 28, 1992), the government moved to inquire "into defense counsels' potential conflicts of interest." *Id.* at *1. The court gave the back of its hand to the government's claim of a right to discovery on this issue, holding that a joint defense agreement "raises no conflict that would not otherwise exist." *Id.* at *5. The court also stated that acknowledging the existence of such an agreement, much less providing a copy of it, would be an unwarranted intrusion into the defense. *Id.* at *6.

You might think that such cases would discourage the government's apparent quest to police the use of joint defense arguments. But prosecutorial zeal runs deep. Despite the lukewarm court reception for this crusade, instances have occurred in which United States attorneys have mailed letters to defense counsel in criminal investigations demanding information on joint defense agreements "in order for us, and the Court, to effectively evaluate the[ir] impact." The letter quoted, which was produced by the United States Attorney for the Eastern District of California, demands information regarding the existence, terms of, and signatories to joint defense agreements, plus copies of all such agreements. It demands that counsel identify whether and from whom they have received information and identify all meetings claimed to be joint defense privileged. It seeks information on witnesses who were interviewed without their counsel, witnesses who declined to sign the agreement, the source of the referral of the case, and the source of payment of legal fees.

Of course, if all that information were provided, there would not be much left of the agreement, or the privilege, for the government to "evaluate." Not surprisingly, defense lawyers decline to provide this information.

Does the government intend to attack joint defense agreements on every front until the issue is decided in its favor? And, whether or not that is the case, what does the government have in mind?

According to Barbara A. Corprew, deputy chief of the Department of Justice (DOJ) Fraud Section, there is no formal or informal DOJ policy to attack defense agreements. She asserts, however, that the government must protect itself from postconviction claims of ineffective assistance of counsel. As a result, she told one of us, "we are seeing more and more efforts [by prosecutors] to bring conflicts issues to the fore." Pointing to *Bicoastal Corp.*, she said that most prosecutors who raise the issue seek a judicial inquiry into potential conflicts under procedures similar to those laid out in Federal Rule of Criminal Procedure 44(c). While Corprew does not believe a court would necessarily view the existence of such agreements as creating a conflict per se, she believes they raise concerns "about the quality and accuracy of witness accounts of the events in question, and whether these accounts may be shaded or varnished by [interdefendant] discussion of facts and legal defenses."

Corprew also notes that corporations wishing to cooperate with the government could find that a joint defense agreement "may be inconsistent with what the corporate volunteer wants to achieve through voluntary disclosure." The responsibilities imposed by the agreement may conflict with a corporation's ability to cooperate with the government, she indicated, and thus limit the benefits available through cooperation. She added that individual employees seeking immunity may find that they are more attractive candidates if they are not parties to a joint defense agreement.

On the civil side, gaining information under a joint defense arrangement also may lead to calls for disqualification. There is even a possibility of indirect disqualification when one of the members of the joint defense group is disqualified. This situation arose in a fairly extreme fashion in *Essex Chemical Corp. v. Hartford Accident & Indemnity Co.*, 1998 U.S. Dist. LEXIS 899 (D.N.J., Jan. 28, 1998). In that case, Essex Chemical sued its insurers to recover for environmental liabilities, and the defendant insurers executed a joint defense and cost sharing agreement to coordinate activities. *Id.* at *4. After years of litigation, Essex realized that the firm representing one of its insurers had previously represented Essex and had gained knowledge of Essex's environmental practices and liabilities, which was directly at issue in the coverage litigation. *Id.*

Essex moved to disqualify not only its prior lawyers, but *all* defense counsel who were parties to a joint defense agreement. *Id.* at *4–5. When Essex's prior counsel, Skadden Arps, voluntarily withdrew from the case, the motion focused on the remaining defense lawyers.

A magistrate judge initially disqualified all defense counsel, finding that Skadden's participation in the joint defense group created a risk that confidential information acquired by Skadden during its prior representation might be used to the detriment of Essex. *Id.* at *6. The magistrate judge presumed confidential information from the previous Skadden, Arps engagement had been shared among defense counsel in spite of their contrary representations. *Id.*

On appeal, the district court reversed the magistrate's decision, finding it unreasonable to reimpute knowledge of the disqualified lawyers to all lawyers who collaborated with them absent "a painstaking factual analysis." *Id.* *33. The district court also found that the magistrate failed to weigh the impact of hardship disqualification and improperly applied the "appearance of impropriety" test. *Id.* at 40–42. The district court remanded the disqualification motion for hearing, leaving open the possibility of indirect disqualification. *Id.* at *44. (At the time this article was prepared, the remand hearing was pending.)

Assume that you now have examined the good parts and bad parts of the joint defense privilege. Assume further that you've taken into account the government's view. You still believe that such agreements provide more benefits than dangers. How do you make such an agreement, and what should be in it?

The first question is fundamental. Should you put it in writing?

A written agreement is not *required* for shared communications to be protected. Most of the leading cases on the subject, such as *Continental Oil, Hunydee,* and *McPartlin,* say nothing about a written agreement, and several recent cases hold that a written agreement does not change the character of the privilege. In *Bicoastal Corp.,* 1992 WL 693384, the court found no merit in the government's attempt to distinguish the common law joint defense privilege and written agreements, stating that "defendants with common interests in multi-defendant actions" may share information without risking waiver of the attorney-client privilege. *Id.* at *5. More directly, in *Sig Swiss Industrial Co. v. Fres-Co System, USA,* No. 91-0699, 1993 WL 82286, at *1 (E.D. Pa., Mar. 17, 1993), the court explicitly stated there is no requirement of a written agreement before joint defense protections apply.

If the law does not require a written agreement, is there reason to have one? Might it not be just another dangerous piece of potentially discoverable paper that could hurt your client? And if the government got hold of the agreement, wouldn't it be a road map to witnesses and, indirectly, to the issues you believe are most important?

Possibly, but despite those concerns, there is good reason to have a written agreement. The law will not get better for you if you do, but written evidence of your agreement may determine whether the law is applied to your situation at all. It is axiomatic that a party claiming a privilege bears the burden of establishing that the privilege applies. In *In re Bevill, Bresler & Schulman Asset Management Corp.,* 805 F.2d 120, 126 (3d Cir. 1986), the claim of a defendant, Bevill, that statements at joint meetings were protected by the joint defense privilege failed because he could produce no evidence "that the parties had agreed to pursue a joint defense strategy." More recently, a district court found that "one party's mistaken belief about the existence of a joint defense does not, and cannot, give rise to a joint defense privilege." *United States v. Sawyer,* 878 F. Supp. 295, 297 n.1 (D. Mass. 1995).

This situation arose with a vengeance in *United States v. Weissman,* No. S1 94 CR. 760 CSH, 1996 WL 737042 (S.D.N.Y., Dec. 26, 1996). In a motion to dismiss a multicount indictment, defendant Jerry Weissman argued that counsel for his former employer, Empire Blue Cross Blue Shield, improperly disclosed joint defense information to the government. In support, Weissman and his lawyers testified that two crucial meetings at which he discussed his allegedly criminal conduct took place under the shield of a joint defense agreement. Unfortunately for Weissman, Empire's counsel denied any agreement.

The court was not impressed by Weissman's contention that a general joint defense agreement should be inferred from the parties' conduct, finding that "[i]n the absence of written documentation of any joint defense agreement," the parties were in a "swearing contest" regarding the existence of an agreement. *Id.* at *22. The court found Weissman could not demonstrate that the actions of the parties amounted to "an agreed-upon joint strategy of representation." *Id.* at *24 (quotations and citations omitted).

Weissman also argued that the two meetings were protected by explicit oral joint defense agreements. His counsel testified that he began the first meeting by stating that Weissman had information to share pursuant to a joint defense agreement, and that Empire's counsel assented. *Id.* at *14. Counsel also testified that the oral agreement was reflected in his contemporaneous notes, though the notes could not be located. *Id.*

Empire's lawyers testified there was no such agreement, and that after the first meeting "the first thing we commented . . . was how amazing it was to us that that confession had been allowed to occur without the protections of some sort of privilege discussion." *Id.* at *15. Moreover, their notes reflected no agreement. In light of this evidence, the court found there was no joint defense agreement. *Id.* at *17.

With regard to a second meeting, the notes of Empire's own counsel stated that the meeting took place "pursuant to an oral joint defense agreement." *Id.* at *18. This clear evidence of the parties' intentions persuaded the court that Weissman's statements at that meeting were privileged (though partly waived). But it was a Pyrrhic victory; Weissman, having cooperated with his employer over several weeks without a written joint defense agreement, was without protection when many of his statements were forwarded directly to the government.

You don't want this to happen to your client. Return for a moment to Judge Mentis's courtroom, where we began. You have overcome the government's bogus claim of a conflict, and you are now listening to Tom Turncoate—your client's former best friend and now the government's star witness—as he testifies about his conspiracy. In response to yet another leading question (is the judge awake?), Tom begins to say how he knows your client is involved: They discussed it—in your office. You jump up.

"Objection, Your Honor. Mr. Turncoate cannot testify about joint defense matters."

Judge Mentis stirs. "Is that right? Did your client and Mr. Turncoate have a joint defense agreement?" You assure him they did. A pause. You see his next words coming. They are in capital letters. "MAY I SEE THE AGREEMENT, PLEASE?"

Consider the possible responses.

Take One. "Well, Your Honor," you stammer, trying to sound well informed. "Of course, the law doesn't require a written agreement. As you know, the witness and my client were indicted together and have common interests or, well, at least they did until Mr. Turncoate turned, and they are—or were—thus entitled to share information in furtherance of their respective defenses."

The prosecutor pounces. "Your Honor, there is no written agreement. And I remind the Court that a common course of conduct is what a conspiracy is all about. Surely Mr. Counsel doesn't challenge the government's right to elicit testimony about preindictment communications between defendants." The judge nods. Your client winces. You begin to sweat.

Take Two. "Of course, Your Honor. May I approach?" At the bench, you produce the agreement. "Your Honor, I ask that you examine this in camera. In it, my client and Mr. Turncoate acknowledge their common defense interests, and Mr. Turncoate and his counsel commit not to disclose information shared in furtherance of these interests. And, of course, such agreements are themselves joint defense material, so the prosecutor really shouldn't see it." In the reverent silence, you cite

Bicoastal Corp. as authority that the provisions of joint defense agreements are privileged. "1992 Westlaw 693384, at *5," you say with a knowing look.

You gaze at the judge confidently as he flips through the pages of the agreement. The prosecutor mumbles that if the law says that, the law is an ass. The judge speaks: "Objection sustained. The United States will not inquire into privileged matters." He informs the jury it is unfair for the government to ask a witness about his trial preparation with counsel.

In which scene would you rather star?

What goes in a written joint defense agreement? What does not? Joint defense agreements are rarely parsed by courts, so there is little case guidance on those questions. The typical agreement is drafted as though the author had passed through the Legalese Cafeteria, picking up this phrase and sampling that one. It is based on something someone found bouncing around the office a few years back, you are not sure from where, and it was changed just enough so that no one will say it was copied. It recites that there is an agreement to share information, defined as "joint defense material," and swears all involved to secrecy, now and forever. Sometimes, to add a note of erudition, it cites *Continental Oil, Hunydee,* and *McPartlin* and says with great formality, "We want what those guys got."

There is nothing wrong with this. However, there are a few basic matters that also should be addressed in your written agreement. First, you should identify clearly the case, the litigation parties, and the parties to the agreement. State that the parties to the agreement intend to share privileged information to further a common defense and that the parties intend all such communications to be, and to remain, confidential.

Nondisclosure Commitments

The agreement should commit each signatory not to disclose privileged communications or documents to anyone who is not a party to the agreement without first getting the consent of all signatories who can claim a privilege as to the requested information. It also is a good idea to require that documents exchanged under the agreement be marked as "Privileged Joint Defense Material."

The agreement should provide that the joint defense materials be used solely for preparation of the defense of the ongoing investigation or case. The parties to the agreement should also agree to notify all other signatories immediately if joint defense information is sought by a nonparty, by subpoena, or otherwise, and they should commit to resisting production. This resistance should include going to court for relief before producing information.

Finally, the agreement should try to guard against future conflict problems. In an ideal world, all parties who expect the protection of the joint defense privilege would sign, as would their counsel. However, trying to get all the defendants in a large criminal case to sign the same document is like herding cats. It can't be done. There is also a danger, albeit remote, that the government would seek, as it did in the *Anderson* case, to treat such an agreement—especially if individually signed by each defendant—as further evidence of a conspiracy.

As an alternative, each lawyer might sign the agreement as "counsel to defendant Bill Blow," and thereafter make a separate written agreement with his client stating that the advantages and disadvantages of the agreement have been discussed and reciting that the client understands. In that separate agreement the client should acknowledge that none of the lawyers except his own owe any duty to him other than as set forth in the joint defense agreement, and that he is aware that he might be subject to cross-examination by other counsel who have signed the agreement. This agreement also should include an acknowledgment that conflict issues may arise through the agreement, but that the client has chosen to enter the agreement despite the potential dangers, and that he expressly waives wholly conflict-free representation.

Likewise, if the parties to a civil action foresee that future litigation between them is likely (for example, for contribution or indemnity), the agreement might also provide that each party may use the same counsel in the future litigation, *notwithstanding that confidential material may have been exchanged in the preceding litigation that could raise a technical conflict.* This bit of foresight may prevent an ugly disqualification motion.

Whether the agreement is embodied in an informal letter or on parchment with the first line stating "witnesseth" or "to all to whom these presents come, Greeting" is a matter of personal taste.

Criminal Discovery for the Civil Litigator

Candace Fabri and Rebecca Cochran

In a civil case, discovery is limited only by the parties' pocketbooks and the lawyers' imaginations. In a federal criminal case, however, this is true for only one party: your opponent, the prosecutor. A federal prosecutor can discover almost anything. With few exceptions, he or she need not share any of it with the defendant until trial. For the uninitiated, criminal discovery may seem like the game of hearts Alice played in Wonderland: The prosecutor has all the cards, and the prosecutor makes up all the rules.

What can you do if you represent a person who has just received a grand jury subpoena or, worse, an indictment? To start, you must understand some things about the federal criminal system, its rules of procedure, and the mentality of the prosecutors who are governed by both.

This knowledge can be helpful even if you never represent a criminal defendant. A prosecutor acquires evidence from many sources, even those not suspected of any wrongdoing. In Chicago's "Operation Greylord" judicial corruption cases, for example, valuable evidence was provided by housekeepers, jewelers, dressmakers, restaurant owners, and car salesmen. Their testimony showed that some judges with $50,000 salaries had $150,000 lifestyles. When the government contacted these witnesses, many called the last lawyer they had encountered. That lawyer could have been you.

Criminal discovery occurs in two phases: preindictment and postindictment. Preindictment discovery is the prosecutor's all-out use of nearly limitless resources to gain information. Postindictment discovery is the defense lawyer's attempt, with imperfect tools, to catch up and

---

Candace Fabri, formerly executive assistant U.S. attorney for the Northern District of Illinois, is a judge of the Circuit Court of Cook County, Illinois. Rebecca Cochran is an assistant professor of law at the University of Dayton Law School.

learn as much as possible about the prosecutor's case. Both phases are governed by the Federal Rules of Criminal Procedure.

The federal prosecutor's principal preindictment tool is the grand jury subpoena. It is a fearsome device, one of the most powerful devised by legal ingenuity. Unfettered by the 100-mile limit of Civil Rule 45(c)(3), or the reasonable notice requirement of Civil Rule 30(b)(1), the federal grand jury subpoena is not limited by narrow time or relevance standards. It can require production of documents or testimony immediately—a "forthwith" subpoena—or at a future date when the grand jury sits. If the government remains solvent and can pay travel expenses, it can demand the appearance of witnesses nationwide, and United States citizens worldwide. Fed. R. Crim. P. 17(e). In certain circumstances, it can reach evidence of assets in offshore banks and in foreign countries.

As white collar crime has become more sophisticated, the use of the grand jury subpoena has too. It is far-reaching and tenacious. Little escapes: Testimony, business documents, bank and telephone records, credit reports, handwriting or voice exemplars, photographs, and hair samples all are fair game. As one president learned, no one's evidence is exempt. *United States v. Nixon,* 418 U.S. 683, 707–13 (1974). (A parenthetical note: Federal grand jury subpoenas differ radically from their state counterparts, which are usually subject to territorial restrictions.)

The most extraordinary aspect of preindictment discovery, particularly for civil litigators, is that it takes place in total secrecy. Neither prosecutors nor grand jurors can disclose what occurs in a grand jury proceeding. Fed. R. Crim. P. 6(e). Grand jury witnesses can, but usually do not. As a result, the target of a grand jury investigation is sometimes the last to know.

Despite its power, you are not defenseless before a grand jury subpoena. Your resources include yourself, your client, your relationship with the prosecutor, and Criminal Rule 17(c).

First, consider the role of the prosecutor. While a subpoena ostensibly issues on behalf of the grand jury, that is often a fiction. The prosecutor, usually acting unilaterally, determines who will get subpoenas and what evidence will be sought. It is the prosecutor, not the grand jury, who can extend subpoena response times or modify the scope of production. Grand juries are not rubber stamps for the prosecutor, but it would be naive to minimize the prosecutor's role.

How the subpoena is served and how your client responds to it are also important. Unlike service under Civil Rule 45(c), most federal grand jury subpoenas are served by an investigating agent—someone from the IRS, FBI, or other government agency. This is intentional. Government officials, just because of who they are, may intimidate many people. This may cause a subpoena recipient to talk before he or she has a chance to consult a lawyer. Confronted by witnesses who take the subpoena and slam the door, these agents usually can get them to open it again. They often say something like this: "If you cooperate now, I'll talk to the prosecutor. You won't even have to come downtown to the grand jury." In subtle ways, agents suggest that cooperation now will divert the full wrath of the federal government.

Because people served with subpoenas often talk first and call later, their lawyers are often left to pick up the pieces. If your client calls while he is being served, and before he has answered any questions, tell him to say good-bye politely to the agents. If he has talked, tell him to stop, and find out what he thinks he has said. Then call the prosecutor or agent to learn what they think your client said.

In representing a subpoenaed person, you *must* get an answer to this question: Is your client the target, a subject, or merely a witness? These terms have special meanings. A "target" is the person the grand jury investigation is aimed at. A target will be indicted if anyone is. A "subject," though not the focus of a grand jury investigation, may have criminal exposure from the matters under investigation. A "witness" is someone the prosecutor believes has no criminal exposure. Ordinarily, the term "witness" is synonymous with "observer": a person with information, but with no role in advancing any criminal conduct.

Which of these three is your client—target, subject, or witness? The only person who knows for sure is the prosecutor.

Before talking with the prosecutor, talk with your client. Remember that people who may have committed crimes are not always totally candid. You may conclude from your client's account that she is just a witness. But, based on what she did not tell you, you may think she is the target. Listen skeptically. Defense lawyers who believe everything they hear find a lot of "witness" clients indicted.

Do not rely on your client's account alone. Talk with the prosecutor. Most grand jury subpoenas list the prosecutor's name and phone number. If not, call the U.S. attorney's office and ask to speak with the prosecutor assigned to the investigation. Most offices catalog investigations by a number, such as 88GJ99, and that number is always on the subpoena.

Whatever you think about your client's status, appear cooperative with the prosecutor. This does not necessarily require real cooperation. But the appearance of cooperation will get you further than hostility or resistance. Ask the prosecutor directly about your client's status. Force the prosecutor to use one of the three key terms—target, subject, or witness. Without these magic words, you will know little more than what your client told you. Most prosecutors know they should tell counsel their client's status. However, because the magic terms are so significant, some prosecutors are reluctant to use them. If a prosecutor will not say your client is a witness, assume that he or she is a subject, or perhaps even the target.

Particularly for a civil practitioner, the best result of a talk with the prosecutor is learning your client is a witness. In fact, this message is bad news only for criminal defense lawyers with mortgages. Remember, however, that the good news of "witness" status is subject to change as the investigation develops. A prosecutor's statement that your client is a witness will usually come with the caveat "at this time." This is not the same thing as immunity or a commitment not to indict, so act accordingly.

Document production for a witness is usually arranged at his convenience; documents are often produced outside the presence of the grand jury. If your client is a witness, he may never see the inside of the grand jury room. If, however, the prosecutor wants to preserve the witness's testimony by a formal appearance, that is usually scheduled at the witness's and your convenience. The appearance itself is often eased by a prepared statement the witness reads to the grand jury.

If the prosecutor says your client is a witness, there is one thing you must do: Get it in writing. Do this *before* producing documents or permitting testimony. Prosecutors usually stand behind their word, even at the cost of losing a possible target, but witness status is too important to leave as an oral representation. Most prosecutors have a form letter, called a "nonsubject letter." Get one. If the prosecutor fails to give you a nonsubject letter, but has said your client is a witness, confirm that by sending your own letter. Specifically state that testimony or documents will be offered only based on the prosecutor's assurance of witness status. If the prosecutor refuses to give you a nonsubject letter or disputes your letter confirming nonsubject status, stop cooperating and be wary.

Preindictment Ploys

If the prosecutor says your client is a subject or target, consider consulting an experienced criminal defense lawyer. No stage in a criminal prosecution is more important to a subject or target than the grand jury phase. Many subjects have made themselves witnesses by providing significant testimony against a target. By providing evidence on bigger targets, even targets themselves may become witnesses. Even if such metamorphoses are not possible, favorable guilty pleas can be negotiated by cooperative subjects and targets during the preindictment phase. In all of this, do not underestimate the value of experience and good lawyering. More criminal cases are won before indictment than after.

If the time comes for testimony, your role will be limited, whether you represent a witness, subject, or target. You, as counsel, may never enter a federal grand jury room during testimony. Your client may leave the grand jury room to consult with you before answering questions, but you cannot go in. (Many state systems are quite different. *See e.g.*, 725 I.L.C.S. 5/112-4.1, the Illinois provision for advice of counsel and presence of counsel in the grand jury room.)

When you represent a target or a subject before the grand jury, the key question is not the content of your client's testimony. It is, instead, whether he should testify at all. For most seasoned defense lawyers, that is an easy question. They assert the Fifth Amendment privilege; they waive it only in return for immunity. Few targets help themselves by testifying before the grand jury. It often compounds their problems and adds an extra count—false declaration before a grand jury—to the indictment.

The question of document production by a subject or a target is not as easy to answer. The Fifth Amendment prohibits compelled testimony. But documents voluntarily created in the past may not be viewed as compelled testimony. In *United States v. Doe,* 465 U.S. 605, 610–11 (1984), the Supreme Court held that a grand jury subpoena for the preexisting records of a sole proprietorship did not require compelled testimony. The only testimonial aspect of the production, according to the Court, would be the actual production and authentication by the sole proprietor before the grand jury. This means that if the government immunizes the act of production itself, the documents themselves are not privileged. They must be produced.

A former Chicago judge learned about *Doe* immunity the hard way. He had to produce originals of his checks, check registers, and other personal financial records. *United States v. McCollum,* 651 F. Supp. 1217, 1221–22 (N.D. Ill.), *affirmed,* 815 F.2d 1087 (7th Cir. 1987). After the government located a handwriting expert and some eyewitnesses to authenticate them, these documents became the cornerstone of the government's case.

Suppose you want to try to make the subpoena go away entirely? A motion to quash can be brought by anyone served with a grand jury subpoena. These motions are, however, rarely seen because they are seldom granted. A motion to quash is governed by Rule 17(c): "The court on motion made promptly may quash or modify the subpoena if compliance would be unreasonable or oppressive." When your client gets a subpoena, the first thing to do—and to do quickly—is to consider whether you can satisfy this rule.

In doing this, forget what you know from civil discovery. The instincts and tactics you developed there will not help you in bringing a motion to quash. What is unreasonable or oppressive in civil discovery may be well within the power of a grand jury subpoena. The grand jury can subpoena documents that previously have been produced to the government or that contain information the grand jury already has. And forget about the civil protective order: Your client must produce embarrassing and humiliating material. *See, e.g., In re Grand Jury Investigation,* 459 F. Supp. 1335, 1345 (E.D. Pa. 1978). Confidential business information is equally unprotected. *See In re Grand Jury Subpoenas Involving Charles Rice,* 483 F. Supp. 1085 (D. Minn. 1979). Even the attorney-client and work-product privileges, ubiquitous mainstays of civil practice, are "strictly confined within the narrowest possible limits." *United States v. Lawless*, 709 F.2d 485, 487 (7th Cir. 1983).

In *theory*, a grand jury subpoena must seek information relevant to the investigation; it must specify the documents sought with reasonable particularity; it must cover a reasonable time span; and it must serve a proper purpose. In *practice*, however, the grand jury is often permitted fishing expeditions unheard of in civil litigation. One circuit does not even require that the subpoenaed documents be relevant to the grand jury's investigation. *In re Grand Jury Subpoena (Slaughter)*, 694 F.2d 1258, 1260 (11th Cir. 1982).

Successful motions to quash—and they are rare—require a showing of an improper use of the grand jury's power, such as an effort to gather information to pursue a civil investigation, *In re Rabbinical Seminary Netzach Israel Ramilis*, 450 F. Supp. 1078, 1085 (E.D.N.Y. 1978), or a request so broad and vague that it cannot conceivably be answered. *In re Grand Jury Subpoena*, 829 F.2d 1291, 1301–02 (4th Cir. 1987), *cert. denied*, 469 U.S. 925 (1990). Although these are uncommon circumstances, do not hesitate to make a motion to quash if there is some basis for it. You might get lucky. The judge might agree.

A better approach is to seek half a loaf. File a motion to modify. These are more promising devices—with good reason. A motion to modify, also governed by Rule 17(c), acknowledges that the grand jury is entitled to something; it disputes only the scope or the volume of the production sought. Since grand jury subpoenas directed to corporate targets can put any civil document request to shame—every corporate record generated within the statute of limitations, for example—the judge may be willing to shave it down to a rational scope. Your years of civil litigation have trained you for this moment. Whittle away, month by month and document by document. Make reasonable written offers to the prosecutor. If the prosecutor remains intransigent, make your motion to modify, using all of your compromise offers as exhibits.

There is a last element of preindictment discovery for the defense, but it cannot be explored at length here. Conduct an aggressive defense-oriented informal investigation. Determine the key documents and be as familiar with them as the prosecutor. Get statements from witnesses before investigating agents reach them. This discovery must be conducted without the benefit of compulsory process, but it must be done.

Suppose the worst has happened. Your client has been indicted. Begin with this principle in mind: The purpose of criminal discovery by the defense is not to determine the truth; it is to find out how much of the truth the prosecutor knows. Given the rules that govern criminal discovery, that is not easy.

Consider a common kind of prosecution: a mail fraud case. Someone is selling something that no one who knew all the facts would want. The defendant has moved beyond the outer limits of sleazy salesmanship. He has lied and used the mails to help him do it. As you read the following account of such a case, think about the discovery you could get if it were a civil suit. Then brace yourself as you fall down the rabbit hole into the Wonderland of criminal discovery.

Your client, Rich Realtor, has created a retirement community on a lake in Arizona. But the lake is missing. Rich's sales pitch, describing the pleasures of spending twilight years fishing and canoeing, has been effective: Thirty people who heard it promptly mailed in checks.

Rich just as promptly mailed out letters saying floods had delayed construction. After getting this letter, one anxious fisherman called a federal agent. The agent, already dreaming of his own retirement, wanted to hear the sales pitch in person. Without disclosing his government affiliation, he met Rich and later prepared a written report. Then he interviewed the 30 purchasers and wrote witness interview statements.

A Scam Uncovered

Ever conscious of the office's win-loss record, the prosecutor was not satisfied with 31 witnesses. He wanted a tape. The prosecutor persuaded Rich's brother-in-law to wear a wire in return for the government's overlooking the ounce of cocaine he had just purchased from a confidential informant. Family ties are not as strong as they used to be.

Rich chatted freely with his brother-in-law. Then his brother-in-law (and his tape recorder) chatted freely with the prosecutor. Rich's references to "suckers" and "the desert" were recorded for posterity and the jury.

Crime is a business. Like all good businessmen, Rich kept lots of records. The grand jury subpoenaed them, as well as his slide show and brochures. Finally, the prosecutor sent the same federal agent back to identify himself and confront Rich with the results of the investigation. Then Rich finally did something right. He took the Fifth and called you.

The civil litigator in you wants to depose the purchasers. But you cannot. You also cannot see their interview statements. You want to serve a document request for records the grand jury got. Again, you cannot. You may not see those records until they are offered in evidence. It almost goes without saying that you cannot serve interrogatories on the ready-to-retire agent or learn the identity of the confidential informant who was so nice to Rich's brother-in-law.

You will not get this discovery because of Criminal Rule 16. If Rule 16 requires production, you will get it. If not, it may never see the light of day.

What can you get under Rule 16? From a generous prosecutor, you will get copies of the lulling letters written by Rich and the tape recording made by his duplicitous brother-in-law. Maybe you will get a terse report on Rich's invocation of the Fifth Amendment when questioned by the government agent. From a parsimonious prosecutor, you will get only a Cheshire cat smile.

Rule 16 is a looking-glass that reflects the Wonderland of postindictment discovery. You cannot learn the identity of the government's witnesses. You cannot obtain pretrial discovery of witness statements and grand jury transcripts. You cannot even see your client's records unless you agree to give the government your own exhibits.

You will also be disheartened—but by now probably not surprised—to learn that Rule 16 does not require the government to identify the 30 purchasers eager to testify against Rich. You can move for a list of government witnesses, but, unless many witnesses are expected to testify, such motions are usually not granted. See *United States v. Jackson*, 508 F.2d 1001, 1006–08 (7th Cir. 1975). You may, in fact, first learn the identity of the government's witnesses when they take the stand and state their names. The only silver lining in this cloud is that the prosecutor gets equally poor notice of the names of your witnesses.

To the civil litigator, a particularly surprising aspect of Rule 16 is that it specifically excludes discovery of the report and interview notes of the investigating agent who heard Rich's sales pitch. 18 U.S.C. § 3500; Fed. R. Crim. P. 26.2. You may not know what the witnesses said to the agent and prosecutor until their direct trial testimony is over. After direct testimony, if the defense asks, the prosecutor must turn over so-called "3500 material" or "Jencks" statements of the witnesses. But, if you fail to make a motion for production following the direct examination, you will lose your Jencks Act rights to the material. *United States v. Benz*, 740 F.2d 903, 915 (11th Cir. 1984), *cert. denied*, 474 U.S. 817 (1985).

In Rich's case, as in most federal criminal cases, there is a problem with Jencks material. The interview statements were actually written by a federal agent. Unless a purchaser adopted or approved the statement after it was written, or unless it was essentially a verbatim transcript, it may be viewed as the *agent's* statement, and not that of the witness who was interviewed. *See United States v. Claiborne*, 765 F.2d 784, 801 (9th Cir. 1985), *cert. denied*, 475 U.S. 1120 (1986). If the investigating agent does not testify, the Jencks Act does not apply, and the witness interviews may never be produced.

In a surprising gesture of evenhandedness, interview statements *you* secure cannot be discovered by the government before trial. If you hired a private investigator who interviewed a government witness—maybe an erstwhile lakefront investor—and prepared a report, that report will not be seen by the prosecutor or the witness until after the witness's direct examination. Fed. R. Crim. P. 26.2. Your investigator's report may give you a basis for impeachment that is a total surprise.

Despite the severe limitations on defense discovery, never give up. Ask for as much as possible, as specifically as possible, as soon as possible. You may never get it, but the fact that you have asked may some day put you in a better position. Virtually every subpart of Rule 16 begins with the phrase "upon request of a defendant." As defense counsel, it is your job to make that request, either in writing to the prosecutor or by motion to the court.

Once you make a request, Rule 16(a) permits you to get two kinds of evidence without having to produce anything of your own: your client's statements and his prior record. Unfortunately, in Rich's case, this information will scarcely help prepare a defense. Still, in other cases, it can be useful.

"Statements of the defendant" are defined in Rule 16 as written or recorded statements made by the defendant. Most prosecutors act as if this means only confessions. Technically, however, the term also covers things like Rich's letters to the retirees and the conversation his brother-in-law recorded. Ask for such things; you are entitled to them.

Under the rubric of defendant's statements, you are also entitled to your client's recorded grand jury testimony if it relates to the charge and to "that portion of any written record containing the substance of any relevant oral statement" made by your client to a person known to be a government agent. Fed. R. Crim. P. 16(a)(1)(A).

Rule 16 thus allows the prosecutor to withhold some of the key evidence that will be offered at trial: the substance of Rich's statements to the purchasers and to the undercover agent during the course of the offense. These statements are the heart of the government's case. They can be devastating, but the first time you hear about them will probably be when the purchasers and investigating agent testify at trial. *United States v. Hoffman*, 794 F.2d 1429, 1432 (9th Cir. 1986).

The other information you can get without giving up anything is the defendant's prior criminal record. You must have this information. You need to determine the risk of impeachment by prior conviction if your client testifies at trial. In fact, if the government fails to disclose a prior offense, you may be able to persuade a court to bar impeachment using it.

Rich does not have a prior record, so you learn nothing about his past. But do not be fooled into thinking that the prosecutor also knows nothing. Rich may have run the same scam in Florida. If Rich was never arrested or convicted in the Sunshine State, however, you will not be told about his previous venture. Even so, the prosecutor may know about these earlier escapades, and may be planning on using them at trial as evidence of prior similar acts under Federal Rule of Evidence 404(b). *United States v. Chaimson*, 760 F.2d 798, 804-07 (7th Cir. 1985). The only way you can find out is to move for all the evidence of other crimes that the prosecutor intends to offer. Rule 404(b) provides that "upon request of the accused, the prosecution . . . shall provide reasonable notice in advance of trial." Without the request of the accused, you run the risk of not receiving it.

Once you have Rich's statements and record, anything else you get will trigger reciprocal obligations: You will have to give something to the prosecution. Still, you must press on. You will want to see copies of Rich's business records subpoenaed by the grand jury and any other documents the government will offer at trial. If you ask, Rule 16 allows discovery of books, papers, documents, photographs, and tangible objects if any of three conditions are met: (1) the items are material to your defense; (2) they will be used in the government's case in chief; or (3) they were obtained from your client. Note well the term "case in chief": This means the government need not produce material obtained from retirement community purchasers that it plans to use to impeach Rich should he testify at trial. It also is not required to produce exhibits that might be used in a rebuttal case.

So much for the good news. Once the government complies with your request, you must reciprocate. The government can now get documents and tangible objects you intend to introduce at trial. Fortunately, reciprocity stops there. If a dragnet grand jury subpoena has not swept up all of Rich's books and records, you need not turn over the ones it missed, unless you intend to use them in your case in chief at trial. Fed. R. Crim. P. 16(b)(1)(A). However, such documents may be subject to subpoena later if Rich waives his Fifth Amendment privilege and testifies.

Even the apparently useful aspects of Rule 16 have limits. One is that the rule sets no deadline for the reciprocal production. Frequently, a prosecutor's production occurs on the eve of trial. Not to be outdone, many defense lawyers produce their exhibits at the start of their case or, better yet, just before each witness testifies. These maneuvers are limited only by the judge's patience and sense of fair play.

A defense lawyer's strongest ally in seeking early disclosure of witness statements and exhibits is usually the judge's calendar. Judges set a limited period for each trial. Your ability to prepare in advance helps the judge meet that goal. Convince the judge that, if you get government witness statements in midtrial, you will need long recesses to prepare your cross-examinations. The judge will convince the prosecutor to speed up production.

Moving Beyond Rule 16

Finally, again if you ask for them, the written results of physical and mental examinations and of scientific tests should be made available, *if* they will be used in the government's case in chief. If the prosecutor is holding an expert for rebuttal, you will not see that expert's report until after his direct testimony. Reciprocity requirements are like those described earlier.

Beyond what Rule 16 offers, you should use your civil litigation skills to try to learn what the prosecutor already knows. A motion for a bill of particulars under Criminal Rule 7(f), for example, can be used to bring meaning to the boilerplate indictment, which simply recites the statute, occasionally inserting the words "Rich Realtor." Persuade the court you need better information to prepare your defense and to avoid prejudicial surprise. The government may be forced to give you details beyond Rich's name and the date of the offense. *See United States v. Kendall*, 665 F.2d 126, 134 (7th Cir. 1981), *cert denied*, 455 U.S. 1021 (1982).

Grand jury proceedings are another element of the prosecutor's knowledge you can try to discover. Move for disclosure of grand jury testimony under Criminal Rule 6(e)(3)(c). Convince the judge that the need for disclosure outweighs the public interest in maintaining grand jury secrecy. The prosecutor also has ex-parte procedures to obtain Rich's tax returns, to tap his telephone, to monitor his outgoing telephone calls, and to record the return addresses of mail delivered to him. Make a motion to get this information. *See, e.g., Alderman v. United States*, 394 U.S. 165, 184–85 (1969). As with certain bad acts material, production of such information is not addressed directly by Rule 16. Your argument should emphasize your unique need for these specific items.

Although not contained in any rule, there is an overarching principle applying to all postindictment discovery. It concerns exculpatory evidence—material that suggests the defendant is not guilty or should not be punished. If such evidence exists, and it is requested by you, the prosecutor must disclose it. *Brady v. Maryland,* 373 U.S. 83, 87 (1963).

Brady and Giglio

So-called "*Brady* material" takes many forms. It can be as obvious as another person's confession to the crime. It can be as subtle as what surveillance agents did *not* see when they were watching the defendant. Whatever form it takes, the prosecutor must produce *Brady* material *before* the end of the trial. But, as in all aspects of postindictment discovery, you should make a specific request. If you do, and the government does not disclose specific *Brady* material, a conviction may be reversed if there is a reasonable chance that the nondisclosure may have affected the outcome. *United States v. Agurs,* 427 U.S. 97, 112 (1976).

A relative of *Brady* material—frequently called "*Giglio* material"—is information that impeaches a government witness. *Giglio v. United States,* 405 U.S. 150, 154 (1972). When the credibility of a witness can determine guilt or innocence, failure to disclose evidence bearing on that credibility is subject to the *Brady* principles. Once again, you should ask promptly and specifically. If the government has promised lenient treatment in return for testimony, you should be told about it. If the government's star witness is a child molester, you should see his rap sheet. If the government has been overly generous with the statutory witness fees, you should get the checks.

Informants are another target for defense discovery. The government increasingly uses informants, usually criminals who have been arrested and are cooperating with the prosecutor. These charming folks often introduce undercover agents to their former partners in crime. Move to obtain the identity and the whereabouts of any confidential informant involved in your client's case. Try to persuade the court that disclosure about the informant is needed to ensure a fair trial and that this need outweighs the public's interest in preserving the informant's anonymity. *Roviaro v. United States*, 353 U.S. 53 (1957). But do not be optimistic. Applying the *Roviaro* test in Rich's case, you should not expect to meet his brother-in-law's cocaine dealer.

Unlike preindictment discovery, postindictment discovery gives both the defense and the government access to compulsory process. Criminal Rule 17 allows both sides to compel the attendance of witnesses at trial. With leave of court, either side may obtain an early return on a subpoena for documentary evidence. But watch out: A Rule 17(c) trial subpoena lacks the secrecy of the grand jury proceedings. Any documents produced become available to both the government and the defense, regardless of who sought the subpoena to get documents. For that reason, prosecutors are reluctant to use early return trial subpoenas. Defense lawyers should be equally cautious. The prosecutor will see whatever you get. Be sure it will not hurt your client.

Again, it is important to say in passing that many state criminal proceedings are different. Many state prosecutors have extensive production obligations, and these requirements have teeth: In state court, failure to list a witness or a document can preclude the prosecutor from using it.

Such an effective and salutary remedy—barring use of withheld evidence—appears less often in federal criminal court. Many judges will permit use of previously undisclosed documents if there is some explanation for the delay. There is one exception: A prosecutor cannot fail to turn over a defendant's statement and then try to cross-examine with it. This is because the absence of the document may have affected the defendant's decision to testify. A court may well conclude that its use in cross would deny the defendant a fair trial. *United States v. Rodriguez*, 799 F.2d 649, 654 (11th Cir. 1986). For other types of documents produced at the eleventh hour, your prospects are dimmer. The thing to do is to point to your prior, specific requests, and argue that your entire defense strategy was predicated upon the documents' absence.

In the same way, even if a pretrial witness list is required, omissions are not necessarily fatal. Again there is an exception: If the defendant has an alibi and the prosecutor has asked for the names of alibi witnesses, the defendant must respond. Otherwise, the alibi evidence may be excluded. Similarly, if there will be an insanity defense, the defendant must tell the government and disclose any proposed expert trial testimony relating to it. The government may then demand that the defendant be evaluated by a government-selected expert.

Given the frustrations for the defense in criminal discovery, Alice might prefer a trial scripted by Lewis Carroll to one conducted in a federal courthouse. But, despite the handicaps, you will get information: Unlike Alice's opponents, yours will play by the rules. Prosecutors take their ethical obligations seriously. They do adhere to *Brady*, for example. Some may in fact give you more than the rules require. Many will identify their witnesses and give you their statements well before trial. A few will even turn over everything the government has. But you should know that this open-file approach is not always just altruism or neighborliness. Many such forthcoming prosecutors believe that a defendant who knows all of the government's evidence is more likely to plead guilty than one who does not. Fortunately, open-file prosecutors are not always right. The discovery you fight for may help you win an acquittal.

Unconventional Strategies in White-Collar Criminal Investigations

Vincent J. Connelly and Tyrone C. Fahner

For a business executive, it may begin with a subpoena requesting any and all financial records relating to a stock purchase or a particular year's tax return. For a bank official, it may be formal interview by investigators who want to know about a series of seemingly unrelated loans. For a prominent political fund-raiser, it may be an invitation to stop by the prosecutor's office for a few questions. Whatever the originating event, clients who are well-regarded—and usually well-heeled—increasingly find themselves the unexpected object of a criminal investigation.

As the distinctions between acceptable business practice and criminal wrongdoing fade, even the most prominent and experienced white collar professionals get an uneasy feeling when a criminal investigator or a prosecutor enters their lives. The concern is not unfounded. As publicized in a variety of investigations stretching from Wall Street to the Silicon Valley, white collar crime is now a major emphasis of law enforcement officials who are armed with a variety of new statutory tools.

Until not long ago, risk analysis in the business sector simply concerned itself with potential civil or regulatory sanctions. Today, that calculus is more discerning and embraces the possibility of indictment and imprisonment, as well. As prosecutors gain experience and grow more comfortable with legislation relating to taxes, money laundering, and fraud in government contracts, their ability and eagerness to affect the white collar segment has increased dramatically. Similarly, tools such as the Racketeer Influenced and Corrupt Organizations Act (RICO) supply prosecutorial weapons that are as effective against business executives as they are against any organized crime figure.

Vincent J. Connelly and Tyrone C. Fahner are partners at Mayer, Brown & Platt in Chicago. Mr. Connelly formerly served as the chief of special prosecutions in the Chicago U.S. attorney's office; Mr. Fahner formerly served as the Illinois attorney general.

In most instances, law enforcement agents and prosecutors initially will view the client as wearing one of three labels:

- the client may be a witness needed to provide factual information for the investigation and potential trial;
- the client may be a target, to be indicted, perhaps along with many others, if the investigation succeeds; or
- the client may have an uncertain status that eventually must be resolved favorably—as a witness or as someone who knows too little to inform the investigation—or unfavorably—as a target.

All three situations offer opportunities for useful lawyering. The lawyer always must learn as much about the investigation as possible, consult (and often console) the client, and offer appropriate strategies for handling the many decisions that affect the outcome. And from the start, the lawyer must recognize that a nontraditional strategy may best keep the client from being indicted.

On the federal level, prosecutors enjoy virtually unlimited investigatory resources and unbridled discretion in choosing which cases to pursue. Thus, it is not unusual to find that United States attorneys' offices convict substantially more than 80 percent of the defendants who go to trial. The truly great defense victories are won in preventing an indictment from being returned in the first place. Although the tactics and techniques used on behalf of the client at the investigatory stage may be known to but a few, they often represent the ultimate service to that client.

There are three pivotal moments in the investigative process: the initial determination that an investigation is being conducted; the decision regarding a client's appearance before the grand jury; and the effort to convince law enforcement officials to follow the course that maximizes whatever realistically attainable benefit the client's circumstances permit.

For clarity, let us consider each of these focal points in the context of those three labels: witness, target, and uncertain status. Defense tactics, of course, can be blended whatever the client's initial status. Every criminal investigation is extraordinarily fact-intensive and, therefore, easily lends itself to combined strategies.

Sometimes the client is no more than a routine witness who will not require extensive legal assistance. For example, consider a bank officer who receives a subpoena requesting all the information on customer John Evader's account. A call to the prosecutor confirms that Evader is under investigation for hiding income. The bank officer has no involvement with Evader and merely has been asked to produce the bank's records relating to Evader's deposits and withdrawals. In this case, the lawyer does not need to engage in lengthy discussions with either the client or law enforcement officials.

Or take the client who has been asked to submit to an interview regarding his outpatient minor heel surgery and one follow-up visit to the doctor. According to the investigators, it seems that Doctor Overbill sought and received insurance payments and Medicare reimbursement for expensive major surgery and a dozen outpatient treatments. Except for explaining the standard procedures followed in the course of an investigation and possible trial, the lawyer need only inform the client that he or she probably will be showing an unscarred foot to a jury.

But some clients may be more—or less—than pure witnesses. They may be something of a hybrid—a witness who nevertheless has possible criminal exposure.

A government lawyer announces that the client, a licensed broker on a national exchange, is needed in the grand jury to explain sales relating to a customer, the notorious James "The Butterfly" Spreads. Spreads is the target of the investigation. After debriefing the client about the Spreads transaction, the lawyer is convinced that the broker has met all professional and regulatory requirements. But the lawyer remains uneasy. The lawyer foresees the potential, under certain circumstances, for a prosecutor to charge that the client might have technically assisted Spreads's fraud.

Whenever the client is exposed to some potential risk, even if unlikely, the lawyer should seek a "witness letter" from the prosecutor's office. The letter should state categorically that the client is sought merely as a witness and is not a target in the investigation. The witness letter has enormous significance, for, as a practical matter, it insulates the client from prosecution.

With good fortune, the client will never cross paths with a zealot or a convoluted prosecutorial theory that would expand liability beyond what the reasonable would believe was possible. But it does not matter. Cases sometimes linger; prosecutors sometimes transfer. Facts expand as investigations continue. Early targets may suddenly "cooperate" and implicate others. To minimize his own predicament, Spreads may someday claim that the licensed broker masterminded the whole scheme.

Witness letters are not uncommon. Ordinarily, they do not exceed one page, and often they are form letters. The introductory language provides a general reference to the investigation, such as "Please be advised that this office is conducting an investigation of alleged marketing manipulation...."

The letter often states that the prosecutor's statement about the client's status responds to the lawyer's desire for clarification:

> You have indicated to me that your client, Licensed Broker, is going to testify truthfully. You requested my assurance that your client is being called to testify as a witness and not as a subject. The government states that it is asking your client to testify truthfully not as a subject, but as a witness to matters and events.

Most letters conclude with a limiting and revocation clause:

> If your client is not completely truthful, he or she could be prosecuted for perjury. Other than the representations in this letter, no commitments or promises have been made to you or your client.

Although such concluding comments are standard, the language may surprise a professional or executive whose integrity and credibility are at least implicitly challenged by the threat of pursuit if the executive does not tell the whole truth.

Because of the importance of the witness letter, the lawyer may want to consider originating the letter rather than merely requesting it. While local custom often dictates that the witness letter be sent by the prosecutor's office to the lawyer and the client, if that precedent is not firmly entrenched, send the prosecutor a summary of your discussions. ("This will confirm our recent meeting and your representation that my client is a witness . . . " and so forth.)

The following true story helps exemplify the significance of the witness letter. A former prosecutor then in private practice represented a prominent businessman who had provided false business invoices for his customers, enabling them to take business deductions for items of personal consumption. The lawyer knew that the prosecutor's office had a policy of requiring supervisory approval for the usual witness letter. When the lawyer learned that an experienced but mediocre assistant prosecutor was handling his client's case, the lawyer offered the client's full cooperation in naming customers, supplying documents, and agreeing to testify. Also, the lawyer offered to send over a letter confirming the status of the client as a witness.

Before the supervising prosecutor reviewed the investigation, the file already contained two extremely self-serving but effective letters thanking the assistant for clarifying the status of the prominent businessman as a witness. As the case developed, it became clear that the businessman had actually created the scheme and actively solicited his customers to participate in it. But the prosecutor's office was foreclosed from proceeding criminally against the businessman; it was confined to charging the customers in a series of tax cases.

Once the client's status as a witness has been established, the client often will be asked to testify before the grand jury. Similar to the strategy of obtaining a witness letter, it helps to prepare a statement for the client to read to the grand jury.

A prepared statement forces the client to focus on the issues and on his or her involvement in the matters under investigation. It permits the lawyer to assist in the recollection process. Particularly important when the lawyer is barred from accompanying the client in the grand jury room (as is true in all federal investigations), it apprises the lawyer of the client's actual testimony.

These benefits usually outweigh the drawbacks to using a prepared statement. One drawback is that the testimony will appear coached. Despite the superficial appeal of that objection, a prepared statement is nothing more than the logical extension of the ordinary witness preparation that occurs in all litigation. Besides, the benefits of focusing the testimony and saving time in the grand jury room outweigh the harm from possible cross-examination about coaching during trial, which usually can be dealt with in a way to make the criticism ineffective.

Sometimes another concern relates to the completeness of the witness's statement. A lawyer can score points in cross-examination of a witness who provided only a four-page statement to the grand jury yet remembered enough to testify at trial for two days. This problem can be blunted by including introductory language in the prepared statement that places the grand jury testimony in a wider context. ("The following testimony is intended to serve as a brief summary of matters about which I have knowledge.")

Similarly, the grand jury statement should conclude with language that permits flexibility in later testimony. ("The foregoing statement is only a summary. Should I have further time to review documents and recollect about events, I would be able to provide greater detail.")

If the client has been assured of witness status but has not received written confirmation of that assurance, the grand jury appearance provides the opportunity to memorialize that understanding. The examining prosecutor can be requested to inform the grand jury that the client's appearance is based on the representation that he or she is only a witness. Also, the client should be instructed to announce to the grand jury (again, better through a prepared statement) that this appearance stems from the prosecutor's assurance that the client is a witness, and nothing else.

The announcement from a law enforcement official that the client is a target of the investigation should cause grave concern, but not despair. Good (that is, effective) prosecutors rarely proclaim categorically that a client will be indicted, particularly if the investigation is not finished. Even the most blunt prosecutors will qualify their remarks by noting that the client is the focus of the criminal inquiry absent "a change of circumstances" or "some revelation of presently unknown evidence." Good lawyering requires that you consider a variety of tactics.

When the client is only a witness, the prosecutor will want both the client and lawyer to understand at least the basic outline of the investigation so that they are better able to provide assistance.

No such incentive exists when the client is a target. To the contrary, most prosecutors want to keep the target in the dark as much as possible. After all, the more the target knows about the investigation, the easier it is to fashion a defense to the anticipated indictment.

Thus, the target's lawyer should gather as much information as possible as early as possible. Identifying the type and number of investigative agencies can tell you something. A case conducted exclusively by the Internal Revenue Service will have different limits from one investigated jointly by an Inspector General's office and the Federal Bureau of Investigation. Learning the nature of the potential charges can introduce added opportunities to convince law enforcement supervisors to rethink whatever initial adverse recommendation they receive from the investigators. Criminal antitrust charges, RICO-based criminal charges, and certain public corruption violations, for example, must be approved by the Justice Department in Washington, D.C., before a local prosecutor can seek an indictment. Similarly, certain criminal tax violations must be approved by the Justice Department and the Internal Revenue Service's "headquarters" before the field office can return the charge. Because an agency's or supervisor's particular habits may affect the outcome, time spent learning about the procedures and the people who will be dealing with your client's case is vital.

If your client is a target, you must decide whether the client should testify before the grand jury. Some prosecutors will subpoena the target to testify, on the articulated theory that, as a matter of balance, the target of the investigation should be allowed to present his story to the grand jury. Be aware, though, that experienced prosecutors often extend this olive branch because of the many pitfalls that the chance to testify creates. Not only will the government gain the possibility of indicting the target (for making false declarations before a grand jury, outlawed by 18 U.S.C. § 1623), but the target's appearance also provides the occasion for unlimited discovery.

Despite the allure of these opportunities, other prosecutors feel that a target should not be harassed by a subpoena. Usually, however, they will allow the target to testify before the grand jury upon request.

Unlike many areas in which facts, personalities, and legal arguments must be balanced against the risks and then evaluated, in this kind of case the legal advice is always simple: The client should never testify. Never. Under any circumstances. Unfortunately, though, clients do not always take this advice. *See, e.g., United States v. Isaacs*, 493 F.2d 1124 (7th Cir. 1974) (prosecution of a judge and former Illinois Governor Otto Kerner).

But isn't it possible that the client's eloquence and logic will convince the grand jury not to return an indictment? Possible, yes, but no more likely than it is that the prosecutor will drop the case against your client out of simple goodness of heart.

Without debating the assertion that grand juries have become nothing more than rubber stamps for prosecutors, efforts to convince grand jurors not to indict are not nearly as effective as presentations made directly to the prosecutor's office. A grand jury simply decides by majority vote that there is probable cause to believe that the client has committed the proposed crime. Although grand jurors do not take their responsibilities lightly, the task often becomes mechanical after a sufficient number of grand jurors have heard a sufficient number of presentations. In most grand juries, the clean slate that the client may believe exists has been written on and erased many times over before the client's case is heard.

Better to address the prosecutor's office. Like all lawyers, prosecutors want to succeed, and that means convicting indicted targets. But convictions result only when proof is marshaled beyond a reasonable doubt, not just to meet the probable cause standard of the grand jury. Moreover, the trial jury must be unanimous. So, if you want to make a case for dropping an indictment, convince the prosecutor.

Most major prosecutorial offices have a policy of supervisory review before indictments are returned or are willing to meet for a review if the target's lawyer requests it.

When should such a request be made? There is no point in presenting your best arguments to an office that has categorically decided to indict. If the client has substantial mitigating circumstances—whether factual, policy, or personal—the lawyer should ask to present the client's case to the decision makers in the prosecutor's office. The decision makers often will include the person assigned to the case, that person's immediate supervisor, and either the first assistant or the United States (or state's) lawyer.

Since you will be giving the prosecutor information about your client and your position that it would not otherwise have, get a commitment that the prosecutor's office will listen with an open mind and will at least consider concluding the case without indictment.

Having obtained the commitment, you must consider how to communicate the client's view to the prosecutors. If the client is sincere, articulate, and able to answer pointed questions (characteristics more common in the white collar target than in the stereotypical street criminal), seriously consider having the client make a presentation directly to the prosecutor (with, of course, your assistance). Or consider a written statement.

Whatever method you use, your presentation should not be a confrontational debate intended to convince the agents and assistant prosecutor that they are incapable of convicting their target. Even if that were true, the prosecutors will not agree, and you will have defeated your aim.

Some lawyers feel that their clients get further protection if their interview statements or prepared remarks are made through a "proffer" (an oral or written statement provided to the prosecutor by the lawyer and client that is treated as a hypothetical outline of information). Once the client's statements are made on the record, they can be put to whatever future use is permitted under the rules of evidence; the proffer creates less exposure for the client because it is not an admission. Frequently, prosecutors request a hybrid statement that, like a conventional proffer, cannot be used in their case in chief if a trial takes place, but unlike the usual proffer can be used to cross-examine a client whose trial testimony varies from the proffer and used in the prosecutor's rebuttal case if the defendant presents evidence that contradicts it.

Although you need not immediately accede to the prosecutor's request that the client interview be conducted under the most favorable prosecutorial conditions, the distinction between a proffer and a transcribed statement that is fully on-the-record is not of paramount importance. The important decision is whether to allow the prosecutor to interview the target client at all. That is the legal equivalent of radical, experimental surgery. It is an extreme measure that should be used only when the interview may persuade the prosecutor to drop the indictment. That decision will not likely turn on concerns about procedural distinctions afforded the client's statement if a trial takes place. Go ahead only if you think you can prevent the trial from taking place.

The radical strategy can succeed. Years ago, a prominent local elected official was accused of having accepted bribes in connection with official decisions that benefited certain real estate interests. The official and his lawyer made themselves available for several days of inquisitorial questions by supervisory prosecutors in the office considering the indictment. Because the official was able to explain his own behavior and to provide information showing that his accusers had a motive to lie, the local official avoided an indictment that surely would have been sought without the interview.

A well-known executive obtained a similarly successful result. He managed a large commercial building, and the investigation focused on his apparent misuse of building funds to improve his personal property. His examination by a number of prosecutorial supervisors over several days resulted in the decision not to indict him. By skillfully explaining the client's personal and family difficulties, and painting an unsympathetic picture of the owners of the building, the lawyer and the client convinced the prosecutors that redress for the client's actions was better left to private civil litigation. Had there been no meeting, the prosecutors unquestionably would have asked the grand jury to return an indictment.

Two examples assure nothing. Yet, they do reveal that unconventional lawyering sometimes provides the safety net for a client falling toward an otherwise inevitable indictment.

Much like the awesome responsibility of defending a truly innocent client at trial, the effort to represent a client whose status is uncertain presents a tremendous opportunity to perform usefully, if not heroically.

In investigations of white collar crime, the gray area between pure witness and announced target is heavily populated. Unlike violent or drug-related crimes, the white collar crime almost always involves a critical unknown that the prosecutor must satisfy, namely, the mercurial element of intent. Frequently, there will be no debate over the facts either internally in the prosecutor's office or between the prosecutor and the client's lawyer. Instead, the argument will center on matters such as the client's willfulness, his fraudulent purpose, or his misrepresentations. These issues often are determined by accumulated, circumstantial evidence rather than by direct testimony.

When the client is a witness, the prosecutor will contact him to learn his testimony. When the client is a target, the prosecutor may contact him either to initiate plea discussions or to provide a final chance to set forth reasons the client should not be indicted.

Unfortunately, the witness whose status is uncertain is not likely to be approached by the prosecutors at all. Instead, the prosecutors will continue gathering evidence about this witness from other sources. Yet it is to the client's advantage if the lawyer can learn as soon as the prosecutors do that the client may face criminal charges, for the "final opportunity" granted to the target is often provided only after the law enforcement officials have concluded, whether tentatively or fully, that indictment will issue unless some extraordinary late-hour argument spares the client.

Is it not certified madness for the client's lawyer to approach a prosecutor and inquire about his client's status? Aren't those inquiries, particularly from lawyers who frequently represent criminal defendants, likely to send out subliminal signals that this client has reason for concern about his conduct? Isn't the best strategy the traditional suggestion that the client remain silent in the nervous hope that the prosecutor will not call?

The answer to these questions often is no.

If contact already has been made by the law enforcement agent through a subpoena or a request for interview, the lawyer should immediately determine the status of the client. If the prosecutor is unwilling to offer more than the uneasy observation that the investigation is too premature, the lawyer must make it clear that any further contact by law enforcement officials should be directed to the lawyer.

The Lawyer Investigates

Similarly, if the lawyer is aware of a criminal investigation that may involve contact with the client, the lawyer should take the initiative and ask the prosecutor to make contact through the lawyer. Arguably, the request may alert the prosecutor to the existence of the client. Still, if a newspaper has announced that a law enforcement agency is examining the Department of Defense contract awarded to OverCharge, Inc., and the client is the executive responsible for cost accounting at OverCharge, there is no reason to pretend coyly that the client may luck out and avoid being contacted.

Once the preliminary discussion with law enforcement officials is over, the lawyer must gather as much information about the investigation from as many sources as possible. Again, before deciding what to do, find out about the type of investigative agencies, the nature of the potential charges, and the personalities of the people conducting the investigation. Particularly in investigations that focus on multiple officers of large companies, information may be obtained from other lawyers representing clients who already have been labeled as witnesses or targets in the case. Although those efforts will build a complete picture slowly, they may provide early warnings about the pace and scope of the investigation. And they will establish a mechanism for hearing news that will one day prove critically valuable.

Here is an example: It is publicly known that criminal investigators are probing Hy Official, believed to have misused his elected office by demanding kickbacks from a variety of businessmen receiving public contracts. From discussions with client Rich Vendor, the lawyer has determined that Vendor may well have acted on the suggestions of Hy Official. The prosecutor has subpoenaed Vendor to testify before the grand jury.

The ritualistic dance of negotiations between the prosecutor and the lawyer follows. The lawyer requests assurance that Vendor is just a witness. The prosecutor replies that no such commitment is possible at this stage of the investigation. The lawyer requests immunity for Vendor, who then will cooperate fully and reveal what he knows about Hy Official's activities. The prosecutor suggests that the lawyer first present a written proffer of Vendor's testimony so that the prosecutor can evaluate it against independent information.

Now the lawyer and the client face a dilemma. Failure to make a proffer runs the substantial risk that events will overtake their position because others will cooperate, strong documentary evidence of wrongdoing will be uncovered, and the client's past conduct will not withstand careful scrutiny. The lawyer knows that if they make a proffer, it must be sufficiently detailed to satisfy the prosecutor's curiosity and sufficiently accurate to block later credibility problems for the client. Additionally, a prosecutor can never unlearn what has been given to him in any proffer. Although the terms of the proffer may preclude its direct use against the client, the underlying information usually can be used by the prosecutor to pursue any leads that are generated independently.

An experienced prosecutor will never bend from the demand that Vendor, through the lawyer, provide information that the prosecutor can evaluate and verify. To make the evaluation, the prosecutor will use information that will not be shared with Vendor or the lawyer. Occasionally, a prosecutor may concede to the lawyer's request for additional information about the case to discuss the matter with the client intelligently. Depending on the relationship between the prosecutor and the lawyer, a good-faith request may well be honored.

Creating a Chinese Wall

If the request is later seen as a ploy to get information for a client who clearly intends not to cooperate, the lawyer's ability to deal with the prosecutor's office in other cases will be hindered. There is an unverified but widely expressed belief that out-of-town lawyers can better afford to make questionable requests, probably because they are less likely to have other matters with the prosecutorial office.

Through inadvertence or mistake, the prosecutor might accept a completely off-the-record statement from the client. But that scenario places a tremendous burden on the prosecutor to convince the court that the evidence against the client came from sources entirely independent of the off-the-record information. Thus, only an inexperienced, foolish, or needy prosecutor would agree to such a statement.

From the client's point of view, a relatively useful but often overlooked compromise to the stalemate can be reached by creating a Chinese Wall around the proffered client testimony. Rather than allowing the prosecutors and agents who actually are conducting the investigation to review the proffer, the lawyer should request that another assistant become involved in the investigation exclusively to evaluate the information.

The argument is that Mr. Ambitious, the assistant conducting the investigation, cannot be expected to hear or read the proffer of a witness whose status is uncertain without its affecting the course of the investigation. Thus, for example, the lawyer representing Rich Vendor would request that another assistant in the prosecutor's office, perhaps Ms. Detached, be briefed by Ambitious about the investigation. Detached would evaluate Vendor's proffer without revealing its contents, especially to Ambitious. Under the terms of the written understanding among all parties, if the proffer convinces Detached that Vendor should be a witness in the case, Vendor receives the witness letter and provides information to the investigators. If Detached concludes that Vendor's conduct is too egregious to ignore, she tells Ambitious that the proffer has been rejected. Theoretically, Ambitious continues his investigation without making any assumptions about Vendor, but certainly he does so without the benefit of Vendor's own information.

If the prosecutors act honorably, Vendor cannot lose. At best, he convinces Detached to award him a witness letter. At worst, he retains his uncertain status. Regardless, Ambitious does not gain any knowledge from Vendor's proffer.

If Vendor becomes a witness, his testimony probably will be sought in the grand jury. If he paid money to Hy Official, even under sympathetic and mitigating circumstances, conventional wisdom dictates that the lawyer seek a grant of immunity for Vendor's testimony. But do not make a knee-jerk grab for immunity without considering all possible ramifications. Vendor has participated in fraud with a public officer. His company not only supplies its product to Hy Official's agency, it also has multimillion-dollar contracts with various federal departments. After Vendor recounts his statements to Official in a highly publicized trial, his federal contracts will be carefully scrutinized or even canceled; or his top-secret clearance will be denied, thereby ending his contracts. Moreover, his professional license may be suspended and possibly revoked. And his carefully nurtured community image may be seriously tarnished.

True, the negative collateral consequences of giving immunized testimony may pale in contrast with the alternative of facing indictment. But not always. If you can effectively argue that Vendor only handed plain envelopes with cash to Hy Official because of the figurative economic gun that Official held to his head, perhaps the prosecutor can be convinced to consider Vendor as a cooperating victim. By avoiding the need for immunity, Vendor may be able to maintain his business and community standing under the perception that he readily assisted law enforcement officials in their efforts to end the infamous reign of Hy Official. The cloak of immunity will forever convince many that Vendor was as much a crook as was Official, but that his slick lawyer kept him out of jail.

A variation on the Chinese Wall sometimes is available to lawyers who have determined that their clients have had low-level participation in a crime unknown to the prosecutors. The lawyer will submit a detailed written proffer that seeks to provide the prosecutor with enough information to whet his appetite for conviction, but camouflages specifics about the actual organization and the people involved so that no road map leads to the actual culprits. For example, the lawyer will describe his accountant-client's knowledge and peripheral participation in a major effort by high-ranking officers in a publicly held company to manipulate assets. But he will not give names, dates, or places.

Prosecutors often will consider these offers if the equities are sufficient—usually, that means that the prosecutors must feel they are not being asked to pass up the big fish only to net the minnows. Most prosecutors will qualify their acceptance of this offer on the absence of the "inevitability factor," meaning that the acceptance is conditioned on making certain that the scenario provided by the lawyer is not already under active investigation by a criminal agency, such that it would inevitably find its way to the prosecutor's desk independent of the lawyer's effort.

The outcome of most trials is largely unaffected by the lawyer's skills. The overlooked truth is that some cases do depend on the lawyer's talents. The same holds true for representing clients before an indictment has been returned in a criminal investigation.

Facts determine the status of most clients, but they do not control everything. In many cases, the lawyer's creative thinking and persistence—especially when imbued with a realistic sense of expectation—can overcome the initial opinion of a prosecutor.

Staying Clean

Donald H. Beskind and David S. Rudolf

If you can't try the case—try the cops.
　　　　　　The last resort for the criminal defense lawyer.
If you can't get the defendant—get his lawyer.
　　　　　　The prosecutor's version.

Going after the defendant's lawyer is an increasingly popular tactic. But unlike the defense strategy of trying the police, it is not a last resort. Neither is it aimed only at criminal practitioners. Most white-collar criminal defendants once had civil lawyers representing them. The result is that some lawyers who think they are working on civil cases find that the government has a different view of the case—and of them.

The increase in investigations of lawyers is partly the result of broader theories of criminal responsibility under the conspiracy statutes and the prosecutor's new favorite—the money-laundering statutes.

To be sure, some lawyers knowingly violate these or other laws, and the government has the duty to investigate and prosecute them. But all too often, prosecutors investigate lawyers whose only crime has been aggressive representation of their clients' legitimate best interests. And, it seems, the more prominent and newsworthy the lawyer, the better.

Even if the lawyer is not the target of such a prosecutor, he may find himself and his records subpoenaed in an investigation of his clients. You must understand that your files are not exempt from the government's reach. The attorney-client privilege generally does not protect information such as a client's identity, the amount and source of fees, and the manner in which the fees have been paid. *See United States v.*

Donald H. Beskind is of counsel with Twiggs, Abrams, Strickland & Trehy in Raleigh, North Carolina. David S. Rudolf is a partner with Rudolf & Maher, P.A., in Chapel Hill.

Blackman, 72 F.3d 1418 (9th Cir. 1995); *In re Shargel*, 742 F.2d 61 (2d Cir. 1984); *In re Michaelson*, 511 F.2d 882 (9th Cir.), *cert. denied*, 421 U.S. 978 (1975). Nor will the privilege protect documents transferred to the lawyer that would not have been privileged if they had been in the hands of the client. *Fisher v. United States*, 425 U.S. 391, 401–05 (1976).

In recent years the government increasingly has used subpoenas and even search warrants to seek leads and incriminating evidence from lawyers' files. When that happens, the evidence may cast suspicion on the lawyer as well as the client.

So how does an honest lawyer minimize the chance of learning criminal law the hard way—from the inside out? Adopting some practices widely accepted by experienced criminal defense lawyers will help.

If you represent criminal defendants, do not:

- socialize with clients;
- do business *with* clients;
- do business *for* clients;
- provide civil legal advice to clients;
- represent more than one witness or party in any one case;
- take the client's property as fees; or
- take fees from someone other than clients or their families.

Civil practitioners may be surprised by some of the rules, particularly the first. In civil practice, business development is important, and socializing with clients is an excellent way of getting new business. It is understandable that civil practitioners may choose not to follow these stringent rules. But understanding why criminal defense lawyers follow them may help civil lawyers avoid a grand jury subpoena, search warrant, or indictment.

To appreciate the risks of socializing with clients, consider the criminal defense lawyer who meets his client in the Caribbean and then uses the client's yacht for a sail from Eleuthera to Miami. A customs search in Miami reveals that the yacht is carrying cocaine. Will anyone, especially a United States attorney, believe the criminal defense lawyer who claims not to know the client was smuggling drugs? After all, he would not need your services if he were not involved in criminal activities. And you are close enough to be a guest on his boat. Add one crewman who thinks he heard an incriminating conversation, and a conspiracy is born.

Criminal defense lawyers should know that any time they are in business *with* one of their clients, they are at risk. If it turns out that the business is illegal, it will be virtually impossible for the lawyer to claim surprise. Nor should criminal defense lawyers ask clients to invest in lawyer's projects.

Criminal defense lawyers also should avoid doing business *for* their clients. They should not buy or sell property for their clients. Nor should they let clients run businesses out of their law offices. Criminal defense lawyers should say no whenever they are asked to do anything for a client that does not relate to the criminal case they are handling. They should not even take business messages for a client.

Do you doubt this?

Consider the lawyer who received a seemingly innocuous telephone call. A client's friend said he had tried to call the client and had been unsuccessful. The lawyer agreed to contact the client with the friend's message, "I'll be in town tomorrow." He passed the message on. The next day the client was arrested with the friend and a kilo of cocaine. When the friend turned out to be an informant, the lawyer was subjected to a lengthy and anxiety-provoking investigation of his "participation" in a conspiracy to import drugs by helping set up the delivery.

Criminal defense lawyers should also avoid advising their clients on civil matters. The obvious risk is that you will give the wrong advice in a field in which you do not regularly practice. But even if you give your clients the right answers, the government may be interested in why you gave any answers at all.

For example, one lawyer advised a client who was charged with running a successful smuggling ring on how the government keeps track of the movement of cash through Cash Transaction Reports, 31 C.F.R. §§ 103.22 *et seq*. He explained only what the law said: that all cash transactions over $10,000 had to be reported by the bank that received the cash. Unknown to the lawyer, the client never again deposited more than $9,000 at one time. Perfectly legal? Perhaps not. At least one lawyer has been indicted for avoiding the statutory reporting requirement by splitting up his cash fees to make sure that $10,000 was never deposited at any one time.

A less obvious example is the lawyer who advised a client charged with RICO violations on how to set up certain kinds of trusts. While this advice may be perfectly proper for civil clients seeking to avoid estate taxation, the government may think the lawyer is assisting in an attempt to obstruct the forfeiture provisions of RICO, 18 U.S.C. § 1963 (c).

It may also be risky to represent more than one witness or client in a case. Even if your clients do not object, the government may. When the government moves to disqualify you, you may lose all of your clients in the case. Much worse, the government may indict you. The theory will be that your representation of Client A was part of a conspiracy to obstruct justice for Client B by keeping Client A from cooperating with the prosecution against Client B.

Finally, there are two questions on fees: what to take as fees and who should pay them. First, criminal defense lawyers should not take clients' property as fees. The automobile or house that you take as a fee may have been used in illegal activities. It is then subject to forfeiture under various laws such as RICO. What was once a large fee turns out to be a large nightmare. That is not all. Because your name is in the chain of title, the government may think your involvement is less than innocent.

Second, do not take fees from anyone other than clients or their families. One lawyer's former client received a grand jury subpoena. He asked the lawyer to represent him again. With him was a "friend" who was willing to pay the retainer that the client could not afford. The lawyer took the money. He vigorously opposed the subpoena and angered the prosecutor. The prosecutor began to think that the legal services had been provided to the client as a part of the cover-up of the original conspiracy. The lawyer received a grand jury subpoena and was faced with answering the question, "Who paid your fees?" or going to jail. No privilege—and not a happy choice.

Even if you take the advice offered so far, and are entirely circumspect and honest in your dealings with clients, the investigation may still focus on you. Generally, this means a subpoena for your records.

What do you do?

Assume the worst and take the matter seriously. At the least, the prosecutor has put you in the unenviable position of having to explain to your client why certain matters that he always assumed were protected by the attorney-client privilege may be disclosed, such as the amount of money he paid you for your legal advice. At worst, the subpoena may mean that the prosecutor has zeroed in on *you* as a target of the grand jury's investigation. Underestimating the seriousness of this situation may prove disastrous.

The subpoena may force you to risk contempt. Until you are held in contempt for refusing to comply, you cannot appeal a denial of your claim of attorney-client privilege. *In re Oberkoetter*, 612 F.2d 15 (1st Cir. 1980); *cf. United States v. Dionisio*, 410 U.S. 1 (1973). The prospect of being cited for contempt is unpleasant and anxiety-provoking, even if imprisonment is extremely unlikely.

You should do what you would advise any client to do: Call another lawyer with experience in this area. It is important to get a second opinion from someone who can be objective and has dealt with such subpoenas before. Such a person may be able to tell, just from looking at what the subpoena requests, whether the government views you as a suspect or just a witness. Even if this is not possible, it is often easier for that person to call the prosecutor and explain your concerns about being subpoenaed to provide information regarding your clients. At the same time, your lawyer can find out what is going on.

In addition to getting independent and objective advice yourself, notify your client of the subpoena. Tell your client to get the advice of an independent lawyer on whether he wishes you to assert the attorney-client privilege. Why should you do that? The chances are that asserting the attorney-client privilege is exactly what your client should do. Why does he need a second lawyer just to tell him that? Because if you are being investigated, the prosecutor may view your advice that your client assert the attorney-client privilege as an attempt to obstruct the investigation and protect yourself.

If your client wants to assert the privilege, it is your ethical duty to protect his confidences. On the other hand, the judge may order you to disclose the information. To avoid this dilemma, the client, through another lawyer, should move to intervene in your subpoena. The client has an absolute right to do this to protect his privilege. *See* Fed. R. Civ. P. 24 (a)(2); *cf. Gravel v. United States,* 408 U.S. 606 (1972). Once intervention is granted, a court order requiring compliance with the subpoena is immediately appealable without the necessity of a contempt citation for the lawyer. *In re Grand Jury Proceedings* (Katz), 623 F.2d 122 (2d Cir. 1980). Finally, it is not enough to get the objective advice of another experienced lawyer. *Listen* to the advice. Your natural inclination will be to cooperate—to show the prosecutor that you have nothing to hide. But cooperation, if it means giving up records over your client's claim of privilege, may violate your ethical obligations. Also, it may be against your own interest to cooperate without a grant of immunity. If you are a target, it may be necessary to assert your Fifth Amendment privilege, even if you believe there is nothing to hide. The line between an innocent act and a criminal one will be drawn by the prosecutor—not by you. If the prosecutor has decided to indict you, what you say *will* be used against you.

Then silence is golden.

These suggestions are intended to make it less likely that the government will try to get you if it cannot get your client. But no matter what you do, all that stands between you and a subpoena, or even an indictment, is a prosecutor who acts in good faith and exercises good judgment. If he does not, you may join the growing list of lawyers who have learned that the term "criminal lawyer" has two meanings—depending on where the prosecutor puts the emphasis.

Creative Defenses and Desperate Defenses

Juanita R. Brooks

Practicing criminal law is different these days. Oh, the initial client conferences sound the same, and the clients look the same, but make no mistake—there is a difference. Chances are that the client who calls tomorrow will have been the victim of surveillance, wiretaps, videotapes, undercover agents, informants, stings, reverse stings, or a transcribed and taped confession. Faced with technological advances, defense counsel have been forced to take desperate measures. But arguing that black-and-white videos can't be used to convict in a colorized world just doesn't seem to cut it.

There is, however, a last bastion of defense that may work. The client who has in fact committed the crime may not be legally guilty. In other words, after all these years, mental defenses are back in style.

Now this is not to say that a *mens rea* defense should be used in all—or even most—situations. But when the case is otherwise indefensible, and there are facts to support a *mens rea* defense, you may not have much choice. It's either plead to the sheet or try the case. The client's state of mind is your glimmer of hope.

Consider these facts from a case I handled. Your client went to the border and appeared nervous. She was referred to secondary inspection, taken into a room, and patted down. A bulge beneath her clothes was felt. When asked what it was, she honestly replied, "heroin," which was found to be strapped to her stomach. Asked what she planned to do with it, she responded, "I was going to deliver it to a man at Tommy's Bar in Redwood City for $3,000."

After remarking about your client's unflinching honesty, you start to evaluate the possible defenses. Somewhere between insanity and "she

---

Juanita R. Brooks is a partner with the firm of McKenna & Cuneo, L.L.P., in San Diego.

should have picked a better lawyer," you come up with the defense that I actually used: battered woman syndrome.

The reasoning process that leads you to this mental defense is simple. First, you go through the list of traditional *mens rea* defenses. Start with the obvious one: She didn't know she was carrying anything (or she didn't know it was heroin). She sent her sweater to the laundry, it came back, it felt a little bulky, she didn't bother to look. The old laundry defense. But it will not work. She told the customs officials that she knew she was carrying heroin.

So how about blaming someone else? Think duress, for example. But for the classic duress defense, the threat must be immediate. There must be no reasonable opportunity to escape. For duress to work, you need a gun held to her head at the border, but the person who prevailed upon her to carry the heroin was 3,000 miles away in Guadalajara.

Don't give up. Consider a less traditional mental defense. If there was no real gun to her head, maybe there was a psychological gun. Hence, the battered woman syndrome defense is born.

Of course, battered woman isn't the only novel mental defense available today. Another example is the imperfect entrapment defense. Your client appears to be entrapped, but his three prior drug convictions go far to demonstrate predisposition. Turn those convictions to your advantage. The fact that your client is a hopeless addict may be the very reason the agents were able to entrap him so easily. His brain may be so addled by drugs that he will do anything anyone asks of him. Or he may have been so desperate for drugs that the informant knew he would be the perfect dupe. Drug dependency syndrome may be the defense you need.

Salvation Through Syndromes

Perhaps you wish to use an insanity defense, but your client just does not meet the legal definition of insanity. He is a war veteran suffering from posttraumatic stress disorder but not to the extent that he is legally insane. Be creative. Because of his experiences during the war, he now needs to live every minute on the edge. In this case, that means dealing drugs.

In desperate times, these creative syndrome defenses may be your salvation. They can shore up what otherwise would be an imperfect traditional *mens rea* defense. And they can add color and drama to a case that the prosecutor may view as a "lock."

With a syndrome defense, the jury is told that there is no dispute about what happened: "Yes, it was heroin. Yes, she knew it was heroin. Yes, she transported it." Then the jury is given a job to do—and a fascinating one at that. "Ladies and gentlemen of the jury, the question is, why? That's what we're here to determine." By admitting all the facts, you take much of the sting out of the prosecution's case. And by using some creativity, you pique the interest of the judge and jury.

Of course, before you mesmerize the jury with your syndrome strategy and accept your colleagues' accolades for your brilliant tactics, you'll need to put your defense together. As you might expect, this is less glamorous—and more tedious—than arguing the defense in court.

Begin by developing the background information to support the syndrome defense you are considering. Speak with family members. Obtain all your client's medical and psychiatric records. In a posttraumatic stress case, get military records. Get anything that might corroborate your client's story.

Sometimes there is no corroborative information. In my battered woman syndrome case, I spoke with family members to verify the beatings that the woman had sustained. But the family members said they had never seen anything. My client never told anyone about the beatings, and although there were some medical records from a hospitalization, she never told her doctors that the injuries were caused by her boyfriend. All I had to go by was my client's word.

The absence of corroboration may make your job more difficult, but it is far from fatal. In fact, one of the fortunate ironies of syndrome defenses is that virtually every syndrome has a built-in explanation for the lack of corroborative evidence. For example, as your expert will testify, the battered woman considers herself responsible for the beatings, which become a terrible secret she must hide. A similar argument is available with posttraumatic stress syndrome. The defendant is a proud former Marine whose pride prevents him from revealing his delusions to others. With defenses like these, an absence of corroborative evidence is almost as good as an abundance.

Once you've obtained as much information as possible from your client or others, you'll need an expert. During my search for the perfect expert, everyone told me, "Well I hope you get Ms. Smith. She is *the* expert in battered women cases." Resist the temptation to follow that kind of advice. Instead, get an expert from the community. (But don't forget about *the* expert. I'll explain why later.)

Find a teacher from the local college or a local practicing physician or psychologist to whom the jurors can relate. I used a psychologist whom the courts often appointed to examine juveniles in custody cases. Time and time again, this man had been given the court's stamp of approval to determine the future of young children. His judgment, talent, and credibility would be beyond reproach. He knew little about battered women when I first consulted him, but that simply forced him to go through the same reasoning process that the jurors would. I think that made him a more effective witness.

Your expert's first job will be to interview and examine the defendant as a general practitioner might evaluate the condition of a new patient: Take a history, talk to the client, give some tests, make some observations, and then consult the *Diagnostic Statistical Manual IV (DSM IV)*. By reaching a conclusion in this fashion, your expert will have additional credibility: A psychologist who does not specialize in cases involving battered woman syndrome but has researched the syndrome will testify that your client is suffering from it. The D.A.'s carefully prepared cross-examination notes will be worthless. She won't be able to sneer: "Oh I see, you're an expert in the battered woman syndrome who has been hired to examine the defendant and who has found the young lady to be a battered woman. What a coincidence!"

The fact that your expert is not *the* expert also enables him to relate to the jurors on their own terms—to take them through the same process he followed to educate himself about the syndrome. That takes the syndrome out of the ivory tower and puts it into real life.

Was It Invented?

At trial, ask your expert whether the syndrome was invented for this case. I did, and the answer was dramatically effective. My expert explained to the jurors that he too was skeptical about the syndrome—until he did his research. He told them about the syndrome's existence. He explained how researchers put puppies in a cage and shocked their paws with electrical current. At first, the puppies tried to escape. But they could not escape. They were trapped. Eventually those little puppies would just lie down in the middle of the cage and allow themselves to be shocked. "Ms. X is just like one of those little puppies."

Be sure to provide your expert with *all* the information you have, both good and bad. Some lawyers think that bad facts hidden from the expert will somehow go away. They won't. In fact, they'll surface when they can hurt you most.

So tell your expert everything. Let him incorporate the worst facts into the basis of his opinion. That way your expert will be ready with the explanation before being confronted on cross-examination. My client told the agents that she was to be paid $3,000 to smuggle heroin across the border. To say the least, this financial motive was less than consistent with my argument that my client smuggled heroin because she was beaten by her boyfriend. But my expert explained that it is not unusual for syndrome victims to lie to hide their real problems.

Remember that I said not to forget *the* expert? You should contact the leading authority on the syndrome you are using. In fact, if you are worried that the prosecution will score points by hiring the expert to rebut your defense, you might want to hire her early to avoid that risk. But also seriously consider using her to back up your local expert's testimony. If you decide to do that, let your local expert bring her into the case for you.

Having both experts on your team gives you the best of both worlds. The local expert is your answer to the charge that a syndrome specialist would be predisposed to finding the syndrome. The expert will deflect any criticism that your local expert is inexperienced in diagnosing the syndrome. The local expert can admit having never diagnosed the syndrome before and can then explain that this is why he contacted the well-known expert to assist him.

Having your local expert contact the expert has advantages for the expert's cross-examination as well. When the prosecutor asks the expert whether she has ever examined someone and found her not to be a battered woman, the negative answer can be easily explained. The expert can simply point out that she is a specialist—like a cardiologist—and the local expert is a generalist—like a general practitioner. A general practitioner makes an initial diagnosis of the patient's problem and, finding heart pathology, sends the patient to a cardiologist. It is therefore not surprising that every patient the cardiologist sees has heart disease. Similarly, it should not be surprising that every patient the expert sees is suffering from the syndrome to some degree. With that explanation, the jury will see the expert less as a hired gun than as a qualified specialist.

In the battered woman case, I had no witnesses other than my client and my experts. There was not a person in the world who would support my client's version of why she did what she did. Under similar circumstances, suggest that your expert's report and testimony include quotes from the client. That way, even if your client does not testify, her story will be before the jury. And if your client is going to testify, her version of the facts will be put before the jury twice.

Before trying the case, consider a dry run with a mock trial. If the funds are available, hire professional jury consultants to conduct the mock trial. They will solicit members of the community to act as jurors. A videotaped miniversion of the trial can be shown to the mock jury. With a camera in the jury room, you can watch the deliberations from another room. As you listen to the jurors' reactions to your case, a profile of the perfect juror may emerge.

If funds are more limited, recruit a class from the local college. Students are often willing to make the mock trial a project for no charge other than the experience they gain.

The unique arguments of a syndrome defense make mock trials particularly valuable in this type of case. Watching the reactions of mock jurors will help reveal what kind of person may be open to the "I did it, but. . . . " defense. A juror who would be terrible in the run-of-the-mill case might be perfect for your syndrome defense. For example, a juror who would be inclined to convict anyone involved in any way with drugs might be sympathetic to your client who was introduced to drugs by the boyfriend who beat her. On the other hand, just because prospective jurors have backgrounds similar to your client's does not necessarily mean they will be sympathetic. Indeed, they may be the harshest judges of all.

Pretrial preparation of proposed jury instructions is a must. You can't know what type of juror is best until the theory of the defense is complete. And the theory of the defense cannot be fully constructed without knowing what the judge is going to say about the law.

Resist the temptation to rely on pattern instructions. Write your own. Pattern jury charges often refer to a syndrome defense as a legal excuse. Duress, necessity, and self-defense are often called legal excuses. Think of how that must sound to the jury. There is your client, caught with five kilos of cocaine, and what is his defense? "I have an excuse. I was in Vietnam. Where were you in 1968?" "Excuse" suggests whining and rationalizing. Eliminate the word.

The Only Just Verdict

If your jurisdiction and judge permit voir dire by the lawyers, use it to address the syndrome defense. Rendering a verdict of not guilty in a syndrome defense case may be very difficult for some jurors. They will have to go home to their spouses and friends and explain why they acquitted someone who had the heroin, knew it was heroin, and confessed to the crime. From the start, suggest to the jury panel that a verdict of not guilty is the *only* just verdict.

For example, in a case of posttraumatic stress syndrome, suggest that a verdict of not guilty is a message to the world that we will protect those who risked their lives to protect us. In my battered woman syndrome case, I told the jurors that a not-guilty verdict told the wife beaters of the world: "You guys are not going to win. You may have put this woman in a cage for ten years, but we're not going to help you do it for another ten."

If you are not permitted to do your own voir dire, don't despair. Opening statement is not too late. In fact, when you use a syndrome defense, you can get instant credibility with the jury by agreeing with the prosecutor. Consider the following excerpts from my opening statement:

> Ladies and gentlemen of the jury, everything the prosecutor just told you is absolutely true. She did come to the border with heroin—it was strapped to her stomach. And she did appear nervous, and she did tell them she was going to be paid $3,000. It's all absolutely true.
>
> But, this is not the issue. This case didn't start on July 22, 1989. This case began on a cold winter night, in a village in the heart of Mexico when Ms. X's mother died during childbirth.

Start painting the whole wretched scene from the beginning.

Cross-examining the prosecution agents in syndrome defense cases is different from cross-examining in most other cases. Instead of a confrontational cross-examination, conduct an informational one. Prosecution witnesses may be privy to facts that will help with your defense.

In my case, two agents testified that they literally had to cut the heroin off my client's body because it was so securely stuck to her with electrical tape. My cross-examination regarding this fact lasted several minutes. By

561

the end it was clear to the jury that even if my client had wanted to throw the heroin away, she could not have. She simply did not have a choice.

By volunteering that they had checked my client carefully to make sure they had not injured her when removing the drugs, the agents opened the door to more questions. Before the defense case ever began, the agents were shown photographs of my client with her front teeth missing (after a beating by her boyfriend). They were also shown photographs of scars on her wrist (from a suicide attempt) and on her legs (from being thrown by her boyfriend through a plate-glass window). They were then asked whether they had noticed any of these marks while conducting their careful examinations. Their answers were irrelevant; the point had been made.

Anticipating the prosecution's only possible rebuttal is easy in syndrome defense cases. Because the facts are not really in dispute, the prosecution must argue that there is no such syndrome or that if there is such a syndrome, your client is not suffering from it, or that if your client is suffering from it, it is not a defense.

Confront the first argument simply and soundly with an authoritative text. For example, the syndrome you will use should be documented in the medical literature and listed in *DSM IV*. The media can help give credibility to your defense as well. For example, if your defense involves drug addiction leading to entrapment, publicity surrounding the evils of drugs may be your strongest ally. And the attention given to syndromes by Oprah and Geraldo will help prepare prospective jurors for the arguments you will make.

The third argument—that the syndrome is not a defense—is just as easy to answer. Incorporating the syndrome into a legally recognized defense, such as insanity or duress, or incorporating the defense into the crime's *mens rea* requirements should be enough to get you a jury charge on the issue. And if you're lucky, the judge may tell the jury that your syndrome in itself is a legal defense.

As might be expected, the case usually comes down to the prosecution's argument that your client is making it all up. Every prosecutor will ask the expert on cross-examination: "Isn't it possible that the defendant just made this up? Your opinion is based only on what the defendant told you. So if the defendant told you a lie, wouldn't your opinion be inaccurate?" Every expert will answer "of course." Redirect may hold the key. In my case, the redirect examination of my expert included the following:

> Q: Dr. Smith, taking into consideration [the client's] verbal I.Q. being a couple of points above mentally retarded, and her reading level being that of a second grader, what are the possibilities or the abilities of someone of that functioning level being able to make this up?

A: I think it would be virtually impossible for her to fabricate a story that would allow myself and another psychiatrist to diagnose her as suffering from battered woman syndrome. It would require her to have read sophisticated books and understand the symptomatology of the battered woman syndrome. She is not a sophisticated woman. She is uneducated. She had very limited experiences in her life. She is a field worker and has worked in a restaurant. For her to falsely describe the level of sadism and to falsely detail the character of Mr. Gonzales in the terms she did, she would have to have a tremendous creative imagination. There is no evidence in the test results that could possibly support that she could make this story up.

To that, I said thank you. And I sat down.

Dress Without Excess

Having prepared your expert to testify, it is now time to prepare the client. Your client's dress, manner, and speech must all be consistent with the defense. If the client is a war-weary veteran, the double-breasted suit and gold Rolex have got to go.

I suggested that my client dress as she would for church. She showed up wearing black stiletto heels and a purple satin dress. I guess her church is different from mine. I toyed briefly with the idea of switching clothes with her, but realized that her apparel might affect my credibility with the jury. Luckily, her grandmother had come to court with her, and they switched clothes. My client looked much more presentable in the orthopedic shoes and knit shawl. And one of the jurors later commented about how sorry he felt for my client when he got a look at her grandmother.

Clothes may help make the client, but clothes alone won't do the trick. Your client's demeanor throughout the trial is crucial. Not that lines should always be delivered with feeling. In fact, it is not unusual for someone suffering from one of these syndromes to have a "flat affect," speaking calmly and unemotionally. Your expert can suggest questions that you can ask your client on direct examination that may break through the barrier. Your expert can explain to the jury why the client appears not to care. The key is ensuring that your client's demeanor is consistent with your theory of defense.

That includes vocabulary. Someone who has a drug-scrambled brain is not going to use words like "aforementioned" or "psychosis inducing."

Despite all your careful planning, once the prosecutors realize that their case has become your case, they will find a new fact to throw at you. It will not be in any of the agents' reports, but you will hear about it at trial. There are two possible responses. One is the classic cross-examination, designed to demonstrate the importance of thoroughness and accuracy in report writing. In essence, you argue to the jury that if it is not in the reports, it did not happen. The other approach is to incorporate the new fact into the defense. Your expert can help do this.

The new fact in my case was that my client was totally calm after being strip-searched. She was not crying; she did not appear frightened; she was not hysterical. As you might expect, my expert helped fit this fact into my theory. Of course she was calm, my expert testified: She was finally safe. She had finally escaped her tormentor. She had found sanctuary. My closing argument began to take its final shape as my expert testified:

> Ladies and gentlemen of the jury, is that consistent with a sophisticated heroin smuggler? They are calm at the border and then panic when arrested. My client's reaction was just the opposite.

By using the new fact to my advantage, I had actually strengthened the defense case.

My experience is that jurors are truly undecided at the close of proof in syndrome cases. They go back and forth in their minds. It is difficult for them. The defendant is an admitted heroin smuggler, an admitted cocaine distributor, or an admitted methamphetamine manufacturer, and the jurors are being asked to set the defendant free. Under the circumstances, you will be under more pressure than usual to sum up effectively.

Make your closing argument as dramatic and powerful as possible. For example, by the time your summation is finished in a posttraumatic stress case, the jurors should be in the foxholes, in the mud with your client, watching their best friends dying around them. They should be able to hear the bombs exploding overhead. They should be uncomfortable and ready to burst—just as your client was.

Anticipate the prosecution's answer to your closing argument. In all these cases, the prosecutor will make arguments such as, "If this defendant is acquitted, you will be giving a license to smuggle" and "The defense is only asking for your sympathy." Challenge those arguments head on. My closing began:

> Before I start discussing with you the law and the facts of this case, I'd like to make one thing very clear so there is no doubt in your mind. Ms. X and I are not asking you to return a verdict of not guilty because you feel sorry for her or because she has had a bad life and because she was beaten by a bad man. What we're asking you to do is to follow the law as the judge gives it to you, and to apply that law to the facts you heard in the courtroom. If you do that, you will find there is only one verdict that you can return. And that's a verdict of not guilty based on the law and the facts, not on sympathy.

Use your summation to paint a vivid picture in the jurors' minds. The expert in my case had already talked about the puppies in the cage, and I didn't want to use that again. But I wanted to get that jury out of the sterile courtroom and onto the streets where my client lived in her private hell.

I used imagery. In California, we have beautiful flowers called birds of paradise, named after a bird that lives in South America. I told the jury about the trappers who catch these birds for zoos or pet shops. Because they are afraid that the birds will die if their cages are too small, the trappers put the birds in a big cage at first. But every day they make the cage a little smaller, until finally the cage is so small that the bird cannot even turn its head from side to side. They leave the bird like that for a long time, until one day they finally remove the cage. Even though the bird appears to be free, it does not move. The bird never tries to escape. For the bird, that cage is always there. It was easy to draw the analogy to my client's pathetic life.

Your last job will be to get your client into the deliberation room with the jury—at least figuratively. The longer the jurors deliberate, the further removed they will be from your client and from their verdict's impact on your client's life. The trick is to leave the jury with the image of your client's sitting with them as they deliberate. There are many ways to do this, of course, including the one I used in my case:

> Ladies and gentlemen, I feel as though I have held Ms. X's life in my hands throughout this trial, and now I must turn that life over to you. You are carrying that life with you into the jury room. I ask you to carry it gently, because no one else ever has. And when you come back out, come back with that life. Give it back to her. Tell her to take her babies and go home.

The wet eyes in the courtroom told me what the jury soon made official.

Making the Most of the Multiparty Defense

John J. E. Markham II

These days, not many federal prosecutors believe that crime is committed by the rugged individual, acting alone. Whatever the suspected crime (and the menu of crimes seems to grow with each session of Congress), prosecutors see group wrongdoing. They eschew the rifle shot at the single suspect and instead use conspiracy, aiding and abetting, and RICO statutes as the criminal law equivalents of the sawed-off shotgun, routinely targeting, investigating, and then prosecuting more—sometimes many more—than one individual for each suspected crime.

The resulting multiparty criminal cases create a series of opportunities—and headaches—for the lawyers involved. Each successive stage of the multiparty criminal process serves up important tactical choices that do not arise in the single-party case. To put it bluntly, how you deal with these matters can determine whether your client goes to jail or walks free. And although there is no single blueprint for how to proceed in the multiparty setting, this article will highlight many of the situations you will commonly encounter if you represent one member of a targeted or indicted group.

When targets of a federal investigation first learn of their status, the smart ones promptly engage the services of a lawyer. Because targets are often co-workers, associates, or even relatives, they frequently approach one lawyer to seek group assistance. The reason for the lawyer's interest in such a group of clients is obvious. But it is almost never a good idea to invite more than one of them to your office, much less to represent more than one. However loyal they are to one another (even parent and child or husband and wife), it is virtually impossible to represent more than one person without prejudice to the rights of each.

John J. E. Markham II practices criminal law in Boston and San Francisco and is a former federal prosecutor and professor of law.

The Supreme Court has held that the possibility of prejudice "inheres in almost every instance of multiple representation." *Burger v. Kemp*, 483 U.S. 776, 783 (1987). And although present ethical norms allow for a waiver of conflicts even in the criminal setting (*see, e.g.*, ABA Model Rule 1.7), the risk of prejudice "is so grave that ordinarily a lawyer should decline to represent more than one co-defendant." Rule 1.7, Comment 7. In fact, even when an informed waiver is obtained from all clients, the trial court is empowered to appoint new counsel if it sees a conflict that, though waived, might prejudice one of them. *Wheat v. United States*, 486 U.S. 153 (1988); *see also* Fed. R. Crim. P. 44(c).

Stay away from this mess. From the very beginning of a criminal investigation, multiple representation significantly reduces your available options. The list shrinks as the case proceeds. The lawyer who represents multiple clients cannot (1) approach the prosecutor before indictment with an offer to give evidence against others in exchange for immunity, (2) negotiate a reduced charge or sentence after indictment in exchange for trial testimony against others, (3) emphasize at trial that there is less evidence inculpating one defendant than there is implicating others, or (4) emphasize mitigating factors at sentencing that highlight the minimal culpability of one defendant at the expense of the others. None of this is possible if the "others" are also your clients.

Resist Temptations

Resist the temptations presented by the early vows of group solidarity (or by the prospect of a higher fee) and send all but one of the group packing before you allow any substantive discussion about the case. But before they leave, recommend some good lawyers with whom you work well. Although you cannot refer the others to a partner or associate in your firm without ethical risk under ABA Model Rule 1.10, it is proper and highly advisable to recommend professional friends or associates to others in the group. The multiparty defense is more likely to go smoothly if the lawyers involved respect and trust one another.

Once you have chosen your client, your first major tactical decision in a multiparty investigation is whether to cooperate with the prosecutor in exchange for favorable treatment of your client. Of course, if you decide to cooperate, you can stop reading here. You will have neither the need nor the ability to participate in joint defense. But depending on the circumstances, cooperation may be the way to go.

If the investigation is in its early stages, your client can explain who did what and save a great deal of time and work for a grateful prosecutor. If the government has not yet settled on your client as the principal wrongdoer, the prosecutor may be quite willing to grant immunity or to give other attractive incentives for early cooperation.

To decide whether and under what terms to cooperate, you must make an early assessment of the extent of your client's guilt, details of proffers, negotiation of formal and/or letter immunity, and nonprosecution and/or plea agreements. Suffice it to say that the prosecutor rarely needs more than one cooperating witness, particularly in the white-collar federal crime setting in which the witness's testimony can usually be corroborated with documentary proof. The longer you wait, the more likely it is that the prosecutor will have made a deal with someone else or discovered other evidence that weakens your client's bargaining position. So if you think you might jump into the prosecutor's arms, jump early. The other good lawyers in the case probably will.

However, cooperation is not always—or even often—the best course. It is not easy to inform on others, particularly loved ones or longtime associates. Taking the stand against them is harder still.

And the government is not always good at keeping its part of the bargain. As indictment and trial approach, a client whose testimony can really help the case is the prosecutorial equivalent of the hot date. But prosecutorial ardor has a short life span; it diminishes appreciably by the morning after the trial. If a sentencing recommendation was part of the initial bargain, don't anticipate that the prosecutor will have the same friendly and appreciative attitude at recommendation time as when your client had something to give. In fact, don't even count on the same prosecutor's showing up. By that time, the prosecutor may be a newly appointed magistrate or chief of another unit within the prosecutor's office or a private practitioner.

What's more, judges do not always follow the glowing recommendations of an appreciative prosecutor who does show up. Keep in mind that in the joint prosecution setting, the cooperating witness has been subjected to one or more searing cross-examinations by the betrayed defendants' lawyers. The effort to discredit your client may impress the judge in a way not to your liking.

Although the path of cooperation is a possibility in every multiparty case, it is much more frequently considered than taken. In most cases, the client wants no part of it, the prosecutor is uninterested, or, even if there is mutual interest, a mutually acceptable deal cannot be reached. In most multiparty cases, you will not be counseling a cooperator.

But before we leave this issue and turn to the matter of working with the lawyers of the other targets, one more point is worth making. It is critically important that all lawyers involved in a multiparty defense remember at every stage that even if no one has jumped ship yet, someone may do so later. It can happen just after you have all agreed to work together, usually with little or no adverse effect. It can happen after you have exchanged defense theories or confidential information, creating serious doubts about the integrity of the previously exchanged confidences. It can happen even after you have given your opening statement at trial, when it can virtually devastate your outline of the case for the jury.

There is simply no way to guarantee that this rug will not be pulled out from under you at some point. About all you can do is to remember constantly that the rug is there and that you must proceed with caution.

It is true that any prosecutor worth her salt can indict a ham sandwich. If a prosecutor believes that a group has committed a crime, an indictment will normally follow and is rarely prevented by preindictment activities of defense counsel. Nonetheless, working together before indictment may be useful. It occasionally results in avoiding an indictment; more often it achieves the more modest—but still useful—result of sharing theories and facts that may help at trial. And when the vast resources of the prosecutor are being secretly used to prepare a case against your client on a timetable not of your making and perhaps not even known to you, it is often helpful to have a group of lawyers collectively building a defense from the earliest possible date. Investigative and research tasks can be efficiently assigned within the group by considering experience, access to witnesses and investigators, and the calendars of the lawyers involved.

Of course, individual defendants must exchange information to maximize the group's collective knowledge and thus its effectiveness. There are risks, however. Another defendant may later disclose exchanged information after switching sides. Or, at trial, the other defendant's lawyer may use the shared information to the advantage of that defendant and the disadvantage of your client.

Before exchanging any information, therefore, it is vital to enter into a "joint defense privilege agreement," providing at a minimum that (1) all information is being exchanged in furtherance of a joint defense and is therefore privileged, (2) the holder of the privilege includes the client whose lawyer disclosed the information to the group, and (3) no person is allowed to disclose exchanged information to people outside the group without a written waiver of the privilege by each holder.

Courts are fairly sympathetic to this privilege. *See Hunydee v. United States*, 355 F.2d 183 (9th Cir. 1965) (ruling that such a privilege protects virtually any information exchanged under a joint defense); *United States v. McPartlin*, 595 F.2d 1321, 1336–37 (10th Cir. 1979) (giving the privilege a broad scope). However, the privilege must be proved by those asserting it. *United States v. Lopez*, 777 F.2d 543, 552–53 (10th Cir. 1985). So be sure to write the joint-defense-privilege agreement carefully and unambiguously.

Even with a written agreement and the helpful case law in the defense arsenal, however, disclose information cautiously. If one member of the group does switch sides, there is little you can do to learn about—much less prevent—disclosure to the prosecutor of facts, legal theories, and defenses. And even if you can show that privileged information was in fact disclosed, the little case law that exists suggests that your remedy is almost never dismissal. At most, you can prevent the prosecutor from using at trial the evidence disclosed in violation of the joint-defense privilege. *United States v. Melvin,* 650 F.2d 641 (5th Cir. 1981).

All clients entering into a joint-defense agreement must be emphatically advised that information be exchanged through the lawyers and never from client to client. What one client says to another is unlikely to be considered privileged unless it is said in a conference room with lawyers present. Informal chats between clients will come back like a bad penny if one of the clients takes the stand in a joint trial, switches sides and cooperates, or is tried separately before being called in the trial of your client.

Moreover, certain communications, although proper if made from lawyer to client, are seen in a very different light if made directly between clients. For example, a lawyer can always advise the client against testifying before the grand jury, but a client who urges another defendant not to testify may be charged with obstructing justice. *See, e.g., Cole v. United States,* 329 F.2d 437 (9th Cir. 1964). Clients should be told not to speak with one another at all about the subject of the investigation.

In addition to protecting the joint-defense privilege as best you can, before sharing your theories and defenses, think about how much you trust the other lawyers. And think about whether your fellow lawyers will take an approach similar to yours in defending the case. If you are skeptical or uncertain whether your co-counsel will be like-minded about airing defenses to attempt to stave off an indictment, you should probably keep your hole card covered. For example, Department of Justice policy requires prosecutors to allow defendants to present exculpatory evidence before the prosecutors present proposed indictments to the grand jury. Although that policy sounds high-minded, it rarely stops an indictment and more often simply gives the prosecutor notice of facts, defenses, and counterarguments the defense will raise at trial. Most capable counsel will therefore save their powder for the trial, unless they have a real showstopper of a defense, such as an alibi, the statute of limitations, a showing that no taxes were owed, or evidence that the material dumped was not in fact toxic. It obviously does no good for you to hide your cards from the prosecutor if someone else in the joint-defense group shows your hand for you. There is no way to prevent this, but you can minimize the risk by obtaining an agreement in advance that no one will volunteer to explain things to the prosecutor unless the entire group consents to the content of the disclosures.

Think Trial Date

Once the agreement has been reached and written and the information and defenses have been exchanged, having enough time for trial preparation is vital, especially in a case with a number of defendants. Unless you have the rare luxury of already knowing the case well enough because of some unique circumstance, an early trial date can all but destroy a good defense and prevent maximum use of the potential advantages of joint preparation. And you may well need more time to prepare a multidefendant case for trial because you have to concern yourself with not only your presentation and the prosecutor's, but also the impact of the other defense presentations on your client.

Therefore, the second thing you should do after indictment (the first, of course, is arranging the best bail possible) is to think trial date. If you do not get the jump on the trial date, you will lose control of it.

The trial court's discretionary powers are nowhere greater than in the context of setting the trial date. "Trial judges necessarily require a great deal of latitude in scheduling trials. Not the least of their problems is that of assembling the witnesses, lawyers and jurors at the same place at the same time...." *Morris v. Slappy,* 461 U.S. 1, 11–12 (1982). Your best chance of getting a comfortable trial date involves strategically approaching the trial judge. It is important to meet with all cooperating counsel before the arraignment (or other court appearance when the trial will be set) and to coordinate a workable trial date. Many judges are quick to lose patience if they suggest a potential trial date and hear something like the following:

> Lawyer A: That's not good for me, Your Honor. I start a murder trial over in superior court a week later. May I suggest three weeks after that?
>
> Lawyer B: Your Honor, on the date suggested by Lawyer A, I have prepaid vacation tickets for me and my wife and four kids. May I suggest....

By the time Lawyer D begs off the fourth proposed date, the judge may simply set the matter and leave your problems to you. Judges are much more likely to accommodate a date if it is the first proposed, it is agreeable to all defense counsel, and everyone has good reasons earlier dates will not do. Earlier dates proposed by the prosecutor sound whiny if they are urged over a later date advanced by four or five grown men and women speaking with one voice.

It is also a good idea to have one of you check with the courtroom deputy or clerk about available dates and the length of gaps between trials that have already been set. This information, along with a realistic assessment of the length of your trial, can provide some helpful ammunition for any arguments about the trial date.

If your trial date is too early, if pretrial preparation is not going well, or if you just have bad vibes about your joint-defense arrangement, you may need to find an exit. One sure way out of the special terrain of a multidefendant indictment is to obtain a severance and separate trial for your client. But such an exit may be difficult to make gracefully.

Rule 8 of the Federal Rules of Criminal Procedure allows liberal joinder of defendants, explicitly permitting joinder if those joined "are alleged to have participated in the same act or transaction or in the same series of acts or transactions constituting an offense. . . ." That allows a single indictment of all alleged co-conspirators, aiders and abettors, and RICO participants. And although Rule 14 permits severance if "it appears that a defendant . . . is prejudiced by a joinder . . . of defendants . . . ," showing such prejudice is not easy.

The court is usually required to grant a severance when (1) there are mutually exclusive or antagonistic defenses (*see United States v. Gonzalez*, 804 F.2d 691, 695 (11th Cir. 1986)); (2) one defendant is willing and able to give exculpatory testimony for a co-defendant but will refuse to do so without a severance to prevent his testimony from being admitted in his own trial (*see United States v. Williams*, 809 F.2d 1072, 1084 (5th Cir. 1987)); or (3) the prosecution seeks to introduce a confession of one co-defendant that would implicate other defendants in the same trial (*see Bruton v. United States*, 391 U.S. 123 (1968)).

If none of these circumstances exists, your only chance will be to argue that it would be unfair to try your client with the others because there is not much evidence against him and the weightier or more prejudicial evidence against others might spill over, to your client's detriment. Unfortunately, courts are increasingly reluctant to sever defendants for this reason, particularly when, as is almost always the case, the prosecution is able to argue that the evidence against all defendants is overlapping and that separate trials would thus waste resources by requiring duplicate presentation. As Judge Friendly explained the stark reality: "[P]ublic considerations of confidence and speed outweigh possible unfairness to the accused." *United States v. Werner*, 620 F.2d 922, 929 (2d Cir. 1980). With crowded dockets on the rise, judicial economy has become all but controlling, and the courts tell us and one another that virtually any potential unfairness from the spillover of evidence can be handled by limiting instructions to the jury. *See, for example, United States v. Peters*, 791 F.2d 1270, 1302–03 (7th Cir. 1986).

Despite the long odds, a severance motion is almost always worth making. For one thing, you might win and thus face a shorter trial unencumbered by co-defendants. If severed, your client may be lucky enough not to be tried first. That gives you the opportunity to attend a dress rehearsal of the case you will have to meet. It also means that at least some of the witnesses who testify at the later trial of your client will already have been cross-examined, allowing you to learn in advance where—and where not—to go when you question them.

Even if your severance motion is not granted, some good will usually result. To defeat the severance motion on the usual evidence-overlap and judicial-economy grounds, the prosecutor must demonstrate the overlap by reciting the evidence against each of the defendants in a fair amount of detail. The recitation often goes well beyond the information that the prosecution is required to give under Rule 16 of the Federal Rules of Criminal Procedure; it may provide you with valuable discovery before trial. It may well help focus the defense of your case.

Few actions in the criminal trial setting are free from all risk, including motions to sever. If severance is granted, the severed defendant tried first can be compelled (by use of immunity granted under 18 U.S.C. § 6002) to testify at the later trial of a co-defendant. Indeed, some aggressive prosecutors even compel a defendant scheduled to be tried to testify at an earlier trial under an order granting use immunity. That does not prevent the defendant's later trial if her compelled testimony is not used directly or indirectly in it. *See Kastigar v. United States*, 406 U.S. 441, 461–62 (1972).

When severed defendants are forced to cross-testify, there is more than one unwelcome twist. Unless all the defendants are falsely accused innocents, the forced testimony will be either perjurious or seriously damaging. It definitely takes the bloom off the joint-defense rose. Working together and testifying against one another are, to say the least, not inherently compatible.

Whether you like it or not, your client will probably be joined with co-defendant cronies for the long haul. So you might as well make the most of the advantages of multidefendant cases. One potential advantage arises in the discovery process. Rule 16(b) of the Federal Rules of Criminal Procedure says the government is entitled to reciprocal pretrial discovery—to physical evidence, diagrams, charts, and the like, that the defendant intends to use during trial—but *only if* the defendant has demanded the same discovery from the government. In the multiparty case, one defendant can demand, and then share with the others, all the government's physical evidence, diagrams, and charts. The other defendants, who may have evidence they wish to use but not disclose in advance, thus benefit by sharing in discovery without assuming the reciprocal duty to disclose their evidence before trial. Of course, the strategic decision regarding which client should demand what information may create some conflict among the co-defendants, but if you can agree on a plan, the advantages can be considerable.

Dividing Responsibilities

If you have confidence in the abilities of your co-defense counsel, you can fully enjoy another of the main benefits of the multiparty defense. You can devise an efficient and effective division of trial preparation responsibilities. After carefully discussing all possible pretrial motions, counsel may divide the ones they agree on according to their familiarity or interest. Once the detailed motions with factual material and/or legal authorities have been filed by the assigned counsel, other individual counsel can file a simple motion joining in the motions already on file. That will save enormous overlap in work.

Preparation for oral argument can be divided along the same lines and offers the same economy. Although many of us truly believe that no one can say it better than we can, allowing other counsel to take the laboring oar on specific motions rarely precludes you from adding your two cents at the end if you have joined in the motion on behalf of your client. And the ability to sit back and listen carefully to the court, your co-counsel, and the government may dramatically improve what you say when you do take the podium. But do not take that opportunity to speak unless you have something genuinely new to add. Judges get annoyed at lawyers who simply repeat arguments.

As with pretrial motions, the remainder of pretrial preparation can be cooperatively organized. Attempts to obtain interviews with known government witnesses can be assigned. Preparation of defense witnesses, sometimes a lengthy task, can likewise be shared. Anticipated *in limine* motions can be divided according to which lawyers have had the most experience with the matter or the best results with that trial judge.

Working together before trial really is the easiest part of the joint defense. There is much to be gained by dividing the work and by brainstorming strategies. Counsel who share with one another their experiences with the assigned judge can prevent many a glitch during trial.

There is little chance of acrimony at this stage. It is rare that a pretrial motion desired by some defendants will cause problems for the others. Sharing investigative tasks rarely causes problems. And very little control is lost to the group because you remain free to undertake any pretrial preparation or to make any pretrial motion, even if the group does not wish to share the work involved.

The going gets rougher as the trial date nears—for example, when you choose defense theories for trial.

In the growth industry of trial practice seminars, there are a few constants. One is the importance of "The Theme" to a successful trial. We are told to pick a theme consistent with the evidence and stick with it, making our point as often as appropriate in opening statement, cross-examination, the defense case, and closing argument. There are many potential themes from which to choose: mistaken identity, thin proof on one or more elements, lack of the requisite state of mind, entrapment, and "the prosecution's chief witness is lying to gain his freedom," to name but a few. As trial nears and the guts of the government's case are revealed, experienced counsel will instinctively know what theme will most likely work.

Most agree that it is countereffective to advance a second, or worse yet, a third, fall-back theme—for example, "it never happened," advanced with "it was not I," advanced with "but if it was, I was entrapped." That will not work with one defendant. And although diverse themes advanced by jointly tried defendants are not always quite as silly on their face, they frequently tend to dilute—if not contradict—one another. Only the prosecutor is left smiling when the first defense lawyer, who opens by telling the jury that her client *never* met with anyone to discuss prices, is followed to the podium by a lawyer who tells the jury, "Sure we talked prices, but we never agreed to anything, so where is the crime?"

Sit down with the other defense lawyers before trial and try to weed out inherently inconsistent themes. Many lawyers are understandably reluctant to give previews, even to co-defense counsel, and are even more reticent about subjecting their proposed trial approach to committee review. Nevertheless, if that is not done by everyone, the results could be discordant openings.

Working together does not necessarily mean that one theme must be found to fit all. This is not always possible, given that evidence against each defendant may vary greatly. Indeed, it sometimes works well when lawyers advance radically different themes. The key is ensuring that the themes do not by their nature undercut or contradict one another.

And this is not meant to suggest that you must always go with the group flow. Of course, "the group" is not your first priority. You must take the approach that is best for your client. And if maximizing your client's chances for acquittal hurts others, your ethical obligation remains clear.

But in the multidefendant setting, you are not in a vacuum. Just as your approach can hurt your client's co-defendants, the approach of other counsel can hurt your case. You must therefore at least try to agree on approaches that lessen the chance that you will trip over one another. Save time close to the start of trial for this important discussion.

Jury selection presents another opportunity for cohesive action. Of course, all counsel involved can submit their standard 50 or so voir dire questions. It is as easy (and mindless) as turning on all counsel's word processors. The result, though, is that the judge must wade through stacks of paper and pick from hundreds of overlapping and differently phrased questions. He will be understandably tempted to abandon the search and devise separate questions. Counsel should make it easy for the judge to choose from the proposed questions submitted. Work together, develop a list of the important questions, and then submit one lean list that the judge can consider with dispatch. That way, more of your questions will make the final cut.

Voir Dire Questions

Working in lockstep will also maximize the chances that you will each get to ask some questions directly to prospective jurors. Rule 24(a) of the Federal Rules of Criminal Procedure allows the judge to decide whether the court or counsel will ask voir dire questions. In some districts, you can plain forget about it. In others, judges are allowing limited questions by counsel as a supplement to the standard questions posed by the court, provided that counsel can be trusted not to start arguing the case.

When judges are considering whether to allow you to examine jurors directly, let them know that all defense counsel have coordinated the questions to be asked and that all intend to stay within the bounds. If all defense counsel make clear that each wishes to ask a few questions different from those asked by the others, the prospects of speaking directly to prospective jurors will increase considerably. But unless you all make your reasonableness known, you will never get permission in the first place. Even worse, if you do not collectively abide by the court's limitations, you may be cut off in midsentence. That is not a good way to introduce yourselves to prospective jurors.

It is also vital to work together and think collectively for cross-examination. The prosecutor who has chosen to indict many defendants together must pay the price of suffering through many cross-examinations of prosecution witnesses. Multiple cross-examination can be very effective. By the time, say, six defense counsel have attacked a witness, the jury may have only a dull memory of the points made on direct. Moreover, the second and subsequent cross-examiners may pick up on points overlooked by those who preceded them. With six good minds working, it is more likely that everything that should be covered will be covered.

The problem with successive cross-examinations is that many cross-examiners going second or later cannot restrain themselves from repeating what has already been effectively covered. There seems to be an almost uncontrollable urge to fix what is not broken.

To take another maxim from the standard trial advocacy seminars, once the point has been made on cross, move on or sit down. Never give a second chance with a subject to a witness who has already been stung. It's never as good as the first time for a variety of reasons.

Every trial lawyer knows this truth. Most of us learned it the hard way. But in the group setting, we often lose the self-control we have learned to exercise when we are alone. It may be that many of our species simply have difficulty controlling themselves once they reach the podium or that our fragile egos cannot accept that the brilliant devastation of the key prosecution witness was done by someone else. Whatever the reason, there is little a prosecutor enjoys more than watching defense lawyer three blur or totally undo a crisp point made 15 minutes earlier by defense lawyer one. There is also little that can create more tension at the defense table than the mucking up of good lawyering in the name of lending a hand. Worst of all, it can hurt your client's chances.

This is not just a technical advocacy point, an anecdote that can provide humor at trial advocacy sessions. It is a major threat to a good defense that can cause someone—perhaps your client—to go to jail. After all, most important government witnesses in federal cases have some weakness—from the government agent whose trial testimony conflicts with earlier statements he made, to the cooperating witness who is testifying for leniency, to the witness who has prior convictions, bad character, bad eyesight or hearing, or a drug or alcohol problem affecting memory. It is important to maximize these weaknesses. Trials are won that way. Cross-examination is the time to do it—and the time to waste the opportunity to do it. Ineffective repetition is not just momentarily annoying; it may weaken what could have been a winning point.

There is no sure way to control this problem, our egos being what they are. Perhaps the best we can do is to discuss it frankly with all counsel before trial and make a sincere effort to subordinate our own interests and desires to the needs of our clients.

The defense team will want to consider assigning the laboring oar for each cross-examination to one lawyer, with the understanding that others may ask follow-up questions but not retreads. It helps to know the talents of all defense counsel. Some lawyers are naturals at cross, and some are not. Some do well attacking cooperators, and others shine with documents or past inconsistent statements. Cross-examination assignments should be tailored to the available skills.

One of the hallmarks of lawyers experienced in handling multidefendant cases is that they are not afraid to insist on being treated separately when it helps. It goes without saying that in some trial contexts it will be necessary to work and act completely separately from the other defendants. Sometimes doing so benefits all defendants, and sometimes only one defendant profits. Nonetheless, separate treatment in the multiparty setting can sometimes make the prosecutor regret insisting on so many defendants.

Defendants tried jointly may be granted extra peremptory challenges. Rule 24(b) of the Federal Rules of Criminal Procedure grants the government six and the defendant ten in noncapital cases. But in the multidefendant case, the rule provides that "the court may allow the defendants additional peremptory challenges and allow them to be exercised separately or jointly."

Greed, Motions, and Timing

The best way to obtain as many peremptories as possible varies with the court or judge, and there is no absolute formula for success. Nevertheless, experience suggests three points to consider unless the judge is known to be persuaded otherwise.

First, do not be greedy. In a six-defendant trial, virtually no judge will allow six times the normal peremptories or anything close to it. Second, do not request additional peremptories by a written motion. It is pointless because there is no persuasive law you can cite and because the longer the judge thinks about it, the more likely he is to deny the motion as wasting time and requiring a larger jury panel. Third, when you do make the oral request, pick the correct moment for it and be ready to show why each defendant's unique circumstances require separate—and therefore additional—peremptories. For example, point out that the defendants are from different backgrounds or will take radically different approaches to the evidence.

Each defendant should again insist on separate treatment when the prosecutor starts to roll out the evidence. Much of that evidence will probably be admissible against only one or some of the defendants rather than all of them. For example, evidence relating to a count in which one or more defendants are not charged, statements of one defendant not made in furtherance of a conspiracy, or co-conspirator statements offered before certain defendants are alleged to have entered the conspiracy will often not be admissible against all defendants. In a multidefendant case, such evidence will be ubiquitous, unless you happen to represent a group of bozos photographed during a group bank robbery with their guns but without their masks.

When your client is not the target of the particular evidence, ask for a limiting instruction advising the jurors that that evidence is not admitted against your client and that they should not consider it when judging your client. Most judges are receptive to such requests, which (1) allow you to distance your client from sometimes damaging evidence and (2) slow the prosecutorial wagon just a bit. And prosecutors get nowhere by complaining, especially when they defeated your severance motion by arguing that any potential unfairness of a joint trial could be cured by the very limiting instructions you seek.

Separate treatment can also help with cross-examination. Remember that the right to cross-examine separately applies not only to government witnesses but to witnesses called by the other defendants as well. In this context you should be able to ask leading questions, which, if not overly repetitive of what has gone before, can sharply focus and effectively emphasize the major points for which the witness was called in the first place.

Separate action can also be effective with objections. You are all free to object as you wish to the prosecutor's questions and should do so as you think appropriate. No defense lawyer alone will come up with all the effective objections to a line of questioning, but the chances improve when more than one counsel focuses on each question the prosecutor asks and joins in the objections of other counsel.

Remember too that you are free to object to the questions of co-defense counsel. Although doing so may momentarily sting your counterpart, the objections are sometimes necessary under the circumstances. Moreover, they may send a message to the jury that each defendant is indeed different and should thus be considered separately.

Independent and separate thinking is never more important than when advising your client whether to testify. When certain defendants cannot take the stand for whatever reasons, pressure is sometimes placed on the others to follow suit. This stems from the quite legitimate concern that the nontestifying defendants will look less than forthcoming when others come forward to explain themselves to the jury. If it is in your client's interest to testify, you should fight any contrary groupthink in the defense camp. Remember that the ability to give independent advice was the reason for your refusal to represent multiple defendants in the first place.

When the other defendant can afford to brave the stand but your client would be foolish to do so, there is nothing wrong with urging co-defense counsel to keep a client off the stand. And you may have something more than past courtesies as a bargaining chip: You can warn that if the defendant takes the stand, your client's interests may force you to cross-examine about some distasteful subject. But do not take this approach lightly. It tends to chill relations and disrupt loyalties just before all defense counsel are most vulnerable to one another—during the closing argument.

The judge in a multidefendant case always instructs the jury in substance to "consider each defendant separately and decide whether each defendant has been proven guilty beyond a reasonable doubt." By the time closing arguments are to be given, this jury instruction looms large in the minds of defense counsel. All the evidence cards have been dealt. The lawyers know which defendants hold the worst hands. And they know whether effective representation of their own clients requires distinguishing them from—or even pointing the finger at—the others.

At that moment, the prospects of acting jointly are at their worst. Each lawyer is sorely tempted (not to mention dutybound) to strike out alone in closing, particularly if she thinks her client has a better case than do the others. That does not always require pointing fingers and naming names. You can point to the most damaging evidence and simply argue that it does not implicate your client. But you can rarely do it without implicitly echoing the prosecutor's point about whom the evidence does inculpate.

At this point, the trial is all but over. There are no future opportunities for co-defense counsel to work together for mutual benefit. It is understandably tempting for defense counsel to abandon the joint defense effort and go it strictly alone, regardless of how much the other defendants may be hurt by a totally self-interested closing argument.

Nonetheless, it is usually a good idea to work together for closings that are not mutually inconsistent or antagonistic. Remember that the prosecutor has the last word and will often use it to damage all defendants by pointing to inconsistencies between your summation and those of your colleagues. In closing, as in opening, it cannot hurt and it often helps to try to work things out so that you damage your co-defendants as little as possible. If you need additional motivation, remember that other defense counsel can often argue your client into jail more easily than you can perform that dubious service for their clients.

When all is said and done, it is the result you get for your client, and not the collective benefit to all defendants, that counts. But sometimes the route to the best individual outcome is a collective effort.

White-Collar Crime: The Defendant's Side

Boris Kostelanetz

The white-collar defendant is usually a first offender, sympathetic in character, pleasant in appearance. This business or professional client does not have the profile of petty thief or forger, and the alleged offenses hardly ever are caused by poverty. Indeed, the defendant may have too much money, or at least more than is shown on the defendant's tax return.

The crimes with which the white-collar defendant is charged encompass substantial controversies and complex facts and law. Tax evasion, stock manipulation, bank fraud, insider trading, antitrust, and the like invariably involve complicated books and records, economic and financial statements, and even scientific formulas and computer technology.

White-collar trials are almost always time-intensive, and are preceded by months, sometimes years, of investigation. In the preindictment stage, squads of state or federal specialists have scoured banks, brokerage houses, present and former customers and creditors, and even neighbors to produce the hundreds of facts necessary to prosecute. In fact, the white-collar defendant usually is well aware of the government's scrutiny over many years and in many transactions. The defendant may be disappointed after viewing the written charges, but hardly surprised.

Whether retained before or after indictment, the lawyer for the white-collar defendant must take charge from the start. So start with the fee.

Over and above the initial—and substantial—retainer, the defendant must be prepared to pay for what in an ordinary criminal case might be termed unnecessary luxuries.

Boris Kostelanetz is of counsel to Kostelanetz & Fink in New York City.

For example, daily transcripts of the testimony should be ordered and available for close analysis. One or two associate lawyers, a legal assistant, an accountant, an investigator, a chemist, and a computer technician may be vital to the case. Certainly, three professionals sitting at the defendant's table ordinarily will not outnumber the prosecutor's team.

Also, the lawyer should not be required to play banker. Except for public corporations or wealthy defendants with impeccable credit, the client should commit to refreshing the retainer as needed and should understand that there is no discount defense. Alternately, a guarantee of a sum certain or an open letter of credit will relieve the lawyer of any concern about having a creditor-debtor relationship with his client.

Although aspects of white-collar litigation are almost indistinguishable from civil litigation, in many ways the lawyer's approach is substantially different. Some strategies that would constitute improper conduct in civil litigation may be required and approved in defense of the criminal.

Guilt or innocence is not decided by counsel, but by courts and juries in adversary proceedings. Absent a private confession of guilt, a lawyer should presume, as does the common law, that the client is innocent. Even where guilt is privately confessed, a lawyer still is obligated to determine the client's defenses with the knowledge that the client, within sanctioned rules, may not necessarily be proved guilty of the charge. The lawyer who fails to take this approach is not performing his or her function. The client can find a way to jail without a lawyer's help.

Trial preparation demands creative thinking and sophisticated techniques. The lawyer cannot rely on genius for persuasion or self-conceived talent for shattering the opponent's case. Instead, the lawyer should concentrate on these tasks:

First, develop alternative and flexible theories for the client's defense. At trial, the lawyer must be able to shift his or her thinking as the emerging evidence requires. Obviously, you will attempt vigorously to pry from the prosecution all the details of the charges. However, alternative theories of defense will help you overcome surprises. Also, your theories will vary, depending on whether the client will testify in his own behalf—a decision that may be made and remade during the course of the trial.

Second, scout the judge. Obviously, any competent lawyer knows something about the judge he or she is appearing before. But the defendant's offensive strategies require having a complete book on the judge. You will have enough problems handling hostile witnesses and a stressed-out client without wondering why the judge's eyes have glazed over during your cross-examination. Likewise, know your opponents' background, attitudes, and favorite procedural ploys. This kind of personal knowledge will give you a better chance of anticipating the prosecution's plans.

Third, consider interviewing all witnesses, including those hostile to the client, and even the outright informers. In dealing with hostile witnesses, adopt the precaution used by government investigators: Have at least two interrogators present who can testify about what was said. This procedure ensures accuracy and obviates claims of improper pressure or undue influence.

Fourth, advance your timetable for trial preparation, so that tasks you would ordinarily handle during a trial are completed well beforehand. Assemble memoranda of law anticipating questions that may arise during trial. Draft alternative sets of proposed jury instructions, paying close attention to changing nuances that flow from your alternative theories of defense. Be sure to comb the judicial opinions on the usual legal propositions for language more favorable to defendants than the standard instruction offered by the prosecutor. Remember that the defendant is entitled to instructions on any theory of defense for which there is evidentiary foundation.

Reproduce all materials, exhibits, and charts that you intend to distribute to the jury and court. Draw up and refine lists of questions for each witness. Repeat your review of discovery materials and analyze anew your reactions and responses.

The defendant's case is not likely to fly without the aid of an expert. The expert—an accountant, for example—must satisfy three criteria. First, the expert must be an active planner in the defense strategy. Second, the expert must help prepare the cross-examination of the prosecutor's expert. Third, the expert—or another expert—must totally support the defendant's contentions, particularly in the opinions testified to in court.

Obviously, the accountant who testifies will not be the one regularly employed by the client. That accountant has given statements to the prosecution, and would face devastating cross-examination. Nor should the witness be the accountant hired to develop the case and whose work product falls within the attorney-client privilege. That accountant has learned a great deal about the case's strong points—and also its weak ones. Under cross-examination, the accountant may be compelled to disgorge secrets revealing that the client's case is a little short of perfect.

In gathering opinion evidence, be prepared to retain an accountant whose personality and qualifications may differ greatly from those of the experts upon whom the client and you have relied up to then. Even an expert accountant with vast substantive knowledge will be ineffective if he or she cannot relate that knowledge personally to the jury.

Accountants as a group are not noted for their expressive articulation, but those who have had both professional and teaching experience generally make the best expert witnesses. That background combines technical experience with the ability to explain and simplify difficult concepts and jargon. So, go to the universities. Find a professor noted for his ability to communicate to students. The ability to clarify the complex will work equally effectively in the courtroom. At the same time, the professional title will enhance the expert's credibility.

Ordinarily, the defendant may choose between trial by court or trial by jury. In federal criminal cases, a jury may be waived with the prosecutor's consent.

I believe that the defendant should never waive a jury; well, almost never. If the judge appears to be predisposed to the defense, then the defendant might as well stand trial by the court alone. Otherwise, remember that our forefathers had something in mind when they provided for juries in criminal cases.

The task of picking a jury differs significantly in state and federal courts. The personal rapport that a lawyer tries to establish with prospective jurors during voir dire—sacred in many state courts—is almost impossible to obtain in most federal courts, where a judge asks the questions. Still, federal judges should ask prospective jurors questions about specific areas, and the information obtained may give cause for challenge.

In tax cases, the government inevitably asks the court to inquire about the prospective jurors' experience in audits of their own returns and similar matters. The defendant may request questions about prospective jurors' knowledge of bookkeeping, accounting, and the preparation of tax returns.

In a case that turned on the testimony of a hostile certified public accountant who had formerly prepared the defendant's tax returns, inquiry by the court disclosed that four prospective jurors were bookkeepers. The defense did not challenge them, reasoning that persons who are supervised generally do not like their supervisors. Neither, for some reason, did the government challenge. As might be expected, in coming to a not-guilty verdict each bookkeeper undoubtedly contributed a nail to the coffin of the prosecution's case.

The opening statement can be a trap for defense counsel. In courts that permit you to reserve the opening statement until the prosecution completes its case, do so. An opening statement by the defense before the government adduces any proof is, in effect, a contradiction to the presumption of innocence; presumably the defendant is not obligated to prove—or say—anything.

In courts that compel the defendant's lawyer to follow the prosecutor's opening statement, be aware of the danger posed by the hundreds of facts in this type of case. Why is this a problem? Because every fact you recite in the opening statement can be used as a test of the defendant's credibility. If you do not prove each statement you offer, you will be in trouble. Here is how the prosecutor's closing statement will sound.

> In his opening statement, Mr. Smithers represented to you that his client was in Buffalo on the key date, November 19th. That is what

he said [prosecutor reads from transcript]. Now, Mr. Smithers is an honorable person. I'm sure he truly believed that his client was in Buffalo on that date. But, members of the jury, we have been sitting here for three months, and we have not heard a single word about where the defendant was on November 19th—not one word. Why is that? The answer is that someone must have lied to Mr. Smithers. Who do you think would lie to him about something so critical?

You can guess the jurors' answer to that question.

Some litigators are fond of recounting how they got their clients acquitted on the basis of a detailed opening statement. Since pretrial discovery is so limited in criminal cases, I think a detailed opening statement usually is unwise. There are only three, rather rare, situations in which I use a full opening statement.

First is in a case that is being retried. Whether the new trial is prompted by a mistrial, a hung jury, or a reversal, the lawyer has a record of sworn testimony. The summation in the first trial can serve as a basis for the opening statement.

Second, there is the unusual situation in which critical adverse facts are indisputable. If the only issue left is whether the defendant acted willfully (or had the requisite *mens rea*), the defense may want to concede some of the factual issues. The emotional impact of the harmful facts is diffused. Instead of listening to time-consuming testimony about the facts, the jury's attention is directed to the issue of willfulness.

The third situation deals with a denunciation of evidence to be offered by the prosecution. Thus, if it is clear that the prosecution will call the complainant-informer and if the facts fit the image, an elaborate and detailed discussion of the informant's uncontradictably bad conduct and scurrilous character may well be in order.

But absent these exceptions, it is better to explain to the jury that the defendant need not prove anything. Say that the defendant's plea of not guilty is a denial of the charges, that the jurors should keep an open mind until the case is concluded, and that in so doing they will be enforcing the law of this Republic. Say this in different ways for five minutes and then sit down.

Of course, everyone likes to enforce the law, and it may be news to jurors that law enforcement, in an appropriate setting, means favoring the defendant instead of the prosecution. So remind the jury at this point and later that when, based on the evidence and the court's instructions, they vote for the defendant, they are rightly enforcing the law.

White-collar defense tactics during the course of the prosecution's case are not much different from those in any criminal trial. In addition to stipulating away part of the government's case in an opening statement, concessions may also be stated for the record when a prosecution witness takes the stand. A prosecutor who tries to prove facts already conceded may succeed only in boring the jury.

A celebrated former governor of Georgia reportedly told the state prison association: "There will never be genuine prison reform in Georgia until we have a better class of prisoners." His remark brings to mind a special cross-examination opportunity unique to white-collar cases. Often, the informer government-witness who has received immunity qualifies as one of the "better class": Depending on the informer's character (which you must assess accurately), the informer may be embarrassed to be in the position of having to tell all. Through a careful and frequently time-consuming cross-examination, defense counsel may be able to exploit the witness's discomfort. An appeal to the informer's ego and natural desire to please the people listening, coupled with the fact that the informer is all alone on cross, may well change the impact of the testimony.

Several times I have been able to cajole the informer into saying that what the informer did and intended to do while engaging in the conduct now alleged to be illicit was actually law-abiding, honest, and decent—just as the informer is. Depending on the facts, this testimony can dissolve the prosecution's prima facie case. At a minimum, such kind words will somehow, in measure large or small, tend to favor the defendant.

During a case with complicated facts, it does not pay to be too polite in registering objections. The defense lawyer never knows for certain when a properly asserted objection will preclude the prosecution from proving some essential part of its case. You should meet every doubtful evidentiary proffer with whatever technical objections are available, particularly if the prosecutor seems poorly prepared or ignorant of the fine points of the rules of evidence.

In the midst of being so "objectionable," you must not forget to preserve your record for appeal by pressing for a decisive ruling from the bench. I have discovered, fortunately only rarely, that the appellate lawyer's view of your record is invariably rich with afterthoughts. Well do I remember a particular judge, now long gone, who would repeatedly say to each side, "Now I will hear you," then listen at length and say, "Proceed," without ever making the actual ruling. The objection without a ruling presents the appellate court with a presumption that the failure to press for a ruling was a withdrawal of the objection.

Equally important to appellate review are your decisive motions to strike items of evidence and to make offers of proof. Without these, the appellate court will be hard put to find an error in admitting evidence or refusing to accept it.

Also, do not worry about the effect of your frequent objections and bench conferences on the jury. In civil trials, objections can be overdone.

But in white-collar defense, proper objections and correct rulings are the beginning of a good offense. Which reminds me of one particular defense.

A few years ago, after days of trial, a co-defendant called me aside during a recess and confidentially inquired, "Boris, who is this guy Wagmore?" I said, "Wagmore? What do you mean?" He said, "He is all over this case. Every time you say something is the law to this judge, the prosecutor gets up and says that Wagmore said exactly the opposite. So I am beginning to notice that this judge wonders who to believe, Kostelanetz or Wagmore, and every time he believes Wagmore." Displaying the kind of thinking that had got him where he was that day, the co-defendant added, "Anyone can see this Wagmore has a real 'in' with the judge."

Often the prosecution's expert witness will use charts, tables, summaries, or models that purport to represent and summarize certain evidence. These visual aids are usually blown up to seemingly life-size models. They develop their own personality, which often is prejudicial to the defense. You can counter this prosecution tactic on two fronts.

First, apply the computer principle of "garbage in, garbage out" to the evidence underlying the charts. Argue that the visual aids must accurately reflect only credible, reliable, and admissible evidence in every detail. Any omission or deviation should be used to disqualify the proffered evidence from the courtroom or, at least, in the minds of the jurors.

Second, remind the jury whenever possible that the visual aids are not evidence in and of themselves, but only a representation of what the prosecution contends is evidence. The snazziest flow chart or model can be flawed by the nagging of a persistent defense counsel, so that the prosecutor wishes he had never heard of demonstrative evidence.

I like to use charts that can be prepared on individual pages and distributed to each of the jurors. Everyone has seen jurors who sleep through explanations of large charts, particularly when they are presented one after the other by a sonorous declaimer. When the same charts are distributed individually to jurors, peer pressure requires them to look at the papers in their hands, turn them over, and follow the expert when he says, "Please look at column 3, line 12." Similarly, you should make copies for each juror of relatively complicated exhibits (such as work papers) that each juror can follow as the witness talks.

Finally, the prosecution's case may present defense counsel with a chance to develop the defendant's contentions from witnesses whose credibility the prosecution has inferentially vouched for. By structuring the defense on cross-examination, you may, by way of maximum result, be able to move for judgment, at least on some counts, before presenting the defendant's case or, even better, to rest his case.

The most desirable defense is that the defendant did not know about the facts claimed to form the charge against him. An alibi defense, though rare in white-collar cases, also is possible.

In an antitrust case celebrated in the late 1950s as the electrical industry conspiracy, we were able to demonstrate that the executive vice president of one of the country's great companies was innocent because he could not possibly have received pertinent knowledge of the conspiracy at the time and place stated, much less have had the opportunity to act on it. When the records of my client's company showed exactly where he and the other company employees (his accusers) were at the time and place charged in the indictment, it was as if the alleged illicit meeting had never happened. The prosecutor declined to proceed with the suit.

Showing a lack of knowledge may involve placing the blame for knowledge and responsibility on others. Or it may involve a showing of plain stupidity, which reminds me of a trial held in Arizona before a jury of farmers. The defendant was an emigre from New York. On direct examination the defendant's lawyer said to his client, "It says in this here indictment that in 1957 you knew the adjusted gross." The defendant replied, "In 1957, Justin Gross I didn't know. I knew Morris Gross." The Arizona jury acquitted this New Yorker.

The defenses related to willfulness vary, depending on the facts. I will only highlight those that crop up most often:

- The questioned conduct that allegedly violated a statute requiring specific intent was motivated by totally lawful or minimally defensible acts. For example, what appeared to be falsification of records or concealment of income may not be connected with the offense charged, but rather motivated solely by an unpleasant relationship with an ex-spouse.
- The defendant's reliance, under proper circumstances, on competent but incorrect advice from experts, sought and received in good faith, is a complete defense.
- Zealous prosecutors may characterize as a criminal sham a business transaction that can be shown to be a lawful scheme of tax avoidance. The defense lawyer should distinguish between the lawful objective of the business deals and the alleged unlawful methods.
- Restitution, either before or after the indictment, is generally no defense. Given special circumstances, however, some courts permit evidence of restitution to show a lack of intent. Certainly courts hearing criminal tax evasion cases have received this kind of evidence.
- The conduct of a defendant when the allegedly fraudulent papers were officially filed with authorities can negate the charge of willfulness. If a problem is openly stated and apparent from supporting documents, no jury is going to believe that the document was willfully falsified. For example, in *Lucien T. Wilcox*, a holding of the Board of Tax Appeals (predecessor of the tax court more than half a

century ago), taxpayer Wilcox found himself charged with civil fraud. On March 15, 1933, the date returns were due in the old days, Wilcox appeared at the office of the collector, picked up a blank income tax return, wrote his name and address on it, and attached to it a check for $10 and a letter. The letter stated in substance that Wilcox was attaching a check for $10 as evidence that he was not trying to evade payments. It recited that he was about to go to Nevada to seek a divorce and, if successful, he would make an amended return. Wilcox added, "Otherwise I will continue to prefer federal to domestic incarceration." Said the Board of Tax Appeals, no fraud. He had a real problem and he revealed it to the collector.

In the same spirit, a defendant's conduct attributable to negligence, even gross negligence, should not be considered equal to the evil conduct that criminal statutes requiring *mens rea* prescribe. Negligence and fraud are mutually exclusive.

Still another defense is mental illness or incompetence. The difficulty is that ordinarily the defendant is an active and successful doctor, lawyer, stockbroker, or executive who does not fit the image of the mentally ill or portray any lack of competence. Given proper facts, however, this defense can raise viable issues negating criminal responsibility.

Should the defendant testify? Every defense lawyer has a theory about the value of the defendant's testimony. It is very easy for a lawyer to say, "I will let them put in their case, then I'll put my client on the stand. If the jury doesn't believe him, it is his fault not mine."

I believe that generally a white-collar defendant should not testify. The defendant's activity covers years and years. The defendant has written letters. The defendant has done things he or she cannot possibly remember and, since his or her testimony is so critical, it must be letter perfect. If it is not, the defendant simply will not be believed.

The defendant's testimony may be further discredited by the manner in which the court instructs the jury about how to test the credibility of witnesses. After the judge describes bias and interest as disqualifying and tarnishing factors, a lawyer may feel ashamed to have called the client to the stand.

Usually the lawyer should prepare the case assuming that the client will not testify. Then the lawyer should prepare alternative theories in case the client does testify, and leave any final decision to be made during the course of the trial.

Naturally, these observations about the hazards of the defendant's testifying do not apply to street crimes, which generally are single occurrences. But white-collar defendants should take them seriously. I prosecuted white-collar crimes for nine years and never lost a case—not because of my brilliance, but because the defendants insisted on removing any reasonable doubt about their guilt by testifying.

The closing argument is the most critical and potentially valuable part of white-collar defense. The jury must be told again and again that they will be fulfilling their function in upholding and enforcing the law if, considering the evidence and the presumptions about which they were charged, they acquit the defendant. The jury should be told in every way possible that no one can be convicted on the basis of suspicion, bias, guesswork, or attractive charts.

Throughout the trial, the closing argument should be taking shape in your mind and on paper. Jot down telling points as they occur to you. Project the defendant's image as you would like the jury to see it. Was the defendant foolish, greedy, pompous—but not a criminal? Did the defendant simply slip up? Does your client deserve to go through life known as Dr. Grandfellow or as Grandfellow the felon? The prosecutor has a version of the defendant. Yours must be more compelling and believable. Particularly if you have access to current minutes and you are able to point to page numbers from the record for your assertions of fact, you can aid your own credibility and be in full control of your case.

In a tax prosecution, if you can convince the jury that the case really belongs in the tax court where tax questions and deficiencies are resolved by experts, then you have won a great point. Similarly, you can argue that a business dispute can be better resolved in civil court where, after all, only money is at stake. Be sure to point out to the jury that a criminal court cannot grant the prosecution a nickel in a criminal trial. Looking ahead, the chances of acquittal on concededly inexact statistics are about one in three, a percentage much more favorable to the defense than the percentage for run-of-the-mill criminal charges.

Whatever the outcome, trials for white-collar offenses will stay in the lawyer's memory with startling detail as rewarding challenges that call for optimal professional effort and skill.

Sentencing the Corporation

Edward F. Novak and Randy Papetti

Jack Travis is the chief executive officer of one of my firm's clients. As with many CEOs, Jack is a straight shooter; he expects his company's employees to follow the law. But employees sometimes do not obey the law or even bosses like Jack. That is why corporations constantly are in trouble.

Federal prosecutors had indicted one of his employees for fraud. Jack wanted to be sure that the corporation did whatever it took to minimize its liability. I asked a few questions, did some quick calculations, and gave Jack some scary news.

Things have changed for corporate criminal defendants, and Jack is learning about these changes the hard way. In case you missed it, too, there has been a bona fide revolution in federal sentencing law for corporations and other organizational defendants, including partnerships, associations, unions, trusts, pension funds, unincorporated organizations, governmental bodies and political subdivisions, and nonprofit groups.

Stiff new federal sentencing guidelines now in effect are intended to take a bite out of corporate crime in America. They just might be nasty enough to succeed.

Here is what naughty organizations—and those of us charged with defending them—have to look forward to under the new guidelines:

- mandatory restitution;
- far stiffer maximum fines;
- required ranges designed to produce fines equal to or greater than even the *highest* fines imposed in the past;

Edward F. Novak is a partner and Randy Papetti is an associate of the law firm Lewis and Roca, L.L.P., in Phoenix, Arizona.

- the "death penalty"—complete divestment of net assets—if the organizational defendant is found to have been operated primarily for criminal purposes; and
- unconventional and highly intrusive probation.

Legitimate fear results. Organizations subjected to the full brunt of the guidelines will endure a sting beyond anything experienced in the past. Of course, fear can be healthy, or at least productive. And the United States Sentencing Commission, which drafted the guidelines, is hoping that organizations will be scared enough to learn about the guidelines and take measures, including those spelled out in the guidelines themselves, to ferret out and discourage crime within their ranks.

These organizational guidelines aptly have been characterized as the most ambitious sentencing laws in American history. The guidelines are so unusual because, through the use of incentives that can be cashed in at sentencing, they affirmatively seek to alter corporate behavior that has nothing to do with the actual underlying substantive crime.

For example, the guidelines provide large rewards—through reduction in fines—to corporations that implement effective compliance programs and self-report employee violations. In essence, corporations have, for the first time, "been conscripted into the fight against crimes." Otto G. Obermaier, "Drafting Companies to Fight Crime," *N.Y. Times*, May 24, 1992, at F11.

But the company cannot wait until it already is in trouble. Taking advantage of the specific incentive found in the guidelines requires that the guidelines be consulted, and that specific measures be adopted *before* trouble hits.

Back to Jack, who understandably did not care for the news I gave him. Jack had a lot of questions—mostly, when and how did all this happen? In particular, he kept emphasizing that his company's code of conduct directs each employee to follow the law, and that he therefore did not understand how the company could be subject to such massive criminal liability. Jack is typical in his naive understanding.

That criminal liability may be imposed on corporations for the acts of their employees is nothing new. In the seminal case of *New York Central and Hudson River Railroad v. United States*, 212 U.S. 481 (1909) *aff'd*, 212 U.S. 500 (1909), the Supreme Court determined that corporations may be held criminally liable for the conduct of their employees if the conduct was within the scope of employment and was done with the intent to benefit the corporation. The Court regarded its holding as just a small extension of vicarious liability rules that already had applied in the civil context.

Although the Supreme Court decision has been vilified throughout this century, it still stands, and its progenies make reasonably clear that a corporation may be criminally liable even if the company expressly forbade and took steps to prevent the misconduct. *United*

States v. Hilton Hotels Corp., 467 F.2d 1000, 1006-07 (9th Cir. 1972), *cert. denied*, 409 U.S. 1125 (1973).

This fairly strict standard of vicarious liability is intended to encourage corporations to do everything possible to prevent criminal misconduct, and ironically may result in its being easier in some cases to convict the corporation than it is to convict the individual employee.

Until recently, however, relatively few organizational defendants had been criminally prosecuted, let alone subjected to stiff criminal sanctions. In fact, lawmakers historically showed little interest in crafting criminal sanctions for corporate misconduct. Federal penalty statutes were drafted principally with individual defendants in mind. They typically imposed significant maximum jail sentences and added modest fine provisions as almost an afterthought.

Perhaps due to the small range of sanctions available, federal prosecutors generally left organizational defendants alone. Indictments usually addressed just the individual employees. The organization, typically, needed to worry only about civil claims against it.

Those days are gone. The Sentencing Reform Act of 1984 raised the ceilings significantly on federal statutes providing for fines. Although the guidelines are more than five years old now, few organizations yet can tell horror stories about them. The latest statistics from the United States Sentencing Commission indicate that as of September 1995, only 244 business organizations had been sentenced under the guidelines and, by the beginning of 1997, only two appellate court decisions had interpreted or applied them. In *United States v. Apex Roofing of Tallahassee, Inc.*, 49 F.3d 1509 (11th Cir. 1995), the court's application of the sentencing guidelines was insignificant, and in *United States v. Eureka Laboratories, Inc.*, 1996 U.S. App. LEXIS 33540 (9th Cir. 1996), the court held that the guidelines do not prohibit a sentencing court from imposing a fine that jeopardizes an organization's viability. In fact, the whirl of attention that surrounded their passage largely, and unfortunately, has subsided.

The primary reason the guidelines have been used so infrequently is that the Department of Justice has declared that the guidelines should be applied only to *criminal conduct* that occurred after November 1, 1991, rather than to all *sentencing* occurring after that date. Given the gestation period that normally precedes prosecutions of corporations, few acts of misconduct governed by the guidelines have come to trial.

Yet, vicarious liability is not that difficult to prove. The alleged misconduct of Jack's employee certainly financially benefited Jack's company and was done in the scope of his employment, rendering the company liable for the same misconduct as DeCarlo. Assuming that the company is indicted and convicted—both realistic possibilities—its exposure under the sentencing guidelines would be great.

Scared clients usually are good listeners, but Jack had heard enough about the history of the guidelines. He understood that they were controversial when promulgated, that they had been in place for a few years now, and that, at least twice since their adoption, my firm had sent to his company information about the guidelines and about implementing compliance programs. At this point, Jack just wanted to know the bottom line.

Jack's company finds itself in its predicament because of William DeCarlo, a project manager on a contract between Jack's company and the Department of Interior. The indictment alleges that DeCarlo fraudulently overstated expenses on a number of different invoices beginning in early 1992 and concluding in 1994, which resulted in the government's overpaying Jack's company nearly $900,000.

Jack's company knew about the allegations long before the indictment. Department of Interior auditors had spotted some of the disputed invoice entries and complained nearly a year ago. Jack's company has dealt with the government for decades; government claims that it is owed money or is being cheated are not unusual.

Upon hearing the auditors' complaints, company officials investigated. They found some mistakes and concluded that some amount, difficult to quantify, should be refunded.

Based on their brief investigation, however, company officials said that they could not determine whether DeCarlo had acted fraudulently. In any event, they said, the government appeared to be seeking much more than that to which it was entitled.

Jack's company, therefore, refunded a small amount to the Department of Interior, stating its position that only a few mistakes had been made, and asking that lines of communication remain open about the other disputed invoice entries. The hope was that the government would be appeased.

Two months later, government investigators contacted the company. They were serious about pursuing the matter. The company denied liability but agreed to cooperate.

Four months later, a grand jury indicted DeCarlo. Prosecutors have demanded that Jack's company make full restitution, and they have suggested that a corporate indictment may follow. After learning more about the government's investigation and findings, Jack is concerned that his company could be held criminally liable.

First, restitution must be made. This is one of the cornerstone principles of the organizational guidelines and generally is mandatory. If convicted of the same counts alleged against DeCarlo, Jack's company would be forced to pay to the Department of Interior more than $800,000 in restitution (the alleged overcharge amount less the already refunded amount). The sentencing judge could apportion the restitution between the employee and the company, but given the employee's probable financial condition by the time of sentencing, the company likely would get hit with the whole bill.

Restitution does not affect whether a fine also will be imposed. Large-dollar restitution catches the company's attention, but big fines deter repeaters and others.

Calculating Fines

Fines were imposed as part of the sentence against 78 percent of the organizations sentenced under the guidelines in 1995. The mean fine was $242,892. Companies convicted of antitrust violations received the largest fines (average of $1.4 million). A fine of $2.26 million was assessed against the one organization sentenced for a racketeering conviction in 1995. Other monetary penalties and the frequency with which they were imposed included: asset forfeiture (7.2 percent); disgorgement (4.8 percent); cost of prosecution (1.8 percent); and cost of supervision (1.8 percent).

Computing the range of possible fines under the guidelines is a little intimidating, mostly because of the jargon, but it is not particularly complex. The first step is to determine what is known as the "base fine," which is the *greatest* of (1) an amount determined from an offense table included in the guidelines; (2) the pecuniary gain to the corporation from the offense; or (3) the pecuniary loss from the offense caused by the organization, to the extent that the loss was caused intentionally, knowingly, or recklessly. Here, the pecuniary gain of nearly $900,000 is the highest amount, and thus it constitutes the base fine.

The base fine presumptively reflects the seriousness of the offense, which is but one of two major considerations. The other consideration is the organization's culpability. This is measured by computing a *culpability score,* which is determined by reference to a table setting forth both a minimum and a maximum multiplier to be applied to the base fine, thus creating the guideline range.

An organization begins with a culpability score of five in a range between zero and ten. Points are added or subtracted based on aggravating or mitigating factors. Each point can be worth thousands of dollars, depending on the base fine amount and multiplier.

It appears that Jack's company might be subject to a two-point addition because it has more than 50 employees and the indicted employee probably was an "individual within substantial authority personnel" who participated in the offense. The higher up the organizational ladder individuals are who commit the offense, the more culpable the organization presumptively is.

Assuming that the company cooperated in an investigation, yet went to trial and lost, no mitigating points would appear to be available. Mitigation points are possible for acceptance of responsibility, but such points probably are not available to companies that lose at trial.

Watch out for the result of the calculation. A culpability score of seven corresponds to a minimum multiplier of 1.40 and a maximum multiplier of 2.80. Jack's company, therefore, if convicted would face a fine of *not less than* $1.26 million (that is, 1.40 × $900,000) and *not greater than* $2.52 million (that is, 2.80 × $900,000).

Remember, any fine would be *in addition to* the required restitution. Jack's company thus is exposed to financial liability of more than $2 million and perhaps nearly $3.5 million!

That is not all. The company also might be placed on probation. The guidelines require that a company of 50 or more employees be placed on probation if, at the time of sentencing, the organization does not have in place an effective program to prevent and detect violations of law.

As conditions of probation, the court may require that the organization quickly develop such a program; that the organization notify its employees and stockholders of its criminal behavior and its new program to prevent future offenses; that the organization submit periodic reports to the court; and that the organization submit to regular or unannounced examinations of its books, records, and employees.

The court may impose even stiffer and more intrusive forms of probation, including appointing experts to oversee aspects of the organization's business, if it concludes that doing so is necessary to prevent future criminal conduct.

The guidelines are tough—really tough—and can be quite literally disastrous for organizations that do not act responsibly in taking steps to limit their exposure.

In that sense, the guidelines create new roles for corporate counsel. The first, of course, is to gain at least general familiarity with the guidelines themselves.

The most important new role for corporate counsel—in-house or outside—is to ensure that the organization implements an effective compliance program. The guidelines provide, with some exceptions, for a three-point reduction in an organization's culpability score if it has in place an effective program. Jack's company had not implemented such a program.

While U.S. Sentencing Commission data indicate that no organization sentenced in 1995 received a reduction in the culpability score under the guidelines for having an effective compliance program, courts are increasingly considering a company's compliance efforts. In at least three 1995 cases, court records show that the judge, before imposing sentence, examined the company's compliance efforts. Additionally, in 13.5 percent of 1995 cases, the judge ordered the company, as part of its sentence, to implement a compliance program to prevent further violations of the law.

Since 1991, companies across America have been implementing compliance programs at a record pace. Merely adopting something called a "compliance program" is not enough. To warrant mitigation under the guidelines, compliance programs must be "effective." No reported cases yet discuss what constitutes an "effective" program.

Avoiding Violations

Here are four hints for organizations to follow to ensure that their compliance programs will be regarded as effective.

- Scrupulously honor the suggestions listed in the commentary to the guidelines about what constitutes an effective program. Admittedly, the commentary is couched in vague standards, but those standards likely will guide any dispute about effectiveness.
- Effective compliance programs always are implemented and administered, not merely drafted. As one article noted, a "company's compliance program is not just another glossy brochure to be tucked away in the credenza. It is a guide to daily living within the hallowed halls of the company." Richard A. Rocchini and Mark S. Olinsky, "Is Your Legal Compliance Program Merely a Paper Tiger? Ongoing Instruction Gives Plan Teeth," *Corp. Legal Times,* June 1994, at 29. Employees questioned once the company is in hot water should have basic familiarity with material aspects of the program. They will not gain that familiarity unless management either requires them to do so or gives them repeated and diverse exposure to the features of the organization's program. More often than not, prosecutors and judges will see through paper tiger programs.
- Larger companies in particular should pay attention to early feedback about what constitutes effective programs. Seminal case law is on the horizon. Organizations need to be ready to adjust their programs based on the first round of judicial decisions or major prosecutorial announcements, which will identify attributes of effective and ineffective programs.
- Make sure everyone knows the stakes. A compliance program is not likely to be effective if company officials and employees think of it as just another justification for lawyers to meddle in their business. Tell them about the company's possible exposure, and keep them abreast of prosecutions of similarly situated organizations. Compliance programs are not a game; they may save the company millions of dollars some day.

Another new responsibility for corporate counsel requires more of an attitude adjustment. Organizational crime often is very difficult for the government to discover. In the past, even when discovery occurred, corporations received relatively small sanctions. Thus, companies had little incentive to investigate vigorously or to self-report criminal conduct.

Now things are different. The guidelines provide a five-point reduction for corporations that self-report violations, cooperate in the ensuing investigation, and fully accept responsibility.

Jack's company conducted only a brief investigation and apparently did so for the primary purpose of determining how much money it might need to refund to the Department of Interior. Had the company dug deeper, as the government investigators later did, it may have discovered that fraud may have occurred. If the company then reported the violation, cooperated with the government, and accepted responsibility, its culpability score would have been reduced by five points. The government might very well have been convinced not to prosecute.

Vague references to reductions in culpability scores may be inadequate to drive home the importance of adapting to life under the guidelines. But culpability scores mean big bucks.

Rethink the calculation for a moment. Jack's culpability score was computed at *seven*, and the resulting fine ranged from $1.26 million to $2.52 million. If the company had in place an effective compliance program (a three-point reduction), and had better investigated and reported the fraud (a five-point reduction), the culpability score potentially could have been reduced to *negative one*. A culpability score of negative one corresponds to multipliers of .05 to .20, implying a fine of $45,000 to $180,000.

Reducing fines is not the only benefit of having compliance programs. An effective compliance program also can result in decreased insurance rates, reduce the likelihood of derivative shareholder suits, and give rise to good publicity. Most important, it may keep the organization from being indicted at all.

Jack's primary hope at this point is that his company's virtually rabid current state of cooperation will convince prosecutors not to prosecute. He asked my opinion about the likelihood of prosecution.

Historically, very few prosecutions of organizations have taken place in federal court. Of more than 40,000 criminal cases sentenced in federal court each year, fewer than 400 involve organizational defendants, and about 90 percent of those prosecutions involved closely held corporations. United States Sentencing Commission, *1993 Annual Report*, at 167–69.

Public Corporations

Jack's company is a publicly traded corporation with about 350 employees. Prosecutions of such corporations are rare.

Thus, had Jack's case arisen even a year ago, my prediction would have been that no prosecution would occur, at least if the company made restitution. Quite simply, prosecutors would have had little to gain by going after a company like Jack's based on the isolated criminal conduct of a single employee. Big companies have far more defense resources than a smaller company or an individual defendant and, more important, the likelihood of obtaining significant sanctions not long ago was minimal.

But, in this current context, outdated experience with prosecution practices rapidly becomes worthless. I felt compelled to tell Jack that prosecution might very well ensue.

The increased sanctions dictated by the new guidelines and the recent amendments to federal law provide prosecutors with greater incentive to prosecute corporate crime. In addition, public opinion appears to be that more must be done to curb corporate crime; the guidelines and new laws reflect the depth of such opinion.

These circumstances strongly suggest that more organizations are going to find themselves enmeshed in criminal proceedings in the coming years. Early indications, in fact, are that federal prosecutors are stepping up indictments of corporations. *See* Jed S. Rakoff, "Corporate Indictment and the Guidelines," *N.Y. L.J.*, Jan. 13, 1994, at 3. As prosecutors become more experienced in prosecuting organizations, and as they start achieving big sentences under the guidelines, prosecution of organizations is likely to increase dramatically.

At this point, CEOs still may have almost as good a chance at personally getting hit by lightning as their corporations do at getting hit by a criminal indictment, but that is changing.

Prosecutors are developing more detailed standards for determining when to indict organizations. One of the leading criteria is that the presence of an effective compliance program counsels against prosecution. Another, predictably, is that cooperation, including self-reporting, also militates against indictment. Thus, the same concepts that permit organizations to limit their exposure under the guidelines also may help to preclude prosecution entirely.

Although the guidelines now cover about 80 percent of the criminal offenses typically committed by organizations, they do not yet apply to environmental crimes. The Sentencing Commission has for some time been looking into promulgating guidelines for environmental offenses committed by organizations.

On November 16, 1993, a distinguished Advisory Working Group on Environmental Offenses submitted a draft of proposed guidelines to the Commission, and public comment on those proposed guidelines has been occurring ever since. The proposed environmental guidelines are detailed and follow a format similar to the other organizational guidelines. They also provide significant mitigation opportunities for compliance efforts and make a focused effort to explain compliance requirements in the environmental context.

Although it is unclear whether these or similar guidelines will become law anytime in the near future, as a prudent counsel, obtain a copy from the Commission. These proposed guidelines provide insight into what leading experts believe compliance really means in this context and, perhaps, into what the law will require in the near future.

The Hidden Penalties of Conviction

Elkan Abramowitz

In simpler times, in the early 1940s, a young waiter working at an Atlantic City nightclub gave a telephone message to a woman who then traveled to Philadelphia for illicit purposes. The waiter was charged with a violation of the Mann Act, 18 U.S.C. §§ 2421–2424.

Presumably not impressed with the seriousness of the charge, but not courageous enough to throw it out, the trial judge convinced the waiter to enter a "technical" guilty plea and immediately sentenced him to sit in the back of the courtroom for the rest of that day.

Two decades later, the waiter had new career ambitions, but his "technical" felony conviction stood in the way. So he went back to court, seeking to vacate his conviction and arguing that before he pled he should have been warned of such collateral consequences as inability to vote or hold public office.

The trial court was unpersuaded, and the appellate court affirmed. The courts reasoned that if a guilty plea were not valid unless the defendant was first apprised of all possible collateral legal consequences, there would be a "a mass exodus from the federal penitentiaries." Furthermore, "[a]ny such requirement would impose upon the judge an impractical burden out of all proportion to the essentials of fair and just administration of the criminal laws." *United States v. Cariola*, 323 F.2d 180, 186 (3d Cir. 1963).

It didn't matter that the so-called "collateral consequences" were more severe for the waiter than the direct sentence he received; if the penalty was "collateral," he had no right to be warned.

Elkan Abramowitz is a member of the New York City firm of Morvillo, Abramowitz, Grand, Iason, & Silberberg, P.C. Alan P. Williamson, an associate at the firm, and Gordon Light, a student at New York University School of Law, assisted in the preparation of this chapter.

Today most white-collar criminals (and crimes) are more sophisticated than the hapless waiter passing a message. But the story is often the same: criminal defendants, corporate and individual, stunned by the consequences of their convictions long after their sentences are over.

It used to be that the sentence itself was the most formidable consequence in the average criminal case. Judges, lawyers, and defendants gave little thought to the hidden consequences of a criminal conviction.

But today white-collar cases often have collateral consequences more severe than a prison sentence, a substantial fine, or restitution—consequences like loss of a professional license, forfeiture, debarment from government contracting, deportation, civil commitment, or subsequent civil litigation with issues predetermined by the prior guilty plea.

As the government more aggressively prosecutes white-collar crime, the threat of collateral consequences is magnified. Yet courts' concern about them apparently is not. Judges continue to advise defendants carefully of the "direct" consequences of a guilty plea without a word about consequences deemed "collateral."

To the defense lawyer goes the lonely job of anticipating collateral consequences, weighing them with the client, and ultimately helping the client to decide whether to enter a plea. To do this you must know which consequences are considered not "direct" but merely "collateral."

Legal Distinctions

The legal distinction between direct and collateral consequences is crucial in federal court: Entering a guilty plea means voluntarily waiving the constitutional right to trial by jury. The defendant who does not understand the direct consequences of a plea is incapable of such a voluntary waiver. On the other hand, whether the defendant understands the collateral consequences of a plea does not affect the voluntariness of a waiver.

The constitutional requirement that a guilty plea be voluntary and a defendant's waiver of rights be knowing and intelligent was explained this way in *Brady v. United States,* 397 U.S. 742, 748 (1970):

> That a guilty plea is a grave and solemn act to be accepted only with care and discernment has long been recognized. Central to the plea and the foundation for entering judgment against the defendant is the defendant's admission in open court that he committed the acts charged in the indictment. He thus stands as a witness against himself and he is shielded by the Fifth Amendment from being compelled to do so—hence the minimum requirement that his plea be the voluntary expression of his own choice. But the plea is more than an admission of past conduct, it is the defendant's consent that judgment of conviction may be entered without a trial—a waiver of his right to trial before a jury or a judge.

Waivers of constitutional rights not only must be voluntary but must be knowing, intelligent acts done with sufficient awareness of the relevant circumstances and likely consequences.

Voluntariness is most often challenged by a motion to withdraw a guilty plea. Under Fed. R. Crim. P. 32(e) the court may permit a defendant to withdraw a guilty plea before sentencing "if the defendant shows any fair and just reason." There is no absolute right to withdraw a plea, however. *United States v. Buckles*, 843 F.2d 469, 471 (11th Cir. 1988), *cert. denied*, 109 S. Ct. 2450 (1989). Courts will not view pleas as "merely 'tentative,' subject to withdrawal before sentence whenever the government cannot establish prejudice." Federal Rule of Criminal Procedure 32, Advisory Committee's note (1983).

The most common ground for a Rule 32 motion is that the plea was involuntary because the defendant was not warned of certain consequences. It is the "direct" consequences that a defendant must understand. "Collateral" consequences are deemed not to affect voluntariness, no matter how serious they are.

Unfortunately for criminal defendants and their lawyers, the attempt to distinguish "collateral" from "direct" has generally expanded the former at the expense of the latter.

For example, in *Cuthrell v. Director, Patuxent Institution*, 475 F.2d 1364 (4th Cir.), *cert. denied*, 414 U.S. 1005 (1973), no one told the defendant that under Maryland law if he pled guilty to assault he could be committed to an institution indefinitely as a "defective delinquent."

The government did not have to be told. Once the guilty plea was entered, the government began civil commitment proceedings against the defendant, who was eventually institutionalized as a "defective delinquent."

The defendant tried to withdraw his plea, but the court denied his motion. Whether a consequence is direct "turns on whether the result represents a definite, immediate and largely automatic effect on the range of the defendant's punishment," the court explained.

"Largely automatic" were the magic words. Because the commitment resulted from a separate civil proceeding, it did not meet the "largely automatic" standard and was therefore a collateral consequence of which the defendant had no right to be warned.

Like the cases, the Federal Rules of Criminal Procedure limit the consequences deemed direct, expanding the "collateral" category.

Rule 11 requires the court to determine whether the defendant understands any mandatory minimum legal penalty, and the maximum possible legal penalty, including the effect of special parole or supervised release, the possibility of a guidelines departure, and possible requirements to make restitution to any victim of the offense. "[I]f the defendant is informed of these critical consequences, he need be informed of no others." *United States v. Dayton*, 604 F.2d 931, 937 (5th Cir.), *cert. denied*, 445 U.S. 904 (1980).

In other words, if it's not in the rule, it's a collateral consequence. No warning necessary.

Realizing now that the sweep of collateral consequences is broad indeed and that defendants may have no inkling of even the most devastating ones except from their lawyers, consider some of the major ones:

Loss of registration or license. A defendant may lose the ability to earn a living in certain fields. For example, under the Securities Exchange Act of 1934, § 15(b)(4), the Securities and Exchange Commission may censure, suspend, or revoke the registration of any broker or dealer who has been convicted of any felony or misdemeanor involving false statements, bribery, perjury, burglary, larceny, theft, robbery, extortion, forgery, counterfeiting, concealment, embezzlement, fraudulent conversion, or the misappropriation, purchase or sale of any security.

Under § 3(a)(39) of the act, a self-regulatory organization may refuse to qualify for membership a person with any such conviction. State "Blue Sky Laws" may have similar provisions. These and other collateral consequences in the securities field are well summarized in Ferrara and Crespi's *Redeeming Fallen Brokers: Managing the Aftermath of Broker-Dealer Enforcement Proceedings* (1988).

After a Guilty Plea

A physician, lawyer, or other professional who depends on a license to practice should expect and prepare for revocation proceedings after a guilty plea. Often the revocation is virtually automatic.

For example, in *United States v. Casanova's, Inc.*, 350 F. Supp. 291 (E.D. Wis. 1972), a corporation and its president were charged with possession of an unregistered firearm. The deal offered by the prosecutor seemed too good to pass up. The corporation pled guilty and was fined $500; the charges against its president were dropped.

It wasn't long before the deal began to sour. As a result of the conviction, the company permanently lost its license to sell weapons. Its $400,000 business went down the drain.

The company moved to withdraw its plea, but the court denied the motion, saying the loss of the "right to operate a business worth a great deal of money . . . [is not] a more serious deprivation than the loss of the right to vote." Both are considered merely collateral consequences.

Loss of government contracts. Another collateral consequence that can go straight to a defendant's pocketbook is debarment from government contracting. A debarment need not be proportional to the severity of the prior criminal sentence; after pleading *nolo contendere* to false statements charges stemming from contracts worth $7,086.75 and paying a $20,000 fine, a meat company that transacted the majority of its business with the government was debarred from contracting with the government for the maximum-allowable period of three years. *Shane Meat Co., Inc. v. United States Dep't of Defense,* 800 F.2d 334 (3d Cir. 1986). The agency may rely solely on conviction and inferences drawn from conviction. *See Agan v. Pierce* , 576 F. Supp. 257 (N.D. Ga. 1983).

Civil forfeiture. For the unwary, federal forfeiture laws have been likened to a house of horrors. *See* "Forfeitures: When Uncle Sam Says You Can't Take It with You," LITIGATION, Vol. 14, No. 2 (Winter 1988), p. 31. Yet civil forfeiture of property may be a collateral consequence of a guilty plea.

This is how one defendant discovered the collateral impact of his guilty plea: He pled guilty to a narcotics charge in state court. Three years later the federal government instituted forfeiture proceedings against the $228,536 seized when he was arrested.

The defendant claimed that his rights under the due process clause of the Fifth Amendment had been violated because the court that accepted his plea had implicitly promised that no such action would be brought. *United States v. United States Currency in the Amount of $228,536.00,* 895 F.2d 908 (2d Cir. 1990), *cert. denied,* 495 U.S. 958 (1990).

The Second Circuit rejected the defendant's argument, holding that civil forfeiture was only a collateral consequence—even if the "factual admissions made during a plea proceeding . . . [were] used to establish probable cause to bring a forfeiture proceeding." *See also Harris v. Allen,* 929 F.2d 560 (10th Cir. 1991).

Further Consequences

Enhancement of criminal liability. A defendant has no right to be told that a guilty plea may lead to enhancement of criminal liability in the future.

One explanation is that a court has a "right to assume that the defendant will not be guilty of a subsequent offense." *Fee v. United States,* 207 F. Supp. 674, 676 (W.D. Va. 1962). Another is that it is too burdensome for the court to have to inform a defendant of sentence enhancing possibilities. *United States v. Garrett,* 680 F.2d 64 (9th Cir. 1982).

Admission of predicate act under RICO. Under the same sort of reasoning, a court is not required to inform a defendant that a guilty plea may also be considered an admission of a predicate act under RICO. *United States v. Persico,* 774 F.2d 30 (2d Cir. 1985).

Federal benefits. The Federal Sentencing Guidelines allow the courts to deny "certain federal benefits" to individuals convicted of distribution or possession of a controlled substance. *See* U.S.S.G. § 5F1.6. The loss of federal benefits is also considered a collateral consequence of pleading guilty. *United States v. Morse,* 36 F.3d 1070 (11th Cir. 1994).

Deportation. A criminal defendant who is also an alien should factor potential deportation into the plea decision. Even in a case in which counsel erroneously advised a defendant that conviction would not subject him to deportation, the court denied a motion to withdraw the plea. *United States v. Parrino*, 212 F.2d 919 (2d Cir.), *cert. denied*, 348 U.S. 840 (1954).

Not all judges agree with this result. In *Parrino*, for example, Judge Frank filed a vigorous dissent, astonished that Parrino's lawyer was so "egregiously derelict" and angry that his colleagues chose to administer "injustice according to law." But even when judges have taken issue with the outcome of such cases, deportation is still deemed a collateral consequence.

Collateral estoppel in subsequent litigation. If a guilty plea in any way acknowledges an injury to a third party—or even to the government—it may have dangerous consequences in subsequent litigation.

Here is a typical scenario from a real case: A defendant pleads guilty to one count of filing a fraudulent tax return. The IRS follows the criminal proceeding with a civil suit to recover the unpaid taxes. The guilty plea follows the defendant to civil court. It may not be withdrawn.

"Although it might be desirable to inform a defendant that his guilty plea would probably have the collateral consequence of estopping him from denying that his tax return was false and fraudulent," the court said, it found no warning legally required. *United States v. King*, 618 F.2d 550, 552 (9th Cir. 1980).

The rationale was that the civil litigation did not follow "directly" from the plea because the government first had to decide to bring the action. The court also reasoned that the defendant would be estopped only from denying that the return was false and fraudulent; the government would still be required to prove the amount of the deficiency. *Accord, United States v. Miss Smart Frocks*, 279 F. Supp. 295 (S.D.N.Y. 1968).

For financial impact, there is surely no more devastating consequence of a guilty plea than the application of collateral estoppel in future civil litigation. Nor is there a thornier question than exactly when this doctrine applies. Collateral estoppel or issue preclusion "prevents re-litigation of all 'issues of fact or law that were actually litigated and necessarily decided' in a prior proceeding. . . . The issue must have been 'actually decided' after a full and fair opportunity for litigation." *Robi v. Five Platters, Inc.*, 838 F.2d 318, 322 (9th Cir. 1988).

Of course, a guilty plea actually decides a number of issues. The question is what impact those decisions have on the issues in the subsequent civil case.

Determining just what facts were necessarily decided in prior litigation seems deceptively simple in theory. The trial judge needs merely to examine the complete record, "including the pleadings, the evidence submitted, the instructions under which the jury arrived at its verdict, and any opinions of the court." *Emich Motor Corp. v. General Motors Corp.*, 340 U.S. 558, 569 (1951).

But what is simple in theory often becomes all but impossible in practice when a prior guilty plea is involved.

Does the language of the indictment control, or can the defendant cut potential losses by bargaining for favorable language in the plea colloquy? If offered an exceptionally good plea, can the defendant agree to pay more restitution than seems warranted and still litigate the amount of damages later in a civil suit? Or does the agreed restitution forever estop the defendant from contending that the amount of actual damages was less? See generally, Cipes, 8 *Moore's Federal Practice* § 11.10[1], n.4. The answers are by no means clear.

In *Alsco-Harvard Fraud Litigation,* 523 F. Supp. 790 (D.D.C. 1981), for example, the government brought a civil suit following the criminal convictions of the president and special counsel of a government contractor that supplied rocket parts to the Navy. The defendants had created a series of dummy corporations and through complex kickback and overbilling schemes defrauded the government. They pled guilty to one count of conspiracy to defraud under 18 U.S.C. § 1001.

In the civil suit, the government contended that the defendants were estopped by their plea from denying their liability. In particular, it argued that because the conspiracy count of the indictment—to which the defendants had pled guilty—described the entire course of the defendants' scheme in detail, the defendants had necessarily admitted each of the allegations.

The defendants argued that the plea of guilty had absolutely no collateral estoppel effect because no issues had actually been litigated.

The court held that the guilty pleas to the counts of making false statements estopped the defendants from contesting liability under the False Claims Act because the elements of the civil cause of action overlapped the substantive criminal charges admitted by the pleas.

However, the plea to the conspiracy charge admitted only the existence of the conspiracy, not the substantive counts incorporated into the conspiracy allegations. "[P]laintiff cannot hope to use defendant[s'] . . . admission to a conspiracy . . . as a catch-all for conclusively establishing the specific manner by which that conspiracy was effectuated." *Alsco-Harvard,* 523 F. Supp. at 804. Consequently, the defendants were free to contest the allegations included in the indictment's conspiracy count. *See also Scheiner v. Wallace,* 832 F. Supp. 687 (S.D.N.Y. 1993) (collecting cases, and holding that insureds' guilty plea to attempted grand larceny, as a matter of law, did not bar civil litigation against their underwriters).

Civil Liability

With the availability of treble damages and the increased popularity of multimillion-dollar allegations in criminal indictments and civil complaints, a guilty plea may be tantamount to an admission of civil liability for three times the amount alleged in the indictment.

Take the lawyer who defrauded a trust held for the benefit of a client and subsequently pled guilty to two counts of a 20-count indictment. Defense counsel agreed that the fraud amounted to at least $495,000 but disputed the government's claim that it was actually $957,000.

The prosecutor told the court "that the parties do in essence agree to disagree, and that the purpose in arriving at the agreed-upon sentence was, in part, to obviate the need for an evidentiary hearing with respect to the material differences in each of the versions." *Appley v. West*, 832 F.2d 1021 (7th Cir. 1987). The court ordered restitution of $957,000.

Meanwhile, the client-victim of the fraud filed a civil RICO suit against the lawyer and, after the guilty plea, moved for summary judgment. The court granted the motion, awarding the client three times the ordered restitution—a total of almost $3 million!

The Seventh Circuit reversed and remanded, pointing out that the actual amount of money that the client had lost was not a material fact alleged in the indictment, so the guilty plea did not estop the defendant from litigating the amount. And because the parties merely "agreed to disagree," the amount of restitution was not "actively litigated." Collateral estoppel did not preclude litigation of damages.

But in an otherwise similar case, where the defendant actually consented to restitution as part of its plea bargain, a New York appellate court held that the defendant was "bound by its plea." *Kuriansky v. Professional Care, Inc.*, 158 A.D.2d +897, 551 N.Y.S.2d 695 (3d Dep't 1990).

Even if a defendant manages to avoid the rigors of collateral estoppel, under Federal Rules of Evidence 801(d)(2)(A) and 410(1), an unwithdrawn plea of guilty is admissible as evidence in a subsequent action. *See* Weinstein & Berger, 2 *Weinstein's Evidence*, § 410[06]. Under Rule 803(22) a final judgment is evidence of the essential facts, not a conclusive demonstration of them. "[T]he defendant is not precluded from offering an explanation based on newly acquired evidence in the second trial." Weinstein & Berger, 4 *Weinstein's Evidence*, § 803(22)[01]. But we all know what admitting the guilty plea is likely to mean at trial.

Theoretically at least, one way of avoiding collateral estoppel is to replace the unseemly "guilty" plea with a plea of *nolo contendere*, which is inadmissible as evidence of guilt in a subsequent civil action. *Duffy v. Cuyler*, 581 F.2d 1059 (3d Cir.), *cert. denied*, 439 U.S. 1075 (1979).

The problem is that there is no right to enter a *nolo* plea. The court has discretion to accept it or not, and courts rarely exercise that discretion in favor of defendants who have all but formally admitted wrongdoing. The government's consent, which weighs heavily with the court, is given only "in the most unusual circumstances." Department of Justice, *United States Attorney's Manual* § 9–16.010.

The harsh fact is that there may be no way around collateral consequences awaiting the defendant who pleads guilty. That should strike fear into the heart of even the most careful criminal lawyer.

As if that weren't bad enough, consider a final chilling thought: Being too careful can backfire. At least it did for poor Congressman Podell and his lawyer in *United States v. Podell*, 572 F.2d 31 (2d Cir. 1978).

Podell was a former U. S. congressman who pled guilty to charges that he conspired to violate, and did in fact violate, the federal conflict-of-interest statute. The Second Circuit affirmed a summary judgment for the government, imposing a constructive trust on the compensation Podell allegedly received from his criminal activity.

In response to Podell's argument that he had not agreed to the amount of money the government alleged was involved, the court acknowledged that ordinarily a plea to a conspiracy count would not preclude subsequent litigation on the amount of money actually involved.

But the court also stressed that in this case Podell and his lawyer "carefully struck the portions of the indictment to which he did not desire to plead guilty" and that "[b]y exhibiting such painstaking care . . . Podell in effect and, indeed in actuality, admitted the truth of the remainder of the paragraph's allegations."

Because one portion of the indictment to which Podell chose to plead referred to a specific amount, he was estopped from challenging that amount in subsequent litigation.

Notwithstanding Podell's predicament, the best way to protect the criminal defendant is to "think collateral" when the government offers a plea bargain that seems too good to pass up. If the client chooses to sign on the dotted line, it should be with eyes open to collateral consequences of conviction.

PART VII

Special Problems in Civil Litigation

Avoiding Problems in Joint Defense Groups

Mark D. Plevin

No one is ever satisfied with joint defense groups. Lawyers for the major defendants fret about keeping the lawyers who represent the minor defendants in line and getting them to do their "fair share." Lawyers for the minor defendants complain about being kept in the dark by the leaders of the group and worry about being left behind if the major defendants settle out.

Consider these scenarios. Each one will be familiar to those who have participated in a joint defense group.

Scenario 1: Becky represents one of the principal defendants in *Mighty Corp. v. Big Insurance Company et al.* For months, she has tried to persuade other members of the joint defense group to take on a greater share of the work. But the other defendants have been content to let Becky's firm take the lead on every significant project. As a result, Becky and her associates drafted and argued the group's joint motion to dismiss, propounded the initial joint discovery requests, and negotiated the case management order with the plaintiff. The deference shown by the other members of the group gave Becky a welcome measure of control over the defense. Now, however, with the plaintiff about to produce more than a million pages of documents, Becky's client, Chuck, has started to complain about the bills.

"What's everyone else up to? Why aren't the other defendants doing any of the work? Can't you twist their arms and get them to help?" Chuck was exasperated, his questions coming rapidly. "I don't want you to be the only one reviewing documents," he warned.

With Chuck's admonition ringing in her ears, Becky convened a meeting of the *Mighty v. Big* joint defense group. She reported what

---

Mark D. Plevin is with the Crowell & Moring L.L.P. firm in Washington, DC.

Mighty's counsel had said about the upcoming document production set to begin next Monday and explained the need for broad participation in the document review effort. Then she asked for volunteers to help in the review. Becky looked around the table expectantly. But she saw only vacant stares. No one wanted to commit any lawyers or paralegals to help.

Suddenly, a hand shot up across the table. It was Frank, a second-year eager-beaver associate at one of the big firms in town. "I'll be glad to talk to the partner about it," he said, earnestly. "He's out of town for a few days, but I should be able to get in to see him early next week. Maybe we can send someone for the last day or two, if the review is still going on then." Frank's offer, meager as it was, was a godsend. At least Becky could tell Chuck someone else might help, if only a little bit.

"I hate joint defense groups," Becky thought.

Scenario 2: The moment had been months in the making. Early on, Julie and counsel for the other defendants in *ABC Corp. v. Huge Corp et al.* had conceived of the novel legal theory that might support summary judgment. Then, Julie carefully crafted and implemented a discovery plan that required the participation of most of the defense group. Finally, the brief was painstakingly drafted, circulated twice for comment, and revised several times to garner the support of all the defendants.

As the principal drafter of the brief and counsel for the lead defendant, Huge Corp., Julie orally argued in support of the motion. And it had gone very well; the judge's comments suggested that he had seen things Julie's way.

As counsel for the plaintiff rose to respond, out of the corner of her eye Julie saw Bob Bumbler, counsel for one of the other defendants, rush toward the podium. Bob only occasionally made it to the monthly joint defense meetings. When he did, he seemed to be on a different page from the rest of the lawyers in the joint defense group. Julie recalled that the brief had to be changed just before filing in order to persuade Bob's client to join it. She began to shudder.

Bob quickly gave his appearance, then said, "Judge, I'd just like to clarify a point made by counsel for Huge." Bob spoke for only two minutes, but his "clarification" was enough to muddy things in the judge's mind. The plaintiff's lawyer never even had to say a word. "Summary judgment denied," the judge ruled from the bench. "I hate joint defense groups," Julie muttered under her breath.

Scenario 3: The letter seemed innocuous, but it was enough to ruin Brian's day, if not his year.

"Please be advised that our client, Massive Corp., has settled with plaintiffs and hereby withdraws, effective today, from the joint defense group in *XYZ Company v. Massive Corp. et al.*"

611

Just then the phone rang. It was Robin, who represented another defendant in the XYZ case.

"What are we going to do now?" he wailed. What, indeed?

Brian recalled how pleased he was last spring when Mary, the general counsel of Minor, Inc., called and asked him to represent the company in a "major piece of litigation." Brian remembered how impressed he was with Massive's counsel at the firm of High & Mighty and his plans for coordinating the defense of the XYZ suit. Every month, Brian sent his junior associate to the meeting of the joint defense group and reviewed his report of all the activity being undertaken by Massive's counsel on behalf of the group. Every once in a while, Brian asked Mary to send a check to cover Minor's share of the group's joint defense costs. Brian was confident High & Mighty would roll over XYZ in the courtroom at trial. Brian would be a hero to Minor, Inc., and Mary would send lots of business in the future. Or so he thought.

Now, with Massive suddenly out of the case, things looked a lot different. Brian realized that he knew next to nothing about the lawsuit. Massive's counsel had taken the lead on reviewing XYZ's document production; to save costs, Brian sent one junior associate to the document review for three days, but she was no longer at Brian's firm. The document imaging system and deposition database were housed at the offices of High & Mighty; besides, neither Brian nor anyone else at his firm knew how to operate the database. No one from Brian's firm attended the dozens of depositions of XYZ's witnesses, or even read the transcripts; instead, Brian relied on the deposition summaries prepared by other defense group members. Brian was not prepared to file any motions for summary judgment even though the deadline was next week; he had been waiting for High & Mighty to circulate a draft group motion. Finally, trial was scheduled to start in only five weeks, and the judge never granted continuances.

How could this have happened? Where did things go wrong?

If no one likes joint defense groups, why do we have them? The answer is easy in some cases: because the court says so. Judges sometimes require defendants to file joint briefs, or serve joint discovery. They sometimes limit the defendants to a specified number of interrogatories or document requests. They sometimes order the defendants to designate a lead questioner at depositions, and they sometimes appoint a "defense liaison counsel," a "defense coordinator," or a defendants' "discovery committee." *See, e.g., Manual for Complex Litigation* 3d § 20.22; *Central Illinois Public Service Co. v. Allianz Underwriters Ins. Co.*, 158 Ill.2d 218, 633 N.E.2d 675, 676–77 (1994). The need to comply with the court's orders forces defense counsel to work together.

But even where the court does not mandate the organization of a joint defense group, it is likely that the defendants will organize one anyway. Joint defense groups, if properly managed, can be a powerful tool. They are frequently the most effective and efficient way of managing and coordinating multiparty litigation from the defense side.

First, joint defense groups enable each defendant to reduce substantially its costs of defense. These cost savings come in two forms. One is sharing of work. The defense firms may divide the legal research tasks in a case, then share the memos. One firm may prepare a joint set of document requests, while another drafts a joint set of interrogatories. A different firm might interview expert witnesses. If the plaintiff is producing a million pages of documents at a distant warehouse, each defense firm can contribute one or more lawyers or paralegals to the on-site review. When depositions begin, the witnesses can be divided among the participating defendants, saving each firm from having to prepare separately for each deposition. A similar division of responsibility can be implemented at trial. The defendants can split up motions *in limine* and witnesses.

Joint defense groups can also provide huge savings in expensive "out of pocket" costs. These can include the costs of experts, consultants, and court reporters. One of the largest costs assumed in "big document" cases is the cost of creating a computerized database of the plaintiff's documents. Typically, all members of the joint defense group have access to the database. This is a significant cost that no single defendant—at least no minor defendant—would take on if it had to pay for the whole thing.

Cost savings are not the only benefit to be gained from joint defense groups. There is also the benefit derived from combining the expertise, knowledge, and skills of the lawyers in the group. Some of the lawyers may have specialized knowledge about the substantive law at issue. Others may have experience dealing with the particular industry or business involved. Perhaps one of the lawyers has recently tried a case before the judge. Taken collectively, the group has better qualifications, deeper knowledge, and more expertise than any single lawyer.

A third benefit of joint defense groups is the ability to coordinate strategy and tactics. A joint defense group enables the defendants, who often face a single (and single-minded) plaintiff, to speak with one voice, staying "on message" and avoiding (or at least reducing) conflict on their side of the case. A joint defense group also can help to ensure that one defendant's strategy doesn't work at cross-purposes with another's.

But the benefits are frequently elusive, as the above scenarios indicate. The biggest reason is that joint defense groups are riven by inherent conflicts between major and minor defendants.

Major defendants are those with the most to lose. They want to control the defense, to protect their large stakes. As a result, major defendants often do most of the group's work. Because the case is riskier for them, major defendants typically invest considerable time and effort in carefully establishing each possible ground of defense. This can be extremely expensive—but for a major defendant, this cost may pale against its potential liability.

Minor defendants, by definition, ordinarily have a lesser stake in the case. They are often comfortable deferring to and relying on the major defendants. This permits the minor defendant to realize significant cost savings and fits well with the major defendant's desire for control. However, the minor defendants sometimes balk at incurring the cost of the gold-plated defense that the major defendant believes is warranted, creating dissension within the group and threatening the major defendant's control.

Major and minor defendants also frequently disagree on strategy issues. The minor defendant may be more willing to risk an early summary judgment motion that has the potential of springing that defendant from the case before it gets too expensive, whereas the major defendant may be more interested in having that issue decided later, after discovery has been completed and the record is fully developed. The minor defendant's desire for an early resolution of a potentially dispositive issue interferes with the major defendant's grand strategic design, again threatening the major defendant's control.

Organizing the Group

There also may be a conflict between the major defendant's interest in control and its desire to spread the workload. The major defendant—Becky's client in the first scenario—wants other defendants to help carry the litigation burden, but may not want to cede or share control of the defense. But if the other defendants respond to Becky's pleas for help by becoming more active, it will become more difficult for Becky to continue controlling the defense, since they will want more say in how the defense is being prepared and presented. Eventually, Becky and her client may be forced to decide which is more important to them, cost savings or control. Finding the right blend may be difficult.

The minor defendant often faces a mirror-image conflict between its interest in cost savings and its opposing desire to participate actively. Minor defendants—Brian's client in the third scenario—want to be involved, but not necessarily so involved that they incur huge costs. On the other hand, too much reliance on the group can be disastrous, as Brian learned. The minor must be active enough to protect its own interests.

Yet another conflict pits the need for group consensus against the need to be proactive. To move forward on any project—whether it is the filing of a motion, the retention of an expert, or the creation of a database—the group must develop a consensus. The larger the group, and the more disparate the interests of its members, however, the harder it is to develop any consensus in a timely fashion. The failure to develop a timely consensus leads to missed opportunities: motions not filed, or filed at the wrong time; depositions not taken; discovery not served; initiatives overlooked. These opportunity costs can be impossible to measure, or even to recognize, even though they may be significant.

Whether you represent a major or minor defendant, navigating through these crosscurrents requires organization, leadership, diplomacy, and diligence. A little bit of luck sometimes helps, too.

First, organize the joint defense group. This means contacting the other defense lawyers as early as possible. Time may be of the essence if you want to remove the case from state court to federal court or persuade other lawyers to avoid raising certain sensitive issues in a motion to dismiss under Rule 12(b)(6) of the Federal Rules of Civil Procedure or comparable state law.

Keep in mind at the outset that your discussions with other defense counsel about joint defense strategy are probably shielded by the "joint defense privilege," a judicial doctrine that protects from disclosure many communications between counsel for similarly situated parties about the litigation. *See, e.g.*, Michael G. Scheininger and Ray M. Aragon, "Joint Defense Agreements," *Litigation*, 20:3 (Spring 1994); Gerald F. Uelman, "The Joint Defense Privilege: Know the Risks," *Litigation*, 14:4 (Summer 1988). As these articles point out, however, the joint defense privilege is not without gray areas as to where and when it applies. One way to make these gray areas black and white is to ask the judge, in a case management order, to include an express recognition of the joint defense privilege and protection for joint defense activities. Particularly where the court is requiring, or at least encouraging, coordination among the defendants, judges and plaintiffs are usually amenable to such a provision.

When you have your first joint defense group meeting or telephone conference call, address head-on the question of whether the defendants want to formulate a joint defense group and, if so, for what purposes. Will the group just talk from time to time about the direction of the case, or will the group meet regularly in an effort to formulate and follow an integrated strategy? Will each defendant review and organize the plaintiff's documents on its own, or will the group contract with a vendor to provide a document management system accessible by all defendants? Will experts and investigators be retained separately or jointly? The answers may depend on the type of suit, the nature of the plaintiff's allegations, and the major issues.

An unstructured group that merely agrees to "keep in touch" might be the best course when one defendant has so much more at stake than the others that it wants to defend the case on its own terms, unfettered by the need to accommodate the interests of a joint defense group. Informal groups sometimes also work well where the members of the group have ties apart from the litigation, and the minor defendants are accustomed to taking their lead from the major defendant. Examples include a manufacturer and its suppliers in a product liability case, or the company and its directors and officers in a securities fraud case. Or, there may be an established protocol or pecking order among the defendants that makes it unnecessary to formalize the joint defense arrangement. For example, high-level excess insurance carriers who are defendants in an insurance coverage case will often take their cues from the policyholder-plaintiff's longtime primary carrier.

In other cases, defendants create joint defense groups with elaborate structures, such as committees (for example, a steering committee, a discovery committee, a technology committee, and an expert committee), formal assignments to "first-chair" or "second-chair" depositions, monthly meetings, and so on. This type of group can work best when there are many defendants, including several having more or less equally large stakes in the litigation; the suit itself is complex, requiring extensive discovery and motion practice; and the stakes are high, justifying the cost of coordinating joint defense activities.

Many joint defense groups enter into two types of written agreements at the beginning. The first is a joint defense agreement, which, at a minimum, declares the parties' intent to share work, share costs, and maintain the confidentiality of information shared in connection with the common defense. To promote unity, joint defense agreements frequently provide that the defendants will refrain from asserting contribution or indemnity claims against one another until the plaintiff's claim is finally resolved. These agreements may toll any applicable statutes of limitations for cross-claims or third-party claims. If there is a prospect of later litigation among the defendants, consider whether the joint defense agreement should provide that each defendant may use its current counsel without restriction in the subsequent lawsuit. Absent such a clause, there may be a risk that the defendant on the indemnity claim will seek to disqualify counsel for the other defendants on the ground that they learned confidential material relating to the claim during the course of joint defense activities in the original case.

The second agreement is a cost-sharing agreement. This will identify which costs will be shared (for example, shared databases, joint experts, the cost of faxing draft briefs to other members of the group for comment) and which will not (for example, each defendant's lawyer's fees, the costs of serving court papers). The agreement typically will include mechanisms for initiating cash calls, approving expenses and contracts, and obtaining reimbursement. The cost-sharing agreement also will declare what proportion of the shared costs will be paid by each individual defendant.

There are different schools of thought in the negotiation of individual cost shares. Some groups try to closely calibrate each defendant's cost share to its potential exposure in the lawsuit. Other groups are content to try to effect rough justice by arranging the defendants into tiers corresponding generally to their roles in the suit. Whichever method is used, most defendants want the lowest possible cost burden. This is so not only for the obvious reason—lowering defense costs—but also because of the fear that some defendants would later propose using the cost shares for determining how much each defendant should contribute to any group settlement or judgment.

But not all defendants strive for the lowest cost shares. Sometimes, a single defendant or small group of defendants are content to have larger cost shares if that enables them to control joint defense group expenditures.

In other words, if the group has decided that approval by 70 percent of the cost shares is required to fund a major expense, such as the creation of a computerized database of the plaintiff's documents, three defendants who are confident of their ability to work together smoothly may not mind having shares of 25 percent each. That way, the 70 percent approval requirement can be met simply by agreement among themselves, ensuring that worthwhile joint defense projects will be approved, with the costs of such projects being spread to all defendants.

In antitrust cases, where the law imposes joint and several treble damage liability on each defendant but prohibits indemnity and contribution claims, joint defense groups may also enter into a liability-sharing agreement. Such agreements serve to equitably allocate a judgment entered on a joint and several basis against two or more defendants, and are frequently (but not always) based on each defendant's market share percentage. Judgment-sharing agreements also may contain provisions requiring a settling defendant to extract an agreement from the plaintiff to reduce its claims against the nonsettling defendants by the amount of damages for which the settling defendant would have been responsible absent any settlement. *See Cimmaron Pipeline Construction, Inc. v. National Council on Compensation Ins.*, 1992 U.S. Dist. LEXIS 18560 (W.D. Okla. 1992); Cranston & Kingdom, *Judgment Sharing Agreements*, 1985 Research Project of the Civil Practice and Procedure Committee, ABA Section of Antitrust Law (1985).

Don't make the all-too-common mistake of spending too much time on these preliminary organizational matters. Defense groups often become so consumed with these internal issues that they overlook the need, which may be especially critical at the outset, to direct their primary efforts to planning the defense. If the group is not careful, by the time the cost-shares have finally been agreed to, the plaintiff's summary judgment motion will be filed and the group may not be ready to respond.

Major defendants generally want one thing above all else: control. But this usually is not completely achievable. There are too many other group members, there may be several other defendants with significant stakes who are unwilling to cede control, or there may be an assertive minor defendant who refuses to follow the major defendant's lead. If the major defendant can't have control, then it wants substantial influence and discipline among the group's members.

Cost savings are often less important to major defendants than to minor ones. This is good, because a major defendant typically does not realize the same cost savings from participation in a joint defense that a minor defendant does. This is particularly true if the major defendant does a great deal of the group's work to better maintain control.

In fact, a major defendant may incur significant additional costs from its participation in the group. There are the direct costs of coordination, which can be considerable: attending meetings, sending and reviewing faxes, communicating constantly with other defendants. In addition, counsel for the major defendants are often treated by minor defendants as a sort of on-call information clearinghouse, expected to answer questions and provide documents and other support essentially on demand.

If, as a major defendant, you want control, it is presumably because you have a strategy that you want the group to follow. The key is to persuade the group to follow your plan. Some lawyers representing major defendants think they can rule by fiat, but most defense groups won't knuckle under. No one likes a bully. If you dictate to the group, no one will follow you, at least not for long.

You Don't Know Everything

In most cases, persuading the group to follow your plan requires communication. As one of the major players, you will likely know more than the smaller players. You will have thought more about the case, spent more time considering the pros and cons of any strategy, and spoken more often with plaintiff's counsel. If you want the group to go along, you must share your knowledge and your thoughts.

Be honest with the group; otherwise no one will trust or follow you. Report developments fully and promptly. Let the others know what you and plaintiff's counsel discussed. Give other defendants a chance to react to developments in a timely fashion. Discuss the pros and cons of any proposed action thoroughly, particularly if you are purporting to speak on behalf of the group.

Listen to what other lawyers in the group have to say. You don't know everything. Especially as the case goes on and your role deepens, you may become even more sure that your strategy is best. But the other members, if they've been doing their jobs, have also been thinking about the case. Often, they've been looking at it from different angles. When you discuss strategy and tactics in meetings, they may have useful ideas and suggestions. Don't ignore them. Use them. If you don't, you'll be failing to capitalize on a principal benefit of being part of a group.

Listen carefully for signs that the minor defendants are dissatisfied with their roles. Find out what is bothering them, and allow them to air their concerns. Be responsive by developing a consensus that keeps them working with you; the last thing you want is for a frustrated minor defendant to break with the group on an important issue. Make accommodations where you can, keeping your eye on the major strategic issues.

A significant part of the communication takes place in formal group meetings. Prepare a detailed agenda for the meeting, and distribute it to all participants ahead of time. The agenda should make clear what issues will be discussed, so that all of the group's members can contemplate the issues and, if necessary, discuss them with their clients. That way, when the meeting occurs, the group can take action and make timely decisions, not simply defer decisions to the next meeting. Joint defense groups frequently place themselves at a disadvantage relative to the plaintiff by repeatedly tabling items that need prompt action.

Follow-up is essential as well. Without it, the brilliant thoughts expressed, the assignments agreed to, the grand strategies hatched, often evaporate as soon as the meeting ends.

Within a few days after the meeting, the group's leader should circulate minutes to all, including those who did not attend. The minutes should list all of the assignments, and their deadlines. That way, there can be no disagreement over who agreed to do what, or on what schedule. This, too, helps to avoid drift and inaction, the natural enemies of defendants. At the next meeting or conference call, the progress of the projects should be addressed. This will ensure that assignments are completed.

These same principles—communicate early and often—apply to the preparation of group briefs. Discuss the strategy and the positions well in advance of circulating the brief for comments. Help other defendants become comfortable with where you want to lead them. Give them a chance to provide input. Then, circulate the draft well before the filing date so others can, if necessary, secure client approval. If possible, circulate a revised draft that reflects the comments you've incorporated. Your goal is to persuade all defendants to sign onto a single brief. It will be easier for the judge to read one brief joined by the defendants than to plow through multiple briefs or even numerous separate joinders in a main brief.

Achieving group consensus on a brief or other filing can sometimes be difficult when dealing with institutional litigants, such as banks and insurance companies, which may have well-established positions on specific issues. You can, of course, change the brief to accommodate their concerns, but the change they want may make it difficult for a defendant already happy with the brief to continue its support. One solution is to add a footnote advising the court that not every defendant necessarily agrees with every point. This may give the defendant concerned about the position being asserted just enough distance to be able to join the group's brief. Another alternative is for a defendant to file a joinder advising the judge that it is joining the group's motion or opposition "substantially for the reasons set forth" in the group's brief.

Defense groups tend to follow the first law of physics: A body at rest tends to remain at rest. A difficult task will be to overcome the problem of inertia. Don't let the group miss opportunities because of a failure to act. Force the consensus to develop. Everyone will be looking to you, the group's leader, to be the principal source of ideas and strategies for defending the case. Don't let them down. Assume that if you don't direct the group, no one else will.

One way to avoid the inertia problem is to just go ahead and do the work. But that can be expensive, and your client may chafe at paying for projects that others ought to be doing. If you're going to ask others to help, don't wait until the monthly joint defense meeting, like Becky did in Scenario 1. Raise the issue ahead of time. Work the phones. Call the lead lawyers for the other defendants. Tell them what you want to do. Explain why your idea is good. Enlist their support. Assign projects, then check on everyone's progress to make sure things get done. Remember what President Reagan said to Chairman Gorbachev: Trust, but verify.

Use the right people in the right places. Think of yourself as the general counsel of the group. Honestly evaluate the strengths and weaknesses of the group's lawyers. Don't assign a project that needs many people to a firm that's shorthanded. Don't ask the lawyer who's known for shoddy writing to prepare the group's brief. If a particular lawyer is a poor questioner, don't assign him the important deposition.

And don't ask for volunteers for projects that are important. Match each project to the right lawyer. Get on the phone before the meeting and ask your preferred person to accept the assignment. Tell her why you need her help, and why she's perfect for the task. Only rarely does someone object when a particular project is assigned to another. On the few occasions that happens, ask the disappointed lawyer to work together with your first choice. It takes effort to coordinate the litigation of a large joint defense group, but the cost of not initiating or completing important projects is huge.

If you're not able to persuade someone to accept a particular task, you have two choices: (1) do it yourself, or (2) don't do it at all. If it's important enough, go ahead and do it yourself. Make sure it gets done. But if you're not receiving help from the others, think again about whether membership in the group is serving your client's interests.

Controlling the Renegade

Despite your best efforts to develop a consensus and maintain defense group discipline, there will be times when counsel for some minor defendant will feel strongly opposed to the group's consensus on a particular issue. Recognize that there are times when it does not undermine group unity, at least not in any important way, if the members of the group take different positions. Don't try to enforce unity when it really doesn't matter: If you can, give a little. Both the renegade's lawyer and his client will remember that you accommodated them, which may give you more influence over them the next time, on something more important.

If a particular lawyer insists on following his own agenda, the group may have to decide whether to permit that lawyer to remain in the group or cut him loose. Often, people like to keep the renegade in the group to maintain the lines of communication, on the theory that the group may be better able to respond to the renegade's actions if the group has advance warning and understands the renegade's objections. Even if the group decides not to expel the renegade, there may be times when the group wants to discuss how to deal with him or his issues. Save that part of the discussion for the end, and ask the renegade to leave the room for that part of the meeting.

In deciding whether to let a renegade remain, don't let your decision be ruled by emotions such as anger and betrayal. Focus on important issues: How important is the issue on which the renegade has chosen his own course? Will information disclosed during meetings advance the renegade's position at the expense of the group? Is the renegade paying a large share of joint defense costs? By focusing on such issues, the group may be willing to tolerate an occasional departure from the group's consensus.

If you know in advance that the renegade is going to take a contrary position, you might head him off by going over his head. Ask your client to call her counterpart in the general counsel's office of the renegade's client. She may be able to reason with that person and persuade him to instruct his counsel to agree. This is a particularly effective option for group leaders whose clients have some relationship with the renegade defendant besides being co-defendants. For example, if you represent the manufacturer in a product liability suit and one of your suppliers is about to take a position that will undermine the joint defense, your client may be able to use its business relationship to bring about a reassessment of the supplier's original position.

Don't assume you can repeatedly use this back-channel communication. You and your client may have to expend considerable political capital to achieve a change of position, particularly since the whole episode may be somewhat embarrassing to the renegade's counsel. This action is best saved for the rare time when you absolutely must maintain group discipline and unity.

Sometimes incompetence, rather than a conscious strategy choice, threatens to wreck your carefully constructed strategy. There's only so much you can do if, as in Scenario 2, Bob Bumbler offers to "clarify" your already persuasive summary judgment argument. You can whisper in Bob's ear, pull on his suit coat, or pass him a note telling him to shut up. But if Bob won't listen, you may simply have to wait and then repair the damage as best you can.

I once saw a defense lawyer named Phil make an unexpected but brilliant save when faced with his own Bob Bumbler. During cross-examination, Phil purposefully avoided a troublesome area. Then Bob stood up. His first question asked the witness to comment directly on the topic Phil had so carefully avoided. We were all dumbfounded. All except Phil, who leaped to his feet. "Objection," he shouted. "Asked and answered."

Everyone in the courtroom, including plaintiff's counsel, began giggling at the spectacle of one defendant objecting to another's cross-examination. Finally, as the laughter died down, the judge spoke. "Sustained," she said. Everyone laughed again. But Phil's quick instincts had saved the day.

Be alert that your role as counsel for a major defendant may give you added settlement leverage that you can use to your client's advantage, particularly if plaintiff's counsel knows (or suspects) that you've been doing most of the work—if, for instance, all of the group's briefs have come from your office, and you've taken most of the depositions.

Don't Rely on Reputation

Removing you and your client from the case may be very important to plaintiff's counsel if it would be easier to litigate successfully against the remnants of the group following your departure. After all, plaintiff may conclude, if you're not in the case, the group suddenly will be left without its workhorse. And if the plaintiff believes that other members are less able or have less expertise, the plaintiff is likely to believe that it will be easier to win without your presence. This may give you settlement leverage. You may be able to settle at a discount from the plaintiff's original assessment of the value of its claims, the discount reflecting the plaintiff's evaluation of its greater chances of success against the other defendants if you are gone.

Be aware, however, that making yourself seem indispensable in the plaintiff's eyes can sometimes backfire. If you're doing all the work—or at least all the work visible to the plaintiff—the plaintiff may conclude that you have more exposure than it previously thought. The plaintiff could increase its settlement demand to make it commensurate with what you appear to believe is your central role.

The chief benefit of joint defense groups to the minor defendant is the ability to save costs by relying on the work and resources of the major defendants. But it is possible to rely too much.

First, neither you nor your client should rely on lawyers who are not up to the task. To avoid this, constantly evaluate the lawyers who, in their roles as counsel for the major defendants, are leading the group. In making this evaluation, don't jump to conclusions based merely on the name of the law firm or the identity of the lead lawyer. A firm's reputation may be obsolete. The first-listed partner may be past his prime or may be planning to delegate most work to someone far less qualified. In such cases, counsel for a minor defendant may need to be more active than if a first-rate lawyer were personally heading the major defendant's defense team. Conversely, don't blithely assume you have to take over leadership just because you don't know the major defendant's law firm or the lead lawyer. After all, the firm you haven't heard of may be populated exclusively by knowledgeable, experienced lawyers who are particularly well-suited to lead, and the junior partner or senior associate taking day-to-day responsibility may be a rising star. The key for you, as counsel to a minor defendant, is to make an independent evaluation of the major defendant's lawyers.

Don't relax just because the major defendant has retained first-rate, qualified lawyers who are obviously capable of leading effectively. You can't lie back and assume that the group is going to win the case for your client. Take Brian in Scenario 3. He thought he was doing a good job for Minor, keeping its litigation costs down by relying on the work being done by Massive's counsel. Brian assumed that Massive and its counsel would always be there, through the end of trial, representing the interests of the group. He was wrong. Even in a smoothly functioning, cohesive group, plan for the contingency that the workhorse defendants may drop out, leaving your client alone.

This is not to say that Brian should have matched High & Mighty lawyer for lawyer or abandoned his concern for controlling Minor's costs. Indeed, the skillful joint defense group lawyer relies on other members for as much as possible. You need to pick your spots. Here, Brian and the other lawyers at his firm might have spent more time helping review XYZ's documents. He could have become familiar with the databases maintained at High & Mighty. If he'd gone to the joint defense meetings, he might have suggested that the databases be maintained at a more accessible location than High & Mighty's office, such as the vendor's office or a document depository. Brian should have attended—or at least read—the key depositions and the key cases. In short, Brian should have been prepared to continue litigating, even if Massive settled. After all, in a litigation system in which more than 90 percent of all civil cases settle, the odds were that Massive would.

A Favorable Settlement

Lawyers representing minor defendants often make a related mistake: They forget that their clients may have defenses that are completely distinct from those available to the rest of the group. In representing a minor defendant, you must pursue a separate litigation and settlement strategy focusing on the issues and defenses unique to your client. Never assume that the group is going to think of everything. After all, no other defendant is going to examine Minor's documents, interview Minor's witnesses, or research legal issues unique to Minor. If Brian fails to do these things, he may overlook potentially dispositive defenses that neither High & Mighty nor any other defendant's counsel will advance because they did not know about them and had no incentive to search for them. If only Brian had done his job and spotted that defense sooner, he might have attended a few of the XYZ depositions to ask five minutes of questions that could have nailed the issue down and ensured early summary judgment. Or, he could have used that testimony as leverage to negotiate a favorable settlement with XYZ. Now, of course, it's too late; the discovery cutoff has passed. If Brian wants to ask those questions, he'll have to do so at trial.

The same goes for settlement. Be cognizant of your own client's interests at all times. If XYZ was willing and able to settle with its main antagonist, Massive, it is likely that it would have been able even sooner to settle with a small player like Minor. If Brian had been on top of the case, and better able to exploit the strengths of Minor's defenses to XYZ's claim, XYZ might have viewed settlement with Minor as worth exploring. Now, with Massive out of the case, it may be significantly easier for XYZ to prevail against Minor. Thus, another lesson: Look for opportunities to settle before the big players do, because the price may go up once the workhorses are gone.

While it may seem that advice to keep your client's interests in mind is too obvious to mention, far too many defense lawyers forget that they are counsel for a specific client, not for the joint defense group. In some ways, this is a natural reaction: The other lawyers in the group are knowledgeable and experienced, they're friendly, and (collectively at least) they appear to have great wisdom. The one thing they don't have is perspective—the perspective of your client. Your client, not the group, is paying your bills. Never forget that.

To protect the minor defendant's interests, participate actively in the group's efforts. First, attend some meetings to learn what strategies and tactics your co-defendants are planning, and to help direct the defense. If you can't be there, send someone from your office who's capable of contributing. And don't be afraid to speak up. Defense group meetings sometimes resemble stage performances: 20 lawyers may be in the room, but only five or six talk. The rest appear to be merely "monitoring" the meeting, taking copious notes that presumably are later turned into a "report" to the client. From time to time, they may mutter the seemingly magic phrase, "I'll need client approval before I can respond," but otherwise they contribute little.

Lawyers who repeatedly send notetakers to meetings miss a valuable opportunity to influence the defense. Well-run joint defense groups use their meetings to discuss strategy and make tactical choices. Should we move to dismiss or file answers? Should the defense take corporate designee depositions under Rule 30(b)(6) before the documents are produced or after? What third-party discovery should be served? What experts and consultants are needed? What issues should we target for summary judgment?

For a modest investment of time and effort, an experienced lawyer can make a significant contribution to the group's consideration and evaluation of these issues in a way that a mere notetaker cannot. He can make suggestions based on his deeper litigation experience, steer the group away from dumb ideas, and support useful contributions by other lawyers. But if the experienced lawyer stays home, the strategy decisions will be made by others, who may not be attuned to the minor defendant's interests. Lawyers and clients who save money by sending junior notetakers to meetings are often being penny-wise but pound-foolish.

A lawyer's influence is not usually affected by whether she represents a "big" player or a "small" player. Helpful and insightful comments are always appreciated, and frequently acted on. But beware: The loud, self-assured lawyer is often accorded more influence than he deserves. The notetakers sometimes mistake a smooth presentation for erudition. Perhaps if you had been there, you might have recognized immediately that Mr. Smooth's ideas were bad ones.

Attending the group's meetings is only the tip of the iceberg. Participate, at least in some fashion, in the group's other efforts: discovery, motions, trial preparation. The best tasks to volunteer for, of course, are those that best advance your client's particular interests. If the group is planning a series of summary judgment motions, and the statute of limitations is your pet issue, volunteer to write that brief. That way, you can be confident that the brief will adequately present your client's views. If you're interested in a particular witness, volunteer to take the lead at his deposition instead of asking a few mop-up questions.

Participate in the group's work even if it doesn't touch directly on your pet issues. When a draft brief that may affect your client is circulated, review it and provide input. A comment that improves a brief is a valuable contribution and one that benefits your client. It's also an extremely efficient way of enhancing the defense. Counsel for minor defendants are sometimes content to let counsel for other defendants litigate issues without their involvement. They reason that they can take advantage of a favorable ruling under principles of offensive collateral estoppel. On the other hand, if the other defendant loses, they think the ruling shouldn't bind their client because collateral estoppel cannot be used offensively against parties who didn't participate in the matter.

This line of reasoning is hazardous. First, it ignores human nature: Once the judge has made up her mind, it is not likely she will later be persuaded to adopt a contrary view.

Second, the very fact of your participation in a joint defense group may lead the court to conclude that your client should be bound by the results of the other defendant's litigation effort. *Central Illinois Public Service Co. v. Allianz Underwriters Ins. Co.*, 158 Ill.2d 218, 633 N.E.2d 675 (1994). In that case, the case management order required the 47 defendants to engage in collective activity, such as joint discovery and joint motions. The trial judge scheduled trial on a discrete subissue in the case. Several defendants, who saw their interests as conflicting with the interests of the single defendant who was directly involved in the discrete subissue, asked if they could also take part in the trial. The judge said they could not.

Eventually, the jury ruled in favor of the plaintiff on the discrete subissue. The plaintiff then argued that the defendants who were not permitted to participate in the trial were bound by the jury's verdict. The trial judge agreed, finding that the single defendant who appeared at trial was the "virtual representative" of the others. "I find that American Empire was, in effect, surrogate for the Joining Defendants, advancing legal theories and proofs on behalf of all defendants . . . . That is substantial participation in the presentation of the case. That is a full and fair opportunity to litigate fact issues in this case." *Id.* at 681.

Eventually, the trial judge was reversed by the Illinois Supreme Court. The Supreme Court suggested that it ordinarily would reject the request of defendants who did not participate in trial to "relitigate" the jury's verdict but held that it would not bind the nonparticipating defendants by the verdict, given the "special circumstance" that "the trial court barred [them] from participation in the trial process." *Id.* at 678. (A dissenting judge argued strenuously that the nonparticipating defendants should have been bound anyway, because they failed to point to any new or different evidence they would introduce at a second trial.)

The lesson is clear. Any lawyer who merely sits back and watches other members litigate must be prepared for the possibility of being held to an adverse ruling or verdict. Whether you represent a major or minor defendant, get involved.

Defending the Multiparty Civil Conspiracy Case

W. Donald McSweeney and Michael L. Brody

Why conspiracy co-defendants should work together is simple: Most of the time, they are more likely to mount an effective defense together than alone or working at cross-purposes. There are exceptions. Occasionally a conspiracy defendant may end-run a coordinated defense and succeed where others have failed, but that is rare. Usually all defendants will stand or fall together. At least three considerations common to most conspiracy suits favor cooperation.

First, if knowledge is power in litigation, then shared knowledge is power multiplied. Even a moderately complex civil conspiracy case involves an extensive cast of characters interacting for a long time in a variety of transactions. The result is at least a small mountain of correspondence, memorandums, computer runs, and invoices. By cooperating, conspiracy co-defendants get to look at more documents sooner and to look with one another as friendly guides.

Second, co-defendants can often make better use of nonparty witnesses, who may be friendly with some of them but hostile or indifferent to others.

Third, they may benefit from their collective memory and their broader view of the litigation.

Consider this case.

A discount electronics store sells a manufacturer's goods at 15 percent below the price charged by his competitors. The competitors complain to the manufacturer. So do retail customers, who dislike the discounter's high-pressure sales tactics and his incompetent and uncooperative service department. Ultimately, the manufacturer termi-

---

W. Donald McSweeney and Michael L. Brody are partners at Schiff Hardin & Waite in Chicago.

nates the discounter's dealership. The discounter sues the manufacturer and competing dealers, alleging that they have entered into a resale price maintenance agreement in violation of the Sherman Act.

How can these defendants help one another?

Working together, they can, in a short time, assemble a more complete record of pricing, sales, and promotions for all electronics brands in the plaintiff's market than any one of them could alone. Their joint recollection is likely to generate a more comprehensive account of the relevant sales meetings and promotional events than any single defendant could construct.

They can learn more from nonparty witnesses than any defendant could learn alone. For instance, another electronics manufacturer with useful information about the market will be hesitant to talk with the defendant-manufacturer but happy to cooperate with a defendant-dealer who carries his brand. Similarly, a defendant-dealer's former sales manager is more likely to talk with the company he left on good terms than with the manufacturer with whose line he now competes.

More important, though, the events leading up to the dealer's termination may look very different to the defendant-manufacturer than to the defendant-dealers. The manufacturer will see a conflict between the discounter's way of doing business and the manufacturer's nationwide strategy of seeking a premium price by maintaining the product line's high reputation for quality and courteous service. The local dealer will focus on the difficulties of maintaining a highly skilled sales force and service department despite the pressure the discounter has put on his profit margin. Putting these perspectives together makes a stronger defense than is possible from either perspective alone, because it provides a broader range of evidence that more persuasively explains why each defendant did what he did.

Now consider a second case.

A pension trustee is accused of masterminding a fraudulent scheme to siphon off pension-fund assets for his own benefit. The trustee is charged with investing in a series of shell corporations that transfer funds back to the trustee's own business. When a local newspaper exposes the scheme, the beneficiaries of the pension bring a class action against the trustee, his company, his co-trustees, and the plan's independent accountants, alleging violations of the RICO Act.

This kind of case is usually brought as a class action or as an individual case by an unsophisticated plaintiff. Either way, the moving force is likely to be a lawyer. The plaintiff typically begins with the facts in the newspaper article that sparked the suit and then uses his own money to finance further investigation. Inevitably, the plaintiff relies partly on inference and conjecture to hold his case together. As discovery proceeds, he plays catch-up. He never assembles the comprehensive record that a coordinated defense team has from the start; yet he must examine the defense witnesses who have been prepared for their depositions on the basis of a comprehensive record and a unified theory of the case.

When the case comes to trial, a coordinated defense can offer the jury a theory that accounts for the complex relations between the various groups and subgroups of defendants: trustees, accountants, and the various corporations that are allegedly part of the scheme. The defendants may have a host of concerns that innocently explain their cooperation. But to prove the conspiracy, the plaintiff must argue that the diverse conduct, actors, and motives are part of a unified scheme with a single goal to loot the pension plan. The richer the description of events that cooperating co-defendants offer the jury, the starker the contrast to the plaintiff's one-dimensional interpretation of the facts.

The most important benefit of this cooperation is a unified defense. This is important in every complex commercial case. The case is tried to an unsophisticated jury that may be bored and even confused. That jury will form its own understanding of what happened. It is dangerous for defendants to present a hodgepodge of fragmentary theories based on each defendant's parochial view of the events. Absent cooperation, the defendants speak with a babble of voices that gives a jury no alternative but to accept the only version of the case that makes sense to them—the plaintiffs'.

Sometimes the plaintiffs are in disharmony. This can happen, for example, when several opt-out cases follow a class-action suit. Then the defendants can turn the tables on the plaintiffs by picking apart the plaintiffs' uncoordinated description of events. But once again, the defendants need to stick together to take advantage of the plaintiffs' disunity.

Finally, cooperation among co-defendants forces the plaintiff to prove his case. Assuming equally solvent defendants, the plaintiff usually does not care who is caught in the conspiracy net, so long as somebody is. The plaintiff's fondest hope is that he will face an uncoordinated defense, with defendants blaming one another for an undisputed wrong. With the defendants proving the plaintiff's case, the issue no longer is whether someone will pay, but who and how much.

Given these advantages, cooperation among co-defendants would seem inevitable. In fact, it is not. Achieving a unified defense creates challenges throughout litigation.

Sometimes the crush of events will force civil defendants to establish a working relationship quickly. A classic example is a civil case following the compressed proceedings in injunction hearings or criminal trials (or not at all).

When there is no emergency, defendants have a chance to find formal ways to ensure their cooperation. A good way to begin is to negotiate a sharing agreement.

A sharing agreement is any arrangement among co-defendants allocating their responsibilities. Ideally, the agreement should be a formal written document, and ideally it should divide up all the principal responsibilities.

The most important purpose of the sharing agreement is to determine responsibility for an adverse judgment, including the responsibility of defendants who settle. If the defendants can agree on this at the outset, they have resolved the issue that is most likely to threaten their ability to work together. Cooperation does not come easily. It is particularly difficult when some defendants are more likely to be found liable than others.

The defendant who is peripheral to the conspiracy and whose risk of liability is comparatively small may be tempted to turn on the other defendants and go it alone. Take the pension case, for example. Suppose the outside auditor of the plan is named as a defendant for having failed to uncover an ongoing fraud allegedly masterminded by one of the trustees.

The auditor may want to defend himself by asserting that the fraud was so thorough that nothing could have uncovered it including the rigorous examination he says he conducted. The risk to this argument is that the jury may not believe the auditor did not know what was happening. By confirming there was a fraud, the auditor has created a problem he did not contemplate. Once the auditor defects, nothing will stop the other defendants from attacking the turncoat and arguing that the auditor knew everything there was to know. If the auditor failed to make the appropriate disclosures, he is just as much to blame as anyone else. But despite these risks, the centrifugal force pulling the peripheral defendant away from cooperation may be strong.

For the defendant at the center of the alleged conspiracy, the incentive to abandon the coordinated defense comes from a different quarter. In any multidefendant case, the plaintiff will try to settle with one defendant at a comparatively low figure. The point is to cause panic among the remaining defendants for fear they will be held responsible for more than their fair share of the liability. The defendant whose risk of liability is high—like the mastermind in the pension case—is tempted to get out cheaply. But there are risks here, too.

For one thing, the plaintiff and the defendant may disagree about what is a cheap settlement. Because negotiations have a way of leaking out, the injury to continued cooperation among the defendants can be substantial, as is the incentive for other defendants to leave the failed settler out on a limb by making deals of their own. Further, if contribution or indemnity actions are available—antitrust is a notable instance where they are not—a cheap settlement may ultimately be undone by a later suit holding the settling defendant liable to its "co-conspirators." Although such a settlement just postpones the inevitable, when the exposure is high, the temptation to settle and get out is strong.

Deciding to allocate responsibility for an adverse judgment is not easy. Indeed, if one or more defendants decides from the outset that long-term cooperation is not in its best interest, agreement will be impossible.

Still, if the defendants share a genuine initial commitment to cooperation, some circumstances may ease such an arrangement. In particular, if contribution will be available down the road, failure to enter a sharing agreement may merely postpone a future battle over degree of responsibility. Moreover, since an early agreement strengthens the defense alliance, it also minimizes the defendants' view of their potential joint liability. They will find it easier to allocate this sum if they think about the larger amount that would come from an adverse verdict following an uncoordinated defense. The odds of reaching agreement will also increase if the risk of exposure is similar for all the defendants or if there is an objective way to measure their risk (as in an antitrust price-fixing case, where exposure is based on market share or dollar volume of sales).

Even if the defendants cannot agree on how to share liability, a formal agreement can still be valuable. The defendants may be able to allocate responsibility for many common expenses. The sharing agreement should specify the principal expenses covered, such as fees for jointly retained experts, rent for a central office, and the expenses of joint data processing.

The sticking point is apt to be how to figure each defendant's share. Large defendants will favor a per capita rule. Small defendants will want a rule weighted toward size. Everyone will take offense at a rule based on relative fault. Once again, the most promising approach is a neutral standard based on an objective determination of the parties' relative exposure such as market share.

Once the sharing agreement is negotiated, the second step is creating a coordinating committee. This committee defines joint defense tasks and policies, assigns responsibilities, and coordinates and oversees joint defense activities. Typically, the committee members represent the defendants with the greatest exposure, since they are most willing to commit the necessary resources. If the court has not already appointed a liaison for the defendants, the committee should do so. This lawyer can distribute communications from the court and circulate the defendants' shared work product. The coordinating committee should also establish any other committees needed to deal with common problems.

A typical example is a joint experts committee. Whereas each defendant could present its own expert testimony—and many will have special needs for expert help—the expert testimony on joint issues should be provided by jointly retained and prepared witnesses. Otherwise the defendants risk providing the jury with conflicting testimony. Besides, too many experts may overwhelm the jury with an avalanche of mind-numbing discussions of downward-sloping demand curves and chi-square tests, leading the jurors to fall asleep or even suspect they are being bamboozled.

Finally, defendants should think about establishing a central office. It will help to have it located near the courthouse. Before trial, this office provides a central document and deposition depository, a centralized computer, an office for specially retained joint staff, and a work space for out-of-town counsel.

Once this central office and the committees are in place, the key to using them effectively is to have regular, well-organized meetings. The defendants will need to identify and assign responsibility for researching legal issues, drafting motions, interviewing witnesses, and handling depositions. The coordinating committee must decide how to handle depositions of hostile witnesses without foreclosing anybody from asking questions. Computerizing the discovery record should be a joint project. As individual defendants settle out, their tasks will need to be reallocated. Finally, the results of all of this work need to be shared, reviewed, and criticized.

One typical result of these meetings is that each defendant becomes responsible for its own employees as witnesses. If former employees have left on good terms, the defendant employer is responsible for them as well. If there is hostility, other defendants will need to step in. Developing other third-party witnesses will depend on the abilities or circumstances of each defendant and its lawyers. Thus, the lawyers should recognize and use a client's special relationship with a third party or a lawyer's unusual sophistication in a particular area.

While the desire to create a united front is central in these efforts, inevitably one or more defendants cannot agree about something. The goal is unity, but not at the price of strait-jacketing the nonconforming defendant. Small disputes can mushroom into charges of bad faith and recalcitrance, harming cooperation. Regular and candid communication is the only antidote.

In planning for trial, the principal tasks are allocating responsibilities for primary direct and cross-examination and sequencing the presentation of testimony and the order in which the co-defendants participate.

Responsibility for the witnesses will largely parallel the assignments made during discovery, with adjustments made to accommodate last-minute settlements. A joint strategy should cover which witnesses to display prominently, which ones to sandwich in, and which to omit. These decisions, and decisions about the order of witnesses, must be based on agreement about how to present the most comprehensible and persuasive narrative of events and how to explain the overarching policy and economic issues.

The defendants must also decide when each lawyer will participate. Should opening and closing statements be sequenced to reflect counsels' rhetorical skills or the significance of their clients? Should the lawyer who opens first and closes last also be prominent during cross-examination of the plaintiff's principal expert? Instead, should a lawyer with greater analytic skills be featured? Who should argue motions that concern all defendants, such as the unavoidable dispute about the admissibility of co-conspirators' admissions? The answers depend on the lawyers' strengths and weaknesses. The subject is touchy, and the coordinating committee must take care to avoid a clash of egos.

During trial, as during discovery, the key to cooperation is communication. Lawyers should use the central office to eat lunch together, so that they can discuss problems that came up during the morning session, finish plans for the afternoon, and assign tasks to be performed out of court. The group should meet at the end of the trial day, too. Besides being a site for these joint meetings, the central office should be the work space for trial counsel and their staffs, where everyone has access to the computer and document depository and to one another.

A unified defense is not a guarantee of success, but failing to unify comes close to ensuring failure. Given the odds, the effort is worth it.

Thinking About Class Actions

Christopher T. Lutz

Class actions have a peculiar fascination for lawyers. They may be the most confused, abused, overpraised, and overanalyzed aspect of procedure. But—despite all the scrutiny—class actions are never boring. They evoke strong reactions. This is partly because the existence of a class increases the stakes; it multiplies the risks and rewards. However, the lure of class actions is also that they seem so different; they go beyond the parties immediately in court, affecting the rights of hundreds or thousands. The effect is almost magical.

Unfortunately, the special quality of class litigation too often produces only emotion and reaction, but not much thought. Some in the plaintiffs' bar seem to add class allegations to every complaint they file, while some defense counsel would not sit in the same room with a copy of Rule 23. Neither response is sensible.

The first thing to consider is whether you really want a class action at all. If you represent a plaintiff, should you file a class complaint? If you are defense counsel answering a class complaint or motion, should you adamantly oppose any class whatsoever? If you think either answer is simple, you probably have not thought enough.

For plaintiffs' counsel, careful thought is an absolute necessity. Blithely filing a class complaint can be a bad mistake. You may find you do not know what to do or do not have the resources to do it. You may find yourself with the wrong plaintiffs. You may not have enough time, or your interest may wane. In short, if you do not think before you begin, you may find yourself overwhelmed by the endeavor, wanting to return to the simple world of individual plaintiffs. *But*—and this is a

---

Christopher T. Lutz, a former editor-in-chief of LITIGATION, *is a partner with Steptoe & Johnson L.L.P. in Washington, D.C. This chapter was updated in mid-1997 during the pendency of the discussions about substantial proposed revisions to Federal Rule 23, and does not reflect the outcome of those discussions.*

critical point—once you begin a class action, you cannot just switch it off. Even voluntary abandonment of class allegations may require court approval. Once you have filed a class suit, you may well have to live with it. Think first.

The most obvious question for prospective class counsel is whether the suit has real substantive potential as a class action. Groups of people rarely form a class and then find a lawyer. Rather, lawyers deal with individuals who have their own personal problems in mind and not those of a whole group.

How do you decide whether you should move from representing the client sitting in your office to a whole class? Think about his complaint. Can it be generalized? Is your client complaining about a problem that concerns him or her alone or about actions that affected many others in about the same way? Is she complaining about a slur from a particular supervisor or instead an employment test that she—and many others—failed? If you cannot generalize, if your client is not talking about a course of conduct that affected many others in about the same way, hesitate to suggest a class action.

If you have a client whose problem seems to be one that many might have, you next need to determine if you have the right plaintiff. Class representatives have a fiduciary duty to class members: fellow employees, security holders, or businesspeople. Especially during the certification battle, they will be subject to uncomfortable scrutiny. Your opponent will depose them, possibly more than once, and may try to depict them as unaware, unprincipled, poor, or otherwise defective. Class plaintiffs will be asked what they know about the law and the facts and whether they will pay "thousands of dollars" in court costs if the class loses. In light of this, class representatives need to have commitment and fortitude. Pursuing a class suit will undoubtedly delay resolution of their own individual claims; a person whose claims could have been tried to judgment in one year may have to wait five times that long if he represents a class. Explain these things to your client.

The facts behind your plaintiff's claim are as important as his personal qualities. Even though a brokerage house may have consciously misrepresented a stock, a plaintiff who purchased on the brokers' oral advice will have difficulty securing a class, while one who relied on a written representation is more likely to succeed. In an employment discrimination case, a plaintiff who assails generally applied educational requirements for promotion but who has a history of discipline and absence problems may have a hard time qualifying as a class representative. Be sure there is nothing so unique, peculiar, or personal in your client's claims that it overwhelms the general. In addition, it always helps if your client's personal story is one that will engage the court's sympathy. Since the judge may hear in person only from a few class members, how he reacts to their concerns will certainly affect his attitude toward the class.

If you want to be class counsel, the third thing you should think about is yourself. Can you prosecute a class action? Obviously, you should know Rule 23 and the substantive law you will sue under; a judge considering certification will require that as a minimum.

But there is more.

Have you ever participated in a class suit? Do you know how to manage one? Do you want to be a fiduciary for hundreds or thousands of class members? Are you ready for their phone calls at home? Where will you get the support staff to deal with discovery, with notice and the like? Think about how big the case will be: If you seek a nationwide class, can you manage nationwide discovery?

Think about your practice: Successful class-action lawyers can make lots of money in court-awarded fees, but they are rarely paid on a monthly basis. Will your banker support you? Can you pay the expenses you will incur? If the class does not win or settle, and you get nothing, can other cases in the office maintain you? You have to think about what the case might require and what you can handle before you start.

All this may seem like an ordeal of self-examination from which no class suit will ever emerge. That is not so. If you have the right plaintiff with the right claims, if you know what will be required, and if you can handle and want a class suit, forge ahead. But think first.

After being served with a thick class complaint, the defense lawyer's analysis need not be as involved as that of prospective class counsel. But it must be done. Unfortunately, many defense lawyers scarcely think at all. They—and their clients—simply react. Many defense counsel approach a proposed class much like they would a proposed case of smallpox.

That kind of reaction can be counterproductive. It is true that even thoughtful defense counsel end up opposing most class allegations. But opposition should not be automatic. Occasionally, a class may offer long-term protection instead of risk. Are your defenses strong? Is the putative class counsel less than skillful? Do you think you have a good chance of winning? Are there likely to be other, more formidable attempts at a class suit in less attractive forums if this one is not certified? Could your client be nibbled to death by a series of individual suits? If these things might happen, you and your client should consider accepting a class.

Why?

Because, if there is a class and if you win, the whole class loses. Everyone will be barred from litigating about the supposed securities fraud, price fixing, or unconstitutionality that produced the suit. The case will be over.

The advantages for the defendant are not always so great. Normally, there will be little reason to fear future individual suits. Few individuals have the resources to start another class, or even individual, action.

Besides, the sheer cost of defending a class suit may exceed the cost of repeated individual defenses. In addition a class judgment may not provide protection against such subsequent litigation.

In employment discrimination cases, the Supreme Court's decision in *Cooper v. Federal Reserve Bank of Richmond*, 467 U.S. 867 (1984), seems to eliminate most class judgment protection against individual suits. And, of course, if you accept a class, you might lose on the merits. Accepting a class as alleged is a high-stakes gamble. The combative, conservative nature of most lawyers leads them to take up the fight and avoid the gamble. That is very often the right decision, but be sure you reach it for the right reasons.

Defense counsel should also ask themselves a second question: Is no class at all the only alternative to the class alleged? This is a more difficult and more important inquiry. In some cases, a fair-minded look at the facts and Rule 23 will strongly suggest that a class is going to be certified. Often it also will indicate that the class the plaintiffs want is insupportably broad. This happens most often in employment discrimination actions; a plaintiff whose claim could justify a class within a single department or facility seeks to represent all of the defendant's comparable employees, nationwide. In cases like this, you face a tough question: Should you deny the propriety of any class or suggest a smaller class than the one the plaintiffs want?

The answer depends as much on litigation style as on logic. Some lawyers believe in taking extreme positions to get intermediate results and that any concession signals weakness. Others take aggressive but reasonable positions, because they believe that doing otherwise risks losing the court's goodwill and attention.

Whatever your basic approach, suggesting a reduced class can be good strategy for a number of reasons. It may simply be right. It often has the advantage of novelty. Judges who daily read one virulent class opposition after another may be shocked to greater attention by a less extreme approach. In addition, carving a class down to a more appropriate size may also mean you have carved unfavorable facts out of the case.

After thinking about whether to have a class, a plaintiff's lawyer next needs to determine *where* the class should be. It is not so much a question of detailed venue rules—which have to be considered—but rather the more basic question of whether to file in federal court or state court.

To most lawyers, this may seem pointless inquiry. Class actions are almost always federal actions based on federal laws. A few states do not even have class-action rules, and others have restrictive rules. Federal discovery is not as geographically confined as state discovery.

Federal judges may be somewhat more comfortable and familiar with class practice than state judges. And if you file in federal court, you can be sure a federal court can extend jurisdiction over class members in other states. That question is unsettled for state class actions.

But, once again, thought should precede reflex. If you think you can file a diversity-based class action in federal court, think again: To satisfy the jurisdiction requirements, *every* class member must have a $10,000 claim; that is rare. Besides, some state court judges—those in California, for example—are quite familiar with class actions. And some states, such as Pennsylvania, have liberal class-action rules. Most important, a variety of important class-based causes of action—such as suits by the beneficiaries of a trust or victims of nuisance—are almost entirely matters of state law. Therefore, before you rush into United States District Court, be certain state court is not a better destination.

The final major topic for careful thought is how you convince the judge you are right. Certainly, you always need to think about the best way to make your points. In class-action battles, this preliminary thought is doubly important. Class-action motions and oppositions have a deadening sameness. Usually too long and too shrill, they often merely consist of fracturing Rule 23 into its subparts, quoting them, asserting they are or are not met, and attaching a string of citations. To avoid such problems, consider a few points, which apply equally to plaintiffs and defendants.

First, some ground rules. Some courts have time limits for filing class motions ranging from 30 to 90 days. The court may deny certifying a class simply because you missed the time limit. And even if the court is lenient, you will always erode your claim to be an "adequate" class lawyer. Even absent such time limits, Rule 23 requires that class questions be decided "as soon as practicable." This admonition should lead both sides to focus discovery mostly (if not exclusively) on class matters. Depose class representatives early on—both sides should prepare for that.

Finally, especially if you are plaintiffs' counsel, even at an early stage, remember the overall case record. Even if you have a class certified and you win at trial, you might still have the whole thing torn apart on appeal because the record is barren of class findings and evidence. Most circuits encourage a class hearing, and you should seriously consider proposing one. If there is not a class hearing, be sure affidavits, discovery excerpts, and the like are introduced with the class papers. This can be time-consuming but is a valuable insurance policy.

Having considered such preliminary matters, plaintiffs' and defense counsel can think about the themes they want to emphasize in seeking or opposing a class. I begin with a heretical observation: Do *not* be guided very much by the text of Rule 23 or comparable state rules. The rules themselves provide little guidance. Class-action arguments relying only on what the rules say can get bogged down in extended, academic, semantic debates:

- Rule 23(a) requires the claims of named plaintiffs to be "typical" of those of class members, but how are "typical" and "atypical" claims distinguished?
- In (b)(3) actions, common claims must "predominate." Is that judgment made by counting claims or weighing them, or by some other process?

Of course, volumes of case commentary try to answer these questions, and you will have to discuss and meet the rule's requirements. Nonetheless, large parts of the class-action rules are, by themselves, not prescriptive. They grow out of but do not illuminate a variety of practical concerns. They are built on but do not explain years of equity practice and experience under joinder and intervention rules. Because their operative language is slippery—"adequate," "typical," "common," "superior," "predominate"—they normally do not provide a basis for compelling argument.

A more effective approach is to talk about concerns and policies underlying Rule 23. Rather than simply asserting that common claims do not predominate, explain what the lack of predominance will lead to in your case and facts. Instead of merely saying the class representative is inadequate, show how his inadequacy will affect prosecution of the case. By tying facts to policies, you should be able to avoid the semantic hairsplitting that plagues many class-action papers.

What are the concerns underlying Rule 23? Judges considering whether to certify a class seem mainly concerned with four questions: First, does a "class" *really* exist here? Second, will class litigation in this case lead to the efficiencies Rule 23 is meant to achieve? Third, is it fair to bind class members by the actions of the lawyers and named plaintiffs? Fourth, if certified, is this case likely to spin off into an unmanageable snarl? Each of these concerns finds expression in Rule 23's various subparts, but relying solely on the text of the rule will not allow you to explain them in your case.

The first question—does a class really exist?—may seem silly. After all, defining the characteristics of a class is what Rule 23 is meant to do. The existence of common questions, typical claims, and the like are what Rule 23 and classes are all about. Nonetheless, I have more than once seen a judge after he has listened to an hour of rarified discourse on Rule 23(a) and (b) lean over the bench and ask, "But does a class *really* exist?"

There is more at work here than the technical fine points of Rule 23. Most judges want to have a deeper sense, based on evidence, that there exists a definable group of people, tied together by common concerns, experiences, or claims. The court usually wants to know whether the class is a unified group. So, if you want a class, try to show that you represent people who have suffered the same harm and experienced the same facts and who share important unifying characteristics. Try to show that the group is sharply defined: You can tell who is in and who is not; you can determine roughly how many class members there are.

Defense counsel, on the other hand, will want to try to convince the court that the class is not defined at all, that it is possibly limitless and has no sharp boundaries (for example, "all Americans affected by air pollution"). Defense lawyers should also try to show that the plaintiffs' class definition ties people into a class by accident or sleight of hand. No one would expect an antitrust class to be certified consisting of those who purchased from two separate companies. Marketing policies of a single corporation in various regions may make it equally inappropriate to include all the company's purchasers in the same group. The goal is to point to differences in the class that will *make* a difference; distinctions that will make litigation about the named plaintiffs' claims inapplicable to the class as a whole. All of these points should surely be clothed in the trappings of Rule 23, because the rule requires it and has meaning. But never forget the court's basic concern: Is there *really* a class?

The second concern—efficiency—is more straightforward. One of the aims of Rule 23 is to provide a means for resolving, once and for all, factual and legal questions affecting many people. This prevents similarly situated people from experiencing different results in court. Properly applied, it also means that only one court needs to decide the common questions.

The rule's—and court's—concerns for efficiency mean you will help yourself to become class counsel if you can convince the judge that certifying a class and trying its claims will prevent him and other judges from hearing the same kinds of claims, case after case. The "commonality" and "typicality" sections of Rule 23 touch on this issue. You should talk about them. But it is even better if you can show concretely that there are many suits or administrative complaints pending that could be resolved in one class suit. If you are suing about a well-publicized occurrence likely to spawn lawsuits—a spectacular corporate failure, an antitrust violation prosecuted by the government, or (possibly) a widely known disaster—say so.

Defense counsel, on the other hand, want to demonstrate that no real efficiencies would come from a class suit. You should show—relying (if appropriate) on the rule's predominance standard—that the questions common to the class are not central to the problems of the individual class members. Later suits would be required to decide significant, individual questions. A related approach is to demonstrate that the facts affecting class members vary so much that follow-up suits would be needed to determine how the results of a class action should apply to the individual class members. Finally, if you decide to argue that a class suit will be an ungovernable mess, argue that the protraction and complexity of class litigation will be far more costly and time-consuming than all the individual suits.

There is one "antiefficiency" argument defense counsel should *not* make. It may be tempting to say that the courts will not be burdened by individual litigation because the cost of litigation exceeds what is at stake on an individual basis. This might be the case in an antitrust suit challenging relatively modest overcharges or an action attacking imposition of a few percentage points of excess interest. But such an argument would be a mistake. There is a very respectable view that class actions are designed in part to make the righting of such wrongs feasible. Arguing that economics make an inefficient proliferation of individual cases unlikely may very well convince a judge that a class suit is the only efficient way to right the wrongs alleged.

The third point of argument about certification—fairness to class members—is probably the most important. I have never encountered a judge who was not acutely concerned about the proper treatment of class members. This concern exceeds any solicitude for named plaintiffs, defendants, and lawyers. Most courts want to be sure that, by certifying a class, they will not be doing a disservice to hundreds or thousands who will not be present in court to protect their rights.

If you have filed a class motion, your job as to fairness is clear. Relying on the rule's "adequacy" standard, show the judge you know what you are doing. Prove you are a capable lawyer, well-versed in the substantive law and familiar with class actions. Show that your individual clients are committed and aware of the burdens they might face. Here is where thinking before filing will pay off: If you have the right plaintiff, you should have an adequate class representative. If you have thought about the burdens you may face as class counsel, you should be able to satisfy the court during a class certification hearing.

Defense counsel should think doubly hard before arguing that class members may be inadequately represented. Professional attacks on opposing counsel and personal attacks on their clients can backfire. In extreme cases, however, such tactics may be proper. If your opponent has been suspended from practice or has frequently mishandled class suits, you can plausibly argue he is a dubious fiduciary for the class. The same is true if the proposed named plaintiff in a securities suit has been convicted of stock fraud.

A defense argument about inadequate representation need not always involve personal attacks, however. In some ways, Rule 23's "typicality" requirement guarantees fairness. It embodies the principle that a true class representative will litigate in a way that matches the concerns of the class as a whole. For example, in a discrimination suit, a class of rejected applicants with claims about testing or educational requirements might not have their interests well represented by a person who was rejected in part because he got into a fight with a hiring officer. A class suit directed by such a person might tend to focus more on his personal vendetta than on the interests of the class. So if you perceive an odd or unusual plaintiff—perhaps one who says he is interested only in money and not injunctive relief—or you see that his claims arise out of unusual facts, consider a fairness argument.

The last concern of Rule 23 is manageability. While manageability is explicitly a requirement only in classes certified under Rule 23(b)(3), it is a real concern for many courts in *any* class suit. The reason is simple. No judge wants a class albatross that will live on his docket for many years. So, if you are prospective class counsel, show the court that class issues can be proved relatively simply, without scores of individual anecdotes. Demonstrate that you know how to use mailing firms, statistical sampling, and other techniques that simplify case management and proof. In general, show that you will be in control of your part of the case.

The agenda for defense lawyers is obvious. Discovery will take years; there will be thousands of motions and scores of intervenors. The trial—if it ever comes—will never end. If all this is likely and can be shown crisply, do it.

But beware the perils of sameness. Judges hear bone-chilling manageability arguments from defense lawyers almost every week. If you write the usual ten-page "parade of horribles" on manageability, the court will very quickly resort to reading only the topic sentences of your paragraphs, if that much. Be short, specific, and concrete. If your opponent flubbed a past suit into a protracted mess, say so. If discovery suggests that 500 witnesses will be called, say so. Whatever you say on manageability, remember that the judge has heard most of it before. Novelty is critical. Remember also that saying a case is unmanageable comes close to saying your judge will not have the skill to manage it. Be careful.

That ends my list of things to think about, but some qualifications are in order. Rule 23 does, of course, matter. It is a highly structured, complicated set of requirements. Understand it. You need to satisfy the rule or show it cannot be met. Because Rule 23 treats specific kinds of class suits differently, not all of my observations apply with equal force in all cases. The important point is this: The rule's surface complexity hides years of common law and statutory history, volumes of case commentary, and many important practical considerations. To deal with class suits successfully, you need to understand the themes that run through that background, using them in an effective, specific way.

Most of all, you need to *think*.

Checkmate: Takeover Litigation Strategy

Jonathan J. Lerner

In the frenetic world of high-stakes corporate takeovers, litigation is the legal equivalent of a championship chess tournament played at ultrasonic speed for megabuck prizes. Masters of strategy confront each other (often flanked by cadres of kibitzers), while knights of all shades—white, black, and grey—maneuver to checkmate the target and capture its crown jewels. As the rapidly unfolding events are featured daily in the financial press, trial counsel for the target of the hostile takeover and for the acquiring company (sometimes pejoratively called the "raider") must coordinate and manage a host of simultaneous proceedings. These often involve federal and state actions as well as administrative proceedings. Virtually all include demands for emergency injunctive relief.

As a general rule, the acquiring company has the white pieces and moves first. Until that opening move, all information concerning the prospective takeover strategy is secret. The bidder must be cautious, because any breach in the confidentiality concerning a planned takeover, such as premature disclosure of the identity of the target company, could result in misuse of inside information to trade in the target's stock.

Once the acquirer picks its target, it may choose a conventional opening and announce a "formal" tender offer. Or it may select a different gambit, such as obtaining enough stock through open-market purchases and block trades to gain control of the target.

Which opening move the acquirer plays depends on a number of factors, including its budget. Unless a formal tender offer is commenced for all the target's stock at a preemptively high price, the target's reaction is likely to be hostile. Usually the acquirer must assume that litigation will be one of the target's defenses.

Jonathan J. Lerner is a member of Skadden, Arps, Slate, Meagher & Flom L.L.P. in New York City.

As in any chess game, the target's litigation moves will be governed by the kind of acquisition threat it faces. One common takeover strategy is to acquire a large stock position in the target (sometimes exceeding 20 percent of the target's voting stock) in open-market and privately negotiated purchases. By this method, sometimes called a "creeping tender offer," an acquirer may accumulate enough shares to block (or at least deter) other companies from competing for control, gain representation on the target's board of directors, or even get control over the entire board in a proxy fight.

Confronted with this threat, targets often resort to the courts. Most often, the case is brought in federal court and attacks the adequacy of the acquirer's disclosure of information that is required by § 13(d) of the Securities Exchange Act of 1934, as well as the legality of the open-market and block purchases. Section 13(d) requires any person who acquires 5 percent of any class of shares of an issuer to file a Schedule 13D within ten days after reaching that level of ownership. The information required includes the number of shares owned by the acquirer and anyone acting in concert with him, the purpose of purchases, and the identity of persons who "control" the acquirer.

Despite these disclosure requirements, it is possible that an acquirer intent on controlling a target may try to obscure its purpose, especially if it wants to buy additional shares of the target's stock without paying the increased price that might come from word of a possible takeover. The result is that compliance with the disclosure obligations of § 13(d) has been a popular subject of litigation. But even though hundreds of actions have been filed under § 13(d), the results have been mixed. Only a handful of targets have gotten any injunctive relief beyond correcting the acquirer's Schedule 13D disclosure.

To be sure, litigation under § 13(d) can be a formidable weapon with a severe bite, as demonstrated by the action brought by General Steel Industries against Walco National Corporation and its founder, former Congressman Frederick W. Richmond. General Steel not only succeeded in obtaining an order requiring Walco to *rescind* the sale of all shares acquired after its Schedule 13D was filed, but also got an injunction halting Walco's tender offer for additional General Steel stock until divestiture of the unlawfully acquired shares.

Walco's attempt to control General Steel began on a promising note when Walco acquired a 25-percent block of General Steel shares. With an additional 4 percent that Walco had already surreptitiously purchased, Walco now owned nearly 30 percent of General Steel's outstanding stock.

Walco's Schedule 13D stated that this substantial position was "purchased for investment." Walco, however, kept buying General Steel stock and acquired an additional 4 percent. Walco filed several amendments to its Schedule 13D; each stated that the purchases were made purely for "investment" and disclaimed any present intention to acquire control. On November 2, 1981, Walco abruptly commenced a formal tender offer to acquire an additional 17 percent of General Steel's stock. If successful, Walco would own more than 50 percent of General Steel's stock and control the company.

General Steel filed suit in the Eastern District of Missouri, where its headquarters were located, claiming that Walco's Schedule 13D and amendments were false and misleading. Chief Judge Kenneth Wangelin ordered expedited discovery to begin on November 11, 1981. Under the provisions of the Williams Act, which regulates tender offers, the right of General Steel shareholders to withdraw any shares they had tendered to Walco in its tender offer expired on November 24. Unless an injunction was obtained by that time, Walco could have bought enough shares to control General Steel. A hearing on General Steel's preliminary injunction application was scheduled for November 23, only hours before the deadline. Thus, even under the expedited schedule, General Steel had less than two weeks to prove its case.

Walco's strategy was to delay discovery so as to capitalize on the limited time available to General Steel. Consequently, Walco moved to adjourn discovery until November 16, which would have left General Steel only one week to review documents, conduct depositions, and prepare its moving papers. Walco's plan backfired when the court not only granted its requested adjournment but also extended the withdrawal date of Walco's tender offer for five business days. Before General Steel's lawyers could breathe a sigh of relief at this short reprieve, the Court of Appeals for the Eighth Circuit vacated the portion of the order extending the withdrawal date because no hearing had been held.

One week before the withdrawal deadline, discovery finally started. Smoking guns are rare, but Walco's document production literally radiated heat. On the same day that Walco had stated in an amendment to its Schedule 13D that its purchases were for "investment" and that it had no intention of seeking control, Walco's controlling shareholder and former chairman (then Congressman) Richmond, had written a memorandum to the company's chief executive officer unequivocally admitting that "our aim is to own 51 percent of the company." *General Steel Indus., Inc. v. Walco Nat'l Corp.*, [1981–82 Transfer Binder] Fed. Sec. L. Rep. (CCH) ¶ 98,402 at 92,413 (E.D. Mo. 1981).

On November 23, the court determined that Walco had willfully violated § 13(d). The court issued an order requiring Walco to rescind its unlawful purchases and also enjoined it from further purchases of General Steel stock pending rescission "to deter future violations of law and to prohibit Walco from taking advantage of a position it has illegally obtained." *Id.* at 92,418.

When the threat is a tender offer and when the target's directors decide to resist a takeover, the target often turns to § 14(e) of the 1934 act. The challenge is to the disclosures made in the bidder's offer to purchase. This broad antifraud provision applies to all tender offers, whether or not the target's shares are publicly traded. Section 14(e) requires the offeror to disclose to the target's shareholders information material to the tender offer.

Usually an injunction under § 14(e) in a tender-offer case is likely to be temporary—lasting only until corrective disclosures can be made. For a permanent injunction against a tender offer, a target generally must look to the antitrust laws, specifically § 7 of the Clayton Act, or find a violation of some regulatory statute. But increased disclosure under § 14(e) still can have value. In addition, even a brief extension under § 14(e) may be enough for a target to find another bidder willing to pay a higher price—a "white knight"—or to take some other defensive action.

Although the relief obtained by the target under § 14(e) can be limited, the information about a bidder that a court may deem "material" can be wide-ranging. This means, from the acquirer's standpoint, the litigation issues must be identified and evaluated before—not after—the offer becomes public.

This rule, evaluate before the offer is public, is illustrated by General Steel's complaint attacking Walco's tender offer under § 14(e). In addition to its holding that Walco had violated § 13(d), the court made a preliminary finding that General Steel had shown a probability of success in demonstrating that Walco's largest shareholder, Congressman Richmond, had:

- diverted Walco's corporate funds to satisfy obligations by the Richmond Foundation (his personal foundation) and to benefit himself politically;
- regularly received secret and substantial subsidies from Walco for his use of an apartment in New York City;
- caused Walco to make "charitable" contributions in Richmond's name (rather than Walco's) for his political aggrandizement.

General Steel Indus., Inc. v. Walco Nat'l Corp., supra at 92,417.

Apart from the adverse publicity created by these preliminary factual findings, a federal grand jury began a criminal investigation into Richmond's activities. Even though Walco finally abandoned its effort to control General Steel and sold its shares to General Steel's white knight, the damage to Richmond was more lasting. After an investigation by the United States attorney's office, he pleaded guilty to tax evasion stemming from failure to report benefits that Walco had provided as taxable income. The case demonstrates that any skeletons a bidder has in the closet may be exposed by litigation and that the consequences can transcend the particular transaction.

To be sure, the *General Steel* case was decided on extraordinary facts, and the relief awarded under § 13(d) was unusual. Nevertheless, the annals of takeover jurisprudence do contain a number of other decisions in which courts have issued lengthy injunctions. For example, in *Essex Chemical Corp. v. Gurit-Heberlein AG*, Civil No. 88-2478 (D.N.J. June 24, 1988), *aff'd without opinion*, 857 F.2d 1463 (3d Cir. 1988), the court enjoined a tender offer by a joint-venture party, which had received material inside information about an Essex subsidiary pursuant to a confidentiality agreement, until completion of a lengthy arbitration process. Similarly, a district court halted a tender offer for Caesar's World by an individual based on a margin violation during the pendency of Caesar's World's suit under the securities laws. *Caesar's World, Inc. v. Sosnoff*, C.V. 87-1622 W.J.R., 1987 U.S. Dist. LEXIS 14293, at *3-4 (C.D. Cal. June 8, 1987). The suit settled five months later. *Caesar's World, Inc. v. Sosnoff*, No. 87-1622 W.J.R. (PX), 1987 WL 48212 (C.D. Cal. Nov. 13, 1987).

The central themes of the federal securities laws, the requirement of full disclosure, and the creation of a level playing field "militate against injunctive remedies, such as a permanent ban against a takeover, that go beyond correction of past violations and unduly favor incumbent management." *ICN Pharmaceuticals, Inc. v. Khan*, 2 F.3d 484, 491 (2d Cir. 1993). In keeping with this view, Ludlow's unsuccessful case seeking to enjoin Tyco under § 13(d) from purchasing any more of its stock is more typical than cases resulting in lengthy injunctions.

Tyco had first tried to control Ludlow through a tender offer for 100 percent of the company. Immediately after this offer was aborted, Tyco acquired approximately 10 percent of Ludlow's stock, which it held passively—in the beginning.

Then, two years later, after its takeover attempt failed, Tyco began to accumulate additional Ludlow shares and soon owned 28 percent of Ludlow's stock. According to the amendments Tyco filed to its Schedule 13D, these purchases of Ludlow stock were for the purpose of "investment." After its share ownership exceeded 28 percent, however, Tyco amended its Schedule 13D to disclose that it was considering the possibility of acquiring control of Ludlow.

Ludlow sued Tyco in the District of Massachusetts where Ludlow's executive offices were located. Ludlow claimed that Tyco's series of "investment" amendments were false and asked for an injunction against further purchases by Tyco as well as an order directing Tyco to offer to rescind its open-market and block purchases.

Ludlow's immediate objective—stopping Tyco from buying more of its shares—was successful. The district court granted Ludlow a temporary restraining order and ordered expedited discovery, holding that "the large volume of purchases involved here over a relatively short period of time, the past history of tender offers on the part of Tyco, and the current position of Tyco as the largest stockholder of Ludlow raises sufficient question as to the accuracy of the 13D filing and sufficient likelihood of success on the merits to warrant further inquiry into the defendant's purpose in purchasing large amounts of Ludlow stock." *Ludlow Corp. v. Tyco Laboratories, Inc.*, [1981–82 Transfer Binder] Fed. Sec. L. Rep. (CCH) ¶ 98,382 at 92,302–03 (D. Mass. 1981).

But, Ludlow's victory was short-lived. After a preliminary injunction hearing, District Judge Rya W. Zobel ruled that Ludlow was not entitled to a permanent injunction because of what happened in the interim. Tyco had made a detailed public proposal to acquire all Ludlow's stock, "curing" any prior omissions. As the court said, "Whatever ambiguity or confusion may have been created by Tyco's [earlier] Schedule 13Ds was dispelled by its recent filings...." *Ludlow Corp. v. Tyco Laboratories, Inc.*, 529 F. Supp. 62, 66 (D. Mass. 1981). In reaching this conclusion, Judge Zobel followed other courts that have denied rescission or other injunctive relief beyond ensuring that misleading statements are corrected. The Tyco theory is that the interests to be protected "are fully satisfied when the shareholders receive the information required to be filed."

Given the difficulty in getting an injunction, a target must maximize its chances for success should it choose to sue. Picking the most receptive forum is critical. One possibility is the target's own headquarters. For the target's executives, this may be the most convenient court in which to testify. In addition, the target may draw a judge who is familiar with the company and its operations and who may be more sensitive to the target's argument that a takeover would be disruptive. Not surprisingly, home court is a favorite choice for a target. Virtually every case in which rescission has been granted as a remedy for a violation of § 13(d) has been tried in a target's home court.

On the other hand, a target that makes a mad dash into the local federal courthouse may find that it has rushed into the wrong one. There may be adverse case law in the circuit relating to the available relief or other key issues. For example, the Supreme Court has not ruled on whether a takeover target has standing to raise an antitrust challenge to the proposed acquisition. Most district courts have denied targets standing, reasoning that a target that will become a part of the entity that will have a monopolistic advantage cannot claim antitrust injury. However, in *Consolidated Gold Fields PLC v. Minorco, S.A.*, 871 F.2d 252 (2d Cir.), *amended by* 890 F.2d 569 (2d Cir.), *cert. dismissed*, 492 U.S. 939 (1989), the Court of Appeals for the Second Circuit concluded that even though a target company "may enjoy the benefits of the cartel" that the merger helps to create, a target has standing to assert an antitrust challenge to takeovers, because of the target's potential loss of "one of the vital components of competition—the power of independent decision-making as to price and output." 871 F.2d at 258.

A target intending to sue also must consider the district's case law interpreting key provisions of the recently enacted Private Securities Litigation Reform Act of 1995, Pub. L. No. 104-67, 109 Stat. 737 (codified at scattered sections of 15 U.S.C. and 18 U.S.C.), which modifies the Securities Act of 1933 and the Securities Exchange Act of 1934. Among other provisions, the reform act mandates the stay of "discovery and other proceedings" pending motions to dismiss, except in cases where the court finds "that particularized discovery is necessary to preserve evidence or to prevent undue prejudice to [a] party." 15 U.S.C. § 78u-4(b)(3)(B). As the initial reform act cases make their way through the judicial system, the courts will be busy hammering out the scope of the discovery stay. So far, courts have been reluctant to allow discovery to proceed in the face of the reform act's stay on the grounds of "undue prejudice." *See Novak v. Kasaks,* [Current] Fed. Sec. L. Rep. (CCH) ¶ 99,307, at 95,862 (S.D.N.Y. Aug. 15, 1996); *Medical Imaging Ctrs. of Am., Inc. v. Lichtenstein,* 917 F. Supp. 717, 720–22 (S.D. Cal. 1996).

Meanwhile, in an opinion that may become an anomaly, a district court held that the phrase "discovery and other proceedings" in the reform act does not include disclosures under Fed. R. Civ. P. 26. *Hockey v. Medhekar,* 932 F. Supp. 249, 251–53 (N.D. Cal.), *vacated, mandamus granted per curiam,* 99 F.3d 325 (9th Cir. 1996).

However, this restrictive interpretation was short-lived. The Ninth Circuit granted the defendants' petition for a writ of mandamus and vacated the district court's opinion, ruling that disclosures pursuant to Rule 26 and similar local rules do constitute "discovery" or "other proceedings" for the purposes of the reform act. *Medhekar v. United States District Court,* 99 F.3d 325, 328–29 (9th Cir. 1996) (per curiam).

Although the reform act was aimed at stemming "the tide of abusive litigation in the form of large class action 'strike' lawsuits, rather than injunctive actions by a corporation," one court has applied the act's discovery stay provision to a situation in which a corporation was attempting to fend off a proxy contest. *Medical Imaging Ctrs. of Am., Inc. v. Lichtenstein,* 917 F. Supp. 717, 721 (S.D. Cal. 1996).

In *Medical Imaging Centers,* the plaintiff corporation sued a group seeking to replace the board of directors for proxy solicitation violations under the Williams Act. The district court affirmed a magistrate's order staying discovery by the corporation pending the resolution of the defendants' motion to dismiss under the reform act.

Despite the plaintiff's protest that a discovery stay is of questionable appropriateness in a fast-paced battle for corporate control, and the fact that "[t]he SEC has echoed this sentiment, suggesting that the Reform Act was aimed more at suits claiming damages for *past harms* than at suits aimed at continuing or future violations," the court upheld imposition of the stay, since the nature of the particular case was "but one factor" for the court to consider in determining the reform act's applicability. *Id.* at 721.

The art of selecting the most favorable forum is not simple. Although it may not be difficult to choose the most favorable forum in which to challenge the bidder's conduct—and one need not be a rocket scientist to determine whether standing to sue will be sustained in that jurisdiction—a choice of forum based solely on these criteria may yield the right answer to the wrong question. These factors may point to the best court for the target *to sue* an acquirer, but that forum may not be the most favorable place for the target to *be sued*, should its own defensive actions become the subject of litigation by the bidder.

Like a chessmaster, the legal strategist must look beyond the first move and evaluate potential defensive tactics as well.

Traditionally, litigation had been considered primarily a weapon in the target's arsenal. But the conventional wisdom has faded as a result of the development of diverse corporate defensive actions by targets, which may or may not be protected by the "business judgment" rule. These defenses, sometimes characterized as "scorched earth" tactics, may involve any number of corporate actions by the target. The target may attempt to make itself less attractive to a hostile bidder by selling a key asset or "crown jewel," or it may try to keep the bidder from proceeding by acquiring a competitor of the bidder to create an antitrust obstacle, just to name two techniques.

The mother of all defensive tactics available to a target is the adoption of a "poison pill," or shareholder rights plan. Poison pill rights are triggered when a bidder acquires a threshold percentage of outstanding shares in the target. Although rights plans take several forms, they are usually securities in the form of dividends on common stock, which the board of directors retains the right to redeem for a token sum.

A typical pill enables its holder to purchase stock in the target company or the acquiring company at a highly discounted price. When shareholders take advantage of these rights, the resulting purchases greatly dilute the acquirer's stake in the target. As a result, unless the board redeems the pill, the acquirer may be effectively blocked from consummating the acquisition of the target's shares. This affords a target board tremendous leverage in negotiating with hostile acquirers, which the board can use to maximize shareholder value.

As long as a board can convince a reviewing court that a pill "continues to serve a legitimate stockholder interest in maximizing the value of [the company] for its shareholders," a court is not likely to order redemption of a pill. *In re Holly Farms Corp. Shareholders Litigation*, 564 A.2d 342, 351 (Del. Ch. 1989). However, courts also have "recognized that at some point, the failure to redeem a poison pill can constitute a fiduciary breach," *Moore Corp. v. Wallace Computer Services, Inc.*, 907 F. Supp. 1545, 1562 (D. Del. 1995), and will not hesitate to order redemption of pills that "serve no purpose . . . other than to preclude shareholder acceptance" of a lucrative offer. *Grand Metro. Pub. Ltd. Co. v. Pillsbury Co.*, 558 A.2d 1049, 1060 (Del. Ch. 1988).

Before selecting a forum, the target should evaluate how the judges view "defensive" corporate tactics. There can be significant differences in evaluating these transactions, and the target may argue that any subsequent claim by the bidder against a defensive maneuver by the target is a compulsory counterclaim and must be brought in the forum selected by the target to challenge the bidder's conduct.

For example, whereas courts today generally use an enhanced business judgment rule to test the legality of target boards' use of takeover defenses, courts in certain jurisdictions still adhere to the traditional business judgment rule. Though its exact phrasing varies among jurisdictions, in substance the business judgment rule requires that a director discharge his duties in good faith and with the degree of care of an ordinarily prudent person in similar circumstances. *See, e.g., In re Munford*, 98 F.3d 604, 611 (11th Cir. 1996); *Stephens v. National Distillers & Chem. Corp.*, Nos. 91 Civ. 2901, 2902 (JSM), 1996 WL 271789, at *6 (S.D.N.Y. May 21, 1996).

In *Unocal Corp. v. Mesa Petroleum Co.*, 493 A.2d 946 (Del. 1985), the Delaware Supreme Court enhanced the standard of review for target boards' responses to takeover bids under Delaware law. Under *Unocal*, the target's directors have the initial burden of proof in litigation involving defensive measures. Specifically, the directors must demonstrate that they had "reasonable grounds for believing that a danger to corporate policy and effectiveness existed," and that their response was "reasonable in relation to the threat posed." *Id.* at 955. Once the board satisfies this burden, its action "is entitled to be measured by the standards of the business judgment rule." *Id.* at 958.

In a series of cases following *Unocal*, the Delaware Supreme Court further detailed the path for Delaware courts to follow in evaluating the conduct of a target board. For example, in *Revlon, Inc. v. MacAndrews & Forbes Holdings, Inc.*, 506 A.2d 173 (Del. 1986), the Delaware Supreme Court held that if the sale of a corporation becomes inevitable, the "directors' role change[s] from defenders of the corporate bastion to auctioneers charged with getting the best price for the stockholders at a sale of the company." *Id.* at 182.

If the directors do not seek to maximize the price received by stockholders from the sale, their actions are not judged under the deferential business judgment rule. In *Paramount Communications Inc. v. QVC Network Inc.*, 637 A.2d 34 (Del. 1994), the Delaware Supreme Court succinctly articulated the gist of a decade of case law employing the enhanced scrutiny test: "The directors have the burden of proving that they were adequately informed and acted reasonably." *Id.* at 45.

Many courts outside of Delaware, construing the law of other states, have followed *Unocal* and its progeny. *See, e.g., International Ins. Co. v. Johns*, 874 F.2d 1447, 1458–59 (11th Cir. 1989); *Dynamics Corp. of Am. v. CTS Corp.*, 805 F.2d 705, 708 (7th Cir. 1986). However, the Second Circuit has kept the initial burden of proof upon the plaintiff attacking the board conduct. *See Hanson Trust PLC v. ML SCM Acquisition Inc.*, 781

F.2d 264, 273 (2d Cir. 1986). In addition, several states have enacted legislation that rejects the *Unocal* standard and retains traditional business-judgment-rule standards. *See, e.g.,* Ohio Rev. Code Ann. § 1701.59(C)(1) (Anderson 1992); Ind. Bus. Corp. Law § 23-1-35-1(f) (Michie 1995).

There also may be differences among those courts that test certain "defensive" transactions under the business judgment rule. Under the internal affairs doctrine, the application of the business judgment rule generally has been based on interpretation of the law of the jurisdiction in which the target is organized. *See, e.g., Atherton v. FDIC,* No. 95-928, 1997 WL 9781, at *7-8 (U.S. Jan. 14, 1997). This doctrine may be undergoing erosion, however, especially in states whose statutes apply provisions of that state's corporation law to corporations doing business there, even though incorporated elsewhere.

Such a statute made the difference in *Norlin Corp. v. Rooney, Pace Inc.,* 744 F.2d 255 (2d Cir. 1984), a case that shows even the best strategy sometimes will not work. When Norlin became aware that large blocks of its stock were being acquired by Rooney, Pace, it rushed into the United States District Court for the Southern District of New York, claiming that the rapid accumulation of more than 30 percent of its shares was an unlawful "creeping tender offer." After its applications for a temporary restraining order and expedited discovery were denied by District Judge David N. Edelstein, Norlin unleashed its doomsday defense.

Norlin issued nearly a million shares of voting-preferred stock to a wholly owned subsidiary and to an employee stock option plan. These transactions would have effectively diluted the acquirer's holdings from almost 45 percent to 27 percent and would have allowed Norlin's management to vote nearly 49 percent of all outstanding shares and perpetuate itself forever.

Although voting of shares issued to a wholly owned subsidiary is barred by the laws of virtually every state in the United States, Norlin tried to sustain defense by relying on the law of Panama, under which it was incorporated. Panama corporate law requires that shareholders adopt a resolution before a derivative action for breach of duty can be brought against the directors. Panama also permits (under limited circumstances) a subsidiary to vote shares that it holds of its own parent. Norlin hoped to avoid the New York corporation law and public policy by using these quirks of Panamanian law.

Norlin's reliance on Panama law was strained, especially since its headquarters were in New York and its stock was listed on the New York Stock Exchange. So refusing to follow Panama law, the district court enjoined Norlin from voting the new shares. The Court of Appeals for the Second Circuit affirmed.

Although a target contemplating litigation must think like a possible defendant as well as a plaintiff in picking the best forum, it is the bidder who may be in a position to preempt the choice of forum. When a formal tender offer is made, it is a ritual for the bidder's first move to start a suit in every state that has a state takeover statute that might apply to its tender offer, seeking to enjoin enforcement on constitutional grounds. *See, e.g., Edgar v. MITE Corp.*, 457 U.S. 624, 634–46 (1982) (Illinois statute that favored management and reduced investor autonomy preempted by Williams Act and invalid under the Commerce Clause); *CTS Corp. v. Dynamics Corp. of Am.*, 481 U.S. 69, 78–94 (1987) (Indiana statute did not conflict with the Williams Act or Commerce Clause, and was therefore constitutional); *United Dominion Indus. Ltd. v. Commercial Intertech Corp.*, 943 F. Supp. 857, 873–74 (S.D. Ohio 1996) (preliminary injunction denied, because bidder not likely to demonstrate successfully that Ohio takeover statute provision is preempted by the Williams Act); *WLR Foods, Inc. v. Tyson Foods, Inc.*, 861 F. Supp. 1277, 1284–89 (W.D. Va. 1994) (challenged Virginia takeover statutes did not conflict with the Williams Act or the Commerce Clause, and were therefore constitutional), *aff'd*, 65 F.3d 1172 (4th Cir. 1995), *cert. denied*, 116 S. Ct. 921 (1996); *Batus, Inc. v. McKay*, 684 F. Supp. 637, 639–40 (D. Nev. 1988) (Nevada takeover statute provision preempted by the Williams Act and violated the Commerce Clause).

Some bidders have attempted to use these state statute actions (so far unsuccessfully) to contend that a target's subsequent challenges to the actual tender offer must take the form of compulsory counterclaims to the bidder's action and therefore must be asserted in the bidder's chosen forum. *See, e.g., Koppers Co., Inc. v. American Express Co.*, 689 F. Supp. 1371 (W.D. Pa. 1988); *General Steel Indus., Inc. v. Walco Nat'l Corp.*, 527 F. Supp. 305 (E.D. Mo. 1981).

In other cases, a bidder has forced any challenge to its tender offer to be made in a court it selects. A bidder does this by suing first, before suit is brought against it by the target corporation. Usually the claim is based on press releases prematurely issued by the target, which comment on the tender offer. In such cases, the acquirer has immediately started suit in the forum it prefers, attacking the press releases as false and misleading and has claimed that any later action by the target under the securities or antitrust laws must be brought as counterclaims in the same action. *See, e.g., H.K. Porter Co. v. Fansteel, Inc.*, [1975-1976 Transfer Binder] Fed. Sec. L. Rep. (CCH) ¶ 95,546 at 99,741 (S.D.N.Y. 1976) (enjoining subsequent action). Given the current split on the right of targets to sue under the Williams Act, a bidder that succeeds in forcing a target to maintain its securities claims in an Eleventh Circuit court might preclude any viable challenge by the target to its disclosures.

Even when a target succeeds in enjoining a tender offer from proceeding, an acquirer may countermove to attempt to stalemate the target, thereby neutralizing its victory. A few courts have granted requests by bidders that have been enjoined to maintain the status quo for *both sides* by keeping the target from engaging in any defensive transaction while an injunction is pending. *Muskegon Piston & Ring Co. v. Gulf & Western Indus.*, 328 F.2d 830 (6th Cir. 1964); *Dan River, Inc. v. Icahn*, Civ. Action No. 82-2014 (W.D. Va. 1983), *rev'd on other grounds*, 701 F.2d 278 (4th Cir. 1983).

Though much of the action in takeover litigation takes place in federal courts, state courts often play an important role as well. Because review of a target's substantive conduct is traditionally a matter determined under state law, many important decisions have shifted to the states, especially the state of Delaware, the state of incorporation of the largest number of targets. When targets are engaged in heavily regulated businesses such as insurance, the application of the relevant statutes often is thrashed out in state courts. Similarly, battles over the application and constitutionality of state takeover statutes, especially when they are invoked in the context of creeping tender offers, have been fought in state courts. Bidders would rather challenge state statutes in the federal courts, but, if they do not sue early, they may be forced to litigate in the state courts preferred by state officials and target companies.

The state forums may play an increasingly important role in litigation over the validity of defensive transactions in cases where diversity of citizenship does not provide an independent basis for federal jurisdiction. The recent spate of state laws regulating hostile takeovers as well as the Supreme Court's decision in *Schreiber v. Burlington Northern, Inc.*, 472 U.S. 1 (1985) (to violate § 14(e), misrepresentation of nondisclosure must be involved), may force a bidder challenging such a transaction into state court. And, absent an independent basis for federal jurisdiction or a basis of pendent jurisdiction, the bidder may be limited to a state court action. *See Anago Inc. v. Tecnol Med. Prods., Inc.*, Civ. A. No. 3-92-250-H, 1992 WL 387242 (N.D. Tex. Nov. 27, 1992); *Data Probe, Inc. v. CRC Info. Sys.*, N.Y. L.J., Dec. 28, 1984, at 7 (N.Y. Sup. Ct. Dec. 27, 1984).

Finally, selecting an appropriate forum is only the opening gambit. Whether a takeover ends in a checkmate or a stalemate will depend on any number of additional factors, including the skill, planning, and master strategy developed by the players throughout the match.

Derivative Litigation: A Primer

Robert J. Kopecky

Acme Technology Company, a small but successful firm, has encountered its first setback. It invested more than $100 million to develop a process for making low-cost ethanol out of recycled grass clippings. The company has just announced that the project is a complete failure and has been abandoned. The company's entire $100 million investment must be written off. Acme is broke. Not surprisingly, Acme's shareholders are unhappy. They feel that the company's management and directors have betrayed them. One of the shareholders calls his lawyer and says he wants to sue.

After reviewing the facts, the lawyer decides that there isn't any claim for securities fraud, but he suggests bringing a derivative suit. "What you're really saying," he explains to the disgruntled shareholder/client, "is that the company's officers and directors breached their fiduciary duties." Ordinarily, that kind of claim belongs to the corporation, not its shareholders, and can be brought only by the corporation. As with any legal rule worth relying on, however, there are exceptions. The exception here is the derivative suit—an action brought by a shareholder "in the right" and on behalf of a corporation.

Derivative suits have been recognized in the United States since at least 1832. The Supreme Court specifically recognized them as a mechanism for aggrieved shareholders in 1856. For the first hundred years or so, shareholder derivative suits were used primarily to assert corporate claims against third parties, often the government. Since the 1930s, however, derivative suits have aimed increasingly at the corporation's own officers and directors.

Robert J. Kopecky practices law with Kirkland & Ellis in Chicago.

The number of derivative cases increased substantially in the 1980s, partly as a side effect of the upsurge in takeovers, leveraged buyouts, and other corporate consolidations. But derivative suits are by no means limited to such corporate warfare. A 1991 study of 535 publicly held corporations showed that 20 percent had faced at least one derivative suit in the previous two decades. Romano, "The Shareholder Suit: Litigation Without Foundation," 7 *J. Law Econ. & Organiz.* 55 (1991). Derivative suits can have many targets: alleged self-dealing by corporate executives, alleged mismanagement or waste of corporate assets by officers and directors, and failure to assert claims against dishonest corporate employees or agents. One particularly popular basis for derivative suits in the past 15 years has been the proliferation of highly publicized guilty pleas by corporations to charges of defense contracting fraud and other corporate crimes.

State Law Controls

The ability of a shareholder to bring a derivative suit is governed by the law of the state in which the corporation is chartered. Despite efforts by the ABA to create uniformity with its Model Business Corporation Act, there are many variations from state to state in the rules governing such suits. *See generally* DeMott, *Shareholder Derivative Actions* (1992). The law of Delaware dominates, however. Roughly half the corporations listed on the New York Stock Exchange are incorporated in Delaware. As a result, Delaware has by far the most developed body of precedent in this area, and courts in other jurisdictions often look to Delaware decisions to fill gaps in their own law.

Despite variations from state to state, there are elements common to derivative cases in almost all jurisdictions. The central shared characteristic is the theory of the action: A derivative suit is one to enforce a claim belonging to the corporation. As a result, any recovery—whether by settlement or judgment—goes to the corporation, not the shareholders. A related requirement, since the action is premised on wrong to the corporation, is that the plaintiff must have been a shareholder at the time of the challenged act or omission.

The most important aspect of derivative litigation—a key battleground—is the "demand requirement." The decision to bring—or not to bring—a lawsuit on the corporation's behalf is a business decision entrusted to the board of directors. The demand requirement implements this basic principle of corporate governance. *Kamen v. Kemper Financial Serv., Inc.*, 500 U.S. 90, 101 (1991). Before a shareholder can establish standing to assert a derivative claim, he must either (1) make a demand on the board and allow the board to decide what to do with the claim, or else (2) show that demand is excused because it would be "futile." A few states (such as Georgia, Michigan, and Wisconsin) have statutory provisions requiring a demand in all cases. And the Pennsylvania Supreme Court recently held that it would follow the approach of the American Law Institute to require a demand in all cases. *Cuker v. Mikalauskas*, 692 A.2d 1042 (Pa. 1997).

A demand generally takes the form of a letter addressed either to the board or to the corporation's general counsel. It must identify the wrongdoers, state the factual basis for the claim, and specify the relief sought on the corporation's behalf. After making a demand, the shareholder must give the board time to consider the action requested, conduct whatever investigation is necessary, and make a written response. Only after giving the board this opportunity and having his demand rejected may the shareholder pursue a lawsuit challenging the board's decision.

A board may have a number of reasons for rejecting a shareholder's demand. The most obvious is that the board concludes the claim has no merit and would therefore be a waste of the corporation's assets to pursue. The board may also conclude that the likely recovery from a potentially meritorious claim, discounted for the possibility of losing, does not justify spending the resources required to pursue the claim. Finally, the board may conclude that a claim should not be pursued because of adverse effects the litigation may have on the corporation. These may include disruption of the corporation's business, bad publicity, or adverse impact on customer or supplier relationships.

A shareholder who asserts that a demand need not be made because it would be futile faces a high hurdle. As the Delaware Supreme Court recently explained, "futility does not mean that there is no likelihood that the board will agree to the demand." *Heineman v. DataPoint Corp.*, 611 A.2d 950, 952 (Del. 1992). Rather, a demand will not be excused as futile unless the shareholder establishes that the board is tainted by self-interest or is otherwise disqualified from deciding whether to pursue litigation on the corporation's behalf. To make that showing, a plaintiff must allege specific facts raising a reasonable doubt either (1) that a majority of the board is interested in the conduct or transaction at issue in the suit or (2) that the directors did not exercise proper business judgment in connection with the challenged transaction. Unless a demand is excused, the board, and the board alone, has the right to decide whether to pursue the litigation, and the shareholder lacks standing to pursue his claim any further.

Self-Dealing and Self-Interest

The demand requirement most often is excused where the plaintiff can allege that a majority of the corporation's directors were engaged in self-dealing or were otherwise tainted by self-interest. For example, if the directors made use of corporate opportunities to benefit another company they have set up on the side, most courts would find that they are disqualified from making a decision about whether to pursue the corporation's claims against themselves concerning that activity. But the self-interest must be clear and pronounced: The courts in Delaware (and most other jurisdictions) hold that a demand will not be excused simply because a majority of the directors are alleged to have some liability to the corporation. As the Delaware Supreme Court stated in *Aronson v. Lewis*, 473 A.2d at 815, "mere threat of personal liability for approving a questioned transaction, standing alone, is insufficient to challenge either the independence or disinterestedness of directors."

Absent facts reflecting director self-interest, courts hesitate to take control away from the board. Allegations that directors breached their fiduciary duties and are therefore disqualified from acting on the corporation's behalf are often insufficient. A notable example is the derivative suit brought against E.F. Hutton's directors in the aftermath of that firm's guilty plea to more than 2,000 incidents of mail and wire fraud. The shareholder plaintiff alleged that, because they received monthly operations reports and attended a meeting with the corporation's auditors, the directors should have been aware of the firm's illegal scheme. Despite this, the court concluded that the plaintiffs had "failed to allege sufficient involvement on the part of a majority of Hutton's board" to disqualify them from responding to a shareholder demand. The court thereupon dismissed the complaint for failure to make a demand. *In re E.F. Hutton Banking Practices Litigation*, 634 F. Supp. 265 (S.D.N.Y. 1986).

The high stakes involved, combined with the significant role of directors and officers (D&O) insurance, tend to move many derivative suits against officers and directors toward settlement if the shareholder can establish standing. Such settlements are not purely private matters, however. As with class actions, settlement of a derivative suit requires court approval. (For derivative suits in federal court, Rule 23.1 makes this explicit.) Shareholders generally get notice of the proposed settlement and an opportunity to object. The court holds a fairness hearing that is usually either combined with or followed by a hearing on the plaintiffs' lawyer's fee petition. As noted earlier, any settlement money goes to the corporate treasury; the plaintiffs' lawyers' fees come out of this common fund.

With this framework in mind, let's return to Acme—the formerly fine little company that lost its way in grass clippings and ethanol. The disgruntled Acme shareholder files a derivative suit purportedly on behalf of Acme. The suit names as defendants each member of the board. It seeks to recover from them the $100 million squandered on the ethanol project. The complaint alleges that the directors of Acme (1) wasted corporate assets on a project no one could have believed would work, and (2) were grossly negligent in managing the corporation's affairs because most of the money allocated to the project was squandered.

Acme's CEO reads the complaint, calls the general counsel, and says: "This sounds bad; what do we do now?" The general counsel explains that decisions made by directors in managing the corporation's affairs are generally protected by the "business judgment" rule. That rule is a presumption that, in making a business decision, the officers and directors of a corporation act (1) on an informed basis, (2) in good faith, and (3) in the honest belief that the action taken was in the best interests of the corporation. The burden is on a shareholder challenging such business decisions to overcome this presumption.

Special Litigation Committees

The chairman says: "But this complaint seems to be trying to get around that rule. It alleges that the whole board was grossly negligent; that we wasted corporate assets; that none of us is protected by the business judgment rule; and that we're disqualified from acting on this claim. Shouldn't we appoint a special litigation committee to avoid this whole question of taint?"

The chairman's reaction is perceptive and timely. The answer to his question—Should there be a special litigation committee?—is the most important strategic decision for the board in responding to a shareholder derivative suit.

What is a special litigation committee (SLC)? Delaware law permits directors to delegate authority to committees of the board. In Delaware (and most other states to consider the issue), a board may delegate its authority over litigation to such a committee *even though* the board itself may be disqualified (on self-interest or other grounds) from exercising its authority over the litigation. If the SLC decides a litigation is not in the company's interests, the company may move to have it dismissed. Thus, even if the demand requirement is excused, a corporation can still retain an element of control by appointing an independent SLC to act for the board.

In *Zapata v. Maldonado*, 430 A.2d 779 (Del. 1981), the Delaware Supreme Court created a special procedure governing attempts to dismiss derivative litigation based on the recommendation of an SLC. The *Zapata* procedure has two significant components.

First, and most significant, the decision of the SLC is *not* afforded the presumption of the business judgment rule. Instead, the *corporation* has the burden of proving: (1) that the SLC was independent, (2) that it acted in good faith, and (3) that it had a reasonable factual basis for its conclusion. To satisfy these criteria, the SLC must produce a thorough written record of the investigation and its findings and recommendations. Under *Zapata*, a plaintiff can take limited discovery on the SLC's independence and good faith.

Second, even if the court is satisfied about the independence and good faith of the SLC, it may still exercise its own independent judgment to determine whether dismissal is really in the best interests of the corporation. In other words, the court can overrule the SLC's business judgment.

The standards governing dismissal of derivative cases by special litigation committees vary from state to state. For example, New York law has a procedure like that in *Zapata,* but with two important differences. First, under New York law, the plaintiff (not the board, as in Delaware) has the burden of proof on the issues of independence, good faith, and reasonableness. Second, the court does not have discretion to exercise its own business judgment and overrule the SLC's determination. *See Auerbach v. Bennett,* 419 N.Y.S.2d 920 (1979).

Against this legal background, a corporate board must consider the advantages and disadvantages of appointing an SLC to deal with a derivative suit alleging that the demand requirement should be excused.

The most obvious advantage of an SLC is that it provides a convenient way for a corporation to dispose of litigation that is meritless or otherwise not in its best interests. If there is a question about whether litigation serves the company's interests, the SLC can reach a conclusion that is objective, well informed, and fair to shareholders. If the suit is one that *should* be pursued, the SLC can take control of the litigation from plaintiffs' counsel, who are less likely to be concerned about the broader interests of the corporation.

The principal *dis*advantage of an SLC is that, by delegating authority to the committee, the board loses control. To ensure judicial deference, the SLC should consist of *independent* directors. The blessing afforded by this independence may become a curse when the SLC views as meritorious a claim management thought was not. In addition, the SLC's investigation—which must be thorough—is likely to disrupt the corporation's regular business. That means many interviews, often consuming much time of corporate executives. The SLC's investigation, including production of its report, is also likely to be expensive. More than that, the SLC's investigation and deliberation probably will be discoverable.

Most important, the corporation may lose a significant procedural advantage by creating an SLC. The problem is illustrated by the decision in *Abbey v. Computer & Communications Technology Corp.,* 457 A.2d 368 (Del. Ch. 1983). In that case (like our Acme example), the plaintiff filed suit alleging that a demand was excused. In response, the board immediately created an SLC with full authority to act for the corporation. A few days later, the company—through its board—moved to dismiss the complaint on the ground that plaintiffs had not alleged facts sufficient to excuse a demand. However, the court in *Abbey* held that, by creating an SLC, the board *conceded* that it was disqualified from acting and that the demand requirement was not excused. As a result, the court said, the board could not seek dismissal except in accordance with the stricter *Zapata* procedure.

One federal decision applying Delaware law underscores the importance of timing in creating an SLC. In *Peller v. Southern Company,* 911 F.2d 1532 (11th Cir. 1990), the plaintiff brought a derivative suit alleging that all the directors of a large electric utility had breached their duty of care and had wasted corporate assets in connection with construction of a nuclear power plant. The defendants did not move to dismiss; instead they immediately created an SLC. After the SLC had investigated and decided that the litigation was not in the company's interests, the company moved to dismiss. The district court applied the *Zapata* test and held that the *company* had the burden of proof. The court then held that the company had not met its burden of showing that the SLC had conducted a good-faith investigation. The appeals court, following *Abbey*, agreed that the more stringent *Zapata* test applied and affirmed denial of the motion under that standard.

Timing Is Everything

Abbey and *Peller* show that the standard governing a company's effort to dispose of a derivative case may depend on how the company first responds to the complaint. So, to return to Acme and its inquisitive chairman, the company should *not* create an SLC, at least not immediately. Instead, it should move to dismiss the complaint on the ground that a demand is not excused. If the case is handled that way, the burden stays on the plaintiff to overcome the presumption of the business judgment rule, whereas the burden would be on the company to satisfy the *Zapata* criteria if it begins by appointing an SLC. If the court denies the motion on the need for a demand, the company can *then* create an SLC. And remember this: If the company creates an SLC immediately, that guarantees plaintiffs will get some discovery; if the corporation simply moves to dismiss, plaintiffs should not be able to get any discovery until after the motion is decided.

Assume the court has determined that a demand is excused because the complaint alleges in great detail that the money supposedly spent on the ethanol project went to the directors themselves. This decision is generally nonappealable; the shareholders now control litigation on the corporation's behalf against its directors. *Now* is the time for the board to form an SLC. By delegating authority over the case to an independent SLC, the corporation can reclaim that control.

The key issue for the board then becomes this: How can the company fulfill the purpose for using the SLC—having the corporation maintain control over litigation on its behalf—*and* do what is in the corporation's best interests? With that problem in mind, there are three key considerations in using an SLC: (1) the membership of the committee, (2) the scope of the SLC's authority, and (3) the SLC's role in settlement.

The main guidelines for SLC membership are simple. The safest course is to pick new directors with no prior connection to the company. At minimum, SLC members should not have been on the board when the challenged transaction occurred, and they should not have had any financial connection to it.

It is better to have more than one SLC member, especially if there is any question of independence. In *Lewis v. Fuqua*, 502 A.2d 962 (Del. Ch. 1985), for example, the court rejected the conclusion of a one-member SLC for lack of sufficient independence. That sole SLC member had been a director at the time of the challenged transaction, had financial and political dealings with the CEO, and was president of a university receiving substantial grants from the company. Without other SLC members to offset these factors, the conclusion of the "committee" had little weight.

It is important to find directors who will spend time on the investigation. These are not honorary positions. SLC members should review the key documents and take an active role in interviewing witnesses. In *Peller v. Southern Co.*, mentioned earlier, the Eleventh Circuit found that the SLC had not conducted its investigation in good faith because it relied too much on lawyers to plan, conduct, and summarize witness interviews.

An SLC must be truly independent. If the board tries to reserve some control or authority over the litigation, the SLC may well be found not to be independent—thus defeating its purpose. Nonetheless, at the beginning, the board must make two significant decisions about the scope of the SLC's authority.

The first is what claims the SLC should evaluate. Against whom are they made? In the case of Acme Technology, for example, the plaintiffs claim that funds were diverted from the ethanol project. They have sued the directors, but no one else. Other possible defendants *could* include the corporate controller, the manager in charge of the project, or the company's outside auditors.

Should the SLC investigate claims against these possible, but not named, defendants? That could make sense for several reasons. Having authority to investigate beyond the scope of the complaint, to reach additional claims or defendants, promotes finality (both of settlement and dismissal), and it may eliminate future derivative actions. And, remember, the shareholders may be onto something. There may be a genuine problem, and the board should know its full dimensions. Expanded scope may increase recovery for the corporation, by pursuing parties with additional assets or D&O insurance. Failure to charter an expansive investigation risks having the statute of limitations run on other claims the corporation may have.

The second major SLC authority question is whether the committee should be granted authority to decide if, and on what terms, the litigation should be settled. The argument for doing so is that, since the board is disqualified, *someone* must have authority to approve a settlement on the corporation's behalf. The argument against settlement authority is that, since plaintiffs must accept, and the court must approve, any settlement, an independent board need not approve it. As a practical matter, a case probably can't be settled if the SLC opposes the settlement. And, once an SLC has begun its investigation, a settlement probably cannot be concluded until the investigation is final.

The SLC can play a key role in the settlement process. One main benefit of the SLC is that it buys time: Courts often will grant a stay of discovery until the committee finishes its work. This can provide a relatively placid period in which to pursue settlement.

An SLC at work can by itself provide a powerful incentive for parties to negotiate in good faith. An ongoing investigation creates uncertainty. Plaintiffs' counsel have to be concerned that the SLC either will have the case dismissed or will take over its prosecution. Defendants' D&O carrier will be concerned that the SLC may decide to pursue claims against directors and officers it insures. A settlement can end such mutual uneasiness.

The SLC generally should not participate directly in settlement negotiations, however. If talks break down, the company will have risked compromising the independence of the committee and, therefore, its ability to end the litigation. If the parties (plaintiff, directors, and insurance carrier) come to terms on a proposed settlement, *then* the SLC should get involved. It can review the settlement and identify any aspects it finds unacceptable from the corporation's standpoint.

Once the parties reach a final agreement, the SLC can consider whether to approve the settlement. If it does, the committee should prepare a written report analyzing the merits of the claims, damages incurred, recoverability, and other factors. This report should be submitted to the court, along with a recommendation that the settlement be approved. By having negotiations conducted in parallel with the SLC's investigation, the committee preserves its integrity and can make an informed judgment about the merits of the settlement that is likely to carry substantial weight with the court.

Return for a minute to Acme and its troubles. Assume that the plaintiff in Acme's case *does* make a demand before he files suit. He decides *not* to argue that a demand would be futile. What should the company do? In this situation, the company runs little risk of conceding something by creating an SLC.

Spiegel v. Buntrock, 571 A.2d 767 (Del. 1990), shows why. In that case, the Delaware Supreme Court held that a shareholder who makes a demand "*can no longer argue that demand is excused*," because making the demand is a concession that the board is independent. The effect of the demand is "to place control of the litigation in the hands of the board." In *Spiegel*, the plaintiff first alleged that a demand was excused and then made a demand after the company moved to dismiss the complaint. In response to the demand, the board created a special litigation committee. The court ruled that the SLC's decision was entitled to deference under the business judgment rule, and should not be evaluated under the stricter *Zapata* standard.

The Plaintiff Makes a Demand

A federal appellate court decision in California, applying Delaware law, reached the same conclusion. *Litton Industries, Inc. v. Hoch*, 1993 U.S. App. LEXIS 16992 (9th Cir. 1993). There, the plaintiff shareholders filed a derivative suit against the officers and directors of Litton Industries; the suit was dismissed for failure to make a demand or to allege facts sufficient to excuse a demand. Plaintiffs then *did* make a demand on Litton's board. The board created a special litigation committee composed of three outside directors to investigate the demand. The committee concluded that the case should not be pursued. The Ninth Circuit held that the only relevant question remaining was the due care and good faith of the SLC because, by making demand, the plaintiff had conceded the board's lack of self-interest.

So, where a plaintiff makes a demand, the decision to reject it will be reviewed under the business judgment rule—not the *Zapata* standard—whether the full board decides or the decision is delegated to an SLC.

In deciding whether to accept or reject a demand, the board has a duty to act in good faith and to inform itself of material information essential to an evaluation of the demand. Delegating full decision-making authority to an SLC does not help in these circumstances, and it creates the practical problems previously discussed by taking control of the litigation from the full board of directors.

If the demand raises complex issues that require further investigation, the best course may be to create an investigatory committee of the board. It can report to the full board, which can then decide. Such a committee can have salutary effects. It relieves most of the directors of detailed involvement in an investigation. In addition, the record developed will strengthen the company's hand in defending a later claim that the demand was wrongfully rejected.

If the board determines, following its investigation, that the action demanded by the shareholder plaintiff would not be in the best interests of the corporation, it will inform the shareholder in writing that his demand has been rejected.

How much of an explanation should be included with the rejection? That is a recurring problem for corporation lawyers. It is useful to offer more than just the board's ultimate conclusion. At a minimum, the response should state explicitly that the board has considered the demand, looked into the relevant facts, and concluded that the action sought is not in the corporation's interest. If the board has retained an expert to assist it or conducted a formal, detailed investigation, that should be mentioned. The reason for giving some explanation is that the board's response will likely become part of the court record; it will be part of the support for a motion to dismiss the plaintiff's almost certain complaint alleging wrongful rejection of the demand. The board's recitation and explanation of what it did may ultimately play a key role in determining whether the board acted in good faith.

Once the board rejects the demand, the only remaining issue is the good faith and reasonableness of the board's investigation and conclusion. To pursue a derivative claim if the board rejects the demand, a shareholder must show that refusal of the demand was in bad faith or was based on an unreasonable investigation. *Levine v. Smith*, 591 A.2d 194 (Del. 1991). Faced with those standards, to get past a motion to dismiss, the plaintiff must allege with particularity facts sufficient to establish "reasonable doubt" that the board's decision is not protected by the business judgment rule. In most cases, the plaintiff must meet this burden without the benefit of any discovery. If the plaintiff fails to do so, the board's decision not to pursue the claims raised by the demand is final.

The interplay of demand, lack of demand, investigation, and response can be confusing, so here is a terse summary: If the complaint alleges that a demand is excused, a corporation generally should not create an SLC immediately; instead it should move to dismiss for failure to make a demand. If the court agrees that a demand is excused (thus letting the suit proceed), the corporation can then set up an independent SLC with broad authority. If a shareholder chooses to make a demand, the corporation can, but need not, create an SLC. The better course is to create an investigatory committee but not delegate full authority to it.

Those are the core strategic decisions in derivative litigation. If the case is dismissed (because a demand was not excused or rejection of the demand is upheld), then the battle is largely over. If it is *not* dismissed, then the fight continues, with shareholders battling corporate management or other defendants on the corporation's behalf. The directions such litigation can go are endless and beyond this article, which will not—despite the possible expectations of some readers—wade into the details either of ethanol or grass clippings.

Patent Litigation

Laurence H. Pretty

Today's patent litigator has a buffed-up image compared with 20 years ago when the widespread (if even then unfair) perception was of a "techie" more at home with technology than trial arts. Two reasons have driven the change. One reason is that, as patent trials in the last decade have changed to more than 50 percent jury trials, patent law firms specializing in litigation have been at the leading edge of trial lawyers in using electronic media and jury litigation consulting to make technology issues understandable to laymen. The other reason is that, during the same years, a number of business trial lawyers have brought their jury trial skills into patent litigation. Polished by the fused skills of both types of trial lawyer, patent litigation is a contest now performed at the most accomplished level.

Precomplaint Considerations

A patent lawsuit is nearly always a major undertaking. The size of the economic interests necessary to justify the high cost of a patent lawsuit, the variety of defenses requiring discovery, the numerous documents, and the often widespread separation of the parties and witnesses add up to serious business. The climate alone can cause classic mistakes. Too often litigators file first and worry about the facts when they get into discovery. Dangerous in any practice, it is taboo in patent litigation. Before you file, you need to study your client's position meticulously for any weaknesses. Do not waste your client's time and money with a premature complaint. A recklessly filed patent lawsuit can expose the patent owner to an adverse award of the defendant's lawyer fees, counterclaims for

---

Laurence H. Pretty is a member of the Los Angeles patent law firm of Pretty, Schroeder & Poplawski and is an adjunct lecturer in law at U.C.L.A. Law School.

unfair competition, and, in extreme circumstances, even to an antitrust claim. *Zenith Radio Corp. v. Hazeltine Research*, 395 U.S. 100 (1969).

Some patent suits begin like this: Your client, Cucamonga Gadget, comes into your office screaming with anger that his prime competitor, Pocatello Widget, has just knocked off a copy of Cucamonga's hottest-selling new product. After calming your client down with sympathetic outrage, your first step is to get a sample of Pocatello's product (or whatever other information is available) and make a comparison with the patent claims to determine whether there is an infringement. In addition, your patent owner, Cucamonga, should investigate the prior art, its own files, and available witnesses to find whether the patent has any incurable defects that would cause a court to hold it invalid or unenforceable.

If there are other patent infringers (unrelated to Pocatello), you have to make some early choices: Whom do you sue first? Do you go against more than one simultaneously? These are important questions in any kind of case. But in patent litigation, they are crucial because of collateral estoppel. Why?

If your first lawsuit results in the patent's being held invalid, the patent is also invalid in any later cases. *Blonder-Tongue Lab. v. University of Illinois Found.*, 402 U.S., 313 (1971). So it is important to bring the first case against the infringer that offers the best prospects for a win. Winning the first case does not legally insulate the patent from further attack, but it helps. If the patent is once sustained, it improves the chances for getting favorable settlements from the other infringers or a favorable outcome in later trials.

Choice of venue used to be narrowly limited by a special patent venue statute, 28 U.S.C. § 1400(b). Its restrictive effects for corporate defendants, however, have been overridden by an amendment to 35 U.S.C. § 1391(c), which has been construed to enable an infringer to be sued in any district in which it is "doing business." *VE Holding Corp. v. Johnson Gas Appliance Co.*, 917 F.2d 1574 (Fed. Cir. 1990). A patent owner can now feel quite confident in filing in its own judicial district against a remotely located infringer who is doing business in the district. Of course, there still can be a risk of transfer to the infringer's district if the patent owner chooses some forum primarily for its inconvenience to the defendant, with little connection to either party. 35 U.S.C. § 1404(a) or 1406(a).

After the initial analysis of whether the patent is infringed and likely to withstand an attack on its validity, another early question is whether to file the lawsuit or try threats of litigation to persuade the infringer to stop. Often it is tempting to save your client expensive litigation fees by merely sending Pocatello Widget a form demand letter. But be careful.

That demand letter can backfire. Instead of rolling over and giving up the product that infringes on your patent, Pocatello Widget may seize the initiative, and, in its home court in Idaho, file a declaratory judgment action to determine that your patent is invalid and not infringed, 28 U.S.C. § 2201.

Don't Be Provocative

Your demand letter can also haunt you later on in litigation. Often the letter is a demand that Pocatello cease infringement, turn over its entire inventory, and account to your client for the damages suffered. Do not be surprised if your opponent waves that letter in front of the jury to make you look ruthless and overbearing. So if you send a demand letter, word it carefully to cast your patent owner as one who has been provoked to the last resort of litigation by the infringer's theft of the owner's invention.

Where you file your suit includes what court. While patent infringement is exclusively the jurisdiction of the federal district courts, 28 U.S.C. § 1338(a), other cases involving patents (such as an action to quiet title to a patent or a suit for patent license royalties) may need to be brought in the state court. An action for compensation for unauthorized use of a patent by the U.S. government can be brought only in the U.S. Claims Court, 28 U.S.C. § 1498. No separate action can be taken against the government's supplier in the district courts, *Western Electric Co. v. Hammond*, 135 F.2d 283 (1st Cir. 1943). Notably, no injunction against patent infringement is available against the U.S. government or its supplier.

Another consideration can be which defendant to sue first since patent litigation often presents multiple choices. If there are multiple independent infringers, the patent owner is not required to dissipate his resources by suing all of them simultaneously. The patent owner can select a target infringer and insulate itself against laches defenses by the others by giving them notice of the first suit and letting them know their turn will come later. *Vaupel Textilmaschinen KG v. Meccanica Euro Italia S.P.A.*, 944 F.2d 870 (Fed. Cir. 1991). If the infringers are related in a chain—for example, the U.S. manufacturer or importer of noninfringing items, a distributor, wholesalers, retailers, and an ultimate customer/user—any link in the chain is an infringer who can be sued. While the choice for the first to be sued may most commonly be the source highest in the chain, venue and tactical considerations can sometimes favor a downstream infringer in the infringing chain.

Whether to Demand a Jury

Always be careful to check your judge's past patent cases as there are a few federal judges who have a record of invalidating almost every patent that comes before them in bench trials. Another question is whether the patent owner should make a jury demand. Before 1982, most patent cases were tried to the bench. During the 1980s, the tide changed to the current situation in which more than 50 percent of patent cases that actually go to trial are tried before juries. The impetus for patent owners to shift to jury trials was the discovery that juries were much less likely than district judges to find a patented invention obvious and overturn the statutory presumption that a patent is valid. Jurors are also perceived to be willing to make damage awards that are significantly higher than are made by district judges who are viewed by many patent owners as having a parsimonious view of what constitutes a "reasonable" royalty or the quantum of lost profits.

Even so, there will still be occasions where a patent owner will choose not to make a jury demand. Examples would be where the judge who drew the complaint has previously tried and sustained the patent, or has a strongly propatent record of reported cases, or the defendant has "hometown" appeal against a patent owner that is out-of-state or is likely to be perceived by jurors as Goliath beating up on David. Another situation favoring a bench trial might be where the invention is one that, in hindsight, appears so deceptively simple that it would be more vulnerable to being underestimated by lay jurors than by a judge more nuanced in the burdens of proof and legal complexities, who could resolve whether an invention was obvious at the time it was made.

If you choose a jury, can it handle the case? My own experience has been that jurors are extremely conscientious and quite well able to understand issues of technology if those issues are explained clearly enough. Of course, a defendant usually has a greater interest than the patent owner in the jurors' understanding the technology for there to be much hope of them finding the invention obvious or the patent not infringed.

Discovery in a Patent Case

Discovery in patent cases can be expensive and time-consuming. A patent's national reach leads to disputes between litigants separated by great distances. Making an invention frequently involves many people, from conception through development to marketing. On the infringer's side, there can be a chain of people from copying to sales. There can be years between the acts surrounding the making of an invention and the time of trial. The documentation, created by many people in different places over a long period of time, is frequently extensive and hard to track down. So you must be imaginative, persistent, and economical in using the tools of discovery to develop the evidence needed for trial.

And discovery may have its own rewards—totally aside from the case itself. You learn many interesting things in discovery for patent lawsuits. I have traced the history of the first aluminum beer can and discovered a still surviving beer-filled can from the first-ever production run in this country in 1959. I have visited the last field of ramie—a tall, Asian hemp—growing in the United States, surviving wild in Florida more than 40 years after several of America's largest corporations walked away from their multimillion-dollar attempts to commercialize nature's strongest natural textile fiber. Anyone who thinks patent litigation lacks human interest has no appreciation for the fascinating human endeavors into which it reaches.

Confidentiality is usually a mutual concern of both sides in patent lawsuits. Discovery can reach technical and business information that each side wants to shield from its opponent and from the eyes of other competitors. This concern is accommodated, in most patent cases, by a protective order under Rule 26, Fed. R. Civ. P., often by stipulation. The order may provide, for example, that discovery information will not be used by the receiving party for purposes other than the lawsuit and is to be kept in confidence, with any confidential information filed with the court to be under seal. Sometimes a "Counsels' Eyes Only" confidentiality provision will be appropriate. Sometimes a confidentiality order may be necessary to protect the privacy of witnesses, particularly when medical inventions are involved. In one case, I had to depose nine women concerning breast-implant operations involving a patented breast prosthesis. Under a carefully drafted protective order, the depositions were taken in a way that got the key information on which I won the case while assuring the patients anonymity and lack of embarrassment.

The length, range, and frictions of discovery in patent cases often can be eased by trying liability and damages separately. Unless there has been a demand for a jury (which would cause the plaintiff and the court to resist bifurcation), the parties may be able to stipulate to an order under Rule 42(b), Fed. R. Civ. P., that infringement and validity will be tried first and damages will be left to a second trial if liability is established. The defendant will usually be the party to move for bifurcation, if agreement cannot be reached. Whether bifurcation will be granted is within the court's discretion—there is no shortage of reported cases coming down on either side of the bifurcation issue. A problem can remain even after bifurcation, if the patent owner intends to prove commercial success at the liability trial to support its position that the patented invention was not obvious. That will require discovery of the extent of the patent owner's sales of the patented product and the infringer's sales of its version.

Sometimes it is not the product but the method of creation that is patented. There are some method patent cases in which it can sometimes be helpful to obtain an order for an entry on land under Rule 34, Fed. R. Civ. P. The purpose is to inspect the details of the defendant's manufacturing process. If you do, take along a photographer and your expert witness so that you can gather enough evidence for trial. The expert can be very valuable in a plant inspection. Some years ago, in a case involving a food manufacturing process, my sharp-eyed expert saw that some of the pipe joints in the defendant's plant were suspiciously bright and shiny. That led to the discovery that the pipe runs had been changed around to a noninfringing arrangement for the day of inspection.

Like any complex case, organizing information for a patent trial can be a nightmare. It is, perhaps, a more serious problem in patent cases because of the unusually wide variety of defenses. I have been able to use a microcomputer effectively to keep track of discovery information and to sort it according to the issues of patent litigation in chronological format, or by other fields. L. Pretty, "Harnessing a Personal Computer to Win Cases," 69 *ABA J.* 1438 (1983). In recent years, I have used a commercially available program called "Summation"® in most of my cases and found it very effective.

Defenses Against Patent Liability

As the case develops in discovery, you will start to learn your adversary's defensive strategy, drawn from the wide range of defenses in patent cases. It sometimes comes as a surprise to laymen to learn that a patent validity issued by the U.S. Patent and Trademark Office can be struck down as invalid by a judge or jury on a variety of defensive grounds. These grounds start with the following statutory defenses:

- The defendant will deny infringement in most cases, asserting that its product or process does not come within any patent claim.
- The most frequently invoked invalidity defenses arise because of anticipation or obviousness, under 35 U.S.C. §§ 102 and 103, respectively, based on "prior art," a term used to denote earlier relevant devices, products, or processes. "Anticipation" means that the claimed invention is entirely found in a single, earlier, publicly known device or method. "Obviousness" means that the claimed invention would have been obvious from combining two or more known earlier devices or methods.
- Less frequently, the defendant will claim that your patent fails to meet the statute's requirements for patentability. For example, the defendant may claim that, under 35 U.S.C. § 101, the patent is invalid because it is for subject matter outside the classes of patentable subject matter or that the invention is not useful (which usually means that, as disclosed in the patent, it would not work).
- Other invalidity defenses (known as "statutory bar" defenses) invalidate the patent if the invention was placed in public use or on sale in this country more than a year before the application for the patent was filed.

There are also equitable defenses. One type is known as "inequitable conduct before the Patent Office." Its theory is that the patent should be invalidated because the patent owner concealed or misrepresented facts to the Patent and Trademark Office to secure the patent. Another line of equitable defenses, known as "patent misuse," is based on the theory that the court should withhold enforcement of the patent because the patent owner has acted in some improper manner in its commercial activities involving the patent, such as tying, price fixing, or package licensing. Laches and equitable estoppel are further equitable defenses available in patent cases.

Then there are technical defenses. The plaintiff's title to the patent may be defective, or an indispensable party—such as the exclusive licensor or license—may have been omitted. The defendant may assert that the patent is inadequate because it does not sufficiently teach how to practice the invention or that its patent claims are not definite enough to enable the public to understand what the patent covers. Other defenses go by such shorthand names as double patenting, misjoinder or nonjoinder of inventorship, and foreign filing without a license. You have to be ready to respond to any of them.

What Is a "Markman" Proceeding?

At this point, I must detour into the crucial subject of "patent claims" because much of what occurs in patent litigation can often be fathomed only when the concept of a "claim" is understood. At the end of a patent is at least one numbered statement called a claim. Each claim is a word picture of the invention defining what will be protected by a court in a way that distinguishes the invention from the closest previously known devices. A claim can be thought of, simplistically, as like a parts list. To decide whether a competitor's device infringes on your client's patent claim, you compare the claim with the device to see whether each part listed in the claim has a counterpart in the device, literally or equivalently. If so, infringement exists. If a claim element is wholly missing from the accused device, there is no infringement.

The other function of a patent claim is to distinguish the claimed invention from already known devices. An accused infringer will usually attack the validity of the patent claim. One way is to show that the claim covers a single device in the prior art, in which case the claim is said to be anticipated under 35 U.S.C. § 102(a). Another way is to show that the patent claim covers a combination that would have been obvious to an ordinarily skilled worker in the relevant art from combining different earlier devices at the time the invention was made. Each claim in a patent constitutes a separate invention under 35 U.S.C. § 282. Since most patents contain a range of claims from broad to narrow, it is possible for a broadly worded claim in a patent to be anticipated or obvious in view of the prior art relied on by the patent and therefore to be invalidated, whereas another more narrowly worded claim retains its validity over the same prior art.

In view of the central part in litigation played by patent claims, a major issue in many patent lawsuits involves construing the meaning to be given to a disputed term in a patent claim. For example, if a claim to a patented cake mix recites "an egg product" as one element of the mix, should that term be construed to require a constituent that is entirely natural egg, a constituent that has a majority of natural egg, or a constituent containing only a minor fraction of natural egg? Sometimes the meanings of all of the elements in a claim are so plain from the ordinary meaning of the English language, or from a definition in the patent specification, that no issue of claim construction needs to be resolved. More commonly, there will be at least one claim term that can be construed in different ways—a meaning advanced by the patent owner permitting the claim to be applied to the accused device for infringement and a more limited meaning advanced by the defendant that would avoid infringement. Where such a dispute exists, the correct construction of the claim can quite often be the determinative issue of the lawsuit.

Who should construe claims—the court or the jury—was definitely resolved as being a matter of law exclusively for the court in 1995. *Markman v. Westview Instruments*, 52 F.3d 967 (Fed. Cir. 1995), *aff'd* 116 S. Ct. 1384 (1996). As a result, it has now become common in patent litigation for the construction of disputed patent claims to be determined by the court in advance of trial in a so-called *Markman* hearing. Sometimes, if presented in the context of a motion for summary judgment of infringement or noninfringement, the *Markman* hearing can resolve the infringement issue. In other cases, the context of a *Markman* hearing may be for an order constructing a claim term to be given as a jury instruction at the trial. In that situation, the jurors can then apply the construction in the second step of the infringement analysis—determining if the accused device satisfies the properly construed claim.

Determining Infringement

As just mentioned, the determination of claim construction is an issue of law solely for the court. However, the second step of the infringement issue, applying the properly construed claims to the accused device, is a question of fact to be determined by the jury. If comparison of the properly construed claim to the accused device shows that there is literal satisfaction of every claim requirement, then infringement exists and that is the end of the inquiry. *Graver Tank & Mfg. Co. v. Linde Air Products Co.*, 339 U.S. 605 (1950).

Sometimes, however, there will be some semantic difference, between the words defining a claim element and its nearest counterpart in the claim, that avoids literal infringement. For example, the patent claim requires a "nail" as one element for joining two other elements, and the defendant uses a screw. In that event, the owner may be permitted a second chance to establish infringement by a rule of patent law called "the doctrine of equivalents." Infringement exists under the doctrine of equivalents if the patent owner can show that, despite the semantic difference that avoids literal infringement, there is no substantial difference between the device defined in the patent claim and the accused device. One formulation for analyzing the substantiality of the difference is to examine whether the accused device and the patented device (1) perform substantially the same function, (2) in substantially the same way, (3) to achieve the same result (sometimes called the "F-W-R test"). *Hilton Davis Chem Co. v. Warner-Jenkinson Co.*, 62 F.3d 1512 (Fed. Cir. 1995), *cert. granted* 116 S. Ct. 1014 (1996). The doctrine of equivalents law is currently in a state of judicial unsettlement, requiring close attention to the most recent precedents.

There is an important limitation on a patent owner's ability to rely on equivalents to compensate for lack of literal infringement, imposed by a countervailing rule called "prosecution history estoppel." This rule requires examination of the proceedings before the patent examiner, recorded in the publicly available patent prosecution file. That file will often reveal whether the patent owner made any changes to his claim or presented any arguments about its scope to obtain its allowance. If the patent owner surrendered an expansive interpretation of a patent claim in order to get the patent allowed, that decision should estop the patent holder from seeking to recapture in a later litigation the coverage it surrendered in the patent and trademark office to obtain the patent. *Mark I Mktg. Corp. v. R.R. Donnelley & Sons*, 66 F.3d 285 (Fed. Cir. 1995).

Jury Instructions and Special Interrogatories

As in any case, jury instructions will be needed. A problem for patent cases is that the judges often feel ill at ease in the unfamiliar territory of patent law and have a tendency to look first to the "canned" instruction of the circuit in which they sit. Since 1982, however, the regional circuits have been deprived of appellate jurisdiction over patent cases by the creation of a new appellate court with exclusive jurisdiction of all appeals from the district courts in cases arising under the patent laws, the U.S. Circuit Court of Appeals for the Federal Circuit based in Washington, D.C. Since the Federal Circuit seldom cites any of the old precedents of the regional circuits and is rarely reviewed itself by the Supreme Court, its jurisprudence should be looked to primarily in preparing jury instructions on patent issues. Most regional circuit jury instructions in patent cases now draw from Federal Circuit authority.

The Federal Circuit has issued opinions that favor submitting to the jurors special interrogatories on which the case is to be decided. Various sets of form interrogatories are available as a starting point for use in preparing a set for your case. *See* "Verdict Forms—A Peek Into The Black Box," Kornitsky and Martens, 23 *AIPLA Quarterly Journal*, No. 4, 617 (Fall 1995).

The Patent Trial

As trial approaches, the patent lawyer must focus on his trial planning and how to present complex questions of fact, rambling expert testimony, and myriad blueprints, diagrams, computer printouts, and the like to a jury composed of truck drivers, housewives, shopkeepers, and—maybe, if he is lucky—a high school physics teacher.

Advanced technology is not the sole preserve of patent lawsuits, and there are patent cases that involve technology well within a layman's general knowledge. Nonetheless, many patent cases do involve inventions beyond the level of technical knowledge possessed by laymen. Also, few federal judges have a scientific or engineering background, and many of them approach patent cases with less confidence than they do more familiar matters.

That means the patent trial lawyer has a delicate task. He must educate the judge or jurors well enough so that they feel comfortable with the technical principles necessary to find infringement and validity. Yet he must do so without creating a false illusion of simplicity that blurs the distinctions between the invention and the prior art.

There is a subjective character to the core issues in a patent trial of (1) obviousness of the patented invention and (2) equivalency of the infringing product to the patent claims. The relative persuasiveness and credibility of each party's witnesses can determine the outcome of many patent cases in which closely balanced facts on these issues would let the case go either way. For the patent owner, testimony on these issues often can be most effectively provided by the inventor. Because of the inherent interest of his role, he is well placed to explain the technology, describe the evolution of his invention, show how it differs from what existed before, and point out how the defendant's product embodies his patented invention.

Unfortunately, a common problem for the patent owner's lawyer is the inventor who is unable to carry this central role because of unavailability, poor ability to express himself, or other failings as a witness. The central role must then be shifted to a technical expert witness. In choosing a technical expert in an advanced field, I usually like to use an expert who has significant hands-on experience in the industrial application of the relevant technology rather than a pure theoretician. A good place to look for technical experts is a university because professors may have status in the local community, good explaining skills learned from teaching experience, and hands-on experience gained in the workplace or as a consultant. Find the expert early. A good expert can help early in discovery in analyzing technical issues affecting infringement and the prior art and in making suggestions.

The patent law expert is another type of special witness. His testimony goes to the significance of actions taken in the examination of the application for the patent, the training of patent examiners, the search for facilities available to them, and other fact issues bearing on the patent. A patent expert is usually needed in a jury trial, if only to guide the jurors through the patent file. In a trial before a judge who is experienced in patent cases, it is sometimes better to dispense with a patent expert. Some judges view a patent expert as no more than a talking brief for the side that calls him.

A third type is the accounting expert, who may be needed to testify about lost profits or reasonable royalties.

Choosing a defense expert is not easier. If the designer of the accused device did not know about the patented device, he may be the best one to explain that the product was nothing more than what was obvious to those in the field. But when there was some actual copying, choose a less-tainted, outside expert witness, such as a university professor.

Patent cases are tailor-made for interesting exhibits. Large, colorful graphics can literally decide your case before a jury. I like:

- Professionally prepared color graphics showing the accused device and other important technical items.
- 40-by-60-inch photo-enlargements of the drawings of the patent-in-suit, mounted on foam board and colored by hand.
- Drawings of principal items of the prior art.
- Retyped versions of the patent claims in issue.
- Drawings or photographs of the defendant's product.
- Diagrams of the steps of defendant's process.
- Time charts showing important dates in sequence.
- Educational exhibits that illustrate technical subjects that would be hard to grasp from oral testimony alone.

Overhead projectors and transparencies made by electrostatic copying machines are helpful for displaying exhibits that are not of sufficient importance to justify the expense of enlargements.

It is becoming quite common nowadays in patent cases to use various electronic image display systems for displaying exhibits, animations, or portions of video depositions to jurors and the court. One common type of system stores the images on a video disk and uses a bar code and wand technology to locate and display described images on the screen. Another system, called Elmo, simply uses a TV scanner, analogous to an overhead projector, to display on the video screen any image placed under the scanner, and it has a zoom-in capability.

Physical exhibits can include prototypes of the invention and its current commercial embodiments. The contrast between the homemade nature of an inventor's first devices and the commercial version on the market brings home the extent of his achievement. Other physical exhibits usually will include the infringing product and, when they help, machines and products from the prior art. If the infringer has made a look-alike copy of the patent owner's product, showing it helps to convince a jury that the inventor has been wronged.

There must, inevitably, be documentary exhibits. Usually they will include the patent itself, the patent office file, the inventor's notebooks, the infringer's project memoranda and drawings, summaries showing the commercial success of the patented invention, and documentation of the infringer's sales.

Do not overdocument the trial and lose the excitement and pace of your plaintiff's case in a morass of paper.

An important problem for the patent owner's lawyer is overcoming the insidious effect of hindsight on the issue of obviousness. The patent statute, 35 U.S.C. § 103, requires that obviousness be resolved by the test of what would have been obvious to a person of ordinary skill in the art at the time that the invention was made. A judge or juror at trial has had the solution to a technical problem made obvious to him by reading the answer provided by the inventor's patent. He may not recognize the difficulty in appreciating why others, with their eyes unopened by hindsight, did not find it obvious to make the invention when the inventor did years before the trial.

To offset the power of hindsight, the patent owner's lawyer must bring the state of technology as it was five, ten, or 15 years ago back to life in the courtroom. The inventor's early models and tools; the inventor's false starts, insights, and eventual success; his wife's account of the help she provided in his tests and experiments; faded newspapers or trade journals of the time describing reaction to the invention in its field; the testimony of elderly men who remember the impact that the inventor's contribution had on their trade at the time; experts who said his invention would never work—these are the tools of a powerful trial presentation.

Damages

Twenty years ago the patent owner who recovered damages would be relegated most often to the modest return of a "reasonable royalty" assessed by judges whose idea of "reasonable" hovered with depressing frequency at about the level of 5 percent of selling price. This was inadequate recompense to a patent owner who might have lost sales of a product on which he would have obtained profits at a marginal rate of 30 percent or more.

Those skinflint days are gone. In most patent cases now, damages are sought—and often granted—on the higher basis of the patent owner's own "lost profits" calculated by the incremental profit. On top of this, additional lost-profits damages have been awarded for price erosion on the sales the patent owner did achieve, where the patent owner was forced to reduce the selling price to meet the infringer's competition. Lost profits have also been expanded beyond the patented product itself to an entire, larger product of which the patented product formed an indispensable part, under what is called "the entire market value rule." Lost profits have also been awarded to compensate for profits lost on unpatented "convoyed" products that the patent owner would normally obtain in conjunction with a sale of the patented product, e.g., special camera accessories usable only with the patent owner's patented camera. For a convenient source of discussion and citation to the various precedents supporting these various lost-profits theories of product damages, see "Proof of Lost Profits Damages Following *Rit-Hite v. Kelley*," Brown, *AIPLA Quarterly Journal*, Vol. 23, No. 4, p. 557 (Fall 1995).

Even when a patent owner cannot establish his right to a lost-profits measure of recovery and must fall back to a "reasonable royalty," juries are usually perceived as more likely than not to choose a figure of at least 10 percent—better than the more Scroogelike judges.

Increase of damages, up to three times, is available in an "exceptional case" under 35 U.S.C. § 284, although an increase of damages is the exception rather than the norm. To justify increased damages, the patent owner must show that the infringement was "willful"—a conclusion that usually involves two factors. One factor is showing that the defendants' infringement was the result of copying the patented product rather than independently developing it. The other factor is showing that, after the defendant learned of the potential infringement of the patent by its product, it failed to obtain a competent opinion of counsel that the defendant would have no liability either because its product was noninfringing or the patent was invalid. The importance of an opinion of counsel to refute willfulness creates a dilemma for the defendant about whether to produce the opinion and waive its privilege or to refuse to produce the opinion and risk an increase of damages if the case goes against it. To relieve the defendant of having to waive privilege before its liability has been established, the Federal Circuit has recommended bifurcation of damages from liability, *Quantum Corp. v. Tandon Corp.*, 940 F.2d 642 (Fed. Cir. 1991).

Injunctions

In many patent lawsuits the most important remedy for the patent owner is a permanent injunction for the remaining term of the patent following a successful adjudication of validity and infringement. The right to a permanent injunction under a patent, once the case has been won, is not normally limited by a weighing of equitable factors but is absolute. The only exception to the granting of a permanent injunction to a winning patent owner has been in a few rare cases where a severe health or safety hazard would be imposed on the public. Whether the permanent injunction will be entered following judgment, or will be stayed until the outcome of an appeal, is within the trial court's discretion.

Preliminary injunctions are also available in patent litigation. Before the advent of the Federal Circuit in 1982, preliminary injunctions were rarely granted in patent cases. The Federal Circuit eliminated some judicially created doctrines that had accounted for the exceptional difficulty in obtaining preliminary injunctions, and it has held that preliminary injunctions in patent cases are judged by the same principles as preliminary injunctions in any other civil litigation. *High Tech Medical Instrumentation v. New Image Indus.*, 49 F.3d 1551 (Fed. Cir. 1995). Nowadays, a number of successful preliminary injunction patent cases are reported every year.

Conclusion

Imagination, drama, and America's fascination with the efforts of its inventors throughout history provide strong emotional hooks for the successful trial of a patent owner's claim. Maybe it is time for you to join the fray.

Planning Fees Fights

Christopher T. Lutz

If a contest were held to determine the kind of lawsuit that puts the parties in the sourest frames of mind, lawyers' fees litigation would come in first. It is easy to understand why.

If you are a defense lawyer, there are few things more difficult than telling your client that, for the privilege of losing or reaching a grudging settlement, he must pay the very lawyers who have been a source of irritation for years. Plaintiffs' counsel, for their part, see fees litigation as an indignity and sometimes an insult. For them, a fees battle delays already delayed compensation and creates a gauntlet of criticism and second-guessing that few defense lawyers face.

These attitudes can make fees litigation bitter. A defendant who was temperate toward the plaintiffs in the merits litigation may want to take off the gloves with the plaintiffs' lawyers. Plaintiffs' counsel may conduct fees litigation like a full-scale crusade. Parties who settle the merits sometimes litigate fees for years.

Emotion can be a good thing in litigation. Small amounts of anger can give arguments a punch they would otherwise lack. But emotion by the bucketful—a standard dose in fees fights—can be harmful. It blocks clear thinking. Too much emotional engagement in lawyers' fees litigation keeps the participants from soundly planning their course in the controversy.

Careful thinking is especially important in conducting discovery in fees fights. Fees discovery has features and pitfalls different from those usually encountered in merits discovery.

In planning the parry and thrust of a fees duel, first get your bearings. Think about what the merits litigation was like. Was it a bitter fight or

---

Christopher T. Lutz, a former editor-in-chief of LITIGATION, *is a partner in Steptoe & Johnson L.L.P. in Washington, D.C.*

relatively decorous? Was it a civil rights case or a commercial litigation? The tone and the substance of a case are important clues to the course of a fees battle.

If defense conduct was tough, even obstreperous, or if plaintiffs' lawyers have vindicated fundamental rights of thousands, dogged, detailed resistance to a fees request may be unwise. On the other hand, if the suit was a purely commercial battle between two corporations, plaintiffs' counsel should expect steely-eyed scrutiny of their request.

As important as the nature of the case is the nature of the judge. Normally, lawyers do far too much handicapping and psychoanalysis of judges. These efforts are usually a waste of time or, worse, highly misleading. But it is useful to review your judge's past fees opinions and other evidence of his attitude toward fee awards. The reason is that most people—judges particularly—have strong feelings about fees litigation.

Many judges' feelings about fees litigation seem like the sentiments of Justice Brennan in a related context: They view such disputes as "one of the least socially productive types of litigation imaginable." *Hensley v. Eckerhart*, 461 U.S. 424, 442 (1983). It is not hard to understand why. Fully occupied in deciding pressing criminal and civil matters, the last thing most judges want is a battle between lawyers about how much plaintiffs' counsel should be paid. If you think you have been pressured to settle in lawsuits on the merits, wait until you try fees litigation.

But not all judges share this blend of impatience and hostility toward fees litigation. Some seem to like it. These are the judges you want to know about in advance. Such enthusiasts fall into two polar groups. Some react to fees petitions in the manner of an accountant who feels stiffed by his own lawyers. They, or their clerks, review page upon page of time and expense records with a jeweler's eye. They ferret out vague time descriptions, duplicate efforts, and unreasonable copying charges. That kind of scrutiny seems motivated by a belief that petitioning lawyers—either in general or in a particular case—invariably pad their records and requests.

Far different are those judges who wade hip-deep into fees litigation because of a concern that plaintiffs' lawyers may be underpaid. These judges believe, often deeply, in the policies underlying antitrust, securities, and antidiscrimination laws, and they think that plaintiffs' counsel, who act as private attorneys general, should be very well paid to enforce those laws. Such attitudes usually result in less quibbling about details, a greater inclination to grant a substantial award, and impatience with anything, including discovery, that might delay petitioning counsels' payday.

After reviewing the nature of the case and sizing up the judge, consider the stakes. If you have represented the plaintiffs, you should already know what you are going to ask for. If you are defense counsel, the plaintiffs may have already told you what they expect. If not, look at your own bills to your client. They are a very rough guide to what your opponent may seek.

As in most disputes, the size of the likely request is a good measure of the intensity of the fight and the resources you should expect to commit to it. If the request is less than $50,000, settle. If the request is under $100,000, settle almost all the time. It is simply not worth anyone's time to wage full-scale war over such sums. Even if you think such litigation is time well spent, the court will not.

All rules have exceptions, and these observations on settlement are themselves no exception. If you represent a defendant, there are a few circumstances in which you should vigorously resist the fees' application: (1) when plaintiffs' counsel want to be paid even though they lost, or got almost nothing; (2) when the requested fees, though small, exceed the money recovery by a factor of two or more; (3) when your client wants to fight on principle and there are good-faith grounds for doing so; and (4) when the petitioning lawyers have sued your client in other cases in which fees might be awarded. In the latter circumstance, your fight over a small fee request will inevitably affect rates and other issues in the larger battle.

A special comment may be in order about fee requests that significantly exceed the underlying money recovery. The Supreme Court has held that, so long as the hours compensated and rates awarded are reasonable, a fee award may be proper even though it dwarfs the money recovery. *City of Riverside v. Rivera*, 477 U.S. 561 (1986). This may be especially true in civil rights cases, where much of the value of the relief lies in injunctive remedies. However, the Court has also held that a nominal money recovery ($1) justifies denial of any fee. *Farrar v. Hobby* 506 U.S. 103 (1992). In any event, disproportionate fee requests can be red flags for two reasons. First, they will surely inflame the defendant. Second, and more significantly, their size may be a symptom of unreasonable rates, padded time claims, and similar defects.

If a fee request is large, and will likely lead to extended litigation, what next? If you are a defense lawyer, have a heart-to-heart talk with your client. The news will not be good, but your life will be easier later if you deliver it now: The fees litigation could take months, maybe years. It will likely require discovery, principally document requests and depositions. There could be a long hearing.

The whole thing will cost money. The client will have to pay your fees, whether he wins or loses the fees battle. If resistance to the fee request proves unsuccessful, your client will have to pay not only the fees sought but also the fees incurred by plaintiffs' counsel in conducting the fees litigation.

Fees on Fees

The "fees on fees" potential of lawyers' fees litigation cannot be overemphasized. It affects most strategic considerations, and it complicates settlement analysis. The defendant's potential liability, and therefore the appropriate settlement level, can become ever-receding horizons. No matter how fast and long the parties run, they never approach the end of the road. It is like owing money to a loan shark: The longer you take to pay, the more you owe, until you owe more interest—or fees on fees—than principal.

Both sides have one more decision before embarking on discovery. Should they retain special counsel for the fees litigation? Ninety-five percent of the time, from a defense perspective, the answer is no. The lawyers who litigated the merits will understand the suit—and the efforts of plaintiffs' counsel—in a way outside counsel cannot without a lot of catching up, which would be expensive and time-consuming.

But there are certain cases in which defendants should consider retaining fees counsel. Ask yourself these questions: Has the defendant's lawyer so botched the litigation that he has lost his client's confidence? Has he done a good, tough job, but, in the process, utterly alienated the judge? Will the fees battle be so complex that special expertise in fees law might be required? If the answer to any of these questions is yes, and the fees request is likely to be large, a defendant should consider hiring new lawyers.

For the petitioning lawyers, retention of separate counsel is more common, though far from universal. Aside from the adage that the lawyer who represents himself has a fool for a client, there are often other sound reasons to get new counsel.

Petitioning counsel usually have to testify—live or by affidavit—in support of a fees petition. In this situation, the canons of ethics may require separate representation. There is also a practical consideration: An argument for big fees often involves lavish praise of plaintiffs' counsel and their litigation handiwork. It is often more comfortable—and seems less vain—to have someone else deliver the panegyric.

Two warnings for plaintiffs' counsel contemplating a new fees lawyer: First, not all judges will view another lawyer as a reasonable expense, especially if the amount in dispute is small. If you win, you can probably get the defendant to pay your lawyer, but that is not guaranteed.

Second, and more important, be absolutely certain the lawyer you pick, aside from knowing fees law, knows something about litigation under the law that produced the merits dispute. The tone and approach of securities litigation, antitrust disputes, and employment discrimination cases differ. These differences are reflected in the fees disputes that grow out of each. If your fees lawyer does not appreciate the distinctions, he may try to sell the wrong thing in the wrong way.

Before diving into discovery, think again about settlement. By now, you should know the stakes. Plaintiffs' counsel have probably filed their petition, and, even if they have not, they have probably announced what they will seek. Now is the time to try to resolve the dispute. It really is only money. Rarely should it be a matter of principle.

Even if you do not want to talk settlement, the court will probably force you to. Most judges do not want to hold a fees hearing, and the pressure to force a settlement can be intense.

Here is a favorite technique: The court calls a chambers conference on fees matters. He looks at the parties and says: "Don't come back until you settle." He then issues an order that no fees discovery may be conducted until the parties have had a reasonable time to discuss settlement. This may last for months. Especially for plaintiffs' counsel, a little delay can sharply focus the mind on compromise.

Even if a complete settlement is impossible, try to settle pieces of the problem. Fees litigation is usually susceptible to piecemeal resolution. Fees requests are based on several discrete elements: expenses incurred; hours worked; hourly rates claimed; and a multiplier. In theory, any of these elements can be settled without compromising anybody's position on the others. If your real dispute is over hourly rates, try not to spend a lot of time fighting about copying charges or time-sheet legibility. By settling in pieces, you can focus the dispute on the real points of conflict.

Not all fees differences can be amicably resolved, though. If settlement is impossible, how do you plan for discovery? First, consider whether you *can* conduct discovery.

Judges who do not like fees litigation like fees discovery even less. They can do many things to restrict it. An order suspending discovery to allow settlement talks is just one restriction you may face. Another approach the judge may take is to set a hearing or final briefing date 30 or 60 days after the formal fees petition is filed. In that little time, not much discovery is possible. Finally, courts often sustain objections to especially probing inquiries. You can try to conduct discovery, but you may not get anything in the face of resistance.

But why worry about discovery? Who needs it? If a petition with supporting documentation is filed, what more does the defendant need? And why would the plaintiffs ever need discovery from the defendant?

For a defendant, the answer is that a petition is often uninformative. While a petition should be intelligible and contain sufficient supporting detail, some counsel unfortunately take a notice-pleading approach to fees requests: Expenses may be uncategorized and reduced to a single figure. Lawyers' hours may be cumulated, and not broken down by either lawyer or activity. In such cases, a defendant has three choices: accept the request on faith; resist it as facially insufficient; or conduct discovery to see if the conclusory demand can be supported by a detailed accounting.

Few defendants choose the first course, and none should. An uninformative fees petition is very often a sign that detailed supporting documentation is not available. Time and expenses may have been reconstructed or invented. Hourly rates may have been plucked from the air. You need to ask to know.

Defendants rarely take the second course—attacking the petition on its face—because that is a big risk. You may think the petition is unsatisfactory, but the court may disagree. If this happens, and you have had no discovery, you are stuck.

Even with very detailed petitions, there are usually good reasons for a defendant to conduct discovery. For example, petitioning counsel may intend to present witnesses or affidavits to show what great lawyers they are. Who are the witnesses? What will they say?

The petition may say that $225 is an appropriate rate for lawyers' services. What is that based on? Counsel may want the court to double their usual hourly rate to reward them for the great result they say they got. Will they present any evidence to show that this multiplier is justified? What will it be? None of these questions can be answered well without discovery.

There are also reasons for petitioning counsel to conduct fees-related discovery. Defendants may present rebuttal witnesses, affidavits, or other evidence. Plaintiffs will often need discovery into this material. And plaintiffs' counsel can use requests for admissions to narrow the points in dispute if the defendant unreasonably wants to fight everything.

Another kind of discovery that plaintiffs sometimes seek in fees litigation is more controversial. It might be called reciprocal discovery. It might also be called embarrassment discovery.

Suppose you represent a defendant opposing a $1 million fees request as excessive. You open your mail. Out drops a set of interrogatories from plaintiffs' counsel asking your client for detailed information on all fees and expenses paid in defense of the underlying suit. Through a fog of disbelief, you see the envelope also contains a document request demanding that you produce copies of all your bills.

Most defense lawyers' reaction is predictable: outrage. Such discovery, they think, pries into the minute details of the financial relationship between them and their clients. It seems to compromise the lawyer-client relationship. And their first instincts tell them that the information plaintiffs are after is irrelevant to boot.

But petitioning counsel have an argument for the discoverability of such material: If the question is what level of fees is reasonable for handling a lawsuit, what better measure is there than the amount that the defendant invested in the case? Surely, plaintiffs would say, how much the defendant spent to litigate the same facts and issues is highly germane. How can $1 million be too much if the defendant spent $4 million?

Despite defense outrage, such arguments sometimes win the day. The propriety of reciprocal discovery varies depending on the component of a fees request that it concerns. The important point is that such counterpunching is possible. A similar risk exists in almost any kind of dispute, but, in fees battles, boomerang discovery can seek out especially sensitive information: what defense counsel charge, what they collect, what they make, and the like. If you are a defense lawyer planning a no-holds-barred discovery program, do not forget the kinds of questions you and your client might have to answer in return.

The specific pattern of discovery in a fees battle depends on the contested issues. Remember that fee requests are made of four main elements: expenses, lawyer and paralegal hours, hourly rates, and a multiplier. Each of these elements can be the subject of discovery.

Take expenses first. Litigating about the costs and expenses incurred by plaintiffs' counsel is one of the duller things a human being can do. Reviewing messenger charges, plane tickets, and copying slips is no fun. More important, from a defense standpoint, it is often uneconomic: If you spend five paralegal hours (at $40 per hour) finding, and one lawyer hour (at $100 per hour) writing about, a dubious $250 copying bill, your client has lost money.

For a defendant, a gradual approach to getting expense information is advisable. First, look at the petition. Add up all the expense items. Compare the total with the expenses your client incurred. If plaintiffs ask for what your clients spent or less, it is unlikely you will be able to chip much off the request. Extensive discovery probably will not make sense. As a check, look at the categories of expenses claimed. If plaintiffs want to be paid for the same kinds of things your client paid for, again extensive reduction of the expense bill is unlikely.

A defendant seeking expense information now has a hard question to answer: How much further should he go?

At least go far enough to be sure there is documentary support for the expenses claimed and that no individual items are scandalously high. You may be able to do much of this with the petition itself. A competently assembled petition will often include attachments listing expenses item-by-item. If the petition lacks such information and it is not produced voluntarily, a defendant should go after it through discovery.

But what discovery device do you use? The logical answer would seem to be interrogatories or requests for production of documents, but Rules 33(a) and 34(a) provide that those discovery devices may be directed only to parties. Are the petitioning lawyers—who almost certainly have the information you need—"parties"? As a technical matter, probably not, even though the fees petition is really their request.

In statutory fees cases, the relevant statutory language usually provides reasonable fees and costs to "prevailing parties" in the underlying litigation. But, like it or not, petitioning counsel *are* the parties for all practical purposes in a fees litigation. Whatever the statutory fiction, it is usually *not* the case that the award goes to the plaintiff, who passes it along to the lawyers. This blurring of who the real party is has caused courts some concern. *See, e.g., Rainsbarger v. Columbia Glass and Window Co.*, 600 F. Supp. 299, 301 (W.D. Mo. 1984). In practice, though, fees petitions are routinely filed by the lawyers themselves, with little or no reference to their clients.

So what does the uncertainty over whether petitioning lawyers are "parties" mean in the conduct of fees discovery? A defense lawyer who wants expense details and records and who wants to be technically correct has a choice: Either serve a Rule 45 subpoena *duces tecum* on the lawyers or direct a document request or interrogatories to the plaintiffs. The first approach will work, but it is cumbersome, unless it prompts voluntary production. The second route—service on the plaintiff—should also work, and also often leads to voluntary production.

Unfortunately, occasionally the plaintiff's response to a Rule 34 document request will be, "I don't know the answers to your questions and I don't have the stuff you want. Maybe my lawyer knows." Again, the defendant has two alternatives: Serve a Rule 45 subpoena on the lawyers, or, sometimes better still, get the court involved, by way of a motion to compel or to strike the plaintiffs' request for expenses (if that is what the discovery concerned). Such a motion can be a good way to show the judge that petitioning counsel are playing games. Plaintiffs' counsel decidedly do not want the judge to see them in that light. As a result, if there really are expense records to produce, the game playing usually stops short of a court order.

The compelling practical incentives for petitioning counsel to provide back-up information mean that defense counsel rarely have to worry about who the "parties" are in planning discovery. But that issue can be important when *petitioning* counsel want to conduct discovery.

Defendants and their lawyers do not have to be as concerned about whether their discovery positions bother the judge. Because many judges are skeptical of attempts to secure fees information from defense counsel, objections to discovery of defendants' expenses are often sustained. So petitioning counsel should remember that the defendant is a party but its lawyers are not. The form of discovery must vary depending on who the target is.

Having decided on what form of discovery to use, you need to figure out what information to go after. If you represent a defendant, the first step is to ask for an itemized breakdown of expenses and the supporting invoices and other original documents. If you get a list, you can scan it to determine what underlying material you want to examine. Often, though, there will not be a list. Having described expenses in broad categories, petitioning counsel will rely on Rule 33(c), or its equivalent, and invite you to examine the records.

If you get such an invitation, what you do depends on the number and location of the documents. If the expenses claimed are small and the records are few and nearby, have a paralegal spend an hour or two examining them. But if there are thousands of expense records, do not spend weeks with them. Sample instead. Look at every third or sixth item, and look particularly at records supporting very big expenditures.

If the records seem to be in order, stop. If you have grounds for contesting significant expense claims, you will know it by now. There may be a dubious charge lurking in the mountain of paper, but it will likely cost more to find it than you will save.

Expense discovery by petitioning counsel is far less common. It is most likely to occur when the defendant has argued that the plaintiff's expenses in general were too high, or that the plaintiff spent too much on certain projects. If the defendant bridles at paying 15 cents per page for copying, for example, plaintiff may want to know what defense counsel's firm charges.

Such reciprocal discovery ordinarily produces a flurry of objections. Besides snorts of indignation and claims of privilege and confidentiality, the defendant's main argument will be based on relevance considerations. Defendants and plaintiffs do different things, they say; there is no necessary relationship between the amounts that the two sides spend. And, some defendants may argue, what defendants and their lawyers voluntarily decide to spend may be more than the "reasonable" expenses an adverse party can be forced to reimburse.

Such arguments have met with mixed success. Whether discovery of the defendant's expenses is allowed will depend less on the law than on the judge's attitude toward fees litigation.

After disbursements, the next major element of a fees petition is the number of hours that the lawyers and paralegals spent on the case. Petitioning counsel will say the time spent was reasonable. Defendants will look for inefficiency, duplication, excess, and invented time.

Like disputes over costs, arguing about time claims can be dull and expensive. Settlement is usually advisable. When the parties cannot get together on the time that plaintiffs' lawyers reasonably spent on the case, the battle over hours is usually hard fought. And, once the fighting gets going, truces are less common on this front.

Judges tend to get more deeply involved in reviewing the reasonableness of hours claimed. The subject is slightly more interesting than the propriety of a $57 messenger charge. Judges often have strong feelings about what lawyers ought to do and how much time it should take them to do it. For their part, petitioning counsel often have a strong personal interest in justifying the reasonableness of work they have done.

Because of the parties' stronger feelings and the judge's greater interest, the parties usually exchange a considerable amount of information on hours claimed. For defense counsel, the task is much as it is with expenses.

Begin with the petition. See if it gives you enough detail to make judgments about the kind of work performed and the efficiency of plaintiffs' staffing. Compare the hours and tasks listed with what you did.

Use Rule 45 subpoenas, if necessary, to get a more detailed breakdown of lawyers' and paralegals' hours. Try to get the original time sheets, so you can sample them and satisfy yourself that they exist and appear to be contemporaneous. As always, how much discovery the defendant conducts has to be sensibly related to how much is at stake and how plausible the hours claimed seem to be.

The issue of hours claimed can be usefully explored in depositions of petitioning counsel. If the time records look fishy—showing, for example, a single 30-hour entry for three days of work, or 50 hours of undifferentiated legal research or client consultation—it may be useful to quiz petitioning counsel about how they kept their time records. If they testify that they "reconstructed" or estimated their time, probing examination is the only effective way to understand how they did it, if that *can* be understood at all.

If you want to conduct a deposition of petitioning counsel, remember these points: First, use a Rule 45 subpoena. Second, remember that deposing a lawyer can be frustrating—he will know the case as well as you do, is likely to be well schooled in the techniques of deposition testimony, and may raise a cloud of privilege objections. Before you conduct a deposition, reflect on whether you are likely to get much. Do not do it simply for the pleasure of grilling—or yelling at—your adversary.

Finally, and most important, judges can be very impatient with fees depositions of lawyers. They may quash Rule 45 subpoenas and sustain privilege or work product objections. Judges sometimes give aid and comfort to plaintiffs' lawyers, it seems, not because plaintiffs' objections are analytically sound, but because of a general feeling that, at some point, enough is enough.

Petitioning counsel frequently attempt discovery related to time claims. Sometimes they get it. The logic of such discovery is much as it was for expenses. If the defendant complains that the 600 hours that plaintiffs' counsel says he spent on the case is too much, for example, it might be relevant to determine whether defendant's lawyers spent 2,000 hours defending the same suit. Some courts have agreed with this logic. *See, e.g., Blower v. Lawyers Coop. Publishing Co.*, 526 F. Supp. 1324, 1326 (W.D.N.Y. 1981).

Other courts may reach the contrary conclusion, reasoning that defendants and plaintiffs do different things, and so even the time spent on similar work may properly be quite disparate. For example, most plaintiffs invest less time drafting interrogatories than defendants do answering them. *See Ohio Sealy Mattress Mfr. Co. v. Ohio Sealy Inc.*, 776 F.2d 646, 659 (7th Cir. 1985); *Johnson v. University College of the Univ. of Ala.*, 706 F.2d 1205, 1208 (11th Cir.), cert. denied, 464 U.S. 994 (1983).

Also, some courts, rightly or wrongly, seem to regard discovery of defendants' counsel's time records as harassment and excess. They believe they can judge the efficiency of plaintiffs' efforts based on the petition and what they know about the litigation. As a result, defense objections on grounds of the work product rule, the attorney-client privilege, and irrelevance, though sometimes just barely plausible, may be sustained.

Discovery on the question of hourly rates is more often sought and allowed, though there are limits. Usually, petitioning counsel just state a series of hourly rates for lawyers and legal assistants. There is normally little or no explanation. Among other things, defense counsel will want to know: How were the rates selected? How do they compare with what petitioning counsel charge, or collect from, other clients? What evidence will counsel present to show that the rates are appropriate charges in the market? What is the relevant market?

The need for defense discovery on such points is obvious. Usually it is permitted. The first step is easy: See if there are reported decisions on fees awards to your adversaries. If the cases are old, be sure to adjust the rates for inflation.

Next, a good way to begin formal discovery on rates—providing opposing counsel do not quibble—is with interrogatories. At minimum, ask who will testify, by affidavit or in person, that the rates claimed are appropriate. Think about deposing those witnesses, but remember that, because they may qualify as experts, you may have to dance the procedural minuet required by Rule 26(b)(4). Remember also that, because rate witnesses are often prominent local lawyers, they may be frustrating to question. Try to find out if petitioning counsel expect to rely on a survey of prevailing rates in the market; if they do, request a copy and consider deposing whoever did the survey. If plaintiffs' counsel themselves will be the only sources of rate testimony, consider deposing them on that topic (as well as hours claimed).

Attempting discovery of further information on the rates that plaintiffs' lawyers have requested can lead to extended battles, because that information usually concerns the internal finances and management of their law firm. Say plaintiffs want $150 per hour for a particular lawyer's time, but you think he normally bills only $110. Can you ask for copies of bills to other clients? If you got them, would that be enough? Not all lawyers collect what they bill. Can you ask for canceled checks from clients? The list of documents and other information requested could be extended almost indefinitely and ever deeper into the recesses of law firm management.

The only reliable answers to the questions about how much defendants can poke around behind petitioning counsel's claimed hourly rates are: *Yes*, you can ask for such information; *yes*, it is all sufficiently relevant to be discoverable; but *no*, a court will not compel answers to all such questions if petitioning counsel resist. At some point, the judge will conclude that, though the material is somewhat relevant, he can determine a proper rate without further scrutiny of otherwise private financial matters. How far a defense lawyer should test the judge's tolerance in this area depends on the stakes and the tenor of the dispute.

What about discovery of hourly rate information from defense counsel? This can be an especially touchy question. Some courts simply bar it. *See, e.g., Samuel v. University of Pittsburgh*, 80 F.R.D. 293 (W.D. Pa. 1978). But others permit it, at least to a limited extent.

The argument for such discovery is by now familiar. If the defendant paid $175 per hour to a lawyer with ten years of experience to defend the case, why should the defendant not pay the same rate to comparably experienced plaintiffs' counsel?

Whether such information is discoverable will depend mostly on how much information petitioning counsel want and where defense counsel are located. If all that is sought is a list of rates, that discovery may be permitted. If petitioning counsel have demanded copies of defendant's bills, records of payments, or depositions of defense counsel, discovery will probably not be compelled. And if the court and petitioning counsel are in Dallas, but defense counsel are in New York City, it will be hard to convince the judge that what the defendants paid their lawyers has any bearing on the rate prevailing in Dallas. Overarching all these points is the court's attitude. Some judges believe they can decide an appropriate rate for plaintiffs' counsel without knowing anything about what defense counsel charge.

The final topic for fees discovery—and often the most disputed—is the multiplier. A few words of background are needed on this point.

The Multiplier

Instead of simply seeking the product of rates times hours, most petitions multiply that product—the "lodestar"—by a number larger than one. A 1.25 multiplier thus produces a 25 percent premium over market rates. A 3.0 multiplier—and some have been sanctioned, though rarely—awards a 200 percent premium to plaintiffs' counsel. Multipliers are what produce awards of $300 to $600 per hour worked. Though the Supreme Court has held that multipliers should be reserved for "rare" and "exceptional" cases, *Pennsylvania v. Delaware Valley Citizens' Council for Clean Air*, 478 U.S. 546 (1986), *rev'd on reh'g*, 107 S. Ct. 3078 (1987), they are routinely sought.

Discovery on multipliers for years revolved around the two justifications most often given for their appropriateness. One of those justifications—which the Supreme Court has now recognized as valid—is the result. *See Blum v. Stenson*, 465 U.S. 886 (1984). If a lawyer achieves a very special result —"exceptional" relief in the Court's words—perhaps accomplishing more than a lawyer at his hourly rate level might be expected to achieve, a bonus may be appropriate.

A second, and more hotly debated, ground for a multiplier—risk—is now largely a historical curiosity in fee-shifting cases. Plaintiffs' counsel advocated a risk-based multiplier because, when they lose, they receive no fees. They said that the laws require that they receive the same average income as defense counsel, who assertedly are paid in every case, win or lose. To prevent plaintiffs' work from being less attractive economically than defense practice, said the advocates of risk-based premiums, there has to be an enhancement of fee awards to account for the time spent on unsuccessful cases where plaintiffs' counsel receive nothing.

Many defendants believed such reasoning was oversimplified and had legal shortcomings, but many courts had accepted it in some form. The Supreme Court first addressed the question in an unclear set of opinions. However, by 1992 the Court was explicit; "risk" enhancement is not permitted in fee-shifting cases. *Burlington v. Dague*, 505 U.S. 557 (1992).

In discovery on multipliers, a defendant's first task is to determine why plaintiffs believe their lawyers are entitled to any premium at all. If this is not spelled out in a brief accompanying the petition (and usually it will be), the rationale can be discovered through interrogatories and, rarely, depositions of petitioning counsel. Almost always, you will quickly learn that plaintiffs' counsel think that the relief achieved justifies a multiplier. Typically, other factors—such as delay in payment and preclusion of other work—will also be mentioned.

Discovery on the success justification for enhancement is fairly simple. Besides generously praising their own work and deprecating results in past cases, petitioning counsel will likely rely on just a few kinds of evidence: their own testimony; testimonials from other lawyers and experts; and, occasionally, testimony from economists about the economic value of the injunctive portions of the relief.

If defense lawyers believe that evidence like this might justify a multiplier, the answer is depositions. Serve a Rule 45 subpoena on petitioning counsel and find out why they think the result is exceptional. How does it compare with the results in other specific cases? What unusual legal hurdles did lead counsel face?

Notice the depositions of noneconomist experts (after complying with Rule 26(b)(4)) and probe their familiarity with the details of the case. Determine how much they know about the issues, the evidence, and the plaintiffs' strengths and weaknesses. Find out what they think "exceptional" means, and determine whether—especially if they are plaintiffs' counsel themselves—their testimony has been shaped by their economic self-interest.

Deposing economists who purport to value nonmonetary relief can be entertaining. Plaintiffs' lawyers—especially those who handle civil rights litigation—present such testimony because they fear some judges may give them insufficient credit for securing complex injunctive relief, and may look exclusively at the money payout. Some judges have been impressed by such appraisal evidence. *See, e.g., Arenson v. Board of Trade,*

372 F. Supp. 1349 (N.D. Ill. 1974). Others have not. *See, e.g., EEOC v. Burlington Northern Inc.,* 618 F. Supp. 1046, 1059–60 (N.D. Ill. 1985), *aff'd in part, rev'd in part, sub nom, In re Burlington Northern, Inc. Employment Practices Litigation,* 810 F.2d 601 (7th Cir. 1986), *cert. denied,* 108 S. Ct. 82 (1987). The main aim in deposing relief appraisal experts is, not surprisingly, to determine how the appraisal was done and what assumptions it is based on.

Besides trying to find errors and illogic, the goal of such a deposition should be to show that the expert's analysis is alien to the subject of the suit. This may be difficult in antitrust and securities suits, which are awash in economic analysis. But it can be productive in civil rights suits.

In a large employment discrimination class action, for example, plaintiffs' money valuation of hiring quotas in a consent decree depended on how many people the defendant would hire in the coming years. The parties differed sharply about this issue. Plaintiffs presented an expert who had constructed an econometric model to predict hiring over the course of six years and to value the settlement.

The expert's prediction for the first year exceeded the actual hiring by 1,000 percent. This inaccuracy did not faze the expert. He insisted that his model was as good as anything the defendant itself had to say about its future hiring needs. He said at the deposition he could meaningfully forecast hiring without knowing anything about the defendant's business. In fact, he testified, he needed to know only two things to forecast hiring for the particular defendant: the year and the Gross National Product. When asked how he could account for all the variables affecting the defendant's industry and business, he said basically just this: "Add a quadratic term to the equation."

The judge, who was used to thinking of hiring levels in terms of people and business needs, seemed unimpressed. He gave no weight to a valuation exercise based on hiring predictions based on the year, the GNP, and a "quadratic term."

Even though the multiplier is usually a hotly contested issue, there is rarely any occasion for plaintiffs' counsel to conduct discovery on this issue. There just is not much to ask. Neither the defendant nor its lawyers will have much useful information about the degree of success achieved. If you ask them, they will probably say that any settlement was "appropriate" and will simply observe that they disagree with the propriety of any judgment they resisted.

Because there is little benefit to discovery by petitioning counsel on the issue of the multiplier to be applied, they should almost never conduct such discovery. In fact, petitioning counsel will have their hands—and minds—full with the developing case law, which seems to pose ever-higher barriers to the use of multipliers for any reason.

A final thought: Discussing the planning of fees litigation discovery does not mean that I necessarily endorse extensive fees discovery in all cases. Justice Brennan had it right when he observed that many aspects of lawyers' fees litigation are not very "socially productive." Discovery is no exception.

If you can settle the controversy, or if you can litigate it without discovery, do so. There will, however, be occasions when discovery, sometimes extended, is unavoidable. If you encounter such a case, do everything you can to make discovery crisp, efficient, and quick. Target your inquiries. And don't let your frustration, or your client's bitterness, get the upper hand. As in all kinds of litigation, control is essential. If you do not impose it in fees litigation, the court will.

Representing a Victim of Employment Discrimination

Barry L. Goldstein

You earned your stripes in litigation combat five years ago. Your career is a litany of litigation's varieties: the claims and defenses of two dozen businesses, your share of consumers' complaints, and a trio of contested divorces. You followed some of these cases on to the state supreme court and your federal circuit court, winning and losing along the way.

But this morning brings a case the likes of which you have only heard: the claim of a young African-American worker who was fired and did not get a promotion he thinks he deserved. More than likely, the case comes to you by way of a very Senior Partner who received a call from his old law school buddy, now a federal judge. The pro se plaintiff came before the judge, and the judge knew there was a better way.

This client's story stirs a sense of justice in you, and you think the story will appeal to a judge and jury.

The question right now is not the character or appeal of the case, but whether you can succeed in a complex and intricate legal arena unknown to you. There is no doubt that your experience as a litigator will benefit your client. It is also true that as a result of fee provisions in the fair employment laws, you may well turn a profit for the firm, with or without payment from the client.

My advice as a regular and enthusiastic practitioner in employment discrimination is: Go For It.

You can count on the support of your litigation experience and considerably broaden and deepen the quality, if not the satisfaction, of it by taking up what the Supreme Court has called the mantle of the "private attorney general." *Newman v. Piggie Park Enterprises, Inc.*, 390 U.S. 400 (1968).

Barry L. Goldstein is a partner in Saperstein, Goldstein, Demchak & Baller, Oakland, California. Linda Dardarian contributed to the editing of this chapter.

There is no doubt that this litigation arena requires decision making each step along the way, and requires matching preceding steps and decisions with succeeding steps and decisions.

It requires an intricate and subtle dance.

The federal employment laws, such as Title VII of the Civil Rights Act of 1964, 42 U.S.C. § 2000e *et seq.* and the 1991 amendments thereto, and the Civil Rights Act of 1866, 42 U.S.C. § 1981, are "separate, distinct and independent." *Johnson v. Railway Express Agency, Inc.*, 421 U.S. 454 (1975). They run parallel to each other: They do not dovetail, but sometimes overlap, and you can move them in harness for the benefit of your client. You will not necessarily sacrifice one cause of action by electing another. Your client may allege many causes of action and an aggregate of potential remedies sufficient to raise the stakes and force the boss to defend on different fronts. To get the benefit of those overlapping remedies, you must meet precise procedural and timeliness requirements for each cause or remedy. Tolling or other equitable arguments will not fill this bill.

The fair employment laws provide a potential plaintiff with a collection of claims. The best first step is to create an inventory of them, noting the following by each:

1. Procedural and time requirements;
2. Standard of proof;
3. Potential forums; and
4. Available remedies.

As the positive thinkers say, visualize the case on a long-term basis, from the pleading possibilities through strategy, on toward realization of the remedy and its satisfaction.

First, you must deal with the administrative agency and overcome initial procedural hurdles. A plaintiff must file administrative charges with the existing state or local fair employment agency and with the Equal Employment Opportunity Commission (EEOC) before bringing a federal action under Title VII (for job discrimination based on race, color, gender, national origin, or religion); under the Age Discrimination in Employment Act (for job discrimination against people over 40); or the Equal Pay Act (which bars paying women less than men for performing substantially the same work). To ensure that the local and federal filing requirements are met, the plaintiff should personally file with both the local fair employment agency and the EEOC.

The EEOC charge must be filed within a certain period—for example, under Title VII—180 days from the alleged illegal act. By filing first with a state or local government fair employment agency, the period for filing with the EEOC may be extended to 300 days.

Once the charge is filed with the EEOC, the plaintiff is required to wait at least 180 days before bringing a lawsuit. This allows the agency to investigate, determine, and attempt to resolve the charge. After the expiration of the waiting period, the plaintiff requests a "right to sue" letter from the EEOC. Having filed a charge and waited the required period, your client has an absolute right to file the lawsuit even if the EEOC or the state agency did not investigate or process the charge, or if the agency found that there was no "reasonable cause" to believe that the law has been violated.

Some practitioners ignore the administrative process, thinking that their representation will truly commence with the filing of a complaint. This is a serious mistake. The administrative stage provides the best opportunity to avoid the procedural wrangles that profit defendants and delay the plaintiffs' day in court—or deny it altogether.

The charge should include a broad statement of all employment practices your client may want to litigate. For example, it should include not just the discharge that brought the client to you, but also the denial of a promotion or the harassment before the client was fired. If appropriate, assert that your client was not alone in suffering the discrimination, that what happened was not an isolated incident but part of a continuing pattern. In *Bazemore v. Friday*, 478 U.S. 385, 395 (1986), the Supreme Court stated, "[e]ach week's pay check that delivers less to a black than to a similarly situated white is a wrong." Your client may recover under Title VII even though the discriminatory pattern began years before a charge or suit was filed, even before Title VII became law.

A broad, clear charge warns of potential and significant relief through a possible class action, and denies the defense argument that a court should limit the federal action because the claims raised are not "like or related to" those presented to the administrative agency.

You must monitor the administrative process to prevent the officer from paring down your charge. Because about 80,000 charges are filed with the EEOC each year, there is a strong bureaucratic tendency to push charges to resolution quickly. The philosophy is: The more narrow the charge, the less work—and the more likely a voluntary settlement. Unfortunately, the settlement often will have only nuisance value.

If the boss wants to settle, do not get excited yet. His or her desire does not have much to do with the quality of the case or your stature as a lawyer.

The truth is that there is a bias toward settlement, and it principally works to the benefit of the employer.

The people who run the system—whether union or company, whether grievance negotiators or administrative agency officers—will pressure you and your client to settle early. The perceptive defense lawyer will make an offer at the "going rate" for a minimal settlement early in the process to thwart development of an effective class action or jury trial lawsuit. Recognize the speedy resolution bias of the process and how the defendant's lawyer takes advantage of the bias, and advise your client accordingly.

The investigation will need your spurring. Commonly, there is only "desk investigation," which means that stock questions are asked and stock answers are given. Yet, private counsel can prod some investigators to prepare penetrating questions, request detailed documentation, and, at the "fact-finding" conference attended by both parties, permit the plaintiff's lawyer to question the company's managers. Since a charging party has access to the investigation record before filing suit, the administrative process offers inexpensive discovery and an opportunity to preview the merits of the lawsuit.

Under Title VII, a plaintiff may receive back pay covering the two-year period before the administrative charge is filed. Note that the filing of a Title VII charge does not toll the running of the statute of limitations for a claim brought under another act such as 42 U.S.C. § 1981, one of the Reconstruction Civil Rights Acts, which the Supreme Court has interpreted as prohibiting racial discrimination in employment. The applicable statute of limitations for a § 1981 case is determined by state law. Many state statutes provide more than a two-year recovery period and, accordingly, if a plaintiff waits to file his or her § 1981 lawsuit until after the completion of the Title VII administrative process, the recovery period for back pay may be reduced. Therefore, consider filing a federal lawsuit under § 1981 when the Title VII administrative charge is filed and perhaps, as suggested by the Supreme Court in *Johnson v. Railway Express Agency, Inc.*, request the court to stay the suit until the administrative process is completed.

There are two principal standards of proof for fair employment laws. Under the "disparate treatment" standard, the plaintiff proves discriminatory motive, that is, that the employer purposefully denied the promotion to the African-American or female because of race or gender. You may show discriminatory purpose by indirect or circumstantial evidence, for example, by a difference in the application of rules or by statistical proof.

Under the "disparate impact" standard, the plaintiff demonstrates that an employment selection procedure, such as a written or physical test or a height or educational requirement, excludes a disproportionate percentage of the protected group. If you show this disproportionate impact, the burden of proof shifts to the employer using the selection procedure. The employer must show that the practice is "job related" or, in other words, that the procedure produces better job performance.

A plaintiff may establish a Title VII violation under either the treatment or the impact theory. But your client receives a greater remedy when malicious intent is proved than when an inadvertent impact claim is shown. The 1991 amendments to Title VII award each victim of intentional discrimination up to $300,000 in compensatory damages and $300,000 in punitive damages (depending upon the size of the employer); these caps do not apply to or limit the scope of relief available under § 1981. 42 U.S.C. § 1981a(b)(4). Title VII also gives broad discretion to the district court to impose affirmative and injunctive relief to end discrimination practices and to remedy the consequences of these practices.

In addition to compensatory and punitive damages, monetary relief under Title VII includes lost "back pay," which may include all actual earnings lost, such as pension, vacation benefits, and interest, for the two years before the charge was filed. As a general rule, injunctive relief is restricted by the so-called "rightful place" principle, because the courts have decided that it is improper to "bump" white job incumbents even if they hold those jobs as a result of racial discrimination. This means that a discrimination victim is not entitled to immediate reinstatement, but must wait until a vacancy occurs.

Finding the Forum

There are alternative or additional claims to Title VII that give the victim of employment discrimination remedies somewhat comparable to successful tort or contract claims. The Federal Equal Pay Act and Age Discrimination in Employment Act provide for a limited amount of liquidated damages. The reliance on § 1981 or pendent state claims may provide an effective jurisdictional basis for claiming significant sums, including compensatory and punitive damages. To establish a violation of § 1981 or a state claim for compensatory damages, however, you must prove "disparate treatment."

By choosing to expand beyond a straight Title VII disparate impact claim, you may change forums or triers of fact from federal to state and from judge to jury. It is a decision that requires looking ahead carefully.

Traditionally, civil rights lawyers have steered away from juries and toward the federal court because of that court's role in the history of civil rights enforcement. However, that is not a hard-and-fast approach anymore. Analyze this case as you would a case in your regular practice, selecting the forum and trier of fact best suited for the client. The 1991 amendments to Title VII provide that if the plaintiff seeks compensatory or punitive damages for intentional discrimination, *any* party may demand a jury trial. Thus, if you want to stick with tradition and have your case heard by a federal judge, request only equitable relief.

Alternatively, you may take a flier: Request compensatory and punitive damages under Title VII and 42 U.S.C. § 1981. If the defendants do not make a timely request for a jury, you have the forum, trier of fact, and remedy package you want. The defense bar does not fall asleep often, but it might this time.

A combination of factors has led some lawyers to file fair employment cases before juries or in state courts, or both.

First, the potential for extensive, uncapped legal damages available under federal or state causes of action other than Title VII is a strong incentive to put your money on a jury.

Second, fair employment plaintiffs have had some notable successes before juries, and not just before predominantly African-American juries. If the plaintiff is an elderly worker and age discrimination is a factor, take advantage of the truth that we all grow old. Juries may respond favorably to a story of a big company or a union unfairly treating a struggling worker, whether the worker is African-American, Hispanic, or female.

Third, not every federal judge is receptive to civil rights claims. Not long ago, a colleague who has practiced law for years in the South tried an individual race discrimination case before a jury. The jury awarded more than $100,000. The lawyer says that he has never won a race case before that presiding federal judge, and he believes that he would not have won this case either without a jury.

For similar reasons, some lawyers have brought cases in state court. In some jurisdictions, the staff jury panels or judges are more sympathetic to plaintiffs' civil rights cases than are the area's federal panels or judges. Moreover, federal appellate courts are increasingly reversing favorable lower court judgments for civil rights plaintiffs. Consider the track record of the area's federal and state appellate courts in choosing your forum.

Of course, other considerations not particularly related to fair employment cases, such as docket congestion or availability of discovery, may influence your choice of forum.

Tie your discovery plan to trial or settlement strategy as tightly as you can. In fair employment cases, the boss controls the relevant records and thus the objective proof. At the same time, he or she will raise cries that your demands are unduly burdensome or irrelevant.

You can expose defense protestations for the smoke screens that they are through efforts that start at the beginning of your representation. By using the administrative process to get copies of company documents, attending interviews of company managers, and exploring different channels of possible discovery, you can lay the groundwork for justifying more extensive discovery.

You have the opportunity to get the first jump in discovery; take it. Consider filing carefully focused interrogatories or a request for production of documents as soon as local rules of court allow. A broad set of first interrogatories regarding all relevant employment selections is less useful than a request for company documents (including those kept in computer-readable form); examples of each type of document; and a description or copies, if written, of all the company's relevant employment policies. If the documents are not self-explanatory after the initial request, follow up with a deposition limited to obtaining a description of the documents, what the codes mean, how the information is recorded, and how it is used.

This approach reaps genuine benefits. First, you are not depending on interrogatory answers prepared by the defense lawyer, nor are you faced with reviewing an unnecessarily large mass of paper in a windowless room pursuant to Fed. R. Civ. P. 33(d). When defense protests sound, you can show the court that you are proceeding along the least burdensome route for gathering the relevant information.

Often you will discover one document or computer file that has significant information and substantially reduces the time and cost of obtaining and analyzing information.

The human drama and harm caused by discrimination is submerged at a trial focused on statistics, job patterns, and document fights. Confusion and complexity will work against your client, bore the jury, and may convince the judge to avoid any involvement in this mud wrestle. Develop discovery in a manner that simplifies the trial and moves it quickly past detailed explanations of job structure and employment patterns directly to the critical issues.

A thorough analysis of the company's documents and careful interviews with your client and other workers will prepare you to depose company personnel managers, supervisors, and others. The documents and the depositions spawn requests for admission of facts or stipulations that put your case in sharp focus, and perhaps establish a prima facie case.

You should know the relevant operation of the employer's workplace better than the employer's witnesses or lawyer's advisers. This is not hard to do.

The personnel manager relies on the contract or policy manual and what supervisors tell her; usually she is not familiar with the personnel records or the "common law" of how the company runs. Learn how the company works from the perspective of the worker, the supervisor, the personnel manager, the personnel documents—and most important—from the contract or manual that says how it should work. This knowledge will provide opportunities during trial to demonstrate that the system operates inconsistently and unfairly, and that the managers do not know what really occurs at the local level.

It is critical to discover the nondiscriminatory reason the company will use. The Supreme Court emphasized in *Texas Dept. of Community Affairs v. Burdine*, 450 U.S. 248 (1981), that, although substantial relevant evidence is controlled by the defendant, the "liberal discovery rules" should permit "the plaintiff meriting relief to demonstrate intentional discrimination." Use this rationale to lock the defendant into its justification. The company can easily use a legitimate reason for a selection decision: not enough education, not the right kind of experience. But it is just as easy for you to undercut the company's stated reason by using factual examples. An affirmative answer (which you ensure by having a copy of the relevant personnel record) to the question, "Isn't it true that your supervisor selected Joe Jones for the same position two years ago, even though Jones had less experience than the plaintiff?" devastates a defense based on the plaintiff's lack of experience.

Your case also may depend on expert testimony. A labor economist determines the availability of qualified minority or female workers in the labor market, an industrial psychologist analyzes whether a selection procedure that disproportionately excludes the protected class is used appropriately, and a statistician calculates and describes the significance of employment patterns. Consider whether an expert is required early in the case and, if so, consult experts as soon as possible. Frequently, if an expert is retained late in the process, you will discover (when there is little time to change direction) that the wrong emphasis or theory has been developed or that you have failed to uncover important information.

For example, a statistician's testimony that the average African-American employee's salary is significantly lower than the average white employee's salary may support a discrimination claim until the employer presents evidence, which the plaintiff neither discovered nor scrutinized before trial, that the salary disparity is due to differences in relevant job experience.

Many defendants depose the plaintiff as soon as allowed by local rule or Rule 26(d). That deposition will be the most crucial event of the litigation. By striking early, defendants often catch the plaintiff unprepared. Begin preparing your client for this deposition at the first interview, well before the filing.

The Supreme Court has issued six opinions on the burden and order of proof in fair employment cases brought by an individual. A thread running through them is that the plaintiff may establish a prima facie case of intentional discrimination by inferential or circumstantial evidence, as overt evidence is unlikely. Therefore, "the burden of establishing a prima facie case of disparate treatment is not onerous," the Court wrote in *Texas Dept. of Community Affairs v. Burdine*, 450 U.S. 248 (1981).

A Prima Facie Case

The Court indicated in *McDonnell Douglas Corp. v. Green*, 411 U.S. 792 (1973), its first opinion on the issue, that a plaintiff establishes a prima facie case when he or she proves four points:

1. that he or she belongs to a protected class;
2. that he or she applied and was qualified for a job for which the employer was seeking workers;
3. that he or she was rejected for employment; and
4. that, after the plaintiff's rejection, the position remained open and the employer continued to seek applicants from persons with the plaintiff's qualifications.

The Supreme Court's use of circumstantial evidence is a guide for establishing a prima facie case, not a mold into which the factual circumstances of every case must fit. You should also convey to the judge or jury why the Court established this minimal standard for the prima facie case. Given the prevalence of racial discrimination and Congress's determination to end it with a broad fair employment law, the Court deemed that a plaintiff has established a prima facie case once he or she has demonstrated at least that the rejection did not result from the two most common legitimate reasons, lack of a job vacancy or lack of the necessary job qualifications.

When the prima facie case is established in a disparate treatment case, the defendant has the burden to produce evidence that "articulates" a "legitimate nondiscriminatory reason" for rejecting the plaintiff, according to *Texas Dept. of Community Affairs* and *St. Mary's Honor Center v. Hicks*. If the defendant offers such evidence, then the plaintiff must present evidence showing that the reason is a pretext to mask unlawful discrimination. The plaintiff may show pretext by establishing that the employer's proffered reason was not the real reason or the entire reason for the employment decision.

The burden of proof never shifts in an individual disparate treatment case. Once all the evidence is submitted, the question for the trier of fact is whether the employer intentionally discriminated.

Add "Something Else"

What this means to your trial strategy is that your prima facie case is easy to establish, but it is very fragile. Build into the trial strategy the prima facie case plus "something else." The something else can be evidence of historical discriminatory practices that have ceased in name but not effect, incidents of insensitivity or hostility toward minorities or women, or statistical evidence showing marked disparity between the promotion of minorities and whites or males and females.

The prima facie case will get the merits to the judge or jury, but the something else will convince the trier of fact to rule for the plaintiff. In one particular case, a white city employee testified that he had overheard a supervisor state to another employee, "I finally got accomplished what I've been trying to do a long time. We fired the nigger." The jury ruled for the plaintiff, but the district court entered a judgment notwithstanding the verdict because the employer had introduced evidence that the plaintiff had wrongfully used city equipment to improve his home. In reversing and reinstating the jury verdict, the appellate court expressly relied upon the testimony about the supervisor's candid comment. *Abasiekong v. City of Shelby*, 744 F.2d 1055 (4th Cir. 1984).

Of course, the critical evidence often is less dramatic. Supervisors sometimes embellish their testimony with factual assertions that careful discovery may show to be wrong or misleading. In one case, a supervisor asserted that he had expressly directed that social workers not take files home. In a civil service proceeding held several years earlier, however, the same supervisor had testified that social workers were not prohibited from taking files home in order to catch up on their work. The inconsistency in this testimony, which was not essential to the employer's case, discredited the supervisor, undercut the proffered nondiscriminatory reason, and led to a jury verdict for the plaintiff.

Anecdotal testimony brings cold numbers to life and the order of witnesses puts that life into perspective.

Follow the bumbling presentation of a company supervisor with an earnest, well-spoken plaintiff or a minority or female employee who works in a similar situation. The search for this juxtaposition of evidence should commence early in the case preparation.

The testimony of an African-American worker and white supervisor about the operation of the seniority system in a foundry is a good example. The African-American worker had learned the machinist trade in the army, worked as a supervisor in installations throughout the Pacific, and had received an army certification as a machinist. In returning to the plant, he was placed in a job category that did not allow for promotion to machinist positions. The white supervisor entered the plant straight from high school as a trainee with no previous machinist experience. During his training, the African-American worker showed him many of the tricks of the trade. The seniority system permitted the white worker, but not the African-American worker, to advance as he learned the job. The contrasting careers of the two workers showed the irrationality of the system and led the trier of fact to conclude that the seniority system was created and maintained with an intent to discriminate.

Let us assume you have tried the fair employment case and won. Now you file an application for lawyers' fees. You should have considered fees from the start of the representation, for lawyers' fees are recovered for work performed during the administrative agency process.

If you are to recover fair and reasonable fees, keep careful records of your time and the work performed. Many lawyers, especially those who work on a contingency basis, are not in the record-keeping habit and find their compensable hours substantially reduced because they lack record proof. A lawyer who fails to keep contemporaneous records risks losing a significant amount of his or her entitlement to fees.

Remedying Sexual Harassment: A Primer

Michael B. Reuben and Isaac M. Zucker

Anita Hill and Clarence Thomas. Many have debated what did or didn't happen between them, but no one can deny that Professor Hill's testimony before the Senate Judiciary Committee elevated public awareness of sexual harassment in the workplace (much as the O.J. Simpson case focused attention on domestic violence). In a sense, though, sexual harassment was already on Congress's agenda. While Professor Hill and Justice Thomas were telling their respective stories to the Judiciary Committee, Congress was busy debating the Civil Rights Act of 1991, the most significant civil rights legislation since the enactment of Title VII in 1964.

Title VII has long applied to sexual harassment claims. But before the 1991 Act, Title VII claimants could get only a bench trial and could seek only back pay and job reinstatement. The 1991 Act let plaintiffs tell their story to a jury. And it allowed them to ask jurors for compensatory and punitive damages (subject to a cap that varies with the size of the employer, up to a maximum of $300,000).

These changes, coupled with a spate of state statutes and local ordinances providing remedies for sexual harassment (e.g., Cal. Gov't Code § 12940 (West 1993); 8 N.Y. City Charter and Code § 502), have inspired a boom in sexual harassment litigation. Unfortunately, as with any newly popular cause of action, the medley of meritorious suits is liberally sprinkled with questionable claims. Some are simply frivolous; others are little more than strike suits. As a result, many employers are quickly growing suspicious of every claim of sexual harassment.

Employers are confused about how to respond to employees' complaints of harassment, and recent court decisions have not helped mat-

Michael B. Reuben is a partner in the New York firm of Gordon Altman Butowsky Weitzen Shalov & Wein and an associate editor of LITIGATION. *Isaac M. Zucker is of counsel at Koenigsberg & Genova in New York City.*

ters. Courts have yet to define the outer boundaries of an employer's liability under Title VII. In a recent opinion, the Second Circuit held that an employer may be liable for a supervisor's acts of sexual harassment even though the employer took corrective action by relieving the supervisor of authority over the employee and subsequently firing the supervisor. *See Karibian v. Columbia University*, 14 F.3d 773 (2d Cir. 1994). Employers may be pardoned for wondering whether they've become strictly liable for any harassment that occurs in the workplace.

Sexual harassment is a grave problem and deserves serious attention—a point that can get lost in the rush of plaintiffs and their lawyers seeking to exploit this latest litigation bonanza.

First, the legal underpinnings. Title VII prohibits discrimination in employment on the basis of sex. 42 U.S.C. § 2000e-2 (1981). Under applicable regulations of the Equal Employment Opportunity Commission (EEOC), discrimination on the basis of sex includes sexual harassment. *See* 29 C.F.R. § 1604.11. Harassment generally falls into one of two categories: "quid pro quo," in which an employer/supervisor demands sexual favors in exchange for compensation, advancement, or even just keeping the job; and "hostile environment," which the Supreme Court has stated exists "when the workplace is permeated with 'discriminatory intimidation, ridicule, and insult,' that is 'sufficiently severe or pervasive to alter the conditions of the victim's employment.'" *Harris v. Forklift Sys. Inc.*, 114 S. Ct. 367, 370 (1993). *See also* 29 C.F.R. § 1604.11(a).

Problems of Proof

Proof or disproof of quid pro quo harassment can be difficult, because, almost by definition, it generally occurs in private between two people. Frequently, though, it is not an isolated incident. Someone in a position to demand sex in return for employment rewards is likely to have done so more than once. While a plaintiff may not be able to corroborate the specific incident she has reported, she has a good chance of establishing a pattern of similar behavior toward other employees.

Harassment by hostile environment covers a broad range of behavior and may well involve the kind of group participation that makes it easier to prove. For example, in *Carr v. Allison Gas Turbine Division*, 1994 WL 387091 (7th Cir. July 26, 1994), plaintiff's co-workers displayed pornographic materials in the office, placed plaintiff's hands on their bodies in a sexually suggestive manner, and often made lewd suggestions in her presence. It was not difficult for the court to determine that the plaintiff had been the victim of sexual harassment.

Until recently, courts in hostile environment cases have focused on whether the plaintiff has actually suffered psychological harm. In *Harris v. Forklift Systems, Inc.*, 114 S. Ct. 367, 371 (1993), however, the Court held that "[s]uch an inquiry may needlessly focus the fact-finder's attention on concrete psychological harm, an element Title VII does not require." According to *Harris*, as long as the working environment "would reasonably be perceived, and is perceived, as hostile or abusive, there is no need for it to also be psychologically injurious." *Id.*

Courts have traditionally applied different standards in determining liability where the alleged harasser is a supervisor as opposed to a coworker. In "co-worker cases" the Sixth Circuit has held that the plaintiff must prove "that the employer, through its agents or supervisory personnel, knew or should have known of the charged sexual harassment and failed to implement prompt and appropriate corrective action." *Rabidue v. Osceola Refining Co.*, 805 F.2d 611 (6th Cir. 1986). The court specifically stated that the "knew or should have known" standard applies *only* to co-worker cases. In "supervisor cases," by contrast, the Sixth Circuit has held that the plaintiff must prove that the supervisor's action fell within the scope of the supervisor's employment or that the harassing actions were *foreseeable. See Kaufman v. Allied Signal, Inc., Autolite Div.*, 970 F.2d 178 (6th Cir. 1991).

Another developing area is employer liability for acts of sexual harassment by nonemployees. EEOC regulations provide that an employer may "be responsible for the acts of nonemployees in the workplace, where the employer (or its agents or supervisory employees) knows or should have known of the conduct and fails to take immediate and appropriate corrective action." 29 C.F.R. § 1604.11(e). The regulations further provide that in reviewing such cases the EEOC "will consider the extent of the employer's control and any other legal responsibility which the employer may have with respect to the conduct of such nonemployees." *Id.*

In at least one case, the EEOC has upheld a claim for "third-party harassment." As reported in a 1984 opinion, a waitress complained to her employer, a restaurant owner, that four male patrons had grabbed at and propositioned her. Witnesses later confirmed the waitress's story, but the restaurant owner advised her that the patrons were his friends and meant no harm. A few days later, the waitress told the restaurant owner that she had consulted a lawyer. He fired her. The EEOC found reasonable cause to believe that the restaurant owner had violated Title VII when he discharged a waitress almost immediately following her complaint of being sexually harassed by four male patrons. *See* EEOC Decision No. 84-3, 1984 EEOC LEXIS 3 (Feb. 16, 1984).

We are aware of, and are currently acting as counsel for the respondent in, a case in which an employee is attempting to press a novel third-party harassment claim. In 1989, an employee of a New York City hotel was allegedly touched and propositioned by a hotel guest; when she complained to her supervisor, the hotel took corrective action, even though the guest denied the incident. Then, in early 1990, the hotel fired the employee for insubordination and poor work performance. The employee responded by filing a claim against the hotel with the New

York State Division of Human Rights (NYSDHR) alleging sexual harassment and discrimination based on sex. The thrust of the employee's claim was that the hotel terminated her employment to protect an alleged relationship with the guest. The NYSDHR proceedings are still pending.

What is the best remedy for sexual harassment? Ask any doctor how to avoid a heart attack, and the answer will probably be something like, "Eat right and exercise." Preventive care works for sexual harassment, too. If done correctly, it helps protect an employer from liability, and it also discourages behavior that may cause liability.

Every employer should adopt an anti-sexual harassment policy. The policy should be posted, published in any employee handbook, distributed to every current employee, and included in the materials given to new employees at every level, including top management. Model policies are available from various employment service organizations as well as the American Bar Association. The ABA model is a good example and can be adapted to meet the needs of most employers. According to the ABA's Commission on Women in the Profession, which drafted the ABA model policy, a comprehensive sexual harassment policy includes the following:

1. A strong statement on the employer's philosophy concerning sexual harassment;
2. A clearly articulated definition of sexual harassment, which includes examples of behavior constituting verbal and physical sexual harassment;
3. Identification of individuals covered under the policy;
4. Procedures to be followed in response to sexual harassment complaints, including guidelines to ensure confidentiality and protect complainants from retaliation;
5. A statement of disciplinary consequences;
6. An explanation of the appeals process;
7. A mechanism for implementing and monitoring the policy;
8. Educational and training programs, regularly repeated; and
9. A commitment to act *sua sponte* against known harassers rather than to wait for complaints.

Promulgating a policy is a good start, but it is usually not enough. Employers should also hold mandatory seminars or training sessions on sexual harassment for all employees. For one thing, such sessions let everyone know that an employer is serious about its anti-sexual harassment policy. Just as important, many people remain genuinely ignorant about what constitutes harassment in the workplace. Some still believe, for example, that repeatedly importuning a reluctant fellow employee for a date is innocent behavior. (It isn't, and even when the two employees are of equal authority, such conduct may form the basis of a hostile environment claim.) Laying out ground rules so that employees know what they can and can't do helps avoid trouble in the future.

Employers should form a committee on sexual harassment and empower it to investigate all claims. The committee's membership should be as diverse as possible to maximize the likelihood that an aggrieved employee will find a member with whom he or she feels comfortable. A committee composed solely of men, or solely of very senior management, is unlikely to encourage many of the most likely targets of harassment to report their problems.

A committee is no good unless employees know about it. The existence, purpose, membership and procedures of the committee should be publicized as part of the anti-sexual harassment policy. Update and republish the policy every time there's a change in the composition of the committee, and at regular intervals in any case.

The committee must investigate *every* complaint, no matter how improbable it may seem. It is far easier and less painful to investigate thoroughly what turns out to be a frivolous complaint than to ignore a claim and risk a later finding that the employer knew of the behavior in question and allowed it to continue. If the multimillion-dollar punitive damage verdict against Baker & MacKenzie in the *Weeks* case taught us anything, it is that juries are offended by employers who appear to have looked the other way while an alleged harasser plied his trade.

The committee must be able to protect its confidentiality. Many sexual harassment victims are reluctant to come forward within the company, whether through fear of reprisal or simple embarrassment. They will be even more reluctant if they fear that the details of their complaint will be bandied about the office. Employees must be assured that, apart from confronting the alleged harasser and interviewing witnesses, the committee will keep the complaint confidential.

Interviewing the Parties

Although you must interview the alleged harasser, it is imperative to separate him from all other aspects of the investigation, especially if the complaint is against a member of senior management. People who are used to exercising broad authority over a company's activities may feel fully entitled to involve themselves in the committee's inquiries. Allowing them to do so will taint the investigation and open the employer to charges of a whitewash.

Besides interviewing the complainant and the alleged harasser, the committee should interview any witnesses to any of the events complained of. Witnesses should be advised that there is an investigation pending, and no more. However, because the very questions will probably tip off interviewees to the subject of the investigation, they must be firmly advised that the investigation is confidential and that failure to maintain confidentiality may result in disciplinary measures.

The committee should maintain a record of each interview. This not only facilitates review of the complete record when all interviews have been finished, but it also serves as evidence that the committee fulfilled its obligation to conduct a thorough investigation. If the employer is later accused of ignoring a sexual harassment complaint, that evidence could be crucial.

Although no one should sacrifice accuracy and thoroughness for the sake of speed, the investigation should be completed as quickly as possible. The longer it drags on, the more likely the complainant may conclude that she isn't being taken seriously and decide to seek a remedy outside the company. This is especially so if the complainant has already retained a lawyer. (More and more often, they do.)

Sometimes an employee will approach a committee member (or a member of management, whether or not on the committee) to report an incident of sexual harassment but then decline to lodge a formal complaint. To protect against any subsequent charge that the employer failed to respond, a memo should be prepared as soon as possible reciting the employee's approach and her subsequent refusal to proceed with a formal investigation. If possible, obtain the employee's signature on the memo.

When the committee has completed its fact-finding work, it must meet and come to a formal decision on the claim's validity. Perhaps the most important guideline is imagining how the claim would look to a group of outsiders. Someday, such a group—a jury—may well be looking at the same evidence that is before the committee. A jury is not likely to care that the accused harasser is powerful or well liked in the company, or contributes materially to the company's success, or that the accuser is a problem employee with a history of poor performance. Indeed, considerations like these will probably make a jury *more* suspicious of a committee finding in favor of the accused, not less. Like any trial judge, the committee must always bear in mind that its work is subject to review by a "higher court" (and a potentially expensive one at that).

If the committee finds that no harassment has occurred, no further action is necessary. (Of course, the complainant may disagree and file a legal action.) If, on the other hand, the committee determines that the complaint is valid, it must decide on an appropriate sanction. The punishment should fit the crime. It may be as mild as a reprimand or as severe as termination of employment. Whatever the sanction, the committee's written record of its decision should reflect the rationale for the particular sanction chosen. Especially where the sanction is severe, the harasser may turn around and challenge it. Thus, for example, a manager fired for repeatedly asking a subordinate for a date could dispute the committee's decision to fire him and sue the employer for wrongful termination or breach of an employment contract.

Whatever the committee's decision, a member of the committee should promptly communicate it to the complainant and explain the reasons—preferably in person. It is important to show the complainant that the company took her complaint seriously and investigated it thoroughly.

The public's increased awareness of sexual harassment has led to a phenomenon which we call "the preemptive strike." Employees who believe they will soon be fired, demoted, or subject to discipline have taken to asserting sexual harassment claims against a superior in the hope of diverting attention from their own predicaments and protecting their jobs. When an employee tries a preemptive strike, there are two major traps into which employers all too easily fall.

The first trap is to settle quickly. Employers who do this a few times risk acquiring a reputation as a cash register for disgruntled employees. That kind of reputation quickly becomes self-fulfilling.

The second trap is to treat the claim as the ploy that it is and promptly proceed with firing, demoting, or disciplining the complainant. The complainant now has a welcome gift from the employer: a valid cause of action where none existed before. Both federal and state statutes protect employees from retaliation for asserting charges of sexual harassment. *E.g.,* 42 U.S.C. § 2000e-3; N.Y. Exec. Law § 296(e) (McKinney 1993). These statutes typically do not require a showing that the charges were meritorious; the employee may only have to show that an adverse change in her employment followed shortly upon her assertion of sexual harassment charges. *See EEOC v. Virginia Carolina Veneer Corp.,* 495 F. Supp. 775, 777. ("Title 42 U.S.C. protects employees from employer retaliation for filing complaints with the Commission, even if the charges alleged are false and malicious.")

Defusing the Crisis

You can neutralize the preemptive strike if the employer proceeds with care. The first thing is to handle a preemptive claim of sexual harassment just like any other claim: Refer it to the committee and let it investigate. There is always the possibility the complaint is justified, and the complainant simply was afraid to pursue it until her own employment status was in jeopardy and she no longer had as much to lose.

Second, if possible postpone the contemplated action (firing, demotion, etc.) against the complainant until the committee has completed its investigation. Unless the complainant is disrupting the workplace, leaving her status unchanged is a small price to pay, especially if the committee proceeds quickly. If it becomes clear that the complainant must be promptly separated from other employees, consider putting her on paid leave until the committee's work is done.

Third, be alert to possible changes in the complainant's behavior. Employees sometimes make the mistake of thinking themselves invincible once they've lodged a sexual harassment complaint. They take liberties in the workplace they wouldn't have dared before. Document such behavior wherever it occurs. It will help support any action taken against the employee later on.

When the sexual harassment committee has finished its investigation and taken any appropriate action, the employer should proceed as it would have in the absence of the preemptive strike. Employers don't lose their ability to discipline or terminate an employee just because the employee has complained of sexual harassment. They just have to be sure there's a clear record of legitimate, independent grounds for their action.

But in legal matters as in health care, prevention isn't always enough. Even a company with a rigorous anti-sexual harassment policy and a diligent sexual harassment committee can't be certain of heading off every lawsuit. Policies and procedures don't always succeed (although they may lay the foundation for a good defense). Some employers can't or won't devote the administrative resources to the kind of anti-sexual harassment regimen we've outlined. Some harassers are simply too senior or powerful to be controlled. Some complainants just aren't satisfied with having a harasser disciplined internally. And, of course, there are situations where the facts, or the interpretation of the facts, are in sharp dispute and the complainant is genuinely dissatisfied with the employer's response to her complaint.

There's always litigation.

One of the gifts that Congress bestowed upon employers in the 1991 Act is the personal injury bar. Now that compensatory and punitive damages are routinely available in Title VII cases, the virtuosos of the contingency fee have rushed in to offer their skills.

We don't mean to disparage personal injury lawyers. They play a vital role in our legal system. But much of the recent boom in sexual harassment litigation has been fueled by the discovery that many companies will pay substantial blackmail to avoid being portrayed in the public arena as a haven for sexual predators. And when settlements come so quickly, a one-third share can be an enticing lure.

Damages aren't the only remedy available under Title VII. The traditional remedies of back pay and reinstatement are still available if they apply. Note that back pay is distinct from compensatory damages and is not subject to any cap. Thus, an employee who was denied a promotion because she refused to sleep with her boss may be entitled to receive back pay equal to the higher salary she should have been earning, *plus* compensatory damages for such items as emotional distress and loss of reputation. Both before and after the 1991 Act, however, back pay is limited to a period of two years before the filing of formal charges with the EEOC. 42 U.S.C. § 2000e-5(g).

The procedures for asserting claims under Title VII are byzantine in the extreme. Claims must be filed, in the first instance, with the EEOC.

No Title VII claim can be filed in federal court without first passing through the EEOC. 42 U.S.C. § 2000e-5(f).

Title VII is governed by relatively short statutes of limitation. An EEOC claim must be filed within 180 days of the occurrence of the discriminatory act. 42 U.S.C. § 2000e-5(e). If the discrimination occurred in a state that has laws against sexual harassment and an agency empowered to adjudicate claims and grant relief, then technically the claim must first be filed with the state agency. 42 U.S.C. § 2000e-5(c). The state agency then has 60 days to act on the claim, and any complaint submitted to the EEOC will not be deemed to have been filed until the 60-day period has run. *Id.* In that case, the complainant has 300 days from the date of the occurrence or 30 days from the date notice is received by the individual that the state proceedings have concluded (whichever is earlier) to file with the EEOC. 42 U.S.C. § 2000e-5(e).

State Agencies

Generally, though, the EEOC has work-sharing agreements with state agencies, so that the complainant can file a single charge with the EEOC and have it automatically forwarded to the appropriate state agency. The charge is then deemed filed with the EEOC when the 60-day period expires.

Plaintiffs who live in a deferral state have no choice about filing with the state agency. Under 29 C.F.R. § 1601.13, a complaint filed with the EEOC in a state that has an agency with jurisdiction over the claim will not be deemed to be filed with the EEOC until 60 days after it has been filed with the state agency (or until the state agency waives the 60-day exclusivity period). In the interim, the statute of limitations continues to run. This is true even if the complaint is physically filed with the EEOC and never filed with the state agency.

The dual state/federal role has created some interesting problems with statutes of limitations. Suppose that Edna Employee files a sexual harassment claim with the EEOC against Contumely Company 250 days after her boss fires her for refusing to date him. Edna and Contumely are in a "deferral" state with its own agency for sexual harassment claims. After allowing the 60-day period of exclusive state jurisdiction to run, the EEOC filing is deemed to have occurred 310 days after the act of discrimination, and it is now time-barred.

To avoid this problem, most states waive the period of exclusivity so that the claim can be deemed timely filed. The U.S. Supreme Court has approved this practice. *See EEOC v. Commercial Office Products,* 486 U.S. 107 (1988).

Of course, this statute of limitations problem is unique to deferral states and only arises when the complainant files charges with the EEOC after the passage of 240 days following the alleged harassment. If the complainant lives in a nondeferral state, charges may be filed directly with the EEOC. Upon filing, the EEOC can act on the charges immediately. For complainants living in a deferral state, use the following formula: If "days elapsed since harassment" plus an additional 60 days are greater than 300 days, then, unless the EEOC and the state agency have an agreement waiving the exclusivity period, the claim will be time-barred.

An EEOC charge is a simple one-page form designed to be filled out by an individual and not by counsel. (Today, though, counsel is more and more frequently involved.) The charge doesn't lead to an adversary proceeding before the agency. Instead, it asks the agency to investigate. Since the agency will investigate only what is in the complaint (at least at the outset), it is important to include as much information as possible. We have found that the best approach is to write the equivalent of a lengthy "speaking" complaint and attach it to the EEOC's form as an addendum.

The EEOC has the power to direct the employer to produce documents. 29 C.F.R. § 1601.16. The documents it requests will probably be based on the allegations in the charge. If you believe that certain company records will help prove the employee's claim, be sure to draft the charge in a fashion that will prompt the investigator to ask for those records. The investigator will often go on-site to conduct an inspection and interviews. If that is something you want to encourage, draft the charge with this possibility in mind.

Ultimately, the investigator issues a report, which will form the basis for the EEOC's decision on the merits. If the EEOC determines there is probable cause to find a violation of Title VII, it will likely initiate a process of conciliation. In conciliation, the EEOC attempts to negotiate with the employer a "just resolution of all violations found" and an "agreement that the [employer] will eliminate the unlawful employment practice and provide appropriate affirmative relief." 29 C.F.R. § 1601.24(a).

The EEOC has substantial clout in a conciliation because it can sue if conciliation does not work. Under 29 C.F.R. § 1601.27, the EEOC may commence a civil action against any respondent named in a charge (other than a government agency) within 30 days from the date of filing unless there has been a conciliation agreement acceptable to the EEOC.

If the EEOC does not find probable cause that a violation exists, it will generally give the claimant a so-called "right to sue" letter. This "right to sue" letter is the claimant's entry ticket to the federal court system. With it the claimant may commence a federal court action. 42 U.S.C. § 2000e-5. Although Title VII supplies the basis of federal jurisdiction, the usual rules governing personal jurisdiction and venue apply. *E.g., Weldon v. City of Detroit*, 403 F. Supp. 436 (D. Mich. 1975).

Several points are important here. If the EEOC is unable to investigate a charge within 180 days after it has been filed—and given the agency's workload, that is not uncommon—the complainant may request immediate issuance of a right to sue letter. Moreover, once a right to sue letter has been issued, for whatever reason, the complainant has a mere 90 days to commence a federal court action. This 90-day limit is strictly enforced. *E.g., Noe v. Ward,* 754 F.2d 890 (10th Cir. 1985). Finally, once a federal court action begins, state agencies will generally terminate any pending investigations, provided there has not been a hearing at which testimony has been taken. *E.g.,* N.Y. Comp. Codes R. & Regs. tit. 9, § 465.6.

A plaintiff in a federal sexual harassment case has all the usual tools of discovery at her disposal. But she needn't wait until the action is commenced to begin gathering information. A complainant has wide-ranging access to the EEOC files regarding her complaint, including documents produced to the EEOC by the employer. These files can be useful in preparing the complaint.

Note, however, that a complainant has access only to her own EEOC file, not to files of any other EEOC complaints against the employer. To obtain those, the only recourse is a request under the Freedom of Information Act. Such a request should be made as early as possible, since a response will typically take several months. The request should be as specific as you can make it; otherwise, the EEOC may, after reviewing the request, claim that it is too broad.

Employers are in the same boat. They are not entitled to review charges that the same complainant has filed against other employers, or any EEOC files relating to such charges. (Of course, once litigation begins, either side can propound discovery requests to the other seeking documents or information in the party's actual possession about other EEOC proceedings.)

A few of the strategies for trying sexual harassment cases (whether for the prosecution or the defense) deserve mention. The 1991 Act amending Title VII imposed a cap on the total amount of compensatory and punitive damages an employee may recover; the cap varies with the employer's size, with an upper ceiling of $300,000. The 1991 Act also provides, however, that a jury hearing a Title VII case must *not* be advised of the statutory cap. 42 U.S.C. § 1981a(3)(c)(2). As a practical matter, the point may not matter, since a Title VII action can also include a claim under any applicable state or local antidiscrimination laws, many of which have no cap. *E.g.,* 8 N.Y. City Charter and Code § 502.

The issue of the 1991 Act's cap, and indeed the whole issue of allowing punitive damages under Title VII, continues to be a hot topic of debate. A bill was pending in Congress in 1993 that would have eliminated the cap on punitive damages. *See* H.R. 2790, 103d Cong., 1st Sess. 1993. At the opposite end of the spectrum, a different bill was introduced in September 1994 to eliminate punitive damages from Title VII altogether. *See* H.R. 5145, 103d Cong., 2d Sess. (1994). Given the new majority in Congress, there may well be other proposals, or even a change in the law.

Claimants considering litigation should pause to consider the employer's possible response. While the claimant may be thrilled at the prospect of putting the alleged harasser on trial, the thrill may come at a price. Once a plaintiff has put personal and intimate matters into issue, the employer may strike back by attempting to make the plaintiff's sex life a central issue in the case. The threat of having to discuss these matters in public may in and of itself provide a claimant with ample motivation to settle or abandon a claim, regardless of the merits.

At a trial in federal court in Virginia, for example, a plaintiff was asked whether or not she and her husband watched X-rated films. Another witness at the same trial was asked whether the plaintiff and her husband had engaged in premarital sex. In other actions, plaintiffs have been asked whether they have experienced sex with animals, other women, or a variety of men. *See* "Plaintiffs' Sex Lives Are Being Laid Bare in Harassment Cases," *Wall St. J.*, Sept. 19, 1994, at A1.

Federal Remedies

Congress has already provided some measure of protection for plaintiffs in sexual harassment cases. The Violent Crime Control and Law Enforcement Act of 1994 amended Rule 412 of the Federal Rules of Evidence to protect plaintiffs in civil actions based on sexual misconduct. Rule 412 now provides that evidence offered to prove the sexual behavior or predisposition of a plaintiff in a civil case will be admissible only if its probative value substantially outweighs the danger of harm to the plaintiff and of unfair prejudice to any party. *See* Violent Crime Control and Law Enforcement Act of 1994, Pub. L. No. 103-322, 108 Stat. 1796.

Rule 412 also establishes the procedure to determine the admissibility of evidence of a plaintiff's sexual behavior. The party seeking to introduce such evidence must file a motion at least 14 days before trial specifically describing the evidence and stating the purpose for offering it. Before ruling on admissibility, the court must hold a hearing in camera and allow the plaintiff the right to attend and be heard. The motion, all related papers, and the transcript of the in camera hearing must be sealed unless the court orders otherwise. *Id.*

However, the 1994 crime bill only barred such evidence at *trial*. It does not necessarily preclude an employer from seeking such evidence in *discovery*. Several states, including California, have already adopted statutes limiting even the discovery of this type of information. *See* Cal. Civ. Proc. Code § 2017 (West 1993). The California statute requires that a defendant in a sexual harassment action seeking discovery of the plaintiff's sexual conduct with individuals other than the defendant must seek leave of court. The court may grant leave only if the defendant establishes (1) specific facts showing good cause for the discovery and (2) that the information is relevant to the subject matter of the litigation and reasonably calculated to lead to the discovery of admissible evidence.

State Court Alternatives

The EEOC and the federal courts are not the sole forums for resolving sexual harassment claims. Many state and local agencies have enforcement powers beyond those of the EEOC, and state courts can hear claims under state human rights statutes (but not Title VII). In New York, for example, the NYSDHR is empowered to hold hearings on the merits and award damages. NYSDHR hearings are somewhat similar to arbitration. Both sides are entitled to call witnesses and to cross-examine each other's witnesses. By statute the NYSDHR hearing examiner is not bound by rules of evidence. N.Y. Exec. Law § 297(4)(a). Within 180 days following the commencement of the hearing, the NYSDHR hearing officer must issue findings of fact and an order. The NYSDHR may order employers to pay compensatory damages (without limitations) and to reinstate the employee (with or without back pay). N.Y. Exec. Law § 297(4)(c). The losing party may appeal to the local trial court. N.Y. Exec. Law § 298.

Most states with comprehensive human rights statutes require an election of remedies. *See, e.g.*, N.Y. Exec. Law § 298. Complainants have the option of proceeding through the state's administrative agency (such as the NYSDHR) *or* going directly to court. By choosing the administrative remedy, which theoretically (often *very* theoretically) results in a quicker resolution, the complainant gives up the option of filing a civil complaint in state court.

A plaintiff who chooses to proceed in state court does not forgo the right to proceed before the EEOC. But because state remedies are commonly broader than those provided by Title VII, e.g., unlimited punitive damages as opposed to a cap on punitive damages, there may be no advantage to pursuing a claim before the EEOC once an action has been commenced in state court.

Then there's arbitration. More and more employers are requiring employees to agree, at the time of hire, to resolve employment disputes, including claims of sexual harassment, through arbitration. Reflecting the popularity of this trend, the American Arbitration Association (the AAA) has established a three-step "Model Sexual Harassment Claims Resolution Process." The first step is a Request for Fact-Finders, where a team of two independent fact-finders investigates the claim and issues a report reciting the facts as they see them. The second step is a Request for Mediation, where a mediator is appointed to help resolve the claim. If a satisfactory resolution is reached after either of these first two steps, the process ends there. If no resolution is reached, the parties proceed to the third step: a Demand/Request for Arbitration. As with all forms of alternative dispute resolution, both sides must agree to the process in advance.

As a general rule, employers prefer arbitration because it is quick and quiet. Some employees, by contrast, have challenged the adequacy of an arbitral forum to hear and resolve sexual harassment claims. In September 1994, a former NCR Corp. employee commenced a class action suit in Texas against the AAA, alleging that the AAA does not provide neutral or impartial tribunals because the arbitration panels are stacked with lawyers who represent management rather than employees. The employee has further alleged that most arbitrators are male and white and are therefore biased against the claims of women or minorities. *See* "Dallas Woman Claims Arbitration Panel Favors Employers," *Dallas Morning News*, Sept. 6, 1994, at 4D.

Alternative Forums

The AAA is not the only institution facing controversy over sexual harassment arbitrations. Because many employers in the securities industry include general arbitration clauses in their employment contracts, most sexual harassment claims in the industry are arbitrated before the National Association of Securities Dealers (NASD). In September 1994, as a result of numerous complaints about its arbitration procedures, the NASD appointed a nine-member panel to review the NASD's arbitration procedures and issue a report. Some plaintiffs' lawyers have attacked the panel, which is being chaired by former SEC Chairman David S. Ruder, as unfairly biased in favor of management. *See* "The 'Old Boys' Run the Street, Panel Is Told," *Nat'l L. J.*, Oct. 3, 1994, at A25.

Sexual harassment litigation is relatively new, and it may be years before the boundaries of actionable and nonactionable conduct are clear. Meanwhile, creative plaintiffs' lawyers will continue to explore new territory. Consider the case of *Carrasquillo v. D'Amato & Lynch*, No. 94 Civ. 4195 (S.D.N.Y. filed June 1994), in which a legal secretary at a New York law firm claimed that a lawyer at the firm pressed into her back, sat on her desk "intently eyeing her body up and down," asked whether the secretary was "one of those women" who could not conceive because she was "allergic to male semen," and made other sexually explicit remarks. The lawyer alleged to have committed these acts was another woman.

What to Do When a Defendant Goes Bankrupt

Martin L. Grayson and Douglas D. Dodd
Tactics

Answer 1: Consider suicide.
Answer 2: Ignore it.
Answer 3: File a proof of claim and then ignore it.

Ask an experienced trial lawyer how to deal with a bankrupt debtor who is a defendant or co-defendant in litigation. His answer, probably one of the above, will reflect despair. Even Answer 3, a course of action that at least registers the claim in the bankruptcy court record, is one of resignation rather than hope.

But one can do more than merely file a proof of claim and notice of representation in the bankruptcy court (see "A Primer on the Law," later in this article) and then await a fate unquestioned and unchallenged by most litigants.

You might think that it would be an exercise in futility to press a claim against a party when the return might amount to ten cents on the dollar. But not always. Consider the potential benefits for plaintiffs and co-defendants who must deal with a bankrupt defendant:

1. For the plaintiff, getting the debtor into court eliminates the "empty chair." Other defendants will not be able to point a finger at the missing party and attempt to place all liability there at your client's expense. On the other hand, when liability is based on the conduct of the debtor (as with an indemnitor or surety) the co-defendant might want to take the lead in getting the debtor to respond because the plaintiff will be more than willing to lay blame on the empty chair.

Martin L. Grayson practices law in Long Beach, California, and is a former associate editor of LITIGATION.
Douglas D. Dodd is a partner with Stone, Pigman, Walther, Wittmann & Hutchinson in New Orleans.

2. Getting the debtor into court may result in a judgment. A judgment might improve your client's prospects for recovery in bankruptcy—a real consideration if large sums are involved and even a small percentage return would be worth the chase. At the very least, a judgment will liquidate the claim and defuse any later attempt to dispute it or the amount in question.
3. A litigant's time, effort, and energy, and the client's money, often will be better served by pursuing a debtor in a civil action rather than in bankruptcy proceedings. If, for example, a debtor avoids civil litigation, in bankruptcy another adversarial procedure might be required to determine liabilities. Another time-consuming alternative would be to require the bankruptcy court to make a complete, independent evaluation of the estimated claim. (See "A Primer on the Law," later in this article.)
4. Getting the debtor into court may prompt his insurer to answer and defend the action.

Perhaps the last item is the real bargain. For many causes of action, the bankrupt party may have insurance coverage that would answer your demand. Major casualty cases, almost all maritime filings, and many corporate actions involve claims for which an insurer stands behind the bankrupt party.

What a comforting thought. Especially because the major hurdle to clear in the bankruptcy court is convincing the judge to lift the automatic stay. This stay goes into effect whenever a person or company files for bankruptcy. The stay bans all pending and prospective litigation, collection attempts, amicable demands, and other actions against the debtor. Judgments already recorded against a debtor are still valid. However, execution of judgment is halted.

The court will look more favorably on a motion for relief from the automatic stay that names an insurance company, rather than the bankrupt, as the real party in interest, because the debtor's assets available to satisfy his creditors will not be depleted. On the other hand, if the debtor has no insurance coverage or only a limited amount and claims are substantial, the bankruptcy court might wish to supervise the distribution of insurance proceeds. If it does not, then proceeds might quickly be exhausted by one set of claims, requiring a subsequent claim to be paid from the assets that otherwise would have been available to satisfy creditors. Supervision by the bankruptcy court means maintaining the stay of the action in the court in which the suit is pending and bringing the dispute (or the part of the dispute that involves the debtor) to bankruptcy court.

Finding out if a party is insured and the name of the insurer is usually not very difficult. The bankruptcy court record will reveal the name of the debtor's counsel or trustee, and one phone call will often produce the necessary information. In fact, if schedules (see "A Primer on the Law," later in this chapter) have already been filed, insurance premiums may be listed as outstanding items, and the name of the insurer would be in the record. One can also contact the creditor's committee, usually comprised of major creditors who know a good deal about the debtor or are in the process of learning fast. With the name of the insurer available, you can move the court for relief from the automatic stay to allow you to name the bankrupt party in an attempt to bring the insurer to the debtor's defense.

In direct action states (Louisiana and Wisconsin), finding the name of the insurer is all that you require to draft or amend your complaint to name the insurer rather than the bankrupt. In other states, the route is a bit circuitous, but the result should be the same.

If the insurer is not readily identifiable, then you may have to back up a step. Rather than petitioning the bankruptcy court to lift the automatic stay so you can sue the debtor (and its insurer), you must move the court to lift the stay to allow discovery against the debtor concerning its insurer. Such a request should not be burdensome for the debtor. Because the court may be suspicious that discovery might proceed into areas that address the claim itself or even the bankrupt's capacity to respond directly, you should be careful to draft a specific motion and supporting memorandum seeking only the identity of the insurer and insurance limits and coverage.

Once you learn the availability of insurance, you may then proceed with a second motion to lift the stay for the purpose of bringing suit. Assuring the debtor has insurance, what arguments and points of law should you advance to convince a bankruptcy court to lift the automatic stay?

The motion may request a lifting of the stay to proceed with a suit against the debtor, to enter judgment against the debtor, or even to allow an execution of judgment, although this last request would almost certainly be denied. Whatever the purpose of seeking to lift the stay, however, courts have found the following arguments to be persuasive.

First, material harm to the litigants, and perhaps other creditors, may result from delay. The failure to institute or proceed with the suit in a timely fashion might result in the invocation of coverage defenses by insurers. You should submit to the court copies of the relevant insurance policies with limiting language. Alert the court to the potential of an added burden on the debtor's bankruptcy estate if the policy defenses stand and insurers are released from their obligation to indemnify the debtor. At the same time, full redress may be denied innocent claimants. Also, if the debtor emerges from bankruptcy or for some reason is unable to avoid a judgment, the debtor may be forced to defend the suit and satisfy a judgment alone, without benefit of insurance. Such a result would hinder any attempt at economic recovery by the debtor already in difficult financial straits and deprive him of the benefit of his insurance.

Second, you can argue to the court that there may be insurance coverage adequate to satisfy any judgment. In other words, you should stress that the assets of the debtor, if any, would not be at risk. This argument should be soothing to the bankruptcy court, trustees, debtors, creditors, and others whose primary concern is the conservation of the assets of the struggling, or moribund, bankrupt. So long as the bankruptcy estate of the debtor will not be invaded, there should be no viable objection to allowing suit to proceed against the debtor.

Third, you must point out that the rights and interests of plaintiffs, co-defendants, or third parties, who might seek indemnity, contribution, or recovery against the bankrupt and its insurers, are also entitled to some consideration and protection. Those rights and interests cannot be protected except by timely institution or completion of suit against the debtor. This is an argument based in equity rather than a strict reading of the Bankruptcy Code, but it would be cynical to assume it must fall on deaf ears.

Finally, in some cases you can argue that the stay should be liked because of special circumstances. For example, the Code does not prohibit the filing and prosecution of suit against a debtor on claims that arise from activity undertaken before a filing for reorganization under Chapter 11 of the Bankruptcy Code. For example, say a small oil exploration company files for Chapter 11 protection. While the company continues its operations, one of its dredges strikes and bursts an oil pipeline causing extensive pollution and loss of product. Because the incident occurred *after* the bankruptcy court had approved the activity resulting in the loss, the debtor should not be permitted to interpose the automatic stay as a shield against suit. The court should allow the company's business to proceed with the understanding that obligations thus incurred, whether in tort or contract, would have to be discharged in full.

You should also remind the bankruptcy court that lifting the stay for the purpose of allowing a claim to be liquidated is different from allowing a judgment to be executed. The court automatically stays execution of judgment. However, if the court allows a suit to proceed to judgment, the creditor-adversary would have a liquidated claim to bring to the bankruptcy court. No harm to the bankrupt, a bit of equity for the injured adversary, economy for the courts.

There are probably other ways to lever the automatic bankruptcy stay off your client's claim to allow that claim to be heard. Those noted above can give you a start without the expenditure of a lot of time. The results may be surprising and gratifying.

Now, what about those folks we dismissed earlier? The ones with the suit on open account? Definitely file a proof of claim in the bankruptcy action. Waiting a long time and lowering expectations is also a perspicacious approach. Answer number one (consider suicide) is always available.

A Primer on the Law

As soon as trial counsel learns that an opposing party has sought refuge under the bankruptcy laws, he should consult members of his firm who are familiar with the Bankruptcy Code and Bankruptcy Rules.

But even if the firm has no lawyer familiar with the bankruptcy laws and rules, there are several simple steps that trial counsel should take to protect his client's interests. These steps will cost the client little and will protect the client from prejudice in the bankruptcy proceedings. Although the advice applies to claims generally, it is more directly relevant to holders of unsecured claims.

1. *Prepare and File a Proof of Claim.* Clerks at bankruptcy court and legal stationers have preprinted proof-of-claim forms, or one can retype the appropriate Official Bankruptcy Form (i.e., 19, 20, and 21) with the necessary insertions. A properly executed and filed proof of claim is prima facie evidence of the validity and amount of a claim under Rule 3001(f). Bankruptcy Rule 3002(a) states that unsecured creditors must file a proof of claim for their claims to be allowed, except as otherwise provided in Rules 3003–3005. In "no asset" Chapter 7 cases, consult Rule 2002(e).

Regardless of whether your client's claim is scheduled (See 5. *Review the Schedules*.) or your belief that there will be no distribution of bankruptcy estate assets to unsecured creditors, you *always* should file a proof of claim on behalf of your client. This is inexpensive insurance that the client will participate in distribution and receive notice of other aspects of a bankruptcy case.

2. *Estimation of Claims.* Under § 502(c) of the Bankruptcy Code, the bankruptcy court must estimate for the purpose of allowance any contingent or unliquidated claim when the precise fixing or liquidation of that claim would unduly delay the administration of the case. The court also must estimate any right to payment from an award of an equitable remedy for breach of performance. Your proof of claim should reflect clearly that it is your own estimate of the amount owed your client, including the fact that the claim may be contingent on another event (such as, if you are co-defendant, the granting of your third-party demand or cross-claim against the debtor). The bankruptcy court makes the ultimate estimate. Consult Section 502(e) for the treatment of claims of co-debtors.

3. *Time for Filing.* In cases under Chapter 7 (liquidation) and Chapter 13 (reorganization of personal finances), Bankruptcy Rule 3002(c) provides that a proof of claim usually must be filed within 90 days after the first meeting of creditors. Such a meeting usually takes place within 45 days of the filing for relief. In the more common Chapter 11 (corporate reorganization) cases, the rules require the court to fix a date within which claims must be filed. Check the record for orders establishing claim bar dates.

4. *File a Notice of Representation.* This should ensure that you receive all notices distributed by the clerk. There is no particular form for this document. In some cases, local practice will permit counsel to indicate on the rear of the proof-of-claim form information about your claim that is not indicated elsewhere. This could include an appearance as counsel of record on behalf of the claimant. When in doubt, check with the bankruptcy court clerk about the need for filing a formal notice. It is prudent to notify the debtor's counsel of your appearance apart from filing a notice with the clerk.

5. *Review the Schedules.* Either you or your client can do this. The Bankruptcy Code requires the debtor to file schedules listing all assets and liabilities, including debts. Rule 3003(b)(1) states that the schedules filed in Chapter 9 and 11 cases are prima facie evidence of the validity and amount of the claim, *unless* the claim is scheduled as disputed, contingent, or unliquidated. Because by their very nature, claims involving litigation are contingent, unliquidated, or disputed, trial counsel should *never* rely on a listing in the debtors' schedules. A proof-of-claim should always be filed. If the case is converted to one under Chapter 7, creditors must file a claim anyway. The consequences of improperly relying on the schedules that reflect your client's claim as contingent, unliquidated, or disputed are severe: Under Rule 3003(c)(2), a creditor whose claim is scheduled as contingent, unliquidated, or disputed is not entitled to treatment as a creditor for purposes of voting or distribution.

The schedules, if properly prepared, are full of information that you and your client will need to evaluate the desirability of becoming more active in the bankruptcy or of obtaining relief from the stay proceedings in the trial court. The cost of obtaining copies of the schedules and statement of financial affairs, in all but the largest and most complex bankruptcies, is worth the investment. Contact the clerk to obtain information on copying.

6. *Review the Bankruptcy Court Record.* Aside from the schedules, there are other documents filed by a debtor that may enable you to determine its financial health and the wisdom of pursuing your client's claim. Moreover, there may be documents that reveal the existence and identity of insurance carriers available to respond to your demands. Also, there may be orders pertaining to the constitution and appointment of a committee of creditors. Depending on the size of your client's claim, trial counsel or the client may wish to serve on that committee.

7. *Always Attend the First Meeting of Creditors.* There must be a meeting of creditors within a reasonable time after the order for relief in a bankruptcy case. Rule 2002(a) provides that creditors who are listed in the schedules or have filed proofs of claim must receive 20 days' notice of the meeting. Section 343 of the Code requires the debtor to appear and submit to examination under oath. Bankruptcy Rule 2004(b) governs the scope of the examination, which is broad, although not without

limit: it may relate "only to the acts, conduct, or property or to the liabilities and financial condition of the debtor, or to any matter which may affect the administration of the debtor's estate, or to the debtor's right to a discharge." In Chapter 13 and most Chapter 11 cases, the examination may also inquire into the "continued operation of and desirability of continuance of any business" and other topics including "any other matter relevant to the case or to the formulation of a plan." You may also use the meeting to determine the debtor's attitude toward your claim. In rare cases, the debtor may admit the validity and amount of your claim.

To maximize the value of the first meeting of creditors as a source of information, counsel (or the client, if the client will attend the meeting) should review the bankruptcy schedules well before the meeting.

The meeting of creditors and the information set forth in the schedules should enable you and your client to decide whether it is worth the time and expense of more aggressive action to pursue the client's claim within the bankruptcy. Alternatives include the possibility of obtaining bankruptcy counsel or seeking relief from the automatic stay to continue the nonbankruptcy litigation.

These simple and relatively inexpensive steps, some of which can be undertaken by the client rather than trial counsel, describe the basic moves to protect a litigant's interests should an opponent file for relief under the Bankruptcy Code. They also will help you and your client decide how best to proceed to recovery.

Bankruptcy Litigation: More Than Voodoo

Robert A. Julian

"Bankruptcy voodoo." That's what an opponent called my oral argument. The comment was bred of frustration, and I could understand it. His clients were limited partners with a multimillion dollar claim against a general partner that was in bankruptcy. For two years, their claim had been batted back and forth between the district court and bankruptcy court on a series of motions—to transfer claims, to enter injunctions, to authorize sales of assets, to lift the automatic stay in bankruptcy, and to approve settlements. Many of the motions, not to mention the different courts' differing responses, seemed inconsistent. At the end of all of this activity, my opponent's clients were only a little closer to recovering on their claim than they had been at the outset.

I also could understand his calling it "voodoo." Bankruptcy lawyers and judges do seem to be a cult, intoning about arcane rules and practicing obscure rituals. And those rules and rituals do seem to put outsiders into a trance. But the bankruptcy laws reflect a consistent set of federal policies that create the procedures and inform the strategies that lead to success in bankruptcy litigation.

First, some basics. The United States district courts have jurisdiction over all bankruptcy cases and related litigation. With authority 28 U.S.C. § 157(b)(1) grants, the district courts may refer their jurisdiction over bankruptcy matters to bankruptcy judges. Each of the country's district courts has made that reference automatic. The bankruptcy judges operate autonomously from the district courts, subject only to rules for withdrawing the automatic reference and appeals of matters that Congress and the courts have determined are to be tried first in bankruptcy court, and then reviewed de novo in district court.

Robert A. Julian is a partner of the San Francisco firm of Murphy, Weir & Butler.

The most common bankruptcy cases are reorganizations under Chapter 11 of the United States Bankruptcy Code and liquidations under Chapter 7. When a bankruptcy begins, the bankruptcy court has jurisdiction over all proceedings that "arise under" the Bankruptcy Code, "arise in" the bankruptcy case, or are "related to" the case. See 28 U.S.C. § 1334(b).

There are two principal sorts of bankruptcy litigation. An "adversary proceeding" resembles a "civil action" under the Federal Rules of Civil Procedure; it has a plaintiff and a defendant. Bankruptcy Rule 7001 provides that any suit to recover money or property or to obtain an injunction or other equitable relief is to be commenced as an adversary proceeding. The Federal Rules of Civil Procedure concerning service of process, pleading, joinder, substitution of parties, discovery, entry of judgment, entry of findings of facts and conclusions of law, and motions for new trial apply in adversary proceedings.

A "contested matter" is any dispute that must be resolved in a bankruptcy case, other than an adversary proceeding. Parties often ask the bankruptcy court for relief available under the Bankruptcy Code or Rules. If someone else opposes the motion, a contested matter has begun.

In contested matters, Bankruptcy Rule 9014 applies most of the rules that apply in adversary proceedings, but a contested matter typically does not require the commencement of a formal adversary proceeding and thus avoids many of the delays that are typical of civil litigation. Contested matters include the debtor or a creditors' committee's application for authority to retain counsel or other professionals; debtor motions to use cash collateral; and creditor motions to lift the automatic stay of Bankruptcy Code § 362(a) to permit foreclosure against the debtor's property.

Bankruptcy litigation can take many forms: A party may try to avoid preferential or fraudulent transfers of the debtor's property; there may be disputes over the assumption or rejection of contracts between the debtor and third persons, or the retention and payment of professionals, or the right to file and the adequacy of disclosure statements leading to confirmation of a plan of reorganization. Confirmation of the plan itself may be litigated, and there may be motions for the appointment of a trustee to run the debtor's business, or for an examiner to investigate the business. Also arising are adversary proceedings to settle the nature, extent, and priority of liens and interests in the debtor's property; injunction actions to protect the debtor's business or a transaction in which the debtor has an interest; and actions for damages by or against the debtor, even if they involve third parties without claims against the debtor.

In civil lawsuits, there typically are two parties or at least two clearly defined sides. Even when there are more than two parties, the adverse positions usually are clear and fixed. But large Chapter 11 cases have many parties in interest, and their positions change with each contested matter. In each case, there usually are at least four core interest groups: the debtor; a committee of unsecured creditors; an equity security holders' committee, representing the interests of one or more classes of shareholders; and one or more secured creditors, whose interests often differ from those of the other groups.

Other important parties include federal government agencies. The Office of the United States Trustee oversees such issues as the debtor's retention of professionals and the allowance of their fees, as well as the dissemination of a disclosure statement and plan. The Securities and Exchange Commission has the right under Bankruptcy Code § 1109 to intervene in any matter, and the Internal Revenue Service often has a claim with greater priority than that of many unsecured creditors.

All of the parties should have the same goal—to reorganize the debtor's business so that prebankruptcy contracts may be reaffirmed or rejected and distributions may be made to creditors, or to liquidate the bankruptcy estate for the benefit of all creditors. Even the litigation that arises in a bankruptcy case is supposed to promote the prompt achievement of these goals. Thus bankruptcy litigation is always open to arguments based on the unique policies of the bankruptcy laws.

Bankruptcy courts are courts of equity, and many litigated matters can be resolved on equitable grounds. To succeed, a litigant must show that its positions are consistent with the core policies of the Bankruptcy Code.

The first principle is that the debtor is entitled to a "breathing spell" from the business pressures and legal claims that forced it to seek bankruptcy court relief. This is the automatic stay of litigation under Bankruptcy Code § 362(a). It enjoins most creditor actions, permits the debtor to attempt a repayment or reorganization plan, and allows the debtor to be relieved of its financial pressures.

A related goal of the automatic stay is to protect creditors. The automatic stay stops creditors from a "race to the courthouse" to obtain a preference over other creditors. This highlights another policy of bankruptcy law—to promote an orderly liquidation in which all similarly situated creditors are treated equally. A rush to judgment against the debtor's assets would undermine that policy.

Any time that litigation threatens to involve a debtor or close associates of the debtor, or assets in which the debtor has an interest, a party may invoke the policy behind the automatic stay to call for a stay of the litigation. Because this bankruptcy policy is so fundamental, the stay has been extended beyond the debtor itself—to protect key employees of a corporate debtor, as well as guarantors of a debtor's obligations and even insurers of a debtor, from litigation during the bankruptcy case.

Another basic principle is the "absolute priority rule," which holds that junior classes, such as shareholders, are to be paid only after senior classes, such as unsecured creditors, are paid in full. The rule recognizes that shareholders bargain for equity returns and assume the risk of losing that investment. Because unsecured creditors do not bargain for the same returns and do not take on the same risks, they should be paid before equity holders. This concept supports Bankruptcy Code § 510(b), which permits the court to subordinate equity holders' claims to the claims of general unsecured creditors.

The absolute priority rule may be invoked in litigating claims by controlling shareholders in the bankruptcies of their corporations. In hopes of gaining equal treatment with unsecured creditors in a bankruptcy, the controlling shareholder may characterize her investment as a loan and not as equity. She may even pledge the debtor's assets to secure the "loan." If the controlling shareholder misuses her control, her claims in bankruptcy may be subordinated to the claims of all creditors under Bankruptcy Code § 510(c). Such litigation typically focuses on whether the insider (the controlling shareholder) engaged in "inequitable conduct." The shareholder will argue that she should not be penalized for investing more money in the company in the form of a loan. Other creditors will respond that the shareholder expected to receive equity returns on all investments in the company, and under the absolute priority rule, should not be treated in the same way as senior classes. That response should not dispose of the shareholder's claim, but it will tend to tip the equities toward the senior creditors.

A related concept is that of "ratable distribution"—that creditors in the same class should be treated similarly. For example, a creditor who has a claim to impose a constructive trust on the debtor's assets, but who has not yet litigated the claim to judgment, usually will not be able to obtain a constructive trust lien during the bankruptcy and will not receive a lien priority over unsecured creditors in the same class.

A host of rules, including the Bankruptcy Rules, the Federal Rules of Civil Procedure, the local district court rules, and the local bankruptcy court rules, govern bankruptcy litigation. Many bankruptcy judges even have their own rules.

Because bankruptcy lawyers and judges work continually with the same statute and rules, they often use a shorthand for the issues and principles that will be covered. In preparing for a hearing, the nonbankruptcy lawyer should become familiar with the relevant statutes, case law, and rules. Since bankruptcy judges rule repeatedly on the same issues, litigants often can learn much about a judge's leanings by reading her previous decisions.

When preparing for a hearing, check the local bankruptcy court rules to see if any special procedures will apply. Some courts, for example, have streamlined the presentation of evidence by requiring direct testimony in the form of written declarations and limiting cross-examination to the direct testimony declarations. These rules may even bar the lawyer from expanding on the direct testimony at the hearing.

Parties may not receive notice of all bankruptcy proceedings. Bankruptcy Rule 2002 specifies the form of notice for some, but not all, matters. In a large Chapter 11 case, the court may limit notice to the debtor, governmental entities, committees, and secured creditors. Other parties who want notice will have to ask for it. If the lawyer wants notice of all matters, she should file a request, obtain updated docket sheets, and ask the principal parties to give notice of all proceedings.

Prepare for the unexpected in discovery and at trial. In formal adversary proceedings, the discovery, pretrial proceedings, and trial usually follow the format of the federal district courts. But the litigation of contested matters will differ. Many contested matters are brought on quickly, with little time for formal discovery. Discovery is permitted under Bankruptcy Rule 9014, but the press of time may prevent it.

It is common, for example, to hold a hearing on a key issue, such as use of cash collateral or appointment of a trustee, without formal discovery. Yet one or more parties may elect (or be ordered by the judge) to put on witnesses, and the opposing lawyer will have to cross-examine without the benefit of discovery. Thorough preparation is essential.

That preparation includes obtaining as much information as possible about the debtor and its operations. Useful sources of information are the debtor's statement of affairs (which includes information on the debtor's officers, bank accounts, prebankruptcy transactions, and other matters); the debtor's statement of assets and liabilities; lien searches; applications for retention by the debtor's professionals; information about the corporation and its officers filed with state officials; and declarations filed by the debtor and other parties in other litigations in the case.

Even when no litigation is pending, Bankruptcy Rule 2004 permits an examination of any person concerning "the acts, conduct, or property or . . . the liability and financial condition of the debtor, or . . . any matter which may affect the administration of the debtor's estate, or . . . the debtor's right to a discharge." This rule is so broad that it even covers business that the debtor conducted before filing for bankruptcy. Most courts permit Rule 2004 subpoenas to be issued, without court approval, after 21 or 30 days.

Despite the breadth of Rule 2004, one should not overuse these examinations. Bankruptcy judges are trying harder than ever to reduce the costs of each case. Unless there is a good reason to conduct the examination, the court may grant a motion to block it.

To keep your expenses down and to impress the court of your concern for conserving the debtor's assets, coordinate discovery with other parties. For example, you can use evidence obtained in a Rule 2004 examination against any party who had notice of the examination and thus was able to attend and cross-examine. At least one court of appeals has held that testimony offered in one contested matter may be used in any later contested matter in the case, if adequate notice of the earlier examination had been given to the litigants in the later proceeding.

The Federal Rules of Evidence will apply in all hearings and trials, but the proceedings may be less formal than in federal district court. Because many routine proceedings in bankruptcy are informal, bankruptcy lawyers may not make as many objections to evidence as in a district court matter. At one time, bankruptcy judges seemed to admit all of the evidence that was offered. In the early 1980s, I appeared in bankruptcy court on a debtor's motion to approve its sale of property. One of the issues was whether the buyer could perform on the contract of sale. The debtor's president testified on the buyer's statements about the buyer's bank balances. I raised foundation and hearsay objections to these questions, and the court overruled each one. When I persisted, the bankruptcy judge said that, unless he admitted some hearsay, there would be no evidence to support his ruling approving the sale. But today, most bankruptcy judges rule on evidentiary issues as carefully as district judges do.

Beware of the trap of who has the burden of proof. In many kinds of bankruptcy litigation, the moving party does not bear the burden of proof on the ultimate issue. As a result, the moving party may get the last word in briefing, presenting evidence, and making oral argument on that issue, even though it does not carry the burden of proof.

Consider claims litigation. Under Bankruptcy Code § 502(a), a creditor's filing of a claim is prima facie evidence that the claim is valid. If a debtor or other party objects to the claim, that party must make a motion to disallow the claim. As the moving party, the objector has the burden of presenting enough evidence to put in issue the validity of the claim. But after that, the party that filed the claim has the burden of proving finally that the claim is valid. This makes sense, because the person who filed the claim resembles a plaintiff who has filed a complaint against a defendant—here, the debtor—and the plaintiff must prove the validity of its claim. But in the bankruptcy case, the objector to the claim, as the moving party, is likely to get the last word at the hearing.

A similar case is a debtor's request to subordinate an insider's claim, such as a shareholder loan, under § 510(c) of the Bankruptcy Code. Insider transactions are subject to strict scrutiny. The insider must prove both that its claim is valid and that its transactions with the debtor were inherently fair. Thus the debtor will make the motion to subordinate the insider's claim, but the insider will bear the burden of proving both that the claim is valid and that his transactions did not breach any fiduciary duty to the company.

A final example is a motion for relief from the automatic stay under § 362(d). One would expect the moving party—such as the creditor who seeks relief from the stay in order to foreclose upon the debtor's property—to have the ultimate burden of proving that relief from the stay is proper. But Code § 362(g) provides that the party requesting such relief from the stay has the burden of proof only on the question whether the debtor has any equity in the property; the debtor or other opponent of the relief has the burden of proof on all other issues. To take advantage of these rules, debtors who are resisting relief from the stay should try to have the final say, both in briefing and arguing all of the issues on which they have the burden of proof. When I face this problem, I try to discuss the burden of proof with the parties and the court, and suggest that the party with the ultimate burden of proof should have the final say on the issue.

Bankruptcy Negotiations

Bankruptcy lawyers are known for negotiating rather than litigating. To the uninitiated, the hallway outside of a bankruptcy court seems most like a bazaar. In litigating relief from the stay, for example, the debtor's lawyer often negotiates for a period of time in which the stay will remain in effect before the creditor may seek the right to pursue state law remedies. This emphasis on negotiations results from the fact that the bankruptcy court is a court of equity: In reaching its decision, the court will balance the parties' competing interests and equities, and experienced lawyers usually are able to balance those differing views in their own negotiations.

Lawyers who resist negotiating before the hearing may find the judge sending them to the hallway soon after oral argument to focus their arguments, address the court's concerns, and resolve some aspect of the dispute. After that, lawyers should not be surprised to see elements of their negotiations played out in the court. Although the bankruptcy rules respect the confidentiality of settlement discussions, bankruptcy cases provide many chances for those negotiations to be revealed in court. Two parties in a multiparty dispute may settle and then inform the court of their discussions in order to obtain court approval of the compromise. In relief from stay litigation, the debtor's offers of "adequate protection"—to protect the creditor's financial position while the automatic stay is in place—are relevant in the stay litigation itself to show that the debtor is trying to protect the creditor's interest.

Negotiations may be described in a disclosure statement as part of the effort to generate support for the proponent's plan. Settlement discussions also may be relevant to an award of fees when the lawyer is compelled to explain the difficulties in the litigation as a way to justify his fees.

The district court is a presence in every bankruptcy case. The district court is likely to defer to the bankruptcy court's resolution of bankruptcy issues, but is as likely to withdraw the reference of a bankruptcy proceeding that is related to one in the district court, or if the proceeding is one typically tried in the district court, such as antitrust claims and securities suits.

Most district judges appear to respect the bankruptcy judges who were appointed in the past decade, and they often work closely with them on matters in which the two courts share jurisdiction. For example, if a district court action may become moot, the district court may stay that action while a related case proceeds in the bankruptcy court. Because bankruptcy judges are adjuncts of the district court, communications between the two courts are entirely proper under the reference mechanisms adopted by most district courts.

Success in bankruptcy litigation results from tailoring one's positions to the principles that make bankruptcy law coherent. The bankruptcy judge wants to balance creditor interests and move the case promptly toward a reorganization or liquidation. Create a plan to handle all issues that may arise. The case develops gradually, and positions taken early in the case will shape positions your client may have to take later. Evaluate how your client's position affects other parties, and make sure your position promotes the reorganization efforts. Because bankruptcy judges will look favorably on strategies that reduce costs, try to take the positions that will streamline the case.

Fashion your arguments to meet the policy considerations that support the bankruptcy laws. Remember that the bankruptcy process favors the debtor's reorganization over its liquidation; the debtor is entitled to reasonable relief from the pressures that forced it into bankruptcy; the rules that favor the debtor (such as the automatic stay or the exclusive right to file and obtain consent to a plan of reorganization) also have limits as fairness requires; the absolute priority rule requires that senior classes be paid before junior classes; one creditor should not obtain a preference over another of equal status or in the same class; and, to the extent the debtor is a taxpayer, the reorganization should consider the concerns of employees, shareholders, and the community.

The purpose of bankruptcy law is the equitable readjustment of debts. If the rules and procedures of the bankruptcy courts seem like "voodoo" at first, it is only because they are unfamiliar. With a little study and practice, any seasoned litigator can become a skilled bankruptcy shaman.

The Client's Suffering

Kenneth P. Nolan

Initially it's anger.

It's anger at the airline for running out of fuel, crashing onto a hill, tearing the four-month-old child from his mother's arms to his death. The mother, whose injured left arm was rendered useless, sadly survived, tormented by incessant demons and inexplicable guilt, unable to share these with anyone, including her husband.

Or it's anger at the drunk driver with the 24 previous license suspensions who runs a red light at 70 mph without headlights, dragging and mutilating a mother and her two teenage girls to horrific deaths. The perfect family is destroyed. The father, injured as well, talks of wishing to die except for the needs of his teenage son. In a home filled with family and graduation photos, he reminds you that his daughters were active in Students Against Drunk Driving. The house, and its cruel reminders of the once-bright future, must be sold. Between tears, he curses the driver to a slow death.

Sometimes it's not only anger: it also becomes depression, apathy, or a combination of emotions. It's always, however, tragedy—permanent, heart-searing tragedy. Death. Paralysis. Brain damage. Amputation. From plane crashes—car accidents—medical malpractice—defective products. The kind you read about, the kind you see paraded on *Geraldo*, the kind you pray you never experience. The crown of thorns that some must endure in this life, making it truly a vale of tears.

But you are a lawyer. You know that the damage can never be altered. You know that the client and family look to you for assistance,

---

Kenneth P. Nolan, a partner at the New York City firm Speiser, Krause, Nolan & Granito, was the 1996–98 editor-in-chief of LITIGATION.

for guidance, and, occasionally, for unattainable revenge. Your job is to counsel, to explain, to litigate.

Emotionally, you empathize with their troubles. You yearn to make the person, the family, whole again. Legally, you want to right the wrong, eradicate the financial worry for this family, change their lives, allow them to move from the railroad-flat tenement in Brooklyn to the sunny respectability of a house and pool in Port St. Lucie, Florida.

But, truth be told, not all your thoughts are so noble. Late at night when you are alone, you even admit to yourself that there's some ego involved here. After all, this is the case that you have been seeking, the one you have deserved but that until now has eluded you. This is the case that will pay those college tuitions, purchase that summer home in Nantucket, put your mug on the six o'clock news, and prove to all what you already knew—that you are the equal (if not the better) of Gerry Spence, F. Lee Bailey, and the rest of your colleagues whose names are household words. Once this case is won, your name will be added to that number. The bar lecture circuit will come begging, and your war stories will be the talk of cocktail parties. Then judges will seek your counsel, and those young trial lawyer wannabes will laugh at your jokes.

Internal Conflict

This case evokes the best and the worst of your personality: the sympathetic, caring side your mother (but no one else, especially your spouse and partners) sees, and the dark side—formed by the greed, the hubris, the cynicism that you have acquired in the years since law school. These two sides will compete through the litigation, as you decide whether to settle or to try, to value the case honestly or to allow your client to dream in a world of multimillion-dollar headlines reinforced by neighborhood gossips.

And your internal conflict isn't the only problem. The pressure is on. The family and the community expect Lotto results. "If a woman can recover $2.9 million for spilling some McDonald's coffee on herself...." The courthouse regulars are already jealously critiquing your strategy. And your partners are busily spending your fee before the lawsuit has been filed.

Even worse, while the expectations of your client and your partners become more unrealistic, the opposition is gearing up. The experienced defendants do not panic. Instead, they retain top guns to represent them. And they are ready to fight, not only for the millions at risk, but also for the reputation of the defendant's product and perhaps the continued existence of the defendant corporation.

And so, despite the fact that your client commands as much sympathy as any juror can give, you have your work cut out for you. In order to defeat these formidable adversaries, fulfill your dreams, justify your ego, satisfy your partners, and serve your client, you must do the following:

Litigate the Case. You will be tempted to rely on the client's catastrophic injuries or on the tears of the widow and her children, and convince yourself that the defendants will be paralyzed by fear of a runaway verdict. They will throw money at you to settle. No jury, you believe, can ever look at this wheelchair and mutter, "Defendants' verdict," or even "$600,000." The sympathy is almost unbearable. Five million dollars, $10 million maybe, but nothing less. It is incomprehensible, you think. It is impossible, you are told.

Do not believe it. Do not delude yourself. The defendants are cornered and their lawyers will battle to save their clients' assets and reputation. Instead of rolling over, the defendants will spend more, work harder, and explore every aspect of the case. You never know what that ten-year-old medical record will reveal, what the high school records will illuminate, what the co-worker will expose.

The defendants will use all their resources to prevent the $25 million verdict, the punitive damages, the newspaper and TV headlines that will send their stock spiraling. Just as your reputation is at stake, so too is the defense lawyer's. With a victory in a case perceived to be impossible to win, the professional and financial rewards garnered by defense counsel are immense—especially because the insurer or corporation always has more business to send his way, always has another huge case.

To get the handsome result your client deserves, your mind-set must be on work, not glory. Preparation must start immediately—preparation not for settlement but for trial. Investigation must be commenced, legal research performed, documents obtained, experts hired. Money must be spent and clients counseled.

Some tasks can be delegated; the essential ones, however, you must do. You must know the facts, the clients, the witnesses, the law. Complete and thorough knowledge of all aspects of the case is paramount. Remember that the defense has more resources, and often more people—since there are usually numerous defendants and therefore several defense lawyers, each of whom has an insurance adjuster looking over her shoulder.

If the case is prepared with the false hope of settlement, maximum recovery will not be attained. Defendants and their principals are not nice guys. To pay as little as possible, every tactic will be utilized, and the ethical envelope will be pushed. Every weakness will be exploited. In the hardball world of million-dollar personal injury and death cases, most defendants respond to nothing less than a foot on the neck. Only the strength that comes from preparation for trial will enable you to effect such a maneuver.

Trust for the other side is a luxury that you cannot afford. Unless you are sure through experience that your opponent can be trusted, take no chances. Maintain a healthy amount of New York City paranoia—trust no one all the time. "You don't mind if I get that in writing, do you, Mom?"

Know Your Clients. In the ordinary personal injury case, you may meet the client when you are retained and once or twice after that—before depositions and then before trial. Younger partners and associates can fill in the gaps.

In a large case, this is inadequate. Since the emotional loss is much greater, you must meet with the client, her family, and close friends regularly to sustain your relationship and to understand their needs and desires. You must become involved in their lives and learn their fears, their hopes, their histories. Do this to nurture them emotionally, to gain their trust and to know them. After one of my partners settled a case involving the death of a teenager, the mother told him: "I want to thank you for your legal work, but more important, I want to thank you for saving my husband's life." Sometimes the emotional component of your representation outweighs the legal.

Any competent defendant will insist on obtaining all of the relevant documents, will interview dozens of co-workers, will perform extensive surveillance on an injured plaintiff. Because the defendants will read every record—medical, financial, school, work—you must learn more. Visit your clients' homes, talk with their friends and relatives. Learn the good and bad. Open those skeleton closets and take a long, hard look inside. Be skeptical of your client's answers. Ask probing questions about the marriage and the job. Ask even embarrassing questions about that arrest for DUI. In short, learn all you can from your clients.

Then investigate, if for no other reason than to rule out any problem before trial. The last thing you need at trial is a surprise. If there is something bad out there, you'll have to deal with it sooner or later. Learn about it sooner, not later. To pretend that it doesn't exist or won't be discovered is naive.

If there is a past problem with law enforcement, for example, learning about it early will enable you to find a way to minimize it. Having it thrust upon you at depositions or at trial, on the other hand, can be devastating. In one death action handled by our office, defense counsel sent a young associate to rummage through our client's hundreds of canceled checks. Each unknown payee was tracked down; one was a marriage counselor. Although the situation turned out to be rather innocuous, the defense argued that the marriage was not the bed of roses we suggested. Diligence is an asset that can translate into savings for the defense. The only way to combat that is to be more thorough.

By the time of trial, you should know more about the client's family than they do. Spend time with them, even time you would rather spend on other matters, or on other issues in this case. You will find that prior problems, physical and emotional, will be mentioned either in discussions with the client or in interviews with others who are potential fact witnesses.

No one voluntarily reveals dirty little secrets. Ask about them. Forewarned is forearmed. And if none exist, then you can confidently provide the endless discovery that the defendants will demand.

Determine who pulls the strings. People who have suffered loss usually look to others for advice. In educated families, a parent, uncle, or cousin might provide financial guidance. In uneducated families, someone outside the family, perhaps someone who has more education or a position of power in the community, might help make important decisions. Learn the motivation of these people. If their goals are selfish or corrupt, you may have to confront these influences. And, regardless, learning who is making the calls will give you insight into the goals and desires of your client.

A continual battle will be fought during the litigation between what is fact and what your client is told by "well-meaning" friends. The more you are with your client, the more you build rapport and the ability to help your client distinguish fact from fiction. And the more you learn.

Think About Venue. Where you bring the action often determines success—and if you win, by how much. Plaintiffs prefer state courts in urban areas. Juries and judges are more liberal there. Defendants prefer federal courts in conservative jurisdictions. There, discovery is usually broader, the judges—usually from large firms that represent corporate America—are more sympathetic to the defense, and the jury pool will include the suburban or rural conservative juror.

The law is secondary. Generally, an Idaho jury with liberal wrongful death law will award less than a Bronx jury with conservative New York wrongful death law. A suburban Atlanta jury will award your client less than an urban Miami jury.

Of course, there are exceptions. In the Pan Am/Lockerbie trial, for example, a white juror from the suburbs assumed the role of Henry Fonda in *Twelve Angry Men* convincing a divided jury to decide in favor of the plaintiffs, while two black elderly women from the city, clutching their Bibles, were the last holdouts for the defense. Hey, you never know.

Research the law as to liability and damages. Is precedent favorable to a finding of fault on your theory? Enumerate the items of damages—particularly in death actions where some states allow recovery for grief and loss of affection, while others permit recovery only for pecuniary loss. Learn the law of all potential jurisdictions before venue is selected. If a plane crashes in Indiana and the defendants include a joint Italian/French manufacturer and an air carrier that is incorporated in Delaware, has a principal place of business in Virginia, and is a wholly owned subsidiary of a Delaware corporation with a principal place of business in Texas, where do you bring suit if your client is an English citizen with a green card, teaching in Montreal, whose wife is from California, teaching in Indiana, but thinks of New York as home?

And once you choose venue, what liability law will be applied? What damage law? Is it the law of Indiana on liability, and the law of Quebec on damages, determined by a Texas jury? Is the foreign manufacturer entitled to a nonjury trial pursuant to the Foreign Sovereign Immunities Act? Can the case be kept in state court? You need to know the answers to all these questions to practice the art of forum shopping.

Substantive law and jury history are not the only considerations; tort reform and its effects must be evaluated as well. Are there caps on noneconomic damages? In a case involving a victim without dependents, such as an infant, the loss of society, and the grief of the survivors, define the damages. There is little, if any, economic loss. Therefore, a jurisdiction with a cap on such items of damage will be disastrous.

Choosing the Law

Is there joint and several liability in any of the potential jurisdictions? If the primary defendant has limited insurance, then you want a jurisdiction where the deep pocket can be forced to pay the entire award, even if found only one percent at fault. Must future damages—loss of earnings, for instance—be structured? If so, then the value of the award will be less in that jurisdiction.

All procedural and substantive tort reform changes must be studied and applied to your facts. If you represent the estate of a wage-earner who is survived by a spouse and children, tort reform may have no effect. On the other hand, if you represent Mrs. Peets, a mother of three who doesn't receive a paycheck for her 110-hour week, then a cap on noneconomic damages will minimize the strongest part of the case—the loss of her presence and care of her children.

These issues must be evaluated and debated. Choice of law must be analyzed. The history of the jurisdiction must be investigated. The background and approach of the potential judges must be ascertained.

Speak to the local clique. Absorb the courthouse gossip. Amass the jury verdict reports. Canvass the local bar for verdict history.

Discover. Learn everything you can about the case. Master the intricacies of the product or procedure that injured your client.

In an obstetrical medical malpractice case, learn how to read the fetal monitoring strips, when to use Pitocin, the differences between internal and external fetal monitors. Read the texts, purchase the forceps. Find all publications by government oversight agencies. Obtain any standards set by national associations, such as the American College of Obstetricians and Gynecologists. These standards are often changed periodically, so make sure that the edition that you have was in effect on the date of the malpractice. Then mark the standards at the doctor's deposition and cross the defendant on whether they were followed during the labor and delivery of Mrs. Abel. If not, watch her squirm to justify her noncompliance.

Research the history of the product. Search for similar incidents. Interview current and former employees. A disgruntled former employee can be the gold you're looking for.

Begin your investigation as soon as you have been retained. I was once called by a friend who told me of a 55-year-old man who went to the emergency room with chest pains. Instead of being admitted or observed for a while, he was diagnosed as having heartburn, given Mylanta, and discharged. That evening he died in bed from a heart attack. The family rightfully believed that he should have been admitted to the hospital. Because I feared that the emergency room EKG tracing would disappear, I immediately went to the hospital to secure the records. While there, a young resident—call her Dr. Ponciroli—pulled me aside and told me that she was the physician who had examined Mr. Newbower and discharged him. When I eventually obtained the hospital records, the name of the examining physician was illegible. The formal response to my demand for the names of all physicians in the emergency room did not include Dr. Ponciroli. And at depositions, no one knew who had treated Mr. Newbower in the hectic emergency room. Without my running to the hospital, I would have never been able to question the physician who was responsible for the treatment. Speed is essential.

Formal discovery must be extensive. Everyone involved must be deposed. When in doubt, take the deposition and request the document. At one damage trial, defendant's psychologist was innocently asked on direct "if there were anything else pertinent in the record of the family doctor." The expert replied that there was a notation of "neurosis." There was no follow-up question and the direct ended a few minutes later. Only because I had scoured every line of the record was I able to locate the word. On cross, I demonstrated that the notation had been written eight years before the event at issue, had resulted in absolutely no treatment, was not even written clearly enough to read with certainty, and might actually have been a totally different term.

Never rest. If you know the file and the law and have a sympathetic client, defendants will respect you. Sometimes they may even fear you.

Find the Best Experts. Hire them early and often. No one is as knowledgeable as the surgeon or the mechanic or the crane operator who devotes his life to a daily routine. If the plane crash involved ice on the wing, hire a meteorologist to analyze the weather pattern, warnings, and technology available to predict the problem. Hire a pilot who flies the particular type of plane to provide you with his experience, his training, and the "hangar talk" among similar pilots. Hire a former NTSB investigator to provide insight into the cause of the crash and to analyze any government findings. Hire an ex-air traffic controller to tell you whether the plane was properly held in the air and whether any procedures were disobeyed. The list goes on. Select those experts who will educate you. You need not use them at trial, but it's always better to have more than less.

The Good Old Days

In the good old Tammany Hall days of New York City, there was "honest graft." Initially, you need "honest experts" to advise you not only of the strengths, but the weaknesses of your case. Maybe the expert is not articulate and does not look like Sean Connery, but use him during discovery to educate you, prepare you for depositions, and interpret documents. If the expert is qualified and will devote time to your case, then he is valuable regardless of whether he will ultimately testify.

At trial, the appearance and jury appeal of the expert are important. Experts must teach, jurors must translate scientific lingo into everyday language. On cross, experts cannot afford to become angry or disconcerted under any circumstances. An experienced expert never becomes combative or flustered, no matter how heated the cross: "Doctor, isn't it true that you're a child molester, a mass-murderer, and smoke smelly cigars?" Turning to the jury, he smiles sweetly and replies with a confident "of course."

Pedigree and education are important, but real hands-on experience is paramount. The truck driver, the 747 pilot, the machine press operator are impressive—especially in uniform with lapels or in grease-stained overalls. Of course, star quality is a real plus. Try cross-examining an astronaut who walked on the moon about his testimony that the pilot of a 727 that crashed was not at fault. Even the judge was excited and had his photo taken with this hired gun.

Pursue Settlement. Be open to resolution at any time. Obtain client authority for a demand. But be patient if your client is unreasonable early on. Any competent defense lawyer or insurance adjuster will understand if you respond, "$100 million." Let your client's anger subside during the litigation. Usually the demand will become more reasonable.

Examine your client's financial needs and find out whether a slightly smaller settlement early in the case might be financially advantageous. Consider structured settlements if your client is financially unsophisticated. Do not let your ego intrude on what should be a business decision in your client's best interest. Sure you would like to stick it to the arrogant slobs, but the client's needs are your priority. Your reputation is secondary. And your cash flow problem is no reason to settle cheaply. Communicate offers in writing and likewise confirm their rejection if you believe that the jury will award less. Be honest with your client and yourself.

Try Your Case. This is the shoot-out, the championship fight, the clash of the titans. Like all battles, it begins with preparation. As you walk through the courthouse door, have your briefs ready on the legal issues and the scientific issues. Educate the judge and her law clerk. The first pages of your scientific brief should be a glossary. Is an aileron something from outer space? Define the technical terms, use illustrations or photos to make the difficult simple. Remember, the judge spends most of her time either on slip-and-fall cases or on drug cases. It is rewarding when the judge thumbs through your brief while the experts testify.

Prepare your jury instructions for the judge before trial begins. Although they may have to be amended as the trial unfolds, the law clerk may use these as a reference from which to draft the final jury charge. Their preparation will also force you again to examine what you must prove to win your case.

Make your motions in limine before jury selection so that you know what is admissible. This is especially true for demonstrative evidence. Do not focus your case around a "Day-in-the-Life" film only to have the judge rule in the middle of trial that it is inadmissible. Have the judge rule before trial so you can adapt your strategy, your witnesses, your proof.

Consider presenting your case to a shadow or mock jury. You have engulfed your life in this action—you know more about myocardial biopsies than the chief of the cardiology department at Einstein Medical Center, your children call you the "heart doctor daddy," and your partners seek your advice on their cardiac problems. But your immersion in the case and its issues may skew your communication—and even your understanding—of the facts. A run-through of your evidence and argument before one or more mock juries may surprise you and may color your judgment about what is effective. Have professionals organize these mock trials. But be sure to have them select jurors from the area of the jury pool.

During trial, remember that jurors are suspicious of lawyers—especially plaintiff's lawyers. They believe you are a shyster. You must convince them otherwise. Either in jury selection or opening, establish rapport. It is always more effective to address the jurors during jury selection. But if not permitted, do it in opening. Admit weaknesses. Inform them of the warts—the messy divorce, the DUI, the history of heart disease. Be honest. Discuss sympathy before the defendant uses it as a club. Tell them that justice—not sympathy—is your goal and their responsibility.

Always understate damages. A momentary view of a brain-damaged infant is infinitely more articulate and persuasive than your 15-minute description. A mother sitting with her children alone on a wooden bench shouts volumes. Let witnesses describe the 65 seconds of terror as the plane plunged to the earth, the lack of any appreciable remains, the nightmares, the loneliness, the fear of raising a family alone.

If your client is catastrophically injured, you do not want him present in the courtroom every day of a month-long trial. With familiarity comes callousness. A few appearances in court are sufficient.

Timing of witnesses is important. By establishing liability first, you will gain the jurors' trust. They will understand that you are not relying on the sympathy generated by your tragically injured or widowed or orphaned client to prove your case.

Then proceed to damages. Use the experts to establish the cost of medical and custodial care. Ask the doctor how many times a week Mr. Gutman must be treated by a therapist, and for how long. Have the doctor testify about the daily cost of such services. If necessary, bring in a therapist or a rehabilitation expert to discuss specific amounts.

Be conservative with your numbers. Do not destroy the economist's credibility by having him testify to projections without support or foundation. When you project lost earnings of a young executive or medical care of an invalid infant, the real numbers are astronomical enough to shock the juror scraping by on $30,000 a year. Do not endanger your case by trying for that extra $50,000.

Use demonstrative evidence: photos, graphs, blowups—whatever works for you. But, again, be a minimalist. Too much is a turnoff. Keep the "Day-in-the-Life" film to under 20 minutes. Let your experts use the demonstrative evidence to teach, to highlight, to convince. We are a visual generation, raised on film and television. The technology is there—use it.

Your client, whether the widowed or the orphaned or the injured, should testify. Keep it short and to the point. Avoid dramatics. With any significant loss, tears flow without prompting. Have other relatives, friends, the boss confirm what a great mother, wife, teacher, worker she was. Again, keep their testimony short. But be sure to have a few individuals who have no interest in the outcome testify to emphasize the goodness, the beauty, the joy that has been lost forever.

In closing, be assured. Look the jurors in the eye and tell them what you want. Do not be apologetic if you ask for an amount that the jurors will collectively never earn in their lifetimes. If you are hesitant, it will be perceived as lack of conviction. If you do not believe in your case, why should the jury? If you are permitted to, write it down. Fill out the jury questionnaire with the jurors, but always remind them that the final determination is theirs. Speak in language that they can understand. Be positive.

And then wait for the jury's decision with the quiet confidence of someone who has done his job well. Because if you have worked hard in preparing and trying your case, the jury will want to ease the pain of your client's devastating loss. And more often than not, that will mean success for you both.

Litigating Cases Before Administrative Law Judges

Lawrence P. Postol

For many lawyers, knowledge of the administrative process starts and ends with a law school course that touches lightly on the Administrative Procedure Act, 5 U.S.C. § 551 *et seq.*, and surveys the few landmark cases setting out the powers of administrative agencies. Many others have even less knowledge of the administrative process. As the administrative process invades more aspects of everyday life, more litigators will need to know as much about administrative adjudication as they know about litigating in traditional courts.

Whether your clients are pensioners or multinational corporations, an active litigator today needs to know how to conduct proceedings before an administrative law judge. To handle this litigation, you must know about the rules, practices, and customs used by administrative law judges. The variety of administrative agencies seems almost endless, ranging from local school boards to massive federal departments. And even though the rules and practices vary from agency to agency, and indeed from judge to judge, certain principles are universal and must be understood.

The Administrative Procedure Act is the starting point. It sets the outer limits for administrative law judges. Agency rules give further shape to practice before administrative law judges, and custom and tradition regulate the inner core of the proceedings. Also, most states have their own versions of the Administrative Procedure Act, many of which are patterned after the federal act. Thus, practitioners who have dealt with state agencies already may have some familiarity with the basics.

Matters get before an administrative law judge in one of three ways. When an agency denies a benefit—such as a license, permit, or a welfare

---

Lawrence P. Postol is a member of the national law firm Seyfarth, Shaw, Fairweather & Geraldson; his office is in Washington, D.C.

entitlement—the action can be appealed to an administrative law judge within the agency. Second, numerous agencies have power to regulate individual conduct, but can do so only after notice and hearing before an administrative law judge. Finally, agencies must give notice and conduct hearings before administrative law judges as part of rule making.

Interested parties can participate in and can even initiate the rule making. They must be given notice of hearings and an opportunity to present evidence and arguments. 5 U.S.C. § 554(b) and (c). Administrative law judges may exclude "irrelevant, immaterial, or unduly repetitive evidence," and decisions must be based on the evidence in the record, which must be "reliable, probative and substantive." 5 U.S.C. § 556(d). The proponent of an order has the burden of proof. 5 U.S.C. § 556(d).

The agency may review and change the decision of the administrative law judge, although in some instances statutes and regulations impose a substantial evidence test as the standard of review. 5 U.S.C. § 557(b). On appeal, an agency's decision must be upheld by the reviewing court if it is based on substantial evidence in the record; is not arbitrary, capricious, or an abuse of discretion; and accords with the statutory mandate. 5 U.S.C. § 706.

Judging the Judge

An administrative law judge must be disinterested and impartial. 5 U.S.C. § 556. In cases where the agency acts as the prosecutor, such as enforcement proceedings before the Federal Trade Commission, there is an inherent conflict between the administrative law judge's role as an employee of the prosecuting federal agency and his role as a judge. Defenders of the system argue that the judge's association with the agency and his familiarity with the cases coming before him provide a level of expertise that far outweighs the possible prejudice. Of course, such conflicts should not arise when the judge rules on a dispute between two private parties, such as in workers' compensation claims.

Nevertheless, in cases where the agency is a party, an argument can be made for having a pool of administrative law judges with no loyalty to any particular agency, and some states have adopted such a system. In most cases, however, the inherent conflict is never a real factor and is far outweighed by the benefit of the administrative law judge's expertise. The best safeguard may be the selection of high quality and fair-minded lawyers as administrative law judges.

Knowing the limits set by the Administrative Procedure Act is important, but the act tells very little about how a particular administrative law judge will act or rule in a case. Like all trial judges, administrative law judges have wide discretion in what discovery and evidence is allowed. Indeed, since the Federal Rules of Evidence usually do not apply, and there is no jury, the administrative law judge has more power than a district court judge.

Will the judge follow the spirit of the Federal Rules of Evidence? Will he sequester witnesses? What type and form of discovery will he allow? The search for answers begins with the agency's enabling statute and regulations, and ends with the individual practices of each judge.

The enabling statute determines how the administrative law judge will rule on the merits of the substantive issues. For example, the National Labor Relations Act determines what conduct constitutes an unfair labor practice before the National Labor Relations Board. Enabling statutes may even regulate some procedural questions, such as who is an interested party and the agency's standard for reviewing the judge's decision. More than likely, however, the agency will have promulgated regulations governing most procedures. Enabling statutes are found in the United States Code, and regulations in the Code of Federal Regulations.

Unfortunately, some lawyers appear before administrative law judges without becoming familiar with the statute and regulations. Such omissions lead not only to procedural failures, but also to situations in which the judge and the client lose confidence in the lawyer. Administrative law judges, like traditional judges, are human—they distrust lawyers who are not well prepared. If you do not know the law and regulations, administrative law judges may well assume that your substantive legal and factual arguments are weak, too.

Knowing the substantive statute is especially important when practicing before an administrative law judge specializing in cases governed by that statute. He knows the statute intimately. He easily detects the lawyer's errors, is reluctant to excuse mistakes, and may well be insulted if it seems that the lawyer has not taken the time to read the statute. Examples of such blunders are endless—they range from mistakenly informing the judge that the other party has the burden of proof, to misciting the judge's jurisdictional limits. If you do not read the statute, you do not know where, when, or how you will falter. If a case is worth trying, it is worth a cover-to-cover review of the statute and regulations.

While agency regulations are not uniform, they generally adhere to a central core of principles and rules. In discovery, regulations are often relaxed versions of the Federal Rules of Civil Procedure. Almost all federal agencies provide for using subpoenas and depositions. About half have the full arsenal of discovery tools, including interrogatories, requests for production of documents, and requests for admissions.

No Fishing Expeditions

The administrative proceeding is supposed to be a streamlined adjudication process. Discovery should only take months, not years. Administrative law judges do not tolerate fishing expeditions. Thus, discovery requests should be specific and precise. Administrative law judges are less tolerant of requests that "may eventually lead to relevant evidence" or that deal with collateral issues. The judges tend to require that discovery seek only relevant, admissible evidence, or that it at least clearly lead to such evidence.

Lawyers should limit the number of interrogatories to fewer than 30 and request only specifically identified documents. Broad-based, shotgun-type requests are not well received.

The same is true for depositions. Do not try to depose every conceivable witness in the case; rather, limit yourself to the main actors. Limit formal discovery by using informal discovery first. Where possible, witnesses first should be interviewed instead of deposed, and documents should be requested through voluntary channels.

Most administrative cases turn on facts, not law. Indeed, the primary purpose of having an administrative law judge is for him to gather facts and to produce a record for the reviewing agency or board, which establishes the policy (the law) that must be applied to the facts of the case. Of course, a lawyer must be aware of what policies, i.e., precedents, have already been established. Yet, many practitioners try a case before an administrative law judge without researching agency case law until preparing the posthearing brief.

This foolish practice can be costly. A lawyer must know the pertinent case law to know what facts are relevant and how they should be presented. A lawyer should not discover the precedent "on all fours" after the record has been made. This will not impress the judge.

I have seen an administrative law judge interrupt an otherwise fine opening statement because the lawyer's argument was based on a case that had been reversed. I could not see the client's expression, but I am sure the client was no more impressed with his lawyer than was the judge. Likewise, I have seen lawyers cite cases in their briefs that had been reversed by the United States Supreme Court two years earlier.

Obviously, you must know relevant case law before trying a court or administrative case; yet the administrative process presents additional hazards to the unprepared lawyer. First, for reasons that are not completely clear, many lawyers take administrative proceedings too lightly. The same lawyer who spends hours researching the case law before going before a district court judge may somehow feel comfortable doing no research prior to appearing before an administrative law judge.

Second, the administrative proceeding may involve unusual legal doctrines, and the agency precedent is hard to find and digest. Many libraries do not carry agency decisions, and you may need to go to a law firm that has a specialized library, or to the agency's own library. Finally, since administrative law judges specialize in one field of law, they are more likely to know the relevant case law than will a district court judge. For example, an administrative law judge in a National Labor Relations Board case understands the difference between an economic strike and an unfair labor practice strike, and knows that fights, picketing, and tire slashing often accompany strikes. Keep the judge's expertise in mind if you contemplate trying to "wing it."

Except for decisions reviewed by a court of appeals, administrative cases are not published in the West system. Some agency decisions, however, are published in well-known private services, some in more obscure ones. A call to the agency's library usually will locate the publisher.

Often it is also important to know if the agency maintains an index or digest of cases that are not published by private services. The administrative law judge will know about such decisions, and many law firms practicing before a particular agency collect all agency opinions, including administrative law judge opinions. You do not want to be the only participant in a case who does not know about a critical agency decision. Indeed, the cost of collecting and analyzing agency decisions is one of the main reasons that practitioners often specialize in handling cases before only one agency. Still, agency libraries may be open to the public, which gives you access to all the decisions available to the most experienced practitioners.

Often it helps to read several opinions written by the administrative law judge assigned to your case: Get a feel for the type of evidence he considers relevant, and for the way he analyzes the facts and the law. The wise lawyer then tailors his case to the pattern the judge has accepted before.

Most administrative law judges are extremely informal about motions. They usually have no prescribed form, often accepting letters as motions. Similarly, they usually will rule on motions without a hearing, or will hold hearings by telephone. If you have a question about the judge's procedures and practices, call his secretary or law clerk.

Administrative law judges usually are more interested in the facts and the equities of discovery disputes than in case citations. They often allow broad discovery in terms of relevance, as long as the requests are specific and not overly burdensome. But they are sensitive about the need to avoid building an unmanageable record, especially since they have to read the record: Under the Administrative Procedure Act, the judge must issue a written opinion discussing all the evidence in the record.

For that reason, many judges do not tolerate lawyers who use the "dump and run" technique—offering piles of paper into evidence and letting the judge figure out what the case is about and which documents are relevant. Rather, when faced with a stack of documents, the judge may make the lawyers go through the stack, eliminating the irrelevant documents and marking the ones they want the judge to consider in making his findings of fact.

Many problems that arise in civil litigation appear in practice before the administrative law judge, but in a different context. First, discovery disputes will be decided on the papers or after a telephone conference call. Administrative law judges do not have a motions day; rather, the administrative case usually involves only one hearing—the trial.

How does a lawyer deal with these limitations? To begin with, since the judge may rule on the pleadings, make sure that your motion papers are complete. Any documents necessary to rule on the motion, such as interrogatories, should be attached to the motion papers.

Taking the initiative also helps. If you want an oral argument, call the judge's law clerk offering to set up a telephone conference with the judge and opposing counsel. Government operators are difficult to deal with, and most administrative law judges are happy when the lawyer offers to set up the conference call. Also, try to limit discovery motions, and try to be the first to file. Finally, offer to draft a proposed order, a step that makes the judge's life easier since his secretarial help may be limited.

Administrative law judges are quite liberal about receiving evidence, but are careful not to let the record become too large and not to violate principles of due process. Since there is no jury, the judge does not have to worry about jurors being confused by irrelevant information or swayed by prejudicial evidence of limited relevance.

Judges do, however, become bored or tired, particularly at the end of the day. Relevancy objections are more likely to be sustained then, although the judge may merely suggest that the lawyer move on to a more relevant area.

Always follow that advice unless the evidence is critical. Except to preserve the point for appeal, there is no sense in continuing if the judge thinks the evidence is not relevant. He is the trier of fact, and thus if he believes the evidence is not relevant, then by definition it is not.

Unless their regulations provide otherwise, administrative law judges are not bound by technical rules of evidence. Documents usually will be admitted without proof of authenticity, even though technically they are hearsay. Nevertheless, administrative law judges follow the central requirements of due process on which the Federal Rules of Evidence are based.

Administrative law judges almost always protect the right of cross-examination. However, they will effectively shift the burden of proof on evidentiary objections. For example, they may ask the objecting party to prove that the offered document is not authentic, instead of making the offering party prove admissibility.

Yet some judges sustain hearsay objections, particularly when the offering party controls the person who made the original statement. These judges reason that if the witness can easily be produced at the hearing, it is unfair to admit a hearsay statement and make the opposing party chase after the witness to exercise his cross-examination rights. If you do not know the judge's view about this, you should have the witness available to testify if needed.

In using leading questions on direct examination, most administrative law judges allow more latitude than would a district court judge. For example, many judges allow leading questions on direct examination of an expert witness whose opinion already is in a report. But when a lay witness's testimony is at the heart of a party's case, leading questions will not be allowed.

Even if you think you will be allowed to lead your witness, you should prepare the witness so that you do not need to ask leading questions. It is always more impressive when the answer seems to come from the witness, and not the lawyer. Conversely, properly phrased leading questions produce a clear, concise transcript, which then can be liberally quoted in the posthearing brief; but be careful of overdoing the technique.

The difference between administrative and court proceedings can easily be seen by looking at the results. Testimony in district court usually is designed for a jury, while the administrative process is designed to create a hearing transcript that the judge reads and evaluates before issuing a decision. Thus, most administrative law judges will exercise broad discretion in helping produce a record that is organized, complete, and fair.

If a party produces a surprise witness or document, an administrative law judge usually will allow the other party an opportunity to offer rebuttal evidence, even if the lawyer did not make the proper discovery request to require disclosure of the witness or document before the hearing. Since a decision is not rendered at the hearing, many judges will keep the record open for a posthearing deposition in place of live testimony. On the other hand, some judges do not like posthearing evidentiary submissions, since they may prejudice the opposing party. Because preferences differ, counsel must know what the presiding judge allows. Finally, most judges appreciate an organized set of exhibits and like the testimony to be presented logically and clearly.

Most judges allow the parties great latitude in compiling the record. Opposing counsel should work together to agree on certain evidentiary issues such as authenticity of documents, and the use of prehearing or posthearing depositions. Indeed, in ruling on most motions or requests, the judge usually begins by asking if the other party opposes the request. If not, the judge usually grants any reasonable request.

You may be confused about whether to treat the administrative law judge like a jury or as a district court judge. An administrative law judge is neither.

Lawyers must recognize that the administrative law judge is not only the trier of fact, but also has the job of deciding legal questions and resolving discovery disputes.

The first rule is to treat the judge with respect. Too many lawyers think they can treat the judge like just "one of the boys" or worse. No matter how friendly the judge, no matter how informal the hearing room and surroundings, never forget the judge is just that: a judge.

Of course, this does not mean that you must knuckle under. If you disagree with the judge, do not be afraid to say so; just be polite and respectful about it.

Another way of showing respect is by making the judge's life easier—be cooperative and provide whatever information or case law the judge needs to rule in your favor. For example, if you cite to cases or statutes that the judge may not have nearby, provide him with a copy. While many agencies have access to their own decisions, they often do not have standard references such as Federal Supplement and the U.S. Code Annotated.

Since many lawyers take administrative law judges for granted, the judges are especially sensitive to improper behavior. Be as polite as possible to opposing counsel, be fair in your arguments, and never, never mischaracterize a fact to the judge.

One of the prime advantages of trying a case before an administrative law judge is the judge's expertise—after a judge has tried 100 black lung cases, he has learned a lot about lungs. Federal Trade Commission judges know more about economics than many economics students. Keep this in mind when formulating your evidence. Confront hard questions and try answering them; the administrative law judge will not overlook them. Where appropriate, expert witnesses, at least the good ones, can be particularly effective. Since the judge usually will understand the field, he will appreciate a truly impressive expert witness. University professors often make the best witnesses because of their uncontroverted expertise and their lack of bias. Administrative law judges who have heard and seen many experts in a particular field are better equipped than a lay jury to distinguish a good expert from a bad one.

Although administrative law judges are educated specialists, they are still human. If they dislike a lawyer, they will find a way to make him pay the price. If you make the judge's life hard, he will return the favor.

Most important, the judge wants to "do justice." Too often, lawyers plead "the law" to the judge. Rather, the lawyer first should convince the judge that justice requires his client to win. Once the "justice" question has been addressed, you can argue "the law" and present the judge with the tools for ruling for your client.

Starting with your opening statement, and ending with your posthearing brief, give your evidence in a clear, logical order, demonstrating that your client has acted fairly and properly, and that the other side is the villain, the liar, or the cheat. Naturally, you should tie the evidence together with legal principles the judge already knows. Juries get legal instructions at the end of the case, but administrative law judges know the law right away. Once the evidence is set out and the judge is convinced that you should win, you can show him the way the law requires ruling in your favor. If the judge believes you should lose as a matter of fairness, the law usually allows him sufficient leeway to reach that result.

Smoothing the Road

Administrative law judges often have heavy case loads. Like all of us, if they are faced with a road that is smooth and easy, they will follow that path and not be swayed. Do everything in your power to make the judge's trip easy. Beginning with discovery disputes, offer to arrange a telephone conference call and provide the judge with the relevant pleadings (which often are lost in the agency bureaucracy, sometimes labeled a filing office). In your opening statement, show the judge the clear path to follow, and provide him with sufficient information so that he will understand the testimony. Documents should be legible and logically organized. Finally, the posthearing brief should be a fully annotated guide for the judge.

The posthearing brief is to an administrative law judge what the closing argument is to the jury, only much more so. Many judges do not listen closely to testimony during the hearing, knowing that they can rely on the hearing transcript. However, in many cases the record is massive. The posthearing brief is your final chance to convince the judge that your client is right and to make it easy for him to rule in your favor. Go over the evidence fairly, as if the judge will write the decision from your brief. Discuss both sides of the evidence—note why your evidence is persuasive and the other party's evidence is not. Give the judge the reasons for making credibility determinations in your favor—point out the inconsistencies in the other side's testimony, explain why your expert is the better expert, and why your client acted fairly.

Finally, make the judge's life easy. Do not just cite a page in the record, forcing the judge to pull the record out. Quote the record liberally in your brief. In fact, if the judge indicates he would not be offended by a proposed decision and order, draft one. Provide him with a computer disk of the proposed decision and order, "for ease of editing." More and more judges like this option. However, do not be presumptuous. First ask the judge if he would like a proposed decision and order in lieu of, or in addition to, a brief. Otherwise, draft your brief in a form from which the judge can easily write his opinion—perhaps taking whole sections from your brief.

The administrative law judge is the trier of fact, but his decision may be appealed within the agency. There are two possible standards for agency review of administrative law judges' decisions. Many agencies use the usual substantial evidence test that many civil appellate courts adhere to. Some agencies, however, provide for a de novo review on the record created by the administrative law judge. If the agency's standard of review is substantial evidence, then the agency must affirm the administrative law judge's decision if there are no errors of law and there is substantial evidence in the record to support the judge's decision. That the agency might have weighed the evidence differently is not a ground for reversal. If the agency does not follow the substantial evidence test, then the agency can reweigh the evidence, although it is bound by the record created by the judge. The agency normally cannot accept new evidence on appeal.

The standard of review may be part of the agency's statute or set out in regulations. After review, the next level is to the United States court of appeals, normally on a substantial evidence test.

Administrative law judges provide the expertise to handle administrative adjudications in a fair and efficient manner. However, to get the most out of the system, the lawyer must know and follow the rules, regulations, practices, and customs of the administrative law judges. In many ways, a trial before an administrative law judge is tougher than one before a district court judge, since the lawyer must cope with strange agency rules and customs, as well as the peculiarities of the particular administrative law judge he is appearing before. The judge is ultimately the trier of fact, and all dealings with him, beginning with discovery disputes, must bear that reality in mind. While agency case law is difficult to find, it is imperative that counsel know the applicable precedent as well as the evidentiary rules and customs the judge follows.

Finally, written skills can be as important as oral skills, since a post-hearing brief can be the key to winning a case before an administrative law judge. Instead of taking administrative proceedings for granted, trial counsel must be totally prepared.

Collecting a Judgment

James J. Brown

You win the big one: a $5 million judgment. With it comes rave reviews from clients, colleagues, friends, and relatives. You have the judgment framed and hang it on your wall.

But wait a second. "Where's the money?" the managing partner asks. The real world rears its ugly head. It dawns on you that the defendant isn't going to stroll into your office with a certified check for five million bucks.

You close your door, take the judgment off your wall, and replace it with the certificate you got for coaching your daughter's little league team. You stop taking phone calls and start looking for the rules on collecting judgments.

Begin with Federal Rule of Civil Procedure 69. It says that procedures for enforcing judgments follow state law, except when a federal statute specifically governs.

Under state law, the first step is to record the judgment in the county where the debtor resides or owns property. A federal judgment may be recorded in the same manner as a state judgment in any locality within the federal district where the judgment was entered. File a certified copy of the judgment in the county land records, usually at the registry of deeds or county recorder's office, and pay the filing fee. The judgment becomes a lien on the debtor's property in the county where you record it. 28 U.S.C. § 1962.

Say you have a federal judgment from the United States District Court for the District of Maryland at Baltimore. If the debtor owns property in Howard County, Maryland (which does not encompass Baltimore, but is

---

The Honorable James J. Brown, formerly with the firm of Weinberg & Green in Baltimore, was deputy chief of the Judgment Enforcement Unit, U.S. Department of Justice, Washington, D.C., and is now a U.S. administrative law judge in Raleigh, North Carolina.

in the same federal district), you would record the judgment by filing a certified copy with the appropriate office of Howard County. The judgment will then be a lien against the debtor's Howard County property.

You can encumber property in other jurisdictions as well. Before the judgment can be recorded in another jurisdiction, it must be properly enrolled on the court docket there.

If you know the debtor has property in other counties in the same state but outside the federal district where the judgment was entered, follow the state procedures for registering the judgment there. Registering the judgment means enrolling it on the court docket. Then record the judgment in the new county so it becomes a lien on any real property the debtor owns there.

Judgments obtained in a federal district court may also be registered in other federal districts once they become final by appeal or otherwise. 28 U.S.C. § 1963. In addition, there are statutory procedures for registering judgments of the Court of International Trade and the United States Claims Court in the district courts. 28 U.S.C. §§ 1963A, 2508.

Judgments registered in a new jurisdiction have the same effect as in the original jurisdiction and are treated the same way. *Stanford v. Utley*, 341 F.2d 265 (8th Cir. 1965). *United States v. Palmer*, 609 F. Supp. 544, 547 (E.D. Tenn. 1985). So once you register the judgment in another district, you can record it and get the resulting lien against the debtor's property in any county within the registering district.

As a practical matter, some court clerks do not understand that, once a judgment has been registered, you do not need to follow state law procedures for enforcing "foreign" judgments. If you have trouble with the clerk on this point, talk to the chief clerk and walk him through the pertinent cases and statutes, giving him copies for comfort.

Now you have liens on the debtor's property in various places. That is a good start, because it will establish your priority interest in that property if you get into a scuffle with creditors who come along later. But how do you get your money?

If the debtor has property in the jurisdiction where the judgment was entered or registered, have the court clerk issue a writ of execution against the property (sometimes called an attachment writ or a garnishment writ). Then present the writ to the U.S. marshal, who will attach the property to satisfy your judgment. Federal Civil Procedure Rule 69 says that the procedure on execution follows the state practice.

You should describe the property to the marshal as specifically as possible. If there are different kinds of property, request different writs from the clerk. For example, in the federal district courts, there are usually separate forms of writs for: Attachment on Judgment (personal property, goods, chattels); Attachment on Judgment (credits); and Attachment on Judgment (garnishment of wages, earnings, salary, commissions and pensions). Consult the clerk on what writs should be issued.

If the debtor's property is in the hands of a third party such as a bank, proceed in accordance with state law (unless a particular federal statute applies) to attach (or garnish) those credits and have them applied against your judgment. (You should check applicable state and federal law on exemptions, especially when garnishing wages.) Writs of attachment on a judgment may be obtained from each court where your judgment is registered, and the process can be repeated until your judgment is satisfied.

Federal administrative agencies have a way around registering a judgment in other districts. A writ of execution obtained for the use of the United States may be executed in any state or territory, or in the District of Columbia. 28 U.S.C. § 2413; see *United States v. Thornton,* 672 F.2d 101 (D.C. Cir. 1982).

This procedure, commonly called long-arm execution, is a very effective collection device. Although it is normally available only to the agencies of the United States, there are exceptions. In some situations, a private party can use long-arm execution if the basic cause of action is in the United States and the judgment is "for the use of" both parties. *See United States ex rel. Marcus v. Lord Elec. Co.,* 43 F. Supp. 12, 13 (W.D. Pa. 1942); *United States v. Palmer, supra,* 609 F.2d at 547.

If the debtor owns personal property, recording the judgment in the county courthouse or registry of deeds may not be enough. For example, if the property is an aircraft, the U.S. marshal should attach it in accordance with state law, but the attachment and levy should be recorded with the Federal Aviation Administration Aircraft Registry Division in Oklahoma City, Oklahoma, following the procedures of the Federal Aviation Act (49 U.S.C. § 1403).

To attach a ship, follow admiralty law and procedure. (These procedures are contained in Rules B and C of Supplemental Rules for Certain Admiralty and Maritime Claims.) If, in settling a judgment, the debtor gives your client a ship's mortgage on a vessel weighing more than 21 tons, follow the procedures set out in the Ship's Mortgage Act (46 U.S.C. § 921), and record the ship's mortgage at the home port of the vessel with the Collector of Customs or U.S. Coast Guard Vessel Documentation Office.

Be sure you instruct the U.S. marshal on the proper method of attaching and levying on each item of the debtor's property, researching any special procedures that might apply to anything big or unusual. Once the marshal has attached and levied on the property, he will auction the property, sell it, and apply the sale proceeds, after expenses, to the judgment. Any excess proceeds are distributed to other lienholders in the order of their priorities, and, if there is anything left, to the debtor. (In many cases, you should consult a creditor's rights lawyer to assist you in sorting out priorities and handling related problems.)

To find the debtor's assets, you may use the same discovery devices available in prejudgment litigation, and more. Fed. R. Civ. P. 69 entitles a judgment creditor to use the discovery procedures found in Rules 26 through 37. In addition, you may use applicable state discovery procedures and state supplementary proceedings. As usual, the timing and sequence of discovery is your choice. An examination of the judgment debtor in supplementary proceedings is an excellent way to begin postjudgment discovery.

To start the process, file a petition for supplementary proceedings. In that petition, recite the facts concerning your judgment, and include a request to examine the judgment debtor and have him bring documents. Along with the petition, file an order authorizing the procedures you want to use. If the debtor is a business, you should normally request at least these documents:

- All documents relating to any leasehold or freehold interest of the debtor in real property and tangible or intangible personal property, including any options to purchase and any property that the debtor owns or leases as a member of a partnership or with any other person or business entity.
- All canceled checks, check stubs, bank statements, ledgers, and correspondence showing disbursements and receipts over the last five years.
- Copies of all federal and state tax returns for the last five years.
- All records relating to any transfer to others of title to or any other interest whatsoever in any real or personal property within the last five years.
- All documents relating to any cause of action pending against debtor, or any loans or advances of money to the debtor.
- Master payroll file.
- All documents relating to the funds, other assets, liabilities, ownership, capitalization, and incorporation of the debtor.

The list can be expanded or contracted depending on what information you already have and whether the debtor is an individual, a partnership, or a corporation. If the debtor is a publicly held company, your request should call for quarterly and annual reports filed with the Securities and Exchange Commission. If the debtor is required to file other disclosure documents with local, state, or federal agencies, get those too.

In postjudgment discovery, more than one examination of the debtor is often necessary, and you may have to move for sanctions under Rule 37 to get all the necessary documents from a recalcitrant debtor. You should also go after other sources of information about the debtor and his finances.

If the debtor has an accountant, subpoena the accountant and his records concerning the debtor. In cases applying federal privilege law, such as bankruptcy cases, there is no accountant-client privilege, even though there may be such a privilege under state law. *See* Fed. R. Evid. 501; *United States v. Arthur Young & Co.*, 465 U.S. 805 (1984).

Even if the debtor has "lost" his financial statements or tax returns, you will find them in the accountant's files. If the debtor does not have an accountant and still has not produced tax returns, move the court for an order requiring the debtor to give you written authorization to obtain copies of his returns from the Internal Revenue Service.

In some cases, you may suspect that the debtor has not produced all his bank records. When that happens, go right to the source. If you know where the debtor banks, subpoena the records from the bank.

A few years ago, I was involved in enforcing a judgment against a corporation. I subpoenaed records from the bank where the corporation maintained a checking account. The documents that the bank turned over demonstrated that, at the time the corporation was indebted to my client, it had repaid certain debts due its president by an unusual and circuitous method, and had made transfers to related corporations, violating my creditor's priority. Without the bank records, I would have been unaware of the potential claim my client had against the corporation's president and the other corporations.

Armed with the information I got from the bank, I filed a new action in federal court to recover fraudulent transfers and pierce the corporate veils of the related companies to satisfy my judgment. I eventually recovered about two-thirds of the judgment debt by settling the action against the company's president and the related companies.

Credit card records are another source of information about the debtor and his activities. In cases where the debtor has little personal income, but is employed by a corporation he controls, you may find that he uses corporate credit cards to maintain his lifestyle.

Some debtors use corporate credit cards to pay for such "business expenses" as suits, socks, microwave ovens, tennis rackets, panty hose, and stereo sets. Credit card account statements are clues to the debtor's spending patterns, and they can help you trace exactly where he was on a given day. The records might show that the debtor stopped at a marina for food and gas, using a boat you did not realize that he or his alter ego corporation owned. Such items are usually obvious personal expenses, which may demonstrate that the debtor uses the corporation as his alter ego.

Judges find it hard to stomach that kind of corporate abuse and will usually allow you to pierce the corporate veil when the corporation is merely a shell to protect the debtor's personal assets from creditors. Or the court may give you a monthly payment order on your judgment based on the debtor's noncash "income" from the corporation.

The debtor's family members are also good sources of information. Sometimes apparently uncollectible judgments become collectible when you uncover fraudulent transfers of valuable assets without adequate consideration to the debtor's close friends or relatives.

The biggest debtor I ever went after (he was six-feet-two and weighed about 350 pounds) was a poultry farmer. In reviewing documents I had subpoenaed from a bank, I discovered that, before the judgment, the debtor had transferred his liquid assets to a trust "for his children." It was amazing how his children's trust paid for his home mortgages, his car, and other personal expenses. Subsequent fraudulent-transfer litigation resulted in my client's recovery of almost all the debt, which was more than $100,000. That's a lot of chickens, even for a big poultry farmer.

During postjudgment litigation, you can often get injunctions or writs to freeze or attach assets that the debtor has transferred to others. This will prevent the assets from being further dissipated while your postjudgment litigation proceeds.

In a recent case, we got an injunction preventing the transfer of several hospital buildings, a mortgage note, and bank accounts. At the same time, we proceeded to litigate whether a successor corporation was the alter ego of three corporations against which we had obtained a $1.4 million judgment. We knew the three companies were mere shells, without assets.

After two years of discovery, the case was finally tried. We won the alter ego suit, getting a judgment for about $1.3 million against the successor corporation. Because the property had been frozen during the litigation, our client was able to satisfy its judgment from the assets still in the hands of the successor corporation.

You should consider restraining asset transfers during a postjudgment appeal by invoking Fed. R. Civ. P. 62. If the debtor is unable to post a supersedeas bond, you can move the court to set other conditions for securing the judgment pending appeal. *Trans World Airlines, Inc. v. Hughes*, 314 F. Supp. 94 (S.D.N.Y. 1970). This will make it easier to collect the judgment if the debtor's appeal is unsuccessful. If the debtor does post a bond, the judgment can be satisfied against the bond.

A few years ago, I was enforcing a $38 million judgment against an oil refinery company and its president. The company owned various properties in four different states. The president owned a cattle ranch and livestock in another state. The judgment debtors were unable to post a bond for such a large judgment amount.

I moved the federal district court under Rule 62 to set other conditions to secure the judgment pending appeal. The court ordered that all corporate stock was to be escrowed at a national bank; the creditor was to be given security interests in all oil refinery and ranch properties; the creditor could file its judgment as a lien against the refinery's real property, and could file deeds of trust or notices of interest in real property against various parcels of land that the corporation and its president owned in several other states; the creditor was to be given periodic access to the books and records of the refinery and the ranch; the salaries of corporate officers and ranch managers would be fixed at an agreed rate of compensation during the appeal; the corporation and its president were prohibited from paying notes, debts, or other obligations to one another, or incurring any debts except in the ordinary course of business; and the corporation and the ranch were prohibited from making any major capital improvements or additions.

After the debtors lost their appeal, I filed in the federal district court for the appointment of a receiver for the refinery and the ranch. Under certain state and federal laws, receiverships may be established to administer the affairs and conserve the assets of financially troubled companies. More often than not, bankruptcy is the preferred method of administering and reorganizing insolvent companies. In our case, we proceeded under federal receivership statutes, 28 U.S.C. §§ 754 and 959, to give us quick access to the debtor's business and to prevent further dissipation of assets.

Later, the individual debtor filed a bankruptcy petition, claiming the ranch and the corporate stock of the refinery as his individual assets. During the following three years, we fought a battle that included nine postjudgment appeals and a jurisdictional struggle between a bankruptcy judge and a chief district judge. *See In re Dalton,* 733 F.2d 710 (10th Cir. 1984), *cert. dismissed,* 469 U.S. 1185 (1985). Throughout the skirmishing, it was a great comfort to have the security of the stringent conditions set pending the initial appeal. The case illustrates that a judgment does not end the litigation and may be the beginning of longer and more complex proceedings.

The postjudgment litigation may be lengthy and expensive. There is no easy way at the beginning to assure your client that the money he spends in postjudgment discovery and litigation will produce an even bigger recovery. Usually the preliminary postjudgment discovery, if done properly, will tell you how much of the judgment you can collect. In other cases, further litigation against third parties may be necessary.

Humanizing the Corporation

Elizabeth Runyan Geise and David J. Katz

> Jurymen seldom convict a person they like or acquit one they dislike. The main work of a trial lawyer is to make a jury like his client.—Clarence Darrow

> Corporation, n. An ingenious device for obtaining individual profit without individual responsibility.—Ambrose Bierce, *The Devil's Dictionary* 57 (1911)

Clarence Darrow was right. Juries are reluctant to find against defendants they can identify with. The problem is that most people don't believe they have much in common with corporations. They often view corporations as artificial beings conceived in law, born on paper, and run by greedy capitalists, who rank in popularity somewhere around lawyers and politicians. Americans, raised to value individualism and the can-do spirit, will favor a determined David suing a corporate Goliath almost every time. Therefore, one of the main tasks of a lawyer defending a corporation is to recast the client in human form, with a likeable human face.

As with most of the conjuring arts, it is far easier to describe the result than to explain the process. Three elements are involved in any successful "humanization," each with its own challenges: formulating an appealing human story, telling that story in a human way, and humanizing the lawyers who tell it.

The first element—formulating an appealing human story—may be the most important. The defense witnesses and lawyers may be as charismatic as Ronald Reagan, but the defendant itself remains unblinking, unsmiling, and faceless. Without a touching human story to tell, the

---

Elizabeth Runyan Geise is a partner, and David J. Katz is an associate at Shea & Gardner in Washington, D.C.

defense team's reliance on charisma may be misplaced. Storytelling requires building up, not tearing down. Too often, defense lawyers squander precious time cross-examining plaintiffs' witnesses, hoping their skillful efforts will carry the day. Other times, defense lawyers work hard developing a coherent defense theme that rests on legal rights instead of personal relationships, ultimately making the corporation appear cold and unfeeling. These corporate counsel may be in for a rude surprise when the verdict is reached, because they overlooked job number one. They should have tied the facts together for the jury into some sort of appealing human story or theme.

Storytelling follows factfinding. There is never a substitute for knowing all the relevant facts to the claim at issue. For example, in a products liability case, relevant questions might include: Did prior testing of the product reveal safety problems? Has the company received notices of accidents similar to the plaintiff's? Was a different design for the product considered and rejected? Has the company made any changes since learning of potential dangers in the product? In other words, to paraphrase Senator Howard Baker's often-repeated line from the Watergate hearings: What did the corporation know, and when did it know it?

Getting the Facts

Finding out the relevant facts, however, is usually easier said than done, particularly when a corporate client is involved. Corporations do not divulge facts easily. Corporate managers may be embarrassed by what happened and reluctant to admit all the details. They also may fear having someone hold them accountable for poor decisions in the past or failure to consult counsel at an earlier date. One defense lawyer told us about a corporate client whose inside counsel gave her—only reluctantly and after great probing—a memorandum that had been written years earlier advising the corporation not to put a warning label on a particular product. The memorandum was not helpful because it showed that the corporation had considered and decided against the warning. Yet the memo was far easier to deal with at an early stage in the litigation than if the plaintiff's lawyer had found it on the eve of trial. The moral of the story: Never be surprised at inside counsel's reluctance to share all the facts with outside counsel because of embarrassment or some other motivation.

In other cases, facts are not concealed on purpose; it is simply too difficult for the corporate managers or counsel to ferret them out. Corporate managers or lawyers may not have worked at the corporation long enough to have a personal memory of the facts. It is sometimes easier for current management to conclude that facts are unknowable, rather than expending the enormous effort required to dig them up. They may conclude after a cursory search that all relevant documents were destroyed pursuant to a document retention policy. They may say that formerly knowledgeable employees are now retired, infirm, lost without a forwarding address, or unwilling to talk.

In any of these situations, outside counsel must be patient but not discouraged in their efforts to piece together as many of the relevant facts as possible. Many plaintiffs' counsel have an uncanny ability to stumble upon documents or witnesses with "bad" facts. Some former or retired employees usually can be found who will talk to plaintiffs' counsel—either voluntarily or under threat of a subpoena. And despite document retention policies, crucial records may still exist. It is essential that a corporation's own counsel discover unhelpful facts first, so that defense counsel have time to figure out how to deal with these facts. The defense lawyer, therefore, must tenaciously push the corporation to find documents, to produce employees to interview, and to think about how to discover the relevant facts. One experienced trial lawyer always tells her corporate clients that she can figure out how to handle any set of facts, if she is given enough time, but she cannot make the same guarantee when "surprise" facts are involved. So the first rule is simply to find out everything that is relevant to the case at hand—corporate skeletons included.

Next, take your facts and build them into an appealing story with a human perspective. Perhaps the plaintiff is mistaken about when and where the injury occurred. Maybe the fault lies elsewhere, or nowhere. The plaintiff may have chosen the corporation as an easy target or a scapegoat, when the alleged injury was caused by some outsider or was an "act of God."

Another common theme involves changing times. The corporation's alleged actions may have been the justifiable product of an earlier age, when technology, law, and social attitudes were less advanced. Now, the plaintiff is arguing with 20-20 hindsight, asking the jury to indulge in the worst kind of "Monday-morning quarterbacking." This defense can be especially persuasive if the corporation's past acts complied with some external set of guidelines, such as then-existing government regulations, and if the corporation changed its practices to keep pace with evolving standards and expectations.

A riskier approach involves embarrassing candor. Imagine a corporation blushing, as its employees confess past mistakes and show how they have worked hard to correct them. If you really enjoy mixing metaphors, you might say your corporation has turned over a new leaf with new people. But don't be too quick to laugh. In some jurisdictions, this is respectfully called the "redemption defense" (or in Washington, D.C, the "Marion Barry defense").

Obviously, infinite variations on these themes are possible. But remember that the corporation's defense story has to be more than thematic—it has to appeal to the humans on the jury.

For graphic accounts of corporate defense strategies that crashed in the courtroom, simply pick up a newspaper. One memorable case involved the 81-year-old woman who bought a cup of hot coffee at a McDonald's. The jury awarded her $2.9 million (including $2.7 million in punitive damages) for third-degree burns caused when the coffee spilled in her lap. According to press reports, much of McDonald's defense involved blaming the plaintiff for spilling the coffee and not removing her clothing more quickly, and arguing that the plaintiff's age contributed to her injuries, since older skin is thinner and more susceptible to injury. McDonald's also asserted that most coffee can cause serious burns. A defense expert, labeled a "human factors engineer," testified that the plaintiff's burns "were statistically insignificant when compared to the billions of cups of coffee McDonald's sells annually." The final nail in the defense's coffin was the testimony of one corporate executive, who said the company did not intend to warn future customers about the danger of serious burns or to change any of McDonald's policies concerning coffee, because "[t]here are more serious dangers in restaurants." In short, while McDonald's defense had a certain theme—buyer beware—it surely had little appeal.

Finally, a coherent defense theme or story collapses if the facts do not support it. You cannot win by fighting the facts. So expect to play the hand you're dealt, no matter how much you feel like cursing the dealer.

The *Exxon Valdez* trial, resulting from the 1989 oil spill in Prince William Sound, provides an illustration. That trial resulted in a $5 billion punitive award against Exxon—to our knowledge, the largest punitive damage verdict in litigation history. To award punitive damages, the jury first had to find that Exxon was reckless. According to a lawyer involved in the trial, Exxon presented a parade of corporate witnesses who all testified that alcohol had not impaired the ship's captain, Joseph Hazelwood, the night that the ship ran aground, and that, because of Hazelwood's prior alcohol problems, Exxon had closely monitored him for years and had no knowledge that his drinking problem had continued. All of the corporate witnesses consistently presented this defense to the charge of recklessness on Exxon's part. But Exxon wasn't taking a realistic look at its cards. The defense theme did not match the facts. The plaintiffs' lawyers anted up press releases and other evidence showing that, shortly after the *Exxon Valdez* grounding, Exxon had fired Hazelwood for drinking on the job, and had blamed the accident on alcohol-induced impairment on Hazelwood's part. Finally, with respect to Exxon's claim that it had no knowledge of Hazelwood's continued drinking problem, the plaintiffs' lawyers called this bluff with a series of witnesses who testified that Hazelwood's drinking problems had been reported to Exxon management for years, including one report just two or three days before the *Valdez* oil spill. In summation, if the defense theme does not fit the facts, you lose all your chips.

Telling the Story

Once the defense theme has been developed, the corporation's counsel can turn to the next task—figuring out how to tell the story as often as possible, from every possible angle. For example, one lawyer told us that he always uses interrogatory answers to emphasize the defense themes. He drafts them in long paragraphs, with any incriminating facts couched and cushioned by the most positive exculpating language. This forces plaintiffs' counsel to read the entire paragraph to the jury, with the bad facts buried in the good.

Prepare corporate witnesses to echo the same defense themes consistently at their depositions. Everyone should be singing the same song. At trial, opening and closing statements should resonate with the same theme. The most effective defense closing marshals every scrap of useful evidence into one last verse of the corporation's appealing defense.

The importance of consistency cannot be overemphasized. For example, in a General Motors truck case that resulted in a $105 million verdict, the defense lawyer's argument during the punitive damages phase of the case included penitent comments about how the truck manufacturer was "changing" and "got the message" from the jury's verdict on compensatory damages. But when the plaintiff's lawyer rose to respond, he held in his hand a press release that General Motors reportedly had just issued, which rejected the jury verdict and accused the jury of being motivated by sympathy for the plaintiff. See "GM Burns Itself," *The American Lawyer* (April 1993).

Another example of a fatal inconsistency comes from the *Exxon Valdez* trial. After determining that Exxon had been reckless and thus liable for punitive damages, the jury took on the chore of deciding how much Exxon should pay. According to a lawyer involved in the trial, the Exxon officials—who had previously denied any recklessness on Exxon's part—expressed total and absolute contrition during this phase of the trial. They told the jury that Exxon had learned its lesson, had accepted responsibility, and had already been punished severely by the cost of the cleanup and the unfavorable publicity after the spill. But when these same officials were asked on cross-examination if their contrition meant that they acknowledged Exxon's recklessness, they hemmed and hawed, obviously worried about the effect of such an admission on any appeal. Even more damning, when the corporate representatives were asked what lessons Exxon had learned, they offered little in reply. They appeared to have only limited knowledge of the evidence received at trial that led to the jury's finding of recklessness. Even worse, they could not offer concrete examples of how Exxon had "learned its lesson" or would do better in the future. These corporate witnesses may have thought—mistakenly—that a *mea culpa* on Exxon's part, however insincere, would be enough to carry the day.

These cases illustrate that when a *mea culpa* is appropriate, it must be sincere and expressed to everyone. In other words, you can't tell one story to the jury and another to the press or to the shareholders.

The medium is always an important part of the message, and your corporation's best "voice" for telling its story is a believable witness. As a defense lawyer, you should be on the lookout for potential witnesses from the corporation while ferreting out the relevant facts. At the conclusion of each witness interview, ask for the names and whereabouts of others who potentially might be helpful. Finding and developing the best witnesses may take weeks or months of painstaking effort.

The most persuasive witnesses are not always the most important or high-ranking corporate officials. In a products liability case, for example, the most knowledgeable and believable witness may be someone who worked on development of the product or the person in charge of quality control. Juries respect witnesses who have in-depth knowledge of the product or the matter in dispute, and who obviously know and perform their jobs well.

The best corporate witnesses are earnest and sincere. They must believe in the corporation's story and convey that belief to the jury. The witnesses need not be polished. After all, the jurors are not, and the defense lawyer's objective is to find a way for the jurors to relate to the corporate witnesses on a personal level. Indeed, some evident nervousness on a corporate witness's part may go a long way toward dispelling the notion of the corporation as a legal abstraction controlled by cold-hearted businessmen.

The most useful corporate witnesses often have spent many years with the company and are proud of their service. Long-standing corporate loyalty implies corporate reliability. Let's say you need a custodian of records. Your choice is an older woman, who has maintained the company's records for 35 years, or her young supervisor, who has an MBA degree. All else being equal, choose the older woman as the company's witness called at trial.

Spend some time developing each corporate witness's personal background during direct examination—his education, military service, and history with the corporation. Ask how he was hired, what jobs he has performed, why he is proud of his company and his job, and possibly even why he has volunteered to testify for the company. You can then remind the jury of these facts about each witness in closing argument. For example: "You remember Mr. Smith, the bald gentleman who started in the mailroom in the 1950s and worked his way up to chief of quality control?"

In the appropriate case, show the jury that the corporation also has shareholders. These shareholders are not necessarily rich people who bark at their stockbrokers over the phone. They include current and former employees of the corporation, retirees, and parents saving for their children's educations. All of these people have a vested interest in the success of the corporation and a stake in the outcome of a lawsuit. If a lower-level corporate witness owns stock in the corporation, such as the custodian of records, for example, bring this fact up in the witness's direct examination. While stock ownership might suggest that a corporation witness is financially biased, this probably is presupposed because the witness is an employee as well as an investor. But this information about stock ownership also helps show the corporation's human side.

Consider portraying the corporation as a good corporate "citizen." Have at least one corporate witness tell the story of the corporation itself—how it came about, what it makes, and its tradition of doing the best job possible. For example, in a products liability case against an automobile company, the corporate witnesses should be able to paint a word picture for the jury of the mighty American automaker—founded in Detroit with American "know-how" and "can-do" spirit, helping to win wars and cover the globe with reliable, economical automobiles. In a defective drug case, the witnesses should sketch for the jury a picture of the defendant's research and development laboratory, where white-coated technicians squint through microscopes, looking for the cure for cancer or a pill to vanquish the common cold. After all, corporations spend millions creating similar images through advertising. General Electric "brings good things to light." Archer Daniels Midland Company is the "supermarket to the world." The defense lawyer's job is to bring some of these same images to the jury.

Other aspects of corporate citizenship should also be mentioned. Examples include charitable donations, scholarships, environmental cleanups, or other participation by the corporation in efforts to improve the community. Sometimes the opposition will try to exclude as irrelevant a wealth of positive information about the corporate defendant. Then the ultimate challenge may be to establish the needed relevance.

Using Voir Dire

Some of these positive background facts may be injected during voir dire, when you first introduce the corporation and its representative to the jury panel. Ask prospective jurors if they are familiar with the corporation through its scholarship program or its sponsorship of community events. Bring out links between prospective jurors and the corporation's witnesses—such as common professions, educational institutions, or hometowns.

Some lawyers even recommend using a corporate video at trial, depicting a "day in the life" of the defendant corporation. To be admissible, such video presentations have to be relevant to some issue in the case and authenticated by a witness for the corporation. In one recent breast implant trial, the defense presented a slide show graphically illustrating how the implants were manufactured. Narrating the slides was a long-time company employee, who pointed out other employees in some of the slides. Another corporate defendant showed a movie that described how the corporation began, what it makes, and how it operates. The purpose of these presentations is simple: to put a human face on the corporation, which the jury will like and remember.

While the corporation itself has no emotion, its people do. So let corporate witnesses show their emotions, if it is appropriate. The jury needs to understand what the case means to those who make up the corporation. For example, a retired general counsel anxiously volunteered to testify for his former company in an insurance coverage case, where the insurer was trying to deny coverage on the ground of fraud. The retired counsel explained that he and his company never did business that way, and he was outraged that anyone could accuse him of fraud. In another case, the retired CEO of a defendant corporation wanted to tell the jury why his company had never thought to place warnings on its products. He explained that, as far as he was aware, every purchaser knew about the hazards and had taken steps to protect product users. To do more had never occurred to him or his company.

Obviously, feigned emotion will not convince a jury of anything. Unjustified anger or a sense of victimization also are unappealing. But sincere and strongly felt emotion can be powerful evidence indeed. After all, much of a plaintiff's case is an emotional appeal. Similar feelings on the other side help counterbalance the jury's natural inclination to favor the injured underdog.

As in all litigation, visual cues are important. Put another way, clothing makes the corporation. Guard against even little things that might create the image of a wealthy, aloof corporate entity. For corporate witnesses, leave monogrammed shirts, expensive jewelry, Italian suits, suspenders, or any other "corporate" clothing in their closets.

The same corporate representative should attend court every day. This shows that the corporation takes the case seriously, and the jurors are not the only ones who have to disrupt their lives and schedules to resolve the plaintiff's case. Along these same lines, the corporate representative should be attentive to the proceedings; she should never be seen reading the paper, doing a crossword puzzle, or playing tic-tac-toe while a juror is within view.

The corporate representative should also be wary of acting self-important. The representative should not rush out at every break in the proceedings to use the phone. Have her leave her cellular phone at the office. Also have absent the laptop computer, beeper, and other high-tech gadgetry that tend to indicate indispensability (and thus self-importance). On the other hand, visits from family (especially children) during breaks in the proceedings may be a welcome sight.

Finally, it is important that the corporation not appear to have money to burn. There should not be hordes of defense lawyers in attendance at trial. Too much high-tech equipment for presentation of the case might appear too slick. An easel and a pointer may be more effective than an elaborate video setup.

Avoid expert witnesses who act like "spin doctors," testifying in their umpteenth lawsuit. Jurors will often be suspicious of anyone authoritatively spouting the corporate line. A good expert witness should appear independent and unbiased, not wedged deeply into the deep pocket's pocket. The best expert has not been overused and can convey to the jury a sincere and considered belief in the company's defense. A rumpled, unpolished academic testifying for the first time may be rough around the edges, but much more believable than the overly polished and overused expert.

Dressing the Part

Even you, as the defense lawyer, should heed the message about avoiding a corporate image. After all, next to the corporate representative, you are the closest in-court representative that the corporation has. It is natural for jurors to transfer their feelings about a lawyer to her client.

Like the corporate representative, avoid cuff links, Italian suits, and suspenders. Leave expensive jewelry or large diamond rings at home for the duration of the trial. One such lawyer limits her courtroom wardrobe to five outfits, rotated each week, during lengthy trials. She does not want the jury to think that she is wealthy.

As with the corporate representative, avoid appearing self-important. Treat associates and paralegals as colleagues, not high-priced gofers. Don't run to the phone at every break, and leave the cellular phone at the office. And, obviously, be attentive to the case at all times.

Convey a sincere belief in the corporation's version of the facts and an intense desire to convey those facts to the jury. Some humor is fine, particularly if the humor is at your expense. But humor cannot be allowed to diminish the seriousness with which the corporation regards the plaintiff's allegations.

Make an effort to be likable—even to the other side, as painful as that might be. From the beginning of the case, this means keeping on cordial terms with the opposing lawyer. Procedural issues such as extensions of time, discovery disputes (to the extent possible), and other minor matters should be worked out by consensus rather than by confrontation. There is no substitute for a perception on the jury's part that the court respects the defense lawyer and finds her conduct reasonable and appropriate. And if the jury perceives that the lawyers on each side have respect for one another, the jury may have a more difficult time finding against the corporation.

Too many objections to the plaintiff's evidence will make a jury believe the corporation has something to hide. Thus, objections should be guided by the same rule applicable to most things in life: Moderation is the best policy.

Finally, take care never to dehumanize the plaintiff. Humor or a cavalier attitude are out of place if an injured plaintiff is involved. Avoid combative cross-examination with little purpose other than combat. A successful defense of a corporation will rarely involve denigration of the plaintiff or undisputed injuries. The verdict against McDonald's in the coffee spill highlights this point. Instead, all the corporate witnesses need to express reasonable concern for the welfare of the plaintiff, while reminding the jury that its job involves deciding whether the defendant is truly liable.

Putting a human face on a corporate defendant demands creativity, foresight, tenacity, and attention to detail. But Clarence Darrow was right: When a corporate client is involved, humanizing that client is the main work of the trial lawyer.

Simple Lessons from a Complex Case

Norman J. Wiener

Big, complex cases usually do not teach useful lawyering skills. The huge securities and antitrust suits that live for years in some unfortunate courts are just too unusual to teach much of general benefit. You may know the standards for multidistrict consolidation by heart, but will you ever use them again? You may be the world's greatest expert on the treatment of discovery "waves" in the *Manual for Complex Litigation*. So what? Young lawyers in big firms often avoid big cases. Their aversion shows great wisdom.

There are times, however, when even a big case reveals important truths. If this happens, pay attention. If a lesson fights its way through the tangle and clutter of multidistrict, multiyear litigation, it must be very hardy.

This article describes some of those hardy truths, from the perspective of a defense lawyer involved in one of the more unusual parts of a most complex proceeding: the "opt-out trial" in *In re Corrugated Container Antitrust Litigation*, 756 F. 2d 411 (5th Cir. 1985).

Corrugated, like many antitrust cases, began as a criminal proceeding. In 1975, a Texas grand jury started an investigation into the pricing practices of the corrugated box industry in the United States. Three years later, price-fixing indictments were returned against 14 manufacturers and 26 individuals. Some of the defendants pleaded nolo contendere and were fined. Those that went to trial were acquitted in April 1979.

Plaintiffs' antitrust lawyers can detect big-money grand jury proceedings a thousand miles away. The *Corrugated* grand jury investigation was no exception. Even before indictments were handed out, civil suits sprouted nationwide. There were ultimately 55 treble-damage class

---

Norman J. Wiener is a partner in the Portland, Oregon, law firm of Miller, Nash, Wiener, Hager & Carlsen. He represented one of the defendants, Willamette Industries, Inc., in all stages of the Corrugated Container *litigation.*

action suits aimed at 37 corrugated box manufacturers. All were consolidated for pretrial proceedings and trial in the Southern District of Texas. All were assigned to Judge John Singleton, who also presided over the criminal price-fixing action. In late 1978, Judge Singleton certified a nationwide class under Rule 23(b)(3) of the Federal Rules of Civil Procedure.

The *Corrugated* class action was massive in every way. There were 200,000 class members. Scores of lawyers represented the class and its subclasses. They were grouped into committees rivaling the organization chart of a major corporation. There were 39 pretrial hearings, 205 pretrial orders, and 15 appeals. Millions of pages of documents were copied. Hundreds of depositions were taken.

The scope of *Corrugated* made a ruinous judgment a troubling possibility, even for manufacturers certain that their actions had been proper. This risk increased when the class was certified. There was a chance that, if the jury concluded some defendants had violated the law, it would find that all the defendants were part of a large, ill-defined conspiracy. This concern was heightened for some of the largest defendants that—at about the same time the *Corrugated* class was certified—were found liable in a separate case for conspiring to fix prices in the plywood market.

Settlements inevitably followed. By manipulation, selection, and timing, the capable plaintiffs' lawyers achieved settlements in 1979 and 1980 with all but three of the defendants. These settlements totaled almost $400 million. The three remaining defendants went to trial in June 1980. Two settled before a verdict. One—Mead Corporation—went through three and one-half months of trial, only to be found in a jury special verdict to have taken part in a price-fixing conspiracy with 18 other manufacturers. Thirteen companies were found in the special verdict *not* to have violated the law.

After many lengthy, expensive skirmishes, including legislative efforts, Mead also settled for $45 million, before judgment was entered on the special verdict. All that remained was to distribute the settlement money, which had accumulated to $550 million, and to award plaintiffs' counsel lawyers' fees, which were more than $40 million. By the end of 1983, the great *Corrugated* class action was over.

But *Corrugated* was not yet dead. Because the *Corrugated* class was certified under Rule 23(b)(3), class members could opt out of the action and pursue their own lawsuits. Nineteen of the largest purchasers of corrugated containers—companies like Pillsbury, Kraft, and Armour Foods—did just that. Eleven of the 19 lawsuits they filed settled before trial, but eight proceeded on. Thus, after extensive criminal and civil litigation, the question of whether there was a price-fixing conspiracy in the corrugated container industry was to be litigated again—not once, but in eight different lawsuits. Despite all that had gone before, more massive discovery occurred. More than 500 new depositions were taken. Hundreds of thousands of pages of documents were produced—some for the second or third time.

The eight opt-out cases were not identical. Not all five remaining defendants were named in each case. Despite these differences, all eight opt-out cases were consolidated for one trial before a single jury. Judge Singleton presided again.

The opt-out trial began in October 1982. Plaintiffs' cases lasted two and one-half months. Defendants' evidence took another month. After seven hours of closing arguments, the jury retired. In less than a day and a half, it returned with dispositive answers to the first two questions on the special-verdict form: *Yes*, there had been a national price-fixing conspiracy, but *no*, none of the plaintiffs had been damaged by it. These answers meant the jury never had to answer whether any of the defendants had been part of the conspiracy. Plaintiffs' posttrial motions and appeals were unsuccessful. This defense victory was sustained at all levels. By April 1985, the *Corrugated* opt-out litigation was over.

Cases as complex, interwoven, and overlapping as those in *Corrugated* produce one novel dilemma after another. Procedural complications, scheduling conflicts, and discovery disputes never seem to end. These are all tough problems. They were important to the litigation. But they are the stuff of law reviews: abstract, complicated, and sometimes unique. This is not surprising. As hard cases make bad law, complicated cases make odd law. What *is* surprising, though, is that even the *Corrugated* litigation—and especially the opt-out trial—taught some bigger lessons. A few of those follow.

One of the clearest lessons is that juries like people, not paper. To an unusual extent, the parties in the opt-out trial learned how jurors think. Judge Singleton permitted interviews of the alternate jurors while the regular jury was deliberating; the jury itself was interviewed after it reached a verdict.

These discussions with jurors suggest that what is evidence to lawyers is not to jurors. In two and one-half months of evidence, the unsuccessful plaintiffs presented 142 witnesses, but only six were flesh and blood. The remaining 136 were deposition transcripts, read into the record. Of these, 55 were from people who took the Fifth Amendment and refused to testify. Only one employee of any plaintiff corporation testified.

Defendants, by contrast, put on 28 live witnesses, along with 35 depositions. Representatives of most of the defendant companies testified.

Jurors Want Real People

The jury's preference was obvious. They were bored by the reading of depositions. They wondered why so few representatives of the plaintiff companies had the fortitude to testify. They were unimpressed by readings of the Fifth Amendment. It is one thing to see a witness—perhaps visibly nervous, perhaps arrogant—refuse to answer. Among other things, this can prompt memories of organized-crime hearings. It is quite another thing to hear someone's lawyer read the invocation of the Fifth Amendment 55 times. That has no impact.

Jurors expect, and want to see, real people. They expect human interest and drama, even in the most complex case. They cannot evaluate transcripts, and what they cannot evaluate they will discard.

Apart from the sheer dullness of listening to depositions, and apart from the jury's desire to see human beings, the opt-out trial also suggests that people speak on behalf of corporations better than paper does. Lawyers representing corporations before juries must try to humanize their clients. It can be easy for a jury to believe a large, faceless corporation took part in a vague, formless conspiracy. Conversely, it is hard for jurors to have sympathy for a company that appears only through deposition transcripts. But jurors can sympathize with people. They may find it harder to believe that the pleasant, articulate man or woman who spoke to them could do anything illegal.

A word of warning: Though juries like people, even the driest transcript is better than a dumb, evasive, weak, or unprepared witness. In fact, almost the only virtue of transcripts is that they neutralize such human failings, burying them under pages of faceless ink and paper. A stenotype machine does not record hesitation, tone of voice, or nerves. So, if certain facts can be proved only through one person, and he is a clod, read in the deposition, if possible. But remember, in its own way, the jury may think the presence of a deposition and the absence of a person mean something is being hidden.

Although jurors prefer human witnesses, they do not like expert witnesses very much. In complex litigation, experts are inevitable: Damages must be proved, markets defined, and economics explained. Very often, however, experts are just the kind of witnesses who—when possible—should appear in writing and not in person. Abstractions, complexity, and even pedantry punctuate much expert testimony. Jurors—and judges—do not like any of it.

The *Corrugated* opt-out trials illustrate the perils of basing a complex case on expert testimony. Both sides had experts. The plaintiffs had two, but since they had only six live witnesses in all, expert testimony was a major human element of their case. A much higher proportion of the defense case was fact testimony and not expert opinion. Worse yet for the plaintiffs, the testimony of their experts was complex and inconsistent. One thought price fixing had added as much as 10 percent to container prices, the other 26.1 percent. One relied on multiple regression techniques, the other on something he called "contribution" data.

All this left the jury skeptical and bored stiff. The substance of the testimony had no intrinsic interest. The spectacle of obvious disagreement in approach and result by experts on the same side of the case was not compelling. This was compounded by the virtual failure of any plaintiff-employee to testify in commonsense terms about the injury his company suffered. And, of course, many jurors believed that an expert would say anything he was hired to say.

Not all of these problems could be avoided. Experts are an intrinsic element of complicated cases, especially antitrust litigation. But they should not be a major element of such litigation. An important lesson of the opt-out trial was this: Use experts as little as possible. Above all, do not use experts as first-line witnesses or—worse yet—as spokesmen for your client. If possible, have employees explain in everyday terms how their company was hurt, where it sells or buys, what it does, and the like. Experts should fill in the gaps only, and the gaps should be small.

Once the jury has heard live witnesses, it should be able to record its conclusions on a special-verdict form. In *Corrugated*, the use and design of a special-verdict form played a major role in the defendants' opt-out trial success. Few lawyers—especially defense lawyers—should fail to use such a form in a complex case. Some of the reasons are familiar and help both sides: A special-verdict helps organize the jury's thinking. It lets you know what you have when the case is over; you can tell what facts were found and what were not. It helps focus any appeal. It permits different treatment for different defendants.

For defendants, there is another, less noble, but important, reason for using a special-verdict: It can give a defendant a lot of chances to win. Usually a special-verdict form asks a yes-or-no question for each of the facts related to each element of the cause of action. To win, a plaintiff usually needs to get all "yeses." A defendant only needs one "no." Relying on a general verdict is much less desirable from a defense standpoint; jurors who simply dislike a defendant may find for the plaintiff even though they could not honestly answer "yes" to every question on a special-verdict form.

When using a special-verdict form, pay careful attention to the organization and number of the questions. A defendant will want some of the earliest inquiries to be knockout questions: If the jury can answer "no" to the question, then it need not proceed to any others. In the *Corrugated* opt-out trial, the organization of the form meant the jury had to answer only two questions—"Was there a conspiracy?" and "Were the plaintiffs damaged?"—instead of the 300-plus questions on the 17 pages that followed. Had the jury been asked a series of relatively innocuous questions at the beginning of the form and had they answered them "yes," the psychological momentum for affirmative answers might have been irresistible.

Order Is Important

The arrangement of particular questions on a special-verdict form can also be important, and was in the opt-out trial. There, as noted, the order of initial questions was basically: (1) existence of conspiracy; (2) damage to plaintiffs; (3) involvement of defendants in the conspiracy. Because the jury answered "no" to the second question, they did not need to answer the third. Had the second and third questions been reversed, the defendants' position might not have been strong. The jury might have found some were conspirators. Minimally, this would have been embarrassing. Worse, it would have produced a less favorable setting for appeals and postjudgment motions. And it might have caused later battles over the collateral estoppel effect of the verdict.

Along with controlling the formalities of proof—witnesses, verdicts, and the like—*Corrugated* shows it is important to give attention to more informal attempts to gain an evidentiary advantage. In particular, lawyers in complex litigation must try to control references to related cases.

By the time the opt-out cases were tried, the alleged corrugated container price conspiracy already had been litigated twice. The opt-out plaintiffs may have left the *Corrugated* class and may have had no direct involvement in either previous action, but they nonetheless referred to those proceedings repeatedly in the opt-out trial. Particularly common were references to some of the defendants' indictments and to the fact that employees of some of the defendants had invoked the Fifth Amendment in earlier testimony. The plaintiffs also sometimes mentioned evidence in the class litigation that put other manufacturers—not parties in the opt-out trial—in a bad light. These seemed to be efforts to prove guilt by association. The plaintiffs apparently believed that, by referring to criminal matters and refusals to testify, they would give the jury a generally poor impression of the defendants.

Such innuendoes are a threat in any case that is part of a pattern of overlapping lawsuits. Parties—particularly defendants—should be alert to it. The problem, however, is easier to describe than it is to solve. The *Corrugated* opt-out defendants tried a bit of everything: motions *in limine,* arguments at pretrial conferences, and objections during trial. Unfortunately, none of these was completely effective. Judge Singleton—perhaps because of conclusions he reached during the criminal or class proceedings—was unwilling to take a hard line on the problem. In fact, although the judge allowed the references to indictments and invoking the Fifth Amendment, he barred defense attempts to point out that some defendants had *not* been indicted and that some had been found *not* to be involved in a conspiracy during the *Mead* trial.

All a party faced with this related-case problem can do is to raise it early, often, and forcefully and hope for the best. Be careful, however: Try to restrict these arguments to the pretrial stage of the case. Unless very artful, trial objections about references to other cases may at best seem picky to the jury and could suggest there is something to hide.

More troubling than references to related cases was the use of testimony from those earlier cases as evidence in the opt-out trial. By the time the opt-out cases were tried, earlier incarnations of the *Corrugated* case had produced mountains of testimony. Not all of the opt-out defendants had been present—or even parties—when such testimony was given. This created a host of problems: Transcripts of testimony in the *Mead* trial, to which few of the defendants had been parties, were introduced against them in the opt-out case. Testimony of persons taking the Fifth Amendment in depositions was introduced against defendants who did not employ those witnesses and had not been indicted by the grand jury.

Of course, depositions can sometimes properly be used as trial evidence. Rule 32 of the Federal Rules of Civil Procedure provides for it in appropriate circumstances. But using depositions and trial transcripts against a party that had no opportunity for cross-examination should not be countenanced. This is particularly true in a consolidated proceeding before a jury that may not be able to remember or determine which strand of evidence pertains to which party. It is doubly true when one of the previous proceedings is a criminal case. Again, the remedies are clear but not certain: motions *in limine*, objections, and the like. Success depends on the disposition of the trial judge.

For all their reliance on the fallout from related cases, the opt-out plaintiffs that went to trial lost. Careful examination of this result may explain why—except possibly in employment discrimination litigation—opt-out trials are uncommon: Opting out can hurt plaintiffs on the merits.

There are many reasons why staying in the *Corrugated* class should have made sense. The plaintiffs' essential allegation in *Corrugated* was that a nationwide price-fixing conspiracy had injured most purchasers of corrugated containers. The case was thus an effort by a large group of alleged victims to redress wrongs committed by a large group of alleged conspirators. The nature of the litigation almost inherently suggests a class. It may be easier for a trier to grasp the theory of a multiparty dispute when most of those parties are in the case. In this way, a procedural step—class certification—can reinforce the substance of the case.

There is another psychological advantage to having a class. Juries may well believe that class counsel is a "private attorney general" protecting the common good. They are more likely to think those representing a few companies are motivated by narrower—mostly monetary—corporate interests.

There are also more practical reasons why nationwide price-fixing cases can benefit from class treatment. Often, a defense tactic in antitrust conspiracy matters is to chip away at the case, party by party, to argue that *this* defendant could not have been involved in a conspiracy or *that* plaintiff could not have been harmed. In a class trial, there is often little patience with this splintering. There are simply too many individual situations for an efficient trial. Few judges will abide the clutter. In fact, there is a respectable view that a class trial is meant to deal only with common class-wide matters. In this view, individual questions are relegated to a second, relief stage. For most defendants, that is cold comfort. No one wants to be in a fight about who will pay a multimillion-dollar judgment.

Finally, a class action can provide unintended proof advantages for antitrust plaintiffs. It is, bluntly, a very good setting for proving guilt by association. The law on the admissibility of evidence against co-conspirators is complex. Lots of defendant parties can be confusing. Evidence on three or four bad actors may stain ten or fifteen much less involved co-defendants. Even the most attentive jury or intelligent judge will have trouble keeping the evidence straight. What they will often remember is the bad news—the smoking guns—not the good. A class proceeding is a major opportunity for this bad news to be spread uncritically. With a broad brush, class plaintiffs can make a big smear.

Despite all these potential advantages, the *Corrugated* opt-out plaintiffs went their own ways. They may have had sound reasons. They probably thought they could make more money on their own. Nonetheless, at trial the absence of a class seemed to hurt them. The opt-out defendants tried to focus the evidence on the purchasing practices of individual plaintiffs, in an attempt to disconnect them from any of the defendants and from any conspiracy. This approach was successful. Though it found a conspiracy, the jury concluded that none of the plaintiffs had been harmed by it. This would have been far less likely if a class comprising every purchaser had been the plaintiff group.

There are sometimes good reasons for opting out of a plaintiff class. The *Corrugated* plaintiffs may still believe they did the right thing: They were, after all, able to negotiate $60 million in pretrial settlements with some of the opt-out defendants. Even after expenses, their settlement share in the class proceeding might not have been as large. In other cases, there are even better reasons for opting out: A class member, on principle, may not support the suit. A class member may not have confidence in class counsel. It may dislike the named plaintiffs. There may be an unbridgeable strategic gap between class counsel and counsel for the class member. Intervention can sometimes solve such problems, but not always. Opting out may be the proper choice. But before taking such a step, a class member should always analyze how procedure could affect the merits.

Corrugated is a paradigm example of the wasteful, needless consequences of opt-out litigation. Litigation costs simply for the *Corrugated* opt-out suits exceeded $8 million. If a case like *Corrugated* is to be litigated at all, every effort should be made to achieve maximum efficiency. Given the limited resources of the courts and the expense of discovery and trial, it makes no sense to litigate the same allegations more than once. Quite apart from the criminal proceeding, the *Corrugated* class action produced mountains of paper. Because the opt-out proceeding involved theoretically—but not really—different cases, much of that discovery had to be done all over again. In fact, there was so much to do that depositions were taken while the trial was underway. None of that makes sense. No rational system should permit such unnecessary repetition.

Repetition was not the only flaw in the *Corrugated* opt-out litigation. Multiple litigation of the same questions created layer on layer of testimony on the same points. Though they left the class case, plaintiffs were, as noted earlier, unfortunately allowed to use testimony from it and from grand jury proceedings, in the opt-out trial. The defendants thus not only had to spend time and money on repetitive discovery and testimony, they also had to defend against material generated in proceedings of which some of them were not a part. That is not simply nonsense. It is unfair.

Of course, the opt-out provisions of Rule 23 are not whimsical. The draftsmen of the rule had reasons for what they did. They thought class members locked into class actions—like some of those certified under subsection (b)(3)—in which class members' interests varied might be denied due process. Such rights are fundamental. They must be protected. But surely such protection need not take the form of an automatic right to opt out and to create duplicate litigation. Even in a (b)(3) proceeding, if only common issues are tried, if class counsel are capable (as certification is supposed to signify), and if there are no issue conflicts between class members and named plaintiffs, then there seems little danger of violating due process. This is particularly true since class members are entitled to intervene as parties in (b)(3) actions. Given the need to conserve resources and make big cases manageable, Rule 23 should be changed to give courts discretion to permit, bar, or condition opting out. In such situations, a class member ought to have the burden of showing why it needs to opt out. Such a flexible approach is more efficient, and no less fair, than the automatic opt-out right now contained in the rule. If *Corrugated* teaches anything, it demonstrates that there must be a better way.